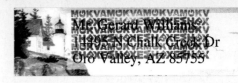

Learn Office 2011
for Mac OS X

D0619957

Guy Hart-Davis

Apress®

Learn Office 2011 for Mac OS X

ISBN-13 (pbk): 978-1-4302-3333-6

ISBN-13 (electronic): 978-1-4302-3334-3

Printed and bound in the United States of America 9 8 7 6 5 4 3 2 1

Trademarked names, logos, and images may appear in this book. Rather than use a trademark symbol with every occurrence of a trademarked name, logo, or image we use the names, logos, and images only in an editorial fashion and to the benefit of the trademark owner, with no intention of infringement of the trademark.

The use in this publication of trade names, trademarks, service marks, and similar terms, even if they are not identified as such, is not to be taken as an expression of opinion as to whether or not they are subject to proprietary rights.

Distributed to the book trade worldwide by Springer Science+Business Media, LLC., 233 Spring Street, 6th Floor, New York, NY 10013. Phone 1-800-SPRINGER, fax (201) 348-4505, e-mail orders-ny@springer-sbm.com, or visit www.springeronline.com.

For information on translations, please e-mail rights@apress.com, or visit www.apress.com.

Apress and friends of ED books may be purchased in bulk for academic, corporate, or promotional use. eBook versions and licenses are also available for most titles. For more information, reference our Special Bulk Sales–eBook Licensing web page at www.apress.com/info/bulksales.

This book is dedicated to the memory of Paul Raven.

Contents at a Glance

Contents

■ Chapter 14: Creating Powerful and Persuasive Charts 421

■ Chapter 15: Crunching Numbers with Formulas and Functions................. 451

About the Authors

 Guy Hart-Davis is the author of more than 60 computer books, including *Beginning Microsoft Office 2010* and *Integrating Macs into Windows Networks*.

About the Technical Reviewer

Jennifer Ackerman Kettell has written and contributed to dozens of books about software applications, web design, and digital photography. She has worked for Microsoft and other top companies, and has done freelance web design and online community management. Jenn has lived all over the United States, but currently calls upstate New York home.

Acknowledgments

My thanks go to the many people who helped create this book:

- Michelle Lowman for signing me to write the book
- Tom Welsh for developing the manuscript
- Jenn Kettell for reviewing the manuscript for technical accuracy and contributing helpful suggestions
- Kim Wimpsett for editing the manuscript with care
- Adam Heath for coordinating the book project and keeping things running
- MacPS, LLC for laying out the chapters of the book
- John Collin for creating the index

Introduction

Do you need to get your work done with the Office:Mac 2011 applications—smoothly, easily, and quickly? Good! You've picked up the right book.

Who Is This Book For?

This book is designed to help beginning and intermediate users get up to speed quickly with the Office:Mac 2011 applications and immediately become productive with them.

If you need to learn to use Word, Excel, PowerPoint, and Outlook to get everyday tasks done, at work or at home, you will benefit from this book's focused approach and detailed advice. You can either start from the beginning of the book and work through it, or use the Table of Contents or the Index to find the topic you need immediately, and then jump right in there.

What Does This Book Cover?

This book contains five parts that cover the shared Office features and the four applications.

Part 1 of the book brings you up to speed with the common features that the Office applications share:

- Chapter 1, "Getting Started with Office 2011," introduces you to Office's four applications—Word, Excel, PowerPoint, and Outlook—and what you can do with them. You learn how to open and close the applications; you meet key features such as the new Ribbon interface; and you create, save, close, and reopen documents.

- Chapter 2, "Learning Common Tools Across the Office Suite," shows you how to control the Office applications using the menus, the toolbars, and the Ribbon, and how to make the most of the tools in the Toolbox. This chapter also explains Office's common ways of sharing a document with others, how to save time and effort by using the AutoCorrect and AutoFormat features the smart way, and how to use the spelling and grammar checkers. You'll also learn how to print documents.

- Chapter 3, "Working with Text," shows you how to do everything from entering text (using the keyboard or other means) to creating tables and hyperlinks. Along the way, you'll learn how to work with cut, copy, and paste, and how to use the Find and Replace features.

- Chapter 4, "Using Pictures and Shapes in Your Documents," teaches you how to add visual interest to your Office document by adding pictures and shapes. You'll learn how to insert clip art, pictures (such as photos), and shapes; how to rotate and position graphical objects; and how to use Office's tools for making pictures look the way you want them. This chapter also covers inserting SmartArt diagrams and arranging graphical objects to control which is visible.

- Chapter 5, "Customizing Office to Suit You," walks you through customizing the toolbars, the Ribbon, and keyboard shortcuts to make the applications easier and faster to use. You'll also learn how to set essential preferences in the applications, such as the General preferences and the Save preferences.

Part 2 of the book covers using Microsoft Word, the powerful word processing application:

- Chapter 6, "Entering Text and Using Views," shows you how to enter text quickly in Word documents. You'll learn how to select text in advanced ways with the mouse and the keyboard, how to move around your documents, and how to tell Word where to find your custom templates. You'll also learn to create backup documents automatically, and to make the most of Word's seven different views of a document.

- Chapter 7, "Adding Style: Formatting Your Documents," teaches you the right way to format a document quickly and consistently by using styles rather than applying direct formatting bit by bit. It also shows you how to get around your documents by using the Sidebar and the Find feature, and how to harness the power of the Replace feature.

- Chapter 8, "Creating Complex Documents and Layouts," starts by showing you how to use Word's extra features for creating tables. The chapter then explains how to break a document into multiple sections; how to add headers, footers, and page numbers; and how to create newspaper-style columns of text. You'll learn to use bookmarks and cross-references, develop your documents using Word's powerful Outline view, and add footnotes and endnotes to your documents.

- Chapter 9, "Creating Business Documents with Mail Merge," shows you how to use Word to create business documents swiftly and efficiently. You'll learn to set up mail merge documents (such as letters or labels), connect them to data sources, and save or print the results.

- Chapter 10, "Revising and Reviewing Documents," covers how to use Word's features for working with your colleagues on documents. You'll learn how to edit a document either simultaneously or separately, how to use the Track Changes feature to mark revisions, and how to integrate changes into a document. You'll also see how to add comments to a document and compare two document versions that contain untracked changes.

- Chapter 11, "Printing, Sharing, and Securing Documents," explains how to print an entire document or just parts of it, with or without markup, and how to print markup without the document. You'll also learn how to remove sensitive information from documents, create a document you can open with earlier versions of Word, and create PDF files from documents.

Part 3 teaches you to create spreadsheets and charts with Excel:

- Chapter 12, "Creating Workbooks and Entering Data," covers creating different types of workbooks in Excel and entering data in them. You'll learn how to navigate the Excel interface, use workbooks and worksheets, and use Excel's views and features to see the data you need.

- Chapter 13, "Formatting Your Worksheets," explains how to insert, delete, and format rows and columns in worksheets; how to format cells and ranges; and how to use the advanced conditional-formatting and data-validation features to identify unusual values or erratic input. This chapter also shows you how to format quickly and consistently with styles, how to add headers and footers to worksheets, and how to share workbooks effectively with your colleagues.

- Chapter 14, "Creating Powerful and Persuasive Charts," teaches you how Excel's charts work and how to add them to your workbooks. You'll learn how to lay out a chart effectively, how to make it look good, and how to hide any components you don't want to display. You'll even learn how to save time by reusing the custom chart formatting you create.

- Chapter 15, "Crunching Numbers with Formulas and Functions," makes clear the difference between a formula and a function, and shows you first how to create custom formulas and then how to use Excel's built-in functions.

- Chapter 16, "Creating Simple Databases and Solving Business Problems," shows you how to use Excel to create databases for storing and manipulating your information. You'll learn how to enter information into a database, how to sort the information, and how to filter it to find only the results you want. You'll also learn how to use the Goal Seek feature and scenarios to work out solutions to business problems.

- Chapter 17, "Manipulating Data with PivotTables," explains how to use Excel's powerful PivotTable feature to manipulate your data so that you can discover the information you need. PivotTables take a few minutes to grasp, but you'll be surprised how easy they are to use.

Part 4 of the book takes you through creating good-looking, persuasive presentations with PowerPoint:

- Chapter 18, "Starting to Build a Presentation," gets you started by creating a presentation document using either a design template or a content template. The chapter then shows you how to add, delete, and rearrange slides; how to use PowerPoint's views effectively; how to develop the outline of a presentation; and how to break a presentation into separate sections. You'll also learn how to collaborate with your colleagues on creating a presentation.

- Chapter 19, "Creating Clear and Convincing Slides," guides you through the toughest part of creating a good presentation: creating slides that convey your meaning clearly and powerfully. This chapter shows you how to plan a presentation, choose suitable layouts (or create your own), and add text and other content to your slides.

- Chapter 20, "Adding Life and Interest to a Presentation," shows you ways of spicing up a presentation by using graphics, movies, sounds, animations, and transitions. You'll also learn how to hide slides to keep them up your sleeve and how to build custom slide shows that enable you to reveal only part of a larger presentation.

- Chapter 21, "Delivering a Presentation Live or Online," explains how to deliver the presentation you've created. You can deliver the presentation live in person, broadcast it across the Internet, or create a version of the presentation that you can share via e-mail or in other ways. You'll also learn how to use PowerPoint's Presenter view and how to create a handout for a presentation.

Part 5 of the book shows you how to manage your e-mail, schedule, contacts, and tasks with Outlook:

- Chapter 22, "Using E-mail Effectively," first shows you how to set up Outlook to work with your ISP or e-mail provider's servers. Once Outlook is working, you'll learn how to get around its complex user interface, how to send and receive e-mail, and how to manage your messages.

- Chapter 23, "Keeping Your Contacts in Order," covers creating contacts either from scratch or importing them from your address books, spreadsheets, or other sources. The chapter also shows you how to view and sort your contacts, add or update their contact information, and quickly create communications to your contacts.

- Chapter 24, "Managing Your Calendar," brings you up to speed with Outlook's Calendar interface, shows you how to customize it, and teaches you to use its views. After that, it explains how to create one-shot appointments and repeating appointments, schedule meetings, and respond to meeting requests.

- Chapter 25, "Working with Tasks and Notes," shows you how to use Outlook to define the tasks you need to complete and track your progress on completing them. This chapter also explains how to use Outlook's Notes feature to jot down information as you work.

Conventions Used in This Book

This book uses several conventions to make its meaning clear without wasting words:

- *Ribbon commands and menu commands*: The ➤ sign shows the sequence for choosing an item from the Ribbon or a command from the menu bar. For example, "Choose Home ➤ Paragraph ➤ Decrease indent from the Ribbon" means that you click the Home tab of the Ribbon (displaying the tab's contents), go to the Paragraph group, and then click the Decrease Indent button. Similarly, the ➤ sign indicates a menu sequence. For example, "Choose Insert ➤ Photo ➤ Picture from File from the menu bar" means that you click the Insert menu on the menu bar to open the menu, click the Photo item to open the Photo submenu, and then click the Picture from File item on the Photo submenu.

- *Special paragraphs*: Special paragraphs present information that you may want to pay extra attention to. Note paragraphs contain information you may want to know; Tip paragraphs present techniques you may benefit from using; and Caution paragraphs warn you of potential problems.

- *Check boxes*: The Office applications use many check boxes—the square boxes that can either have a check mark in them (indicating that the option is turned on) or not (indicating that the option is turned off). This book tells you to "select" a check box when you need to put a check mark in the check box, and to "clear" a check box when you need to remove the check mark from it. If the check box is already selected or cleared, you don't need to change it.

- *Keyboard shortcuts*: In the Office applications, you can often save time and effort by using a keyboard shortcut rather than a Ribbon command. This book uses + signs to represent keyboard shortcuts. For example, "press Cmd+S" means that you hold down the Cmd key, press the S key, and then release the Cmd key. "Press Cmd+Option+T" means that you hold down the Cmd key and the Option key, press the T key, and then release the Cmd key and the Option key.

Building Essential Office Skills

To save you time and effort, the Office:Mac 2011 applications share many common features. This part of the book shows you how to get started quickly with the applications and learn to use these common features.

In Chapter 1, you'll quickly meet Office's four main applications—Word, Excel, PowerPoint, and Outlook—and learn what you can do with them. You'll grasp essential moves, such as opening and closing the applications; and you'll create, save, close, and reopen documents.

In Chapter 2, you'll take control of the applications using the menus, the toolbars, and the ribbon. You'll learn how to share a document with others, how to save time and effort by using the AutoCorrect and AutoFormat features the smart way, and how to use the spelling and grammar checkers. You'll also learn how to print documents.

In Chapter 3, you'll study how to work with text—everything from entering text using the keyboard to creating tables and hyperlinks. By the end of the chapter, you'll also know how to work with cut, copy, and paste, and how to use the Find and Replace features.

In Chapter 4, you'll add visual interest to your Office document by inserting pictures and shapes. You'll learn how to insert clip art, pictures (such as photos), and shapes; how to rotate and position graphical objects; and how to use Office's tools for making pictures look the way you want them. When you need more complex illustrations, you can add SmartArt diagrams and arrange graphical objects to overlap each other, with fine control over which object is visible.

In Chapter 5, you'll make the Office applications easier and faster to use by customizing the toolbars, the Ribbon, and keyboard shortcuts. You'll also learn how to set essential preferences in the applications, such as the general and save preferences.

Getting Up to Speed with the Office Applications

You're probably in a hurry to start being productive using Office 2011, so this chapter gets you moving quickly. First, you'll meet each of the applications, find out what you can do with them, and come to grips with key features such as the Ribbon and the toolbars. Then, I'll show you how to launch the applications or make them launch themselves. Finally, you'll look at how to create, save, and close documents, as well as how to reopen them when you need to work on them again.

Meeting the Office Applications and Learning What You Can Do with Them

Microsoft Office 2011 comes in two versions and includes either three or four main applications, which this section briefly introduces. The basic version, Microsoft Office Home & Student, includes Microsoft Word, Microsoft Excel, and Microsoft PowerPoint; the more expensive version, Microsoft Office Home & Business, adds Microsoft Outlook to those three applications. This book shows you how to become proficient with these four applications.

> **NOTE:** Apart from the four main applications, Office also includes the Microsoft Messenger instant messaging application, the Microsoft Communicator telephony and conferencing application, the Remote Desktop Connection application for connecting remotely to Windows computers, and the Microsoft Document Connection application for connecting to SharePoint sites and Windows Live SkyDrive. This book focuses on the four main applications and doesn't cover the others.

For ease of use and to save time, the four main applications share many features, from the ways in which you create, save, and open documents to common actions you perform in them, such as copying text from one part of a document and pasting it in at another part.

Part 1 of this book discusses these common features. Parts 2 through 5 of the book then examine each of the applications in turn.

Microsoft Word

Microsoft Word (see Figure 1–1) is a word processing application that you can use to create everything from a single-page letter to a 1,000-page book complete with a table of contents, an index, and cross-references between different parts of the book.

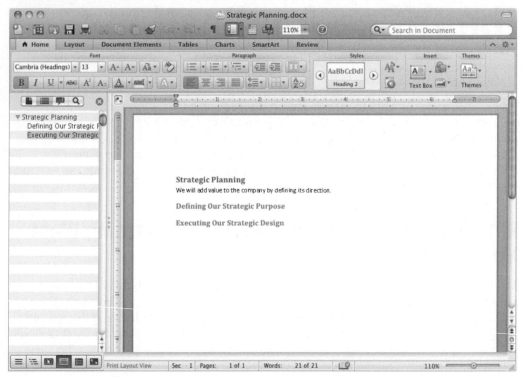

Figure 1–1. *Microsoft Word is the Office application for creating text-based documents.*

Part 2 of this book explains how to make the most of Microsoft Word.

Microsoft Excel

Microsoft Excel (see Figure 1–2) is a spreadsheet application that you can use to record, calculate, and analyze data. Excel includes features for creating many different types of charts for presenting your data clearly and effectively.

Figure 1–2. *Each Microsoft Excel workbook contains as many worksheets as you need for entering and analyzing your data.*

Part 3 of this book shows you how to work quickly and effectively in Microsoft Excel.

Microsoft PowerPoint

Microsoft PowerPoint (see Figure 1–3) is an application for creating and delivering presentations. Each presentation consists of slides, to which you can add any data from straightforward text to charts and movies. You can also add animations and transition effects to provide visual interest.

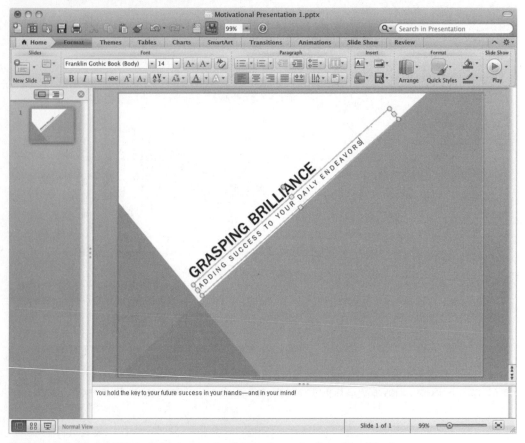

Figure 1–3. *In Microsoft PowerPoint, you create slides and organize them into slide shows.*

Part 4 of this book covers creating persuasive presentations in PowerPoint and delivering them to your audience either in person or online.

Microsoft Outlook

Microsoft Outlook (see Figure 1–4) is an application for e-mail and managing your contacts, calendar, and task list. If you have multiple e-mail accounts, you can manage them all within the single application, which saves large amounts of time and effort.

Figure 1–4. *Microsoft Outlook makes it easy to work with multiple e-mail accounts and to schedule your business and home life.*

Part 5 of this book shows you how to send e-mail and organize your life with Outlook.

Understanding the Common Features of the Applications

As you can see from the figures on the past few pages, the Office applications share a common look and several common features. Some of the features are standard for Mac OS X applications, but others are peculiar to the Office applications.

Figure 1–5 shows the Mac OS X menu bar and a Word window with a document open and the major features labeled. The following sections explain what the features are and what you use them for.

Figure 1–5. *The major features of an Office application window, shown with the Mac OS X menu bar*

The Title Bar and the Close, Minimize, and Zoom Buttons

The title bar at the top of the window shows the name of the open document and its file extension—for example, Strategic Planning.docx.

At the left end of the title bar are the following three buttons:

- *Close.* Click this button to close the window. The application stays open even if you close the last window; to close the application, quit it by pressing Cmd+Q or by clicking the application's menu and then clicking the Quit command (for example, choose Word ➤ Quit Word).

- *Minimize.* Click this button to minimize the window to the Dock. By default, Mac OS X displays each minimized window as an icon on the right side of the Dock divider bar; click this icon to restore the window to its former size.

> **TIP:** To save space on the Dock, Ctrl+click or right-click the Dock divider bar (the dashed white line), click Dock Preferences to display the Dock pane in System Preferences, and then select the Minimize windows into application icon check box. Press Cmd+Q or choose System Preferences ➤ Quit System Preferences to quit System Preferences. Now, when you minimize a window, Mac OS X puts it in the application's icon in the Dock. To restore a window, Ctrl+click or right-click the application's icon, and then click the window you want.

- *Zoom.* Click this button to make Mac OS X enlarge the application's window to the amount of space Mac OS X estimates will make its contents fit just right. This works better for some windows than for others; you'll often need to adjust the window size (by dragging the lower-right corner) after zooming. Click the Zoom button again to restore the window to its previous size.

The Toolbars

Below the title bar, each application by default displays a *toolbar*—a bar containing icons for frequently used commands, such as creating or opening documents, saving them, and printing them.

Word, Excel, and PowerPoint each have a Standard toolbar and a Formatting toolbar.

- *Standard.* This toolbar appears by default, *docked* (attached) to the application window. You can hide it by choosing View ➤ Toolbars ➤ Standard, removing the check mark from the Standard item.

- *Formatting.* This toolbar doesn't appear by default, but you can display it (by choosing View ➤ Toolbars ➤ Formatting) when you need it.

NOTE: You can also display or hide toolbars by Ctrl+clicking or right-clicking a displayed toolbar and then using the Toolbars submenu on the context menu that appears.

Word also has a Database toolbar, and PowerPoint has an Outlining toolbar; Figure 1–6 shows PowerPoint with the Standard toolbar, Formatting toolbar, and Outlining toolbar all displayed at the top of the application window. In Word, Excel, and PowerPoint, you can create other toolbars as needed and put on them the commands you want, but you can't dock these toolbars to the application window.

Figure 1–6. *Each application has one or more toolbars to give you quick access to important commands. PowerPoint has the Standard toolbar, Formatting toolbar, and Outlining toolbar, which you can see at the top of this window.*

Outlook has a single toolbar called simply the Toolbar. You can hide the Toolbar by choosing View ➤ Hide Toolbar and display it again by choosing View ➤ Show Toolbar.

TIP: In any of the applications, you can toggle the display of the toolbars on and off by clicking the jellybean button (the oval-shaped button) at the right end of the title bar.

The Ribbon

Below the title bar and any toolbars the application is displaying, the Ribbon runs across the top of the window. The Ribbon is a control bar that contains multiple tabs. You can display one tab's contents at a time by clicking the tab at the top.

Each Office application has a Home tab that contains some of the most widely useful commands—for example, applying the most popular types of formatting. Beyond this tab, each application has other tabs to cover its needs. For example, PowerPoint's tabs include the Slide Show tab, the Transitions tab, and the Animations tab, none of which Word, Excel, or Outlook need.

NOTE: When you need as much space as possible for working in a document, you can minimize the Ribbon by clicking the tab that's currently active, clicking the Hide Ribbon button (the ^ button) at the right end of the Ribbon, choosing View ➤ Ribbon, or pressing Cmd+Option+R. To display the Ribbon again, click the tab you want to see, click the Show Ribbon button (the ∨ button) at the right end of the Ribbon, choose View ➤ Ribbon, or press Cmd+Option+R.

In Word, Excel, and PowerPoint, each tab contains several groups of controls, divided into different types of actions. For example, the Home tab in PowerPoint contains a Slides group for creating and laying out slides, a Font group for applying font formatting, a Paragraph group for applying paragraph formatting, and several other groups. Unlike the other three applications, Outlook's tabs don't use groups.

You'll look at the details of how to use the Ribbon in Chapter 2, but the basic method is straightforward. You click the tab for the type of action you want to take and then click the button or control for the action you want to take. For example, to insert a picture in a Word document, you click the Home tab to display its contents, go to the Insert group, and then click the Picture button.

NOTE: If you find the Ribbon awkward to use, you can turn it off in Word, Excel, and PowerPoint and use the menus and toolbars instead. See Chapter 2 for instructions on turning the Ribbon off. Outlook doesn't let you turn the Ribbon off.

The Status Bar

At the bottom of the application window is the status bar, which shows information about the document and what you're currently working on and provides controls for changing the view and zooming in or out. For example, in Word, the status bar shows the view the document is using, the current page number, the number of words in the document, and the proofing status (whether the document contains spelling or grammar errors).

Opening Applications

To get anything done in the Office applications, you'll need to open and close the applications. You can open an application from the Dock or the Applications folder or by opening a document associated with that application. You may also want to open one or more applications when you log in to your Mac.

Opening an Application from the Dock

Usually, the easiest way to open one of the Office applications is by clicking its icon on the Dock (see Figure 1–7). The Office installer automatically adds an icon for each Office application to the Dock, so the icons should be there unless you remove them.

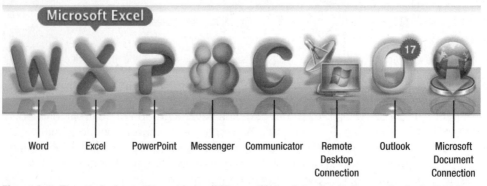

| Word | Excel | PowerPoint | Messenger | Communicator | Remote Desktop Connection | Outlook | Microsoft Document Connection |

Figure 1–7. *The standard way of launching an Office application is to click its icon on the Dock. Hold the mouse pointer over an icon to display its name, as for Microsoft Excel here.*

NOTE: If the Dock doesn't contain icons for the Office applications, you can add them easily. Click the Finder icon at the left end of the Dock (or the top end if you've displayed the Dock vertically), and then choose Go ➤ Applications from the menu bar to display the Applications folder. Microsoft Communicator is in the Applications folder itself; to reach the other applications, open the Microsoft Office 2011 folder to display the applications. Then click an application's icon and drag it to the Dock, dropping it to the left of the Dock divider bar (the dashed white line); if the Dock is vertical, drop the icon above the Dock divider bar.

Opening an Application from the Applications Folder

If you choose not to place icons for the Office applications on the Dock, you can run the applications from the Applications folder. To do so, follow these steps:

1. Click the Finder icon on the Dock to activate the Finder.

2. Choose Go ➤ Applications from the menu bar to display the Applications folder.

3. Open the Microsoft Office 2011 folder.

4. Double-click the application you want to launch.

Making a Application Launch Automatically

If you work in one or more of the Office applications every time you use your Mac, set the application to run automatically when you log in. For example, you may want to run Word, Excel, and Outlook each computing session so that you can work on documents, update your spreadsheets, and check your e-mail.

To make Mac OS X launch an application automatically when you log in, follow these steps:

1. If the application's icon doesn't appear on the Dock, launch the application from the Applications folder as described in the previous section. Mac OS X adds the application's icon to the Dock.

2. Ctrl+click or right-click the application's icon on the Dock to display the context menu.

3. Click or highlight the Options item to display the Options submenu.

4. Click the Open at Login item on the submenu (see Figure 1–8) to place a check mark next to this item.

Figure 1–8. *To make an application launch automatically when you log in, Ctrl+click or right-click the Dock icon, and then choose Options ➤ Open at Login.*

Now log out and then log back in. Check that Mac OS X automatically starts the applications you chose.

> **NOTE:** You can set up any application to launch automatically as described in this section. The more applications you set to launch automatically, the longer the login process will take—but once it is finished, you'll be ready to work fast.

Creating a Document

In Word, Excel, and PowerPoint, you create individual documents and save them in separate files. For example, in Word, you create word processing documents such as reports or letters. In Excel, you create workbooks containing worksheets of data. In PowerPoint, you create presentation documents containing slides.

> **NOTE:** Documents work differently in Outlook. While you create individual messages and other items (such as tasks and appointments) in Outlook, the application automatically stores most of your data for you.

Word, Excel, and PowerPoint come with *templates*, files that contain the basic structures of different kinds of documents. For example, Word includes templates for letters, reports, faxes, and other types of documents. A template can contain anything from the paper size, margins, and layout of a document up to an almost complete document in which you need to fill in only a few pieces of information to get a complete document. For example, in a customer letter template, you may need to fill in only the customer's name, address, and product type to produce a complete document.

When you want to work from a blank slate, you can create a new Word document, Excel workbook, or PowerPoint presentation that has no contents and no special formatting.

To create a new document based on a template, follow these steps:

1.   Open the Gallery dialog box in one of the following ways:

     ■   *Launch the application.* The application displays the Gallery dialog box automatically. Word displays the Word Document Gallery dialog box (see Figure 1–9), Excel displays the Excel Workbook Gallery dialog box, and PowerPoint displays the PowerPoint Presentation Gallery dialog box.

     ■   *Choose File ➤ New from Template.* If the application is already running, click the File menu on the menu bar, and then click New from Template. Alternatively, press Cmd+Shift+P.

Figure 1–9. *Use the application's Gallery dialog box—for example, the Word Document Gallery dialog box shown here—to create a new document. You can choose between having the document be blank or basing it on a template. You can also open a recent document from the Recent pane in the lower-left corner.*

2. Click the template or design. For a blank document, click the Word Document icon, the Excel Workbook icon, or the PowerPoint Presentation icon.

> **TIP:** To get a better view of the previews, drag the Zoom slider at the bottom of the Gallery window. If the template contains multiple pages or the design contains multiple slides, click the > and < buttons below the preview in the third column to move among them.

3. Choose options for the template or design as needed:

- *Colors.* If the Colors pop-up menu appears in the preview column, open it and choose the set of colors to use for the document.

- *Fonts.* If the Fonts pop-up menu appears in the preview column, open it and choose the font or fonts to use.

- *Slide size.* If the Slide size pop-up menu appears in the preview column in the PowerPoint Presentation Gallery, open it and choose the aspect ratio for the slides: Standard (4:3), Widescreen (16:9), or Widescreen (16:10).

4. Click the Choose button. The application closes the Gallery dialog box and creates the document.

> **NOTE:** You can create a new blank document in Word, Excel, or PowerPoint by pressing the Cmd+N keyboard shortcut.

Saving a Document

As soon as you've created a document, save it. When you save a document, you choose the folder in which to store it and specify the file name to give the document. After that, you can quickly save changes you make to the document, and you can close it and reopen it as needed.

> **CAUTION:** If you don't save a document, it disappears for good when you close the application. This is occasionally useful when you create a document you don't want to keep, but normally you'll want to save each document when you create it and then delete it using Finder when you no longer need it. When you close an application, it displays a dialog box prompting you to save any unsaved documents (and any unsaved changes in saved documents), but it's easy enough to click the wrong button and lose the document (or the changes).

To save a document, follow these steps:

1. Click the Save button on the Standard toolbar, or press Cmd+S to display the Save As dialog box (see Figure 1–10). You can also choose File ➤ Save from the menu bar.

Figure 1–10. *The Save As dialog box at first appears at its smaller size, with the folder area hidden. To change folders, either pick a folder from the Where pop-up menu or click the button to the right of the Save As box to expand the dialog box.*

2. Choose the folder in which you want to store the document:

    •   You can move quickly to one of the main folders on your Mac (such as the Desktop folder or the Documents folder) or a recent folder by opening the Where pop-up menu and then clicking the folder.

    •   To display the folder area, click the button to the right of the Save As box. The Save As dialog box expands, as shown in Figure 1–11. You can then navigate through your Mac's drives and folders using the same techniques as in a Finder window. If you need to create a new folder to save the document in, click the New Folder button, type the folder name in the New Folder dialog box, and then click the Create button.

NOTE: The Office applications come configured to save your documents in your Documents folder. You can switch to any other folder needed for any document, but you can also change the default location. See Chapter 5 for how to do this.

Figure 1–11. *Expand the Save As dialog box if you need to use the folder pane to navigate to a different folder. You can drag the shaded handle at the lower-right corner of the expanded Save As dialog box to resize the dialog box.*

3. In the Save As text box, type the name you want to give the file. The application suggests the first few words of the document, but you'll often want to use a different name.

4. In the Format pop-up menu, choose the file type you want the document to have.

    ■ The Format pop-up menu suggests the application's default format at first: Word suggests the Word Document (`.docx`) format, Excel suggests the Excel Workbook (`.xlsx`) format, and PowerPoint suggests the PowerPoint Presentation (`.pptx`) format.

    ■ You may need to use a different format for sharing a document with people using earlier versions of Office or other applications. We'll discuss this in more detail in the chapters on the individual applications.

    ■ You can change the default format as discussed in Chapter 5.

5. If you want to display the file extension (for example, `.docx` for a Word document) in the Save As box, clear the Hide extension check box.

6. Click the Save button. The application closes the Save As dialog box and saves the document. The document's name appears in the application window's title bar so that you can easily identify it.

After saving a document as described here, you can save it again at any point by clicking the Save button on the Standard toolbar, by pressing Cmd+S, or by choosing File ➤ Save from the menu bar.

> **TIP:** Save your documents frequently. Any time you've made changes that you don't want to have to make again, press Cmd+S or click the Save button on the Standard toolbar.

Closing a Document

When you have finished working on a document, close it. Use one of these methods:

- Click the Close button (the red button) at the left end of the window's title bar.

- Open the File menu and click Close.

- Press Cmd+W.

If the document contains unsaved changes, the application prompts you to save them (see Figure 1–12). Click the Save button to save the changes, the Don't Save button to jettison them, or the Cancel button to return to the document to remind yourself what you've changed.

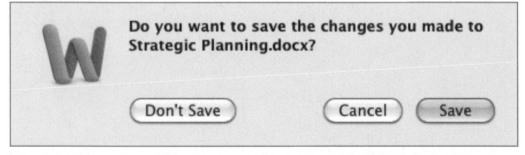

Do you want to save the changes you made to Strategic Planning.docx?

Don't Save   Cancel   Save

Figure 1–12. *When you close a document that contains unsaved changes, the application checks whether you want to save them.*

> **NOTE:** Even though the applications prompt you to save unsaved changes when you close a document, it's a good idea to save the document before closing it. This eliminates the possibility of you clicking the Don't Save button in the prompt dialog box by mistake.

Opening a Document

You can open a document in the Office applications in various ways. The following list shows you the four most useful ways:

- *Open a recent document from the Apple menu.* Click the Apple menu at the left end of the menu bar, and then click or highlight Recent Items to display the list of recent items (see Figure 1–13). In the Documents list, click the document you want to open. If the application associated with the document isn't already running, Mac OS X launches it automatically.

TIP: Because the Documents list in the Recent Items submenu contains all kinds of documents, other recent documents may have knocked your recent Office documents off the list. You can improve matters by increasing the list of recent documents and reducing or removing the Applications list and the Servers list. Click the Apple menu, and then click System Preferences to display the System Preferences window. Click the Appearance icon to display the Appearance pane, go to the Number of recent items section, and adjust the numbers in the Applications pop-up menu, the Documents pop-up menu, and the Servers pop-up menu as needed. For each, you can choose None, 5, 10 (the default setting), 15, 20, 30, or 50. If you usually launch applications from the Dock, choose None in the Applications pop-up menu to give yourself more space for the Documents list. When you've chosen settings, click the Close button (the red button at the left end of the title bar), press Cmd+Q, or choose System Preferences ➤ Quit System Preferences.

Figure 1–13. *You can quickly open a recent document .*

- *Open a document from Finder.* Open a Finder window to the folder that contains the document, and then double-click the document. Mac OS X opens the document in the application associated with the document type. For example, if you double-click an Excel workbook document in a Finder window, Mac OS X opens the document in Excel. Mac OS X launches the application if it's not currently running.

NOTE: You can also open a document that you've received as an attachment to an e-mail message in Outlook. See Chapter 23 for instructions on doing this.

■ *Open a document with the Open dialog box.* With the application
   running, click the Open button on the toolbar, press Cmd+O, or
   choose File ➤ Open from the menu bar. The application displays the
   Open dialog box (see Figure 1–14). Navigate to the folder that contains
   the document, click the document, and then click the Open button.

Figure 1–14. *Use the Open dialog box to open a document from within one of the Office applications.*

■ *Open a document from the File ➤ Recent submenu.* With the
   application running, open the File menu, and then click or highlight the
   Recent item. On the submenu (see Figure 1–15), click the document
   you want to open. If the document doesn't appear on the menu, you
   can click the More item to display the Gallery dialog box with the
   Recent pane open in the lower-left corner.

| PowerPoint | File | Edit | View | Insert | Format | Arrange | Tools | Slide Show | W |

New Presentation	⌘N
New from Template...	⇧⌘P
Open...	⌘O
Open URL...	⇧⌘O
Open Recent	▶

Public Speaking 1.pptx
Executive Briefing.pptx
Brewery info.pptx
PowerPoint Temp
Motivational Presentation 1.pptx

More...

Clear Recent

Close	⌘W
Save	⌘S
Save As...	⇧⌘S
Save as Pictures...	
Save as Movie...	

| Share | ▶ |

| Reduce File Size... | |

| Restrict Permissions | ▶ |

| Page Setup... | |
| Print... | ⌘P |

| Properties... | |

Figure 1–15. *When you're working in a application, you can use the File ➤ Recent menu to open a document you've worked on recently.*

TIP: You can also open a recent document from the application's Dock icon. Ctrl+click or right-click the Dock icon, click or highlight Open Recent to display the submenu, and then click the document. If the document doesn't appear, click the More item to display the Gallery dialog box.

■ *Open a document from the Gallery dialog box.* Open the Gallery dialog box by either clicking the More item on the Open Recent submenu (as just described) or choosing File ➤ New. In the Recent pane in the lower-left corner, click the time frame for the documents you want to see: All, Today, Yesterday, Past Week, or Past Month. The main part of the Gallery dialog box lists the documents. Click the document you want, and then click the Choose button.

NOTE: If the Recent Documents pane, Recent Workbooks pane, or Recent Presentations pane doesn't appear in the Gallery dialog box, click the Open or Close Recent Documents button in the lower-left corner of the Gallery dialog box to display the pane.

Closing an Application

When you have finished using a application, close it by quitting it. Quitting the application removes it from your Mac's memory so your Mac can use the memory to run other applications.

The standard way of quitting an application is to press Cmd+Q or open the application's menu and then click the Quit command. This command includes the application's name—for example, Quit Excel. The application closes any documents that are open, prompting you to save any unsaved changes, and then closes.

You can also quit an application by Ctrl+clicking or right-clicking its Dock icon and then clicking Quit on the context menu.

NOTE: If you plan to use an application again later, you can simply hide the application until you need it rather than close it and restart it. To hide the application, open its application menu and then click the Hide command (for example, choose Word ➤ Hide Word, or Excel ➤ Hide Excel) or press Cmd+H. When you need to see the application again, click its Dock icon.

Summary

In this chapter, you met each of the Office applications—Microsoft Word, Microsoft Excel, Microsoft PowerPoint, and (in the Home & Business version of Office for Mac) Microsoft Outlook. You learned what you can do with the applications, and you met several of their key features, such as the Ribbon and the toolbars. You know how to launch the applications; create, save, and close documents; and reopen documents as needed.

In the next chapter, you'll learn how to work quickly and smartly with common tools in the Office applications.

Chapter 2

Learning Common Tools Across the Office Suite

To save you time and effort, the Office applications have many common features, starting with the three elements you use to give most commands: the menu bar, the toolbars, and the Ribbon control interface.

This chapter starts by showing you how to control the applications using the menus, the toolbars, and the Ribbon. After that, it covers using the Toolbox, the free-floating control panel containing tools such as the Scrapbook palette, the Reference Tools palette, and the Compatibility Report tool. The chapter then explains the common ways of sharing a document with others, how to save time and effort with the AutoCorrect feature, and how to turn off AutoFormat features that can cause surprises and waste time. Lastly, the chapter shows you how to check spelling and grammar, customize the spelling checker and grammar checker for better results, and print your documents.

Using the Menus, the Toolbars, and the Ribbon

To give most commands in the Office applications, you use three forms of control interface:

- *Menus.* Like most Mac OS X applications, each Office application uses the menu bar that appears across the top of the screen. The menus provide access to most of the commands in the applications.

- *Toolbars.* Each application has one or more of these button bars that appear either across the top of a document window or floating free on the Desktop. The toolbars let you quickly reach some of the most widely used commands in the applications.

- *Ribbon.* Each application uses this Office-specific control strip that appears across the top of each document window. The Ribbon lets you give many (but not all) of the commands that the application offers.

Figure 2–1 shows the menu bar, two toolbars, and the Ribbon in a Word document window.

Figure 2–1. *To give commands in the Office applications, you use the Mac OS X menu bar, the toolbars, and the Ribbon.*

There's a considerable amount of overlap between the menus, the toolbars, and the Ribbon. Here are some examples:

- To open a document (in Word, Excel, or PowerPoint), you can choose File ➤ Open from the menu bar or click the Open button on the Standard toolbar.

- To apply formatting to cells in an Excel workbook, you can use the controls on the Home tab of the Ribbon, use the controls on the Formatting toolbar, or choose Format ➤ Cells from the menu bar and work in the Format Cells dialog box.

- To insert a slide in a PowerPoint presentation, you can use the New Slide command in the Slides group of the Home tab on the Ribbon or choose Insert ➤ New Slide from the menu bar.

You can use whichever method of giving a command you find most convenient. The underlying commands are the same—it's just a question of how you give them.

> **NOTE:** Beyond the commands that appear on the menus, the toolbars, and the Ribbon, each application has specialized commands that you can reach only by customizing the application. See Chapter 5 for instructions on customizing the applications.

Using the Menus

If you've used most any other Mac OS X application, you'll know how to use the menus:

1. Make sure the application is active so that the menu bar shows its menus. If it's not, click the document window to make the application active.

2. Click the menu you want to open. For example, click the View menu to reveal its commands.

3. If the command you need is on a submenu, click or highlight the submenu. Figure 2–2 shows the View menu and its Toolbars submenu open in PowerPoint.

Figure 2–2. *As in most Mac OS X applications, you can give commands using the menus in the Office applications.*

4. Click the command. The application closes the menu and performs the command.

Using the Toolbars

The toolbar or toolbars that appear at the top of the document window, below the window's title bar and above the Ribbon, are also easy to use. Click the button for the command you want to give; or, if the button produces a pop-up menu, click the button, and then click the command on the menu. To identify a button, hold the mouse pointer over it until the application displays a ScreenTip explaining what it does (see Figure 2–3).

Figure 2–3. *To see a ScreenTip showing what a toolbar button does, hold the mouse pointer over the button for a moment.*

NOTE: If you want to customize the toolbars, turn to the section "Customizing the Toolbars" in Chapter 5.

Using the Ribbon

As you learned in Chapter 1, the Ribbon is the control strip that appears across the top of each document window, below any toolbars the window is displaying. The Ribbon contains tabs, groups, and controls:

- *Tab.* A tab is one of the major groups of controls on the Ribbon and takes the whole width of the Ribbon. The Ribbon displays only one tab at a time; this tab is the *active tab*. You switch from tab to tab by clicking the small named tab at the top. For example, to display the Home tab of the Ribbon, you click the Home tab at the left end. Figure 2–4 shows the Home tab in Word.

Figure 2–4. *The Ribbon contains tabs, groups, and controls.*

NOTE: Unlike Word, Excel, and PowerPoint, Outlook doesn't divide its Ribbon tabs into groups.

- *Group.* Each tab consists of several groups of controls. Each group is a vertical division of the Ribbon, with the group's name appearing at the top. For example, the Home tab in Word contains the Font group, the Paragraph group, the Styles group, the Insert group, and the Themes group by default (you can customize the Ribbon; see Chapter 5 for details).

- *Controls.* Each group consists of one or more controls—buttons, control boxes, or pop-up menus that you click to give commands. For example, the Text Layout group on the Layout tab in Word (shown in close-up in the middle of Figure 2–5) contains the Direction pop-up menu, the Columns pop-up menu, the Line Numbers pop-up menu, and the Hyphenation button.

Figure 2–5. *The controls on the Ribbon include buttons, pop-up menus, and boxes for entering quantities or measurements.*

NOTE: The Ribbon automatically resizes its groups and their controls to make the best use of the space available in the application window. For example, if you make the window narrower, the Ribbon hides the names of buttons to make them fit in the space. If you make the window narrower still, the Ribbon can collapse an entire group into a single button that you click to produce a pop-up panel containing the group's buttons.

Giving Commands from the Ribbon

To give commands from the Ribbon, click the tab that contains the command, go to the group, and then click the control. For example, to give the Hyphenation command in Word, click the Layout tab (if it's not already displayed), go to the Text Layout group, and then click the Hyphenation button.

To see information about what a button does, hold the mouse pointer over the button for a moment until a ScreenTip appears. Move the mouse pointer away when you no longer need to see the ScreenTip.

NOTE: This book presents Ribbon commands by tab, group, and command name. For example, "choose Tables ➤ Table Options ➤ New" means that you click the Tables tab to display it, go to the Table Options group (you don't need to click it), and then click the New button.

Minimizing the Ribbon

When you need as much space as possible to work on a document, you can minimize the Ribbon so that only the tabs appear (see Figure 2–6). You can minimize the Ribbon in these ways:

- Click the tab that's currently active.
- Click the Minimize the Ribbon button to the right of the tab bar (the ^ button).
- Press Cmd+Option+R.

Figure 2–6. *You can minimize the Ribbon so that just its tabs appear to give yourself more space in the document window.*

To restore the display of the Ribbon, use one of these moves:

- Click the tab you want to display.

- Click the Expand the Ribbon button (which replaces the Minimize the Ribbon button when you minimize the Ribbon).

- Press Cmd+Option+R.

NOTE: See Chapter 5 for instructions on how to customize the Ribbon or make it vanish completely in Word, Excel, or PowerPoint.

Using the Toolbox

Each application has a tool palette called the Toolbox. The Toolbox floats freely rather than being docked to the application window, so you can position it wherever is best for you.

In each application, the Toolbox contains the Scrapbook palette and the Reference Tools palette. In Word, Excel, and PowerPoint, it also contains other palettes:

- *Word.* The Toolbox also contains the Styles palette, the Citations palette, and the Compatibility Report palette. Figure 2–7 shows the Scrapbook palette open in Word.

Figure 2–7. *Use the Scrapbook palette in the Toolbox to collect items you want to include in your Office documents.*

- *Excel.* The Toolbox also contains the Formula Builder palette and the Compatibility Report palette.

- *PowerPoint.* The Toolbox also contains the Custom Animation palette and the Compatibility Report palette.

The following sections explain how to use the three common palettes—the Scrapbook palette, the Reference Tools palette, and the Compatibility Report palette. You'll meet most of the other palettes later in the book—the Styles palette (but not the Citations palette) in the chapters on Word, the Formula Builder palette in the Excel chapters, and the Custom Animation palette in the PowerPoint chapters.

To display the main palettes of the Toolbox, choose View ➤ Scrapbook, View ➤ Reference Tools, or View ➤ Compatibility Report from the menu bar. The Toolbox opens, showing the palette you chose.

To hide the Toolbox, you can click its Close button (the red button in its title bar) or give the View menu command again—for example, when the Reference Tools palette is displayed, choose View ➤ Reference Tools to hide the Toolbox. But you may want to make the Toolbox collapse, fade, or close after you've left it unused for a number of seconds. To set the Toolbox to take one of these actions, follow these steps:

1. Click the Toolbox Settings button, the curling-arrow button in the upper-right corner of the Toolbox. The Toolbox flips over and displays the Toolbox Settings palette (see Figure 2–8).

Figure 2–8. *In the Toolbox Settings palette on the back of the Toolbox, you can make the Toolbox collapse, fade, or close automatically after a period of inactivity.*

2. In the Close Effect pop-up menu, choose the effect you want to use for closing the Toolbox: Genie, Scale, or None. (Genie and Scale are the same effects used for minimizing applications to the Dock.)

3. Select the When inactive for check box.

4. Drag the slider to set the number of seconds of inactivity—from 1 to 60.

5. Select the appropriate option button:

- *Collapse.* Select this option button to make the Toolbox collapse to just its title bar and the tab bar. The Toolbox then expands again when you click a tab button.

- *Fade.* Select this option button to make the Toolbox fade. Drag the slider to set the fade percentage—from 10 percent (almost invisible) to 100 percent (fully there). The Toolbox reappears when you move the mouse pointer over it.

- *Close.* Select this option button to make the Toolbox actually close.

> **NOTE:** In the lower part of the Toolbox Settings palette, you can choose which items appear in the Reference Tools palette. Make sure that Reference Tools is selected in the Palette pop-up menu, and then select or clear the check boxes in the Show Panels list box as needed. Select the Allow online access check box if you want the reference tools to be able to look up material on the Internet.

6. Click the OK button to close the Toolbox Settings palette. The Toolbox flips over and displays the palette that was displayed before.

Using the Scrapbook to Collect Items

When you need to collect clippings and files into a single handy location so that you can quickly insert them in your documents, use the Scrapbook palette in the Toolbox. The Office applications share the Scrapbook, so you can collect items in one application and use them in another.

Adding an Item to the Scrapbook

You can add an item to the Scrapbook in any of these ways:

- *Add a selection.* Select the text or other item you want to add to the Scrapbook. Then click the Add button in the middle of the Scrapbook palette.

- *Add a graphics file.* Click the Add drop-down button, and then click Add File to display the Choose a File dialog box. Select the file you want, and then click the Choose button.

- *Add whatever you've copied to the Clipboard.* Copy the item to the Clipboard as usual—for example, by selecting it in an application and then pressing Cmd+C. Then click the Add drop-down button in the Scrapbook palette, and click Add from Clipboard.

■ *Add everything you copy to the Clipboard.* If you use the Scrapbook extensively, you can make Office add a clipping of everything you copy in Mac OS X while the Scrapbook palette is open. To do so, click the Add drop-down button in the Scrapbook palette, and then click Always Add Copy, placing a check mark next to this item. The application displays the Always Add Clipping Selected dialog box to warn you that this feature may slow your Mac down or gobble up its disk space. Click the OK button.

NOTE: To make your clippings easier to find, you can add keywords to them. Click a clipping, type one or more keywords in the Keywords pane, and then click the Apply button. You can then open the pop-up menu in the upper-left corner of the Scrapbook palette, choose Keyword contains, and type the keyword by which you want to search.

Inserting an Item from the Scrapbook

To insert an item from the Scrapbook, position the insertion point or selection at the appropriate point in the document. Then click the item in the Scrapbook palette, and click the Paste button.

If you want to paste the item as plain text (without formatting) or as a picture, click the item, and then click the Paste drop-down button. On the menu, click Paste as Plain Text or Paste as Picture, as needed.

Deleting an Item from the Scrapbook

Chances are you'll want to keep some items permanently in your Scrapbook, but you'll need to get rid of others once their shelf life passes. Here's how to get rid of items:

■ *Delete a single item.* Click the item, and then click the Delete button.

■ *Delete all the items currently displayed.* Display the items you want to delete, click the Delete drop-down button, and then click Delete Visible.

■ *Delete all the items from the Scrapbook.* Click the Delete drop-down button, and then click Delete All.

Using the Reference Tools Palette to Look Up Information

When you need to look up information quickly, use the Reference Tools palette of the Toolbox (see Figure 2–9). Choose View ➤ Reference Tools to display the Reference Tools palette, type the word in the Search box at the top, and then press the Return key. The Thesaurus displays the word's meanings and synonyms; in the Meanings pane, click the meaning whose synonyms you want to display. You can then click a synonym and click the Insert button to insert it in the document, or you can click the Look Up button to look up the synonym.

To find out more about the word, click the title bar of the four other collapsible panes—Dictionary, Bilingual Dictionary, Translation, and Web Search—to display its contents.

Figure 2–9. *Use the Reference Tools pane in the Toolbox to quickly look up a word, translate it, or search for information about it on the Web.*

Using the Compatibility Report Pane to Check a Document's Compatibility with Older Versions of the Application

Over the years, Microsoft has added many features to the Office applications and has changed the file formats the applications use to save documents. As a result, a document you create in (say) Word 2011 may not display correctly in an older version of Word.

To help you identify potential problems and (if you want) root them out, the Office 2011 applications include the Compatibility Report palette in the Toolbox. You use it like this:

1. Open the document if it's not already open.

2. Choose View ➤ Compatibility Report to open the Toolbox with the Compatibility Report palette at the front.

3. Open the Check compatibility with pop-up menu, and then click the version of the application with which you want to make sure the document is compatible. The Results box shows a list of possible problems (see Figure 2–10).

Figure 2–10. *In the Compatibility Report palette, choose the application with which to check the document's compatibility. You can then choose which problems to fix and which to ignore.*

4. To see the details of a problem, click it in the Results box. The Explanation box displays an explanation of the problem.

5. To fix a problem, click it in the Results box. If the Fix button is available, click it to fix this instance of the problem. To fix all the instances, click the Fix drop-down button, and then click Fix All on the menu.

6. To ignore a problem, click it in the Results box, and then click the Ignore button. To ignore all the instances, click the Ignore drop-down button, and then click Ignore All on the menu. To teach the application not to bother you with this problem again, click the Ignore drop-down button, and then click Don't Show Again on the menu.

Sharing a Document with Other People

Word, Excel, and PowerPoint all enable you to share a document with other people in several different ways. This section covers the three ways common to all three of these applications:

- Send using e-mail
- Save to SkyDrive
- Save to SharePoint

NOTE: For coverage of the other ways of sharing documents that the individual applications offer, see the chapters on those applications.

Sending a Document via E-mail

You can send a document via e-mail by starting a message in Outlook (or another e-mail application) and then attaching the document's file. But if you're working from one of the Office applications and have the document open, you can start a message directly from the application. This saves a bit of time and effort, because you use the application to identify the document—you don't have to navigate to the document in your Mac's file system like you usually must when attaching a file to a message.

CAUTION: Before sending a document via e-mail, make sure you've saved it. The applications will let you send an unsaved document, but doing so isn't a good idea.

To send a document using e-mail, follow these steps:

1. Make the document the active document. If the document is already open, click in its window; if the document isn't open, open it.

2. Choose File ➤ Share to display the Share submenu (see Figure 2–11).

Figure 2–11. *Open the File ➤ Share submenu when you need to send a file via e-mail, save it to SkyDrive, or save it to SharePoint.*

3. Click the E-mail (as Attachment) item on the Share submenu. The application launches your default e-mail application (for example, Outlook) if it's not running, or activates it if it is running, and creates a new message with the document attached.

4. Address and complete the message, and then send it as usual.

> **NOTE:** If you're sharing a document saved on Windows Live SkyDrive or a SharePoint site and you want to send the recipient only a link to the document rather than sending the document itself, choose File ➤ Share ➤ E-mail (as Link). The application creates a new message in your default e-mail application (for example, Outlook) and inserts in it a link to the document. You can then complete the message, address it, and send it.

Saving a Document to SkyDrive

If you have a Windows Live account (including a Hotmail account or an MSN account), you can save documents to SkyDrive, Microsoft's online document service. You can use SkyDrive either to share documents with other people who have Windows Live accounts or to access and work on your documents from other computers.

> **NOTE:** You can sign up for a free Windows Live account at the Windows Live web site (`http://home.live.com`).

To save a document to SkyDrive, follow these steps:

1. Make the document the active document. If the document is already open, click in its window. If the document isn't open, open it.

2. Choose File ➤ Share ➤ Save to SkyDrive.

3. If the application displays the Windows Live Sign In dialog box (see Figure 2–12) prompting you to log in to SkyDrive, type your Windows Live ID and password. Select the Save password in my Mac OS keychain check box if you want Mac OS X to save your password so that you don't have to enter it in the future. This is usually a good idea when you're using your own Mac; if you're using someone else's Mac, don't save the password. Then click the Sign In button to sign in.

> **NOTE:** The Windows Live Sign In dialog box doesn't recognize most password-collection applications—so even if you use such an application, you will need to type in your password.

Figure 2–12. *When you sign in to Windows Live, you can select the Save password in my Mac OS keychain check box to make Mac OS X store the password and provide it automatically in future.*

4.   In the Save As dialog box that the application displays (see Figure 2–13), select
     the folder in which to save the document. Change the file name as necessary in
     the Save As box, and then click the Save button to save the document.

NOTE: At first, SkyDrive gives you a Public folder (which you share with everyone) and a private
My Documents folder. You can create other folders as needed by working in a web browser, but
not directly from the Save As dialog box.

Save As:	Commitment Drive| .docx

▼ Personal Folders

   📁 My Documents

   📁 Office Live Documents

▼ Shared Folders

   📁 Public
       Shared with: Everyone (public)

Learn about SkyDrive   (Cancel)   (Save)

Figure 2–13. *In the Save As dialog box for Windows Live SkyDrive, choose the folder in which to save the
document, and change the file name if necessary.*

Saving a Document to a SharePoint Site

If your company or organization has a SharePoint site, you can save documents to it to
share them with your colleagues.

To save a document to a SharePoint site, follow these steps:

1.   Make the document the active document. If the document is already open, click in
     its window; if the document isn't open, open it.

2.   Choose File ➤ Share ➤ Save to SharePoint. The application displays the Save As
     dialog box shown in Figure 2–14.

Save As: Commitment Drive   .docx

▼ Recent Locations
▼ Saved Locations

\+   −

Learn about saving to SharePoint   (Cancel)   (Save)

Figure 2–14. *When you've connected to a SharePoint site, you can save in a Recent Location or a Saved Location. You can also click the Add (+) button to add a new location.*

3. In the Save As box, change the file name if needed.

4. In the main area of the dialog box, navigate to the folder in which to save the document, and then select the folder.

NOTE: To add a SharePoint site to the Save As dialog box, click the Add (+) button in the lower-left corner of the dialog box. In the Add a SharePoint Location dialog box that opens, type the URL of the SharePoint server, and then click the Add button. If the site displays the Login dialog box, type your user name and password, and select the Save password in my Mac OS keychain check box if you want to store the password for future use. Then click the Log In button.

5. Click the Save button to save the document in the SharePoint folder.

Saving Time and Effort with AutoCorrect

As you work in a document, the AutoCorrect feature watches the characters you type and springs into action if it detects a mistake it can fix or some formatting it can apply. This feature can save you a lot of time and effort and can speed up your typing substantially, so it's well worth using—but you need to set it up to meet your needs. AutoCorrect also has some features that can cause surprises, so you will want to choose settings that suit the way you work.

To set up AutoCorrect, first open the AutoCorrect preferences pane:

- *Word.* Choose Tools ➤ AutoCorrect from the menu bar to display the AutoCorrect preferences pane in the Word Preferences dialog box.

- *Excel.* Choose Tools ➤ AutoCorrect from the menu bar to display the AutoCorrect preferences pane in the Excel Preferences dialog box.

- *PowerPoint.* Choose Tools ➤ AutoCorrect from the menu bar to display the AutoCorrect preferences pane in the PowerPoint Preferences dialog box.

- *Outlook.* Choose Outlook ➤ Preferences (or press Cmd+,) to display the Outlook Preferences window. Then click the AutoCorrect icon in the Personal Settings area to display the AutoCorrect preferences pane.

The AutoCorrect preferences pane has different contents in each of the Office applications:

- *Word.* Word's AutoCorrect preferences pane (see Figure 2–15) has four tabs: one for standard AutoCorrect, one for Math AutoCorrect, one for AutoFormat as You Type, and one for AutoText.

AutoCorrect: English (US)

◄ ►   Back/Forward   Show All   🔍 Search Word Preferences

☑ Automatically correct spelling and formatting as you type

| AutoCorrect | Math AutoCorrect | AutoFormat as You Type | AutoText |

☑ Show AutoCorrect smart button

☑ Correct TWo INitial CApitals
☑ Capitalize first letter of sentences
☑ Capitalize names of days
☑ Capitalize first letter of table cells

☑ Replace text as you type   (Exceptions...)

Replace: With: ⊙ Plain text   ○ Formatted text

-->	→
:-(	⊗
:-)	☺
:-|	😐

(Add)   (Delete)

☑ Automatically use suggestions from the spelling checker

Description of preference

AutoCorrect
Use AutoCorrect to correct text and formatting as you type.

(Cancel)   (OK)

Figure 2–15. *The AutoCorrect preferences pane contains options that can save you plenty of time but may also give you surprises. Word's AutoCorrect preferences pane (shown here) contains more options than the preferences panes in the other applications.*

- *Excel.* Excel's AutoCorrect preferences pane has no tabs, because Excel has only the standard AutoCorrect feature.

- *PowerPoint.* The AutoCorrect preferences pane has two tabs: one for standard AutoCorrect and one for AutoFormat as You Type.

- *Outlook.* The AutoCorrect preferences pane has two tabs: one for standard AutoCorrect and one for AutoFormat (which includes options for applying formatting as you type and replacing characters with formatting as you type).

TIP: Because Outlook's implementation of AutoCorrect is in a window rather than in a dialog box, you can leave the AutoCorrect preferences pane open as you work in Outlook if you want. Doing this can save you time when you need to create multiple AutoCorrect entries at the same time or test different settings.

The details vary depending on what each application needs, but the basic part of AutoCorrect is the same for each application: AutoCorrect watches as you type and makes changes that are supposed to be helpful. To get the most out of AutoCorrect, you'll need to configure it carefully, as discussed in the following sections.

Choosing Standard AutoCorrect Options

Let's start by looking at what you might call the standard AutoCorrect options—those that appear on the AutoCorrect tab for Word, PowerPoint, and Outlook, and in the tab-free AutoCorrect preferences pane in Excel.

NOTE: Word has a master control for turning off AutoCorrect as a whole. This is the Automatically correct spelling and formatting as you type check box that appears at the top of the AutoCorrect preferences pane. Clear this check box if you want to turn off AutoCorrect.

These are the options you can choose:

- *Show AutoCorrect smart button* or *Show AutoCorrect Options Buttons.* The Show AutoCorrect smart button check box appears in Word, the Show AutoCorrect Options Buttons check box appears in PowerPoint, and Excel and Outlook don't have this check box. Select this check box to have the application display a small button under each item AutoCorrect changes. You can hold the mouse pointer over this button to make the application display a menu of AutoCorrect-related choices, such as stopping making this change. These buttons are usually helpful.

- *Correct TWo INitial CApitals.* Select this check box to have AutoCorrect apply lowercase to a second initial capital—for example, changing "THree" to "Three." This option is usually helpful.

- *Capitalize first letter of sentences.* Select this check box if you want AutoCorrect to automatically start each sentence (and paragraph) with a capital letter. Clear this check box if you prefer to write in fragments and then fix them afterward.

■ *Capitalize names of days.* Select this check box to have AutoCorrect automatically capitalize the first letter of the day names (for example, Sunday). This option is usually helpful.

■ *Capitalize first letter of table cell.* (Word only.) Select this check box if you want AutoCorrect to automatically capitalize the first letter of each entry in a table cell. Some people find this option helpful; others don't.

■ *Replace text as you type.* Select this check box to use AutoCorrect's main feature, replacing misspellings and contractions with their designated replacement text. You will want to use this feature to make the most of AutoCorrect.

■ *Automatically use suggestions from the spelling checker.* (Word only.) Select this check box to let the Replace text as you type feature use suggestions from the spelling checker as well as the entries in the list. This option is usually helpful too.

Choosing AutoFormat As You Type Options

The AutoFormat As You Type options are the ones that cause most surprises to Office users. These features try to apply necessary formatting as you work—without consulting you. You may well want to turn some or most of them off.

All four applications have AutoFormat As You Type options, but they put them in different places. Here are the details:

■ *Word.* Word has the most AutoFormat As You Type options. They appear on the AutoFormat As You Type tab of the AutoCorrect preferences pane (see Figure 2–16).

Figure 2–16. *You may want to turn off some of the AutoFormat As You Type options to avoid surprises. This is the AutoFormat As You Type tab in the AutoCorrect preferences pane for Word.*

- *Excel.* Excel's only AutoFormat As You Type option is the Replace Internet and network paths with hyperlinks check box, which appears in the AutoCorrect preferences pane (rather than on a tab).

- *PowerPoint.* The AutoFormat As You Type tab in PowerPoint's AutoCorrect preferences pane has two Replace As You Type options and two Apply As You Type Options.

- *Outlook.* The AutoFormat As You Type tab in the AutoCorrect preferences pane contains two AutoFormat As You Type options and five Replace As You Type options.

These are the options Word offers in the Apply as you type area of the AutoFormat As You Type tab:

■ *Headings.* Select this check box if you want AutoCorrect to automatically apply Word's heading styles when you create a short paragraph in the right way. For Heading 1 style, press the Return key twice, type the heading, and then press the Return key twice more. For Heading 2 style, press the Return key twice, press the Tab key, type the heading, and press the Return key twice more. For Heading 3 style, use two tabs, and for Heading 4 style, use three tabs. AutoCorrect removes the extra paragraphs and tabs when it makes the change. Chapter 6 shows you how to work with heading styles and other styles.

NOTE: The Apply as you type options can be useful once you know what they do and how they work. Until then, these options tend to cause surprise by making unwanted changes in your documents. If you don't find these options helpful, turn them off, like many people do.

■ *Borders.* Select this check box to have AutoCorrect apply border lines when you type three or more hyphens, underscores, asterisks, tildes, equal signs, or hash marks at the beginning of a paragraph and then press the Return key. Try these out to see the types of lines they produce.

■ *Tables.* Select this check box if you want to be able to create a table by typing a line of plus signs and hyphens. Each plus sign indicates a column border, so +--+----+--+ produces a three-column table. The number of hyphens indicates the relative width of the columns—in the previous example, the left column and right column are narrow (two hyphens each), while the middle column is wider (four hyphens).

■ *Automatic bulleted lists.* Select this check box if you want AutoCorrect to automatically apply a bulleted list style when you start a paragraph with an asterisk, a hyphen, or a greater-than sign followed by a space or tab.

■ *Automatic numbered lists.* Select this check box if you want AutoCorrect to automatically apply a numbered list style when you start a paragraph with a number or letter followed by a period or closing parenthesis and then type a space or tab.

These are the options that Word offers in the Replace as you type area:

■ *"Straight quotation marks" with "smart quotation marks".* Select this check box to have AutoCorrect replace straight-up-and-down quotation marks with smart, or "curly," quotation marks. This is usually helpful.

- *Ordinals (1st) with superscript.* Select this check box to have AutoCorrect apply superscript to the letters of ordinals (for example, 1st, 2nd). This option is useful when you need fully formatted documents. If you don't need superscripted ordinals, clear this check box.

- *Fractions (1/2) with fraction character (½).* Select this check box to have AutoCorrect insert real fraction characters in place of fractions you type. This too is usually helpful.

- **Bold* and _italic_ with real formatting.* Select this check box if you want to be able to apply bold by typing an asterisk before and after a word and to apply italics by typing an underscore before and after a word. These are long-standing Internet conventions for designating formatting in plain text, but usually it's easier to use keyboard shortcuts to apply the bold or italics.

- *Symbol characters (--) with symbols (—).* Select this check box to have AutoCorrect insert en dashes (–) in place of a hyphen preceded and followed by spaces and to have AutoCorrect insert em dashes (—) for two hyphens typed between words. This option is usually helpful.

- *Internet and network paths with hyperlinks.* Select this check box to have AutoCorrect insert a hyperlink when you type a URL (for example, `www.microsoft.com`) or a network path (for example, `\\server1\users`). This option is helpful only if you want live hyperlinks in your documents.

These are the options Word offers in the Automatically as you type area:

- *Define styles based on your formatting.* Select this check box only if you want AutoCorrect to automatically create styles when it thinks you need one. This feature is a recipe for confusion, so you'll probably want to clear this check box.

- *Tabs and backspace set left indent.* Select this check box to have AutoCorrect automatically move the left indent to the left when you press the Backspace key at the beginning of a blank paragraph and to move it to the right when you press the Tab key. This feature tends to cause formatting surprises, so you may want to turn it off. For example, in most word processing applications and text editors, you can press Backspace from the beginning of a paragraph to delete the previous paragraph mark, joining the two paragraphs. When this check box is selected, that Backspace press moves the left indent instead.

- *Format beginning of list item exactly like the one before it.* Select this check box to have AutoCorrect format the second and subsequent items in a list using the same formatting you've added to the beginning of the first item—for example, italic or bold. This setting can be useful when you override the standard formatting of the list, but you may find it easier to apply the formatting overrides yourself.

In PowerPoint, the AutoFormat As You Type tab contains four options:

- *Straight quotes with smart quotes.* Select this check box to have AutoCorrect replace straight-up-and-down quotation marks with smart quotation marks.

- *Internet and Network Paths with Hyperlinks.* As discussed earlier, select this check box to have PowerPoint automatically create links from Internet addresses and network paths.

- *Automatic Bulleted and Numbered Lists.* As discussed earlier, select this check box to have PowerPoint automatically create bulleted lists when you start a paragraph with a bullet-like character (such as *) and to create numbered lists when you start a paragraph with a numbering character (such as 1. or A.).

- *AutoFit body text to placeholder.* Select this check box if you want PowerPoint to automatically reduce the point size of text when it becomes too long to fit in a body placeholder. This option is often helpful, but you may prefer to edit the text down to size to keep it readable.

In Outlook, the AutoFormat tab of the AutoCorrect preferences pane contains two sets of options. The first set, Apply as you type, has two options:

- *Automatic bulleted lists.* Select this check box to make Outlook automatically create a bulleted list when you start a paragraph with a bullet-like character (such as *).

- *Automatic numbered lists.* Select this check box to make Outlook automatically create a numbered list when you start a paragraph with a numbering character (such as 1. or A.).

The second set of options on the AutoFormat tab of the AutoCorrect preferences pane in Outlook is the Replace as you type set, which contains the following options:

- *Dashes with n-dashes and m-dashes.* Select this check box to make AutoCorrect insert en dashes (–) in place of a hyphen preceded and followed by spaces and to make AutoCorrect insert em dashes (—) for two hyphens typed between words.

- *"..." with ellipses.* Select this check box to make Outlook replace three periods with an ellipsis character (…).

- **Bold* and _italic_ with real formatting.* Select this check box if you want to be able to apply bold by typing an asterisk before and after a word and if you want to apply italics by typing an underscore before and after a word. Usually, it's easier to apply bold or italics manually as needed—for example, press Cmd+B for bold or Cmd+I for italics.

- *Replace *** or —— with horizontal line (3 or more characters).* Select this check box to have Outlook create a decorative line when you type three asterisks (***) or three underscores (___) and then press the Return key.

- *Internet and network paths with hyperlinks.* Select this check box to have AutoCorrect insert a hyperlink when you type a URL (for example, `www.microsoft.com`) or a network path (for example, `\\server1\users`). This can be helpful when you need to enter hyperlinks in your messages.

NOTE: In Word, the AutoCorrect preferences pane also includes an AutoText tab. This tab contains options for creating AutoText entries, blocks of text, or other content that you can insert quickly in your documents. Chapter 6 shows you how to save time and effort by using AutoText.

Choosing Math AutoCorrect Options

Math AutoCorrect makes it easy to enter characters and symbols used in math in your Word documents. For example, you can type **\theta** to enter a lowercase theta character (θ) without visiting the Symbol dialog box. Math AutoCorrect comes with a long list of entries for math characters and symbols.

The Math AutoCorrect tab of the AutoCorrect preferences pane in Word (see Figure 2–17) lets you control whether and where to have AutoCorrect replace math terms with math symbols. If you use math in your documents, Math AutoCorrect can be a great time-saver; if you don't use math, turn it off by clearing the Replace text as you type check box on the Math AutoCorrect tab.

If you do use Math AutoCorrect, select the Use Math AutoCorrect rules outside of math regions check box if you want to use Math AutoCorrect anywhere in your documents. If you want to use Math AutoCorrect only in math areas, clear this check box.

Figure 2–17. *If you include math in your Word documents, choose whether to restrict Math AutoCorrect to math regions—areas in which you've inserted equations—and decide which items to replace as you type.*

These are the options you can choose on the Math AutoCorrect tab:

- *Replace text as you type.* Enables Word to replace the text items listed in the main box with their math replacements.

- *AutoCorrect items.* To add an item, type the abbreviation or text version in the Replace box, type or paste the replacement text in the With box, and then click the Add button.

- *Recognized Functions.* To change the list of math expressions that Word recognizes and doesn't automatically italicize, click the Recognized Functions button, and then work in the Recognized Math Functions dialog box that opens.

Creating AutoCorrect Entries

The Replace text as you type feature in AutoCorrect can save you a large amount of time and typing. To make the most of this powerful feature, you'll need to spend some time creating a list of entries that will fix your typing mistakes and expand abbreviations you define.

TIP: You can create standard AutoCorrect entries up to 255 characters long—enough for several sentences. Long AutoCorrect entries are great for quickly entering boilerplate text, such as addresses, company names, set phrases, or standard text for documents such as business letters or contracts. If you need to create longer AutoCorrect entries in Word, you can do so by creating formatted AutoCorrect entries, as you'll see shortly.

The basic way of creating an entry is to type the error or short version in the Replace text box and the replacement text in the With text box and then click the Add button. You can create an entry faster by pasting in the replacement text, which is especially handy if it's long.

NOTE: The quickest way of creating an AutoCorrect entry for a typo is by using the AutoCorrect option when checking spelling, as discussed elsewhere in this chapter.

Regular AutoCorrect entries are plain text, but in Word, you can create formatted AutoCorrect entries as well. A formatted AutoCorrect entry can contain not only formatted text but also other objects, such as tables, graphics, or equations. To create a formatted AutoCorrect entry, follow these steps:

1. In a document, create the replacement text and other items exactly as you want them to appear in the document after the AutoCorrect replacement. For example, type text and format it, add a graphic, or add a table.

2. Select everything you want to include in the AutoCorrect entry.

3. Choose Tools ➤ AutoCorrect from the menu bar to open the AutoCorrect dialog box. The first part of your selection appears in the With text box.

4. Make sure the Formatted text option button is selected. (If not, click it.)

5. Click the Add button to add the entry.

NOTE: Word stores formatted AutoCorrect entries in the Normal template (Normal.dotm), which it loads each time you launch the application. Depending on the options you've chosen for Word, you may see a prompt to save Normal when exiting Word after creating a formatted AutoCorrect entry. If you receive this prompt, click the Yes button to save the changes to Normal.

Creating AutoCorrect Exceptions

As well as AutoCorrect entries, you can create *AutoCorrect exceptions*—specific terms when you don't want AutoCorrect to replace text when it normally would. To create AutoCorrect exceptions, follow these steps:

1. Open the AutoCorrect Exceptions dialog box in one of these ways:

    - *Word or PowerPoint.* Click the Exceptions button on the AutoCorrect tab of the AutoCorrect preferences pane.

    - *Excel.* Click the Exceptions link under the Correct TWo INitial CApitals check box to display the INitial CAps tab) or the Capitalize first letter of sentences check box (to display the First Letter tab).

    - *Outlook.* Click the Exceptions button on the AutoCorrect tab of the AutoCorrect preferences pane.

2. Click the tab for the type of exception you want to work with:

    - *First Letter.* On this tab, list the terms that end with periods but after which you don't want the next word to start with a capital letter. Office starts you off with a list of built-in terms, such as vol. and wk. Figure 2–18 shows the First Letter tab of the AutoCorrect Exceptions dialog box in Word.

    - *INitial CAps.* On this tab, list the terms that start with two initial capital letters that you don't want AutoCorrect to reduce to a single capital—for example, IPv6.

    - *Other Corrections.* This tab appears only in Word. On it, list other terms that you don't want AutoCorrect to fix.

AutoCorrect Exceptions

| First Letter | INitial CAps | Other Corrections |

Don't capitalize after:

| inst. | | Add |

in.
inc.
incl.
incr.
int.
intl.

Remove

☑ **Automatically add words to list**

Cancel   OK

Figure 2–18. *In the AutoCorrect Exceptions dialog box, you can create lists of terms that you want AutoCorrect to ignore.*

3. Add and delete exceptions as needed:

    ■ *Add an exception.* Type it in the Don't capitalize after box or the Don't correct box (depending on the tab), and then click the Add button.

    ■ *Delete an exception.* Click it in the list box, and then click the Remove button.

4. In Word, select the Automatically add words to list check box if you want Word to automatically add exceptions when you undo a correction it has made.

5. When you have finished working with exceptions, click the OK button to close the AutoCorrect Exceptions dialog box. In Outlook, click the Close button.

Working with Smart Buttons

A *smart button* is a little button that an Office application inserts automatically in a document to indicate that you can take actions with a particular type of material. The smart button provides a pop-up menu of actions tailored to that type of content.

For example, Word and PowerPoint can display a smart button after replacing an AutoCorrect entry with its replacement text, in case you need to undo the correction or stop the application from using it in the future. And when you paste in text or other options, Word, Excel, and PowerPoint display a Paste Options smart button that provides different ways of pasting the text—for example, with or without formatting.

Figure 2–19 shows what you'll see when a smart button is available. This example is for AutoCorrect, but other smart buttons work in a similar way.

- At first, the application displays a light-blue line and a downward-pointing arrow below the correction to indicate that it has taken place. This line and arrow appear momentarily when the application makes the correction and then disappear. When you move the mouse pointer near the correction, they appear again.

- When you move the mouse pointer over the correction or the line and arrow, the application displays the AutoCorrect Options button.

- You can then click this button to display the menu of options—for AutoCorrect, undoing the correction, stopping the application from correcting it in future, or opening the AutoCorrect Options to make other changes.

Figure 2–19. *A smart button pops up when you move the mouse pointer over text with which you can perform specific actions. For example, the AutoCorrect Options button appears first as a blue line (top). When you move the mouse pointer over it, the full button appears (middle). You can click the button to display the actions (bottom).*

Checking Spelling and Grammar

To check that your documents are as correct as possible, you can check the spelling in them. Each of the Office applications lets you use the spelling checker, which is shared among the applications. Word and Outlook also have a grammar checker.

> **NOTE:** Computers are great at checking spelling, because in most cases, each word is spelled either correctly or incorrectly—there are few gray areas, and the spelling checker doesn't need to understand what the text means to evaluate the spelling. So, in most cases, it's a good idea to use the spelling checker to remove spelling mistakes from your documents. You still need to make sure that any suggested replacement is the right word—the spelling checker has minimal understanding of context, so don't accept its suggestions blindly.

Checking Spelling

In Word, PowerPoint, and Outlook, you can have the spelling checker check spelling either as you type or when you're ready to check the whole document. Excel doesn't offer on-the-fly checking, only full checking.

Checking Spelling as You Type

Word, PowerPoint, and Outlook can all check your spelling as you type. If you leave this checking turned on, the spelling checker puts a wavy red underline beneath any word whose spelling it thinks is wrong.

To check the spelling of a queried word, Ctrl+click or right-click the word, and then make one of the following choices from the context menu (see Figure 2–20):

- *Help.* Launches the application's Help file. This isn't usually helpful for dealing with spelling queries.
- *Replace the word.* Click one of the suggested words at the top of the context menu.
- *Ignore.* Ignore this instance of the apparently misspelled word, but question other instances.
- *Ignore All.* Ignore all instances of the apparently misspelled word in this document.
- *Add.* Add this word to your custom dictionary so that the spelling checker never queries it again.
- *AutoCorrect.* Create an AutoCorrect entry that will fix this typo in future. Click or highlight the AutoCorrect item on the context menu, and then click the correct word on the submenu. The application creates the AutoCorrect entry and corrects the word in the document.
- *Spelling.* Launch a full-scale spelling check (see the next section).

Rosa liked the sharpness of his mind.

Figure 2–20. *When checking spelling as you type, create an AutoCorrect entry for any spelling mistake you think you may repeat.*

Checking Spelling in the Whole Document

Instead of checking spelling as you type (or in addition to doing so), you can run a spell check at any time.

Before you start, position the insertion point or selection where you want to start the check.

Here are some examples:

- *Word.* Press Cmd+Home to move the insertion point to the start of the document.

- *Excel.* Click the cell in which you want to start the spell-check.

- *PowerPoint.* Click the slide at which you want to start the spell-check.

Open the Spelling and Grammar checker by pressing Cmd+Option+L or giving the appropriate command:

- *Word.* Choose Tools ➤ Spelling & Grammar from the menu bar.

- *Excel.* Choose Tools ➤ Spelling from the menu bar.

- *PowerPoint.* Choose Tools ➤ Spelling from the menu bar.

- *Outlook.* In a message window, choose Edit ➤ Spelling & Grammar ➤ Show Spelling and Grammar from the menu bar, or choose Options ➤ Spelling from the Ribbon.

The spelling checker displays its first query.

Figure 2–21 shows the Spelling and Grammar dialog box in Word. The Spelling dialog box in Excel and PowerPoint has most of the same features.

Figure 2–21. *The Spelling dialog box or Spelling and Grammar dialog box suggests ways to fix any problems it finds.*

NOTE: If the spelling checker finds nothing to query, it displays a dialog box telling you that the check is complete. Click the OK button to dismiss the dialog box.

You can now choose how to deal with each query. These are your options:

- *Ignore.* Click this button to ignore this instance of the word.

- *Ignore All.* Click this button to ignore all instances of the word in this document (but query it in other documents).

- *Add.* Click this button to add the word to your custom dictionary so that the spelling checker never queries it again.

- *Change.* In the Suggestions list box, click the word with which to replace the queried word, and then click this button to change this instance.

- *Change All.* In the Suggestions list box, click the replacement word, and then click this button to change all instances in the document.

- *AutoCorrect.* In the Suggestions list box, click the replacement word, and then click this button to create an AutoCorrect entry and to correct this instance.

> **TIP:** When you check spelling, create an AutoCorrect entry for any misspelling you think you may repeat. Each AutoCorrect entry may help only a little, but taken together, they can make a huge improvement in your typing speed and accuracy.

- *Options.* Click this button to open the Proofing pane in the application's Preferences dialog box or Preferences window with the Spelling options or Spelling and Grammar options displayed.

- *Undo.* Click this button to undo the last spelling change you made.

- *Cancel.* Click this button to end the spelling check before you've dealt with all the queries.

When you've dealt with one query, the spelling checker displays the next query. When the spelling checker reaches the end of the document after starting anywhere but the beginning, it asks whether you want to continue at the beginning. Figure 2–22 shows the dialog box you'll see in Excel. Click the Yes button or the No button, as appropriate.

Figure 2–22. *If you start checking from the middle of a document, the spelling checker prompts you to continue at the beginning.*

When you have dealt with every spelling query, the spelling checker lets you know that the check is complete (see Figure 2–23).

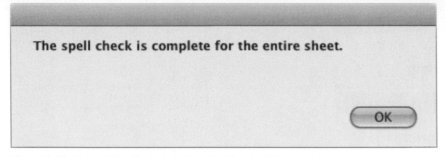

The spell check is complete for the entire sheet.

OK

Figure 2–23. *The spelling checker confirms that the check is complete.*

Checking Grammar in Word and Outlook

For documents you create in Word or outgoing messages you write in Outlook, you can check the grammar as well as the spelling. As with spelling, you can check grammar either as you type or in a separate operation when you're ready to review your document.

> **CAUTION:** Before using the grammar checker, make sure you understand how severe its limitations are. The grammar checker doesn't understand the meaning of the text, but it tries to identify the different parts of speech (nouns, verbs, and so on) and their relationship to each other. Many of the grammar checker's suggestions will not improve your documents. Its best features are identifying minor problems such as unsuitable words or missing punctuation. It is particularly unsuited for creative writing that bends the rules of grammar.

If you choose to use on-the-fly grammar checking, the grammar checker puts a wavy green underline under any text that it queries. This may be a word, a phrase, or an entire sentence or more, depending on what the query is. You can then Ctrl+click or right-click the underlined text and choose from the context menu (see Figure 2–24) what to do:

- *Help.* Opens the Help window. This isn't usually helpful for resolving grammar queries.

- *Replace the text with a suggestion.* If the grammar checker offers one or more suggestions at the top of the menu, as in Figure 2–24, click the one you want to use.

She buy tortillas every Monday.

Figure 2–24. *When using on-the-fly grammar checking, Ctrl+click or right-click a query to see what the problem is and whether the grammar checker has a suitable solution.*

- *Ignore.* Click this item to ignore this instance of the issue.

- *Grammar.* Click this item to open the Spelling and Grammar dialog box.

When you check grammar along with spelling, the grammar checker runs in tandem with the spelling checker, so you see queries from both of them in the Spelling and Grammar dialog box. Figure 2–25 shows an example of a grammar query.

Figure 2–25. *If you choose to check grammar, the grammar checker runs alongside the spelling checker and displays queries in the Spelling and Grammar dialog box.*

From the Spelling and Grammar dialog box, you can take the following actions:

- *Edit the text.* Click in the upper-left text box, and then type your fix for the problem. Click the Change button to apply the change in the document.

- *Ignore.* Click this button to ignore this grammar issue once.

- *Ignore All.* Click this button to ignore all instances of this grammar issue in this document.

- *Next Sentence.* Click this button to move to the next sentence, even if you haven't dealt with the current query.

- *Change.* If the Suggestions box contains a suitable suggestion, click it, and then click this button to replace the text.

- *Undo.* Click this button to undo the last change you've made.

- *Cancel.* Click this button to cancel the spelling and grammar check.

Controlling How the Spelling Checker Works in Word and PowerPoint

In Word and PowerPoint, you can control how the spelling checker works by setting options for it. It's worth spending a few moments doing this to get the spelling checker working the way you prefer.

To make the most of the spelling checker in Word, PowerPoint, or Outlook, spend a few minutes customizing its settings. Follow these steps:

1. Choose Word ➤ Preferences to display the Word Preferences dialog box or PowerPoint ➤ Preferences to display the PowerPoint Preferences dialog box.

NOTE: You can't set spelling options in Excel or Outlook.

2. Display the Spelling and Grammar preferences or the Spelling preferences:

- *Word.* Click the Spelling and Grammar icon in the Authoring and Proofing Tools section. Figure 2–26 shows the Spelling and Grammar preferences pane for Word.

Figure 2–26. *You can choose custom settings for the spelling checker and grammar checker in the Spelling and Grammar pane in the Word Preferences dialog box.*

■ *PowerPoint.* Click the Spelling button on the toolbar. Figure 2–27 shows the Spelling pane in the PowerPoint Preferences dialog box. As you can see, it contains around one-third of the options that Word has.

PowerPoint Preferences

| General | View | Edit | Save | Spelling | Ribbon | AutoCorrect | Compatibility | Advanced | Feedback |

Spelling

- ☑ Check spelling as you type
- ☐ Hide spelling errors
- ☑ Always suggest corrections
- ☑ Ignore words in UPPERCASE
- ☑ Ignore words with numbers
- ☑ Use German post-reform rules

French modes: [Traditional and new spellings ▲▼]

Cancel   OK

Figure 2–27. *PowerPoint has a much smaller selection of spelling options than Word.*

TIP: You can also open the Spelling preferences by clicking the Options button in the Spelling and Grammar dialog box in Word or the Spelling dialog box in PowerPoint.

3. To control the spelling checker, choose options in the Spelling area:

- *Check spelling as you type.* (Word and PowerPoint.) Select this check box if you want the spelling checker to check spelling continually as you type. The spelling checker puts a wavy red underline under any word it queries. Clear this check box if you prefer to check spelling in a separate operation.

- *Hide spelling errors.* (Word and PowerPoint.) Select this check box if you want to hide spelling errors in the document. Outlook doesn't have this option. In Word, this check box is the Hide spelling errors in this document check box.

- *Always suggest corrections.* (Word and PowerPoint.) Select this check box to have the Spelling and Grammar dialog box or Spelling dialog box suggest corrections for spelling queries. This is usually helpful but may slow down an aging Mac that's struggling to run Office.

- *Suggest from main dictionary only.* (Word only.) Select this check box if you want spelling suggestions only from Office's main dictionary file, not from custom dictionaries you create. Usually, you'll want to clear this check box so that the spelling checker uses your custom dictionaries as well.

- *Ignore words in UPPERCASE.* (Word and PowerPoint.) Select this check box if you want the spelling checker to skip words that appear in uppercase. This is usually helpful, because it helps you avoid queries on technical terms.

- *Ignore words with numbers.* (Word and PowerPoint.) Select this check box to have the spelling checker skip any word that includes numbers (for example, IPv6). Clear this check box if you tend to get number typos in words and need the spelling checker to help root them out.

- *Ignore Internet and file addresses.* (Word and PowerPoint.) Select this check box to make the spelling checker ignore any URLs (for example, `www.apress.com`) and file addresses (for example, `\\server2\reference\manual.pdf`). This option too is usually helpful.

- *Flag repeated words.* (Word only.) Select this check box to allow the spelling checker to query a word that appears twice in succession. This option is good at picking up useless duplication, though you may sometimes need to approve a deliberate repetition.

- *Use German post-reform rules.* (Word and PowerPoint.) Select this check box if you need to use post-Reform German spelling rather than traditional spelling in German-language documents.

- *Enforce accented uppercase in French.* (Word only.) Select this check box if your documents use a French dialect (such as Canadian French) that retains accents on uppercase letters rather than removing the accents (as in standard French).

- *Russian: Enforce strict ë.* (Word only.) Select this check box to make the spelling checker enforce the use of the ë character in Russian-language documents.

- *French Modes.* (Word and PowerPoint.) In this pop-up menu, choose which spelling type you want the spelling checker to use: Traditional and new spellings, Traditional spelling, or New spelling.

- *Spanish Modes.* (Word only.) In this pop-up menu, choose whether to use the Tuteo verb forms, the Voseo verb forms, or both for the second person. The choices are Tuteo verb forms only, Tuteo and Voseo verb forms, and Voseo verb forms only.

- *Portuguese Modes.* (Word only.) In this pop-up menu, choose whether to use Post-reform rules, Pre-reform rules, or Both in Portuguese-language documents.

- *Brazilian Modes.* (Word only.) In this pop-up menu, choose whether to use Post-reform rules, Pre-reform rules, or Both in documents that use Brazilian Portuguese.

- *Custom dictionary.* (Word only.) In this pop-up menu, select the custom dictionary you want to add words to when you use the Add command when checking spelling. For information on how to use custom dictionaries, see the section "Taking Control over Spelling Checks with Custom Dictionaries" later in this chapter.

4. To control grammar checking in Word, choose settings for the following options:

- *Check grammar as you type.* Select this check box if you want the grammar checker to raise queries as you work. The grammar checker puts a wavy green underline under items it queries. On-the-fly grammar checking tends to be distracting, so you'll probably want to clear this check box.

- *Show grammatical errors in Notebook Layout View.* Select this check box if you want to display grammatical errors when you're using Notebook Layout view. Often, it's useful to hide the grammatical errors in this view so that you can take notes without the grammar checker hassling you. (Turning the grammar checker off may be an even better choice.)

- *Hide grammatical errors in this document.* Select this check box if you want to hide the display of grammar queries in the document without turning off grammar checking. You can then display the grammar queries when you want to deal with them.

- *Check grammar with spelling.* Select this check box if you want to use the grammar checker. Otherwise, clear it.

- *Show readability statistics.* Select this check box if you want the spelling checker to display the Readability Statistics dialog box when it finishes a spelling check.

> **TIP:** Don't bother with the readability statistics. The counts of words, characters, paragraphs, and sentences can be useful, but you can get the first three more easily in the Word Count dialog box (click the Words readout on the status bar or choose Tools ➤ Word Count from the menu bar). The averages of sentences per paragraph, words per sentence, and characters per word have little relevance. The Passive Sentences, Flesch Reading Ease, and Flesch-Kincaid Grade Level are computed statistics that don't accurately assess how easy or hard the document is to read. If you want to know whether a document is hard to understand, ask a colleague to read it.

5. For Word, you can also choose grammar and style options. See the next section for details.

6. When you've finished choosing options for the spelling checker, click the OK button to close the Preferences dialog box.

Choosing Grammar and Style Options for Word and Outlook

When choosing proofing options for Word in the Spelling and Grammar dialog box, you can also choose options for the grammar checker.

If you turn on the grammar checker by selecting the Check grammar with spelling check box (and the Check grammar as you type check box if you want ongoing error checking as well), you can choose the type of checking you want in the Writing style pop-up menu in the Spelling and Grammar pane or in the Grammar Settings dialog box (see Figure 2–28). Usually, it's easiest to click the Settings button to display the Grammar Settings dialog box, which shows the details of the settings.

Figure 2–28. *Use the Grammar Settings dialog box to control which grammar and style issues the grammar checker raises when checking your documents.*

The grammar checker offers five degrees of checking for different needs:

- *Casual.* Choose this setting to check only for essentials: capitalization issues, commonly confused words, misused words, subject-verb agreement, and verb and noun phrases.

- *Standard.* Choose this setting to check using rules appropriate for standard documents—for example, general writing.

- *Formal.* Choose this setting to check using formal rules. This setting makes the grammar checker check for everything it knows about except for gender-specific words (such as *he* and *she*) and the use of the first person (*I*).

- *Technical.* Choose this setting to check using rules suited to technical writing. This setting makes the grammar checker check for most offenses it knows about, but not for passive sentences, possessives and plurals, contractions, gender-specific words, jargon, more than three successive nouns, more than three successive prepositional phrases, or infinitives split by more than one word.

- *Custom.* Choose this setting to choose which items to check. Word selects all the Grammar and style options check boxes except the Use of first person check box. You can then clear each check box you don't want to use.

- *Grammar Only.* The grammar checker checks for grammatical problems such as fragments of sentences (rather than complete sentences), misused capitalization and punctuation, and verbs not agreeing with their subjects (for example, "if they buys eggs").

- *Grammar & Style.* The grammar checker also tries to assess your document for clichés, gender-specific words, passive sentences, unclear phrasing, and a dozen or so other potential problems.

The Writing style pop-up menu at the top shows the same setting as the Writing Style pop-up menu in the Spelling and Grammar pane. This pop-up menu acts as the master control for the check boxes in the Grammar and style options list box. You can then select or clear check boxes as needed to fine-tune the checking.

Whichever writing style you choose in the Writing style pop-up menu, take a moment to set the three options in the Require area:

- *Comma required before last list item.* Choose the Always setting to make the grammar checker check for the serial comma (for example, "Peter, Paul, and Mary" rather than "Peter, Paul and Mary"), as is widely used in U.S. English. Choose the Never setting if you want to make sure you don't use the serial comma. Choose the Don't check setting if you don't want to check for this.

- *Punctuation required with quotes.* Choose the Inside setting to make the grammar checker check that punctuation appears inside quotes. Choose the Outside setting to make the grammar checker check that punctuation appears outside quotes. Or choose the Don't check setting to skip checking punctuation placement around quotes.

- *Spaces required between sentences.* Choose the 1 setting to make the grammar checker enforce one space between sentences, as is widely used. Choose the 2 setting to use two spaces between sentences, as some style guides recommend. Choose the Don't check setting to prevent the grammar checker from checking this.

When you have finished choosing grammar and style options, click the OK button to close the Grammar Settings dialog box.

Taking Control over Spelling Checks with Custom Dictionaries

The spelling checker uses a dictionary file for the language you've chosen (for example, U.S. English). The dictionary file consists of a list of words that are spelled correctly; unlike a conventional dictionary, the file doesn't contain definitions for the words.

You can't change the main dictionary file, but you can add to it by creating custom dictionaries containing words you don't want the spelling checker to query. For example, you may need to include technical terms in your documents that the main dictionary file doesn't contain.

Understanding How Custom Dictionaries Work

Office starts you off with a custom dictionary named Custom Dictionary. Office stores this dictionary in your ~/Library/Preferences/Microsoft/Office 2011/ folder (where the tilde, ~, represents your home folder) and sets the Office applications to add words to it automatically during spelling checks. So when you give the Add command as described earlier in this chapter, the spelling checker adds the word to your custom dictionary.

You can stick with using just this Custom Dictionary file if you want, but it's often useful to create extra custom dictionaries that contain different types of terms. You can then choose which custom dictionaries to load for a particular project. For example, you may work on some technical documents that need the spelling checker to accept various technical terms, but you may want the spelling checker to query the same terms in your other documents.

Normally, you'll just add words to your custom dictionaries, but you may sometimes need to remove words you've added and no longer want the spelling checker to accept.

Coming to Grips with Your Custom Dictionaries

Office provides the Custom Dictionaries dialog box for creating, editing, and managing custom dictionaries. Here's how to open the Custom Dictionaries dialog box:

1. In Word, choose Word ➤ Preferences to display the Word Preferences dialog box.

2. Click the Spelling and Grammar icon in the Authoring and Proofing Tools section to display the Spelling and Grammar pane.

3. Click the Dictionaries button to display the Custom Dictionaries dialog box (shown in Figure 2–29 with several dictionaries already added).

Figure 2–29. *Use the Custom Dictionaries dialog box in Word to create, edit, and manage your custom dictionaries.*

Creating a Custom Dictionary

To create a new custom dictionary, follow these steps in the Custom Dictionaries dialog box:

1. Click the New button to open the New Dictionary dialog box. Except for its name, this dialog box is the Save As dialog box that you're familiar with.

2. In the Save As text box, type the name you want to give the new dictionary. You can use pretty much any name you want as long as there's no file of that name in the folder you use.

3. If necessary, change the folder. The default folder, the `~/Library/Preferences/Microsoft/Office 2011/`, is usually the best place unless you need to share the dictionary with others—in which case, use a network folder rather than a folder on your Mac.

4. Click the Save button. The application closes the New Dictionary dialog box and creates the dictionary. The dictionary appears in the list box in the Custom Dictionaries dialog box

5. Select the check box next to the dictionary.

The dictionary is now ready for use, but you may need to change its language. Word chooses the (none) setting in the Language pop-up menu, which sets the dictionary for use with all languages (by not restricting it to a particular language). If you want to restrict the dictionary to a particular language, click the dictionary in the list box, and then choose the language from the Language pop-up menu.

> **NOTE:** If you already have a custom dictionary file (for example, one your company has created), click the Add button in the Custom Dictionaries dialog box. In the Add Dictionary dialog box, select the dictionary file, and then click the Open button. The dictionary then appears in the list box in the Custom Dictionaries dialog box, and you can select its check box to make it active.

Adding Words to or Removing Words from a Custom Dictionary

Normally, you'll build a custom dictionary one word at a time by using the Add command when checking spelling. But you can also open a custom dictionary file for editing so that you can make wider-ranging changes to it. This is useful when you need to add a whole list of words to the dictionary or when you need to remove a word that you've added by mistake.

To edit a custom dictionary, follow these steps from the Custom Dictionaries dialog box:

1. Click the custom dictionary in the list box.

2. Click the Edit button to open the dictionary for editing. Word opens the dictionary in a document window, just like any other document (see Figure 2–30).

> **NOTE:** If you're using automatic spell checking, when you open a dictionary for editing, Word displays a dialog box warning you that it will turn off automatic spell checking. Click the OK button to proceed. After editing the dictionary, you'll need to turn automatic spell checking back on—if you don't, Word will leave it turned off.

Figure 2–30. *When you open a dictionary file for editing, Word uses a regular document window rather than a special dialog box. Word turns off as-you-type spelling checking, but if the grammar checker is turned on, it will query errors such as the incomplete sentences this dictionary appears to suffer from.*

3. Change the list of words by using standard editing techniques. Type each entry in a separate paragraph, pressing the Return key to create a new paragraph.

NOTE: If you haven't turned off as-you-type grammar checking, the grammar checker will likely mark each dictionary entry as an incomplete sentence. Either turn off as-you-type grammar checking or grin and bear the wavy green underlines.

4. Click the Save button on the Standard toolbar (or choose File ➤ Save or press Cmd+S) to save the dictionary. Word displays the Continue with Save? dialog box (see Figure 2–31).

Figure 2–31. *The Continue with Save? dialog box, which appears when you save a dictionary file, tries to alert you to a problem that doesn't exist. Click the Yes button to save the dictionary file in the Speller Custom Dictionary format.*

5. Click the Yes button. Word saves the dictionary file.

6. Click the Close button on the title bar to close the dictionary file.

> **NOTE:** If Word turned off automatic spell checking when you opened the dictionary for editing, turn it back on when you've finished editing. Choose Word ➤ Preferences to open the Preferences dialog box, and then click the Spelling and Grammar icon to display the Spelling and Grammar pane of the Preferences dialog box. Select the Check spelling as you type check box, and then click the OK button to close the Preferences dialog box.

Turning Off, Removing, or Deleting a Custom Dictionary

When you want to stop using a custom dictionary for the time being, clear its check box in the list box in the Custom Dictionaries dialog box. The dictionary remains in the list, and you can start using it again at any point by selecting its check box.

If you want to remove a custom dictionary from the list, click it in the list box, and then click the Remove button. The application removes the dictionary from the list, but its dictionary file remains in its current folder. If you need to start using the dictionary again, you can add it by clicking the Add button.

If you want to dispose of a custom dictionary, remove it as just described. Then open a Finder window to the folder that contains the file, and move the file to the Trash.

Printing Documents

These days, you'll probably share documents with others via e-mail frequently, but there will still be times when you need to print out hard copies of documents to share. For example, you may need to print letters or papers you write in Word, print a page of an Excel spreadsheet, or print a handout for a PowerPoint presentation.

In each of the Office applications, you can choose from a wide range of printing options to make the printout look the way you want.

Printing a Full Copy of the Document Quickly

Sometimes you'll need straightforward printing—one copy of the whole document on your default printer. To get this, click the Print button on the Standard toolbar in Word, Excel, or PowerPoint.

> **NOTE:** In Outlook, clicking the Print button on the toolbar displays the Print dialog box rather than printing a single copy of the selected item.

Printing Exactly What You Need

When you need to set options for printing, open the Print dialog box by choosing File ➤ Print or by pressing the standard Cmd+P keyboard shortcut. In Outlook, you can also click the Print button on the Standard toolbar to open the Print dialog box.

At first, each application usually displays the Print dialog box at its smaller size (see Figure 2–32). From here, you can take essential actions such as changing the printer, choosing a preset set of printing options, or previewing the document. But usually you'll want to expand the dialog box by clicking the button to the right of the Printer pop-up menu so that you can see the quick preview and all the available options.

Figure 2–32. *If the Print dialog box opens at its small size, click the button to the right of the Printer pop-up menu to expand it to its full size.*

Figure 2–33 shows the full-size Print dialog box for Word. The Print dialog box in each application is different, because it contains controls suited to the document type that application produces. For example, in Word you can choose which pages to print and whether to include comments and tracked changes, while in PowerPoint you can choose which slides to print and whether to frame the slides. But in each case the basics are the same.

Figure 2–33. *When you need to print only part of a document or print multiple copies, open the Print dialog box and choose the appropriate settings. This is the Print dialog box for Word.*

We'll look at the application-specific options in the chapters on the individual applications. But these are the basic moves that you can use in any of the applications:

- *Choose the printer.* Open the Printer pop-up menu and choose the printer to use. If you need to add a printer, click the Add Printer item on this menu.

> **TIP:** Mac OS X lets you either set a particular printer as your default printer or print to whichever printer you last used. To adjust this setting, open the Printer pop-up menu in the Print dialog box, and then click Print & Fax Preferences to display the Print & Fax pane in System Preferences. Open the Default Printer pop-up menu, and then choose either the printer you want or the Last Printer Used setting. Choose System Preferences ➤ Quit System Preferences to quit System Preferences.

- *Choose a preset.* Open the Presets pop-up menu and choose the preset group of settings to use. Normally, you'll find the Presets pop-up menu contains only the Standard preset and the Last Used Settings preset until you define your own presets.

> **TIP:** When you've chosen a group of printing settings you'd like to use again, create a preset for them. Open the Presets pop-up menu and click Save As to display the Save Preset As dialog box. Type the name for the preset in the Preset Name box. In the Preset Available For area, select the Only this printer option button or the All printers option button. Then click the OK button to close the dialog box. The application adds the preset to the Presets pop-up menu, and it's ready for use.

- *Change the number of copies.* To print more than one copy, type the number in the Copies box. If you want the sheets of each copy in order (1,2,3), select the Collated check box; clear this check box if you want all the copies of each page together.

- *Create a PDF of the document.* To create a file in the widely used Portable Document Format (PDF), click the PDF button, and then click Save as PDF in the pop-up menu. In the Save dialog box (see Figure 2–34), specify the file name in the Save As box and the folder either in the Where pop-up menu or in the navigation pane. Then enter any metadata the document needs: the title, author, subject, and keywords (press the Return key after each keyword to create a keyword button). If you want to secure the PDF with a password for opening or printing it, click the Security Options button, and then work in the PDF Security Options dialog box. When you're ready to save the PDF, click the Save button. The application automatically closes the Print dialog box for you.

Figure 2–34. *In the Save dialog box, you can add a title, author, subject, and any keywords needed to a PDF file you're creating from an Office document.*

> **TIP:** If you just need to e-mail a PDF version of the document without adding metadata or applying a password, you can save a step by choosing the Mail PDF command from the PDF pop-up menu in the Print dialog box. The application creates a new message in your default e-mail application (for example, Outlook) and attaches a PDF file of the document to the message.

- *Preview the document.* In Word, Excel, and PowerPoint, the full-size Print dialog box displays a quick preview unless you clear the Quick Preview check box; in Outlook, the full-size Print dialog box always displays the quick preview. To see more detail, click the Preview button. The application creates a preview of the document and displays it in the Preview application. Choose Preview ➤ Quit Preview when you've finished examining the preview.

- *Print the document.* When you've chosen the settings you want, click the Print button. The application closes the Print dialog box and sends the details of the print job to the print queue for the printer.

Summary

In this chapter, you learned how to use several common features of the Office applications. You now know how to control applications using the menus, the toolbars, and the Ribbon; how to use the common palettes in the Toolbox; and how to share your documents quickly and easily with other people in formats they can read.

You also looked at ways to save time and effort by using the AutoCorrect feature and those AutoFormat options that you find helpful (while turning off any options that cause unpleasant surprises as you work). You can now choose settings for the spelling checker and grammar checker, run one or both, and choose which of its suggestions to accept and which to reject. And you know how to preview your documents and print them.

In the next chapter, I'll show you further vital skills for making the most of the Office applications: how to work with text; use Office's powerful version of Cut, Copy, and Paste; and create tables and hyperlinks.

Chapter 3

Working with Text

In this chapter, I'll show you how to work with text in the Office applications. As you'll see, the operations are almost the same for each application, so once you learn to work with text in one application, you'll be able to work with text in each of the other applications too.

You'll start with entering text itself by using the keyboard or other means. Then you'll move to navigating with the keyboard and selecting objects. You'll then be ready to learn to apply direct formatting to text and objects; use the Cut, Copy, and Paste features; and use the core Find and Replace features that the applications share. I'll then show you how to create tables, enter text in them, and format them to look good. Finally, you'll learn to add to your Office documents hyperlinks that lead the user to another document, take them to a web site, or start a new e-mail message automatically.

Entering Text in Your Documents

The main way of entering text in your Office documents is by typing it with the keyboard, but you can also paste text from other documents, scan documents and use optical character recognition (OCR) to identify the text in them, or use speech recognition. And some documents will likely need symbols that don't appear on the keyboard.

Entering Text in Documents Using Copy and Paste

To enter text using Copy and Paste, copy the text from the document that contains it, and then paste it into the Office document. See the section "Using Cut, Copy, and Paste" later in this chapter.

Entering Text by Scanning a Document and Using Optical Character Recognition

If you have a document that contains the text you want to use in an Office document, you can scan the text using a scanner and then use optical character recognition to get the text out of the picture file that the scanner produces.

To perform the scanning, you'll need a scanner and third-party OCR software such as OmniPage Pro X (www.nuance.com) or Readiris Pro (www.irislink.com). And to use the text from a hard-copy document in a document of your own, you will typically need to get permission from the copyright holder.

CAUTION: When you use OCR to recognize a document, always read through the resulting text and compare it to the original. Although OCR does its best to recognize the text accurately, it often introduces errors—sometimes surprising ones.

Entering Text by Using Speech Recognition

If you have a third-party speech-recognition application such as MacSpeech Dictate (www.macspeech.com), you can use it both to control the Office applications and to insert text in them.

TIP: Always use a headset microphone for speech recognition, because you will get much better results from having the microphone positioned consistently close to your mouth to pick up your voice clearly. Place the microphone to the side of your mouth rather than in front of it so that it doesn't pick up your breath stream.

When you use speech recognition, proofread your documents closely to catch substitutions of words and phrases. Simple mistakes such as substituting *can* for *can't* are usually easy enough to catch, but if the speech-recognition application replaces a whole phrase, you may have a hard time working out how the text should actually read.

Inserting Symbols in a Document

By typing, you can easily insert any characters that appear on your keyboard—but many documents need other symbols, such as letters with dieresis marks over them (for example, Ä or ë) or ligatures that bind two characters (for example, Æ).

You can quickly insert one or more symbols in a Word document, Excel workbook, or PowerPoint presentation by using the Symbol Browser pane in the Media Browser. In Word, you can also use the Symbol dialog box, which gives you access to a wider range of symbols.

NOTE: When you insert a symbol using the Symbol Browser, the application inserts the symbol character in the same font you're currently using—if that font contains that character. If not, the Symbol Browser substitutes a font that does have the character. By contrast, when you use the Symbol dialog box, you can see exactly which symbols are available for a specific font.

Inserting a Symbol Using the Symbol Browser Pane

You can use the Symbol Browser pane in the Media Browser to insert a symbol in Word, Excel, or PowerPoint. To insert a symbol, follow these steps:

1. In the document, position the insertion point where you want the symbol to appear.

2. Open the Symbol Browser (see Figure 3–1) in one of these ways:

    ■ *Word.* Choose Insert ➤ Symbol ➤ Symbol Browser.

    ■ *Excel or PowerPoint.* Choose Insert ➤ Symbol.

    ■ *Any application.* Click the Media Browser button on the Standard toolbar, and then click the Symbols tab.

Figure 3–1. *To insert a symbol in a document in Word, Excel, or PowerPoint, click the symbol in the Symbol Browser in the Media Browser. Choose the All Symbols item in the pop-up menu to browse all symbols (left), or select only the set you're interested in (right).*

3. Find the symbol you want in one of these ways:

   ■ *Browse all symbols.* Choose All Symbols in the pop-up menu at the top of the Symbol Browser, and then scroll down.

> **TIP:** Drag the slider at the bottom of the Symbol Browser if you want to zoom in to see the symbols larger or zoom out to see more symbols at once.

   ■ *Display only a set of symbols.* Open the pop-up menu at the top of the Symbol Browser, and then click the set you want. For example, click the Greek set to display Greek characters.

4. Click the symbol to insert it in the document.

5. Leave the Symbol Browser open if you need to insert more symbols or other media objects. Otherwise, click the Media Browser's Close button (the button at the left end of the title bar) to close it.

Inserting a Symbol or Special Character Using the Symbol Dialog Box in Word

When you want to reach the full range of symbols that Word has to offer, use the Symbol dialog box instead of the Symbol Browser pane. The Symbol dialog box also contains a pane called Special Characters that lets you quickly insert widely used symbols such as dashes and copyright characters.

To insert a symbol using the Symbol dialog box, follow these steps:

1. Choose Insert ➤ Symbol ➤ Advanced Symbol to display the Symbol dialog box (see Figure 3–2).

Figure 3–2. *The Symbol dialog box in Word gives you access to a wide range of symbols and special characters. Click a character to display a larger preview, as shown here.*

2. Open the Font pop-up menu, and then click the font you want to use. The item named "(normal text)" that appears at the top of the list shows the symbol characters in the font you're using.

3. If you need to see a larger version of a symbol, click it to display a preview box.

TIP: After clicking a symbol to display its preview, you can continue to hold down the mouse button and drag in any direction to preview other symbols. This trick is useful when you're looking for a symbol that's hard to distinguish from similar symbols around it.

4. To insert a symbol, click it, and then click the Insert button; you can also simply double-click the symbol. When you insert a symbol, the Symbol dialog box remains open, but the Cancel button changes to a Close button.

5. Insert other symbols as needed.

TIP: You can continue to work in the Word document while the Symbol dialog box is open. For example, you can type some text in the document, or reposition the insertion point, and then click in the Symbol dialog box and use it to insert another symbol character.

6. Click the Close button to close the Symbol dialog box.

To insert a special character, open the Symbol dialog box by choosing Insert ➤ Symbol ➤ Advanced Symbol, and then click the Special Characters tab (see Figure 3–3). Click the character you want to insert, and then click the Insert button—or, as before, double-click the character you want to insert. Click the Close button to close the Symbol dialog box.

Figure 3–3. *The Symbol dialog box includes the Special Characters tab, which gives you quick access to widely used symbols such as em dashes and en dashes, optional hyphens, and fixed-width spaces.*

When you've selected a symbol or special character in the Symbol dialog box, you can click the AutoCorrect button to start creating an AutoCorrect entry for that character or the Keyboard Shortcut button to start creating a keyboard shortcut for it.

> **TIP:** If you often use the same words that include symbols or special characters, create an AutoCorrect entry for each of those words. This is usually much easier than using an AutoCorrect entry to enter a particular character within a word.

Navigating with the Keyboard and Selecting Objects

In Mac OS X, the main means of moving around in a document is by using the mouse. For example, you can click an object to select it, drag the scroll box down the scroll bar to move down the document, or click to place the insertion point where you want to type text.

When you're typing in a document, you may find it handier to use the keyboard to move the insertion point. Table 3–1 explains the standard keyboard shortcuts you can use to move the insertion point in the Office applications.

NOTE: Because Excel's worksheets consist of cells rather than containing paragraphs, many of the keyboard shortcuts have different effects in Excel.

Table 3–1. *Keyboard Shortcuts for Moving the Insertion Point in the Office Applications*

Press These Keys	To Move the Insertion Point Like This
Left arrow	One character to the left
Right arrow	One character to the right
Up arrow	Up one line, paragraph, or cell
Down arrow	Down one line, paragraph, or cell
Home	To the start of the line or object
End	To the end of the line or object
Cmd+Home	To the start of the document
Cmd+End	To the end
Option+Left arrow	To the beginning of the current word (if the insertion point is in a word) or to the beginning of the previous word
Option+Right arrow	To the beginning of the next word

To work with text or an object in a document, you select that text or object by using the mouse or the keyboard:

- *Select with the mouse.* Click at the beginning of what you want to select, hold down the mouse pointer, and then drag to the end of the selection.

- *Select with the mouse and keyboard.* Click to place the insertion point at the beginning of what you want to select. Hold down the Shift key, and click at the end of the selection.

- *Select with the keyboard.* Move the insertion point to the beginning of the selection, hold down the Shift key, and then move the insertion point to the end of the selection (for example, by pressing the arrow keys).

TIP: In Word, you can also select multiple items at once. Select the first item as usual, using either the mouse or the keyboard. Then hold down the Cmd key as you select each of the other items with the mouse.

Applying Direct Formatting to Text and Objects

Each of the Office applications lets you apply a wide range of formatting to the text and objects you add to your documents. Each application has different types of formatting suited to its needs, but all the applications support direct formatting—formatting that you apply directly to text or to an object, such as bold and italic.

NOTE: Direct formatting is easy to use, but in Word and Excel, you can save time by formatting with styles instead. A *style* is a collection of formatting that you can apply in a single click. Not only can you apply formatting more quickly with styles, but you can also change the style's formatting and have the application automatically apply the change to the text that uses the style. This saves even more time and keeps your documents consistent.

The easiest way of applying most direct formatting is by using the controls and buttons on the Formatting toolbar. If the Formatting toolbar isn't displayed, choose View ➤ Toolbars ➤ Formatting to display it (clicking to put a check mark next to the Formatting item on the Toolbars submenu).

Figure 3–4 shows the Formatting toolbar for Word (shown as a floating toolbar so the buttons are easier to see). The Formatting toolbars in Excel and PowerPoint contain many of the same commands.

Figure 3–4. *You can apply direct formatting quickly by using the Formatting toolbar. This is the Formatting toolbar for Word, shown floating rather than docked to the document window.*

You can also apply the most widely used types of direct formatting from the Home tab of the Ribbon. Word, Excel, and PowerPoint all have a Font group on the Home tab, and Outlook has a similar but unnamed group. Word and PowerPoint also have a Paragraph group for applying paragraph formatting. Figure 3–5 shows the Home tab in PowerPoint with the Font group labeled.

Figure 3–5. *The Font group on the Home tab of the Ribbon includes widely used formatting tools.*

The Paragraph group on the Home tab of the Ribbon in Word and PowerPoint contains controls for formatting paragraphs. Figure 3–6 shows the Paragraph group in Word.

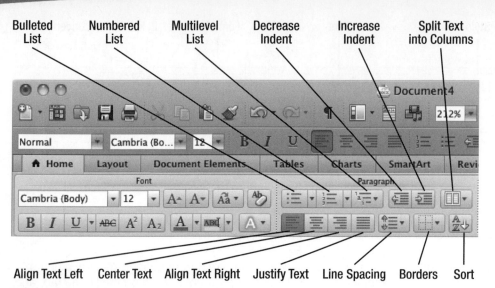

Figure 3–6. *The Paragraph group on the Home tab of the Ribbon in Word and PowerPoint provides essential commands for applying direct formatting to paragraphs.*

With a few exceptions, the controls in these groups are for applying direct formatting. And they're easy to use. In most cases, you select the text or other object you want to affect and then click the button. Here are some examples:

- *Apply bold.* Select the text you want to affect, or click in a single word. Then click the Bold button to apply bold. Click again to remove bold.

- *Change the font.* Select the text you want to affect. Click the Font pop-up menu, and then click the font name you want.

- *Change the font size.* Select the text you want to affect, then click the Font Size pop-up menu, and finally click the point size you want: 8, 9, 10, 11, 12, 14, 16, 18, 20, or whatever. For a quick change, click the Increase Font Size button to move up one of the steps in the Font Size pop-up menu (for example, from 9 to 10 points or from 18 to 20 points), or click the Decrease Font Size button to move down one size.

- *Change the alignment.* Click in the paragraph or click the object you want to affect, and then click the Align Text Left button, the Center Text button, the Align Text Right button, or the Justify Text button, as needed.

You can also apply widely used direct formatting by using keyboard shortcuts. Table 3–2 lists the most useful keyboard shortcuts for applying direct formatting.

Table 3–2. *Keyboard Shortcuts for Applying Direct Formatting*

Formatting Type	Keyboard Shortcut
Bold	Cmd+B
Italic	Cmd+I
Underline	Cmd+U
Subscript	Cmd+=
Superscript	Cmd++ (in other words, Cmd+Shift+=)
Grow font by one increment	Cmd+Shift+>
Shrink font by one increment	Cmd+Shift+<
Align left	Cmd+L
Align right	Cmd+R
Center	Cmd+E

Using Cut, Copy, and Paste

If you've worked with Mac OS X applications before, you're almost certainly familiar with the Cut, Copy, and Paste features. You can use these features as usual in the Office applications, but you can also use the special Clipboard the applications share.

Using Standard Cut, Copy, and Paste in the Office Applications

You can use Cut, Copy, and Paste as usual in the Office applications by using either keyboard shortcuts or the buttons on the Standard toolbar (see Figure 3–7):

- *Cut.* Click the Cut button or press Cmd+X.
- *Copy.* Click the Copy button or press Cmd+C.
- *Paste.* Click the Paste button or press Cmd+V.

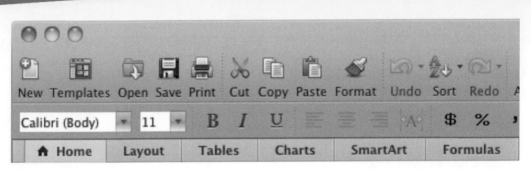

Figure 3–7. *You can perform Cut, Copy, and Paste operations by using the Cut, Copy, and Paste buttons on the Standard toolbar.*

After you paste text or an object, you can use the smart button that the application displays to change the way in which you pasted it. For example, in Word, the smart button's pop-up menu (see Figure 3–8) frequently offers these choices:

- *Keep Source Formatting.* Click this item to maintain the formatting of the item you've pasted.

- *Match Destination Formatting.* Click this item to make the pasted item take on the formatting of the paragraph or object into which you've pasted it.

- *Keep Text Only.* Click this item to keep only the text of the pasted item, discarding all formatting and any nontext objects (such as graphics).

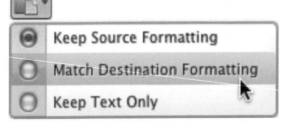

Figure 3–8. *After pasting an item, you can use the smart button to change the formatting used. This is the smart-button menu you'll often see in Word.*

NOTE: When you need to copy (or cut) and paste multiple items, use the Scrapbook. See the section "Using the Scrapbook to Collect Items" in Chapter 2 for details.

Using Find and Replace

When you need to locate specific text quickly in an Office document, use the Find feature. And when you need to replace specific text with other text, use the Replace feature.

Word, Excel, PowerPoint, and Outlook implement Find and Replace in different ways suited to their needs. This section introduces you to the basics of Find and Replace. The chapters on the individual applications provide further details on advanced Find and Replace features you may need to use.

Searching Quickly with the Search Box on the Standard Toolbar

When you need to search quickly for a word or phrase, use the Search box at the right end of the Standard toolbar in Word, Excel, and PowerPoint, and on the toolbar in Outlook. Follow these steps:

1. Click in the Search box to place the insertion point there.

2. If necessary, click the pop-up menu button to the right of the Search icon, and choose options as discussed next. Figure 3–9 shows the pop-up menu for Excel.

   - *Word.* Click the List Matches in Sidebar item if you want to display the Sidebar containing all the matches for the search term. Click the Replace item if you want to display the Find and Replace pane in the Sidebar.

   - *Excel.* Click the Search in Sheet item if you want to search just the displayed worksheet, or click the Search in Workbook item to search the whole workbook (including the displayed worksheet). Excel displays a check mark next to the item you chose so that you can see what you're searching. Click the Advanced Search item to display the Find dialog box (which you'll meet shortly). Click the Replace item to display the Replace dialog box (which you'll also meet shortly).

   - *PowerPoint.* Click the Advanced Find item to display the Advanced Find dialog box, in which you can choose to match the case on searches or find only whole words rather than partial matches.

   - *Outlook.* Outlook has no pop-up menu button.

Figure 3–9. *From the Search box on the Standard toolbar, you can search quickly or access search options. These are the search options for Excel.*

3. Type the search term in the Search box.

4. In Excel, press the Return key to run the search. Word, PowerPoint, and Outlook search automatically as you enter the search term.

5. Click the Next (>) button to move to the next instance of the term, or click the Previous button to move to the previous instance.

When you need to clear the Search box so that you can search for another term, click the × button at its right end.

Locating Text with the Find Dialog Box or Advanced Find Dialog Box

The Search box is easy to use, but often you'll want to locate text with more precision— for example, by matching the case used (rather than using non-case-sensitive matching) or by finding only whole-word matches rather than partial-word matches. To get these extra features, you need to use the Find dialog box or the Advanced Find dialog box, depending on the application you're using.

To open and use the Find dialog box or the Advanced Find dialog box, follow these steps:

1. Open the Find dialog box or the Advanced Find dialog box by using the appropriate command or keyboard shortcut:

    ■ *Word.* Choose Edit ➤ Find ➤ Advanced Find and Replace to display the Find and Replace dialog box with the Find tab at the front (see Figure 3–10).

Figure 3–10. *Word's Find and Replace dialog box at first opens at its smaller size. You can display further options by clicking the arrow button in the lower-left corner. To find single instances of the search term, clear the Highlight all items found in check box*

- *Excel.* Choose Edit ➤ Find to display the Find dialog box (see Figure 3–11).

Figure 3–11. *Excel's Find dialog box lets you choose whether to search the current worksheet or the whole workbook; whether to search by rows or columns; and whether to search in formulas, values, or comments.*

- *PowerPoint.* Choose Edit ➤ Find ➤ Advanced Find to display the Advanced Find dialog box (see Figure 3–12).

Figure 3–12. *PowerPoint's Advanced Find dialog box includes options for matching the case on searches and finding only whole-word matches.*

■ *Outlook.* In a message window, choose Edit ➤ Find ➤ Find to display the Find dialog box (see Figure 3–13).

Figure 3–13. *Outlook's Find dialog box contains no extra options. The right-arrow button finds the next instance of the search term, while the left-arrow button finds the previous instance.*

> **NOTE:** Outlook also has an Advanced Find feature that you can access by choosing Edit ➤ Find ➤ Advanced Find.

2.   In the Find what box, type or paste the text you want to find.

> **TIP:** If you've performed a search earlier in this session of working with this application, you can open the pop-up menu on the Find what box and select the term again.

3.   Choose any options needed. For example, select the Match case check box to make the search find only items that use the same case as the text you've typed.

4.   Click the Find Next button to find the next instance of the search term.

NOTE: In Word, you can select the Highlight all items found in check box to make Word highlight all the instances of the search term in the main document (or the other area you choose in the pop-up menu). This is helpful when you need to get an overview of where the search term appears in the document. When this check box is selected, the Find and Replace dialog box contains a Find All button rather than a Find Next button.

5. Click the Close button when you've finished finding items.

Replacing Text with Replace

To replace text in Word, Excel, or PowerPoint, follow these steps:

1. Open the Search pane in the Sidebar, the Find and Replace dialog box, or the Replace dialog box:

   - *Word*. Choose Edit ➤ Find ➤ Replace or press Cmd+Shift+H to display the Search pane in the Sidebar (shown on the left in Figure 3–14). For more options, you can choose Edit ➤ Find ➤ Advanced Find to display the Find and Replace dialog box and then click the Replace tab (shown on the right in Figure 3–14).

Figure 3–14. *Word provides two tools for replacing text. The Search pane in the Sidebar (left) shows you all the matches for the search term and lets you quickly move among them. The Replace tab of the Find and Replace dialog box (right) provides more search options when you need them.*

■ *Excel.* Choose Edit ➤ Replace to display the Replace dialog box
(see Figure 3–15).

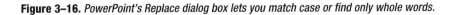

Figure 3–15. *Excel's Replace dialog box includes options for matching case and limiting the replacement to the entire contents of cells rather than partial contents.*

■ *PowerPoint.* Choose Edit ➤ Find ➤ Replace or press
Cmd+Shift+H to display the Replace dialog box (see Figure 3–16).

Figure 3–16. *PowerPoint's Replace dialog box lets you match case or find only whole words.*

2. In the Find what box, type or paste the text you want to find.

3. In the Replace with box, type or paste the replacement text.

TIP: If you've performed a search earlier in this session of working with this application, you can open the pop-up menu on the Find what box and select the term again. If you've performed a replacement, you can open the pop-up menu on the Replace with box and select the term again.

4. If you need to use any other options, choose them. For example, select the Find whole words only check box in Word or PowerPoint to find only whole-word matches rather than partial-word matches (for instance, you may need to replace *hand* without replacing *beforehand* or *underhand*).

5. Click the button for the operation you want to perform:

    ■ *Find Next.* Click this button to find the next instance of the search term.

> **NOTE:** In Word's Search pane, click the Find button to find all the instances of the search term.

    ■ *Replace.* Click this button to replace the current instance of the search term with the replacement term and find the next instance of the search term.

    ■ *Replace All.* Click this button to replace every instance of the search term with the replacement term.

6. When you have finished searching, click the Close button to close the Find and Replace dialog box or the Replace dialog box, or click the Close button (the × button) to close the Search pane in Word. The Close button replaces the Cancel button when you start replacing items.

Creating Tables

When you need to lay out data in a regular grid, create a table. A table consists of cells, which are rectangular areas formed by the intersection of rows and columns. Each table can contain one or more rows and one or more columns.

> **NOTE:** You can use tables in Word and PowerPoint. Excel's worksheets already have a grid structure, so you don't need to create tables for layout in Excel; instead, Excel uses the term *table* to mean a database laid out on a worksheet (see Chapter 16 for details).

Inserting a Table

The most straightforward way of adding a table to a Word document or a PowerPoint slide is to insert it. Inserting a table gives you a regular table with the number of rows and columns you choose. You can insert a table either using the New panel on the Ribbon or using the Insert Table dialog box.

Inserting a Table Using the New Panel on the Ribbon

To insert a table using the New panel on the Ribbon, follow these steps:

1. Position the insertion point where you want the table to appear.

2. Choose Tables ➤ Table Options ➤ New, opening the New panel (see Figure 3–17).

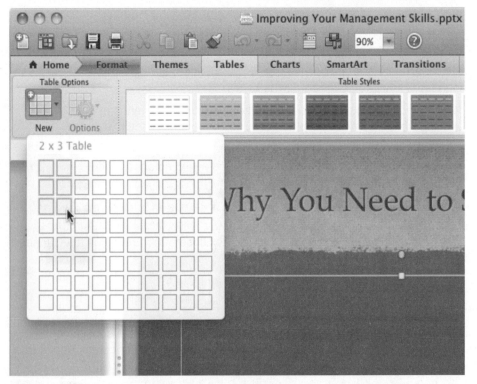

Figure 3–17. *To insert a table, choose Tables ➤ Table Options ➤ New, and then click the square for the table configuration you want to insert.*

3. Click the square for the table configuration you want—for example, a 2×3 table is two columns wide and three rows deep.

Inserting a Table Using the Insert Table Dialog Box

When you need more control over a table's behavior in Word, use the Insert Table dialog box to insert the table. You can also use the Insert Table dialog box in PowerPoint, but it has no advantage over using the New panel on the Ribbon.

To insert a table using the Insert Table dialog box, follow these steps:

1. Place the insertion point where you want the table to appear.

2. Give the appropriate command:

- *Word.* From the Ribbon, choose Tables ➤ Table Options ➤ New, and then click the Insert Table command near the bottom of the New panel to display the Insert Table dialog box (shown on the left in Figure 3–18).

- *PowerPoint.* From the menu bar, choose Insert ➤ Table to display the Insert Table dialog box (shown on the right in Figure 3–18).

Figure 3–18. *Word's Insert Table dialog box (left) lets you control AutoFit behavior and create default settings for new tables. PowerPoint's Insert Table dialog box lets you set only the numbers of columns and rows.*

3. Use the Number of columns box and the Number of rows box to set the dimensions of the table.

4. In Word, select the appropriate option button in the AutoFit behavior area:

   - *Initial column width.* Select this option button to have Word set the width of each column. In the pop-up menu, choose Auto to have Word automatically set the width, or set the precise width you want (for example, 1.25").

   - *AutoFit to contents.* Select this option button to make Word automatically adjust each column's width to fit its contents. This is often a good choice.

   - *AutoFit to window.* Select this option button to make Word automatically adjust each column's width to suit the document window. This option is useful for tables you expect people to view on the screen at different window widths.

5. Also in Word, select the Set as default for new tables check box if you want Word to store these settings for future use.

6. Click the OK button to close the Insert Table dialog box, and insert the table in the document or slide.

Drawing a Table

Inserting a table as described earlier is usually the easiest way of creating a regular table, but you may also need to create irregular tables by drawing tables instead. You can do this in Word and PowerPoint.

To draw a table, choose Tables ➤ Draw Borders ➤ Draw from the Ribbon, and then use the drawing cursor to draw the table layout you want (see Figure 3–19).

- *Draw a cell.* Click with the pen pointer, and drag to draw a cell.

- *Erase a line.* Choose Tables ➤ Draw Borders ➤ Erase to change the pen pointer to an eraser, and then click the line you want to erase. Choose Tables ➤ Draw Borders ➤ Draw when you want to switch back to the pen for drawing more cells.

- *Stop drawing.* In Word, choose Tables ➤ Draw Borders ➤ Draw to deselect the Draw button and turn off the pen pointer; alternatively, press the Esc key. (PowerPoint automatically turns off the pen pointer after you draw a cell.)

Figure 3–19. *When you need an irregular table, give the Draw command, and then use the pen pointer to draw the table layout you need.*

Merging and Splitting Cells in a Table

To change the layout of the table, you can merge cells together to form a larger cell or split a cell into several smaller cells.

To merge cells together, select the cells, and then choose Table Layout ➤ Merge ➤ Merge . The application turns the selected cells into a single cell. Any contents of the previous cells appear as separate paragraphs in the merged cell.

To split a cell into multiple cells, click in the cell, and then choose Table Layout ➤ Merge ➤ Split Cells. In the Split Cells dialog box that the application displays (see Figure 3–20), enter the number of columns and rows you want to create within the cell, and then click the OK button.

Figure 3–20. *Use the Split Cells dialog box to split one existing cell into two or more new cells.*

NOTE: In Word, if you select multiple cells for splitting, select the Merge cells before split check box to make Word treat all the selected cells as one cell. For example, if you select two cells, select the Merge cells before split check box, and specify four columns, you get four columns total. By contrast, if you select two cells, clear the Merge cells before split check box, and specify four columns, you get four columns from each cell, giving eight columns altogether.

Adding Content to a Table

The most straightforward way to add content to a table is by clicking in the destination cell and then typing the text. Press the Tab key the insertion point to the next cell, or press Shift+Tab to move the insertion point to the previous cell.

You can also paste text into a table you've created. Simply click in the cell, and then paste the text (for example, click the Paste button on the Standard toolbar or press Cmd+V).

TIP: In Word, you can copy text that's laid out with a tab between each separate item and then paste it into multiple cells at once. Copy the text from the source, switch to Word, select the appropriate number of cells in the table, and then give the Paste command.

Formatting a Table

To make a table look the way you want, you format it. You can apply formatting either quickly by using a table style or manually by applying only the formatting the table needs.

To apply a table style, click anywhere in the table, and then choose Tables ➤ Table Styles ➤ Quick Styles, choosing the style you want either from the Quick Styles box or from the Quick Styles panel (see Figure 3–21). You can browse the table styles in the box by clicking the left arrow button and the right arrow button, but usually it's easier to use the panel. Move the mouse over the box so that the panel's button appears below it, as shown in the figure, and then click the button to open the panel.

Figure 3–21. *The quick way to format a table is to apply a style from the Quick Styles box or Quick Styles panel on the Tables tab of the Ribbon.*

After applying a table style, you can customize it by selecting or clearing the check boxes in the Table Options group on the Tables tab of the Ribbon. For example, select the Header Row check box to apply different formatting to the table's first row so that it looks like a header, or select the First Column check box to apply different formatting to the first column if it contains headings.

If you prefer not to use a table style, you can format a table manually. These are the main techniques you'll need:

- *Borders.* Select the table or the cells you want to affect, choose Tables ➤ Draw Borders ➤ Borders, and then click the border style you want.

- *Shading.* Select the table or the cells you want to affect, choose Table Layout ➤ Table Styles ➤ Shading, and then click the shading color.

- *Font formatting.* Select the cell or cells you want to format, and then use the controls in the Font group of the Home tab of the Ribbon or the controls on the Formatting toolbar, as for other text.

Creating Hyperlinks

As you know from browsing the Web, a *hyperlink* is text or an object on a web page that's linked to another location—for example, to another web page or to another place on the same web page. You can insert a hyperlink in just about any Office document—a Word document, an Excel workbook, a PowerPoint presentation, or an e-mail message or task you're creating in Outlook. This section shows you how to create a hyperlink in Word, Excel, or PowerPoint.

You can create both text hyperlinks and object hyperlinks. A text hyperlink appears as underlined text. An object hyperlink appears as just the object—for example, a picture or a shape. For either type of hyperlink, you can choose whether to display a ScreenTip when the user holds the mouse pointer over the hyperlink, as in the text hyperlink shown in Figure 3–22.

Display the Surreal Macs website

To read about our products, visit the Learn More page on our website.

Figure 3–22. *When you create a hyperlink, you can include a ScreenTip that appears when the user holds the mouse pointer over the hyperlink.*

To insert a hyperlink, follow these steps:

1. Choose the type of hyperlink you want to insert:

    ■ *New text hyperlink.* Position the insertion point where you want the hyperlink to appear.

    ■ *Hyperlink that displays existing text.* If the document already contains text that you want to use as the display text for the hyperlink, select that text.

    ■ *Object hyperlink.* Insert the object in the document, and then select it. For example, you can insert a graphic as explained in Chapter 4.

2. Choose Insert ➤ Hyperlink from the menu bar or press Cmd+K to display the Insert Hyperlink dialog box (see Figure 3–23).

Insert Hyperlink

Link to: http://www.surrealmacs.com/about/contact_us.html

Display: Contact Us

ScreenTip...

Web Page   Document   E-mail Address

In the Link to box, enter the address (URL) of the Web page that you want to link to.

Anchor:

Locate...

If you want to link to a specific location (anchor) within the Web page, enter the name of the anchor above or click Locate to find it.

Cancel   OK

Figure 3–23. *Use the Insert Hyperlink dialog box to quickly create a link to a file, a web page, an e-mail address, or a document.*

3. In the Link To box, enter the URL (the web address) or network address to which you want to link. You can type in the address, paste it, or use the tabs in the middle of the Insert Hyperlink dialog box, as described next.

- *Web Page.* The easiest way to enter a URL in the Link to box is to copy it from Safari (or another browser) and then paste it by pressing Cmd+V. If you need the link to lead to a particular anchor (a marked spot) on the page, type the anchor's name in the Anchor box.

- *Document.* Click the Document tab to display the Document controls (see Figure 3–24). Click the Select button to open the Choose a File dialog box. Navigate to the folder that contains the document, click the document, and then click the Open button. The application enters the document's address in the Link to box.

Figure 3–24. *To create a hyperlink to a document, click the Select button, and then use the Choose a File dialog box to pick the document. The application enters the address in the Link to box.*

- *E-mail Address.* Click the E-mail tab to display the E-mail controls (see Figure 3–25). You can then type or paste the address in the To box, open the Recent Addresses list and pick an address, or click the Launch E-mail Application button to launch your e-mail application so that you can copy the address. After entering the address, type the subject in the Subject box. The application automatically enters the details of the hyperlink (a mailto: address) in the Link to box.

Insert Hyperlink

Link to: `mailto:sales@surrealmacs.com?subject=Customer%20Query:`

Display: `mailto:sales@surrealmacs.com?subject=Customer Query:`

ScreenTip...

Web Page   Document   E-mail Address

Recent Addresses   Launch E-mail Application

To: `sales@surrealmacs.com`

Subject: `Customer Query:`

Enter the e-mail address and subject for messages that will be created when people click on this link.

Cancel   OK

Figure 3–25. *To create a hyperlink that automatically starts an e-mail message, enter the address and subject line on the E-mail Address tab of the Insert Hyperlink dialog box.*

4. In the Display box, enter the text that you want the document to display for the hyperlink.

   - If you selected text in the document in step 1, that text appears here.

   - If you selected an object in step 1, the Text to display box shows <<Selection in Document>> and is not available for change.

5. To add to the hyperlink a ScreenTip that appears when the user holds the mouse pointer over it, click the ScreenTip button. In the Set Hyperlink ScreenTip dialog box (see Figure 3–26) that opens, type the ScreenTip, and then click the OK button.

Set Hyperlink ScreenTip

ScreenTip text:

`Display the Surreal Macs website`

Cancel   OK

Figure 3–26. *You can add a ScreenTip to a hyperlink to provide a more detailed explanation of where the link goes or why the user may want to click it.*

6. When you have finished specifying the details of the hyperlink, click the OK button to insert it in the document.

You can now test your hyperlink by clicking it.

> **NOTE:** To edit a hyperlink, Ctrl+click or right-click the text or object, and then click Edit Hyperlink on the context menu; the Office application opens the Edit Hyperlink dialog box, which is the Insert Hyperlink dialog box with a different name. To remove a hyperlink, Ctrl+click or right-click the text or object, and then click Remove Hyperlink on the context menu.

Summary

In this chapter, you learned how to work with text in the Office applications. You now know how to navigate with the keyboard; select objects using the mouse, the keyboard, or both; and apply the most widely used types of formatting to text and objects. You can also use the Cut, Copy, and Paste features; find and replace text; and add tables and hyperlinks to your documents.

In the next chapter, I'll show you how to add graphics to your documents and make them look good.

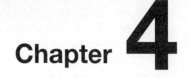

Using Pictures and Shapes in Your Documents

To give your documents visual interest, you can add various types of graphical content to them—graphics themselves (I'll use the term to cover all kinds of pictures and images), shapes (anything from a simple arrow or circle to a complex shape), charts, and even movies.

This chapter shows you how to insert clip art and other pictures, how to insert shapes and format them, and how to position graphical objects where you want them. You'll learn how to wrap text around a graphical object in Word, how to make a picture look the way you want it, and how to illustrate your documents by adding SmartArt diagrams.

We'll start by going over how the Office applications handle graphical objects, because understanding this is essential to mastering how to place objects.

NOTE: See Chapter 14 for instructions on creating charts in Excel.

Understanding How You Position Graphical Objects

Even though an Office document appears to be flat, it actually consists of multiple separate layers. Until you add objects to a layer, the layer is transparent, so you see through the layer to whatever is underneath. One layer contains the text; the other layers contain graphical objects. Having these multiple layers enables you to position graphical objects either in front of the text layer or behind the text layer. You can also position a graphical object in front of another graphical object—for example, to superimpose one graphical object on another.

Word, Excel, and PowerPoint let you position graphical objects in the graphics layers, where you can move them freely. Word also lets you position graphical objects as inline characters in the text layer. When you do this, Word places the graphical object just like a character in the document's text. If you then insert text before the graphical object, it moves further down the document.

Outlook gives you far less control over graphical objects. You can add pictures to a message or attach an audio or video file, but that's about all. We'll look at how to do this in Chapter 22.

Choosing Where to Insert a Graphical Object

Before inserting a graphical object, you need to place the insertion point or selection where you want to insert the object. Place the insertion point or selection like this:

- *Word.* Place the insertion point where you want to insert the object.

- *Excel.* Click the cell where you want to place the upper-left corner of the object.

- *PowerPoint.* Click the slide on which you want to insert the object, or select the placeholder in which you want to place the object. If the placeholder is a standard placeholder, you can click one of the three icons at the bottom—the Insert Picture from File icon on the left, the Clip Art Browser icon in the middle (see Figure 4–1), or the Insert Media Clip icon on the right—to start inserting a graphical object.

Figure 4–1. *Click the Clip Art Browser icon in a standard placeholder on a PowerPoint slide to start inserting a clip art item in that placeholder.*

Inserting Clip Art

When you need a quick illustration in a document, you can insert a clip art item. Office includes a modest but useful set of clip art pictures that you can use in your documents. You can also download other clip art pictures from the Office pages of the Microsoft web site.

Inserting clip art is more complex than it ought to be, because Office gives you two different tools. First, each application has a Clip Art Browser pane that appears in the Media Browser; this pane shows a variety of clip art pictures. Second, there's the separate Clip Gallery application, which you can use to manage your clips and insert them in your documents. The Clip Gallery has a wider selection of clip art pictures than the Clip Art Browser pane, but some of the items are the same.

Let's take it from the top and start with the Clip Art Browser.

Inserting a Clip Art Picture Using the Clip Art Browser

Where you'll probably want to start with clip art is by seeing whether the Clip Art Browser contains a suitable picture. To open the Clip Art Browser and insert an item (if there is a suitable one), follow these steps:

1. Choose Insert ➤ Clip Art ➤ Clip Art Browser from the menu bar to display the Clip Art Browser pane in the Media Browser window. Figure 4–2 shows the Clip Art Browser pane.

Figure 4–2. *Use the Clip Art Browser pane in the Media Browser to insert clip art pictures in your Office documents. You can drag the sizing handle at the lower-right corner to resize the Media Browser.*

2. In the pop-up menu at the top, choose All Images if you want to see all the images available, or choose the category of images you want—for example, Animals or Business.

3. If you want to zoom in to see the pictures at a larger size, drag the zoom slider at the bottom to the right. To zoom out, drag the slider to the left.

4. Browse through the clip art items that appear in the Clip Art Browser to find the one you want.

5. To insert an item, click it and drag it to where you want it to appear in the document.

Instead of inserting a clip art picture in the document, you can Ctrl+click it or right-click it and then click Copy on the context menu to copy it to the Clipboard. You can then use the Paste command (for example, press Cmd+V) to paste the clip art picture where you need it.

Inserting a Clip Art Picture Using the Clip Gallery

If the Clip Art Browser doesn't contain a suitable picture for your document, try the Clip Gallery. Follow these steps:

1. Position the insertion point where you want to insert the item.

2. Choose Insert ➤ Clip Art ➤ Clip Art Gallery from the menu bar to launch the Clip Gallery application (see Figure 4–3).

Figure 4–3. *The Clip Gallery is a tool for managing your clip art and inserting clip art items in documents.*

3. In the Category list box, click the category of pictures you want to display. You can then scroll through the pictures.

4. To search by clip name or keyword, type the search term in the Search box, and then click the Search button. The Clip Gallery adds all matching clips to the Search Results category at the top of the Category list box and displays this category in the main box.

5. Click the clip art item you want to insert in the document.

6. Click the Insert button. The application inserts the clip art item and automatically closes the Clip Gallery.

Managing Your Clip Art Items with the Clip Gallery

To get the most out of the Clip Gallery, you can add your own pictures, motion clips, and sounds to it. You can also download clip art items from the Microsoft Office web site and add them to the Clip Gallery. To keep the Clip Gallery items arranged and make it easy to find the items you need, you can change the categories in the Clip Gallery and tag the items with keywords.

Adding Your Own Pictures to the Clip Gallery

To add your own pictures to the Clip Gallery, follow these steps:

1. Choose Insert ➤ Clip Art ➤ Clip Art Gallery from the menu bar to open the Clip Gallery.

2. Click the Import button to display the Import dialog box (see Figure 4–4).

Figure 4–4. *Use the Import dialog box to add your own pictures or downloaded pictures to the Clip Gallery.*

3. In the Enable pop-up menu, choose the type of items you want to add:

    ■   *All Clips.* Select this item to import any type of item the Clip Gallery can handle.

    ■   *Clip Gallery Images.* Select this item to add picture files to the Clip Gallery.

    ■   *Clip Gallery Movies.* Select this item to add movies.

    ■   *Clip Gallery Sounds.* Select this item to add sound files.

    ■   *Clip Gallery Packages.* Select this item to add gallery packages you've downloaded.

    ■   *Microsoft Office Online Files.* Select this item to add gallery packages you've downloaded in the `.cil` file format from the Microsoft Office web site.

4. Click the file to add to the gallery.

5. In the lower-left corner of the Import dialog box, select the appropriate option button to choose how to add the item to the Clip Gallery:

    ■   *Copy into Clip Gallery.* Select this option button to make a copy of the clip and add that copy to the Clip Gallery. Take this approach when the clip art item is on a removable drive or a network drive.

    ■   *Move into Clip Gallery.* Select this option button to move the clip from its current folder to the Clip Gallery. Use this option when you've downloaded a file but not for your material that you've organized into folders.

    ■   *Add alias to Clip Gallery.* Select this option button to add an alias (a file shortcut) to the Clip Gallery. The alias points to the file in its current location. Use this option for material you've organized into folders but want to add to the Clip Gallery.

6. Click the Import button. The Clip Gallery closes the Import dialog box and displays the Properties dialog box for the item (or the first item if you're importing multiple items). Figure 4–5 shows the Description tab of the Properties dialog box for a picture.

Figure 4–5. *On the Description tab of the Properties dialog box for a clip art item, enter a useful description in place of the file name.*

7. In the Description of this clip box, type a description of what the clip shows. The Clip Gallery suggests the first part of the file name as the description, but you'll often want to improve on this.

8. Click the Categories tab to display its contents (see Figure 4–6).

Figure 4–6. *On the Categories tab of the Properties dialog box, select the check box for each category you want to assign the item to. To add a category, click the New Category button.*

9. Select the check box for each category you want the picture to appear in. If no category is suitable, create one by clicking the New Category button, typing the name in the New Category dialog box, and clicking the OK button.

10. Click the Keywords tab to display its contents (see Figure 4–7).

Figure 4–7. *On the Keywords tab of the Properties dialog box, add keywords to the clip art item so that you will be able to search for it.*

11. Mark the clip art item with the keywords it needs. Use these techniques:

- *Add a keyword.* Click the New Keyword button to open the New Keyword dialog box. Type the keyword, and then press the Return key or click the OK button.

- *Remove a keyword.* Click the keyword in the list box, and then click the Remove Keyword button. In the confirmation dialog box that opens, click the OK button.

12. Click the OK button to close the Properties dialog box. The Clip Gallery imports the picture and adds it to the categories you chose.

Downloading Clip Art Items from the Microsoft Office Web site

The Clip Gallery contains enough items to get you started with clip art, but if you need to use clip art extensively in your documents, you'll probably want to download other items from the Microsoft Office web site and add them to the gallery. To do so, follow these steps:

1. Choose Insert ➤ Clip Art ➤ Clip Art Gallery from the menu bar to open the Clip Gallery.

2. Click the Online button to launch or activate your default browser and display the Images page on the Microsoft Office web site.

> **NOTE:** The first time you click the Online button in the Clip Gallery, the Launch Browser dialog box appears, asking your permission for it to launch your default browser. Select the Don't ask me again check box, and then click the Yes button.

3. Browse to find the images you want.

4. Add each image to your basket by moving the mouse pointer over the image, waiting until the details panel pops up, and then clicking the Add to Basket link on it.

5. When you're ready to download the images, move your mouse over the Selection Basket link in the upper-right corner, and then click the Download link.

6. On the web page that appears, click the Download button to download the clip art items in an archive file.

7. Click the Downloads folder on the Dock, and then click the archive file. Its name starts with ClipArt, and it has the file extension `.cil`, so it should be easy to identify. The Clip Gallery automatically imports the files.

> **NOTE:** If your Dock doesn't contain a Downloads folder, open a Finder window to the Downloads folder in your user account. Then double-click the archive file. Alternatively, click the Import button in the Clip Gallery window, click the file in the Import dialog box, and then click the Import button.

After importing the files, you may want to set their properties and keywords as described in the previous section to make them easier to find.

Organizing the Clip Gallery with Categories

As you saw a little earlier in this chapter, you can create new categories as needed when importing items into the Clip Gallery. You can also create categories or delete categories by clicking the Categories button in the Clip Gallery and working in the Categories dialog box (see Figure 4–8):

- *Create a category.* Click the New Category button to display the New Category dialog box. Type the name for the category, and then click the OK button.

- *Delete a category.* Click the category in the list box, and then click the Delete button. In the confirmation dialog box, click the OK button.

Figure 4–8. *Use the Categories dialog box in the Clip Gallery to delete existing categories or create new categories.*

Inserting Pictures in Your Documents

You can insert your own pictures in your Office documents easily too. You can either insert pictures you've added to iPhoto or insert pictures that are in your Mac's file system but not in iPhoto.

Inserting Pictures from iPhoto

To insert a picture from iPhoto, follow these steps:

1. Click the Media button on the Standard toolbar or choose View ➤ Media Browser from the menu bar to open the Media Browser.

2. Click the Photos button on the toolbar to display the Photos Browser pane (see Figure 4–9).

Figure 4–9. *Use the Photos Browser pane in the Media Browser to add a picture from iPhoto to a document.*

3. In the pop-up menu, choose the source of the pictures. Choose iPhoto to see all pictures in iPhoto, or choose an item such as Events from the iPhoto Albums list.

4. Click the photo you want, and then drag it to the document window, dropping it where you want it to appear.

5. Leave the Media Browser window open if you want to use it further. Otherwise, click the Close button (the red button in its upper-left corner) to close it.

Inserting Pictures from Your Mac's File System

To insert a picture that's not in iPhoto but is stored in your Mac's file system or on a network drive, follow these steps:

1. Position the insertion point or selection where you want the picture to appear.

2. Choose Insert ➤ Photo ➤ Picture from File from the menu bar to display the Choose a Picture dialog box (see Figure 4–10).

Figure 4–10. *From the Choose a Picture dialog box, you can choose whether to link the picture to the document. For some picture types, you can also choose to treat the picture layers as separate objects so that you can manipulate them independently.*

3. Navigate to the folder that contains the file, and then click the file.

4. If you want to link the picture file to the document rather than insert it, select the Link to File check box. When you do this, you can select the Save with Document check box to store the latest version of the picture file in the document. See the sidebar "Linking a Picture to a Document" for advice about linking.

5. If you want to be able to manipulate each layer of the picture separately, select the Treat picture layers as separate objects check box. This feature is available only for some types of pictures, such as JPEGs.

6. Click the Insert button. The application closes the Choose a Picture dialog box and inserts the picture in the document.

TIP: You can also insert a picture file by dragging it from a Finder window to an Office document window.

LINKING A PICTURE TO A DOCUMENT

When you add a picture to a document from your Mac's file system, you can either insert it or link it. Inserting the picture adds a copy of the picture to the document. The application saves the picture in the document, so even if you move the document, the picture stays in it.

If you need to keep the document's file size down or if you need to be able to update the picture easily, you can link the picture instead. Linking makes the application add to the document a link to the picture file. When you open the document, the application loads the current version of the picture from the file. But if you move the document to a different computer, the link will no longer work, because the application will be unable to find the picture file.

To solve the problem of broken links, you can link a picture but also save the latest version of it. To do this, select the Link to File check box and the Save with Document check box in the Choose a Picture dialog box. When you open the document, the application checks to see whether the linked version is available. If so, the application loads the linked picture; if not, it displays the version saved in the document.

Adding and Formatting a Shape

If a document needs a drawing, you can create it from scratch by using Office's shapes. Office provides a wide variety of shapes, from arrows and basic shapes to stars, banners, and callouts.

To insert a shape, follow these steps:

1. Display the area of the document where you want to add the shape. When adding a shape, you don't need to position the insertion point or make a selection.

> **NOTE:** You can also insert a shape by choosing Home ➤ Insert ➤ Shape from the Ribbon to display the Shape panel, clicking the category of shape (for example, Lines and Connectors), and then clicking the type of shape. But in general the Shapes Browser gives you an easier way to access shapes.

2. Click the Media button on the Standard toolbar or choose View ➤ Media Browser from the menu bar to display the Media Browser.

3. Click the Shapes button in the toolbar to display the Shapes Browser pane (see Figure 4–11).

Figure 4–11. *Choose the type of shape from the Shapes Browser pane in the Media Browser. Hold the mouse pointer over a shape to see a ScreenTip showing its description.*

4. In the pop-up menu at the top of the Shapes Browser, click the category of shapes you want to see: All Shapes, Rectangles, Basic Shapes, Lines and Connectors, Block Arrows, Equation Shapes, Flowchart, Stars and Banners, or Callouts.

5. Click the shape you want. The application changes the mouse pointer to a crosshair.

6. With this crosshair, click where you want to place one corner of the shape, and then drag to the opposite corner (see Figure 4–12). It doesn't matter which corner you place first, because you can drag in any direction, but placing the upper-left corner first is usually easiest.

Figure 4–12. *Click and drag with the crosshair to place and size the shape you're inserting.*

When you release the mouse button, the shape appears with selection handles around it, so you can work with it as described in the following sections. When the shape is selected, the application adds the Format tab to the Ribbon, which provides controls for formatting the shape.

Close the Media Browser window by clicking its Close button (the red button in the upper-left corner) unless you need to insert more shapes or other objects.

Applying a Style to a Shape

After inserting a shape, you can apply a style to it from the Shape Styles box or panel in the Shape Styles group on the Format tab of the Ribbon. If the style you want appears in the Shape Styles box, click it; otherwise, move the mouse pointer over the Shape Styles box so that the panel button appears, and then click the button to display the panel (see Figure 4–13). You can then click the style you want.

Figure 4–13. *To change a shape's style, open the Shape Styles panel on the Format tab of the Ribbon, and then click the style you want.*

To refine the shape, open the Fill panel, the Line panel, or the Effects drop-down panel in the Shape Styles group, and then click the option you want. For example, choose Format ➤ Shape Styles ➤ Shape Effects ➤ 3-D Rotation, and then click one of the 3D rotation effects (see Figure 4–14).

Figure 4–14. *Use the Fill panel, the Line panel, or the Effects panel (shown here) to make the shape look the way you want it to look.*

Rotating a Graphical Object

After inserting a graphical object, you can rotate it as needed. Click to select the object, and then drag the green handle to the left to rotate counterclockwise (see Figure 4–15) or to the right to rotate clockwise.

Figure 4–15. *Drag the green rotation handle to the left or right to rotate a graphical object.*

Positioning a Graphical Object

If you don't get a graphical object in precisely the right position when you insert it, you can easily move it afterward.

The quick way to reposition a graphical object is to click it and then drag it to where you want it. This works well most of the time, but for more precision you can also click the object to select it and then press an arrow key (for example, the Left arrow key) to nudge it a small distance in the arrow's direction.

When you need to control exactly where the object appears, Ctrl+click or right-click the object, and then click the Format command on the context menu (for example, the Format Shape command for a shape) to display the Format dialog box for the object. In the left pane, click the Size item to display the controls for resizing the object and controlling its placement. Figure 4–16 shows the Size category in the Format Shape dialog box for Word.

Figure 4–16. *Use the controls in the Size category of the Format dialog box for an object to resize and position the object precisely.*

NOTE: In PowerPoint, use the controls in the Position category in the Format dialog box to control where an object appears on a slide.

Choosing Text Wrapping in Word

In Word, you can place a graphical object either inline with the text or in the graphics layers. It can be hard to tell just by looking at a graphical object how it's positioned, but if you find you can't move a graphical object freely, it's most likely because it's inline.

The easiest way to set text wrapping for an object is to use the object's Format dialog box—for example, the Format Picture dialog box for a picture or the Format Shape dialog box for a shape. To open the Format dialog box, Ctrl+click or right-click the object, and then click the Format command on the context menu. Once the dialog box is open, click the Layout category in the left column to display the Layout options. Figure 4–17 shows the Layout options in the Format Picture dialog box.

Figure 4–17. *The Layout category in the Format dialog boxes (such as the Format Picture dialog box shown here) lets you set basic wrapping. But often it's best to click the Advanced button to reach all the wrapping options.*

In the Wrapping style area of the Format dialog box, you can click one of the wrapping styles to apply it to the picture. Usually, though, you'll do better to open the Advanced Layout dialog box by clicking the Advanced button.

On the Text Wrapping tab of the Advanced Layout dialog box (see Figure 4–18), follow these steps to set wrapping:

1. In the Wrapping style area, click the wrapping style you want: Square, Tight, Through, Top and bottom, Behind text, In front of text, or In line with text.

2. For the Square style, Tight style, or Through style, select the appropriate option button in the Wrap text area: Both sides, Left only, Right only, or Largest only.

3. For the Square style, Tight style, Through style, or Top and bottom style, use the Top box, Bottom box, Left box, and Right box in the Distance from text area to specify how much space to leave between the object and the text.

4. Click the OK button to close the Advanced Layout dialog box, and then click the OK button to close the Format dialog box from which you opened the Advanced Layout dialog box.

Figure 4–18. *Use the options on the Text Wrapping tab of the Advanced Layout dialog box to take precise control over the way Word wraps text around an object.*

NOTE: For a picture, you can also set wrapping by selecting the picture, choosing Format Picture ➤ Arrange ➤ Wrap Text, and then clicking the appropriate item on the panel: In Line with Text, Square, Tight, Behind Text, In Front of Text, Top and Bottom, or Through. You can also Ctrl+click or right-click a picture or shape, click the Wrap Text submenu, and then click the appropriate command: In Line with Text, Square, Tight, Through, Top and Bottom, None, or Edit Wrap Boundary.

After you close the Advanced Layout dialog box, you'll see how well the wrapping makes the text fit the object. Figure 4–19 shows an example of tight wrapping around a picture.

Traffic Management on Rural Highways

In this section, you'll learn about special considerations for managing traffic on rural highways. We'll start by looking at how to deal with pipe bursts in nonurban situations, move on to handling stray animals, and finally consider how to handle dangerous game.

You'll learn how to approach emergency situations, tricks for deciding which tools to deploy and ways of using them effectively, and how to deal calmly with enraged motorists without losing your professional aplomb. We'll also go through how to call in other agencies and how to resolve questions of competing priorities.

Dealing with Burst Pipes

When a pipe bursts on a rural highway, the first priority is safety.

Figure 4–19. *Text wrapped around a picture in Word using the Tight wrapping style.*

If you want to try another wrapping style, Ctrl+click or right-click the object, click or highlight Wrap Text on the context menu, and then click the wrapping style you want. For more options, go back to the Advanced Layout dialog box, as described earlier.

If you need to fine-tune the wrapping, Ctrl+click or right-click the object, click or highlight Wrap Text on the context menu, and then click Edit Wrap Boundary. Word displays a red border around the object with square black handles indicating changes in wrap direction. You can then drag the handles to change the shape of the wrap boundary (see Figure 4–20). Click the red line to place another handle when you need one.

Traffic Management on Rural Highways

In this section, you'll learn about special considerations for managing traffic on rural highways. We'll start by looking at how 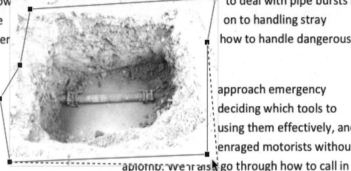 to deal with pipe bursts in nonurban situations, move on to handling stray animals, and finally consider how to handle dangerous game.

You'll learn how to approach emergency situations, tricks for deciding which tools to deploy and ways of using them effectively, and how to deal calmly with enraged motorists without losing your professional aplomb. We'll also go through how to call in other agencies and how to resolve questions of competing priorities.

Figure 4–20. Click and drag the square black wrap handles to adjust the wrap boundary and make the text wrap the way you want it to wrap.

Making a Picture Look the Way You Want It

After you insert a picture, you can use the controls that appear on the Format Picture tab of the Ribbon to make the picture look the way you want it. You can adjust the picture's colors, apply a picture style to the picture, or crop the picture so that only part of it shows.

Adjusting a Picture's Sharpness, Brightness, Contrast, and Colors

To adjust the sharpness, brightness, or contrast in a picture, click the picture to select it, and then choose Format Picture ➤ Adjust ➤ Corrections to open the Corrections panel (see Figure 4–21). Click the color correction you want.

Figure 4–21. *To fix problems with a picture's sharpness, brightness, or contrast, open the Corrections panel and choose the look you want.*

To change the colors in a picture, click it, choose Format Picture ➤ Adjust ➤ Recolor, and then click the effect you want. The Color drop-down panel has different sections for Color Saturation, Color Tone, and Recolor (for example, Grayscale or Sepia).

To apply an effect such as paint strokes or a light screen to a picture, click the picture, choose Format Picture ➤ Adjust ➤ Filters, and then click the effect you want.

To reset a picture to its original look, choose Format Picture ➤ Adjust ➤ Reset.

Applying a Picture Style

To apply a picture style to a picture, click the picture, click the Format Picture tab of the Ribbon to display it, and then click the picture style you want. If the picture style appears in the Quick Styles box in the Picture Styles group, click it there; otherwise, move the mouse pointer over the Quick Styles box so that the panel button appears, click the panel button, and then click the picture style on the panel (see Figure 4–22).

Figure 4–22. *Choose the picture style from the Quick Styles box or panel in the Picture Styles group of the Format Picture tab on the Ribbon.*

Cropping a Picture

If you need the document to show only part of a picture rather than the whole picture, you can crop off the parts you don't want.

The Office applications let you crop a picture in several ways, but this way is usually the easiest:

1. Click the picture to select it. The application adds the Format Picture tab to the Ribbon.

2. Click the Format Picture tab if the application has not displayed it.

3. Choose Format Picture ➤ Adjust ➤ Crop, clicking the top part of the Crop button rather than the drop-down button. The application displays crop handles on the picture (see Figure 4–23).

Figure 4–23. *The quick way of cropping is to drag the crop handles until they encompass the part of the picture you want to keep.*

4. Drag the crop handles to make the cropping area contain the part of the picture you want to show:

   ■ Shift+drag to crop the image proportionally.

   ■ Option+drag to crop the image evenly around its center point.

   ■ Option+Shift+drag to crop the image proportionally around its center point.

   ■ Cmd+drag to crop the image in increments of Word's underlying drawing grid or Excel's worksheet cells.

TIP: If you make the crop area exactly the size you need, you can click and drag within the crop area to make a different part of the picture appear in it. You move the picture, not the crop area—much as if you were to reach through a window and move the landscape until the window displayed the part you wanted to see.

5. Click the Crop button again to turn off the Crop tool, or click elsewhere in the document to deselect the picture. The application applies the cropping to the picture.

> **NOTE:** You can also crop a picture to fit into a shape. To do this, choose Format Picture ➤ Adjust ➤ Crop, clicking the Crop pop-up arrow button rather than the top part of the button. On the pop-up menu that appears, choose Mask to Shape, and then click the shape you want.

Saving Space by Compressing Pictures

When you insert pictures in a document (rather than linking them, as discussed earlier in this chapter), the application saves a copy of each picture in the document. This can greatly increase the file size of the document.

To keep the document's file size down, you can compress the pictures and delete the cropped areas of them. To do so, follow these steps:

1. Click a picture to make the application add the Format Picture tab to the Ribbon.

2. Choose Format Picture ➤ Adjust ➤ Compress to display the Reduce File Size dialog box (see Figure 4–24).

Figure 4–24. *Use the Reduce File Size dialog box when you want to reduce the file size of one or more pictures or when you want to delete the cropped areas of pictures.*

3. In the Picture Quality pop-up menu, select the picture quality you want:

   - *Best for printing (220 ppi).* Compresses the pictures only a bit, leaving them high enough quality for most purposes.

   - *Best for viewing on screen (150 ppi).* Compresses the pictures a bit further but leaves them looking good enough for use on the screen.

   - *Best for sending in e-mail (96 ppi).* Compresses the pictures to the extent that they start to look bad but are OK for viewing on the screen at small sizes.

■ *Keep current resolution.* Keeps the pictures at their current resolution. You'd use this setting for removing the cropped parts of pictures without changing the resolution.

4. In the Apply to area, select the Selected pictures only option button if you want to affect only the picture you've selected. Normally, you'll want to select the All pictures in this file option button to make the application compress all the pictures in the document.

5. Select the Remove cropped picture regions check box if you want to get rid of the areas you've cropped off. This is a good security measure provided you don't need to adjust the cropping of any pictures in the document to reveal more.

6. Click the OK button. The application closes the Reduce File Size dialog box and changes the quality or cropping as you specified.

Inserting SmartArt

When you need to create an illustration such as an organization chart, a flow chart, or a Venn diagram, use Office's SmartArt feature. Follow these steps:

1. Position the insertion point or the selection where you want to insert the SmartArt object.

2. Click the SmartArt tab on the Ribbon to display its contents. You can also display this tab by choosing Insert ➤ SmartArt Graphic.

> **NOTE:** In PowerPoint, if you're inserting the SmartArt on a slide that has a standard placeholder, you can click the Insert SmartArt Graphic icon in the placeholder to display the SmartArt tab of the Ribbon.

3. In the Insert SmartArt Graphic box, click the button for the category of SmartArt graphic you want to create: List, Process, Cycle, Hierarchy, Relationship, Picture, or Other. A panel opens showing the available types. Figure 4–25 shows the Hierarchy panel, which includes various kinds of organization charts.

Figure 4–25. *Open the panel for the category of SmartArt graphics you want, and then click the type of graphic.*

4. Click the type of graphic you want. The application inserts in the document and displays the Text Pane (see Figure 4–26).

Figure 4–26. *When you insert a SmartArt graphic, the application displays the Text Pane next to it.*

NOTE: If the application doesn't display the Text Pane, click the Text Pane button at the upper-left corner of the SmartArt graphic to display the Text Pane. You can also click this button to hide the Text Pane when you don't need it.

5. In the Text Pane, type the text for each item. As you do, the application adds the text to the SmartArt graphic (see Figure 4–27).

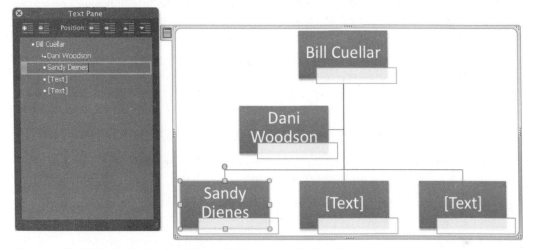

Figure 4–27. *Add the text to the SmartArt graphic by typing in the Text Pane.*

6. Add any other items the SmartArt graphic needs. For example, to add the titles to the org chart shown, click in each title placeholder, and then type the title.

7. Resize the SmartArt graphic to suit the document best. For example, in a PowerPoint presentation, you may want to make the graphic as big as will fit on the slide to enable the audience to read it easily.

8. If you need to change the layout of the SmartArt graphic, choose another layout from the Change SmartArt Graphic group on the SmartArt tab of the Ribbon.

9. Apply a style to the SmartArt graphic by choosing a style from the Quick Styles box or the panel in the SmartArt Graphic Styles group on the SmartArt tab.

When you have finished creating the SmartArt graphic, save the document as usual.

Arranging Graphical Objects to Control Which Is Visible

When you have placed multiple graphical objects in the same area of a document, you may need to arrange the order in which they appear in the document's layers to control how they appear in relation to each other. For example, you may need to move a particular object to the front of the stack of document layers, so that it appears on top of the other objects, or move another object back so that it appears behind one of its companion objects.

In Word, Excel, or PowerPoint, you can rearrange objects by using the Arrange submenu on the context menu. Word and PowerPoint also let you drag the objects into a different order, which is quicker and easier.

Arranging Graphical Objects Using the Arrange Submenu

The old-style way to arrange graphical objects is to use the Arrange submenu. This approach works in Word, Excel, and PowerPoint.

To change where an object appears in the layers, Ctrl+click or right-click the object, click or highlight the Arrange submenu, and then click the appropriate command:

- *Bring to Front.* Click this command to bring the item to the very front of the stack.

- *Send to Back.* Click this command to send the item right to the back of the stack.

- *Bring Forward.* Click this command to bring the object forward by one layer. Give the command again as many times as necessary to bring the object up the stack to where you need it.

- *Send Backward*. Click this command to send the object backward by one layer. As with the Bring Forward command, you may need to give this command multiple times to get the object to where you need it.

- *Bring in Front of Text.* In Word, click this command to move the object so that it appears in front of the text layer.

- *Send Behind Text.* In Word, click this command to move the object so that it is behind the text layer.

Rearranging Graphical Objects with Dynamic Reordering

Word and PowerPoint include a feature called *dynamic reordering*, which enables you to reorder graphical objects quickly.

To use dynamic reordering, follow these steps:

1. Choose Home ➤ Format ➤ Arrange ➤ Reorder Objects. The application displays the page or slide as a sequence of layers. Figure 4–28 shows an example using a PowerPoint slide.

NOTE: To view only the objects that overlap each other, choose Home ➤ Format ➤ Arrange ➤ Reorder Overlapping Objects.

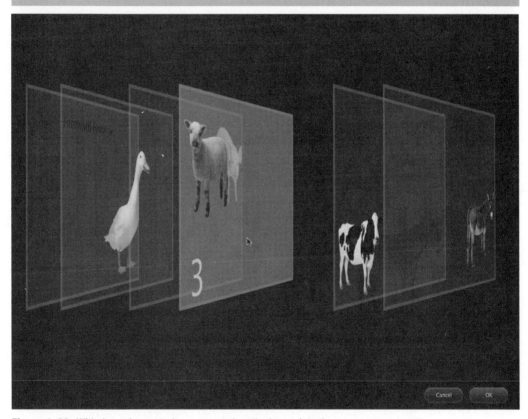

Figure 4–28. With dynamic reordering, you can drag the layers into the sequence you want.

2. Drag the layers into the order you want.
3. Click the OK button to turn off dynamic reordering.

Summary

In this chapter, you learned how to work with graphical objects in the Office applications. You now know how to insert clip art and how to manage clip art items using the Clip Gallery application that comes with Office. You know how to insert your own pictures from iPhoto or your Mac's file system, how to insert shapes and format them, and how to position graphical objects where you want them. You also learned how to control text wrapping in Word; how to recolor, crop, and compress pictures; and how to create SmartArt graphics to illustrate your documents.

In the next chapter, I'll show you how to customize the Office applications to suit your needs.

Chapter 5

Customizing Office to Suit You

Microsoft has put a lot of work into making the Office applications easy to use, but only you know exactly how you work and what you need. To make the Office applications suit you better, you can customize both their looks and their behavior.

In this chapter, you'll learn how to put the controls you need at your fingertips by customizing the three main control features: the toolbars, the menu bar, and the Ribbon. I'll also show you how to create custom keyboard shortcuts in Word and Excel so that you can give commands without moving your fingers from the keyboard.

Beyond these direct customizations to the user interface, each application has hundreds of settings you can use to change how the applications work. In the second half of this chapter, we'll look at two key areas of options common to the applications: the General options, which control vital aspects of the applications' looks and behavior, and the Save options, which control the default formats and folders that the applications use to store your documents.

Choosing Which Toolbars to Display and How to Display Them

The most straightforward step in customizing the Office applications is to choose which toolbars to display. You can also choose whether the Standard toolbar displays icons and text or text only and whether the Formatting toolbar appears within the window or floating outside it.

Choosing Which Toolbars to Display

First decide which of the available toolbars you want to display. To control which toolbars appear, follow these steps:

1. Ctrl+click or right-click one of the toolbars at the top of a document window to display the context menu.

2. Click or highlight the Toolbars item to display the Toolbars submenu. This submenu shows a check mark next to each toolbar that's displayed, as you can see in Figure 5–1.

Figure 5–1. *The easiest way to display or hide a toolbar is to Ctrl+click or right-click a toolbar in the document window and then click the toolbar's entry on the Toolbars submenu.*

3. Click a displayed toolbar's entry on the submenu to remove its check mark and hide the toolbar, or click a hidden toolbar's entry to place a check mark and display the toolbar.

If no toolbar appears in the document window, choose View ➤ Toolbars and use the Toolbars submenu instead.

Switching the Standard Toolbar Between Icons and Text and Icons Only

Next, choose whether to display the buttons on the Standard toolbar as icons with text labels or as icons only (as they appear in Figure 5–1). To switch from one to the other, Ctrl+click or right-click the Standard toolbar, and then click the Icon and Text item or the Icon Only item on the context menu, as appropriate.

Undocking and Docking the Formatting Toolbar

Word, Excel, and PowerPoint at first display their main toolbars docked at the top of the window, between the title bar and the Ribbon (unless you've turned off the Ribbon). The

Standard toolbar remains docked all the time, but you can undock the Formatting toolbar if you prefer to have it floating so that you can position it freely on your Desktop. In PowerPoint, you can also undock the Outlining toolbar.

To undock the Formatting toolbar (or the Outlining toolbar in PowerPoint), Ctrl+click or right-click the toolbar, and then click Dock Toolbar in Window on the context menu to remove the check mark. The application undocks the toolbar and displays it as a floating toolbar (see Figure 5–2) that you can reposition as needed.

Figure 5–2. *You can undock the Formatting toolbar so that you can position it anywhere on the screen—including overlapping the document window if you want.*

NOTE: You can change the size or shape of a floating toolbar by dragging the sizing handle in its lower-right corner. You can also undock or re-dock a toolbar by choosing View ➤ Toolbars ➤ Customize Toolbars and Menus and then clearing or selecting the toolbar's Dock check box in the Customize Toolbars and Menus dialog box, which you'll meet later in this chapter.

To dock the toolbar again, Ctrl+click or right-click empty space in it (where there's no button), and then click Dock Toolbar in Window on the context menu, putting a check mark next to the item. The application snaps the toolbar back into the window.

TIP: If the floating toolbar is packed with buttons, Ctrl+click or right-click outside the Style pop-up menu, Font pop-up menu, or Font Size pop-up menu, where there's a bit of empty space, to display the context menu. Alternatively, drag the sizing handle at the lower-right corner of the toolbar to change the toolbar's shape so that some empty space appears.

Customizing the Toolbars and Menus in Word, Excel, and PowerPoint

In Word, Excel, and PowerPoint, you can customize the toolbars. You can either change the buttons that appear on the main built-in toolbars, such as the Standard toolbar and the Formatting toolbar, or you can create custom toolbars of your own. You can also choose which toolbars to show and hide and decide whether to keep the main toolbars within the document window or allow them to float freely on your screen.

NOTE: In Outlook, you can't customize the menus, and you use a different technique to customize the toolbar. See the section "Customizing the Toolbar in Outlook" later in this chapter for details.

You can also customize both the menus and the menu bar. For example, you can add extra commands to the menus, and perhaps remove commands you don't use, or you can create custom menus of your own. To customize the menus and the menu bar, you use the same techniques as for the toolbar, because the menu bar is technically the same type of object (a "command bar") as the toolbars, even though it looks and acts differently.

TIP: In PowerPoint, you can even customize the context menus that appear when you Ctrl+click or right-click objects.

Preparing to Customize the Toolbars, Menu Bars, or Menus

To prepare to customize the toolbars, menu bar, or menus, open the Customize Toolbars and Menus dialog box and display the toolbar or menu bar ready for customization. Follow these steps:

1. Open the application you want to customize, or activate it if it's already running.

2. Right-click one of the main toolbars, and then click the Customize Toolbars and Menus item on the context menu to display the Customize Toolbars and Menus dialog box. You can also choose View ➤ Toolbars ➤ Customize Toolbars and Menus.

3. If the Toolbars and Menus tab isn't already at the front, click it to bring it to the front. Figure 5–3 shows the Customize Toolbars and Menus dialog box for PowerPoint with the menu toolbar (which you use for customizing the menus and menu bar) above it.

Figure 5–3. *On the Toolbars and Menus tab of the Customize Toolbars and Menus dialog box, select the Show check box for each toolbar or menu you want to display so that you can customize it. The toolbar above the dialog box here is the menu toolbar, which you use for customizing the menus and menu bar.*

4. In the Show column, select the check box for each toolbar or menu bar you want to customize. For example, if you want to customize the menu bar, select the Show check box in the Menu Bar row to make the menu bar appear.

5. In the Dock column, select the Dock check box if you want to dock the toolbar; clear this check box if you want the toolbar to float.

You're now ready to customize the toolbars, menu bar, or toolbars, as discussed in the following sections.

Finding the Commands to Add to the Toolbars or Menus

To find the commands you want to add to the toolbars or menus, follow these steps:

1. Click the Commands tab of the Customize Toolbars and Menus dialog box to display its contents (see Figure 5–4).

Figure 5–4. *On the Commands tab of the Customize Toolbars and Menus dialog box, click the category that contains the command you want to add to a toolbar or menu.*

2. In the Categories list box, click the category of commands you want. For example, click the File category to see the commands associated with the application's File menu.

NOTE: Each category contains more commands than appear on the associated menu. For example, if you click the File category in the Categories list box, you'll see not only those commands that actually appear on the File menu but also those commands that don't appear but perform operations related to files.

3. In the Commands box, locate the command you want to add to the toolbar or menu.

You're now ready to add the command to a toolbar or menu, as discussed in the following sections.

Customizing a Toolbar

You can customize a toolbar by adding to it any of the commands that the application provides, by removing the existing buttons from it, or by repositioning the buttons on the toolbar to suit you better. You can also change the text or icon (or both) that appears on the toolbar to represent the item. And you can add a built-in menu to a toolbar.

Adding an Item to a Toolbar

To add a command to a toolbar, drag the command from the Commands list box on the Commands tab of the Customize Toolbars and Menus dialog box to the toolbar. The application shows a light blue line where the button will appear. If the toolbar is positioned horizontally, as in Figure 5–5, the blue line is vertical; if the toolbar is positioned vertically, the blue line is horizontal.

Figure 5–5. *To add a command to a toolbar, drag it there from the Commands box on the Commands tab of the Customize Toolbars and Menus dialog box.*

Removing an Item from a Toolbar

To remove an item from a toolbar, drag the item off the toolbar and either into the document area of the window or over the Customize Toolbars and Menus dialog box. The item disappears from the toolbar.

Repositioning Items on a Toolbar

To reposition an item on a toolbar, drag it from its current position to where you want it to appear. You can drag an item from one toolbar to another if you want. For example, you can drag a button from the Standard toolbar to the Formatting toolbar to move it from one to the other.

Changing How a Toolbar Button or Menu Item Appears

When you add a button to a toolbar or an item to a menu, the application uses the item's regular icon, text, or both. To make the button or menu item easier to identify, you can change the icon and text. To do so, follow these steps:

1. Ctrl+click or right-click the toolbar button or menu item, and then click Properties on the context menu. The application displays the Command Properties dialog box (see Figure 5–6).

Figure 5–6. *Use the Command Properties dialog box when you want to change the icon, text, or both that appear for a toolbar button or a menu item. The icon to the left of the name box shows the current icon for the command.*

2. In the Name text box, type the name you want to display for the toolbar button or menu item.

> **NOTE:** Some commands display an ampersand character (&) in the Name text box—for example, in Figure 5–6, the Decrease Indent command appears as &Decrease Indent. This character is used in Windows to control the letter used as an access key for the command, like when you press Alt+F to display the File menu (F is the access key). The ampersand character doesn't work like this on the Mac, so you don't need to include it in names you type.

3. In the View pop-up menu, choose how you want the toolbar button or menu item to appear:

- *Default Style.* Choose this item to make a toolbar button appear using the default style you've set for toolbars. (If you've chosen to show icons and text, the button appears as an icon with text beside it; if you've chosen to show only icons, just the icon appears.) A menu item appears as text with an icon if the command has an associated icon.

- *Text Only (Always).* Choose this item to make the toolbar button or menu item appear as text without an icon.

- *Text Only (in Menus).* Choose this item to make a menu item appear only as text.

- *Image and Text.* Choose this item to make the toolbar button or menu item appear as an icon with text beside it.

4. If you want to change the icon, click the arrow button to the left of the Name box, and then click the icon you want on the pop-up menu.

> **TIP:** If you want to use the icon from another toolbar button or menu item, click the Cancel button to close the Command Properties dialog box. Ctrl+click or right-click the item with the icon and click Properties from the context menu to display the Command Properties dialog box for that command. Click the arrow button to the left of the Name box, and then click Copy Button Image. Click the Cancel button to close the Command Properties dialog box. Now open the Command Properties dialog box for the other item, click the arrow button to the left of the Name box, and then click Paste Button Image.

5. Select the Begin a group check box if you want to place a divider line before the item. This is useful when you want to put different groups of items in different sections of the menu or toolbar.

6. Click the OK button to close the Command Properties dialog box.

Adding a Built-in Menu to a Toolbar

One customization that may come as a surprise is that you can add one or more of the built-in menus to a toolbar. You may find this handy if you like to give commands using the menus but you find it awkward moving the mouse all the way up and across to the menu bar—for example, on a large monitor or with a multimonitor setup.

To add a built-in menu to a toolbar, follow these steps:

1. On the Commands tab of the Customize Toolbars and Menus dialog box, scroll down to the bottom of the Categories list box.

2. Click the Built-in Menus item to display the list of menus in the Commands box. The X menu that appears at the top is the application menu—the Word menu, the Excel menu, or the PowerPoint menu.

3. Drag the menu to the toolbar and drop it where you want it to appear.

Figure 5–7 shows a Word window with the File menu and Tools menu added to the Standard toolbar.

Figure 5–7. *You can add the built-in menus to a toolbar to put them within easy reach.*

Customizing a Menu

You can customize a menu by adding an item to it, removing an item from it, moving an item to a different position, or renaming an item.

Adding an Item to a Menu

To add an item to a menu, follow these steps:

1. Drag the item from the Commands tab of the Customize Toolbars and Menus dialog box to the menu toolbar.

2. Hold the item over the menu to which you want to add it. The application opens the menu.

3. Drag the item down the menu until the horizontal blue bar is where you want the item to appear on the menu (see Figure 5–8). Then drop the item.

Figure 5–8. *To add a command to a menu, drag it from the Commands box to the menu toolbar, hold it over the menu until the menu opens, and then drag it where you want it on the menu.*

Moving a Menu Item

To move a menu item to a different position on the menu, display the menu by clicking its name on the menu toolbar, and then drag the menu item you want to move.

Renaming a Menu Item

If you want to change the text or icon for the menu item, Ctrl+click or right-click the item, click the Properties item on the context menu, and then work in the Command Properties dialog box, as described in the section "Changing How a Toolbar Button or Menu Item Appears" earlier in this chapter.

Removing an Item from a Menu

To remove an item from a menu, click the menu on the menu toolbar to display its contents. Then Ctrl+click or right-click the item, and click the Delete Command item on the context menu (see Figure 5–9).

Figure 5–9. *To remove a menu item, right-click it, and then click Delete Command on the context menu.*

Customizing the Menu Bar

If you decide to customize an application extensively, you'll probably want to customize the menu bar. You can do this by adding menus, removing existing menus, or changing the order of the menus.

Creating a New Menu

To create a new menu, follow these steps:

1. On the Commands tab of the Customize Toolbars and Menus dialog box, scroll down to the bottom of the Categories list.

2. Click the New Menu item. The Commands list shows a single command, also called New Menu.

3. Drag the New Menu item from the Commands box to the menu toolbar, and drop it where you want the new menu to appear. Figure 5–10 shows an example of creating a new menu between the Slide Show menu and the Window menu in PowerPoint. Even though the Window menu is open, the new menu lands between the existing menus.

Figure 5–10. *To create a new menu, drag the New Menu item to the menu bar and drop it where you want the new menu to appear.*

4. Ctrl+click or right-click the new menu (which is named New Menu), and then click Properties to display the Command Properties dialog box (shown in Figure 5–6, earlier in this chapter).

5. In the Name box, type the name you want to give the menu, replacing the default name.

6. Click the OK button to close the Command Properties dialog box.

7. Add items to the menu as described earlier in this chapter.

Removing an Existing Menu

To remove an existing menu from the menu bar, Ctrl+click or right-click the menu on the menu toolbar, and then click Delete Command on the context menu. The application removes the menu without confirmation.

Changing the Order of the Menus

To change the order in which the menus appear on the menu bar, click a menu on the menu toolbar and drag it to the new position, just as you would drag a toolbar button on a toolbar.

If you want, you can move a menu from the menu bar onto another menu so that it appears as a submenu. This is occasionally useful if you need to work with low screen resolutions.

Customizing the Context Menus in PowerPoint

In PowerPoint, you can customize the context menus—the shortcut menus that appear when you click objects. Customizing these menus can be a great way to put useful commands right where you need them.

You use the same techniques for customizing the context menus as for toolbars and menus. The only tricky part is that PowerPoint has many context menus, so it may take you a while to determine the name of the context menu you want to customize.

Start by selecting the Shortcut Menus check box on the Toolbars and Menus tab of the Customize Toolbars and Menus dialog box. You can then drag an item to a menu on it (see Figure 5–11), remove items, or reposition items as needed.

Figure 5–11. *To customize the context menus in PowerPoint, display the Shortcut Menus toolbar. You can then drag items to the menus on it, remove items, or reposition items.*

Creating Custom Toolbars Containing the Commands You Need

Customizing the built-in toolbars is often enough to put essential commands where you need them, but if you find yourself giving many commands from the toolbars rather than the Ribbon, you'll probably want to create custom toolbars as well. You can either put all the commands you need on a single toolbar or create different toolbars for different needs. For example, you can create one toolbar with commands for writing your screenplays and another for writing business letters.

To create a custom toolbar, follow these general steps from the Toolbars and Menus tab to the Customize Toolbars and Menus dialog box:

1. Click the New button to display the Add a Toolbar dialog box (see Figure 5–12).

Figure 5–12. *To create a custom toolbar, click the New button on the Toolbars and Menus tab of the Customize Toolbars and Menus dialog box, and then type the name in the Add a Toolbar dialog box.*

2. Type the name for the toolbar.

3. Click the OK button. The application displays an unmarked toolbar just large enough for a single button. The toolbar may appear on top of the Customize Toolbars and Menus dialog box, which can make it hard to see.

4. Click the Commands tab of the Customize Toolbars and Menus dialog box to display it.

5. Locate the first command you want to add, and then drag it to the toolbar (see Figure 5–13). Repeat this process for each command you need on the toolbar.

:Merge Workbooks...

Customize Toolbars and Menus

Toolbars and Menus | Commands

Drag a command into a toolbar or menu bar.

Categories:

All Commands
File
Edit
View
Insert
Format
Tools
Data
Window and Help
Charting

Commands: (Drag to toolbars and menus)

Share Workbook...

Highlight Changes...

Accept or Reject Changes...

Merge Workbooks...

Protect Sheet...

Description

Merge Workbooks (Tools menu)

Combines changes from multiple copies of a shared workbook into one workbook.

Keyboard...   OK

Figure 5–13. *Until you add commands to a new toolbar, it appears at minimum size and can be hard to locate, especially if it's positioned over another object.*

NOTE: To delete a custom toolbar, click it on the Toolbars and Menus tab of the Customize Toolbars and Menus dialog box, and then click the Delete button. In the confirmation dialog box, click the OK button. To rename a custom toolbar, click it on the Toolbars and Menus tab, click the Rename button, type the new name in the Rename a Toolbar dialog box, and then click the OK button.

Resetting a Toolbar to Its Default Buttons

If you decide you don't want to keep the customizations you've made to a toolbar, you can quickly reset it to its default buttons and layout. To do so, follow these steps:

1. Ctrl+click or right-click the toolbar you want to reset. The application displays the context menu.

2. Click the Reset Toolbar item. The application displays a confirmation dialog box (see Figure 5–14).

Figure 5–14. *You can quickly reset a toolbar to get rid of the changes you've made to it.*

3. Click the OK button. The application resets the toolbar to its default buttons in their default order.

Customizing the Ribbon in Word, Excel, and PowerPoint

Word, Excel, and PowerPoint let you turn off the Ribbon if you don't want to use it or customize it if you do use it. You can choose how the Ribbon behaves, which tabs it contains, and the order in which they appear.

Opening the Ribbon Preferences Pane

To customize the Ribbon, first open the Ribbon preferences pane. Follow these steps:

1. Choose Word ➤ Preferences, Excel ➤ Preferences, or PowerPoint ➤ Preferences to display the Preferences dialog box. You can also press Ctrl+, (Ctrl and the comma key).

2. In Word and Excel, click the Ribbon icon to display the Ribbon preferences pane. In PowerPoint, click the Ribbon button on the toolbar.

Figure 5–15 shows the Ribbon preferences pane for Word. The Ribbon preferences panes for Excel and for PowerPoint offer almost the same set of options.

Figure 5–15. *In the Ribbon preferences pane, you can set general options to control the Ribbon's behavior or choose which tabs appear and in which order.*

Choosing General Options for the Ribbon

In the General section at the top of the Ribbon preferences pane, choose settings for these three options:

- *Turn on the ribbon.* Clear this check box (which is selected by default) if you want to turn off the Ribbon. You can then simply use the menus, toolbars, and keyboard shortcuts, as in earlier versions of Office.

- *Expand ribbon when document opens.* This check box, which is selected by default, controls whether the application automatically expands the Ribbon when you open a document. Usually, expanding the Ribbon is handy, because it gives you quicker access to the controls. But if you don't use the Ribbon much, clear this check box to keep the Ribbon collapsed until you click it.

- *Hide group titles.* Select this check box (which is cleared by default) if you want to hide the group titles, such as Font and Paragraph. Hiding the group titles makes the Ribbon take a little less space, but it makes following the instructions in this book (which use the group titles in Ribbon commands) harder to follow.

Choosing Which Tabs and Groups to Display

In the Customize section of the Ribbon preferences pane, choose the look you want for the Ribbon, the tabs to display, and the order in which to display them.

First, open the Appearance pop-up menu and then click the look you want. Each application has its own color: Word Blue, Excel Green, and PowerPoint Orange. The alternative (for all three) is Graphite.

Then, in the "Show or hide tabs, or drag them into the order you prefer" box, set up the tabs. Follow these steps:

1. Clear the check box for each tab you want to hide. You can't clear the check box for the Home tab.

2. In Word, select the check box for any group that's not displayed by default but that you want to display. For example, you can select the Paragraph Indents & Spacing check box to add this group to the Home tab, or you can select the Themes check box to add this group to the Layout tab.

3. If you want to change the order in which the tabs appear, drag them into the order you want.

Closing the Ribbon Preferences Pane

When you've customized the Ribbon to your satisfaction, click the OK button to close the Ribbon preferences pane. The changes to the Ribbon then appear, and you can find out how well they work for you. If you need to change them, just go back to the Ribbon preferences pane.

Customizing the Toolbar in Outlook

In Outlook, you can customize the toolbar in three ways:

- *Change how the buttons appear.* You can choose among showing icons and text, only icons, or only text on the buttons.

- *Switch between normal-size and small buttons.* Using smaller buttons lets you pack more commands on the toolbars.

- *Change which buttons appear on the toolbar.* You can quickly remove buttons you don't need and add those you find helpful.

Changing How the Buttons Appear

At first, Outlook's toolbar displays buttons with both icons and text, as you can see in the top part of Figure 5–16. When you recognize the icons, you can turn off the text by Ctrl+clicking or right-clicking the toolbar and then clicking Icon Only on the context menu; the middle part of Figure 5–16 shows the toolbar with only the icons. If you prefer to show only the text, as shown in the lower part of Figure 5–16, Ctrl+click or right-click the toolbar, and then click Text Only on the context menu.

Figure 5–16. *In Outlook, you can set the toolbar to display icons and text labels, icons only, or text labels only.*

Changing Which Buttons Appear on the Toolbar

To make Outlook easier to work with, you can change which buttons appear on the toolbar. You can do this either quickly by removing a particular button or more formally by using the Customize Toolbar dialog box.

To quickly remove a button from the toolbar, Ctrl+click or right-click the button, and then click Remove Item on the context menu.

> **TIP:** You can quickly rearrange the icons on the Outlook toolbar by Cmd+dragging an icon to where you want it. The other icons move out of the way to make space for the one you're dragging.

To customize the toolbar extensively, follow these steps:

1. Ctrl+click or right-click the toolbar, and then click Customize Toolbar on the context menu; alternatively, choose View ➤ Customize Toolbar from the menu bar. Outlook displays the Customize Toolbar dialog box (see Figure 5–17).

Figure 5–17. *In Outlook, you customize the toolbar by dragging the items you need into it and by dragging from it any items you don't need.*

2. To add a button to the toolbar, drag it from the Drag your favorite items into the toolbar section.

3. To remove a button from the toolbar, drag it from the toolbar into the Customize Toolbar dialog box. The button vanishes in a puff of smoke.

4. To rearrange the buttons on the toolbar, drag a button to the position in which you want it. The other buttons move out of the way to make space.

5. To reset the toolbar to its normal settings, drag the default set of buttons from the bottom of the Customize Toolbar window to the toolbar.

6. In the Show pop-up menu, choose whether how to display the buttons: Icon and Text, Icon Only, or Text Only.

7. Select the Use small size check box if you want to use smaller buttons on the toolbar.

8. Click the Done button to close the Customize Toolbar dialog box.

Creating Custom Keyboard Shortcuts in Word and Excel

The toolbars, menus, and Ribbon can be great for giving commands with the mouse, but if you prefer to keep your hands on the keyboard, you can give commands by pressing keyboard shortcuts instead. Each of the applications comes with many keyboard shortcuts built in, but in Word and Excel, you can also create custom keyboard shortcuts of your own.

> **NOTE:** Keyboard shortcuts can save you time and effort, so it's well worth learning the ones you'll find most useful. The easiest way to learn the keyboard shortcuts for the most widely used commands is to look at the shortcuts listed on the Office applications' menus. For example, the File menu shows you shortcuts such as Cmd+O for the File ➤ Open command, Cmd+W for the File ➤ Close command, and Cmd+P for the File ➤ Print command. You can also find impressively long lists of keyboard shortcuts in the Help files (search for *keyboard shortcuts*).

To create a custom keyboard shortcut, follow these steps:

1. Choose Tools ➤ Customize Keyboard to display the Customize Keyboard dialog box. Figure 5–18 shows the Customize Keyboard dialog box for Word with settings chosen. The Customize Keyboard dialog box for Excel is a different shape (portrait rather than landscape) but has the same controls except for the Save changes in pop-up menu.

Figure 5–18. *Use the Customize Keyboard for Word (shown here) or Excel to set up custom keyboard shortcuts for the commands you need to give most often.*

2. In Word, make sure the Save changes in pop-up menu is showing `Normal.dotm` (see the nearby Note). Choose another template or document only if you want to save the keyboard shortcuts in that template or document rather than have them available for general use. Excel doesn't have this setting.

> **NOTE:** `Normal.dotm`, usually called "the Normal template," is a template that Word opens automatically each time you launch the application and keeps open until you quit the application. The Normal template contains settings for blank documents and also Word-wide settings, such as macros and keyboard shortcuts. By saving your keyboard shortcuts in the Normal template, you make them available to all documents and templates except those containing their own keyboard shortcuts (which override those in the Normal template).

3. In the Categories list box, click the category of command for which you want to create a keyboard shortcut.

   - Both Word and Excel have categories for the main menus that appear on the menu bar all the time: the File menu, the Edit menu, the View menu, and so on.

- Each application has a category for each menu that becomes available only when you work with particular objects. For example, Word has a Drawing category, and Excel has a Charting category.

- Word has an All Commands category. Click this category to see the full list of Word commands. There are more than 1,000, so working with this list is slow going.

- Word has categories for Fonts, AutoText, Styles, and Common Symbols. For example, click Styles to display the list of styles so that you can assign a keyboard shortcut to one.

4. In the Commands list box, click the command. Word or Excel displays information about the command:

- *Current keyboard shortcuts*. The Current keys list box shows any keyboard shortcuts currently assigned to the command (some commands have several shortcuts). If this command has any shortcuts, check that you know them and decide whether you need to create another.

- *Description*. This area shows the description of the command. Read it to make sure you've picked the command you intended. Some command names are clear, but others can be confusing.

5. Click in the Press new shortcut key text box.

6. Press the keyboard shortcut you want to assign:

- You can create keyboard shortcuts that start with the Cmd and Ctrl keys: Cmd, Cmd+Option, Cmd+Ctrl, Cmd+Option+Shift, Cmd+Option+Ctrl, Cmd+Option+Ctrl+Shift, Cmd+Ctrl+Shift, Ctrl, Ctrl+Option, Ctrl+Shift, Ctrl+Option+Shift are all possible.

- You can use pretty much any key on the keyboard—letters, numbers, function keys, and so on.

- A normal shortcut consists of a modifier or modifiers plus one key—for example, Cmd+Option+T. But in Word you can also create modifiers that use two keys in sequence—for example, Cmd+Option+T, S—by pressing the extra key after the key combination. This lets you create many more keyboard and is good for related commands—for example, using the "Cmd+Option+S, 1" keyboard shortcut for one style, the "Cmd+Option+S, 2" keyboard shortcut for another, and the "Cmd+Option+S, 3" keyboard shortcut for a third.

7. Check the Currently assigned to readout to see whether the keyboard shortcut is currently used. If so, press another keyboard shortcut if you don't want to overwrite it.

8. Click the Assign button. Word or Excel assigns the keyboard shortcut to the command.

9. When you've finished assigning keyboard shortcuts, click the Close button to close the Customize Keyboard dialog box.

> **NOTE:** In Word, you need to save the changes you've made to the Normal template. The best way to do this is to Shift+click the File menu and then click Save All. If Word displays a dialog box asking whether you want to save changes that affect the global template, `Normal.dotm`, click the Save button. You can also leave your changes unsaved until you quit Word. At this point, Word either prompts you to save the changes or saves them for you automatically. But if Word crashes before you quit, you will lose the changes.

Choosing Essential Preferences in Word, Excel, and PowerPoint

Each of the Office applications includes several hundred preferences that you can set to make the application behave the way you prefer. That's many more than we can cover in detail here. So, this section concentrates on those settings that are common to Word, Excel, and PowerPoint and make a big difference in the way that the applications behave.

> **NOTE:** You'll find information on important preferences peculiar to individual applications in the chapters that cover those applications, later in the book.

Opening the Preferences Dialog Box or Preferences Window

To work through this section, open the application's Preferences dialog box by choosing Word ➤ Preferences, Excel ➤ Preferences, PowerPoint ➤ Preferences, or Outlook ➤ Preferences. Outlook has a Preferences window rather than a Preferences dialog box; the difference is that you can leave the Preferences window open as you work if necessary, while you have to close the Preferences dialog box before you can continue working in the application.

> **TIP:** You can also press Cmd+, (Cmd and the comma key) to display the Preferences dialog box or Preferences window. This keyboard shortcut works in most Mac applications.

Figure 5–19 shows the Preferences dialog box for Word. Each application not only has different preferences but also divides them up differently among the panes in the Preferences dialog box or Preferences window.

Figure 5–19. *Each Preferences dialog box or Preferences window divides the preferences into different categories.*

In Word and Excel, you can navigate the Preferences dialog box in these ways:

- *Display a category of preferences.* Click the category you want to display—for example, the General category. The application displays the corresponding preferences pane.

- *Return to the main preferences screen.* Click the Show All button on the toolbar. Alternatively, click the Back button on the toolbar.

- *Search for a preference.* Click in the Search Word Preferences box or the Search Excel Preferences box, and then type the term to search for. Highlight the search result that matches, and press the Return key. The Preferences dialog box displays the pane that contains the match.

- *Retrace your path through the preferences panes.* Click the Back button on the toolbar to display the previous pane. Keep clicking the Back button as many times as needed to go back as far as you need.

- *Go forward again through the preferences panes.* After going back, you can click the Forward button on the toolbar to display the next pane. Again, keep clicking to keep going forward.

In PowerPoint, you simply click the toolbar button for the preferences pane you want to display. And in Outlook, you click the icon for the preferences pane you want and then click the Show All button on the toolbar to return to the main preferences screen.

Setting Your User Name, Initials, and Address

If you installed Office yourself, you probably set your user name and initials during setup. If not, you may find that the Office applications think you're called Authorized User or some other generic name. Either way, you may need to add or change your address information.

To change your name, initials, or address information, use Word. In the Word Preferences dialog box, click the User Information icon in the Personal Settings area to display the User Information pane (see Figure 5–20). You can then fill in as many fields as you want: your names and initials; your company name, the city, state, and zip code; and the phone number and e-mail address you want to have associated with the Office applications.

Figure 5–20. *Word is the best application to enter your details in, because it provides fields for the address, phone number, and e-mail address as well as your name and initials.*

Word makes the information you enter available to Excel and PowerPoint, so you don't need to enter your name and initials separately in them. You'll find your user name in the General preferences pane in Excel, and you'll find your name and initials in the Advanced preferences pane in PowerPoint.

Choosing Whether to Display the Gallery Dialog Box When the Application Opens

By default, Word, Excel, and PowerPoint display the Gallery dialog box automatically when you launch the application. The Gallery dialog box can be helpful when you need to create a new document or open a recent document (as discussed in Chapter 2), but you may prefer to have the application open without displaying the extra window. If so, display the General preferences pane for the application and clear the Open Word Document Gallery when application opens check box, the Open Excel Workbook Gallery when application opens check box, or the Open PowerPoint Presentation Gallery when application opens check box, as appropriate.

Choosing Whether to Receive Feedback with Sound

To grab your attention when there's something you need to know, Word, Excel, and PowerPoint can all provide feedback using sound. For example, the application plays a sound to let you know it has finished saving or printing a document. Whether this is helpful depends on how you work and where—for example, whether you're in a cubicle or your own office.

If you want to hear these sounds, select the Provide feedback with sound check box in the General preferences pane; otherwise, clear this check box. In PowerPoint, the control is the Provide feedback with sound to screen elements check box.

Choosing Whether to Confirm Launching Other Applications

Mostly, when you're working in an application, you'll create or open files created in that application or compatible with it. For example, when you're working in Excel, you'll normally create or open workbook files or open text files that Excel can display.

But sometimes you may take an action that creates or opens a type of file that requires a different application. When you do this, the application can warn you that it needs to use a different application. Figure 5–21 shows an example, where PowerPoint (represented by the P icon) asks whether you want to open a document in Word.

The document "Flyer 1.docx" was created in Word. Do you want to open it in Word?

Cancel   Open in Word

Figure 5–21. *Usually, it's a good idea to have Word, Excel, and PowerPoint warn you when you try to create or open a document that requires a different application than the one you're using.*

This prompting is usually helpful. To turn it on in Word and PowerPoint, select or clear the Confirm launching applications in Open and New check box in the General preferences pane. In Excel, select or clear the Confirm before opening other applications check box, also in the General preferences pane.

Changing the Number of Recent Documents the Application Tracks

Word, Excel, and PowerPoint can all track the documents you open and display the list of most recent documents on the File ➤ Open Recent submenu. Usually, the Open Recent submenu is a great time-saver, because it enables you to quickly open any of the last few documents, workbooks, or presentations you worked with.

Each application comes set to track the last 10 documents, but you may want to increase this number to make the Open Recent submenu even more useful. Even if your Mac has a small screen, 25 or so documents will usually fit on the submenu.

Here's how to choose how many recent documents the applications list:

- *Word and PowerPoint:* In the General preferences pane, select the Track recently opened documents check box, and then choose the number in the Display *N* documents in Open Recent box.

- *Excel:* In the General preferences pane, select the Show this number of recent documents check box, and then choose the number in the box.

NOTE: For most people, the only downside to the Open Recent submenu is that it is a potential security threat. If you leave your Mac unlocked and unattended while you are logged on, someone else can see which documents you've been using. You can clear the Open Recent submenu by choosing File ➤ Open Recent ➤ Clear Recent from the menu bar.

Choosing the Default Format for Saving Documents

Word, Excel, and PowerPoint can each save documents in several different formats. Each application comes set to save documents in its preferred format. For example, PowerPoint uses the latest PowerPoint Presentation format by default. But to make sure other people can open the documents you share with them, you may need to change the format. For example, you may need to use a Word document format that colleagues using Office 2004 for Mac or Office 2003 for Windows can open.

When saving a document for the first time, you can save it in any of the formats the application supports. You can also use the File ➤ Save As command to save a new copy of an existing document in a different format. But it's a good idea to set the default format for the documents you create in the application.

Setting the Default Document Format in Word

To set the default format Word uses to save documents, display the Save preferences pane in the Word Preferences dialog box (see Figure 5–22), open the Save Word files as pop-up menu, and click the format you want.

Figure 5–22. *In the Save preferences pane for Word, you can set the default format for saving files, set up AutoRecover backups, and choose other save-related options.*

These are the formats you're most likely to need for Word:

- *Word Document*. Use this format if your colleagues have Office 2011, Office 2008 for Mac, Office 2010 for Windows, or Office 2007 for Windows. Anyone with Office 2004 for Mac or Office 2003 for Windows will need to install converter filters to be able to open the documents.

- *Word 97–2003 Document*. Use this format if your colleagues have Office 2004 for Mac, Office 2003 for Windows, or an earlier version of Office. You can also use this format for greater compatibility with other word processors, such as OpenOffice.org Writer or Google Docs.

- *Rich Text Format*. Use this format if you're creating text-based documents that you need to ensure are fully readable in almost any word processor.

Setting the Default Workbook Format in Excel

To set the default format that Excel uses to save workbooks, display the Compatibility preferences pane in the Excel Preferences dialog box, open the Save files in this format pop-up menu, and click the format you need.

These are the formats you're most likely to need for Excel:

- *Excel Workbook*. Use this format if your colleagues have Office 2011, Office 2008 for Mac, Office 2010 for Windows, or Office 2007 for Windows. Anyone with Office 2004 for Mac or Office 2003 for Windows will need to install converter filters to be able to open the workbooks.

NOTE: Office 2008 for Mac doesn't include VBA. So although you can include macros in an Excel Macro-Enabled Workbook file, Excel 2008 users won't be able to run them.

- *Excel Macro-Enabled Workbook*. Use this format if you need to include macros in your workbooks to perform custom actions. Again, your colleagues will need to have Office 2011, Office 2008, Office 2010, Office 2007, or either Office 2004 or Office 2003 with filters installed to open these workbooks.

- *Excel Binary Workbook*. Use this format if you create large and complex workbooks and need to improve performance. Once more, your colleagues will need to have Office 2011, Office 2008, Office 2010, Office 2007, or either Office 2004 or Office 2003 with filters installed to work with these workbooks.

- *Excel 97–2003 Workbook*. Use this format if your colleagues have Office 2004 for Mac, Office 2003 for Windows, or an earlier version of Office. You can also use this format for greater compatibility with other spreadsheet applications, such as OpenOffice.org Calc or Google Docs.

Setting the Default Presentation Format in PowerPoint

To set the default format PowerPoint uses to save presentations, display the Save preferences pane in the PowerPoint Preferences window, open the Save PowerPoint files as pop-up menu, and then click the format you want.

These are the formats you're most likely to need for PowerPoint:

- *PowerPoint Presentation*. Use this format if your colleagues have Office 2011, Office 2008 for Mac, Office 2010 for Windows, or Office 2007 for Windows. Anyone with Office 2004 for Mac or Office 2003 for Windows will need to install converter filters to be able to open the presentations.

- *PowerPoint Presentation 97–2003*. Use this format if your colleagues have Office 2004 for Mac, Office 2003 for Windows, or an earlier version of Office. You can also use this format for greater compatibility with other presentation applications, such as OpenOffice.org Impress, Google Docs, or Apple Keynote.

Setting AutoRecover to Keep Backups of Your Documents for Safety

Word, Excel, and PowerPoint also let you choose whether to keep AutoRecover files. AutoRecover is a safety net that automatically saves a copy of each open document every few minutes in case the application closes unexpectedly and loses the changes you've made. After the application restarts automatically or you restart it manually, the application opens the latest AutoRecover files for you so that you can choose which versions to keep. If you save your documents and then exit the application, it gets rid of the saved AutoRecover files.

CAUTION: Never rely on AutoRecover as protection against disasters. When AutoRecover works, it can save your bacon, but sometimes it doesn't save everything. So, you should always save your documents frequently while working on them and use AutoRecover only if disaster strikes. You can save a document at any time by pressing Cmd+S, clicking the Save button on the Standard toolbar, or choosing File ➤ Save from the menu bar.

To choose AutoRecover settings, follow these steps:

1. Display the Save preferences pane.

2. Select or clear the Save AutoRecover info every *N* minutes check box (in Word and PowerPoint) or the Save AutoRecover information after this number of minutes check box (in Excel).

3. If you select the check box, enter the number of minutes in the text box. You can set any interval from 1 minute to 120 minutes. An interval of around 3 minutes usually works well, because it saves information frequently enough to avoid disasters but doesn't overly interrupt your work by saving constantly.

NOTE: You can use different AutoRecover settings in each application if you want. For example, you may want AutoRecover to save your Word documents every 2 minutes, your Excel workbooks every 15 minutes, and your PowerPoint presentations not at all.

Setting the Default Folders for Saving Your Documents and Presentations

In Word and PowerPoint, you can set the default folder for saving your documents. The application then displays this folder the first time you display the Save As dialog box after starting the application. (After that, the application displays whichever folder you last saved a document in.)

In PowerPoint, you can also set the folder in which PowerPoint saves narration you record in presentations.

Setting the Default Folder for Saving Word Documents

To set the default folder in Word, follow these steps:

1. Click the File Locations icon in the Word Preferences dialog box to display the File Locations preferences pane (see Figure 5–23).

Figure 5–23. *From the File Locations preferences pane in Word, you can set the default folder for documents and several other types of files.*

> **NOTE:** In the File Locations preferences pane, you can also set the file locations for other types of files. The two settings you're most likely to want to change are the user templates folder (the folder in which Word looks for your templates) and the workgroup templates folder (the folder in which Word looks for templates you share with your co-workers).

2. In the File locations list box, click the Documents item.

3. Click the Modify button to display the Choose a Folder: Microsoft Word dialog box.

4. Navigate to the folder you want to use as the default folder, and then click the Choose button. The dialog box closes, and the folder appears in the Location column alongside the Documents item.

Setting the Default Folder for Saving PowerPoint Presentations

To set the default folder for saving PowerPoint presentations, follow these steps:

1. Click the Advanced button in the toolbar of the PowerPoint Preferences dialog box to display the Advanced preferences pane (see Figure 5–24).

Figure 5–24. *In the Advanced preferences pane for PowerPoint, you can set the default folder for saving files, the default folder for saving narration, and your user name and initials.*

2. Look at the Default file location readout. If you need to change it, click the Select button to display the Choose a Folder dialog box.

3. Navigate to the folder you want to use, and then click the Choose button.

4. Repeat the previous two steps to set the Default narration file location, the folder in which PowerPoint stores files containing the narration you record into presentations.

Summary

In this chapter, you learned essential techniques for customizing the Office applications. You now know how to make the toolbars appear the way you want them and show the buttons you need, not to mention create custom toolbars of your own. You know how to customize the menus and the Ribbon as well—and how to create custom keyboard shortcuts to speed up your work.

You also learned how to open the Preferences dialog box or Preferences window and access the hundreds of settings you can choose in each application. And we went through a handful of essential settings, including those for setting your name, initials, and address; for choosing the default formats for saving documents; and for setting AutoRecover to create automatic backups of your open documents.

This is the end of the first part of the book. You're now familiar with the most important tools and techniques that the applications share, so it's time to dig into using the individual applications. We'll start with Microsoft Word.

Part II

Creating Documents with Microsoft Word

In this part of the book, you'll learn how to harness the power of Microsoft Word to create whichever kinds of documents you need—anything from a short memo or letter to a full-scale book that makes this tome look puny.

In Chapter 6, you'll first learn ways to enter text quickly in Word documents. Next up is selecting text in advanced ways with the mouse and the keyboard, moving around your documents swiftly and smoothly, and pointing Word at the folder that contains your custom templates. You'll also learn to create backup documents automatically, and to make the most of Word's eight different views of a document.

In Chapter 7, I show you the right way to format a document quickly and consistently by using styles rather than by applying direct formatting bit by bit. In this chapter, you'll also learn how to get around your documents by using the Sidebar and the Find feature, and how to harness the power of the Replace feature.

In Chapter 8, you'll first study Word's extra features for creating complex tables—for example, creating a table from existing text. You'll then learn how to break a document into multiple sections; how to add headers, footers, and page numbers; and how to create newspaper-style columns of text. You'll also learn to use bookmarks and cross-references, develop your documents using Word's powerful Outline view, and add footnotes and endnotes to your documents.

In Chapter 9, you'll use Word's Mail Merge feature to create business documents swiftly and efficiently. You'll learn to set up mail merge documents (such as letters or labels), connect them to data sources, and save or print the results.

In Chapter 10, you'll use Word's features for working with your colleagues on documents. You'll learn how to edit a document either simultaneously or separately, how to use the Track Changes feature to mark revisions, and how to integrate changes into a document. You'll also see how to add comments to a document and compare two document versions that contain untracked changes.

In Chapter 11, you'll put your documents to use. First, you'll learn to print an entire document or just parts of it, print a document with or without markup, and even print markup without the document. You'll also learn how to remove sensitive information from documents, create a document you can open with earlier versions of Word, and create PDF files from documents.

Chapter 6

Entering Text and Using Views

In this chapter, I'll show you how to enter text quickly in Word documents by using extra features that Word provides beyond those in the other applications. You'll see how to select text in advanced ways with the mouse and the keyboard, how to move around your documents using keyboard shortcuts and the mysterious "browse object," and how to tell Word where to find your custom templates.

You'll also learn how to make Word automatically create backup documents so that you can recover from disastrous edits or other mishaps and how to exploit the possibilities offered by Word's eight different views of a document.

Entering Text in Your Word Documents

In Word, you can enter text in your documents by typing it in as usual, but you can often save time by entering text in other ways:

- *Paste*. If you have the text in another document or e-mail, you can copy it and then paste it into the Word document.

- *Scan.* If you have the text in a hard-copy document, you can scan it with a scanner and use an optical character recognition (OCR) application such as OmniPage Pro X (www.nuance.com) or Readiris Pro (www.irislink.com) to get the text from the scanned image. You can export or copy the text to Word.

- *Inserting a file*. If you have the text in a Word document or a text file, you can insert it quickly in a Word document. See the "Inserting the Text from a File in a Document" section for details.

- *Using AutoCorrect*. After creating AutoCorrect entries as described in "Saving Time and Effort with AutoCorrect" in Chapter 3, you can insert their contents by just typing their names. AutoCorrect is great for entering sections of boilerplate text with just a few keystrokes.

- *Using AutoText*. As well as AutoCorrect, Word provides AutoText, which is another easy way of inserting preexisting blocks of text. See the "Inserting Prebuilt Blocks of Text with AutoText" section for details.

Inserting the Text from a File in a Document

When you need to put all the text from one document in another document, you can use the Insert ➤ File command instead of opening the document, copying the content, closing the document, and then pasting the content. Follow these steps:

- Place the insertion point where you want to insert the text.

- Choose Insert ➤ File to display the Insert File dialog box (see Figure 6–1).

Figure 6–1. *Use the Insert File dialog box to quickly insert either the entire contents of a document or the contents marked by a bookmark in it.*

- Navigate to the document you want to insert, and then click it.

NOTE: You can also use the Insert File dialog box to insert the contents of a range of cells in an Excel worksheet into a Word document. In the Enable pop-up menu, choose All Office Documents, Excel Workbook (for files with the `.xlsx` file extension), or Excel 97–2004 Workbook (for files with the `.xls` file extension). Then select the workbook, type the appropriate range in the Range/Bookmark text box, and click the Insert button.

- Make sure the Link to File check box is cleared. (If this check box is selected, Word creates a link to the file's data rather than inserting the data itself, which is what you usually want.)
- Click the Insert button. Word inserts the document's text.

TIP: Instead of inserting the entire contents of a document, you can insert the contents of a single bookmark, an electronic marker that you set. To use this feature, set up a document with bookmarks containing the chunks of text you want to use separately, and give the bookmarks names you can remember. Then, in the Insert File dialog box, select the document, and then click in the Range/Bookmark box and type the bookmark's name. Click the Insert button in the Insert File dialog box as usual.

Inserting Prebuilt Blocks of Text with AutoText

If some or many of your documents will include some of the same sections of text, you may be able to save time by using AutoText. This feature gives you an easy way to store prebuilt sections of text so that you can reuse them in your documents. AutoText is like AutoCorrect in a way, but it doesn't replace text automatically—instead, you choose when to insert each AutoText entry, although you can have Word prompt you with available AutoText entries if you like.

An AutoText entry consists of as much text as needed, plus any other objects, such as graphics or tables. Word includes some built-in AutoText entries for standard text items such as "Dear Sir or Madam" and the "Page X of Y" numbering used for headers and footers.

To use AutoText, you first create one or more AutoText entries that contain the text and elements you want. You can then insert these entries as needed in your documents.

To create a new AutoText entry, follow these steps:

1. In your document, enter the material that you want to include in the AutoText entry:

    - Type in the text, and apply any formatting it needs.
    - Add other elements such as graphics or tables.

> **TIP:** Unless you're highly organized, you may find it easier to create AutoText entries when you realize that part of a document you've created would be useful again in the future. If you need to modify the material before creating an AutoText entry from it, copy that part of the document, paste it into a new document, and then change it—for example, removing specific information that you will fill in each time you reuse it. When the material is ready, select it, and then create an AutoText entry.

2. Select the material.

3. Choose Insert ➤ AutoText ➤ New to open the Create New AutoText dialog box (see Figure 6–2).

Create New AutoText

Word will create an AutoText entry from the current selection.

Name: Contact Us

Cancel   OK

Figure 6–2. Use the Create New AutoText dialog box to create a new AutoText entry from the text or other material you've selected in the document.

4. In the Name text box, type the name you want to give the AutoText entry.

> **TIP:** As you'll see in a moment, the easiest way to insert an AutoText entry is by typing enough of its name to identify it. This means it's best to give your AutoText entries distinctive names that describe their contents so that you can type the names without having to look up the entries.

5. Click the OK button. Word closes the Create New AutoText Entry dialog box and adds the AutoText entry to the list Word maintains.

After creating an AutoText entry, you can insert it quickly at the position of the insertion point by typing the first four characters of the name or enough to identify it uniquely among your AutoText entries. When Word displays a ScreenTip containing the first part of the AutoText entry (see Figure 6–3), press Return to insert it.

Figure 6–3 .Word displays a ScreenTip containing the first part of the AutoText entry when you type enough of the name to identify it uniquely. Press Return to insert the entry.

Typing is usually the easiest way to insert your AutoText entries, but you can also browse them by using the AutoText submenu on the Insert menu and the AutoText tab of the AutoCorrect dialog box.

To insert an AutoText entry from the menu bar, choose Insert ➤ AutoText, navigate to the submenu that contains the entry (see Figure 6–4), and then click it. The difficulty here is that Word automatically assigns the AutoText entries to different categories rather than letting you choose the categories, so you may have to hunt down the entry you want.

Figure 6–4. *You can insert an AutoText entry by using the Insert ➤ AutoText submenu and its submenus.*

If you're having difficulty finding the AutoText entry you need, it's usually easier to use the AutoText tab of the AutoCorrect pane of Word's Preferences dialog box. Follow these steps:

6. Choose Insert ➤ AutoText ➤ AutoText to display the AutoCorrect preferences pane with the AutoText tab at the front (see Figure 6–5).

Figure 6–5. *From the AutoText tab of the AutoCorrect preferences pane in Word's Preferences dialog box, you can insert AutoText entries, delete existing entries, or create new entries.*

7. You can then scroll down the list of entries and click the entry you want to see in the Preview box.

8. When you've selected the entry you want, click the Insert button.

From the AutoText tab of the AutoCorrect preferences pane, you can also delete an AutoText entry you no longer need: click the entry in the list, and then click the Delete button. You can also create a new AutoText entry from text and objects you've already selected in your document by typing a name and clicking the Add button, but usually it's easier to use the Create New AutoText dialog box, as described earlier in this section.

Selecting Text in Word-Specific Ways

Apart from the ways of selecting text that you learned in Chapter 3, you can use several shortcuts for selecting text in Word. You can use the mouse, the keyboard, or both.

Selecting Text with the Mouse

When you're using the mouse to move around a document, you can quickly select text by moving the mouse pointer to the left of the text area so that the pointer changes to an arrow pointing up and to the right. You can then use this selection pointer like this:

■ *Select a line.* Click next to the line you want to select.

■ *Select multiple lines.* Click to place the insertion point anywhere in the line at which you want to begin the selection. Then Shift+click in the left margin at the line on which you want to end the selection.

■ *Select a paragraph.* Double-click next to the paragraph you want to select.

■ *Select the whole document.* Triple-click or Cmd+click. (Again, you click to the left of the text area, not in the text.)

■ *Select a column of text.* Sometimes it's useful to select not whole lines but part of several lines—for example, to select the first few blank characters at the beginning of several lines of text you've pasted so that you can delete them all at once. You can do this by Option+dragging with the mouse (see Figure 6–6). When you've selected the text you want, you can format it or delete it.

```
Latest Orders

1 Quick-Erase Marker

1 White Board Cloth, Large

2 Masking Tape, Thick
```

Figure 6–6. *Option+drag when you need to select part of the text on each of several lines—for example, to delete unwanted blank space.*

Selecting Text with the Extend Selection Feature

You can select text in Word using the standard keyboard selection methods discussed in Chapter 4, but Word also provides an odd feature called Extend Selection. You put Word into Extend mode by pressing F8, and you can then continue selecting like this:

- Keep pressing F8. Press once more to select the current word. Press twice more to select the current sentence. Press three more times to select the current paragraph. Press four more times to select the whole document.

NOTE: Depending on how your Mac is configured, you may need to press Fn+F8 rather than F8 on its own to give the Extend Selection command.

- Press the character to which you want to extend the selection. For example, press M to extend the selection to the next letter *m*, press . (the period key) to extend the selection to the end of the sentence, or press Return to extend the selection to the end of the paragraph. You can then press another key to extend the selection further, as needed.

- Press the right arrow key to extend the selection by a single character, or press the left arrow key to reduce the selection by a single character. Press the down arrow key to extend the selection by a line, or press the up arrow key to reduce the selection by a line.

TIP: You can also extend the selection by opening the Find and Replace dialog box and searching for particular text. Make sure the Highlight all items found in check box is cleared.

- With the mouse, click at the point to which you want to extend the selection.

- Press Esc when you've finished selecting and want to work with the selection.

NOTE: The Extend Selection feature can be useful, but it's fine if you decide it's too bizarre to use. But if Word starts behaving oddly and selecting sections of text you're not trying to select, you may have switched on Extend mode by accident. If so, press Esc to switch it off again.

Selecting Multiple Items at Once

Sometimes in Word it's useful to select multiple items at the same time. To do so, select the first item using the keyboard, the mouse, or both. Then hold down Cmd and select the other items with the mouse.

After you've selected multiple objects, you can apply most types of formatting to them all at the same time.

Moving with Keyboard Shortcuts and the Browse Object

As well as the standard keyboard shortcuts discussed in Chapter 3, you can move around a document by using the keyboard shortcuts listed in Table 6–1.

Table 6–1. *Keyboard Shortcuts for Moving the Insertion Point in Word*

Press These Keys	To Move the Insertion Point Like This
Cmd+Up arrow *or* Option+Up arrow	If the insertion point is in a paragraph, to the start of that paragraph. If the insertion point is at the start of a paragraph, to the start of the previous paragraph.
Cmd+Down arrow *or* Option+Down arrow	To the start of the next paragraph.
Cmd+Home	To the start of the document.
Cmd+End	To the end of the document.
Cmd+Page Down	To the next page (or the next browse object).
Cmd+Page Up	To the previous page (or the previous browse object).

To move about a document with the mouse, you can click the scroll arrows or drag the scroll box as usual, but you can also use the three buttons that appear below the vertical scroll bar on the right side of the Word window:

- *Previous button.* This is the button with a double arrow pointing upward.

- *Select Browse Object button.* This is the button with a round gray dot on it. The *browse object* is the type of item by which Word is currently set to move through a document—for example, pages, headings, or tables.

- *Next button.* This is the button with a double arrow pointing downward.

When you first open a document, the buttons are Previous Page and Next Page. Click the buttons to display the previous page or the next page.

When you search using Find, Word automatically switches the Previous and Next buttons to Previous Find and Next Find. You can click the Previous button and Next button to move to the previous or next instance of your search term (if the search term appears more than once).

Similarly, you can move among ten other types of objects in a document, such as comments, tables, and graphics. Table 6–2 explains these items.

Table 6–2. *Word's 12 Browse Objects*

Browse Object	Explanation
Page	Browse from page to page in the document. This is the default setting until you use Find or otherwise change the browse object.
Section	Browse from one section to the next. See Chapter 8 for information on sections.
Comment	Browse from one comment attached to text (or another object) to the next. See Chapter 10 for information on comments.
Footnote	Browse from one footnote to the next. A footnote is a note that appears at the foot of the page that refers to it. See Chapter 8 for information on footnotes.
Endnote	Browse from one endnote to the next. An endnote is a note that appears at the end of a section or document. See Chapter 8 for information on endnotes.
Field	Browse from one field to the next. See Chapter 8 for details on how to use fields.
Table	Browse from one table to the next. See Chapter 3 and Chapter 8 for information on creating tables.
Graphic	Browse from one graphic to the next.
Heading	Browse from one heading to the next. This works with any paragraph you've given a Heading style (see Chapter 7 for details).
Edits	Browse back and forth among the last four edits you've made in the document.
Find	Browse to the next instance of the search term (or other object, such as formatting) you've entered in Find or to the previous instance.
Go To	Move to the next item you've set on the Go To tab of the Find and Replace dialog box. The Go To tab (choose Edit ➤ Find ➤ Go To) lets you move among pages, sections, lines, bookmarks, comments, footnotes, endnotes, fields, tables, graphics, equations, objects, and headings, giving you more flexibility than the Select Browse Object panel does.

TIP: You can also move the insertion point to your last four edits by pressing Shift+F5 once, twice, thrice, or four times.

To choose the browse object, click the round button between the Previous button and the Next button below the vertical scroll bar. This is the Select Browse Object button, and it displays the Select Browse Object panel shown in Figure 6–7. Click the item you want, and you can then click the Previous button and the Next button to move among the instances of that item. You can also press Cmd+Page Down to move to the next item or Cmd+Page Up to move to the previous item.

Figure 6–7. *To browse through a document by comments, fields, or another object, click the Select Browse Object button, and then click the object you want.*

TIP: To open the Select Browse Object panel from the keyboard, press Cmd+Option+Home. You can then use the arrow keys to select the object you want to browse by and press Return to close the panel and start browsing by that object.

Telling Word Where to Find Your Templates

If you have your own custom templates, you may need to tell Word where they're located, or you may need to move them into the templates folder that Word is already using so that you can use them from the Word Document Gallery.

NOTE: Word uses two template folders, the User templates folder and the Workgroup templates folder. When you install Office, the installer automatically sets the User templates folder for you to a folder on your Mac. For a normal installation, the installer does not set the Workgroup templates folder; in a company network, an administrator may set this folder for you. If you share templates with others on your network, you can set the Workgroup templates folder manually to point to this folder by using the technique described in this section.

To set your templates folders or to check which folders Word is using for them, follow these steps:

1. Choose Word ➤ Preferences from the menu bar, or press Cmd+, (Cmd and the comma key), to display the Word Preferences dialog box.

2. In the Personal Settings area, click the File Locations icon to display the File Locations pane (see Figure 6–8).

Figure 6–8. *Use the File Locations pane in the Word Preferences dialog box to check or change the folder in which Word stores your templates.*

3. In the File types list box, click the type of file for which you want to see or change the path. For example, click the User templates item.

> **TIP:** If the folder path is too long to appear fully in the Location column of the File Locations pane, click the Modify button to display the Choose a Folder: Microsoft Word dialog box. You can then click the pop-up menu at the top of the dialog box to see the details of the path to the folder.

4. Click the Modify button to display the Choose a Folder: Microsoft Word dialog box.

5. To change the folder, navigate to the folder you want to use, click it, and then click the Choose button. Word closes the Choose a Folder: Microsoft Word dialog box and displays the new path (or as much of it as will fit) in the File Locations pane.

6. Change any other file paths (for example, you may want to set the Workgroup templates path), and then click the OK button to close the Word Preferences dialog box.

Creating Backup Documents and Recovering from Disaster

Like the other Office applications, Word automatically saves versions of your documents as you work and offers you the chance to recover them when Word restarts after closing unexpectedly (see Chapter 5). But to keep your documents safe, it's a good idea to also turn on Word's feature for creating automatic backups. When you do so, you can also check that a couple of other important options are set correctly. Follow these steps:

1. Choose Word ➤ Preferences from the menu bar, or press Cmd+, (Cmd and the comma key), to display the Word Preferences dialog box.

2. In the Output and Sharing area, click the Save icon to display the Save preferences pane.

3. Select the Always create backup copy check box.

4. If you want Word to automatically save changes you make to the Normal template, such as AutoText entries or new keyboard shortcuts you've created, make sure the Prompt to save Normal template check box is cleared. Select this check box if you want Word to ask you to decide whether to save changes.

5. Click the OK button to close the Word Preferences dialog box.

Now that you've selected the Always create backup copy check box, Word keeps one backup of each document. Here's how it does it:

■ The first time you save, Word saves the document as normal. There's no backup.

- Each time you save the document after that, Word changes the name of the latest saved version of the document to the backup name and then saves the current version under the document name.

Word names the backup file *Backup of* and the document's name and keeps it in the same folder as the document. So if you create a document named `Merlot Tasting.docx`, Word names the backup file `Backup of Merlot Tasting.docx`.

If a document becomes corrupted or if you delete a vital part of it and save the change, you can recover your work by opening the backup document.

Using Views and Windows to See What You Need

To work quickly and comfortably in your documents, you need to understand the eight different views that Word provides and know when to use each of them. You may also need to open multiple windows on the same document so that you can work in different parts of it. Or you may want to split a single document window into two panes so that you can view the document differently in each.

Picking the Right View for What You're Doing

Each of Word's views has a distinct purpose, but you can use each view as much or as little as you want. Most likely, you will find some views much more useful than others for the types of documents you create and the Mac you work on.

You can switch from view to view in these ways:

- *Status bar.* Click the six View buttons at the left end of the status bar and the horizontal scroll bar (see Figure 6–9). You can't switch to Web Layout view this way.

Figure 6–9. *To change views quickly with the mouse, click the view buttons at the left end of the status bar and the horizontal scroll bar. Hold the mouse pointer over a view button to display a ScreenTip showing its name and an explanation.*

NOTE: The View buttons appear only when the horizontal scroll bar is displayed, like it normally is in most views. If the horizontal scroll bar is hidden, you can display it by choosing Word ➤ Preferences, clicking the View icon, selecting the Horizontal scroll bar check box in the Window area, and then clicking the OK button.

- *Menus.* Open the View menu, and then click the command for the view you want: Draft, Web Layout, Outline, Print Layout, Notebook Layout, Publishing Layout, or Full Screen.

- *Keyboard.* Press Cmd+Option+P for Print Layout view, Cmd+Option+O for Outline view, and Cmd+Option+N for Draft view (which used to be called Normal view). The other views don't have built-in keyboard shortcuts, but you can create your own keyboard shortcuts as described in Chapter 5.

Using Print Layout View to See How a Document Will Look When Printed

For most documents, Word opens at first in Print Layout view (see Figure 6–10), which shows you the document as it will appear on paper. You can see each printable element in the document—text, tables, graphics, equations, and so on—in the positions they occupy on the page, along with the white space of the page margins. If you have added headers or footers to the document, you see them too.

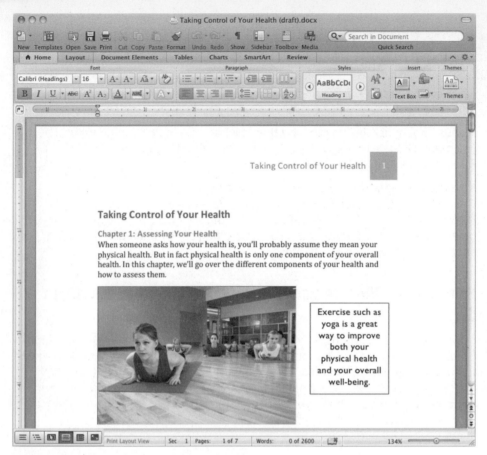

Figure 6–10. *Print Layout view shows the document with headers and footers, margins, and graphics all in the positions they occupy on paper.*

Using Full Screen View to See More of a Document

Full Screen view removes as much of the Word interface as possible to let you see more of your document. In Full Screen view (see Figure 6–11), Word expands to take up the whole screen, hides the Ribbon, and displays only essential controls on a bar across the top of the window. This bar appears at first for a few seconds and then disappears until you move the mouse pointer back to the top of the screen to summon it again.

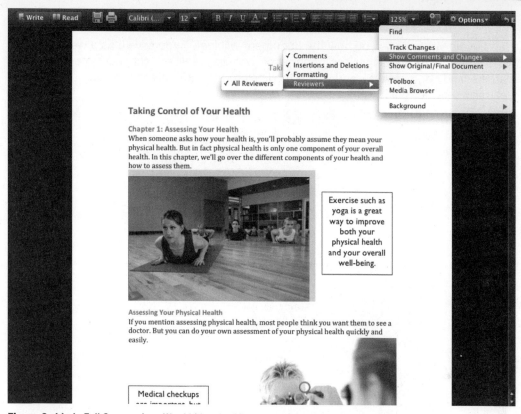

Figure 6–11. *In Full Screen view, Word hides the Ribbon and the menus, but you can give essential commands from the bar across the top of the screen and the Options pop-up menu.*

As you can see in the figure, a Write button and a Read button appear at the left end of the command bar. Word normally opens Full Screen view in Writing view, which you see in the figure and which contains commands for writing and formatting documents. To pare down the interface further, switch to Reading view by clicking the Read button. In Reading view, you can navigate from page to page by clicking the page thumbnails that appear in a column at the left side of the screen.

If the text isn't big enough to read or is too big, use the Zoom pop-up menu to change to a more suitable zoom percentage. From the Zoom pop-up menu, you can also switch among displaying one page, displaying two pages, or displaying multiple pages. Displaying multiple pages can be helpful for getting an overview of how the document looks, even if most of the text is too small to read.

To leave Full Screen view, move the mouse to the top of the screen to display the command bar, and then click the Exit button at the right end. From the keyboard, press the Esc key. Word returns you to the view you were using before you switched to Full Screen view.

Using Web Layout View to Get a Preview of Web Pages

Web Layout view shows you how the document will look if you save it as a web page. Word hides all the items that don't appear on web pages—headers and footers, margins, and page breaks—and wraps the lines to the width of the window, just as a web browser does (see Figure 6–12).

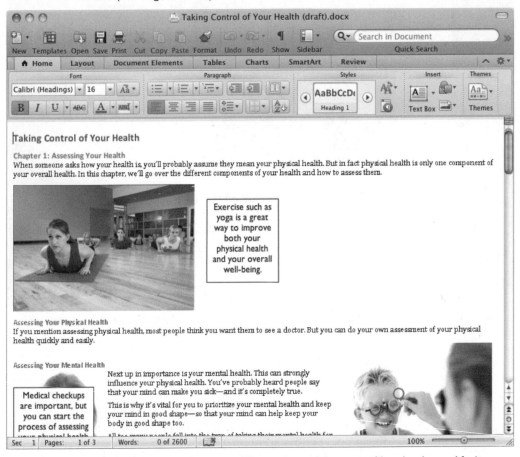

Figure 6–12. *Web Layout view displays the page as if it were in a web browser, with no headers and footers, margins, or page breaks. Some items may appear in unsuitable places, such as the caption box superimposed on a figure in the lower-left corner here.*

NOTE: When you switch to Web Layout view, Word hides the horizontal scroll bar and the View buttons. To switch from Web Layout view to another view, use either the commands on the View menu or a keyboard shortcut.

Developing a Document in Outline View

Outline view is a powerful tool for developing the outline and structure of a document. Outline view displays the document as a structure of headings, each of which you can collapse or expand as needed (see Figure 6–13). See Chapter 8 for instructions on using Outline view.

Figure 6–13. *Outline view is a great tool for working on the structure of a document. You can expand different sections of the document to different levels as needed.*

Using Draft View

Draft view, which used to be called Normal view, is great for working with the body text of a document. You see all the text, but Word hides items such as headers and footers, margins, and objects. Figure 6–14 shows Draft view.

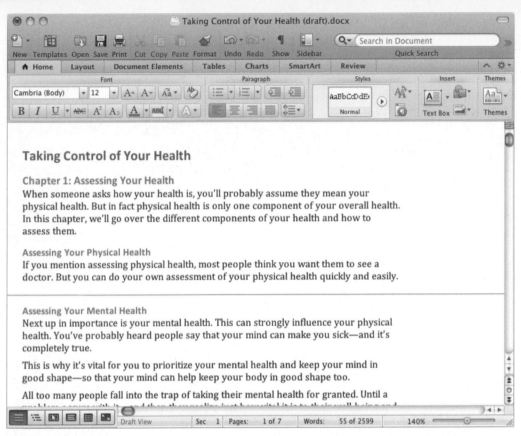

Figure 6–14. *Draft view enables you to concentrate on the text of the document without worrying about layout elements such as headers and footers. To display as much text as possible and avoid having white space on the right side of the window (as shown here), turn on the Wrap to window feature.*

TIP: Draft view is usually easiest to use if you make Word wrap the text to the window so that the text fills the window—otherwise, you'll often get blank space on the right side of the window. Word doesn't do this by default. To make Word wrap the text, choose Word ➤ Preferences, and then click the View icon in the Authoring and Proofing Tools section of the Preferences dialog box. In the View pane, select the Wrap to window check box in the Window area, and then click the OK button.

Taking Notes in Notebook Layout View

When you switch a document to Notebook Layout view, Word displays the document as if it were part of a loose-leaf binder (see Figure 6–15). If the document has only a single section (as many blank documents do at first), Word automatically creates two extra sections and displays tabs for the sections on the right side of the page. You can move from one section to another by clicking these tabs, and you can create a new section by clicking the + button below the last tab.

Figure 6–15. *Notebook Layout view shows the Word document as part of a notebook. You can move from one section to another by clicking the tabs on the right.*

These are the essential moves to use in Notebook Layout view:

- *Give the page a title.* Click above the Title line at the top of the page, and type the title.

- *Rename a section.* Double-click the section name to select it, type the name you want, and then press Return.

- *Display another section.* Click the tab for the section you want to display.

- *Create a new section.* Click the + button below the last section tab.

- *Change the order of sections.* Drag a section tab up or down the tabs to where you want it to appear.

- *Change the workspace background.* Click the Customize Workspace pop-up menu on the status bar, and then click the color or look you want—for example, Oak or Grill.

- *Record audio notes.* Click the Audio Notes tab on the Ribbon to display its contents (see Figure 6–16). You can then drag the Input Volume slider to adjust the input level (shown on the Input Level meter) and click the Record button when you're ready to start recording.

Figure 6–16. *Use the controls on the Audio Notes tab of the Ribbon for a document in Notebook Layout view to record audio straight into the notebook using your Mac's microphone.*

Laying Out a Document in Publishing Layout View

When you need to lay out a document in Word rather than develop or edit a document's text or other content, use Publishing Layout view. This view makes Word act more like a page layout application and less like a word processing application, although you can still enter and edit text much as usual.

When you create a document based on one of the templates that appear in the Publishing Layout View section of the Templates list in the Word Document Gallery dialog box, Word automatically switches to Publishing Layout view. Figure 6–17 shows a new (but saved) document created from one of Word's newsletter templates in Publishing Layout view.

NOTE: If you want to lay out a document from scratch in Publishing Layout view, choose the Blank template in the Word Document Gallery dialog box. You can then add to the document whichever elements it needs.

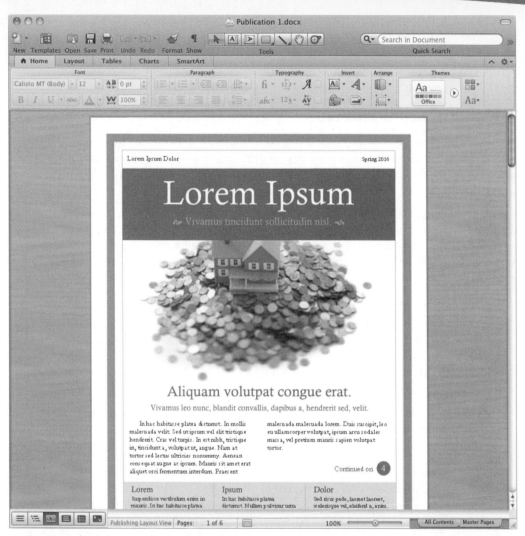

Figure 6–17. *Publishing Layout view hides editing-related Ribbon tabs and displays layout-related tools on the Standard toolbar and on the remaining Ribbon tabs.*

NOTE: You can also switch an existing document to Publishing Layout view by clicking the Publishing Layout view button at the left end of the status bar and the horizontal scroll bar or by choosing View ➤ Publishing Layout. If the document you're switching wasn't originally created in Publishing Layout view, Word warns you of this and offers to create a new document in Publishing Layout view instead. Click the Continue button if you want to continue switching the existing document to Publishing Layout view.

In Publishing Layout view, Word hides the Document Elements tab and Review tab of the Ribbon and displays layout-related groups on the other tabs, together with layout-related buttons on the Standard toolbar. For example, in Publishing Layout view, the Home tab displays the Typography group and the Arrange group that you can see in the figure, and the Layout tab includes the Pages group and the Guides group (for controlling on-screen guidelines, not Girl Scouts).

Opening Extra Windows

At first, Word displays a single window of each document. For short documents, this is all you need, but for long or complex documents, you may find it helpful to open extra windows so that you can see two or more parts of the document at once or use different views.

For example, when you're writing a lengthy report, you may benefit from seeing the introduction as you write the conclusion, to make sure you nail each of your main points. Or you may want to open a window showing the outline of a document so that you can add headings and change its structure even as you write regular text in one of its sections.

Here's how to open and work with extra windows:

- *Open a new window.* Choose Window ➤ New Window from the menu bar. Word adds ": 1" to the document's name in the title bar of the original window to indicate that it's now the first window of the document. The second window's name includes ": 2"—for example, Linguistics Report: 2.

- *Arrange your Word windows.* Click and drag the windows to where you need them.

> **NOTE:** Word includes an Arrange All command (choose Window ➤ Arrange All), but it tiles the Word windows horizontally, which usually isn't what you want. Usually it's best to arrange your windows manually, but you can also use a third-party utility such as Divvy (www.mizage.com/divvy/) or SizeUp (http://irradiatedsoftware.com/sizeup/) or create a macro using Visual Basic for Applications (VBA). If possible, try such a third-party utility before buying it, because the Office applications appear to disagree with some of them.

- *Switch from window to window.* If you can see the window you want, click it. Otherwise, open the Window menu, and then click the window you want on the list at the bottom.

> **TIP:** Press Cmd+F6 or Option+F6 to display the next window (of any open Word document, not just the one that has multiple windows open). Press Cmd+Shift+F6 or Option+Shift+F6 to display the previous window.

- *Close a window.* Click the window's Close button (the red button at the left end of the title bar). The document remains open until you close its last window.

Splitting the Document Window into Two Panes

Sometimes it's useful to split the document window into two panes so that you can work in two different parts of the same document at once. Splitting the document window is like opening a new window except that you don't need more space. Figure 6–18 shows the document window split, with the upper pane showing Print Layout view and the lower pane showing Outline view.

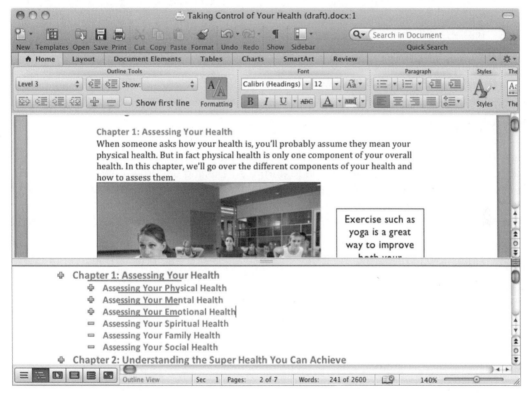

Figure 6–18. *You can split a window into two panes so that you can use two different views at once or work in different parts of the document.*

To split the document window into two equal parts, double-click the split box just above the scroll arrow at the top of the vertical scroll bar. You can then adjust the split by dragging the split bar up or down as needed.

To split the document window into two unequal parts, drag the split box from the top of the vertical scroll bar down as far as needed.

Once you've split the window, you can scroll each pane separately so you can display a different part of the document in each pane. You can also use a different view in each pane—for example, display the document's outline in Outline view in one pane while you write the introduction or summary in Normal view in the other pane.

To switch to the other pane, click in it or press F6.

> **TIP:** You can also zoom out in one pane to get an overview of the document as a whole, and you can zoom in using the other pane so that you can see the detail of a section.

When you want to remove the split, take one of these actions:

- *Mouse.* Double-click the split bar. Alternatively, drag it to the top (to keep the lower pane) or to the bottom (to keep the upper pane).

- *Keyboard.* Press Cmd+Option+S.

- *Menu bar.* Choose Window ➤ Remove Split.

Summary

In this chapter, you learned new tricks for inserting text quickly and easily in Word document, including how to insert the text from an existing document and how to create AutoText entries to reuse boilerplate text. You've also grasped how to select blocks of text using the Option+drag maneuver and the Extend Selection feature and learned new ways of navigating around a document using keyboard shortcuts and the browse object.

Better yet, you now know how to get Word to make automatic backups of your documents, how to make the most of Word's seven views, and how to open extra windows or split a single window into two panes.

In the next chapter, you'll learn how to save any amount of time by formatting your documents the right way—by using Word's powerful styles.

Chapter 7

Adding Style: Formatting Your Documents

To make your documents look good, you must apply formatting to the text and other elements in them.

That's easy to say, but Word gives you such a wide range of formatting options that it's easy to use the wrong ones. This chapter teaches you the right way to format a document quickly and consistently by using styles—collections of formatting—rather than by applying direct formatting piece by piece. It also shows you how to use the Sidebar pane and the Find feature to navigate your documents and how to make the most of the versatile Replace feature.

Before we start, a word of warning: styles are an extremely powerful tool that can save you huge amounts of time—but you will need to invest some time and effort in understanding how they work before you can harness all their power. To complicate things, Word provides several different tools for working with styles, and the way these tools interact and overlap takes some getting used to. But once you get the hang of them, you'll find that you can work swiftly and effectively with them.

Understanding Word's Many Types of Formatting

Word gives you such a wide variety of formatting that it's easy to waste time by using the wrong ones for your needs. This section explains the different types of formatting and shows you the best and fastest way to use them.

Understanding Direct Formatting and When to Use It

Where most people start is by using direct formatting, the kind of formatting that you can apply by using the controls in the Font group and the Paragraph group on the Home tab of the Ribbon or the controls on the Formatting toolbar (see Figure 7–1). For example, you can create a heading paragraph by changing to a different font, increasing the font size, changing the font color, giving it an "outdent" so that it sticks out into the margin, and adding extra space before and after the paragraph.

Figure 7–1. You can easily apply direct formatting such as font formatting and paragraph formatting using the Font group and Paragraph group controls on the Ribbon or using the controls on the Formatting toolbar, but you can save time and effort by applying styles from the Styles group or the Styles pop-up menu first.

Each part of this formatting is easy enough to apply—click this, click that, click the other—but it takes time. And if you need to create another heading of the same type, you need to do it all over again. Or you can copy and paste the formatted text and type the new heading over it (as many people do) or use Word's clever Format Painter feature (which you'll learn about later in this chapter).

Because direct formatting takes extra time and effort, you'll do best to apply it only when you have formatted your documents almost completely using better tools, as discussed next.

Understanding Styles and When to Use Them

To help you apply standard formatting quickly, Word includes a feature called styles. A *style* is a collection of formatting that you can apply all at once. So, once you've set up a style for the heading that contains exactly the formatting you want, you can apply it in a single click.

In fact, in many cases you don't even need to create the styles yourself. Word comes with many styles built in to its Normal template and other templates. As soon as you create a document based on one of these templates, you can start applying styles, formatting your documents swiftly and consistently.

Word gives you four different types of styles:

- *Paragraph style.* This is a style you apply to a whole paragraph at a time—you can't apply it to just part of a paragraph. A paragraph style contains a full range of formatting for that paragraph—everything from the font name, size, and color to the indentation and spacing for the paragraph, and the language used. For example, many documents use a Body Text style that gives the distinctive look to the body paragraphs.

- *Character style.* This is a style you apply to individual characters within a paragraph, usually to make it look different from the style of the rest of the paragraph. For example, within a paragraph that uses the Body Text style, you can apply an Emphasis character style to a word to make it stand out.

- *Table style.* This is a style you can apply to a Word table. Like a paragraph style, the style can contain font and paragraph formatting, but it can also contain table formatting such as borders and shading.

- *List style.* This is a style you can apply to one or more paragraphs to make them into a list—a numbered list, a bulleted list, or a multilevel list. A list style usually contains font formatting and numbering formatting.

Styles enable you not only to apply formatting quickly but also to change the formatting by modifying or replacing the style:

- *Modify the style.* If the style doesn't look right, you can modify it. Each paragraph to which you've applied the style takes on the changes you make immediately.

- *Replace one style with another style.* You can replace every instance of one style with another style in moments, making sweeping changes right through a document.

Formatting Your Documents the Best Way

Here's the best way to format your documents:

- First, format each paragraph with a paragraph style. This style gives the whole paragraph its overall look. If the paragraph is a heading, the Heading style tells Word to include the paragraph in the document's outline.

- Next, use character styles to add extra formatting needed within paragraphs. For example, use a character style such as Emphasis to add impact to a word or phrase that you want to stand out.

- If the document contains lists, apply the appropriate list style to each list. For example, apply a numbered list style to a list that needs numbers, or apply a bulleted list style to a list that needs bullets.

- If the document contains tables, apply a suitable table style to each table.

UNDERSTANDING WHERE WORD KEEPS STYLES

Word keeps styles in templates and documents. As you learned in Chapter 1, a template is a file that contains the basic structure of a document—for example, the structure of a business letter. When you create a new document, you can choose whether to base it on a particular template or on the Normal template that Word uses for "blank" documents.

The styles available from the Styles group and the Styles panel when you first open Word are the ones stored in the Normal template. You can customize these styles as needed, but be aware that the changes carry through to all documents based on the Normal template.

When you create or open a document based on a template other than the Normal template, Word makes that template's styles available in the Styles group and the Styles panel. If the template is one that comes with Word or one that you've downloaded from the Web, it will most likely contain its own styles. You can modify these styles if you need to do so.

When you create a new template, you can create all the custom styles you need. You can also import styles from other templates or documents to save time.

Even though each document picks up the details of the styles from the attached template, the document itself contains information about the styles. This enables Word to display the document correctly when the template is not available.

When you're working in a document and modify a style, you can choose whether to save the changes in that document or in the template attached to the document. Normally you'll want to save the changes in the template, making them available to all existing documents based on the template and any new documents you create based on the template. By contrast, changes you save in the document are available only to that document (and to other documents you base on it).

Applying Styles to a Document

Word 2011 gives you four main ways of applying styles to a document:

- *Ribbon.* Use the Quick Styles box on the Home tab.
- *Formatting toolbar.* Use the Styles pop-up menu.
- *Toolbox.* Use the Styles pane.
- *Styles dialog box.* Open the Style dialog box, and use it to apply a style.

Each method has its pros and cons. Let's look at each method in turn.

Applying Styles from the Quick Styles Box on the Ribbon

Usually, the easiest way to get started with styles is to apply styles by using the Quick Styles box and panel on the Home tab of the Ribbon. Follow these steps:

1. Click in the paragraph to which you want to apply the style. If you want to apply the style to several paragraphs at once, select all or part of each paragraph.

2. Apply the style:

- If the style name is in the Quick Styles box that appears in the Styles group, click it.

- If the style name doesn't appear in the Styles group, hold the mouse pointer over the Quick Styles box to display the panel button, and then click the panel button to display the Quick Styles panel (see Figure 7–2). Then click the style name.

Figure 7–2. *Click a style in the Quick Styles panel to apply the style to the current paragraph or selected paragraphs.*

TIP: Never use the Normal style as the formatting for the body of your documents. The problem is that Word uses the Normal style as the default, so it can be hard to tell whether you've applied the Normal style or Word has applied it because you haven't applied another style. For the body text in your documents, use a style such as Body Text instead, keeping the Normal style only for text you still need to give a style. You can then search (as described later in this chapter) for the Normal style and apply another style to each instance of it as needed.

Applying Styles with the Styles Pop-Up Menu on the Formatting Toolbar

If you keep the Formatting toolbar displayed in Word, you can also apply styles from this toolbar's Styles pop-up menu. Follow these steps:

1. Place the insertion point in the paragraph you want to apply the style to, or select multiple paragraphs.

2. Click the Styles pop-up button to display the pop-up menu (see Figure 7–3).

Figure 7–3. *You can quickly apply a style from the Styles pop-up menu on the Formatting toolbar.*

3. Navigate to the style you want to apply:

   ■ Hold the mouse pointer over the up arrow button at the top to scroll up the list. Hold the pointer over the down arrow button at the bottom to scroll down.

   ■ Type the first letter, or first few letters, of the style name to jump to that point in the list.

4. Click the style to apply it to the paragraph.

> **NOTE:** Because the Styles pop-up menu shows you only a dozen or so styles at a time, it can be an awkward way to apply styles. But you may find the Styles pop-up menu useful even if you don't open it, because it gives you a quick way to see the style applied to the current paragraph.

Applying Styles with the Styles Pane

When you need to work extensively with styles, the best tool is the Styles pane, which is part of the Toolbox.

You can display the Styles pane (see Figure 7–4) in any of these ways:

- *Mouse.* Click the Toolbox button on the Standard toolbar, and then click the Styles button (the left button, with the ¶ symbol) to display the Styles pane.

- *Ribbon.* Choose Home ➤ Styles ➤ Manage Styles. The Manage Styles button is the button with the ¶ symbol in the lower-right corner of the Styles group.

- *Menu bar.* Choose View ➤ Styles.

Figure 7–4. *The Styles pane in the Toolbox is the best choice for extensive work with styles. The ¶ symbol to the right of a style's name indicates a paragraph style; the letter a indicates a character style.*

In the Styles pane, you can take the following actions:

- *Check the current style.* The Current style of selected text box at the top of the pane shows the style of the current paragraph or selected text.

- *Start creating a new style.* Click the New Style button.

- *Select all instances of the current style.* Click the Select All button. By selecting all instances, you can then apply another style easily.

- *Apply another style.* In the Pick a style to apply list box, click the style you want to apply.

- *Choose which styles to show in the list.* Many Word templates contain many styles, so you don't necessarily want all the styles to appear in the Styles pane. Use the List pop-up menu to control which styles do appear. Your choices are as follows:

  - *Recommended.* Click this item to display the styles that Word recommends for widespread use in documents of this type.

  - *Styles in Use.* Click this item to restrict the list to the styles you're currently using in the documents based on this template.

  - *In Current Document.* Click this item to restrict the list to the styles the current document uses so far. This is often a good choice once you've applied most of the styles you intend to use for the document at least once.

  - *All Styles.* Click this item to display the full list of styles. You'll need to scroll up and down to find the styles you need.

- *Toggle styles guides on and off.* Select the Show Styles Guides check box to display a color-coded number next to each paragraph in Print Layout view showing the style. The Styles pane shows the color-coded numbers next to their styles. For example, in Figure 7–5, the Heading 1 style has the number 2 and is applied to the top paragraph.

Show Styles Guides check box in the Styles pane in the Toolbox to display color-coded styles. Select the Show Direct Formatting Guides check box to display boxes around the text ing applied, such as "plan the project" in the last paragraph.

rect formatting guides on and off. Select the Show Direct g Guides check box to make Word display a box around that contains direct formatting. For example, in the figure, the words *office relocation project* in the second paragraph have direct italic formatting applied, and the words *plan the project* in the last paragraph have direct bold formatting applied.

TIP: After displaying the direct formatting guides, click one of the boxes to see the details of the formatting applied. The Current style of selected text box at the top of the Styles pane shows the details—for example, Normal + Bold. If you want to remove the direct formatting, hold the mouse pointer over the Current style of selected text box, click the pop-up button to display the pop-up menu, and then click Clear Formatting.

- *Select all instances of a style.* Move the mouse pointer over the style name in the Pick a style to apply list so that a pop-up arrow appears, and then click the arrow to display the pop-up menu (see Figure 7–6). Click the Select All item on the menu.

Figure 7–6. *Use the pop-up menu for a style to access the Select All command, the Modify Style command, the Delete command, and the Update to Match Selection command.*

- *Open the Modify Style dialog box.* Open the pop-up menu for the style, and then click the Modify Style item.

- *Delete a style.* Open the pop-up menu for the style, and then click the Delete item. This item isn't available for key built-in styles such as Heading 1 and Normal.

- *Update a style to match the selection.* When you've applied a style but then changed it with direct formatting, you can update the style so that it takes on the direct formatting. To do this, select the paragraph, open the pop-up menu for the style, and then click the Update to Match Selection item.

Applying Styles Using the Style Dialog Box

The fourth way of applying styles is to use the Style dialog box. This method is sometimes useful, but generally it's more awkward than using the Styles pane.

To apply a style using the Style dialog box, follow these steps:

1. Click in the paragraph to which you want to apply the style, or select the text that'll receive the style.

2. Choose Format ➤ Style to open the Style dialog box (see Figure 7–7).

Figure 7–7. *You can use the Style dialog box to apply a style, to modify an existing style, or to start creating a new style.*

3. In the Styles list box, click the style you want to apply.

> **NOTE:** If the style you're looking for doesn't appear in the Styles list box, open the List pop-up menu and choose All Styles instead of Styles in Use or User-Defined Styles.

4. Click the Apply button. Word closes the Style dialog box and applies the style.

Applying Different Quick Styles to a Document

When you've applied a style to each paragraph (and perhaps to individual words), you've defined what the different parts of the text are—the headings, the body text, and so on. If you want to change the way the whole document looks, you can now change the look of the styles.

Choose Home ➤ Styles ➤ Change Quick Styles Settings to display the pop-up menu (see Figure 7–8), and then click the style set to apply.

Figure 7–8. *Use the Change Quick Styles Settings pop-up menu in the Styles group on the Home tab of the Ribbon to change a style set.*

From the Change Quick Styles Settings pop-up menu, you can also give these three commands:

- *Reset to Quick Styles from Template.* Click this command to apply the default set quick styles used in the template on which the document is based.

- *Reset Document Quick Styles.* Click this command to reset the quick style sets in the document to their default settings. Doing this removes any customizations you've made to the quick styles.

- *Save as Quick Style Set.* Click this to display the Save Quick Style Set dialog box, in which you can save the current set of quick styles under a name of your choice. Save the quick styles when you've customized them and want to keep the changes.

Changing the Styles in the Quick Style Gallery

The Quick Style Gallery on the Home tab of the Ribbon includes a selection of styles to get you started. But if you apply styles frequently from the Quick Style Gallery, as is handy, you may want to customize the selection of styles.

You can customize the Quick Style Gallery like this:

- *Remove an existing style.* In the Quick Style Gallery, Ctrl+click or right-click the style, and then click Remove from Quick Style Gallery on the context menu.

- *Add an existing style.* In the Pick a style to apply list, hold the mouse pointer over the style, click the pop-up button, and then click the Modify Style item. In the Modify Style dialog box, select the Add to Quick Style list, and then click the OK button.

- *Create a new style and add it.* Follow these steps:

  1. Format some text with the formatting you want the new style to have.

  2. Select the text you've formatted.

  3. Choose View ➤ Styles to display the Styles pane in the Toolbox if it's not already displayed.

  4. Click the New Style button to display the New Style dialog box (see Figure 7–9).

Figure 7–9. *Select the Add to Quick Style list check box in the New Style dialog box to make Word add the new style to the Quick Style Gallery.*

  5. In the Name box, type the name you want the style to have.

  6. Choose other settings for the style as needed. We'll dig into these in the section "Creating Custom Styles" later in this chapter.

7. Select the Add to template check box if you want to add the style to the template. This is usually a good idea.

8. Make sure the Add to Quick Style list check box is selected.

9. Click the OK button. Word closes the New Style dialog box and adds the style to the Quick Style Gallery. You can then apply it like any other style.

Applying Styles Using the Keyboard

You can also apply styles by using keyboard shortcuts, which is useful when you're typing. Table 7–1 shows standard keyboard shortcuts, which work in Word's Normal template and in many other templates.

Table 7–1. *Standard Keyboard Shortcuts for Applying Styles in Word*

Style	Keyboard Shortcut
Normal	Cmd+Shift+N
Heading 1	Cmd+Option+1
Heading 2	Cmd+Option+2
Heading 3	Cmd+Option+3

TIP: If you want to apply other styles from the keyboard, create keyboard shortcuts for them as discussed in Chapter 5.

See Which Styles a Document Uses

To see which style a particular paragraph uses, you can click in the paragraph and look at the style selected in the Styles pane or the Styles pop-up menu on the Formatting toolbar. In Print Layout view, you can also select the Show Styles Guides check box in the Styles pane to display the color-coded numbered boxes to the left of the text, as discussed earlier in this chapter.

To see the style applied to each paragraph in Draft view and Outline view, you can open the style area, which is a vertical strip at the left side of the Word window that displays the style applied to each paragraph (see Figure 7–10).

Heading 1	**Office Relocation Project**
Body Text	Our *office relocation project* consists of three parts:
List Bullet	• Planning
List Bullet	• Approval
List Bullet	• Execution
Body Text	You'll find the details in the following sections.
Heading 2	Planning
Body Text	We must **plan the project** thoroughly to make sure it will work.

Figure 7–10. *In Draft view and Outline view, you can display the style area on the left side of the window to see the style applied to each paragraph.*

To display the style area, follow these steps:

1. Choose Word ➤ Preferences from the menu bar or press Cmd+, (Cmd and the comma key) to display the Word Preferences dialog box.

2. In the Authoring and Proofing Tools area, click the View icon to display the View pane.

3. In the Window area, enter the measurement in the Style area width box. One inch is usually about right.

4. Click the OK button to close the Word Preferences dialog box.

Now click the Draft button at the left end of the status bar to switch to Draft view, or click the Outline button to switch to Outline view. The style area appears on the left of the screen, and you can easily see the style applied to each paragraph.

> **TIP:** To change the width of the style area, move the mouse pointer over the line that divides the style area from the text. When the pointer changes to a double-headed arrow, click and drag the line to the width you want. Drag the line all the way to the left to close the style area.

Creating Custom Styles

If you find that Word's styles don't meet your needs, you can either create custom styles of your own or customize the built-in styles to make them suitable.

The easiest way to create a custom style is by example, and that's the way we'll look at first. After that, you'll also see how to create a new style by specifying its formatting in the New Style dialog box.

Creating a Custom Style by Example

To create a custom style by example, you set up a paragraph or other object with the formatting you want. You then tell Word to create a style from that formatted text so you can then reapply the style wherever you need it.

Type a paragraph of text to use as a sample, or pick an existing paragraph in the document. If Word has an existing style that's similar to the style you want to create, apply that style first so you don't need to make as many formatting changes.

Choosing the Font Formatting for a Style

Often, you'll want to start by choosing the font formatting for the style. You can do so by using any of the standard tools:

- *Font group.* Use the controls in the Font group of the Home tab of the Ribbon.

- *Formatting toolbar.* Select the paragraph or text, and then use the controls on the Formatting toolbar to adjust the formatting.

- *Font dialog box.* Choose Format ➤ Font or press Cmd+D to open the Font dialog box. On the Font tab (see Figure 7–11), choose the font, font style, size, color, underline, and other effects you need (for example, small caps). Click the OK button when you've finished.

Figure 7–11. *You can quickly choose font formatting on the Font tab of the Font dialog box.*

NOTE: On the Advanced tab of the Font dialog box, you can change the scaling, spacing, and position of fonts. For example, you can change the spacing to spread the letters farther apart, or you can choose the Raised position to create a superscript. You can also work with typography features such as ligatures (two letters joined together), which you'll normally need only if you're typesetting a document.

Choosing the Paragraph Formatting for the Style

You can set some paragraph formatting for your sample paragraph by using the controls in the Paragraph group on the Home tab of the Ribbon, but you'll usually want to open the Paragraph dialog box so you can reach all the most useful types of paragraph formatting.

To choose paragraph formatting, follow these steps:

1. Choose Format ➤ Paragraph, or press Cmd+Option+M to open the Paragraph dialog box.

2. On the Indents and Spacing tab (see Figure 7–12), choose settings like this:

    ■ *Alignment.* Choose Left, Centered, Right, or Justified, as needed. Justified text is aligned with both margins.

Figure 7–12. *Choose alignment, indentation, and spacing on the Indents and Spacing tab of the Font dialog box.*

■ *Outline level.* If you want Word to treat this style as a type of heading, click the appropriate level, from Level 1 (a top-level item) down to Level 9. Choose Body Text if you want Word to treat paragraphs of this style as regular body text.

■ *Indentation.* In the Left box and the Right box, set any indentation needed from the margins. To create a first-line indent, choose First line in the Special pop-up menu, and then set the distance in the By box. You can also create a hanging indent (also known as an *outdent*) by choosing Hanging in the Special pop-up menu.

■ *Spacing before and after paragraphs.* In the Before box and the After box, set the number of points of empty space you want before or after each paragraph that uses this style. Select the Don't add space between paragraphs of the same style check box if you want to suppress space between successive paragraphs that use the same style (for example, Body Text style).

> **NOTE:** A point (pt) is $\frac{1}{72}$-inch. Try six points after single-spaced paragraphs if you want a small gap, or try 12 points for a larger gap. Body text doesn't usually need space before it, but you will probably want to add 12–24 points of space before a heading to separate it from the text above it, and about 12 points to separate it from the text below.

- *Line spacing.* In the Line Spacing pop-up menu, choose the line spacing you want: Single, 1.5 lines, Double, At least, Exactly, or Multiple. For the At least setting or the Exactly setting, set the number of points in the At box. For the Multiple setting, set the number of lines in the At box—for example, use **3** to set three-line spacing.

3. Click the Line and Page Breaks tab to display it (see Figure 7–13), and then choose settings like this:

 - *Widow/Orphan control.* Select this check box if you want to avoid a single line appearing at the top of a page (a widow) and a single line appearing at the end of a page (an orphan), each separated from the rest of its paragraph. Normal typesetting practice is to suppress both widows and orphans.

Figure 7–13. *On the Line and Page Breaks tab of the Paragraph dialog box, you can tell Word whether to keep a paragraph with the next paragraph or add a page break before it.*

- *Keep with next.* Select this check box to make Word keep the paragraph on the same page as the next paragraph. Typically, you'll set this option for a heading style to prevent Word from putting it at the bottom of a page with the following paragraph on the next page. Don't use this option for body text paragraphs, or they'll end up bouncing from one page to the following page so that they can stay together.

- *Keep lines together.* Select this check box to make Word keep all the lines of a paragraph on the same page rather than breaking the paragraph across pages. This setting is useful for headings and display paragraphs, but not for body text.

- *Page break before.* Select this check box to have Word start a new page each time the style occurs. You'd normally use this only for styles such as chapter headings.

NOTE: The Line and Page Breaks tab of the Paragraph dialog box contains two other settings. Select the Suppress line numbers check box if you want to suppress line numbers (in automatically numbered documents such as legal papers) for a particular paragraph. Select the Don't hyphenate check box if you want to prevent Word's hyphenation feature from hyphenating the paragraph.

4. If you want to set tabs for the style, click the Tabs button at the bottom of the Paragraph dialog box to display the Tabs dialog box (see Figure 7–14). You can then set tabs like this:

- *Change the default spacing.* Adjust the value in the Default tab stops text box. For example, if you want Word to move 1 inch each time you press Tab in a paragraph that has this style, enter 1".

TIP: Instead of opening the Tabs dialog box from the Paragraph dialog box, you can open it directly by choosing Format ➤ Tabs.

Figure 7–14. *Use the Tabs dialog box to set any custom tab stops that the style needs.*

■ *Set a new tab stop.* In the Tab stop position text box, type the position for the tab—for example, **1"**. Click the appropriate option button in the Alignment area—for example, the Left option button. If you want to use tab leader characters, click the appropriate option button in the Leader area. Then click the Set button.

NOTE: A left tab is the usual kind: the text starts left-aligned at the position of the tab stop. A center tab centers the text around the tab stop and is widely used in headers and footers that have a left section (at the left margin), a center section (with a center tab), and a right section (with a right tab). A right tab makes the right part of the text align with the tab stop, so as you type, the text moves back to the left. A decimal tab aligns the text with the decimal point, enabling you to align numbers with different numbers of decimal places (for example, 123.45 and 678.9). A bar tab is a way of creating a vertical line but is little used these days.

■ *Delete an existing tab stop.* Click the tab in the Tab stop position list box, and then click the Clear button. Click the Clear All button if you want to delete all the tabs.

■ *Move or change a tab stop.* Delete the tab stop you want to change, and create a new tab stop with the position and alignment you want.

5. When you've finished setting tabs for the style, click the OK button to close the Tabs dialog box.

6. Click the OK button to close the Paragraph dialog box.

Adding Bullets or Numbering to the Style

If you're creating a list style, add whichever bullets or numbering it needs.

The quick way to add bullets or numbering is to use the first three controls in the Paragraph group on the Home tab of the Ribbon. Click the Bullets pop-up button, the Numbering pop-up button, or the Multilevel List pop-up button in the Paragraph group to open the panel, and then click the style you want to apply. Figure 7–15 shows the Numbering panel.

NOTE: You can also apply the default style of bullets, numbering, or multilevel list by clicking the button itself (for example, the Bullets button) rather than the drop-down button. If you need to customize bulleted or numbered lists, choose Format ➤ Bullets and Numbering from the menu bar, and then work in the Bullets and Numbering dialog box.

Figure 7–15. *You can quickly apply bullets, numbering, or a multilevel list by using the Bullets pop-up button, the Numbering pop-up button, or the Multilevel List pop-up button in the Paragraph group of the Home tab.*

Adding Borders and Shading to the Style

Next, add any borders or shading that the style needs.

You can apply individual borders by clicking the Home ➤ Paragraph ➤ Borders pop-up button and then clicking the border you want in the panel, but you can get greater control by choosing Format ➤ Borders and Shading from the menu bar to display the Borders and Shading dialog box.

To add borders, display the Borders tab of the Borders and Shading dialog box (see Figure 7–16), and then work like this:

1. In the Apply to pop-up menu, choose Paragraph if you want to apply the border to the whole paragraph. Choose Text if you want to put the border only around the text.

Figure 7–16. *Use the Borders tab of the Borders and Shading dialog box to quickly apply borders to a paragraph.*

2. To apply a standard border, click Box, Shadow, or 3-D in the Setting area. To create a custom border, click the borders in the diagram in the Preview area to place borders where you want them. When you click a border in the diagram, Word selects the Custom item in the Setting area.

3. Change the border's appearance by using the Style list, the Color pop-up menu, and the Width pop-up menu.

NOTE: To move the borders closer to the text or farther away from it, click the Options button. In the Borders and Shading Options dialog box that opens, adjust the Top, Bottom, Left, and Right measurements, and then click the OK button.

4.   Click the OK button to close the Borders and Shading dialog box.

NOTE: A paragraph border is usually the most useful kind of border for a style, but if you're creating a style that will occupy most (or all) of a page, you may want to create a page border in the style. In this case, click the Page Border tab in the Borders and Shading dialog box, select the appropriate document part in the Apply to pop-up menu (for example, select the This section item), and then work with the border controls in the same way as for applying a paragraph border.

To apply shading to a style, click the Shading tab in the Borders and Shading dialog box, and then follow these steps:

1.   In the Apply to pop-up menu, choose Paragraph if you want to apply the shading to the whole paragraph. Choose Text if you want to apply the border only to the text.

2.   In the Fill pop-up menu, choose the shading color you want.

3.   In the Style pop-up menu, choose the shading style—for example, 25% shading or Dk Trellis shading.

4.   In the Color pop-up menu, choose the pattern color.

5.   Click the OK button to close the Borders and Shading dialog box.

Adding Language Formatting to the Style

The final type of formatting that you can include in the style is language formatting. Unlike almost all the other types of formatting, language formatting isn't visual formatting. Instead, it tells Word to treat the text as being in a particular language. For example, if you're writing a paper on French poets, you could create a style for block quotes and set its language to French. The spell checker would then refrain from querying the words as not being in the English language.

NOTE: When you apply language formatting, the text you format doesn't actually have to be in the language you specify, but you're telling Word to treat it as if it is.

To apply language formatting to text, follow these steps:

1. Choose Tools ➤ Language to display the Language dialog box (see Figure 7–17).

Figure 7–17. *In the Language dialog box, you can specify the language used for the text. You can also turn off spelling and grammar checking for the style.*

2. In the Mark selected text as list box, select the language you want to use. Your current language appears at the top of the list to save you from having to scroll to find it.

3. If you want to tell spell checker and grammar checker not to check the text, select the Do not check spelling or grammar check box. This setting is useful for styles you'll use for text that will contain apparent misspellings, such as computer code.

4. Click the OK button to close the Language dialog box.

Creating the Style

Once you have set up the paragraph with all the formatting it needs, you can create a style like this:

1. Select the paragraph.

2. Open the Styles pane in the Toolbox by choosing View ➤ Styles or clicking the Toolbox button on the Standard toolbar and then clicking the Styles tab.

3. Click the New Style button to display the New Style dialog box (shown in Figure 7–9, earlier in this chapter).

4. Type the name for the style in the Name text box.

5. In the Style type pop-up menu, choose the style type: Paragraph, Character, Table, or List.

6. In the Style for following paragraph pop-up menu, choose the style you want Word to apply automatically to the next paragraph when you press the Return key at the end of a paragraph with this style. For a display style (such as a heading), you will normally want a body style next; for a body style, you will probably want to continue with the same body style.

7. Select the Add to template check box if you want Word to add this style to the document's template so that it will be available for other documents. Usually, this is helpful. If you clear this check box, Word stores the style in the document, where other documents can't use it.

8. Select the Add to Quick Style list check box if you want Word to include this style in the Quick Style Gallery. Otherwise, clear this check box.

9. Clear the Automatically update check box unless you want Word to update the style without consulting you when it thinks you've altered the style. Automatic updating is well intended but usually confusing.

10. Click the OK button to close the New Style dialog box.

NOTE: If you need to make any other changes to the style's formatting after you've opened the New Style dialog box, use the formatting controls in the middle of the New Style dialog box or the Format pop-up menu in the lower-left corner. For example, to change the paragraph formatting, click the Format pop-up menu, and then click Paragraph to display the Paragraph dialog box.

Modifying an Existing Style

You can modify an existing style by opening it in the Modify Style dialog box and working from there. You can also change the formatting of a paragraph of text that uses the style and then make the style pick up your changes.

Changing a Style Using the Modify Style Dialog Box

The more formal way of modifying an existing style is to open the style in the Modify Style dialog box, which is a renamed version of the New Style dialog box. You can then use the formatting controls and the options on the Format pop-up menu to adjust the style exactly as you need it.

You can open the Modify Style dialog box from the Styles pane, the Quick Style Gallery, or the Style dialog box:

- *Styles pane.* Move the mouse pointer over the style name, click the pop-up button, and then click Modify Style.

- *Quick Style Gallery.* Ctrl+click or right-click the style name, and then click Modify on the context menu.

- *Style dialog box.* Select the style in the Styles list box, and then click the Modify button.

Updating a Style with New Formatting

Instead of modifying an existing style as described in the previous section, you can apply a style, change its formatting, and then update the style to match the new formatting. This method can be useful when you're developing a template and you need to keep adjusting styles to make everything look and fit right.

To update a style with new formatting, follow these steps:

1. Apply the style using whichever tool you prefer (for example, the Styles pane).

2. Reformat the text as needed.

3. Take one of the following actions:

   - *Styles pane.* Hold the mouse pointer over the style name, click the pop-up button, and then click Update to Match Selection on the pop-up menu.

   - *Quick Style Gallery.* Ctrl+click or right-click the style, and then click Update to Match Selection on the context menu.

Applying Direct Formatting on Top of Styles

After you've applied the style each paragraph needs and you've applied list styles and character styles as needed, you can finish off the formatting by applying direct formatting to any parts of the document that need it. For example, you may need to apply different font formatting to pick out special display elements or add more space before some paragraphs.

> **NOTE:** To get the most out of Word's automatic formatting features, use direct formatting as little as possible. If you need to apply the same direct formatting to several different items, consider creating a style with that formatting so you can apply it instantly in future. If you will need to use the same direct formatting and text, save it as an AutoText entry (see Chapter 6 for instructions).

To apply direct formatting, use the tools you met earlier in this chapter for setting up font formatting, paragraph formatting, bullets and numbering, and so on. Here are some examples:

- *Font formatting.* Use the controls in the Font group on the Home tab of the Ribbon, on the Formatting toolbar, or in the Font dialog box.

- *Paragraph formatting.* Use the controls in the Paragraph group on the Home tab of the Ribbon or in the Paragraph dialog box.

■ *Bullets and numbering.* Use the controls in the Paragraph group on the Home tab of the Ribbon.

> **TIP:** To remove direct formatting from text, select the text, and then press Ctrl+spacebar. If you find this keyboard shortcut doesn't work, it may be because another application is already using it. Choose Apple ➤ System Preferences, click the Keyboard icon, and then click the Keyboard Shortcuts tab. You can then click an application to see which keyboard shortcuts it's using.

Copying and Pasting Formatting Using the Format Painter

When you've painstakingly applied direct formatting to text or another object, you may want to reuse that direct formatting for other text or another object. The straightforward way to do so is to copy the text (or object), paste it in, and then type the new text over it. This works fine for new text items or objects (unless you forget to replace the pasted text), but it's not efficient if the text is already there.

Instead, you can use Word's Format Painter. This feature enables you to pick up the formatting for a selection and then "paint" it on other text or another object. Follow these steps:

1. Select the text or object that contains the formatting you want to copy.

2. Click the Format button on the Standard toolbar (the button with the paintbrush icon) or press Cmd+Shift+C to copy the formatting. Word changes the mouse pointer to an I-beam with a plus sign (+) beside it.

> **TIP:** If you want to apply the formatting to multiple items, double-click the Format button on the Standard toolbar. The mouse pointer becomes the Format Painter I-beam until you turn it off by clicking the Format button again or pressing the Esc key.

3. Drag the I-beam over the text or object to which you want to apply the formatting. Word applies the formatting and then restores the mouse pointer.

Navigating Quickly Around Your Documents

To help you navigate quickly around your documents, Word provides the Sidebar pane, the Find and Replace feature, and the Go To feature.

Using the Sidebar

The Sidebar is a pane that appears at the left side of the Word window and contains four panes that you can switch among by clicking the four buttons at the top of the pane:

- *Thumbnail pane.* This pane (shown on the left in Figure 7–18) displays thumbnail pictures of your document's pages. Click the thumbnail for the page you want to display.

Figure 7–18. *In the Sidebar on the left of the Word window, you can display (from left to right) the Thumbnail pane, the Document Map pane, the Reviewing pane, or the Search pane.*

- *Document Map pane.* This pane (shown second from left in Figure 7–18) displays your document as an outline of collapsible headings. If a heading contains subheadings, a triangle appears next to it. Click the triangle to display the headings or to hide them again. Click the heading you want to display in the main part of the window.

TIP: To control which levels of headings appear in the Document Map pane, Ctrl+click or right-click any heading, and then click the heading level you want—for example, Show Heading 3. From the context menu, you can also expand the section or collapse it, but usually it's easier to use the triangles in the Document Map pane.

- *Reviewing pane.* This pane (shown second from right in Figure 7–18) displays a summary of the tracked changes in the document. You'll learn how to use the Reviewing pane in Chapter 10.

- *Search pane.* This pane (shown on the right in Figure 7–18) lets you search through your documents and see a summary of all search results. We'll dig into how you use the Search pane later in this chapter.

You can open the Sidebar in any of these ways:

- Click the Sidebar button on the Standard toolbar to display whichever pane you used last.

- Click the Sidebar pop-up button on the Standard toolbar to display the pop-up menu, and then click the pane you want to see: Document Map Pane, Thumbnail Pane, Reviewing Pane, or Search Pane.

- From the menu bar, choose View ➤ Sidebar, and then click the appropriate pane on the submenu: Document Map Pane, Thumbnail Pane, Reviewing Pane, or Search Pane.

Once the Sidebar is open, you can resize it by dragging its right border. For example, you may need to make the Sidebar wider so that you can see the page thumbnails at a larger size.

To close the Sidebar, click the Close button (the × button) in its upper-right corner. You can also close the Sidebar by clicking the Sidebar button on the Standard toolbar again.

Using Find and Replace

As you saw in Chapter 3, Word provides three tools for searching within your documents:

- *Search box on the Standard toolbar.* This box is good for quickly finding the next instance or previous instance of the search term you enter in the box. You can also click the pop-up button at the left end to display two options: click the List Matches in Sidebar item to open the Sidebar and show all matches for the search term, or click the Replace item to open the Sidebar ready for replacing items.

- *Search pane in the Sidebar.* This pane lets you quickly search for text you enter in the Search Document box or replace that text with text you enter in the Replace With box. What's less obvious is that you can also search for and replace special characters (such as a paragraph mark or a tab character) by using the pop-up menu at the end of the Search Document box or the Replace With box (as shown on the right in Figure 7–19). And you can also set four search options—Whole Word Only, Ignore Case, Sounds Like, and All Work Forms—by clicking the Action button (the button bearing the cog icon) and then clicking the appropriate item on the Action pop-up menu (as shown on the left in Figure 7–19).

Figure 7–19. *The Search pane in the Sidebar is good for straightforward searches, but you can also choose search options from the Action menu (left) or search for or replace special characters (right).*

- *Find and Replace dialog box.* When you need to access Word's full Find and Replace capabilities, open the Find and Replace dialog box. In this section, we'll look at the extra features this dialog box provides.

You can open the Find and Replace dialog box in either of these ways:

- *From the menu bar.* Choose Edit ➤ Find ➤ Advanced Find and Replace.

- *From the Search pane in the Sidebar.* Click the Action button to display the Action pop-up menu, and then click Advanced Find & Replace.

With the Find and Replace dialog box open, you can search for regular text by using the techniques explained in Chapter 3. But you can also click the down arrow button to display the hidden part of the dialog box (see Figure 7–20) and then choose other search options as described here.

Figure 7–20. *After expanding the Find and Replace dialog box by clicking the down arrow button (which changes to the up arrow button), you can search with wildcards and special characters. You can also search for particular formatting or for styles. The area below the Find what box shows the search options you're using.*

TIP: You can work in the document while the Find and Replace dialog box is open—just click in the document and edit it as needed, and then click in the dialog box when you want to start using it again. This means you can leave the Find and Replace dialog box open until you've finished searching and making any changes needed to what you find.

Highlighting All Instances of a Search Term

To make Word highlight all the instances it has found, select the Highlight all items found in check box, and then choose the appropriate item in the pop-up menu. Normally, you'll want to choose Main Document to search in the main part of the document, but you can also search in other areas the document contains—for example, Headers and Footers, Endnotes, Footnotes, or Text Boxes in Main Document.

Searching Only Part of the Document

When you need to search in just part of the document, select it. You can do this either before opening the Find and Replace dialog box or when the dialog box is open.

When Word finishes searching the selected part of the document, it asks whether you want to search the remainder of the document (see Figure 7–21).

Figure 7–21. *You can search only part of a document rather than the whole document. After searching that part, Word prompts you to search the remainder of the document.*

Changing the Search Direction

When you first search, Word searches from the position of the insertion point to the end of the document, wraps around automatically to the beginning, and continues until it gets back to the insertion point.

If you want to search upward rather than downward, open the Search pop-up menu, and choose Current Document Up; at the beginning of the document, Word asks if you want to continue. To search downward and have Word ask at the end of the document if you want to continue, choose Current Document Down. To search through the whole of the document without prompting, choose Current Document All.

Finding Search Terms That Match the Case You Type

Normally, Find ignores the case of characters, so it finds the search term no matter what capitalization it uses. If you want Find to find only results that match the case you type, select the Match case check box.

Restricting the Search to Whole Words

If you want to find your search term only as a whole word rather than as part of other words, select the Find whole words only check box. For example, you may need to find the word *any* rather than *many* or *anywhere*. This option works only for single words; as soon as you type a space in the Find what box, Word makes this check box unavailable.

Using Wildcards to Find Variable Text

To give your searches more flexibility, select the Use wildcards check box. A *wildcard* is a character or group of characters that represents other characters—a bit like your being able to use a joker as another card in some games or a blank tile at Scrabble. Table 7–2 explains the wildcards you can use for searching in Word.

Table 7–2. *Wildcard Characters for Searching in Word*

Use This Wildcard	To Find This Text	Example
?	Any character	**r?de** finds *rede*, *ride*, *rode*, and *rude*.
*	Any characters, or none	**force*** finds *force*, *forced*, *forceps*, and *forces*.
[*characters*]	Any one of the characters you've specified	**b[aeiou]ll** finds *ball*, *bell*, *bill*, and *bull*.
[*character1–character2*]	Any one of the characters in the alphabetical range you've entered	**b[a-j]t** finds words such as *bat*, *bet*, and *bit*. It does not find *but*, because *u* is not in the range.
[!*character1–character2*]	Any one character that's not in the alphabetical range you've entered	**b[!a-jt]** finds *bot* and *but* but doesn't find *bat*, *bet*, and *bit*.
character{*number*}	The number of occurrences of the character	**20{4}** find *20000*, because it has four zeroes.
character{*number1*, *number2*}	From *number1* instances to *number2* instances of the character	**20{1,4}** finds *20*, *200*, *2000*, *20000*, and similar numbers.
character@	One or more instances of the character	**0@in** finds *10in*, *100in*, and other text with one or more zeroes followed by *in*.

Finding Words That Sound Like Other Words

If you need to find words that sound like other words, select the Sounds like check box. This feature is worth trying if you work in documents that may have unintentional word substitutions (for example, documents entered using speech recognition), but overall it's too hit-and-miss to rely on.

Finding All Forms of a Word

Select the Find all word forms check box if you need to find each different form of the search text. For example, if you search for *go*, Find finds *went* and *gone* as well.

Searching for Special Characters

If you need to search for a character that you can't type with the keyboard, such as a paragraph mark (the normally hidden character that ends a paragraph) or an em dash (—), open the Special pop-up menu (see Figure 7–22), and then click the item you want. Word enters the appropriate code in the Find what text box, and you can then run the search.

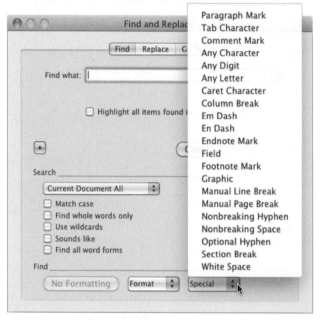

Figure 7–22. *Use the Special pop-up menu in the Find and Replace dialog box to enter a special character, such as the code for a paragraph mark or a graphic.*

Searching Only at the Start or End of a Word

To make Word search for your search text only at the start of words, select the Use wildcards check box, open the Special pop-up menu, and click Beginning of Word. (The Special menu's contents change to wildcard options when you select the Use wildcards check box.) For example, you can search for *after* at the beginning of words to find *afterward* and *afternoon*.

Similarly, you can select the Use wildcards check box and then choose the End of Word item on the Special menu to search for your search term only at the end of words—for example, finding *after* in *hereafter* or *rafter*.

Finding Formatting

As well as finding text, Word enables you to find formatting—either formatting applied to particular text or formatting on its own. For example, you can search for instances of the word *industry* with the Subtle Emphasis style applied to it, or you can search for any text formatted with both bold and italic.

To search for formatting, follow these steps:

1. Type your search text in the Find what box like you've done before. If you want to search for just formatting, delete anything that's in the Find what box.

2. Click the Format pop-up menu, and then click the type of formatting (see Figure 7–23).

Figure 7–23. *Use the commands on the Format pop-up menu in the Find and Replace dialog box to specify the formatting you want to find.*

3. In the dialog box that opens, set up the type of formatting. For example, in the Find Style dialog box, click the style name, and then click the OK button.

NOTE: The Highlight item on the Format pop-up menu doesn't display a dialog box—it just switches on searching for Highlight text. Choose Format ➤ Highlight again to search for Not Highlight; choose Format ➤ Highlight a third time to remove Highlight from the search.

Click the No Formatting button when you want to remove the formatting criteria from the search.

Replacing Text, Formatting, and Styles

Finding text or formatting is great, but what you'll often need to do is replace what you're finding with other text, other formatting, or both. To replace items, display the Replace tab of the Find and Replace dialog box by choosing Edit ➤ Find ➤ Advanced Find and Replace and then clicking the Replace tab. You can also click the Action button in the Search pane in the Sidebar, click Advanced Find & Replace on the pop-up menu, and then click the Replace tab.

The Replace tab (shown in Figure 7–24 with settings chosen for replacing direct formatting with a style) works in much the same way as the Find tab. For a straightforward replacement, type the search text in the Find what box and the replacement text in the Replace with box. For a complex replacement, click the More button to display the lower part of the dialog box, and then choose the options you want.

Figure 7–24. *One of the Replace tool's most useful tricks is to replace direct formatting with a style.*

Once you've set up the replacement, use the Replace button, Replace All button, and Find Next button to run it:

- *Find Next.* Click this button to find the next instance of the search term.

- *Replace.* Click this button to replace the instance Word has found and to find the next instance.

- *Replace All.* Click this button to replace every instance. If you've chosen Current Document Up or Current Document Down rather than Current Document All in the Search pop-up menu, Word asks if you want to continue when it reaches the beginning or end of the document.

Replacing Text

To replace text, simply type the replacement in the Replace with box. But you can also make Word insert the contents of the Clipboard or the Find what box:

- *Insert the contents of the Clipboard.* Type **^c** in the Replace with box to make Word insert the contents of the Clipboard in place of whatever you're searching for. You can use this trick to insert a table, an image, or a section of text that you've copied to the Clipboard.

- *Insert the contents of the Find what box.* Type **^&** in the Replace with box to make Word insert the contents of the Find what box (or what the contents represents). For example, you can type wildcards in the Find what box and then have the Replace with box insert text plus whatever expression matched the wildcards.

Replacing Formatting or Styles

When you need to reformat documents, you can use Replace to replace formatting. You can replace formatting in several ways:

- *Replace text and formatting.* Sometimes you may need to find given text that's formatted in a particular way and replace it with other text formatted differently. (You can also replace it with the same text formatted differently.)

- *Replace text with formatting.* You can find text that's formatted in a particular way and replace it with formatting, getting rid of the text. This approach is useful if you create documents in a text editor (for example, on a portable device) and need to apply formatting in Word. For example, you can replace the text *h1* with the Heading 1 style.

- *Replace formatting only.* You can replace one type of formatting with another type—for example, replacing bold italic 20-point text with a Heading 2 style. Or you can replace one style with another style.

To replace formatting or styles, follow these steps:

1. Open the Replace tab of the Find and Replace dialog box. For example, choose Edit ➤ Find ➤ Advanced Find and Replace, and then click the Replace tab.

2. In the Find what box, enter any text you want to find. If you're searching for formatting, delete anything that's in the Find what box.

3. With the insertion point in the Find what box, specify the formatting you want to find. Open the Format pop-up menu; click Font, Paragraph, Tabs, Language, Frame, or Style; and use the dialog box that opens to specify the details. When you click the OK button, the Format line under the Find what box shows your choices.

4. In the Replace with box, enter any replacement text. To replace only with formatting, delete anything that's in this box.

5. With the insertion point in the Replace with box, specify the replacement formatting. Use the same techniques as in step 3.

6. Run the replacement as usual. For example, click the Replace All button to replace all instances of the formatting.

Navigating with Go To

If you want to get about your documents quickly, it's well worth learning how to use the Go To feature. Go To overlaps with browsing by different objects using the Select Browse Object button (as discussed in Chapter 6), but it can be a handy way of getting around a document.

To use Go To, open the Go To tab of the Find and Replace dialog box (see Figure 7–25) in one of these ways:

- *Mouse.* Click the Pages readout in the middle of the status bar.

- *Ribbon.* Choose Edit ➤ Find ➤ Go To.

- *Keyboard.* Press Cmd+Option+G.

Figure 7–25. *The Go To tab of the Find and Replace dialog box is great for moving quickly to a page by number or for going from one equation or bookmark to another.*

In the Go to what box, click the type of object you want to move by: Page, Section, Line, Bookmark, Comment, Footnote, Endnote, Field, Table, Graphic, Equation, Object, or Heading.

> **NOTE:** A bookmark is an invisible marker you set in the text to mark a point you want to be able to access easily (see Chapter 8). An object is an item such as an audio file or video file that you insert in the document.

Once you've done this, you can move from one object of that type to another in either of these ways:

- If you just want to move to the next or previous object, click the Next button or the Previous button. (The Next button appears in place of the Go To button when you pick an object that has multiple instances.)

- In the box on the right, identify the number or name of the object you want. This box changes depending on the object you've chosen. For example, type a page number or choose a bookmark name, type + and a number (for example, +5) to move forward by that number of objects, or type – and a number (for example, –50) to move backward by that number of objects. Then click the Go To button.

When you've finished using the Go To feature, click the Close button to close the Find and Replace dialog box.

Summary

In this chapter, you learned the best way to format your Word documents—by using styles from start to finish and then adding only such little direct formatting as is absolutely necessary. You saw how to apply Word's existing styles, how to create custom styles of your own, and how to modify a style either directly or by updating it to match an example.

You now also know how to navigate around your documents using the Sidebar, Find, and Go To. And you learned how to find any document item you need, from plain text to characters you can't type—and how to replace it if necessary.

In the next chapter, I'll show you how to create complex documents and complex layouts. Turn the page when you're ready to start.

Chapter 8

Creating Complex Documents and Layouts

Once you've mastered the art of formatting your documents with styles (as described in Chapter 7), you're ready to create long or complex documents in Word.

In this chapter, you'll learn first how to use the extra table features that Word provides over those that the Office applications share. Then I'll show you how to break a document into multiple sections; how to add headers, footers, and page numbers; and how to create newspaper-style columns of text.

After that, you'll see how to mark important parts of a document with bookmarks and how to insert cross-references back to these bookmarks or to other parts. Finally, you'll learn how to develop your documents using Word's powerful Outline view and how to add footnotes and endnotes to your documents.

Working with Word's Extra Table Features

In Word, you can create tables in the following three ways:

- *Insert a table.* As discussed in Chapter 3, choose Tables ➤ Table Options ➤ New, and then click the table arrangement you want on the New grid—for example, five rows of three columns each. This is good for creating regular tables, ones that have the same number of cells in each row.

- *Draw a table.* Also as discussed in Chapter 3, choose Tables ➤ Draw Borders ➤ Draw, and then use the drawing cursor to draw the table layout you want. Drawing a table is good for creating irregular tables.

- *Convert existing text to a table.* If the document already contains the text you want to create the table from, you can convert the text into a table, as discussed next.

Converting Existing Text into a Table

Converting existing text to a table is usually faster than creating a table and moving existing data into it.

First, you need to make sure that the material is laid out regularly, with its contents separated using one of these four items:

- *Tabs.* This is usually the easiest way of separating material, because you can see the different columns that the table will create. Figure 8–1 shows a table laid out with tabs. Notice that because the tab stops aren't optimally positioned, the columns don't align in each row. This doesn't matter as long as there's only one tab between each item destined for a cell.

Department →	Position Needed → Manager → Target Hire Date ¶
Sales·and·Marketing →	Administrative·Assistant → Renee·Williams·4·January·2011 ¶
Operations →	Director·of·Operations→Mauro·Flaherty·11·January·2011¶
HR → Administrative·Support →	[Hiring·Manager] → 11·January·2011¶

Figure 8–1. *When using tabs to lay out text you plan to turn into a table, use only one tab between the contents of each cell. Press Cmd+8 to display the invisible characters including the tabs and paragraph marks.*

NOTE: When converting tabbed material into a table, you must make sure of two things. First, check that each item is separated by only one tab, not by two or more tabs—otherwise, you'll get the wrong number of columns. (But if you need to leave a cell blank, do use two tabs in sequence.) Second, check that the material for each cell is not broken onto multiple lines—otherwise, you'll get the wrong number of rows.

- *Paragraphs.* If each cell's data appears in a separate paragraph, you can quickly convert it to a table. Make sure the data contains no unnecessary blank paragraphs.

- *Commas.* If you have data separated by commas, such as a comma-separated values export from a spreadsheet, you can use a comma as the separator character for a table.

■ *Other character.* If your data is separated consistently by another character (for example, * or |), you can specify that character as the separator character. You need to make sure that this character doesn't appear as part of the regular text, only as the separator character.

When your data is in good order, convert it to a table like this:

1. Select the paragraphs of data. Select right from the start up to the paragraph mark at the end of the last paragraph. (If Word is hiding paragraph marks, you'll appear to have selected a chunk of blank space at the end of the last paragraph.)

2. Choose Tables ➤ Table Options ➤ New ➤ Convert Text to Table from the Ribbon, or choose Table ➤ Convert ➤ Convert Text to Table from the menu bar, to display the Convert Text to Table dialog box (see Figure 8–2).

Convert Text to Table

Table size

Number of columns: 4

Number of rows: 4

AutoFit behavior

⦿ Initial column width: Auto
○ AutoFit to contents
○ AutoFit to window

Separate text at

○ Paragraphs   ○ Commas
⦿ Tabs   ○ Other: -

(Cancel) (OK)

Figure 8–2. *In the Convert Text to Table dialog box, make sure that Word has chosen the right separator character (for example, tabs), and choose the AutoFit behavior you want.*

3. In the Separate text at area, make sure that Word has picked the right separator character. If not, select the Paragraphs option button, the Commas option button, the Tabs option button, or the Other option button as appropriate; for the Other option button, type the separator character in the text box.

4. In the Table size area, make sure that the number of columns is right:

■ If you're using tabs as the separator character and the number of columns is wrong, one or more of the paragraphs contains an extra tab (or is missing a tab). Click the Cancel button, find the extra or missing tab, and then start the conversion again.

- If you're using paragraphs as the separator character, you must tell Word how many paragraphs to use for each row. Enter this number in the Number of columns box.

5. In the AutoFit behavior area, choose whether to fit the column widths automatically to their contents:

- *Initial column width.* Select this option button to use a fixed width for each column. You can then choose Auto to have Word allocate the space equally among the columns or type the fixed width you want.

- *AutoFit to contents.* Select this option button to let Word adjust each column's width to fit its contents. You may need to adjust the widths afterward.

- *AutoFit to window.* Select this option button to have Word make the table automatically fit the window's width.

6. Click the OK button to close the Convert Text to Table dialog box. Word converts the text to a table. Figure 8–3 shows the text from the example in Figure 8–1 converted into a table.

Department¤	Position Needed¤	Manager¤	Target Hire Date¤	¤
Sales and Marketing¤	Administrative Assistant¤	Renee Williams¤	4 January 2011¤	¤
Operations¤	Director of Operations¤	Mauro Flaherty¤	11 January 2011¤	¤
HR¤	Administrative Support¤	[Hiring Manager]¤	11 January 2011¤	¤

¶

Figure 8–3. *The table that Word creates from the tabbed text in Figure 8–1*

Converting a Table to Text

Word also lets you convert a table back to text. This move is useful when you've received material in table form that you need to convert to a different layout.

To convert a table to text, follow these steps:

1. Click anywhere in the table. You don't need to select it.

2. Choose Table ➤ Convert ➤ Convert Table to Text from the menu bar to display the Convert Table to Text dialog box (see Figure 8–4).

Convert Table to Text

Separate text with

○ Paragraph marks
⊙ Tabs
○ Commas
○ Other: [-]

☑ Convert nested tables

(Cancel) (OK)

Figure 8–4. *When converting a table back to text, you can separate the cells with paragraph marks, tabs, commas, or another character of your choice.*

3. In the Separate text with area, choose the character with which to separate the cell contents: select the Paragraph marks option button, the Tabs option button, the Commas option button, or the Other option button (and type the character in the text box).

4. Select the Convert nested tables check box if you want to convert nested tables as well. This check box is available only when you're using paragraphs as the separator character.

> **NOTE:** Word converts a nested table to paragraphs of text like the rest of the table. The nested table's paragraphs appear in their cell order between the paragraphs for the table cells that surround them.

5. Click the OK button to close the Convert Table to Text dialog box and perform the conversion.

Nesting One Table Inside Another Table

When you need to create a complex layout, you can nest one table inside another so that one cell of the outer table contains however many cells the inner table has. Figure 8–5 shows an example of a nested table.

To nest a table, click in the cell in which you want to nest the table, and then insert the table as usual.

Department	Coverage		Contact Information
Anthropology	Biological Anthropology	1-8	
	Cultural Anthropology	1-4	
	Linguistic Anthropology	5-12	
	Social Anthropology	1-12	
Biology			
Chemistry			

Figure 8–5. *You can nest one table inside another table to create complex layouts.*

TIP: You can nest tables several levels deep if necessary, but the further you nest tables, the more confusing working with them tends to become. If you're considering several levels of nesting, see whether merging and splitting cells could give you a similar result with less fuss.

Creating Complex Documents with Multiple Sections

When you need to create documents that use multiple layouts, you have to put each layout in a separate section. Here are three examples of documents that use multiple layouts:

- A newsletter may need different numbers of columns on different pages.

- A report may require different headers and footers for different chapters.

- A business letter may need to contain an envelope page as well.

Word's sections are highly useful, but they're tricky both to see and to grasp. Word makes matters worse by automatically creating sections when your documents need them—for example, when you apply columns to part of a document, as discussed later in this chapter—but not making clear what it's doing.

Here is the essential information you need to know about sections:

- *Each new blank document has a single section at first.* When you create a new blank document, Word creates it as a single section until you add further sections. By contrast, documents you create based on a template contain however many sections the template has.

- *When you need to give part of the document a different layout, you create a new section.* For example, if you need to create a landscape page in a document that uses portrait orientation, you put the landscape page in a separate section so that you can change the layout.

- A section can start on the same page or on a different page. Word gives you four kinds of section breaks:

  - *Continuous.* The new section starts on the same page as the previous section. This type of break is useful for creating multicolumn layouts on part of a page.

  - *Next page.* The new section starts on the next page after the previous section ends. This is the kind of break you use for putting a new chapter on a new page or for changing the layout from portrait to landscape.

  - *Even page.* The new section starts on the next even page after the previous section ends. This may mean having a blank page in the printed document.

  - *Odd page.* The new section starts on the new odd page after the previous section ends. This too may mean a blank page appears in the printed document.

- *A section break divides one section from the next.* When you create a section (or Word creates one automatically for you), you add a section break to the document. A section break is normally hidden, but if you display paragraph marks and other invisible characters, it appears as a blue double line with the words Section Break and the type in the middle—for example, Section Break (Continuous).

Once you know all this, inserting a section break is easy:

1. Place the insertion point where you want the new section to start. It's best to put the insertion point at the beginning of a paragraph.

2. On the Ribbon, choose Layout ➤ Page Setup ➤ Break to open the Break panel, and then click the section break type you want: Next Page, Continuous, Even Page, or Odd Page. Word inserts the break.

> **NOTE:** If you prefer to use the menus, you can choose Insert ➤ Break to display the Break submenu and then click Section Break (Next Page), Section Break (Continuous), Section Break (Odd Page), or Section Break (Even Page), as needed.

To see the break in Print Layout view or Web Layout view, click the Show button on the Standard toolbar. In Draft view or Outline view, Word displays the break all the time. In Full Screen view, Word hides the break; and in Notebook Layout view, Word displays the sections as section tabs in the notebook.

When you start using sections in a document, Word adds the Section readout to the status bar to give you a heads-up on which section you're working in. For example, the readout "Sec 2 Page 4" indicates that the insertion point or selection is in the second section of the document.

Adding Headers, Footers, and Page Numbers

If you're planning to print out a multipage document or to distribute it as a PDF or XPS file, it's often a good idea to add headers, footers, and page numbers to make the pages easy to identify.

Adding Headers and Footers to a Document

A *header* appears across the top of a page, and a footer appears across the bottom of a page. You can use headers and footers to add information such as the document name and file name, author name, date, and page numbers—or any other information that you need to make available to the reader.

> **NOTE:** This section discusses headers and footers for word processing documents. In publishing layouts and in notebook layouts, Word makes the standard header and footer tools unavailable, because these documents don't need standard headers and footers. You can still add page numbers to the footer of a notebook-layout document.

Word gives you plenty of flexibility with headers and footers. If a document needs the same header (or footer) all the way through, you can quickly add one. But you can also use different headers or footers on the odd pages of the document to the even pages, and you can use different headers and footers from one section of the document to the next. You can also prevent the header or footer from appearing on the first page of a document, which is useful for letters and various other documents.

Word's templates come with built-in headers and footers that you can quickly add to give your documents a standard look. These headers and footers range from the straightforward Blank one to stylish designs that can look good in a variety of documents. Many of the headers and footers come with odd-page and even-page versions so that you can create effective page spreads.

> **NOTE:** If you want to create a header or footer completely from scratch, choose View ➤ Header and Footer to open the Header area. In Print Layout view, you can also simply double-click in the header area at the top of the page.

To insert a built-in header or footer, follow these steps:

1. If the document has multiple sections, click in the section you want to add the header or footer to.

2. Choose Document Elements ➤ Header and Footer ➤ Header or Document Elements ➤ Header and Footer ➤ Footer to open the Header panel or the footer panel.

3. Click the header or footer you want. Word then does the following:

   ■ Inserts the header or footer in the document.

   ■ Switches to Print Layout view if the document is in Draft view or Outline view.

   ■ Displays the header or footer area with the header or footer ready for editing. Figure 8–6 shows a header added to a page. The Header tab shows that you're working in the header; if you're in a particular section of the document rather than the document as a whole, the tab shows that too.

   ■ Adds the Header and Footer tab to the Ribbon.

Figure 8–6. *Word adds the Header and Footer tab to the Ribbon to give you access to the commands for working with the header or footer that you've inserted; if the header or footer uses a table, Word adds the Table Layout tab as well. Below the header in the document, Word displays a button identifying the header (here, Odd Page Header) and the Close button.*

4. Fill in the placeholders in the header or footer. For example, in the Type the document title placeholder shown, type the title that you want the header to show. Or if the header or footer includes a Year placeholder, click the pop-up button, and then click the date in the panel that opens.

5. If necessary, adjust the position or alignment of the header:

   ■ To change the header's position relative to the top of the page, alter the value in the Header from Top box in the Position group of the Header and Footer tab of the Ribbon (see Figure 8–7). When you do this, you may also need to change the page margins.

Figure 8–7. *Use the controls on the Header and Footer tab of the Ribbon to change the position or other aspects of the header and footer.*

NOTE: When the Word window is too narrow for the labels to fit, the Header from Top box and the Footer from Bottom box appear unmarked. You can hold the mouse pointer over the controls in the Position group to display ScreenTips identifying each button.

- To change the footer's position relative to the bottom of the page, alter the value in the Footer from Bottom box in the Position group.

6. Click the Close button under the header area or above the footer area to close the header and footer area and return to the main document. You can also press Ctrl+Shift+C or double-click in the main text area.

Creating Different Headers and Footers for Different Pages

Many documents either don't need a header (or footer) on the first page or need a different one there. Likewise, many documents need a different header or footer on their odd pages than on their even pages.

To set up different headers and footers for the first page or for odd and even pages, follow these steps:

1. Open the header area or footer area in one of these ways:

   - In Print Layout view, double-click in the header area or footer area.

   - Choose View ➤ Header and Footer from the menu bar.

2. Click the Header and Footer tab on the Ribbon to display its contents.

3. To create a different first page header or footer, select the Different First Page check box in the Options group on the Header and Footer tab of the Ribbon.

4. To create different headers and footers for odd pages and even pages, select the Different Odd & Even check box in the Options group.

5. Use the Previous Section button and Next Section button in the Navigation group on the Header and Footer tab to move from one header or footer to another, entering the material you want each to have. If you're using Word's built-in headers or footers, try the Odd Page and Even Page ones for your odd and even pages.

Using Different Headers and Footers in Different Sections of a Document

If you break a document into separate sections, you can create different headers and footers in each section or continue headers and footers from one section to the next. As well as making each section's headers or footers different from the other sections, you can also create different first-page and odd- and even-page headers and footers within sections as needed.

Create your sections as described earlier in this chapter, and then go to the beginning of the document and open the header area or footer area. Give the first section the headers and footers it needs, and then go through the remaining sections.

Word automatically carries through the headers and footers from one section to the next until you tell it to stop. You'll see the Same as Previous indicator between the Section indicator and the Close button for the header or footer, as in Figure 8–8.

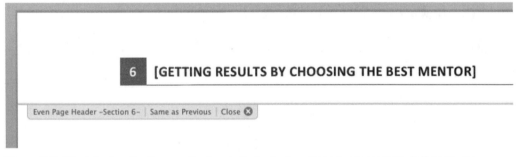

Figure 8–8. *Word displays the Same as Previous indicator to show that a header or footer is linked to the previous one.*

To stop Word from continuing the headers and footers like this, move to the section you want to change, and then clear the Link to Previous check box in the Options group on the Header and Footer tab of the Ribbon. You can then create a different header or footer in this section.

Delete a Header or Footer

When you want to get rid of a header or footer, open it for editing, press Cmd+A to select all its contents, and then press Delete.

Inserting Page Numbers in a Document

To help your readers (or perhaps yourself) keep the pages of a document in the right order, it's often useful to add page numbers. The best way to add page numbers in Word is to put a page number field in the header or footer. Word then repeats the page number on each page, inserting the correct value.

> **NOTE:** If you need to insert in the body of a document a page number that's in fact a reference to another page, insert a cross-reference as discussed later in this chapter. You can refer either to an item such as a heading, table caption, or graphic or to a bookmark that you place exactly where you need it.

To add page numbers to a header or footer, follow these steps:

1. Open the Page Numbers dialog box (see Figure 8–9) in one of these ways:

   - *Ribbon.* Choose Document Elements ➤ Header and Footer ➤ Page #. Note that this isn't the Header and Footer ➤ Header and Footer ➤ Page # button—that button inserts a page number without displaying the Page Numbers dialog box.

   - *Menu bar.* Choose Insert ➤ Page Numbers.

Figure 8–9. *In the Page Numbers dialog box, choose the position and alignment for the page numbers. You can also choose whether to show the page number on the first page.*

2. In the Position pop-up menu, choose Top of page (Header) or Bottom of page (Footer), as needed.

3. In the Alignment pop-up menu, choose Left, Center, Right, Inside, or Outside. Inside and Outside are for facing-page designs—for example, using Inside in a header places the page number at the upper-right corner of the left page and the upper-left corner of the right page. The Preview box shows you where the page numbers will appear.

4. Select the Show number on first page check box if you want the first page to have a number too. To suppress the number on the first page, clear this check box.

5. If you want to set the formatting for the page numbers, follow these steps:

    ■ Click the Format button to display the Page Number Format dialog box (see Figure 8–10).

Figure 8–10. *Use the Page Number Format dialog box to change the formatting of a page number—for example, including a chapter number in it.*

    ■ Open the Number format pop-up menu, and click the number formatting you want—for example, 1, 2, 3; A, B, C; or i, ii, iii.

    ■ If your document has chapters and you want to include the chapter number in the page numbering, select the Include chapter number check box. Then open the Chapter starts with style pop-up menu, and click the style that marks the beginning of each chapter—for example, Heading 1 or a Chapter Title style you've added. Last, open the Use separator pop-up menu, and choose the separator character to use between the chapter number and the page number. Your choices are a hyphen, a period, a colon, an em dash (a long dash), or a en dash (a short dash but longer than a hyphen).

    ■ In the Page Numbering area, choose how to control the numbering. Click the Continue from previous section option button to have the page numbers follow those in the previous section. To start again or start at a specific number, click the Start at option button, and enter the number in the text box.

    ■ Click the OK button to close the Page Number Format dialog box and return to the Page Numbers dialog box.

6. Click the OK button to close the Page Numbers dialog box. Word inserts the page numbers.

NOTE: To remove the page numbers from a document, choose View ➤ Header and Footer, select the page number in the header area or footer area, and then press the Delete key.

Creating Newspaper-Style Columns of Text

If you create newsletters or similar publications, you may want to create multicolumn layouts. Word can do this well, but there are a couple of tricks you need to learn.

TIP: Only Print Layout view and Full Screen view show the columns on-screen, so it's best to use these views to work with columns. Print Layout view is the easiest choice.

To create simple columns, follow these steps:

1. If you want to turn only part of the document into columns, select that part. For example, select existing text, or select a blank paragraph at the point where you want to start the columns.

NOTE: If you want to turn the whole document into columns (and the same number of columns throughout), click anywhere in the document.

2. Choose Layout ➤ Text Layout ➤ Columns to open the Columns panel, and then click the type of columns you want (see Figure 8–11). Word turns your selection into columns.

Figure 8–11. From the Columns panel, choose One, Two, or Three columns. Choose Left for a narrow left column and a wide right column, and choose Right for wide left and narrow right. Click Columns for further options.

If you need to create other types of columns than appear on the Columns panel, such as four columns or columns with a vertical line between them, follow these steps:

3. Select the part of the document you want to apply the columns to.

4. Choose Format ➤ Columns from the menu bar or choose Layout ➤ Text Layout ➤ Columns ➤ Columns from the Ribbon to display the Columns dialog box (see Figure 8–12).

Figure 8–12. *Use the options in the Columns dialog box to create more complex column layouts in your Word documents.*

5. Choose the type of columns you want:

    ▪ To use one of the presets in the Presets area, click it.

    ▪ To specify a different number of columns, enter it in the Number of columns box.

6. If you want a vertical line between the columns, select the Line between check box.

7. Set up the column width and spacing:

    ▪ To make each column the same width, select the Equal column width check box. On the Col # 1 line of controls, set the width and spacing for the columns.

    ▪ To set each column to the width you want, clear the Equal column width check box, and then set the width for each column in the Width box and the spacing in the Spacing box. If you have four or more columns, you'll need to scroll down to reach the last ones.

8. Make sure the Apply to pop-up menu shows the right part of the document—the Selected text item to affect only the selection, the This section item to affect only the current section, the This point forward item to affect the rest of the document from here on, or the Whole document item to affect the whole document.

9. If you chose the This point forward item, you can select the Start new column check box if you want to create a new column layout from the current position of the insertion point.

10. Click the OK button to close the Columns dialog box. Word creates the columns using your choices. Figure 8–13 shows a three-column layout with vertical lines between the columns.

Figure 8–13. *You can include vertical lines between the columns to make a multicolumn layout easier to read.*

Breaking Your Columns with Column Breaks

After you've created the columns, Word automatically flows the text down each column as you enter it. When the first column reaches the bottom of the text area on the page, Word flows it to the start of the second column, and so on.

To end a column early, you can insert a column break. Position the insertion point where you want the break, and then choose Layout ➤ Page Setup ➤ Break ➤ Column from the Ribbon. Word inserts the column break and moves the insertion point to the top of the next column.

TIP: You can also insert a column break by choosing Insert ➤ Break ➤ Column Break from the menu bar or pressing Cmd+Shift+Return.

If you need to remove a column break, delete it. Click the Show button on the Standard toolbar or press Cmd+8 to display invisible characters so that you can see the column break, which appears as a blue line with the words Column Break in the middle. Position the insertion point before the column break, and then press Delete to delete it.

Removing Multiple Columns from a Section or Document

If you want to change a multiple-column section or document back to a single column, click in the section or document, and then choose Layout ➤ Text Layout ➤ Columns ➤ One. Word restores the text to a single column.

Using Bookmarks, Fields, and References

In long documents, you'll often need to mark parts of the document so that you can find them easily or refer to them. You may also want to insert pieces of information that Word can automatically update for you, such as the date and time or the name of the last person to save a document. And you may also find it useful to be able to refer easily to another part of the document and have Word keep its page number, name, or contents automatically updated.

Marking Important Parts of a Document with Bookmarks

To identify parts that you want to return to or refer to, you can place bookmarks in your Word documents. A bookmark is an electronic marker that you can place either at a single point in text (between two characters or other objects) or around text or an object.

NOTE: Use a single-point bookmark when you need to move the insertion point to a particular point or refer to a page number. Use a bookmark with contents when you need to refer to the specific contents—for example, to make a reference automatically display the text that appears in the bookmark.

Insert a Bookmark to Mark Part of a Document

To insert a bookmark, follow these steps:

1. Click the point where you want to place the bookmark, or select the text or other object you want the bookmark to contain.

2. Choose Insert ➤ Bookmark from the menu bar to display the Bookmark dialog box (see Figure 8–14).

Figure 8–14. *Create a bookmark when you need to mark a specific point or an area of content in a document.*

3. Type the name for the bookmark in the Bookmark name text box. You must start the name with a letter, but after that you can use any letters, numbers, and underscores as needed. You can't use spaces or symbols in the name.

4. Click the Add button to add the bookmark, and close the dialog box.

NOTE: If you need to move a bookmark to a different point in a document, position the insertion point or select the new location. Then open the Bookmark dialog box, click the bookmark name, and click the Add button. Word changes the bookmark to the new location without comment.

Navigating from Bookmark to Bookmark

After placing a bookmark, you can move the insertion point to the bookmark. Follow these steps:

1. Choose Insert Bookmark to display the Bookmark dialog box.

2. In the Bookmark name list box, click the bookmark.

3. Click the Go To button. If the bookmark is a single point, Word moves the insertion point to it; if the bookmark has contents, Word selects them.

4. Click the Close button to close the Bookmark dialog box.

Seeing Where Bookmarks Are in Your Documents

Word hides the bookmarks in your documents unless you set it to display them. When you're editing a document, it's often useful to display the bookmarks to avoid deleting them by accident. You may also need to display the bookmarks to make sure they're in the right place.

To display bookmarks, follow these steps:

1. Choose Word ➤ Preferences or press Cmd+, (Cmd and the comma key) to display the Word Preferences dialog box.

2. In the Authoring and Proofing Tools section, click the View icon to display the View preferences pane.

3. In the Show area, select the Bookmarks check box.

4. Click the OK button to close the Word Preferences dialog box.

For a single-point bookmark, Word displays a black I-beam in the document. For a bookmark that contains text or another object, Word displays brackets around the contents. Figure 8–15 shows one single-point bookmark (between "Aerobic" and "Exercise" in the heading paragraph) and two bookmarks with contents ("aerobics class" in the first body paragraph and around the illustration).

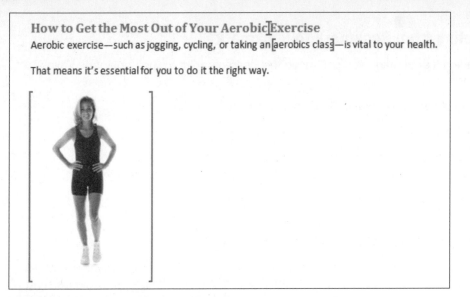

How to Get the Most Out of Your Aerobic Exercise

Aerobic exercise—such as jogging, cycling, or taking an aerobics class—is vital to your health.

That means it's essential for you to do it the right way.

Figure 8–15. *Word displays a black I-beam for a single-point bookmark marker and a pair of black brackets around the text or object in a bookmark that has contents.*

Deleting a Bookmark You No Longer Need

When you no longer need a bookmark, delete it like this:

1. Choose Insert ➤ Bookmark to display the Bookmark dialog box.

2. In the Bookmark name list box, click the bookmark.

3. Click the Delete button.

4. Click the Close button to close the Bookmark dialog box.

Inserting Automated Information with Fields

Many documents need automated items of information that Word can provide for you, such as the date or time, page numbers (discussed earlier in this chapter), or the file name. To add such information to your documents, you use fields—codes that tell Word to insert the information you want and whether to update it automatically.

Inserting a Field

To insert a field in a document, follow these steps:

1. Choose Insert ➤ Field from the menu bar to display the Field dialog box (shown in Figure 8–16 with the Date and Time category selected in the Categories list box and the SaveDate field selected in the Field names list box).

Figure 8–16. *The Field dialog box includes a wide range of fields. Normally, you'll want to start by choosing the type of fields in the Categories list box.*

2. In the Categories list box, choose the category of fields you want (see the following list). Here, I use the Date & Time category as an easy example.

    ■ *(All).* Lists all the fields. This is useful when you know the field's name but not the category that contains it.

    ■ *Date and Time.* Contains fields for entering dates and times, such as the current date or the time the document was last saved, in various formats. You can also insert a date, time, or both more easily by choosing Insert Date & Time from the menu bar and using the Date and Time dialog box.

    ■ *Document Automation.* Contains fields for automating movement around the document, running macros, printing, and similar actions.

    ■ *Document Information.* Contains fields for inserting information contained in the document's properties, such as the author name or file name.

    ■ *Equations and Formulas.* Contains fields for inserting equations and formulas. Use these when the Document Elements ➤ Math ➤ Equation panel on the Ribbon doesn't contain what you need.

    ■ *Index and Tables.* Contains fields for creating indexes and content tables (such as tables of contents and tables of figures). The References group on the Document Elements tab of the Ribbon contains controls for inserting these fields more easily.

- *Links and References.* Contains fields for inserting links (such as hyperlinks) or cross-references. The Insert ➤ Hyperlink, Insert ➤ Bookmark, and Insert ➤ Cross-reference commands on the menu bar provide easier access to these fields.

- *Mail Merge.* Contains fields for creating mail-merge documents. Usually it's easier to choose Tools ➤ Mail Merge Manager from the menu bar and then work in the Mail Merge Manager, as discussed in Chapter 9.

- *Numbering.* Contains fields for inserting automatic numbering in a document. For creating page numbers, it's easier to work in the header or footer, as described earlier in this chapter.

- *User Information.* Contains fields for inserting the user's name, initials, or address.

3. In the Field names list box, click the field you want. In the example, I've clicked the SaveDate field, which inserts the date the document was last saved. The Field codes area shows the code format for the field, and the text box underneath it shows the current version of the field—at the moment, just SAVEDATE.

4. Select the Preserve formatting during updates check box if you want to keep the field's formatting when you update it. This behavior is normally useful.

5. You can insert the field at this point if you want, but you may prefer to choose options for the field first. To choose options, follow these steps:

- Click the Options button to display the Field Options dialog box (see Figure 8–17). The contents of this dialog box vary depending on the field: some fields have many options, while others have few or none.

Figure 8–17. *Most fields have options that you can set by using the Field Options dialog box.*

- Click the option you want, and then click the Add to Field button. For example, in the Field Options dialog box for the SaveDate field, click the format you want in the Date-time formats list box, and then click the Add to Field button. Word adds the option's code to the Field codes text box.

- Click the OK button to close the Field Options dialog box and return to the Field dialog box.

6. Click the OK button to close the Field dialog box and insert the field.

Examining and Updating a Field

Now that you've inserted a field, you can examine it. At first, the field displays the field results—the information that the field produces. For example, the SaveDate field displays a date in the format you chose.

Normally, the field result appears like normal text until you click in it or select it, at which point Word displays gray shading behind it to indicate that it's a field (see Figure 8–18). To update the field, Ctrl+click or right-click it, and then click Update Field on the context menu.

Figure 8–18. *When you click a field result, Word displays gray shading to indicate that it is a field.*

NOTE: If you want to see field shading all the time, choose Word ➤ Preferences to display the Word Preferences dialog box. In the Authoring and Proofing Tools area, click the View icon to display the View preferences pane. In the Show area, open the Field shading pop-up menu, and choose Always. You can also select the Field codes check box if you want to display field codes all the time. Click the OK button to close the Word Preferences dialog box.

If you want to see the field code that's producing the field result, Ctrl+click or right-click anywhere in the field, and then click Toggle Field Codes on the context menu. Word displays the field code, as shown in Figure 8–19. You can edit the field code directly if you know which changes you want to make, but generally it's easier to use the Field Options dialog box.

Last saved date: { SAVEDATE \@ "dddd, MMMM d, yyyy" * MERGEFORMAT }

Figure 8–19. *If you want to see the code that produces a field result, Ctrl+click or right-click in the field, and then click Toggle Field Codes on the context menu. Repeat this move to show the field result again.*

Adding Cross-References to Other Parts of a Document

When you create formal documents, you often need to refer from one part to another. To do so, you can create cross-references to any of several different types of item, including headings, bookmarks, figures, and tables.

To insert a cross-reference, follow these steps:

1. Position the insertion point where you want the reference.

2. Choose Insert ➤ Cross-reference to display the Cross-reference dialog box (shown in Figure 8–20 with settings chosen for referring to a bookmark).

Figure 8–20. *In the Cross-reference dialog box, you can insert a cross-reference to a bookmark, heading, table, or other item in the document.*

3. Open the Reference type pop-up menu and choose the type of item you want to refer to:

- *Numbered item.* An item to which you have applied Word's automatic numbering. For example, a paragraph in a numbered list.

- *Heading.* A paragraph you have formatted with one of Word's Heading styles.

- *Bookmark.* A bookmark you have inserted in the document (as described earlier in this chapter).

- *Footnote.* A footnote you have created in the document, as discussed later in this chapter.

- *Endnote.* An endnote you have created in the document, as discussed later in this chapter.

- *Equation.* An equation you have inserted with the Document Elements ➤ Math ➤ Equation Ribbon command or the Insert ➤ Equation menu command, or as a field.

- *Figure.* A figure that you have marked with an automatically numbered caption using the Insert ➤ Caption command.

- *Table.* A table that you have marked with an automatically numbered caption using the Insert ➤ Caption command.

4. In the For which list box, click the item you want to refer to. (The name of this list box changes to reflect the type of item you've selected—for example, it's the For which numbered item list box when you select Numbered item or the For which caption list box when you select Table.)

5. Open the Insert reference to pop-up menu, and choose the item you want to refer to. The options vary depending on the object you're referring to, but these are the options for a bookmark to give you an idea:

- *Bookmark text.* Inserts the bookmark's contents (whatever that may be). Use this for bookmarks that have contents rather than for single-point bookmarks.

- *Page number.* Inserts the page number on which the first part of the bookmark appears.

- *Paragraph number.* Inserts the paragraph number in which the start of the bookmark appears. Use this only with numbered paragraphs.

- *Paragraph number (no context).* Inserts the numbering for the paragraph in which the start of the bookmark appears, without any other numbering involved in the multilevel list. For example, if you have a three-level list and the bookmark appears in paragraph 2. a. (ii), this choice inserts the (ii) part without the rest of the numbering.

- *Paragraph number (full context).* Inserts the numbering for the paragraph in which the start of the bookmark appears, including the full number—for example, 2. a. (ii).

- *Above/below.* Inserts "above" if the start of the bookmark appears earlier in the document than the reference or "below" if it appears later in the document. This is occasionally useful, but see the next paragraph for a better alternative.

6. If you choose a page number or paragraph number in the Insert reference to pop-up menu, you can select the Include above/below check box if you want to add "above" or "below" to the end of the reference to indicate whether the item falls before or after the reference.

7. Select the Insert as hyperlink check box if you want the reference to appear as a hyperlink. The reader can click the hyperlink to jump to the referenced item.

8. Click the Insert button to insert the reference in the document. The Cancel button changes to a Close button.

9. Click the Close button to close the Cross-reference dialog box.

NOTE: A cross-reference is a field code, so you can update it by Ctrl+clicking or right-clicking in the field and then clicking Update Field on the context menu.

Creating Long Documents with Outline View

To plan, structure, and rearrange long documents, use Outline view. You met Outline view briefly in Chapter 6 when we looked at each of Word's main views in turn. In this section, you'll learn how Word handles outlines, how to create the outline of a document, and how to use Outline view to edit and rearrange a document quickly and easily.

How Outlines Work

Word creates outlines by assigning different outline levels to the paragraphs of a document. There are nine outline levels, with Level 1 being the highest and Level 9 the lowest. Below these is the body text level, which prevents a paragraph from appearing in the outline of the document.

Word's nine heading styles automatically map to the outline levels—Heading 1 to Level 1, Heading 2 to Level 2, and all the way down to Heading 9 mapping to Level 9. But you can also set the outline level of any style to the level you want, which allows you to make other styles appear in the outline as needed. For example, if you want your figure captions to appear at the fifth level of the outline, you can change the Caption style so that it has the Level 5 outline level.

> **NOTE:** You can also set the outline level of an individual paragraph if you want, without assigning that paragraph a style that has an outline level. Promoting a paragraph manually like this can be useful sometimes, but using styles gives you greater consistency in your documents.

Developing the Outline of a Document

To develop the outline of a document, you work in Outline view. You can either start off in Outline view and work in it to structure your document at first, or you can switch to Outline view at any point when you need to work on the outline or get an overview of the structure of the document.

> **TIP:** When you're working intensively on a document, it's often useful to open a second window on the document and keep that window in Outline view. If you prefer to work in a single window, you can either switch views or split the window into two panes and then use Outline view in one pane. To open a second window, choose Window ➤ New Window. To split a window in half, choose Window ➤ Split.

Switching to Outline View

You can switch to Outline view in any of these ways:

- *Mouse.* Click the Outline View button at the left end of the status bar.
- *Keyboard.* Press Cmd+Option+O.
- *Menu bar.* Choose View ➤ Outline.

When you switch to Outline view, Word automatically displays the Outline Tools group on the Home tab of the Ribbon. You use the controls in the Outline Tools group (shown labeled in Figure 8–21) to create the outline and display the parts of it you want to see.

Figure 8–21. *Use the controls in the Outline Tools group to develop your outline. Word displays the Outline Tools group on the Home tab of the Ribbon when you switch to Outline view.*

Creating Headings in Outline View

When you switch a document to Outline view, Word displays the document's headings (or more correctly, its outline levels).

When you press Return at the end of a heading paragraph in Outline view, Word continues the heading style to the next paragraph rather than applying whichever style that paragraph's style specifies for the following paragraph. So when you type a heading, pressing Return creates another paragraph at the same level in the outline. This enables you to create multiple headings quickly without needing to apply a heading style as you would need to in another view.

NOTE: If you create a new blank document and switch it straight to Outline view, Word automatically applies Heading 1 style to the first paragraph. You can then start creating your outline immediately.

Promoting and Demoting Headings

You can quickly promote or demote headings by using the buttons in the Outline Tools group:

- To move the current paragraph down to the next heading level, click the Demote button.

- To change a paragraph to body text, click the Demote to Body Text button.

- To move the current paragraph up to the next heading level, click the Promote button.

- To promote the current paragraph to Heading 1, click the Promote to Heading 1 button.

TIP: From the keyboard, press Tab to demote the current paragraph or Shift+Tab to promote it. You can also select a section and then drag it to the left to promote it or to the left to demote it, but doing so sometimes requires a steady touch.

Expanding and Collapsing the Outline and Headings

One of Outline view's strongest features is that you can expand the outline to different levels so that you can see exactly what you need to see. Figure 8–22 shows a section of outline with three levels of heading displayed and some sections expanded.

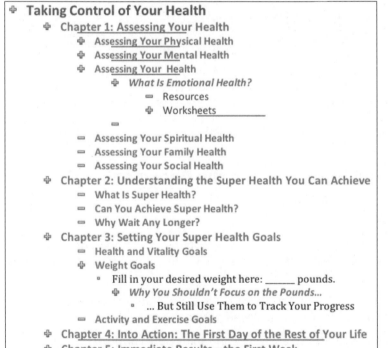

Figure 8–22. *You can expand an outline to different levels so that you can see exactly what you need.*

To choose the overall level of outline levels displayed, open the Show pop-up menu, and click the level you want. Your choices are from Level 1 to Level 9, or All Levels if you want to display every paragraph. For much of your work in Outline view, you'll likely want to show several levels of headings—for example, Levels 1, 2, and 3.

Once you've chosen the outline level, you can double-click the + sign next to a heading to display or hide the headings and other contents below it. A – sign next to a heading indicates that it has no lower-level headings or body text below it, as is the case with the "Activity and Exercise Goals" heading in Chapter 3.

The dotted underline that appears under some headings indicates that the heading has collapsed subheadings under it. The underline starts at the indentation level of the first subheading so you can see which level this is at. For example, the Chapter 4 heading has an underline that starts at the first level of indentation, indicating that the first subheading is a Heading 3-level or Outline 3-level item (the next level below the Chapter heading, which is Heading 3-level).

If you want to expand or collapse multiple sections at once, select the sections, and then click the Expand button or the Collapse button.

> **TIP:** If you want to zero in on the text of your outline without distractions, click the Formatting button in the Outline Tools group on the Home tab of the Ribbon. Clicking this button, so that it no longer appears pressed in, makes Word show all the text in a standard font that lets you see more of the outline at once. Click the button again, pressing it in, when you want to see the formatting again.

When you display all of the text of the document, you may find you lose many of the advantages of Outline view. But you can select the Show first line check box in the Outline Tools group on the Home tab to make Word display only the first line of each paragraph (ending with an ellipsis to show that the rest is hidden). This feature lets you follow the gist of the paragraphs in the document without displaying the full text.

Moving Paragraphs Up and Down the Document

When you have displayed the outline level you want, you can quickly move paragraphs up and down the outline.

Click a + sign to select that item and all its subordinate items, or click and drag in the selection bar to select multiple items. You can then move them up or down the outline in these ways:

- *Ribbon.* Click the Move Up button or the Move Down button to move the selection up or down by one displayed paragraph at a time.

- *Keyboard.* Press Ctrl+Shift+Up arrow or Ctrl+Shift+Down arrow to move the selection up or down by one displayed paragraph at a time.

- *Mouse.* Drag the selection up or down as far as necessary. Word displays a line between paragraphs to indicate where the selection will land when you drop it.

Switching from Outline View to Another View

When you've finished working on the outline, switch to another view by clicking the appropriate View button at the left end of the status bar or by opening the View menu and clicking the view you want.

> **TIP:** If you need to create very long documents, look into Word's Master Document feature, which you access by choosing View ➤ Master Document from the menu bar. This feature, which is beyond the scope of this book, enables you to create a kind of super-document that consists of multiple subdocuments. You can work with the master document in Master Document view, which is similar to Outline view.

Adding Footnotes and Endnotes

If you create professional or academic documents, you may need to add footnotes or endnotes to provide extra information or show your sources.

A *footnote* is a note that appears at the foot of the page that refers to it, while an *endnote* is a note that appears at the end of a section or document. Use footnotes when it's likely the reader will want to read the information and the chunks of information are short enough to fit at the bottom of pages. Use endnotes for information that you think only a few readers will need to consult or for longer pieces of information.

> **TIP:** You can convert footnotes to endnotes, or endnotes to footnotes, if necessary. So, it's not a disaster if you start with one type of note and then realize you need the other type.

Adding a Footnote

To add a footnote to a document, follow these steps:

1. Place the insertion point immediately after the last word of the text you want the footnote to refer to.

NOTE: You can also insert a footnote or endnote using the Footnote or Endnote dialog box, which you'll meet later in this chapter. Normally, you'll use the Footnote or Endnote dialog box to insert a footnote (or endnote) only when you need choose specific settings for the note, such as changing the numbering.

2. Choose Document Elements ➤ Citations ➤ Footnote to insert a superscript footnote number or mark and open the footnote area.

    - In Print Layout view, Word shows the footnote area at the bottom of the page, separated by a horizontal line, as shown in the upper part of Figure 8–23. The footnote area shows only the footnotes that appear on that page.

    - In Draft view, Outline view, or Web Layout view, Word shows the footnote area as a separate pane, as shown in the lower part of Figure 8–20. The footnote pane shows a list of all the footnotes in the document.

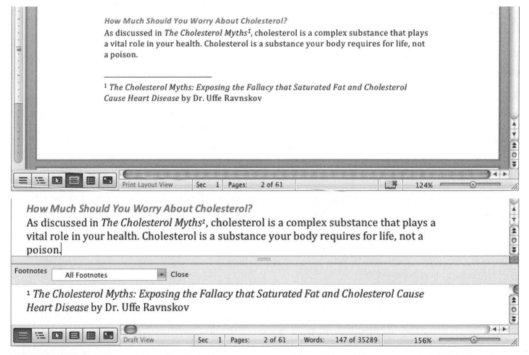

Figure 8–23. *In Print Layout view, the footnote area appears at the bottom of the page (above). In Word's other views that can display footnotes, the footnote area appears as a separate pane (below).*

3. Add the text or other material for the footnote—for example, by typing it in or pasting it.

4. Click in the main text of the document again to resume work in it. You can either leave the footnote pane open so that you can work with other footnotes in it or close it in one of these ways:

   - Click the Close button.

   - Double-click the bar that separates the pane from the main window.

   - Press Ctrl+Shift+C.

Adding an Endnote

To add an endnote to a document, follow these steps:

1. Place the insertion point immediately after the last word of the text you want the footnote to refer to.

2. Choose Document Elements ➤ Citations ➤ Endnote to insert a superscript endnote number or mark and open the endnote area.

   - In Print Layout view or Web Layout view, Word shows the endnote area on the last page of the document or section, separated by a horizontal line, as shown in the upper part of Figure 8–24.

   - In Draft view or Outline view, Word shows the endnote area as a separate pane, as shown in the lower part of Figure 8–24. The endnote pane shows a list of all the endnotes in the document.

You can treat yourself well and boost your health—or you can treat yourself poorly and drive yourself into sickness and death.

Choose wisely!

---

[i] The 2011 *Physical Activity Guidelines for Americans* recommend that active adults perform at least 150 minutes of "moderate intensity aerobic physical activity" each week. Fast walking, running, dancing, bicycling, and swimming all count as this type of activity.

[ii] "Spiritual health" is the foundation of all our health. If you cannot keep your spirit in good condition, what hope is there for your physical manifestation?" William Smith, 1919

[iii] See *The Annals of Complementary Medicine Compendium II* (Wiley, 2010) pages 235ff.

`Print Layout View    Sec  1   Pages:  61 of 61    Words: 35363 of 35387    124%`

You can treat yourself well and boost your health—or you can treat yourself poorly and drive yourself into sickness and death.

Choose wisely!

Endnotes   All Endnotes   Close

[i] The 2011 *Physical Activity Guidelines for Americans* recommend that active adults perform at least 150 minutes of "moderate intensity aerobic physical activity" each week. Fast walking, running, dancing, bicycling, and swimming all count as this type of activity.

[ii] "Spiritual health" is the foundation of all our health. If you cannot keep your spirit in good condition, what hope is there for your physical manifestation?" William Smith, 1919

[iii] See *The Annals of Complementary Medicine Compendium II* (Wiley, 2010) pages 235ff.

`Draft View    Sec  1   Pages:  61 of 61    140%`

Figure 8–24. *In Print Layout view and Web Layout view, the endnote area appears at the bottom of the final page of the document or section (above). In Draft view and Outline view, the endnote area appears as a separate pane (below).*

3. Type or paste in the text or other material for the endnote.

4. Click in the main text of the document again to resume work in it. In Draft view or Outline view, you can either leave the endnote pane open for further use or close it in one of these ways:

- Click the Close button.

- Double-click the bar that separates the pane from the main window.

- Press Cmd+Shift+C.

Customizing Footnotes and Endnotes to Suit Your Document

Word automatically numbers footnotes and endnotes and inserts them using its default placement—footnotes at the foot of the page and endnotes at the end of the document. The default settings work well for many documents, but for others, you may want to change the numbering or the placement. To do so, follow these steps:

1. Click in the section of the document for which you want to change the footnotes or endnotes. (If the document has only a single section, click anywhere in it.)

2. Choose Insert ➤ Footnote from the menu bar to display the Footnote and Endnote dialog box (see Figure 8–25).

Figure 8–25. *Open the Footnote and Endnote dialog box when you need to choose the numbering or symbols for footnotes or endnotes, change the position or numbering, or convert footnotes to endnotes or endnotes to footnotes.*

3. In the Location area, select the Footnotes option button or the Endnotes option to tell Word which type of notes you want to affect.

4. Choose where to place the notes in the document:

   ■ *Footnotes.* In the Footnotes pop-up menu, choose Bottom of page (the default) or Below text (which gives an odd look but helps make the footnotes more obvious to the reader).

   ■ *Endnotes.* In the Endnotes pop-up menu, choose End of document (the default setting) or End of section.

5. In the Format area, choose the numbering you want for the notes whose option button you've selected:

   ■ *Number format.* In this pop-up menu, click the numbering format to use: "1, 2, 3"; "a, b, c"; "A, B, C"; "i, ii, iii"; "I, II, III"; or a series of symbols.

- *Custom mark.* To use a custom note mark, click the Symbol button. In the Symbol dialog box, click the symbol you want, and then click the OK button. The symbol appears in the Custom Mark box; delete it if you want to return to regular numbering.

- *Start at.* In this box, enter the starting number to use for numbering. The default is the first character of the number format—for example, 1, i, or A.

- *Numbering.* In this pop-up menu, choose Continuous if you want to use the numbering sequence throughout the document. Choose Restart each section to start afresh with each section (this is useful for a document with endnotes at the end of each chapter). Choose Restart each page if you want to restart footnote numbering on each page (you can't use this option for endnotes, because it wouldn't make sense).

6. Click the Apply button to apply your choices.

7. Click the Close button to close the Footnote and Endnote dialog box.

> **NOTE:** To insert a footnote or endnote using the Footnote and Endnote dialog box, select the Footnotes option button or the Endnotes option button (as appropriate), choose any other options needed, and then click the Insert button.

Converting Footnotes to Endnotes or Endnotes to Footnotes

To convert footnotes to endnotes, endnotes to footnotes, or each kind of note to the other at the same time, follow these steps:

1. Choose Insert ➤ Footnote to display the Footnote and Endnote dialog box.

> **CAUTION:** Before converting the footnotes or endnotes in a long or complex document that contains many notes, create a fresh backup of the document. The conversion seldom goes wrong, but when it does, the notes can become severely scrambled.

2. Click the Convert button to display the Convert Notes dialog box (see Figure 8–26).

Figure 8–26. *Use the Convert Notes dialog box to convert footnotes to endnotes, convert endnotes to footnotes, or switch each kind of note to the other.*

3. Click the Convert all footnotes to endnotes option button, the Convert all endnotes to footnotes option button, or the Swap footnotes and endnotes option button, as needed.

4. Click the OK button to close the Convert Notes dialog box and perform the conversion.

5. Click the OK button to close the Footnote and Endnote dialog box.

Navigating Among and Viewing Footnotes or Endnotes

You can navigate from one footnote or endnote to another by using either the browse object (as discussed in Chapter 6) or the Go To tab of the Find and Replace dialog box. Here are some examples:

- *Browse object.* Click the Select Browse Object button between the Previous button and Next button at below the vertical scroll bar. On the Select Browse Object panel that opens, click the Footnote icon. You can then click the Next button to select the next footnote or click the Previous button to select the previous footnote.

- *Go To tab of the Find and Replace dialog box.* Click the Pages readout in the status bar to display the Go To tab of the Find and Replace dialog box. In the Go to what list box, click the Footnote item or the Endnote item, as needed. You can then move between footnotes or endnotes by clicking the Next button or the Previous button on the Go To tab.

Once you've located a footnote mark or endnote mark, you can preview the footnote or endnote by holding the mouse pointer over the footnote mark or endnote mark until Word displays a ScreenTip containing the text of the footnote or endnote (see Figure 8–27).

The Cholesterol Myths: Exposing the
Fallacy that Saturated Fat and
Cholesterol Cause Heart Disease by Dr.
Uffe Ravnskov

How Much Should You Worry Ab

As discussed in *The Cholesterol Myths[1]*, cholesterol is a complex substance that plays a vital role in your health. Cholesterol is a substance your body requires for life, not a poison.

Figure 8–27. *The quick way to view a footnote is to preview it in a ScreenTip.*

If the note is short and text only, this may be all you need to do. But if the note is longer or contains other types of contents (such as graphics, tables, or charts), double-click the footnote mark or endnote mark to display the footnote area or endnote area and jump directly to the note whose mark you double-clicked.

You can then move from note to note in the footnote area or endnote area. As you move the insertion point to another note, Word displays the corresponding part in the main document.

NOTE: You can also display the footnote or endnote area by choosing View ➤ Footnotes. If Word displays the View Footnotes dialog box, click the View footnote area option button or the View endnote area option button as appropriate, and then click the OK button. (If the document contains only one kind of note, Word displays the area for that kind of note without opening the View Footnotes dialog box.)

Summary

In this chapter, you learned how to create complex documents and complex layouts. You now know how to convert existing text in a Word document into a table; how to add headers, footers, and page numbers to a document; and how to create a multicolumn, newsletter-style layout.

You also saw how to insert bookmarks to enable yourself easily to access and refer to parts of a document and how to insert cross-references to bookmarks or other document elements. And you learned to develop a document's outline swiftly and easily in Outline view plus the techniques for adding footnotes and endnotes to your documents.

In the next chapter, I'll show you how to create business documents and perform mail merge.

Chapter 9

Creating Business Documents with Mail Merge

In this chapter, you learn how to use Word's powerful Mail Merge feature to create business documents such as form letters, catalogs, mailing labels, and envelopes. Each of these types of documents is built around a common core, the main document, into which you merge variable data contained in records in a data source such as an Excel workbook or an address book.

Mail merge may initially seem daunting, but it's a great way of saving time and effort—so if you can invest some time to come to grips with how mail merge works, you'll soon reap the rewards.

We'll start by running through how mail merge works and the six separate steps Word uses to set up and execute mail merges. We'll then go through each step in turn so that you're comfortable creating mail merge documents. Lastly, I'll show you how to turn a mail merge main document back into a regular Word document.

Understanding How Mail Merge Works

Mail merge works by using a standard document that contains the data that remains constant and a data source that contains the records to be merged into the document.

■ *Main document.* This is the document that contains the body of the merge documents you're creating. For example, when you use mail merge to create form letters, the main document is a letter that contains your address, the text that remains constant for each recipient, and fields into which the variable information (such as the recipient's name and address) slot.

NOTE: In mail merge, the main document is always a Word document. The data source can also be a Word document that contains a table with the records for the mail merge, but it is more often a database-like file: an Excel workbook containing a table of records, your Mac OS X Address Book or Outlook's Contacts, or a query on a "real" database in an application such as FileMaker Pro.

- *Data source.* This is the file that contains the records or data that the merge places in the main document to create each merge document. For example, when you're creating a form letter, the data source will contain each recipient's name and address, nickname or preferred greeting, and other items of information such as the product or query about which you're contacting the recipient. Each record consists of one or more *fields*, discrete items of information. For example, if you create a customer record, you'll usually have separate fields for the last name, first name, middle initial, e-mail address, all the separate components of the physical address, and so on.

TIP: When you're creating a data source, break up your records using a field for each item of data you may want to use separately. For example, instead of having a single field containing the street address, you may find it better to create a field for the street name and a separate field for the house number. This separation enables you to use the street name separately from the house number, which can be useful (for instance, if you need to identify all your customers in a particular street).

Word treats mail merge as a six-step process:

- *Step One: Select Document Type.* In this step, you choose the type of mail-merge document you want to create and create that document.

- *Step Two: Select Recipients List.* In this step, you choose the recipients list to use for the mail merge—for example, a Word document containing a table, or an Excel workbook.

- *Step Three: Insert Placeholders.* In this step, you insert placeholders in the main document to mark the places where the merge will insert fields of information. For example, you insert the Last Name field where you want the recipient's last name to go.

- *Step Four: Filter Recipients.* In this step, you choose whether to merge all the records in the data source or only some of them.

- *Step Five: Preview Results.* In this step, you preview how your merged documents will look so that you can make any changes needed before you proceed.

- *Step Six: Complete Merge.* In this step, you perform the merge, producing one of three end results: a document containing mail-merge letters (or labels or whatever) that you can use like any other merge document; multiple documents that Word sends directly to your printer; or e-mail messages.

In the rest of this chapter, we'll look at each step in turn.

Creating the Main Document for the Mail Merge

The first step in mail merge is to tell Word what kind of mail merge documents you want to create—form letters, labels, envelopes, or a catalog—and create a suitable main document. You can either create a new document from scratch or open an existing document.

To choose the merge document type and create the main document, follow these steps:

1. Open the existing document you want to use or create a new document:

   - *Open an existing document.* Click the Open button on the Standard toolbar to display the Open: Microsoft Word dialog box. Navigate to and select the document, and then click the Open button.

   > **TIP:** When creating form letters, you can often save time either by reusing an existing letter or by basing the main document on a letter template that has the sender address, recipient address, salutation, and so on, in suitable places. Similarly, if you already have the framework for a catalog, you can reuse that. You can also reuse an existing document when creating envelopes or labels, but these are quick and easy to create from scratch using the Mail Merge Manager.

   - *Create a new document.* Click the Templates button on the Standard toolbar, or choose File ➤ New from Template to display the Word Document Gallery dialog box. Click the template on which to base the document, and then click the Choose button. Click the Save button on the Standard toolbar, specify the document name and folder in the Save: Microsoft Word dialog box, and then click the Save button.

2. Choose Tools ➤ Mail Merge Manager from the menu bar to display the Mail Merge Manager palette. If the Select Document type section at the top of the palette is collapsed, click its header bar or its disclosure triangle to expand it (see Figure 9–1).

Figure 9–1. *The Mail Merge Manager palette contains six sections that you can collapse or expand by clicking their header bars or the disclosure triangles on them.*

3. Click the Create New pop-up button, and then click the item you want to create:

- *Form Letters.* Click this item to create merged letters. This is the type of document we'll use in the examples. The documents don't have to be letters as such—you can create anything from party invitations to personalized storybooks.

- *Labels.* Click this item to create labels such as mailing labels for printing on a printer. In the Label Options dialog box that Word displays, you can choose from a wide variety of types of mailing labels.

- *Envelopes.* Click this item to create envelopes for printing on a printer. In the Envelope dialog box that Word displays, you then choose the size and shape of envelope you will use.

- *Catalog.* Click this item to create a catalog containing mail merge data. For example, if you have a data source with records that contain details of machine parts, you can pull those records into a catalog to make them easily readable.

Once you've specified the document type, Word changes the Select Document Type area in the Mail Merge Manager palette to show your choices and automatically expands the Select Recipients List section ready for the next step. Figure 9–2 shows an example.

Figure 9–2. *Word adds the information about the main document and the merge type to the Select Document Type section of the Mail Merge Manager. Word expands the Select Recipients List section automatically.*

Selecting the Recipients for the Mail Merge

Once you've created the main document, the next step in the mail merge is to tell Word which data source to use. To do so, click the Get List pop-up button in the Select Recipients List section of the Mail Merge Manager pane, and then click the appropriate item on the pop-up menu:

- *New Data Source.* Click this item to create a new data source in Word.

- *Open Data Source.* Click this item to open an existing data source in a Word document.

- *Office Address Book.* Click this item to use data from your Outlook Contacts.

- *Apple Address Book.* Click this item to use data from your Mac OS X Address Book.

- *FileMaker Pro.* Click this item to use data from a FileMaker Pro database.

- *Header Source.* You use this submenu to add a different source of headers after selecting a data source. This topic is beyond the scope of this book.

How you use each of these data sources varies, so we'll look at each in a separate section.

Creating a New Data Source in Word

The first option the Mail Merge Manager offers you is to create a new data source in Word. Word creates a data source by inserting a table in a document and then storing the data in the rows of the table.

> **CAUTION:** Creating a data source in Word does work, but you should almost never do it. In many cases, you'll have the information you need in a more easily accessible format, such as a worksheet in an Excel workbook, your Outlook Contacts, or your Mac OS X Address Book. And even if you don't have the information in such a format, you'll do better to put it in a spreadsheet, address book, or database, because you'll be able to keep it updated and reuse it more easily there than if you create a data source in Word.

If you decide to create a data source in Word (see the nearby Caution), follow these steps:

1. In the Select Recipients List area of the Mail Merge Manager palette, click the Get List pop-up button, and then click New Data Source on the pop-up menu. Word displays the Create Data Source dialog box (see Figure 9–3). This dialog box contains a list of standard fields for form letters, labels, and envelopes: Title, FirstName, LastName, JobTitle, Company, and so on.

Figure 9–3. *Use the Create Data Source dialog box to set up the fields for a new data source stored in a Word document. Before you create such a data source, consider alternatives such as an Excel workbook, your Outlook Contacts, or your Mac OS X Address Book.*

2. Customize the list of fields as needed:

- *Add a field.* Type the name in the Placeholder list text box, and then click the Add Placeholder button. Word adds the field to the bottom of the Field names in header row list box. You can move it up by clicking the Move Up button (the button with the up arrow).

- *Remove a field.* Click the field in the Field names in header row list box, and then click the Remove Field Name button. Word doesn't confirm the removal, but it places the field name in the Placeholder list text box in case you need to edit it and add it back to the list.

- *Rearrange the fields.* To change the order in which the fields appear in the Field names in header row list box, click the field, and then click the Move Up button (the button with the up arrow) or the Move Down button (the button with the down arrow).

3. When you've finished customizing the fields, click the OK button to close the Create Data Source dialog box. Word displays the Save Data Source dialog box, which is the standard Save As dialog box with a different name.

4. Type the name for the data source, and select the folder in which to save it.

5. Click the Save button to close the Save Data Source dialog box. Word saves the data source and then displays the Data Form dialog box (see Figure 9–4).

Figure 9–4. *Use the Data Form dialog box to enter data in a new Word data source quickly and easily.*

6. Type the information in each field, pressing Tab to move from one field to the next. (Press Shift+Tab if you need to move back to the previous field.)

7. When you've finished adding a record, click the Add New button to add a new record.

8. When you've finished adding records, click the OK button to close the Data Form dialog box. Word automatically saves the data source document.

EDITING RECORDS IN THE DATA FORM DIALOG BOX

When you're creating a new data source, you'll mostly use the Add New button in the Data Form dialog box. But when you open a data source for updating or editing, you can also take other actions. To open a data source for editing, open the Mail Merge Manager palette, expand the Select Recipients List section, and then click the Edit Data Source button (the button that shows a grid with a pencil sticking out of it).

These are the other actions you can take when editing records:

- *Navigate among records.* In the Record area in the lower-left corner of the Data Form dialog box, click the |< button to move to the first record, the < button to move to the previous record, the > button to move to the next record, or the >| button to move to the last record. Or, if you know the number of the record you want, type it in the text box, and then press Return to display that record.

- *Delete the current record.* Click the Delete button in the Data Form dialog box.

- *Restore the record you're editing.* Click the Restore button to read the record again from the data source, and enter its data into the fields in the Data Form dialog box. Restoring the record wipes out any changes you've made to the record.

- *Find a record.* Click the Find button to display the Find in Field dialog box (see Figure 9–5). Type the search term in the Find what box, entering all the text that will appear in the field (Word doesn't find matches for part of a field). Then open the In field pop-up menu, and click the field to search. Click the Find First button to locate the first matching record. Click the Find Next button (which replaces the Find First button after Word finds a match) to search again. Click the Close button when you've found the record you want to edit.

- *Open the data source.* Click the View Source button in the Data Form dialog box. Normally you don't need to open the source, because it's easier to add and edit records by using the Data Form dialog box; Word keeps the data source document hidden from view, even though it is open for editing. But you may sometimes need to open the data source so that you can make sweeping changes to it—for example, by using Word's Replace features to replace all instances of a particular term.

Figure 9–5. *Use the Find in Field dialog box to quickly locate a particular record in a Word data source.*

Opening an Existing Data Source

If you already have your data in a Word data-source document that you've created before, in an Excel workbook (for example, one that contains a database table), or in a text file, use the Open Data Source command to connect the data source to the main document. Follow these steps:

1. In the Select Recipients List section of the Mail Merge Manager palette, click the Get List pop-up button, and then click Open Data Source. Word displays the Choose a File dialog box, which works like any other Open dialog box.

2. Navigate to the folder that contains the data source, and then click the file.

3. Click the Open button to close the Choose a File dialog box. Word connects the data source to the main document.

Using Contacts from the Office Address Book

If your version of Office:Mac includes Outlook, you'll probably store your contacts in Outlook's Contacts. In this case, you can use your contacts easily in mail merges.

To use your Outlook Contacts in a mail merge, click the Get List pop-up button in the Select Recipients List section of the Mail Merge Manager palette, and then click Office Address Book in the pop-up menu. Word connects the Office Address Book to the main document as the data source.

Using Contacts from the Mac OS X Address Book

If you keep your contacts' data in the Mac OS X Address Book rather than in Outlook, click the Get List pop-up button in the Select Recipients List section of the Mail Merge Manager palette, and then click Apple Address Book in the pop-up menu. Word connects the Mac OS X Address Book to the main document as the data source.

Using Data from a FileMaker Pro Database

If the data you will use for the mail merge is in a FileMaker Pro database, follow these steps to connect the database to the main document:

1. In the Select Recipients List section of the Mail Merge Manager palette, click the Get List pop-up button, and then click FileMaker Pro. Word displays the Choose a File dialog box, which works like any other Open dialog box.

2. Navigate to the folder that contains the data source, and then click the file.

3. Click the Open button to close the Choose a File dialog box. Word connects the database to the main document.

Inserting Placeholders in Your Main Document

Now that you've connected the data source to the main document, you're ready for the third step in the mail merge process. This step is to insert placeholders in your main document to tell Word where to place each field of information from the records.

If the Insert Placeholders section in the Mail Merge Manager palette is collapsed, click its title bar or its disclosure triangle to expand it. You'll see a list of placeholders (see Figure 9–6). Click the placeholder you want to add, and then drag it to the document.

> **TIP:** Remember to add all the necessary spaces and punctuation between the placeholders. It's easy to omit the spaces and punctuation when you're arranging the placeholders, but the resulting merged documents look unprofessional and unconvincing. You've probably received enough of these yourself to know how even a minor mistake in layout instantly destroys the illusion of care that the personalized letter is intended to give. If you can get the spaces and punctuation right when inserting the fields, you're ahead of the game; if not, you can catch errors at the preview stage.

Figure 9–6. *Add fields to your main document by dragging them from the Insert Placeholders section of the Mail Merge Manager palette to the appropriate part of the document.*

NOTE: The More tab in the Insert Placeholders section of the Mail Merge Manager palette contains *Word fields*, fields you can insert in the document to do things such as adding information about the merge itself or inserting data only if a condition is met. For example, the Merge Sequence # field inserts the merge sequence number, and the If… Then… Else inserts one text string if the condition you specify is met and a different text string if it's not. Word fields are beyond the scope of this book, but you can find information on how to use them online or in Word's Help file.

Filtering the Recipients of the Merge Document

The fourth step in the mail merge process is to filter the recipients of your data source to specify which of them should receive the merged documents.

NOTE: If you want to use each item in your data source to produce a document or entry in the mail merge, you don't need to apply filtering.

To filter the recipients of the merge, follow these steps:

1. If the Filter Recipients section in the Mail Merge Manager palette is collapsed, click its title bar or its disclosure triangle to expand it (see Figure 9–7).

Figure 9–7. *Click the Options button in the Filter Recipients section of the Mail Merge Manager palette to open the Query Options dialog box.*

2. Click the Options button to display the Query Options dialog box. Figure 9–8 shows the Query Options dialog box as it appears for the Office Address Book; other types of data source have different controls, but they work in a similar way.

Figure 9–8. *In the Query Options dialog box, set up any filtering needed to identify the records you want to use in the mail merge.*

3. Choose options for filtering the data source. For example, for the Office Address Book:

- In the List mail merge recipients by pop-up menu, choose Categories if you want to see Address Book categories such as Personal, Work, Friends, and Family. Using a category is the quick and easy way to filter records—as long as you've arranged your contacts by categories. Choose Complete Record if you want to be able to choose individual contacts by name.

- In the Select the categories you would like to include list box (when you've selected Categories) or the Select the individual contacts you would like to include list box (when you've selected Complete Record), select the check box for each category or for each contact you want to include.

4. When you have chosen the records you want, click the OK button to close the Query Options dialog box.

Previewing the Results of the Mail Merge

At this point, the merge is set up and ready to run—in theory. In practice, it's all too easy to waste paper or send embarrassing e-mail messages by getting mail-merge fields and text in the wrong places. So, it's always wise to use the preview feature to make sure your merge works the way you intend it to work.

To preview the results, click the Preview Results heading or disclosure triangle in the Mail Merge Manager palette to display the Preview Results controls (see Figure 9–9). You can then click the View Merged Data button to toggle the document between showing the fields you've inserted and the data that will appear in them when you perform the merge.

Figure 9–9. *Use the controls in the Preview Results section of the Mail Merge Manager palette to make sure the merged documents look correct before you create them.*

What you'll normally want to do is click the View Merged Data button to load the data from the first record into the merge fields. You can then move through the records using the Next Record button, Last Record button, Previous Record button, and First Record button, looking to see whether data missing from or present in any of the records shows up problems with the document's fields and layout. With the data in place, it's much easier to see whether you're missing text, spaces, punctuation, or even paragraph marks.

If you need to move to a particular record by number, click the Record Number box to select its current contents, type the number, and then press Return to display it.

You can also click the View All Placeholders button to display the fields as field codes (see Figure 9–10). Doing this can be helpful when you need to see exactly which information is going where. Click the View All Placeholders button again when you want to restore the display of data.

```
{ MERGEFIELD Title } { MERGEFIELD Full_Name }

{ MERGEFIELD Address }



Dear { MERGEFIELD First_Name },

Thank you for your interest in { MERGEFIELD Custom_Property_1 }.
```

Figure 9–10. *You can turn on the display of all placeholders when you need to check which field you've placed where.*

Completing the Mail Merge

After you've previewed the merge results and deemed them satisfactory, you're ready for the sixth and final step: completing the mail merge. In this step, you choose among sending the mail merge documents directly to your printer, creating a document that contains them all (and that you can edit and customize further if need be), or creating e-mail messages to the recipients.

When you're ready to complete the mail merge, follow these steps:

1. In the Mail Merge Manager window, click the Complete Merge heading or disclosure triangle to reveal its controls (see Figure 9–11).

2. In the Merge Data Range pop-up menu, choose which records you want to perform the merge for:

    ■ *All.* Select this item to merge all the records.

    ■ *Current Record.* Select this item to merge just the record you've selected. This setting is useful for merging individual records you've missed in your main merge.

■ *Custom.* Select this item when you need to specify a range of records. Type the start number in the From text box and the end number in the To text box.

3. Follow the instructions in the next three subsections for the type of merge documents you want to create.

Figure 9–11. *Expand the Complete Merge section of the Mail Merge Manager palette so that you can access the commands for completing the mail merge.*

Merging Individual Documents to a Printer

To merge the records to individual documents and send them directly to a printer, follow these steps:

1. In the Complete Merge section of the Mail Merge Manager palette, click the Merge to Printer button. Word displays the Print dialog box.

2. Make sure the correct printer is selected in the Printer pop-up menu.

3. If the Print dialog box appears at its smaller size, click the down-arrow button to the right of the Printer pop-up menu to expand the dialog box to show all its options.

4. Choose any other print options needed. For example, if you need to print two copies of each merged document, enter **2** in the Copies text box.

5. Make sure that the document in the Quick Preview box looks the way it should. Use the First Page button, Previous Page button, Next Page button, and Last Page button below the Quick Preview area to move from page to page, making sure that each page looks right.

6. Click the Print button to merge the documents to the printer and print them.

Merging to a New Document

To merge the records to a new document that contains all the documents together, click the Merge to New Document button in the Complete Merge section of the Mail Merge Manager palette.

Word creates a new document that contains all the merged documents. You can then check through the document, add any extra information needed (for example, you may want to personalize some documents manually), and then save it or print it as needed.

Merging to E-mail Messages

To merge the records and create e-mail messages, follow these steps:

1. In the Complete Merge section of the Mail Merge Manager palette, click the Generate E-mail Messages button. Word displays the Mail Recipient dialog box (see Figure 9–12).

Mail Recipient	
To:	E_mail
Subject:	Can You Afford to Miss This Offer?
Send As:	Text
	Cancel Mail Merge To Outbox

Figure 9–12. *In the Mail Recipient dialog box, enter the subject line for the e-mail messages, and choose whether to send them as text, HTML, or attachments.*

2. In the To pop-up menu, make sure the field containing the e-mail address is selected. Word suggests the E_mail field by default, but you may need to select a different field (for example, one with a home e-mail address).

3. In the Subject text box, type the subject line you want each message to use.

4. In the Send As pop-up menu, choose the format in which to send the e-mail messages:

- *Text.* Choose this item to send the Word document's text without formatting. Using text makes sure the addressee receives the message, but the text loses any formatting. If you use plain text, test how the document looks in a text-only format before sending the merged documents.

- *Attachment.* Choose this item to send the Word document as an attachment to the e-mail message. Sending the document as an attachment ensures that the Word document retains all its formatting in transit, but recipients must have Word (or a compatible word-processing application) in order to read the attachment.

- *HTML Message.* Choose this item to send the Word document as a formatted e-mail message. This works well as long as the recipient's e-mail application can accept HTML-formatted messages; if not, the recipient will see a text-only version of the message and a version with HTML codes studded through it.

5. Click the Mail Merge To Outbox button to merge the documents to your e-mail outbox.

6. Go to your e-mail application. Check that the messages look correct, and then send them.

Restoring a Mail Merge Main Document to a Normal Document

Sometimes you may need to change a main document that you've used for mail merge back to a normal document so that you can use it normally. To do so, follow these steps:

1. Open the document.

2. Choose Tools ➤ Mail Merge Manager to display the Mail Merge Manager palette.

3. If the Select Document Type area is collapsed, click the Select Document Type bar or the disclosure triangle to expand the area.

4. Click the Create New button, and then click Restore to Normal Word Document on the pop-up menu. Word displays a confirmation dialog box (see Figure 9–13).

By restoring Customer Letter 1.docx to a normal Word document, the text of the document will not change. However, Customer Letter 1.docx will no longer be a mail merge main document.

Do you want to continue?

Cancel   Restore

Figure 9–13. *Click the Restore button in this confirmation dialog box to change a Word document back from a mail merge main document to a normal document.*

5. Click the Restore button. Word removes the link to the data source.

6. Save the document. For example, click the Save button on the Standard toolbar, or press Cmd+S.

Summary

In this chapter, you learned how to use Word's powerful Mail Merge feature to create business documents such as form letters, mailing labels, envelopes, and catalogs.

You now know how Word's six-step process for creating mail merge documents works. You can create main documents, build new data sources or connect existing data sources, filter the records to use only those you need, and perform the merge.

In the next chapter, I'll show you how to revise, review, and finalize documents. Turn the page when you're ready to start.

Chapter 10

Revising and Reviewing Documents

Chances are that you'll create some documents on your own, but for other documents, you'll need to work with other people—either sharing the documents on a network or via the Internet or using e-mail to send the documents back and forth.

Word includes strong features for working together on documents. In this chapter, I'll start by reviewing your different options so that you're clear about the different choices. After that, I'll show you how to work on a document simultaneously with your colleagues—if you have the technology required—and how to share documents but work on them one person at a time.

Next, you'll learn how to use the Track Changes feature, also called revision marking, to track all the edits you and your colleagues make to a document so that you can keep an audit trail. You can then review the changes and decide which to keep and which to remove.

Last, I'll show you how to add comments to a document, how to compare two documents to identify their differences automatically, and how to incorporate changes from two or more copies of a document into a single file.

Understanding How You Can Work on Documents with Your Colleagues

In Word, you can work on documents with your colleagues either together or separately:

- *Work on the same copy of the document simultaneously.* If you have a SharePoint site or you store documents on Windows Live SkyDrive, you and your colleagues can store the document on the site, each open it at the same time, and work on it together. Microsoft calls this *coauthoring*.

- *Work on separate copies of the document.* If you don't have a SharePoint site or use Windows Live SkyDrive, Word warns you when you're opening a document that someone else is using. When this happens, you can open the document in a read-only state, save it under a new name so that you can edit it, and then integrate any changes you make back into the main copy.

- *Circulate a copy of the document, and each work on it in turn.* This method is easiest, because you use only a single copy of a document, and each person has free rein when they're editing it—but it usually takes longer than the other methods. To see clearly which changes each person has made to the document, you'll normally use Word's Track Changes feature, as discussed in this chapter.

> **NOTE:** If you have a SharePoint site, chances are you will want to try simultaneous editing and see how well it works for you. But if you find that running into conflicting changes creates more problems than it solves, you may be better off using the older means of collaboration. Coauthoring is technically very impressive, and it can be great in the right situation, but it's not suitable for everyone.

Whichever way you work, you can use three main features for revising and reviewing documents with your colleagues:

- *Track Changes.* When you turn on this feature, Word tracks the insertions, deletions, formatting changes, and most other changes to the document. You can then view the changes, accept the changes you want to keep, and reject the others.

- *Comments.* You and your colleagues can attach comments to items in the document to offer opinions or suggest changes, without actually changing the text itself. You can then view the comments and remove them once you've dealt with them.

- *Document Compare.* This feature makes Word analyze and mark up the differences between two versions of the same document. Document Compare is useful when you need to amalgamate changes from two or more different versions in which you haven't tracked changes.

Editing a Document Simultaneously with Your Colleagues

Word's most advanced way of working on a document with your colleagues is for each of you to open the same copy of the document at the same time and all work on it together. Here's what happens:

- *Create the document.* You create the document as normal (for example, by using a template) and store it on your SharePoint site or on Windows Live SkyDrive.

CAUTION: Unless you have a fast and reliable Internet connection, simultaneous editing of a large document stored on Windows Live SkyDrive can be slow enough to make collaboration difficult.

- *Open the document.* The first person opens the document as normal. When another person opens the document, they see a pop-up message (see Figure 10–1) telling them about the other people already editing the document. The first person also receives a pop-up message as soon as Word notices that other authors have joined in.

Figure 10–1. *When you open a document that others are working on, Word displays a pop-up message to let you know they're editing it.*

- *See who's editing the document.* The status bar displays an icon showing the number of people editing the document. (This number includes you.) You can click the icon to see who the people are (see Figure 10–2) and click a person's name to display information and contact buttons (for e-mail, instant messaging, and audio and video calls) for him or her.

Authors editing this document:
Last update: Sep 9, 2010 3:34 AM

☑ Guy
☑ Derby Gentian

Print Layout View   2   Sec   1   Pages: 1 of 1

Figure 10–2. *To see who the other authors are, click the Authors icon on the status bar.*

■ *Edit the document.* You can work pretty much as normal in Word, except that only one person can edit a particular paragraph or other element at a time. As you work, Word shows you which parts of the document other authors are working on by placing a line to the left of the items and displaying a name box (see Figure 10–3).

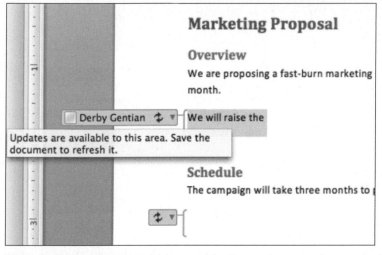

Figure 10–3. *Word shows you which parts of the document your coauthors are working on at the moment and when updates are available.*

■ *Update the document.* When you're ready to save changes and get any updates that are available, you press Cmd+S or click the Save button on the Standard toolbar as usual. The Save button displays a pair of curving arrows to indicate that it's acting as an Update button. Word then updates the copy of the document you're viewing with the changes the others have made (see Figure 10–4), applies shading to the changes to draw your attention to them, and makes your changes available to your coauthors.

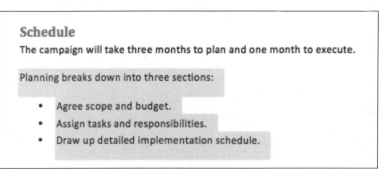

Figure 10–4. *When you save your changes, Word merges in updates your coauthors have saved. Word displays the new items with shading (as in the second body paragraph and three bullet points here).*

- *Resolve conflicts.* Word does its best to show you and your coauthors who's working where, but sooner or later, two or more of you may change the same part of the document in the same cycles of saving and updating. When this happens, Word displays the Upload Failed bar (see Figure 10–5) to the author who tried to save changes over the changes another author had already saved. Click the Resolve Conflicts button to add the Conflicts tab to the Ribbon and display the Conflicts pane (see Figure 10–6). You can then use the controls in the Conflicting Changes group on the Conflicts tab of the Ribbon to resolve the conflicts by accepting or rejecting changes. When you have resolved all the conflicts, Word displays the Conflicts Resolved bar; click the Save And Close View button to save the changes and exit from Conflict Mode back to the normal editing mode.

Figure 10–5. *Word warns you of any conflicting changes when you try to save the document. Click the Resolve Conflicts button on the Upload Failed bar to deal with the highlighted conflicts.*

Figure 10–6. *In the Conflict pane on the left, click the change you want to resolve. Use the controls in the Conflicting Changes group on the Conflict tab of the Ribbon to accept and reject changes and move among them.*

- *Close the document.* When you have finished working with the document, save any unsaved changes, and then close it as usual.

Sharing Documents with Your Colleagues on a Network

You can also share documents with your colleagues on a network without using SharePoint. In this case, you save the document in a shared folder on the network. From there, anyone permitted to use the folder can open the document, edit it, and save it— but only one person can open the document at a time.

If you try to open a document that someone else has already opened, Word displays the This File Is Locked for Editing dialog box (see Figure 10–7). From here, you can take two actions:

- *Cancel opening the document.* Click the Cancel button to cancel your request to open the document. You can then try again at a convenient time.

Figure 10–7. *From the This File Is Locked for Editing dialog box, you can open the document as a read-only file or cancel trying to open the document.*

- *Open a read-only copy of the document.* Click the Read-Only button to open the document in a read-only state. *Read-only* means that you can't save changes to the network copy of the document, but you can save it under a different name, in a different folder, or both. If you want to integrate those changes into the network copy, you'll need to do so either manually or by using the Document Combine feature (discussed later in this chapter). When you open a document in a read-only state, Word displays "(Read-Only)" in the title bar, dims the unavailable controls on the toolbars and the Ribbon, and displays the Server Document bar across the top of the document area (see Figure 10–8). To edit the document, click the Save As button on the Server Document bar and save the document under a different name or in a different folder (or both).

Figure 10–8. *Word displays the Server Document bar and adds "(Read-Only)" to the title bar when you open a read-only document.*

Tracking the Changes in a Document

When you need to work with other people on creating or revising a document, use Word's Track Changes feature. Track Changes can automatically track almost all the changes in the document so that you can review them, see who made which changes when, accept the changes you want to keep, and reject the rest.

You can choose which types of changes to track and which to ignore. For example, you may want to track only the edits to the text of a document and let your colleagues handle the formatting.

Choosing Which Changes to Track

To choose which types of changes Word tracks in a document, follow these steps:

1. From the Ribbon, choose Review ➤ Tracking ➤ Show Markup ➤ Preferences to display the Track Changes pane in the Word Preferences dialog box (see Figure 10–9). You can also choose Word ➤ Preferences from the menu bar and then click the Track Changes icon in the Output and Sharing area of the Word Preferences dialog box.

Figure 10–9. *In the Track Changes pane of the Word Preferences dialog box, choose how to show markup, track moves, and handle changes to table cells and formatting. You can also choose whether to use balloons to display changes.*

2. In the Markup area, choose how to mark insertions, deletions, changed lines, and comments:

- *Insertions.* Open the Insertions pop-up menu, and then click the type of markup you want for inserted text. Your choices are (None), Color Only, Bold, Italic, Underline, Double Underline, Strikethrough, or Double Strikethrough. Use the Color Only setting when you need a subtle indication of added text; use Underline or Double Underline when you need a stronger indication. Open the topmost Color pop-up menu, and choose By Author if you want Word to use a different color for each reviewer's additions; to use a specific color or shading for all added text, click that color or shading.

- *Deletions.* Open the Deletions pop-up menu, and then click the type of markup to use for deleted text. Your choices are (None), Color Only, Bold, Italic, Underline, Double Underline, Strikethrough, Hidden, ^ (Word displays a single caret mark to show where text has been deleted), # (Word shows a single number sign where text has been deleted), or Double Strikethrough. Open the second Color pop-up menu and choose By Author if you want Word to use a different color for each reviewer's deletions; to use a specific color or shading for all deletions, click that color or shading.

TIP: The Hidden item can be a good choice for deletions, because it makes the deleted items disappear from the document, leaving only the text that hasn't been deleted and the text that has been added.

- *Changed lines.* Open the Changed lines pop-up menu and choose whether (and, if so, where) you want Word to display a vertical line in the margin next to each line that has changed. These changed lines help you locate changes in documents that contain changes on only some lines, but if most every line has changed, the changed lines are little use. Choose (None) to skip using changed lines, Left Border to put them in the left margin, Right Border to put them in the right margin, or Outside Border to put the lines in the left margin on left pages and the right margin on right pages. Open the third Color pop-up menu, and choose the color or shading you want; the Auto item applies the default text color and is often the best choice.

- *Formatting.* Open the Formatting pop-up menu, and choose how to mark up items whose formatting has changed. Your choices are (None), Color Only, Bold, Italic, Underline, Double Underline, Strikethrough, or Double Strikethrough. Pick a formatting type you haven't yet used, and then choose the color in the fourth Color pop-up menu.

- *Comments.* Open the Comments pop-up menu, and choose the color or shading to give to each reviewer's comments. Choose the By Author item to have Word use different colors for each reviewer.

3. In the Moves area, select the Track moves check box if you want Word to track text you've moved within a document separately from insertions and deletions. If you select this check box, you can choose settings as follows:

   - *Moved from.* Open the Moved from pop-up menu, and choose how to mark the text that is no longer there because it has been moved to a different location in the document. Your choices are the same as for Deletions, but you'll want to use a different marking so that you can distinguish moved text from deletions. For example, use Strikethrough for Deletions and Double Strikethrough for Moved From text. Open the Color pop-up menu, and choose By Author or the color or shading you want.

   - *Moved to.* Open the Moved to pop-up menu, and choose how to mark the moved text in its new location. Your choices are the same as for Insertions, but you'll want to use a different marking so that you can distinguish the moved text; for example, Underline for Insertions and Double Underline for Moved To text.

> **NOTE:** Word's feature for tracking moved text separately from insertions and deletions works only for documents that use the Word Document format (with the .docx file extension), not for documents that use the older Word 97–2004 Document format (on the Mac) or the Word 97–2003 Document format (on Windows).

4. In the Table cell highlighting area, choose the colors with which to shade cells that have been inserted, deleted, merged, or split in a table. Usually, you'll want to use a different color for each of these changes to a table's structure.

> **CAUTION:** Word provides the By Author setting for the four pop-up menus in the Table cell highlighting area of the Track Changes Options dialog box, but it's best not to use this setting. Otherwise, although you can see who changed the table's structure, you need to dig deeper to see what the person did to the table. Usually, it's easier to see how the table has changed and then find out who made the changes only if you need to do so.

5. In the Balloons area, choose whether to use balloons and the comments pane to display details of tracked changes and comments. These are the settings you can choose:

- *Use balloons to display changes.* Select this check box to turn on the use of balloons for markup.

- *Include reviewer, time stamp, and action buttons.* Select this check box to include in each balloon the name of the person who made the change, the date and time they made it, and buttons for accepting and rejecting the change. These items are usually helpful.

6. Click the OK button to close the Word Preferences dialog box.

Turning On Track Changes for a Document

To turn on Track Changes for a document, choose Review ➤ Tracking ➤ Track Changes, moving the Track Changes switch from the Off position to the On position.

> **TIP:** From the keyboard, press Cmd+Shift+E to toggle Track Changes on or off.

You can also choose Tools ➤ Track Changes ➤ Highlight Changes from the menu bar to display the Highlight Changes dialog box (see Figure 10–10), select the Track changes while editing check box, and then click the OK button.

Figure 10–10. *You can turn Track Changes on by selecting the Track changes while editing check box in the Highlight Changes dialog box and then clicking the OK button.*

When you need to turn Track Changes off again, choose Review ➤ Tracking ➤ Track Changes again, moving the Track Changes switch from the On position to the Off position.

Ensuring Your Colleagues Use the Track Changes Feature

Track Changes is a great feature, but anyone can turn off tracking and rampage through the document making untracked changes unless you force them to use Track Changes. You can do this by protecting the document. Follow these steps:

1. Choose Review ➤ Protection ➤ Document from the Ribbon or Tools ➤ Protect Document from the menu bar to display the Protect Document dialog box (see Figure 10–11).

Figure 10–11. *Use the Protect Document dialog box to ensure that your colleagues use Track Changes when editing the document.*

2. In the Protect document for area, select the Tracked changes option button.

3. In the Password (optional) box, type a password. You'll usually want to make the password at least eight characters long, mix upper- and lowercase letters, and include numbers and symbols.

4. Click the OK button. Word displays the Confirm Password dialog box.

5. Type the password in the Reenter password to open box, and then click the OK button. Word closes both the Confirm Password dialog box and the Protect Document dialog box and applies the protection to the document.

6. Save the document. For example, click the Save button on the Standard toolbar, or press Cmd+S.

Working in a Document with Track Changes On

After you turn on Track Changes for a document, you can work in it much as normal. Word tracks your insertions, deletions, and other changes and displays such markup as you've chosen to show.

For example, in Print Layout view, Web Layout view, and Full Screen view, Word normally displays the markup area and balloons, as shown in Figure 10–12.

Figure 10–12. *In Print Layout view, Web Layout view, and Full Screen view, Word displays the markup area with balloons detailing the changes.*

TIP: To switch quickly among the settings for markup balloons, choose Review ➤ Tracking ➤ Show Markup ➤ Balloons, and then click the command you want: Show Revisions in Balloons, Show All Revisions Inline, or Show Only Comments and Formatting in Balloons.

In Draft view and Outline view, Word shows the changes inline, using the markup specified in the Track Changes pane of the Word Preferences dialog box, such as applying an underscore to each insertion and strikethrough to each deletion, as shown in Figure 10–13.

Chapter 5: Immediate Results—the First Week
We're pretty sure that whatWhat you'll like the most about this approach is the waythat you see results immediately—within a very short space of time. In fact, you'll be able to notice the difference in the very firsta week or less.

Figure 10–13. *Depending on the markup options you've chosen and the view you're using, Word can mark insertions and deletions inline.*

To see information about a change in Draft view or Outline view (or in one of the other views—for example, when you have chosen not to use the markup area), hold the mouse pointer over the change. Word displays a ScreenTip showing the details of the change (see Figure 10–14).

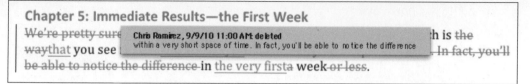

Figure 10–14. *Hold the mouse pointer over a tracked change to display a ScreenTip showing the details.*

NOTE: If Word doesn't display a ScreenTip when you hold the mouse pointer over a tracked change, choose Word ➤ Preferences to display the Preferences dialog box. In the Authoring and Proofing Tools area, click the View icon to display the View preferences pane. In the Show area, select the Comments on rollover check box, and then click the OK button. Word now displays the ScreenTips.

Choosing How to View the Document's Changes and Markup

As you work with Track Changes on, you may find it helpful to change how Word displays the markup for review. For example, you can show the document as it will appear with all the markup accepted or show the document's original version to see how it was before you or other editors let rip.

To choose how to view the document's markup, go to the Tracking group on the Review tab of the Ribbon. Open the upper-right pop-up menu, and then click the setting you want:

- *Final Showing Markup*. Choose this item to see the document's final text with all the markup displayed. This is the default setting and the one you'll probably want to use most of the time while marking up the document. In the layout views with balloons displayed, the insertions appear in the document's text without balloons; the deletions disappear from the document except from markers connected to balloons in the markup pane that show what was deleted.

- *Final*. Choose this item to see the document's final text with no markup appearing. Use this view when you want to read the document without the visual distraction of markup or when you want to see the true page count of the final document.

- *Original Showing Markup.* Choose this item to see the document's original text with the markup displayed. Use this view when you want to focus on the changes made to the original text. In the layout views with balloons displayed, the deleted items appear in the document marked with strikethrough (or your chosen marking); the insertions appear only as markers connected to balloons in the markup pane that show what was inserted.

- *Original.* Choose this item to see the document's original text before any of the changes were made. Use this view when you need to remind yourself of how the document originally read.

Controlling Which Changes Word Displays

When a document contains many changes or when you need to focus only on one aspect of the changes, you may want to turn off the display of some changes so that you see only others. To control which changes Word displays, go to the Tracking group on the Review tab of the Ribbon. Open the Show Markup pop-up menu (see Figure 10–15), and then display an item by clicking to place a check mark next to it or hide a displayed item by clicking to remove its check mark.

Figure 10–15. *On the Show Markup pop-up menu, place a check mark next to each item you want Word to display.*

These are the items you can display or hide:

- *Comments.* Choose whether to show comments inserted in the document (as discussed in the section "Adding Comments to a Document" later in this chapter).

- *Insertions and Deletions.* Choose whether to show text and other items inserted in the document, deleted from it, or moved from one place in the document to another.

- *Formatting.* Choose whether to show changes to formatting, for example the application or a style or the addition of direct formatting.

- *Markup Area Highlight.* Choose whether to show shading on the markup area rather than displaying it as the document's normal background color. Usually it's helpful to show the shading so that you can easily see where the page ends and the markup area starts.

- *Reviewers.* In this submenu, choose All Reviewers to display comments from all reviewers. Otherwise, remove the All Reviewers check mark, and put a check mark next to each reviewer whose changes you want to see.

- *Highlight Updates.* Choose whether to have Word highlight the latest updates to the document so that you can identify them more quickly.

- *Other Authors.* Choose whether to mark updates by other authors.

NOTE: Click the Preferences item at the bottom of the Show Markup pop-up menu to display the Track Changes pane in the Word Preferences dialog box.

Integrating Tracked Changes into a Document

When everyone has made their edits to the document, you can go through the changes and accept those you want to keep and reject the others.

If you're using balloons to display the changes, you can quickly accept and reject changes right from the balloons. Click the check mark in a balloon to accept a change (see Figure 10–16), or click the × button to reject the change.

Figure 10–16. *You can quickly accept a tracked change by clicking the check mark in a balloon or reject a tracked change by clicking the × button.*

Otherwise, to go through the changes, use the controls in the Changes group on the Review tab of the Ribbon. First, select a change by clicking the Next button or the Previous button, clicking the balloon in the markup area, or clicking the change in the Reviewing pane. (Word uses the terms *Review pane* and *Reviewing pane* interchangeably for this pane.)

You can then accept changes by using the Accept button and its pop-up menu (see Figure 10–17):

- *Accept the selected change and automatically select the next change.* Click the main part of the Accept button (or click the pop-up button and then click the Accept and Move to Next item).

Figure 10–17. *Use the Accept button and the options on the Accept pop-up menu to accept tracked changes in the document. To give the Accept and Move to Next command quickly, click the main part of the Accept button in the Changes group of the Review tab.*

- *Accept the selected change.* Click the Accept pop-up button, and then click Accept Change.

- *Accept all changes shown with your Show Markup options.* When you've chosen to show only some markup, click the Accept pop-up button, and then click Accept All Changes Shown to accept all that markup but not markup that's hidden. For example, if you've chosen to show formatting but not show insertions and deletions, clicking Accept All Changes Shown accepts all formatting changes.

- *Accept all the changes in the document.* If the document contains changes light enough that you can review them all without dealing with individual changes along the way, click the Accept pop-up button, and then click Accept All Changes in Document.

Similarly, you can reject one or more changes at once:

- *Reject the selected change and automatically select the next change.* Click the Reject button (or click the pop-up button and then click the Reject and Move to Next item).

- *Reject the selected change.* Click the Reject pop-up button, and then click Reject Change.

- *Reject all changes shown with your Show Markup options.* When you've chosen to show only some markup, click the Reject pop-up button, and then click Reject All Changes Shown to reject all that markup but not markup that's hidden.

- *Reject all the changes in the document.* To get rid of all the changes, click the Reject pop-up button, and then click Reject All Changes in Document.

When you've finished accepting or rejecting changes, save the document. You may want to save it under a different name if the document is now ready for another stage in its evolution.

> **TIP:** You can also accept or reject a change by using the context menu. Ctrl+click or right-click the change in the text, in the markup area, or in the Reviewing pane, and then click Accept Change or Reject Change on the context menu.

Using Track Changes in Full Screen View

If you like to work in Full Screen view, you can work with Track Changes in it too. You can view the tracked changes in either Writing view or Reading view, but to work with the changes, you must use Writing view. To switch to Writing view, click the Write button at the left end of the command bar in Full Screen view.

To control Track Changes in Full Screen view, click the Options button, and then use the following options on the pop-up menu:

- *Track Changes.* Click this item to toggle Track Changes on or off.

- *Show Comments and Changes.* Click this item to display a submenu with commands for controlling which markup items Word shows (see Figure 10–18).

Figure 10–18. *In Full Screen view, use the Track Changes, Show Comments and Changes, and Show Original/Final Document settings on the Options menu to control change tracking and which changes appear.*

- *Show Original/Final Document.* Click this item to display a submenu with commands for switching among Final, Final with Markup, Original, and Original with Markup displays.

Adding Comments to a Document

When you need to give your input on a document without making changes to the text, use Word's comments. A *comment* appears in a floating balloon attached to a word or another object in text, enabling you to comment easily and clearly on a specific item.

> **NOTE:** If you want to ensure your colleagues use comments on a document rather than altering its text, protect the document for comments. Choose Tools ➤ Protect Document from the menu to display the Protect Document dialog box, and select the Comments option button. Type a password in the Password (optional) box, and then click the OK button. Confirm the password in the Confirm Password dialog box, click the OK button, and then save the document.

Adding a Comment

To add a comment to a document, select the text or object you're commenting on, and then give the appropriate command:

- *Ribbon.* Choose Review ➤ Comments ➤ New.
- *Menu bar.* Choose Insert ➤ New Comment.
- *Full Screen view.* Click the New Comment button, the button to the left of the Options button on the command bar at the top of the screen.

> **NOTE:** If you want to attach a comment to a single word, just click in that word or immediately before it. When you insert the comment, Word automatically puts the comment parentheses around the word.

Word then adds colored parentheses around your selection to indicate that it has a comment attached. The way Word displays the comment depends on the view you're using:

- *Print Layout view, Web Layout view, or Full Screen view.* Word displays the markup area at the right side of the page and opens a comment balloon for you to type the comment in. The comment balloon is attached to the comment markers by a thin line, so you can see which part of the document each comment belongs to. Figure 10–19 shows the markup area open with two comments inserted.

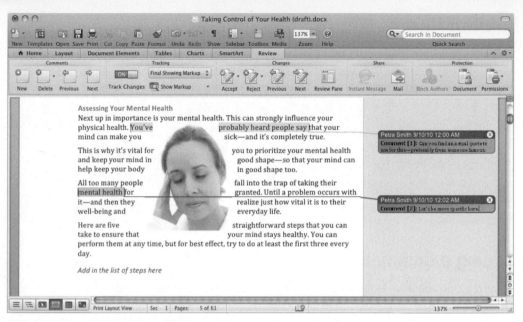

Figure 10–19. *In Print Layout view, Web Layout view, or Full Screen Reading view, Word displays comments in the markup area to the side of the document.*

- *Draft view or Outline view.* Word opens the Reviewing pane, which you use for reviewing comments and other markup. Figure 10–20 shows the Reviewing pane open in Draft view.

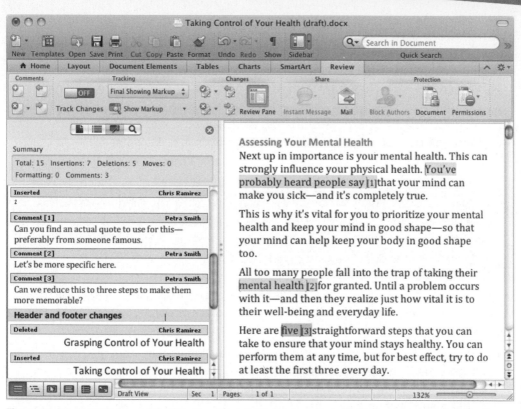

Figure 10–20. *In Draft view and Outline view, Word displays comments in the Reviewing pane and shows the comment number in brackets after the commented item.*

Type (or paste) the text of the comment either in the comment balloon or in the comment's area in the Reviewing pane. Most people leave comments as plain text, but you can apply formatting to a comment if you want. For example, you can apply bold or a style to a word that you want to emphasize. You can also insert elements such as tables and graphics in comments.

If you're using the Reviewing pane, click the Close button (the × button) at the upper-right corner when you've finished using it. You can also choose Review ➤ Changes ➤ Review Pane to toggle the display of the Reviewing pane.

Viewing and Reviewing Comments

To review comments, you normally use the markup area and comment balloons (in Print Layout view, Web Layout view, and Full Screen view) or the Reviewing pane.

You can also hold the mouse pointer over commented text or the comment mark to display a ScreenTip showing the text of the comment, as shown in Figure 10–21.

> **Peta Smith, 9/10/10 12:08 AM:**
> Commented –Can we reduce this to three steps to make them more memorable?

Here are five [3] straightforward steps that you can take to ensure th
can perform them at any time, but for best effect, try to do at least t

Figure 10–21. *Hold the mouse pointer over commented text or a comment mark to display a ScreenTip showing the text of the comment.*

NOTE: If Word doesn't display a ScreenTip when you hold the mouse pointer over a comment, choose Word ➤ Preferences to display the Preferences dialog box. In the Authoring and Proofing Tools area, click the View icon to display the View preferences pane. In the Show area, select the Comments on rollover check box, and then click the OK button.

Most people find the markup area and comment balloons easy unless a document has a huge number of comments, but if you find the balloons awkward, you can turn them off like this:

1. Choose Review ➤ Tracking ➤ Show Markup ➤ Preferences from the Ribbon to display the Track Changes pane in the Word Preferences dialog box. You can also choose Word ➤ Preferences and then click the Track Changes icon in the Output and Sharing area.

2. In the Balloons area at the bottom, clear the Use balloons to display changes check box.

3. Click the OK button.

Even when the markup area is open, you can display the Reviewing pane by choosing Review ➤ Changes ➤ Review Pane from the Ribbon or View ➤ Sidebar ➤ Reviewing Pane from the menu bar.

TIP: You can browse comments by using the browse object. Click the Select Browse Object button between the Previous button and Next button below the vertical scroll bar, and then click Comment on the panel. You can then click the Previous button and Next button to move from comment to comment.

Deleting Comments

You can delete a comment by Ctrl+clicking or right-clicking it in the text, in the comments pane, or in the Reviewing pane, and then clicking Delete Comment on the context menu.

> **NOTE:** If you're using balloons, you can delete a comment by clicking the × button in its balloon.

Alternatively, click the comment in the text, in the comments pane, or in the Reviewing pane, and then choose Review ➤ Comments ➤ Delete (clicking the main part of the Delete button).

To delete only the comments currently displayed, choose Review ➤ Comments ➤ Delete ➤ Delete All Comments Shown (clicking the Delete pop-up button to display the pop-up menu, as shown in Figure 10–22).

Figure 10–22. From the Delete pop-up menu in the Comments group of the Review tab of the Ribbon, you can delete all the comments shown or all the comments in the document.

To delete all the comments from the document, choose Review ➤ Comments ➤ Delete ➤ Delete All Comments in Document. Word doesn't confirm the deletion, but you can use Undo if you give the command by accident.

Comparing or Combining Different Versions of the Same Document

When you need to follow and review the changes in a document, the best approach is to use Track Changes (as described earlier in this chapter) on a single document that each reviewer works on in turn. This way, Track Changes records all the information you need about the changes made to a document and gives you the tools to review the changes and incorporate them easily.

Other times, you may need to circulate a document to various colleagues at the same time, such as to get the review done more quickly. This method gives you multiple copies of the same document containing their different edits marked by Track Changes. To incorporate all the different edits into a single copy of the document, you can use Word's Document Combine feature.

You may also need to compare two copies of a document in which the changes haven't been tracked. For this, you can use the Document Compare feature. This feature isn't as good as Track Changes used consistently, but it's a huge improvement over spending hours poring over different document files and trying to integrate the best changes into a single version.

To use Document Compare to compare or combine two documents, follow these steps:

1. If either or both of the documents are open, close them. Starting with both documents closed is usually easier than starting with either or both open, because it avoids any confusion over similarly named documents you have open.

2. If you have no document open in Word, press Cmd+N to open a new blank document. You need to do this because Word makes the Compare Documents command and the Merge Documents command unavailable when no document is open.

3. Give the command for comparing or combining, as needed:

    - *Compare.* Choose Tools ➤ Track Changes ➤ Compare Documents from the menu bar to display the Compare Documents dialog box (shown in Figure 10–23 expanded to display all its settings).

Figure 10–23. *Use the Compare Documents dialog box or the related Combine Documents dialog box to identify the changes between two documents based on the same document.*

- **Combine.** Choose Tools ➤ Merge Documents from the menu bar to display the Combine Documents dialog box, which is almost identical to the Compare Documents dialog box apart from the title.

4. Choose the documents you want to compare:

- Either open the Original document pop-up menu and click the document in the list or click the Open button next to the pop-up menu, click the document in the Open: Microsoft Word dialog box, and then click the Open button.

- Similarly, either open the Revised Document pop-up menu and click the document in the list or click the Open button next to the pop-up menu, click the document in the Open: Microsoft Word dialog box, and then click the Open button.

5. Tell Word how to label the changes to the document:

- The left Label changes with text box or the Label unmarked changes with text box shows the name of the original document's last reviewer who used Track Changes. Type a different name if necessary. If the text box is blank and unavailable, the document contains no tracked changes.

- The right Label changes with text box or Label unmarked changes with text box shows the last reviewer of the revised document. Again, you may need to type a different name.

6. Click the arrow button on the left to display the lower part of the dialog box so that you can choose comparison settings.

7. In the Comparison settings area, clear the check box for any items you don't want to integrate. For example, if you want to omit the changes to fields, clear the Fields check box. Usually, you'll want to leave most of the check boxes selected.

8. On the Show changes at side of the Show changes area, select the Word level option button to make Word analyze changes at the word level. If you need to dig deeper, you can select the Character level option button instead, but for many documents this produces more detail than is helpful.

9. On the Show changes in side of the Show changes area, select the New document option button if you want to merge the changes into a new document. This is usually clearest, but you can select the Original document option button or the Revised document option button instead if you prefer.

10. Click the OK button to close the dialog box and make Word analyze the changes.

11. If Word displays the dialog box shown in Figure 10–24, warning you that the new document already has changes and that Word may ignore some existing changes, click the Yes button. What this means is that the revised document contains tracked changes; to make the comparison, Word will accept these changes. (The alternative is to click the No button, go back into the documents, and accept or reject the revisions before you compare or combine the documents.)

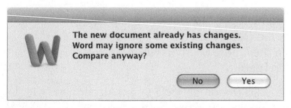

The new document already has changes. Word may ignore some existing changes. Compare anyway?

No   Yes

Figure 10–24. *If Word displays this dialog box when you're comparing or combining documents, click the Yes button to proceed.*

Word then displays the result of the comparison or combination, for example a new document containing tracked changes shown in balloons. You can then review the tracked changes as discussed earlier in this chapter. If you've created a new document that you want to keep, save it.

Summary

In this chapter, you learned essential techniques and tools for revising and reviewing documents. You learned how to edit a document simultaneously with your colleagues and how to share documents via a network. You know how to set up Track Changes to mark the changes you want to track, how to make your colleagues use Track Changes, and how to accept or reject the changes that Word records. You can use comments to add suggestions or requests to documents, and you can use the Document Compare feature and Document Combine feature to analyze documents and automatically incorporate different edits in them.

In the next chapter, I'll show you how to finalize, print, and share your Word documents.

Chapter 11

Printing, Securing, and Sharing Documents

In this chapter, we'll look at how you can share your documents with other people. You'll start by seeing how to print an entire document or the relevant pages or sections of it, how to choose whether to include markup, and how to print other parts of the document, such as markup and document properties. After that, I'll show you how to secure your Word documents by removing sensitive information, locking the documents with passwords, and marking the documents as read-only.

Next, you'll learn how to deal with issues in making a Word 2011 document compatible with earlier versions of Word. Last, I'll show you how to create an electronic version of a document suitable for distributing online or taking to a print shop for specialist printing.

Using Word's Features for Printing Documents

You can print your Word documents by using the standard techniques discussed in Chapter 2, but Word also offers extra features that you may want to use, such as printing a custom range of pages; printing markup with its document or without its document; or printing a document's properties, styles, or custom key assignments.

Printing a Custom Range of Pages

After correcting a document, you may need to print a custom range of pages, such as pages 3, 5, 8–10, 15, and 30. To do so, follow these steps:

1. Choose File ➤ Print or press Cmd+P to display the Print dialog box.

2. If the Print dialog box opens at its small size, click the arrow button to the right of the Printer pop-up menu to expand the dialog box to its full size (see Figure 11–1).

Figure 11–1. *Use the Page Range option button and text box in the Copies & Pages pane of the Print dialog box to print a custom range of pages.*

3. Select the Page Range option button.

4. In the text box below the Page Range option button, type the details of the range you want to print, using the conventions shown in Table 11–1.
For example, **3,5,8-10,15,30** prints the pages mentioned at the beginning of this section.

5. Choose any other print options needed.

6. Click the Print button to print the pages.

Table 11–1. *Specifying a Custom Range of Pages to Print*

To Print These Pages	Type This	Example
Consecutive pages	Starting page number, hyphen, ending page number	**8-10**
Individual pages	Page number, comma, page number	**7,11,15**
Sections	**s** and section number	**s1,s3**
Range of sections	**s** and starting section number, hyphen, **s** and ending section number	**s1-s3**
Pages within sections	**p** and page number, **s** and section number	**p3s5-p8s7**

NOTE: Printing by sections is most useful if you've split up a document into sections, each of which starts on a new page.

Printing Markup and Other Items

To print items such as markup and document properties, you use the Print What pop-up menu in the Microsoft Word pane of the Print dialog box. To display the Microsoft Word pane, follow these steps:

1. Choose File ➤ Print or press Cmd+P to display the Print dialog box.

2. If the Print dialog box opens at its small size, click the arrow button to the right of the Printer pop-up menu to expand the dialog box to its larger size.

3. Open the pop-up menu below the Presets box, and then click the Microsoft Word item to display the Print What pop-up menu and Print option buttons in the Microsoft Word pane (see Figure 11–2).

Figure 11–2. *Choose the Microsoft Word item in the pop-up menu below the Presets pop-up menu to display the Microsoft Word pane, which contains the Print What pop-up menu and the Print option buttons.*

Choosing Whether to Print Markup—or Only Markup

When you print a document, you can choose either to print any markup and comments it contains or to print the document as it appears without the markup and comments.

To tell Word which you want, open the Print What pop-up menu in the Microsoft Word pane in the Print dialog box. Click the Document item on the menu to print the document without markup. Click the Document showing markup item on the menu to include the markup in the printout.

> **NOTE:** Sometimes it's useful to print only the markup for a document. To do so, open the Print What pop-up menu in the Microsoft Word pane in the Print dialog box, click the List of markup item, and then click the Print button.

Printing Document Properties, Styles, AutoText Entries, and Key Assignments

In the same way that you can print only the markup in a document, you can also print four other items by choosing them on the Print What pop-up menu in the Microsoft Word pane in the Print dialog box:

- *Document Properties.* Select this item to print a page showing the document's properties—the file name, directory (folder), template, title, subject, author, and so on.

- *Styles.* Select this item to print pages listing the styles used in the document and their formatting.

- *AutoText Entries.* Select this item to print a list of the AutoText entries stored in the document's template.

- *Key Assignments*. Select this item to print a list of the custom key assignments in the document (there may not be any).

NOTE: Depending on the printer model you have, you may be able to choose other settings—for example, to control layout or paper handling.

Securing a Document

When you are ready to share a document with others, you may need to secure it. Word gives you several tools for securing a document:

- You can remove sensitive information from the document automatically.

- You can protect the document with a password to prevent unauthorized people from opening it or modifying it.

- You can mark a document with a read-only recommendation.

- You can restrict access to the document to only specific people. This topic is beyond the scope of this book.

In this section, we'll look at the first three of these four tools.

Removing Sensitive Information from a Document

Quite apart from any confidential contents, a Word document can include sensitive information about who worked on it, who last saved it, and who added and deleted which parts of it. Before you distribute a document, you can set two options to limit the amount of information others can pick up from the document.

To remove potentially sensitive information from a document, follow these steps:

1. Choose Word ➤ Preferences or press Cmd+, (Cmd and the comma key) to display the Word Preferences dialog box.

2. In the Personal Settings area, click the Security icon to display the Security pane (see Figure 11–3).

Figure 11–3. *To turn on Word's features for helping you avoid distributing documents containing sensitive metadata, select the two check boxes in the Privacy options area of the Security pane in the Word Preferences dialog box.*

3. In the Privacy options area, select the Remove personal information from this file on save check box if you want to make Word remove the author's name and the names of reviewers who have made tracked changes or comments in the document.

4. Also in the Privacy options area, you'll probably want to select the "Warn before printing, saving or sending a file that contains tracked changes or comments" check box. This makes Word display a warning dialog box (Figure 11–4 shows an example) when you go to print, save, or send a file that contains tracked changes, comments, or both.

NOTE: The "Warn before printing, saving or sending a file that contains tracked changes or comments" setting tends to give a lot of false-positive warnings, because when you save a document, Word doesn't know whether you're about to attach it to an e-mail message from your e-mail application or distribute it another way. But if your documents contain comments or tracked changes you need to remove before distributing the documents, these extra warnings are only a minor irritant.

The document being printed contains comments and tracked changes. Continue printing?

Cancel   OK

Figure 11–4. *You can set Word to warn you that a document you're about to print, save, or send contains comments or tracked changes.*

5.   Click the OK button to close the Word Preferences dialog box.

6.   Click the Save button on the Standard toolbar or press Cmd+S to save the document with its new settings.

Protecting a Document with a Password

If you need to keep other people out of a document or let only approved people open it, you can protect the document with a password. Word lets you use two types of password:

■ *Password to open.* This is a password required to open the document at all. Word prompts you to enter this password when you try to open the document (see Figure 11–5).

Password

Enter password to open file

Taking Control of Your Health (draft).docx

••••••••

Cancel   OK

Figure 11–5. *When you set a password to open a document, Word prompts you for the password before you can open the document.*

■ *Password to modify.* This is a password required to open a document in write mode, in which you can save changes to the document. Word prompts you for this password when you open the document (see Figure 11–6). If you don't have the password, you can click the Read Only button to open the document in read-only mode, in which you cannot save changes under the current file name and folder. (You can save a copy of the document using a different file name, folder, or both.)

Password

'Taking Control of Your Health (draft).docx' is reserved by

Enter password to modify, or open read only.

Password: ••••••••

(Read Only)   (Cancel) (OK)

Figure 11–6. *When you set a password to modify a document, Word prompts you for the password when you open the document. You can open the document in read-only mode by clicking the Read Only button.*

Use a password to open when you need to protect the contents of the document against people who shouldn't see them. Use a password to modify when you want to protect this particular copy of the document against unwanted changes. Use both when you need to implement both forms of protection; Word displays the Password dialog box for the password to open first and then (if the user gets that password right) the Password dialog box for the password to modify.

CAUTION: Word's password protection is effective only against casual snoopers. An attacker who uses a password-cracking program (which are widely available on the Internet) can open a password-protected document with minimal effort.

To encrypt a document with a password, follow these steps:

1. Choose Word ➤ Preferences or press Cmd+, (Cmd and the comma key) to display the Word Preferences dialog box.

2. In the Personal Settings area, click the Security icon to display the Security pane.

3. Click in the Password to open text box or the Password to modify text box, as needed.

4. Type the password. As usual, the longer the password, the more secure it is; you should include numbers and symbols, and you should avoid using any real word in any language or any name.

5. Click the OK button. Word displays the Confirm Password dialog box. Figure 11–7 shows the Confirm Password dialog box for a password to open.

Confirm Password

Reenter password to open:

••••••••

Caution: If you lose or forget the
password, it cannot be recovered. It is
advisable to keep a list of passwords and
their corresponding document names in
a safe place. (Remember that passwords
are case-sensitive.)

Cancel   OK

Figure 11–7. *Type the password again in the Confirm Password dialog box to make sure your fingers hit the right keys.*

6. Type the password again, and then click the OK button. Word closes the Confirm
   Password dialog box and the Word Preferences dialog box and applies the
   password.

7. Now that the protection is in place, save the document. For example, click the
   Save button on the Standard toolbar, or press Cmd+S.

NOTE: You (or anyone else who knows the password) can remove it easily. Choose Word ➤
Preferences to open the Word Preferences dialog box, and then click the Security icon to display
the Security pane. Select the password in the Password to open text box or the Password to
modify text box, and then press Delete to delete it. Click the OK button to close the Word
Preferences dialog box, and then save the document (for example, press Cmd+S).

Marking a Document As Read-Only

As well as providing password protection, the Security pane of Word's Preferences
dialog box also contains the Read-only recommended check box. By selecting this
check box (and then saving the document), you can make Word display a dialog box
(see Figure 11–8) to anyone who opens the document. The dialog box recommends that
the user open the document as read-only, but the user is free to click the No button and
open it for editing.

Confidential Memo 1.docx should be opened
as read-only unless changes to it need to be
saved. Open as read-only?

Cancel   No   Yes

Figure 11–8. *When you mark a document as read-only, Word displays this dialog box to recommend that the user open the document as read-only. The user can easily ignore the recommendation.*

CAUTION: Marking a document as read-only is a feeble security measure that is seldom helpful. If you want to force your colleagues to treat a particular document as read-only, apply a password to modify to the document, and share the password with nobody but yourself.

Making a Document You Can Open with Earlier Versions of Word

If you work with people who use versions of Word earlier than Word 2008 for Mac or Word 2007 for Windows or with people who use other word processing programs, you may need to make versions of your documents that will open in earlier versions of Word. This is because earlier versions of Word used a different file format than Word 2007, Word 2008, Word 2010, and Word 2011; Word 2003 for Windows and Word 2004 for Mac can open the new file format only if you install file converters (see the nearby Note), and many other word processing programs can open only files in the older format, which is generally referred to as Word 97–2003 on Windows or Word 98–2004 on the Mac.

NOTE: If you need to get the file converters for Windows, steer your browser to the Microsoft Download Center (www.microsoft.com/downloads/), and download the Microsoft Office Compatibility Pack for Word, Excel, and PowerPoint File Formats file. For the Mac, go to the Mactopia Downloads page (www.microsoft.com/mac/downloads), and download the Open XML File Format Converter.

To save a document in a format compatible with earlier versions of Word, follow these steps:

1. If the document contains unsaved changes, save them.

2. Choose File ➤ Save As or press Cmd+Shift+S to display the Save As dialog box.

3. Open the Format pop-up menu (see Figure 11–9), and click the format you want. These are the file types you're most likely to need:

    - *Word 97–2004 Document (.doc).* Use this format to create a document readable by older versions of Word and by compatible word processing programs.

Figure 11–9. *Use the Format pop-up menu in the Save As dialog box to save a Word document in a format that's compatible with other word processors.*

NOTE: The format listed as "Word Document (.docx)" in the Format pop-up menu is the Word 2011 format. This is the format in which Word 2011 saves documents unless you specify another format—so in most cases you will be changing the document from this format to another format.

- *Word Template (.dotx).* Use this format to create a Word template on which you can base new documents.

- *Rich Text Format (.rtf).* Use this format to create a document with formatting that most word processing programs and text editors can open successfully.

4. Choose any other settings needed for the new document. For example, you may want to give it a different file name or save it in a different folder.

5. Click the Save button to save the document.

6. If you have finished working with the document, close it.

Creating PDF Documents for Digital Distribution

When you want to distribute a Word document digitally (as opposed to printing it and distributing the hard copy), you can choose between sending the document in Word format and sending an electronic file that shows the Word document's contents and layout.

Normally, you'll send the Word document only when the recipient needs to edit the document in Word or a compatible word processor. For other purposes, sending a file of the laid-out document is usually better. Word makes it easy to create a file in the widely used Portable Document Format (PDF).

To create a PDF file from a document, follow these steps:

1. If the document contains unsaved changes, save them.

2. Choose File ➤ Save As or press Cmd+Shift+S to display the Save As dialog box.

3. Open the Format pop-up menu, and click the PDF item.

4. Choose any other settings needed for the PDF file. For example, you may want to give it a different file name or save it in a different folder.

5. Click the Save button. Word creates a PDF file with the name and folder you specified and then returns you to the document you were working in.

Now open a Finder window to the folder in which you created the PDF file. Double-click the PDF file to open it in Preview (or your default PDF viewer), and make sure all the content appears correctly.

Summary

In this chapter, you learned how to use Word's extra features for printing documents or parts of them, such as document properties or details of the styles they contain. You know how to secure your documents with passwords, remove sensitive information from them, and mark them as read-only.

You also learned how to save a Word 2011 document so that it's usable with earlier versions of Word and how to create documents in the widely used PDF format that you can take to specialist printing services or distribute across the Internet.

Part III

Analyzing Data with Microsoft Excel

In this part of the book, you'll learn how to use Microsoft Excel to build powerful spreadsheets and analyze your data.

In Chapter 12, you'll learn to create different types of workbooks in Excel and enter data in them. You'll navigate the Excel interface, work with workbooks and worksheets, and use Excel's views and features to see the data you need.

In Chapter 13, you'll insert, delete, and format rows and columns in worksheets; format cells and ranges; and use the advanced conditional-formatting and data-validation features to identify unusual values or erratic input. You'll also learn how to format quickly and consistently with styles, how to add headers and footers to worksheets, and how to share workbooks with your colleagues.

In Chapter 14, you'll grasp how Excel's charts work and start adding them to your workbooks. You'll learn how to lay out a chart effectively, how to make it look good, and how to hide any components you don't want to display. You'll even learn how to save time by reusing the custom chart formatting you create.

In Chapter 15, you'll first learn the difference between a formula and a function. You'll then grasp how to create custom formulas and how to use Excel's built-in functions to perform preset calculations.

In Chapter 16, you'll start using Excel to create databases for storing and manipulating your information. You'll learn how to enter information in a database, how to sort the information, and how to filter it to find only the results you want. You'll also learn how to use the Goal Seek feature and scenarios to work out solutions to business problems.

In Chapter 17, you'll meet Excel's powerful PivotTable feature and start using it to manipulate your data so that you can discover the information you need. You'll learn to build a PivotTable from a spreadsheet, sort and filter it, and make it show the data you're looking for.

Chapter 12

Creating Workbooks and Entering Data

In this chapter, you'll get started quickly with Excel by creating and saving a new workbook. You'll then look at how to navigate the Excel interface and work with worksheets and workbooks. You'll learn how to enter data in worksheets, how to select and manipulate cells, and how to use Excel's various view features to see the worksheet data you need so that you can work easily with it.

Creating and Saving a New Workbook

When you launch Excel, the application by default displays the Excel Workbook Gallery dialog box automatically so that you can create a new workbook or open one you've recently used. In this section, we'll look at how to create a new workbook and how to save it.

Creating a New Workbook

To create a new workbook, you use the Excel Workbook Gallery dialog box (see Figure 12–1). By default, the Excel Workbook Gallery dialog box opens when you launch Excel, but you can also display it at any other time by choosing File ➤ New from Template from the menu bar or pressing Cmd+Shift+P.

> **NOTE:** If you don't want the Excel Workbook Gallery dialog box to open when you launch Excel, select the Don't show this when opening Excel check box at the bottom of the Excel Workbook Gallery dialog box, and then click the Cancel button. To start displaying the Excel Workbook Gallery dialog box again on launch, choose Excel ➤ Preferences or press Cmd+, (Cmd and the comma key) to display the Excel Preferences dialog box. In the Authoring area, click the General icon to display the General pane. Select the Open Excel Workbook Gallery when application opens check box, and then click the OK button.

Figure 12–1. *From the Excel Workbook Gallery, you can create a blank workbook, a workbook based on a template on your Mac, or a workbook based on an online template. You can also open a workbook you've used recently.*

From here, you have three ways to create a new workbook:

- *Blank workbook.* To create a blank workbook, click the Excel Workbook item, and then click the Choose button. The Excel Workbook item appears first in the All category in the Templates list.

- *Template on your Mac.* To create a new workbook based on a template that's stored on your Mac, follow these steps:

  1. Click the appropriate category in the Templates list in the left pane—or click the All category if you want to see all the templates.

  2. In the middle pane, click the template you want. A preview appears in the right pane. If the workbook has multiple sheets, you can preview them by clicking the Previous (<) button and Next (>) button in the right pane.

  3. Click the Choose button to create a workbook based on the template.

- *Online template.* To create a workbook based on a template from Microsoft's Office.com site, follow these steps:

    1. In the left pane, click the disclosure triangle to the left of the Online Templates item to expand it.

    2. Click the category of templates you want—for example, Budgets. The middle pane displays the available templates.

    3. In the middle pane, click the template you want. The right pane displays details about the template.

    4. Click the Choose button to download the template and create a workbook based on it.

> **NOTE:** If you need to base a new workbook on an existing workbook, choose File ➤ Open to display the Open: Microsoft Excel dialog box. Select the existing workbook, click the Open pop-up menu and click Copy, and then click the Open button. Excel opens a new workbook containing the same contents as the existing workbook. You then use the File ➤ Save command to save the workbook under a name you specify, just as when you create a new workbook. (By contrast, if you don't choose Copy in the Open pop-up menu, you open the original workbook. You can then use the File ➤ Save As command to save it under a different name or in a different folder—but it's easy to get distracted, forget to use Save As, and then save changes to the original file by mistake.)

Saving a Workbook

To save a workbook for the first time, give the Save command in any of the usual ways—by clicking the Save button on the Standard toolbar, by choosing File ➤ Save from the menu bar, or by pressing Cmd+S. In the Save As dialog box that Excel opens, select the folder in which to save the workbook, type the workbook name, and then click the Save button.

The one complication is the file type. By default, Excel uses the format called Excel Workbook, which the four latest versions of Excel—Excel 2011 and Excel 2008 for Mac, and Excel 2010 and Excel 2007 for Windows—can open. Earlier versions of Excel for Mac used a different format, called Excel 97–2004 Workbook format on the Mac and Excel 97–2003 Workbook format on Windows. Excel 2004 for Mac and Excel 2003 for Windows users can install converters to enable Excel to handle the new file formats, but many people don't have these converters, even though they're available for free from the Microsoft web site.

TIP: If you start recording or writing macros to automate your work in Excel, you need to use a workbook format that can contain macros, because the Excel Workbook format cannot. Use the Excel Macro-Enabled Workbook format if the workbook is for Excel 2011, Excel 2010 for Windows, or Excel 2007 for Windows; use the Excel 97–2004 format if the workbook is for Excel 2004, Excel 2003, or an earlier version. Excel 2008 for Mac doesn't run macros.

So if you want to be able to share the workbook with colleagues who use Excel versions released before 2007, open the Format pop-up menu in the Save As dialog box and click the Excel 97–2004 Workbook item before you click the Save button to save the workbook. Your colleagues will then be able to open the workbook in Excel 2004 or Excel 2003 without installing the converters.

NOTE: The latest Excel file format (the one called simply Excel Workbook) is technically superior to the earlier file format (Excel 97–2004 Workbook or Excel 97–2003 Workbook). Using the Excel Workbook format, you can create workbooks containing more worksheets, and each worksheet can have many more rows and columns. The file format is also more resilient to data corruption. But for normal-size spreadsheets, such as those most business users and home users create, the earlier file format works just fine.

Navigating the Excel Interface, Worksheets, and Workbooks

When you've created a new workbook or opened an existing one, you see the worksheets in the workbook. Figure 12–2 shows a new workbook with some data entered.

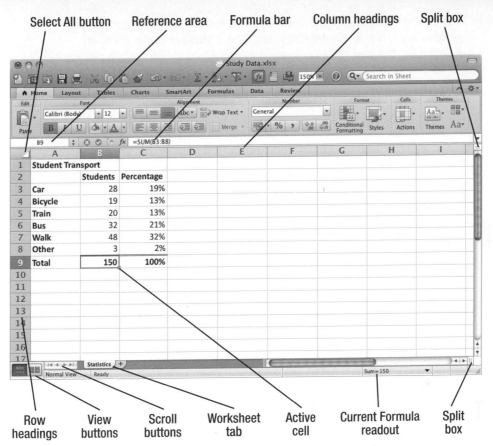

Figure 12–2. *The main elements of the Excel application window and a workbook*

Apart from regular Office application elements such as the Ribbon, the Standard toolbar, the scroll bars, and the status bar, these are the main elements of the Excel application window and workbooks:

- *Formula bar.* This is the bar below the Ribbon. This area shows the data or formula in the active cell and gives you an easy place to enter and edit data.

- *Reference area.* This area appears at the left end of the formula bar. It shows the active cell's address (for example, B9) or name.

- *Row headings.* These are the numbers at the left side of the screen that identify each row. The first row is 1, the second row 2, and so on.

- *Column headings.* These are the letters at the top of the worksheet grid that identify the columns. The first column is A, the second column B, and so on.

- *Cells.* These are the boxes formed by the intersections of the rows and columns. Each cell is identified by its column letter and row number. For example, the first cell in column A is cell A1, and the second cell in column B is cell B2.

- *Active cell.* This is the cell you're working in. Excel displays a blue rectangle around the active cell.

- *Select All button.* Click this button at the intersection of the row headings and column headings to select all the cells in the worksheet.

- *Worksheet tabs.* Each worksheet has a tab at the bottom that bears its name. To display a worksheet, you click its tab in the worksheet tabs area.

- *Scroll buttons.* Click these buttons to scroll the worksheet tabs so that you can see the ones you need. Click the leftmost button to scroll all the way back to the first tab, or click the rightmost button to scroll to the last tab. Click the two middle buttons to scroll back or forward by one tab.

- *View buttons.* Click these buttons to switch between Normal view and Page Layout view. You'll learn how to use these views later in this chapter.

- *Split boxes.* You use these boxes when you need to split the worksheet window into two or four areas. You'll learn how to do this in the section "Splitting the Window to View Separate Parts of a Worksheet," later in this chapter.

Understanding Workbooks, Worksheets, Columns, and Rows

Each workbook consists of one or more worksheets or other sheets, such as chart sheets or macro sheets. To display the worksheet you want to use, you click its tab in the worksheet tab bar (see Figure 12–3); if the worksheet's tab isn't visible in the worksheet tab bar, you click the scroll buttons to display it (unless you've hidden the worksheet).

TIP: If you want to make the worksheet tab bar wider so that you can see more tabs at once, drag the divider bar to the right. Excel makes the horizontal scroll bar smaller to compensate.

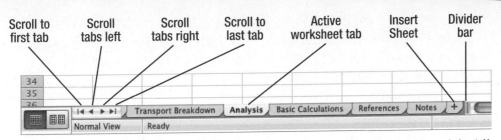

Figure 12–3. *Use the worksheet tab bar to display the worksheet you want or to insert a new worksheet. You can drag the divider bar to change the length of the tab bar.*

Each worksheet contains 16,384 columns and 1,048,576 rows, giving a grand total of 17,179,869,184 cells. (This is a worksheet in the Excel Workbook format; the older format uses smaller worksheets.) Normally, you'll use only a small number of these cells—perhaps a few hundred or a few thousand—but there's plenty of space should you need it for large data sets.

> **TIP:** You can quickly move to the next worksheet by pressing Cmd+Page Down or to the previous worksheet by pressing Cmd+Page Up.

Each column is identified by one, two, or three letters:

- The first 26 columns use the letters A to Z.

- The next 26 columns use AA to AZ, the following 26 BA to BZ, and so on.

- When the two-letter combinations are exhausted, Excel uses three letters: AAA, AAB, and so on, up to XFD.

Each row is identified by a number, from 1 up to 1048576.

Each cell is identified by its column lettering and its row number. For example, the cell at the intersection of column A and row 1 is cell A1, and the cell at the intersection of column ZA and row 2256 is ZA2256.

Moving the Active Cell

In Excel, you usually work in a single cell at a time. That cell is called the *active cell* and receives the input from the keyboard.

You can move the active cell easily using either the mouse or the keyboard:

- *Mouse.* Click the cell you want to make active.

- *Keyboard.* Press the arrow keys to move the active cell up or down by one row or left or right by one column at a time. You can also press the keyboard shortcuts shown in Table 12–1 to move the active cell further.

TIP: If your Mac's keyboard doesn't have the Home key, End key, Page Up key, and Page Down key, you'll need to use function-key shortcuts. Press Fn+left arrow for Home, Fn+right arrow for End, Fn+up arrow for PageUp, and Fn+down arrow for PageDown.

Table 12–1. *Keyboard Shortcuts for Moving the Active Cell*

To Move the Active Cell Like This	Press This Keyboard Shortcut
First cell in the row	Home
First cell in the active worksheet	Cmd+Home
Last cell used in the worksheet	Cmd+End
Down one screen	Page Down
Up one screen	Page Up
Right one screen	Option+Page Down
Left one screen	Option+Page Up
To the last row in the worksheet	Cmd+down arrow
To the last column in the worksheet	Cmd+right arrow
To the first row in the worksheet	Cmd+up arrow
To the first column in the worksheet	Cmd+left arrow or Home
To the next corner cell clockwise in a selected range	Ctrl+. (Ctrl and the period key)

To access a cell, click it with the mouse or use the arrow keys to move the active cell's rectangle to it. Excel makes that cell the active cell, the cell that receives input from the keyboard.

Selecting and Manipulating Cells

To work with a single cell, you simply click it or use the keyboard to move the active cell to it. When you need to affect multiple cells at once, you select the cells using the mouse or keyboard.

Excel calls a selection of cells a *range*. A range can consist of either a rectangle of contiguous cells or various cells that aren't next to each other. The left illustration in

Figure 12–4 shows a range of contiguous cells, while the right illustration shows a range of separate cells.

Figure 12–4. *You can select either a range of contiguous cells (left) or a range of individual cells (right).*

You can select a range of contiguous cells in any of these three ways:

- *Click and drag.* Click the first cell in the range, and then drag to select all the others. For example, if you click cell B2 and then drag to cell E7, you select a range that's four columns wide and six rows deep. Excel uses the notation B2:E7 to describe this range—the starting cell address, a colon, and then the ending cell address.

- *Click and then Shift+click.* Click the first cell in the range, and then Shift+click the last cell. Excel selects all the cells in between. This technique tends to be the easiest to use when the first cell and last cell are widely separated; for example, they don't appear in the same window.

- *Hold down Shift and use the arrow keys.* Use the arrow keys to move the active cell to where you want to start the range; then hold down Shift and use the arrow keys to extend the selection for the rest of the range. This method is good if you prefer using the keyboard to the mouse.

You can select a range of noncontiguous cells by clicking the first cell (or dragging through a range of contiguous cells) and then holding down Cmd while you click other individual cells or drag through ranges of contiguous cells. Excel uses commas to separate the individual cells in this type of range. For example, the range D3,E5,F7,G1:G13 consists of three individual cells (D3, E5, and F7) and one range of contiguous cells (G1 through G13).

NOTE: You can quickly select a row by clicking its row heading or pressing Shift+spacebar when the active cell is in that row. Likewise, you can select a column by clicking its column heading or pressing Ctrl+spacebar. To select all the cells in the active worksheet, click the Select All button (where the row headings and column headings meet). You can also either press Cmd+A or press Shift+spacebar followed by Ctrl+spacebar (or vice versa).

To deselect a range you've selected, click anywhere outside the range.

Enter Data in Your Worksheets

You can enter data in your worksheets by typing it, by pasting it, or by using drag and drop to move or copy it. Excel also includes a feature called AutoFill that automatically fills in series data for you based on the input you've provided.

Typing Data in a Cell

The most straightforward way to enter data is to type it into a cell.

Once you make a cell the active cell by clicking it or moving the selection rectangle to it, you can start typing in it. When you start typing, Excel displays an insertion point in the cell.

When you've finished typing the contents of the cell, move to another cell in any of these ways:

- *Press Return.* Excel moves the active cell to the next cell below the current cell (but see the next Tip). If you select a range of cells, Excel moves the active cell down until it reaches the bottom of the range and then moves it up to the first cell in the range's next column.

- *Click another cell.* Excel moves the active cell to the cell you click.

- *Press an arrow key.* Excel moves the active cell to the next cell in the direction of the arrow. For example, press the right arrow key to move the active cell to the next cell to the right.

TIP: To change the direction Excel moves the active cell when you press Return, choose Excel ➤ Preferences or press Cmd+, (Cmd and the comma key). In the Excel Preferences dialog box, click the Edit item in the Authoring area to display the Edit preferences pane. Make sure the "After pressing RETURN, move selection" check box is selected, then open the Direction pop-up menu, and finally choose Down, Right, Up, or Left, as needed. (If you don't want Excel to move the active cell when you press Return, clear the "After pressing RETURN, move selection" check box.) Click the OK button to close the Excel Preferences dialog box.

Editing a Cell

When you need to edit the existing contents of a cell, open it for editing in one of these ways:

- Double-click the cell. Excel displays an insertion point in the cell.

- Move the active cell to the cell, and then press Ctrl+U. Excel displays an insertion point in the cell. Figure 12–5 shows an example of editing in a cell.

Figure 12–5. *Double-click in a cell or press Ctrl+U to edit its contents in place. In this example, cell B3 is open for editing.*

- Click the cell (or move the active cell to it), and then click the cell's contents in the formula bar. Excel displays an insertion point in the formula bar (see Figure 12–6).

Figure 12–6. *You can also edit a cell by clicking in the formula bar. This method is often easier for editing entries longer than their cells.*

When you're editing a cell, pressing an arrow key moves the insertion point within the cell's contents rather than finishing the entry and moving to another cell:

- *Left arrow key.* Press this key to move left by one character.

- *Right arrow key.* Press this key to move right by one character.

- *Down arrow key.* Press this key to move to the end of the cell's contents.

- *Up arrow key.* Press this key to move the insertion point back to where it was before you moved to the end of the cell's contents by pressing the down arrow key.

To finish editing a cell, press Return, click the check-mark button on the formula bar, or click another cell. To cancel editing a cell and restore its previous contents, press Esc or click the cross button on the formula bar.

TIP: Instead of editing a cell's existing contents, you can simply replace them by making the cell active and then typing new contents. Replacing tends to be faster than editing when a cell contains a short entry that you can easily retype.

Entering Data Quickly Using AutoFill

When you need to fill in a series of data, see whether Excel's AutoFill feature can do the trick. To use AutoFill, you enter the base data for the series in one or more cells and then select them and drag the AutoFill handle in the direction you want to fill. AutoFill checks your base data, works out what the other cells should contain, and fills in the data for you. For example, you can fill in a series of numbers or a range of days, months, or years.

Using AutoFill's Built-in Capabilities

Open a test workbook, or add a test worksheet to your current workbook by clicking the Insert Sheet button, and then try using AutoFill.

> **TIP:** You can also insert a new worksheet by pressing Excel's Shift+F11 keyboard shortcut—but only if your Mac isn't set to use F11 as the keyboard shortcut for Exposé's Show Desktop command. This is a standard setting in Mac OS X, so if you want to be able to insert new worksheets from the keyboard, you must either change the Show Desktop keyboard shortcut (in the Exposé & Spaces pane in System Preferences) or assign a new keyboard shortcut in Excel (see Chapter 5 for instructions).

Type **Monday** in cell A1, press Return to enter the data, and then click cell A1 again. Then drag the AutoFill handle—the blue square that appears at the lower-right corner of the selection—down to cell A7. As you drag past each cell, AutoFill displays a ScreenTip showing the data it will fill in that cell (see Figure 12–7). When you release the mouse button on cell A7, AutoFill fills in the days Tuesday through Sunday.

Figure 12–7. Drag the AutoFill handle down or across to fill in a series of data derived from one or more existing entries. In this case, AutoFill fills in the days of the week and repeats the series if you drag farther.

Now drag through the range to select it, and then press Delete to clear it. Then follow these steps:

1. Click cell B2, and type a date such as **2-15-11** in it.

2. Press Return, and you'll see that Excel changes it to a full date—for example, 2/15/11.

3. Ctrl+click or right-click the AutoFill handle and drag it to cell G2. As you drag, AutoFill displays dates incremented by one day for each column (2/16/11, 2/17/11, and so on), but when you release the mouse button, AutoFill displays a context menu (see Figure 12–8).

Figure 12–8. *To reach more AutoFill options, Ctrl+drag or right-drag the AutoFill handle, and then choose the option you want from the context menu.*

4. Click the Fill Months item, and Excel fills in a separate month for each column: 3/15/11, 4/15/11, and so on.

Now clear your data again, and then follow these steps:

1. Click cell A1, and type **5** in it.

2. Press Return to move to cell A2, type **25** in it, and press the up arrow to move back to cell A1.

3. Press Shift+down arrow to select cells A1 and A2.

4. Click the AutoFill handle, and drag downward. AutoFill fills in a series with intervals of 20—cell A3 gets 45, cell A4 gets 65, and so on—using a linear trend.

Delete the data that AutoFill entered, leaving 5 in cell A1 and 25 in cell A2. Then follow these steps:

1. Select cells A1 and A2.

2. Ctrl+click or right-click the AutoFill handle, and drag downward. As you drag, you'll see ScreenTips for the same values as in the previous list.

3. Release the mouse button, and then click Growth Trend on the context menu. AutoFill enters a growth trend instead of the linear trend: because the second value (25) is 5 times the first value (5), Excel multiplies each value by 5, giving the sequence 5, 25, 125, 625, 3125, and so on.

NOTE: The AutoFill context menu also contains items for filling the cells with formatting only (copying the formatting from the first cell), filling the cells without formatting (ignoring the first cell's formatting), and filling in days, weekdays, months, and years.

Creating Your Own Custom AutoFill Lists

If you need to enter the same series of data frequently, you can create your own AutoFill lists. Follow these steps:

1. If the data for the series already appears in a worksheet, select the cells that contain it.

2. Choose Excel ➤ Preferences or press Cmd+, (Cmd and the comma key) to display the Excel Preferences dialog box.

3. In the Formulas and Lists area, click the Custom Lists item to display the Custom Lists pane (shown in Figure 12–9 with settings chosen). If you selected cells in step 1, the references appear in the Import list from cells text box; move ahead to step 6.

Figure 12–9. *You can supplement Excel's built-in AutoFill lists by creating your own data series that you need to enter frequently in your worksheets.*

4. In the Custom lists box, click the NEW LIST item.

5. Click in the List entries box, and then type your list, putting one item on each line.

6. If you've just entered a list, click the Add button to add the list to the Custom lists box. If you imported a list from a worksheet, click the Import button.

> **TIP:** If you need to create another list from worksheet data at this point, you don't need to close the Excel Preferences dialog box. Instead, click the Collapse Dialog button to the left of the Import button to collapse the Custom Lists dialog box to a shallow dialog box, and then drag through the list on the worksheet. Click the Collapse Dialog button to restore the Excel Preferences dialog box, where the range appears in the Import list from cells text box. Then click the Import button to bring in the data.

7. Click the OK button to close the Excel Preferences dialog box.

Pasting Data into a Worksheet

If the data you need to add to a worksheet is already in another document, you can copy it and paste it into the worksheet using the techniques explained in Chapter 3. You can also use Excel's Paste Special command to paste only some of the data—for example, the values of formulas rather than formulas themselves.

Using Paste and Paste Options

To paste data, position the active cell at the upper-left corner of where you want the data to land. In most cases, you don't need to select the right number of cells for the data, because Excel does that for you automatically; if you find Excel prompts you to select the destination range, do so.

After positioning the active cell, you can either simply give the Paste command or choose one of the available Paste Options:

- *Paste.* Press Cmd+V, click the Paste button on the Standard toolbar, choose Home ➤ Edit ➤ Paste from the Ribbon (clicking the main part of the Paste button rather than the pop-up button), or choose Edit ➤ Paste from the menu bar. If you don't get the result you want, click the Paste Options button that appears near the lower-right corner of what you pasted, and then click the option button you want on the Paste Options menu (shown on the left in Figure 12–10).

- *Paste Options.* Choose Home ➤ Edit ➤ Paste (clicking the Paste pop-up button), and then click the appropriate item on the Paste pop-up menu (shown on the right in Figure 12–10).

Figure 12–10. *If pasted data arrives in the wrong format, click the Paste Options button, and choose a different option from the Paste Options menu (left). You can also use the Paste pop-up menu on the Home tab of the Ribbon to choose the format while pasting (right).*

Which Paste Options are available depends on the data you're pasting, but in most cases you have at least the choice of Keep Source Formatting (retaining the formatting the data had wherever you copied it from) and Match Destination Formatting (making it look like the worksheet you're pasting it on).

Controlling Pasted Data with the Paste Special Command

Sometimes you'll want to paste less than all of the data you've copied. For example, you may need to paste all the data and formatting except for cell borders, or you may want to retain only the values and number formats rather than other information.

For these needs, Excel provides the Paste Special command. You can access most of these options from either the Paste pop-up menu in the Edit group of the Home tab or from the Paste Options pop-up menu, but in most cases it's clearest to use the Paste Special dialog box.

To display the Paste Special dialog box (see Figure 12–11), use one of these commands:

- *Ribbon.* Choose Home ➤ Edit ➤ Paste ➤ Paste Special.

- *Menu bar.* Choose Edit ➤ Paste Special.

- *Context menu.* Ctrl+click or right-click the destination cell, and then click Paste Special.

- *Keyboard.* Press Cmd+Shift+V.

Figure 12-11. *Use the Paste Special dialog box when you need to paste only some of the data, when you need to perform an operation on the data, or when you need to transpose its rows and columns.*

You then choose the option button you want in the Paste area:

- *All.* Select this option button to paste all the data and all its formatting. Normally, you'll want to do this only if you're using the Skip blanks check box, the Transpose check box, or the Paste Link button— otherwise, it's easier to use the Paste command.

- *Formulas.* Select this option button to paste in all the formulas and constants without formatting.

- *Values.* Select this option button to paste in formula values instead of pasting in the formulas themselves. Excel removes the formatting from the values.

- *Formats.* Select this option button to paste in the formatting without the data. This option is surprisingly useful once you know it's there.

- *Comments.* Select this option button to paste in only comments. This option is handy when you're integrating different colleagues' takes on the same worksheet.

- *Validation.* Select this option button to paste in data-validation criteria.

- *All using Source theme.* Select this option button to paste in all the data using the theme from the workbook the data came from.

- *All except borders.* Select this option button to paste in all the data and formatting but to strip out the cell borders.

- *Column widths.* Select this option button to paste in only the column widths—no data and no other formatting. This option is useful when you need to lay one worksheet out like another existing worksheet but put all different data in it.

- *Formulas and number formats.* Select this option button to paste in formulas and number formatting but no other formatting.

- *Values and number formats.* Select this option button to paste in values (rather than formulas) and number formatting.

- *Merge conditional formatting.* Select this option button to copy all data and formatting and to merge in any conditional formatting. See Chapter 13 for details on conditional formatting.

If you need to perform a mathematical operation using the data you're pasting, go to the Operation area of the Paste Special dialog box and select the Add option button, the Subtract option button, the Multiply option button, or the Divide option button, as needed. For example, if you want to multiply the current values in the cells by the values you're pasting, select the Multiply option button. Otherwise, leave the None option button selected to paste the data without performing math with it.

In the bottom section of the Paste Special dialog box, you can select or clear the two check boxes as needed:

- *Skip blanks.* Select this check box to prevent Excel from pasting blank cells.

- *Transpose.* Select this check box to transpose columns to rows and rows to columns. This option is much quicker than retyping data that you (or someone else) have laid out the wrong way.

When you've chosen the options you want, click the OK button. Excel closes the Paste Special dialog box and pastes the data or formatting you chose.

> **NOTE:** If you need to link the data you're pasting back to its source, click the Paste Link button in the Paste Special dialog box instead of the OK button. This makes Excel create a link to the source data so that when the source data changes, the linked data changes too. If the source data is in the same workbook, Excel updates the links automatically. If the source data is in another workbook, Excel updates the data when you open the workbook that contains the links.

Copying and Moving Data with Drag and Drop

When you need to copy or move data within Excel, you can use drag and drop. Follow these steps:

1. Select the data you want to move or copy.

2. Move the mouse pointer over an edge of the section so that the pointer turns to a hand icon (see Figure 12–12).

	A	B	C	D
1	**Student Transport**			
2		*Students*	*Percentage*	
3	Car	28	19%	
4	Bicycle	19	13%	
5	Train	20	13%	
6	Bus	32	21%	
7	Walk	48	32%	
8	Other	3	2%	
9	Total	150	100%	
10				

Figure 12–12. *To move data using drag and drop, select the data, and then move the mouse pointer over one of its edges to display the drag-and-drop pointer, which is the hand icon that appears at the bottom here.*

3. Click and drag the data to where you want it to appear. If you want to copy the data rather than move it, Option+drag rather than drag; the hand icon shows a plus (+) sign to indicate you're making a copy.

Normal drag and drop moves or copies all of the data and all of its formatting, much like pasting the material. To reach more options, such as copying only the values or the formats or creating a link or a hyperlink to the source, Ctrl+click or right-click and drag instead of left-clicking and dragging. When you release the mouse button, Excel displays a context menu of choices (see Figure 12–13). Click the choice you want.

Figure 12–13. *Use the Ctrl+drag or right-drag context menu to transfer only some of the data or to create a link.*

Inserting, Deleting, and Rearranging Worksheets

When you create a workbook, Excel puts a single worksheet in it by default. For many workbooks, this may be all you need, but for other workbooks, you'll need to insert further worksheets to give yourself space to work in.

For most workbooks, you'll want to give the worksheets custom names instead of the default names. You may also need to rearrange the worksheets into a different order.

> **TIP:** To change the number of worksheets that Excel includes in a blank workbook, choose Excel ➤ Preferences or press Cmd+, (Cmd and the comma key) to display the Excel Preferences dialog box. In the Authoring area, click the General icon to display the General preferences pane. Change the number in the Sheets in new workbook box to the number of worksheets you want, and then click the OK button.

Inserting and Deleting Worksheets

You can easily insert a new worksheet in a workbook in either of these ways:

- *Insert a new worksheet after the last existing worksheet.* Click the Insert Sheet button that appears on the tab bar after the last worksheet tab.

- *Insert a new worksheet after a particular worksheet.* Ctrl+click or right-click the existing worksheet, and then click Insert Sheet on the context menu.

TIP: You can also press Shift+F11 to insert a new worksheet after the worksheet that's currently selected—as long as Mac OS X isn't using F11 for a different purpose, such as the Show Desktop feature in Exposé. If Mac OS X is already using F11, you can map the Insert Sheet command to a different keyboard shortcut using the technique explained in the section "Creating Custom Keyboard Shortcuts in Word and Excel" in Chapter 5.

After inserting a worksheet, double-click its tab to select the default name, type the name you want, and then press Return. You can use up to 31 characters in the name. If you want to make the tab stand out, Ctrl+click or right-click the tab, click Tab Color to display the Tab Color window, and then click the color for the tab. Click the Close button (the button at the left end of the title bar) to close the Tab Color window.

To delete a worksheet, Ctrl+click or right-click its tab, and then click Delete on the context menu. Excel displays a dialog box (see Figure 12–14) to double-check that you're prepared to delete it; click the Delete button to go ahead.

Figure 12–14. *Excel confirms the deletion of one or more worksheets in case you've given the Delete command by accident.*

Rearranging the Worksheets in a Workbook

You can rearrange the worksheets in a workbook into the order you need.

The quick way to move a worksheet is to click its tab, drag it left or right until Excel displays a downward arrow between the worksheets where you want to place it, and then drop it.

TIP: To move two or more worksheets, select them first. To select a range of worksheets that appear next to each other, click the first worksheet's tab, and then Shift+click the tab for the worksheet at the other end of the range. To select worksheets that aren't next to each other, click the first worksheet's tab, and then Cmd+click each other worksheet's tab in turn.

This method works well for moving a worksheet a short distance along the tab bar, but for moving larger distances, you may prefer to use the Move or Copy dialog box. You can also use the Move or Copy dialog box to move or copy worksheets to a different workbook. Follow these steps:

1. If you want to move or copy the worksheets to a different workbook, open that workbook.

2. In the source workbook, Ctrl+click or right-click the worksheet's tab to display the context menu. To move multiple worksheets, select them, and then Ctrl+click or right-click one of the selected tabs.

3. On the context menu, click the Move or Copy item to display the Move or Copy dialog box (see Figure 12–15).

Figure 12–15. *Use the Move or Copy dialog box to move one or more worksheets farther than you can comfortably drag within a workbook or to move or copy worksheets to another open workbook.*

4. In the To book pop-up menu, make sure the current workbook is selected unless you want to move the worksheet to another workbook—in which case, select that workbook.

5. In the Before sheet list box, click the worksheet before which you want to position the worksheet you're moving. If you want to put the worksheets at the end of the workbook, select the (move to end) item.

6. Select the Create a copy check box if you want to copy the worksheet to the destination rather than move it. Copying tends to be most useful when the destination is another workbook, but you can copy within a workbook as well.

7. Click the OK button to close the dialog box. Excel moves or copies the worksheet to the destination you chose.

Making Excel Display Worksheets the Way You Need

To work quickly and easily in your workbooks, you need to know how to make the most of Excel's three views and how to use Full Screen view. You also need to know how to split the window into two or four parts, how to hide windows when you don't need to see them, and how to use Excel's features for freezing parts of a window that you need to keep in sight.

Understanding Excel's Views

Excel gives you two views for working in your workbooks:

- *Normal view.* This is the view in which workbooks normally open and is the view in which you'll do most of your data entry, formatting, and reviewing. Normal view is the view in which you've seen Excel so far in this chapter.

- *Page Layout view.* This view shows your worksheets as they will look when laid out on paper. You use it to adjust the page setup. You'll learn how to do this in Chapter 13.

To switch view, click the Normal View button or the Page Layout View button at the left end of the status bar (see Figure 12–16) or choose View ➤ Normal or View ➤ Page Layout from the menu bar.

Normal   Page
View   Layout
         View

Figure 12–16. *Use the View buttons at the left end of the status bar to change views quickly.*

TIP: When you want to see as much of a worksheet as possible, choose View ➤ Full Screen from the menu bar. Excel hides the Ribbon and displays the worksheet full screen but doesn't hide the menu bar or the Dock the way Word's Full Screen view does. You can use Full Screen view in either Normal view or Page Layout view. When you want to leave Full Screen view, click the Close Full Screen button on the Close Full Screen toolbar (which Excel displays automatically when you switch to Full Screen view), choose View ➤ Full Screen again, or simply press Esc.

Splitting the Window to View Separate Parts of a Worksheet

Often, it's useful to be able to see two parts of a worksheet at the same time as you work in it—for example, to make sure that your notes correctly describe your data, or when you're copying information from one part to another.

When you need to see two parts of the worksheet in the same window, you can split the window either horizontally or vertically. To do so, you use the horizontal split box at the right end of the horizontal scroll bar, the vertical split box at the top end of the vertical scroll bar, or the Split button in the Window group of the Layout tab of the Ribbon (see Figure 12–17).

Figure 12–17. *The Window group on the Layout tab of the Ribbon contains several essential commands, but most of the button names appear only when the Excel window is very wide.*

Double-click the horizontal split box to split the window horizontally above the active cell, or double-click the vertical split box to split the window vertically to the left of the active cell. If the active cell isn't in the right place for splitting, click the horizontal split box or the vertical split box, and then drag it until the split bar appears where you want the split.

If you want to split the window into four panes, split it in the other dimension as well. For example, if you've already split the window horizontally, split it vertically as well. Figure 12–18 shows the Excel window split into four panes.

> **NOTE:** You can also split the window into four panes by choosing Layout ➤ Window ➤ Split from the Ribbon or Window ➤ Split from the menu bar.

Figure 12–18. *Split the Excel window into two or four panes when you need to work in separate areas of the worksheet at the same time.*

Once you split the window, you get a separate scroll bar in each part, so you can scroll the panes separately to display whichever areas of the worksheet you need.

NOTE: When you split the window, you may find it helpful to freeze certain rows and columns, as discussed later in this chapter, to keep them visible even when you scroll to other areas of the worksheet.

To reposition the split, click the split bar, and drag it to where you want it. If you've split the window into four panes, you can resize all four panes at once by clicking where the split bars cross and then dragging.

To remove the split, either double-click the split bar or click the split bar and drag it all the way to the left of the screen or all the way to the top. You can also choose Layout ➤ Window ➤ Split from the Ribbon or Window ➤ Remove Split from the menu bar.

Opening Extra Windows to Show Other Parts of a Workbook

Instead of splitting a window, you can open one or more extra windows to show other parts of the workbook.

Choose Layout ➤ Window ➤ New from the Ribbon or Window ➤ New Window from the menu bar to open a new window on the active workbook. Excel distinguishes the windows by adding :1 to the name of the first and :2 to the name of the second—for example, General Data.xlsx:1 and General Data.xlsx:2.

> **NOTE:** Opening extra windows has two advantages over splitting a window. First, you can display other worksheets (or workbooks) in the windows if you want rather than just other parts of the same worksheet. Second, you can zoom each window by a different amount as needed or use a different view in each window.

Changing the Window and Arranging Open Windows

The easiest way to change the window you're working in is to click the window you want to use—either click the window itself (if you can see it) or click its button on the Taskbar. You can also choose open the Window menu on the menu bar and then click the window in the list at the bottom.

When you've opened several windows, you can arrange them by using standard Mac OS X techniques, such as by dragging them to the size and position you want. You can also use Excel's Arrange Windows dialog box or Arrange pop-up menu to arrange Excel's windows.

To arrange windows using the Arrange Windows dialog box, follow these steps:

1. Choose Window ➤ Arrange from the menu bar or Layout ➤ Window ➤ Arrange ➤ Arrange Windows from the Ribbon to display the Arrange Windows dialog box (see Figure 12–19).

Figure 12–19. *Use the Arrange Windows dialog box to tile or otherwise arrange all the Excel windows or only those from the active workbook.*

2. Click the option button for the arrangement you want:

- *Tiled.* Select this option button to make Excel resize all the nonminimized windows to roughly even sizes so that they fit in the Excel window. If you have several windows open, tiling tends to make them too small for working in, but it's good for seeing which windows are open and closing those you don't need.

- *Horizontal.* Select this option button to arrange all the windows horizontally in the Excel window. This arrangement works well for two windows in which the data is laid out in rows rather than columns.

- *Vertical.* Select this option button to arrange all the windows vertically in the Excel window. This arrangement works well for two windows in which the data is laid out in columns rather than rows.

- *Cascade.* Select this option button to arrange the windows in a stack so that you can see each one's title bar. This arrangement is useful for picking the window you want out of many open windows.

3. To arrange only the windows of the active workbook, select the Windows of active workbook check box. This option is good for the Horizontal and Vertical arrangements.

4. Click the OK button to close the Arrange Windows dialog box. Excel arranges the windows as you chose.

> **TIP:** When you don't need to see a particular window, you can hide it to get it out of the way. Click the window, and then choose Window ➤ Hide. To display the window again, choose Window ➤ Unhide, click the window in the Unhide dialog box, and then click the OK button.

To arrange windows quickly using the Arrange pop-up menu, choose Layout ➤ Window ➤ Arrange, and then click the Vertical item or the Cascade item on the pop-up menu, as needed. You can also click the Arrange Windows item to display the Arrange Windows dialog box.

Zooming to Show the Data You Need to See

You can zoom in or out on your worksheets to make the data easier to read or to display more of a worksheet at once.

The easiest way to zoom in or out is by opening the Zoom pop-up menu on the Standard toolbar and then clicking one of the items on it: 200%, 150%, 125%, 100%, 75%, 50%, 25%, Selection, or (in Page Layout view only) One Page.

You can set a custom view percentage by clicking the Zoom box or opening the Zoom pop-up menu, typing the percentage you want, and then pressing Return.

When you need to zoom just the right amount to display a particular area of the worksheet as large as it will fit in the window, select the area, open the Zoom pop-up menu, and then click Selection.

NOTE: If you choose not to display the Standard toolbar, use the other way of setting the Zoom percentage—by using the Zoom dialog box. Choose View ➤ Zoom from the menu bar, choose the appropriate option button, and then click the OK button.

Freezing Rows and Columns So That They Stay On-Screen

To keep your data headings on-screen when you scroll down or to the right on a large worksheet, you can freeze the heading rows and columns in place. For example, if you have headings in column A and row 1, you can freeze column A and row 1 so that they remain on-screen.

You can quickly freeze the first column, the top row, or your choice of rows and columns:

- *Freeze the first column.* Choose Layout ➤ Window ➤ Freeze Panes ➤ Freeze First Column from the Ribbon.

- *Freeze the first row.* Choose Layout ➤ Window ➤ Freeze Panes ➤ Freeze Top Row from the Ribbon.

- *Freeze your choice of rows and columns.* Click the cell below the row and to the right of the column you want to freeze. For example, to freeze the top two rows and column A, select cell B3. Then choose Layout ➤ Window ➤ Freeze Panes ➤ Freeze Panes from the Ribbon or Window ➤ Freeze Panes from the menu bar.

Excel displays a gray line along the gridlines of the frozen cells. Once you've applied the freeze, the frozen columns and rows don't move when you scroll down or to the right. Figure 12–20 shows a worksheet with rows 1 and 2 and column A frozen.

Figure 12–20. *Freeze the heading rows and columns to keep them in place when you scroll down or across the worksheet.*

When you no longer need the freezing, choose Layout ➤ Window ➤ Freeze Panes ➤ Unfreeze from the Ribbon or Window ➤ Unfreeze Panes to remove the freezing.

Summary

In this chapter, you learned how to create and save a workbook and start entering data in it. You came to grips with the Excel interface, and you know how to add, delete, and rearrange the worksheets in a workbook. You also learned how to select cells and ranges, not to mention essential techniques for making Excel display worksheets the way you need them—everything from splitting a window into separate parts to opening and arranging multiple windows and freezing any heading rows and columns you want to keep on-screen when you scroll.

Chapter 13

Formatting Your Worksheets

In this chapter, you'll learn how to format your worksheets so that they show the information you need and present it clearly.

We'll start by looking at how to work with rows and columns—inserting, deleting, and formatting them so that your worksheet is the right shape. I'll then show you how to format cells and ranges, how to apply conditional formatting to quickly flag values that need attention, and how to use data validation to check for invalid entries.

After that, we'll look at how to format worksheets quickly using table formatting or Excel's styles, how to add headers and footers to worksheets, and how to print worksheets and workbooks.

Lastly, you'll learn to use Excel's features for sharing workbooks with your colleagues. You can protect a workbook against unwelcome changes, and even share a workbook so that both you and your colleagues can edit it at the same time.

Working with Rows and Columns

In this section, you'll learn how to insert and delete rows, columns, and cells; change the width of columns and the height of rows; and hide rows or columns when you don't need to see them.

Inserting and Deleting Rows, Columns, and Cells

To accommodate the data in your worksheets, you'll often need to insert or delete entire columns or rows. Sometimes you may also need to delete a block of cells without deleting an entire column or row.

The easiest way to insert a column or row is to Ctrl+click or right-click the heading of the existing column or row before which you want to insert the new one and then click Insert on the context menu.

To insert more than one column or row, select the same number of columns or rows first. For example, to insert three columns before column F, drag through the headings of columns F, G, and H to select those columns; then Ctrl+click or right-click anywhere in the selected headings, and click Insert on the context menu.

You can also insert a column by selecting a cell in the column before which you want to add the new column, and then giving either of these commands:

- *Ribbon.* Choose Home ➤ Cells ➤ Insert ➤ Insert Columns.

> **NOTE:** If the Excel window isn't wide enough for the Insert button, Delete button, and Format button to appear in the Cells group, an Actions pop-up button appears instead. Click this button to display a pop-up menu with an Insert submenu, a Delete submenu, and a Format submenu. Click the appropriate menu, and then make your choice from it.

- *Menu bar.* Choose Insert ➤ Columns.

Similarly, you can insert a row by selecting a cell in the row before which you want to add the new row and then giving either of these commands:

- *Ribbon.* Choose Home ➤ Cells ➤ Insert ➤ Insert Rows.

- *Menu bar.* Choose Insert ➤ Rows.

As before, if you want to insert multiple columns or rows, select cells in the corresponding number of columns or rows first.

> **NOTE:** What the Insert button in the Cells group on the Home tab of the Ribbon inserts depends on what you've selected. Select one or more columns to make the Insert button insert columns; select one or more rows to make the Insert button insert rows; or select one or more cells to make the Insert button insert cells. If you haven't selected the appropriate item, click the Insert pop-up button rather than the main Insert button, and then choose the item you want from the pop-up menu.

To insert just some cells, follow these steps:

1. Select the range before which you want to insert the cells.

2. Choose Home ➤ Cells ➤ Insert ➤ Insert Cells to display the Insert dialog box (see Figure 13–1).

Figure 13–1. *When you insert a block of cells, click the Shift cells right option button or the Shift cells down option button in the Insert dialog box to tell Excel which way to move the existing cells.*

3. Select the Shift cells right option button to move the existing cells to the right. Select the Shift cells down option button to move the existing cells down the worksheet. You can also select the Entire row option button to insert a whole row or select the Entire column option button to insert a whole column, but it's usually easier to insert a row or column by using the methods described earlier.

4. Click the OK button to close the Insert dialog box. Excel inserts the cells.

The easiest way to delete a column or row is to Ctrl+click or right-click its heading, and then click Delete on the context menu. Alternatively, you can select the row or column and then choose Edit ➤ Delete from the menu bar or Home ➤ Cells ➤ Delete (clicking the main part of the Delete button) from the Ribbon.

Instead of selecting the column or row, you can click a cell in it, choose Home ➤ Cells ➤ Delete (clicking the Delete pop-up button), and then click Delete Columns or Delete Rows, as needed. Usually, it's easier to select the row or column first.

To delete just some cells, select them, and then choose Home ➤ Cells ➤ Delete ➤ Delete Cells. In the Delete dialog box (see Figure 13–2) that Excel displays, select the Shift cells left option button or the Shift cells up option button, as appropriate, and then click the OK button.

Figure 13–2. *When you delete a block of cells, click the Shift cells left option button or the Shift cells up option button in the Delete dialog box to tell Excel how to fill the gap in the worksheet.*

NOTE: In the Delete dialog box, you can select the Entire row option button to delete the row the selected cell is in, or select the Entire column option button to delete the column. This is useful when you realize you need to delete entire rows or columns rather than just a block of cells. Otherwise, you don't need to open the Delete dialog box to delete rows or columns.

Setting Row Height

Excel normally sets the row height automatically to accommodate the tallest character or object in the row. For example, if you type an entry in a cell, select the cell, and click the Increase Font Size button in the Font group of the Home tab a few times, then Excel automatically increases the row height so that there's enough space for the tallest characters. You can also choose Home ➤ Cells ➤ Format ➤ AutoFit Row Height to force automatic fitting if Excel doesn't set the row height automatically.

You can also set row height manually in either of these ways:

- *Drag the lower border of the row heading.* Move the mouse pointer over the lower border of the row heading so that the pointer changes to an arrow pointing up and down, and then click and drag the border up (to make the row shallower) or down (to make the row deeper).

- *Use the Row Height dialog box.* Ctrl+click or right-click the row heading, and then click Row Height on the context menu to display the Row Height dialog box (see Figure 13–3). Type the row height you want, and then click the OK button.

Figure 13–3. *Use the Row Height dialog box when you need to set a row's height precisely.*

NOTE: You can also display the Row Height dialog box by choosing Home ➤ Cells ➤ Format ➤ Row Height from the Ribbon or Format ➤ Row ➤ Height from the menu bar.

Setting Column Width

Unlike with row height, Excel doesn't automatically adjust column width as you enter data in a worksheet. But you can quickly set column width in any of these ways:

- *AutoFit a column.* Double-click the right border of the column heading. Excel automatically changes the column's width so that it's wide enough to contain the widest entry in the column.

- *AutoFit several columns.* Select cells in all the columns you want to affect, and then double-click the right border of any of the selected column headings. Excel automatically fits each column's width to suit its contents. You can also select the cells and then choose Home ➤ Cells ➤ Format ➤ AutoFormat Column Width from the Ribbon or Format ➤ Column ➤ AutoFit Selection.

TIP: AutoFit is usually the best way to resize a worksheet's columns. But if some cells have such long contents that AutoFit will create huge columns, set the column widths manually and hide parts of the longest contents. You can also wrap the text within a cell so that it occupies as many lines as it needs; you'll learn how to do this in the section "Setting Alignment" later in this chapter.

- *Resize a column by hand.* Drag the right border of the column heading as far as needed.

- *Resize a column precisely.* Ctrl+click or right-click the column heading, and then click Column Width on the context menu to display the Column Width dialog box (see Figure 13–4). Type the cell width, and then click the OK button.

Column Width

Column width: `1.74"`

Cancel   OK

Figure 13–4. *Use the Column Width dialog box when you need to set column width precisely.*

- *Resize several columns precisely.* Select the columns by dragging through their column headings or by selecting cells in each column. Ctrl+click or right-click in the selected column headings, and then click Column Width on the context menu to display the Column Width dialog box. Type the column width, and then click the OK button.

Hiding Rows and Columns

Sometimes it's helpful to hide particular columns and rows so that they're not visible in the worksheet. You may want to do this to hide sensitive data from your printouts or simply to make the part of the worksheet you're actually using fit on the screen all at once.

To hide a column or row, Ctrl+click or right-click its column heading or row heading, and then click Hide on the context menu. You can also click a cell in the row or column and choose Home ➤ Cells ➤ Format ➤ Hide Row or Home ➤ Cells ➤ Format ➤ Hide Column from the Ribbon or Format ➤ Row ➤ Hide or Format ➤ Column ➤ Hide from the menu bar.

TIP: To quickly hide the active row or selected rows, press Ctrl+9. To hide the active column or selected columns, press Ctrl+0.

To unhide a row or column, select the rows above and below it or the columns on either side of it. Then Ctrl+click or right-click the selected row headings or column headings and click Unhide on the context menu.

NOTE: You can also hide and unhide items by choosing Home ➤ Cells ➤ Format ➤ Unhide Row or Home ➤ Cells ➤ Format ➤ Unhide Column from the Ribbon or by choosing Format ➤ Row ➤ Unhide or Format ➤ Column ➤ Unhide from the menu bar.

Formatting Cells and Ranges

In Excel, you can format cells in a wide variety of ways—everything from choosing how to display the borders and background to controlling how Excel represents the text you enter in the cell. This section shows you how the most useful kinds of formatting work and how to apply them.

Each cell comes with essential formatting applied to it—the font and font size to use and usually the General number format, which you'll meet shortly. So when you create a new workbook and start entering data in it, Excel displays the data in a normal-size font.

> **TIP:** To control the font and font size Excel uses for new workbooks, choose Excel ➤ Preferences or press Cmd+, (Cmd and the comma key). Click the General icon in the Authoring area of the Excel Preferences dialog box to display the General pane. Open the Standard font menu, and click the font you want; the Body Font choice at the top of the list gives you the body font set in the workbook's template. Then choose the size in the Size pop-up menu. Click the OK button to close the Excel Preferences dialog box.

Understanding the Three Main Tools for Applying Formatting

Excel gives you three main tools for applying formatting to cells and ranges:

- *Formatting Toolbar.* If you display this toolbar (choose View ➤ Toolbars ➤ Formatting from the menu bar), you can quickly apply some of the most widely used formatting. Figure 13–5 shows the Formatting toolbar (displayed undocked so you can see it more easily) with its controls labeled.

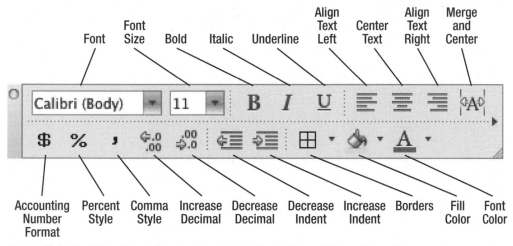

Figure 13–5. *The Formatting toolbar provides controls for applying widely used formatting.*

■ *Home tab of the Ribbon.* The Font group provides widely used font formatting; the Alignment group offers horizontal and vertical alignment, orientation, indentation, wrapping, and merging; and the Number group gives you a quick way to apply essential number formatting. Figure 13–6 shows the Font group with its controls labeled. Figure 13–7 shows the Alignment group and Number group with their controls labeled.

Figure 13–6. *You can quickly apply essential font formatting, borders, and fills from the Font group on the Home tab of the Ribbon.*

NOTE: The Increase Font Size button, Decrease Font Size button, and Borders pop-up menu appear in the Font group on the Home tab of the Ribbon only when the Excel window is wide enough to accommodate them.

Figure 13–7. *From the Alignment group on the Home tab of the Ribbon, you can set horizontal and vertical alignment, orientation, and wrapping. From the Number group, you can apply number formatting.*

- *Format Cells dialog box.* When you need to apply formatting types that don't appear on the Standard toolbar or on the Home tab of the Ribbon, open the Format Cells dialog box and work on its six tabs, which you'll meet later in this chapter. The easiest way to display the Format Cells dialog box is to Ctrl+click or right-click a cell or a selection and then click Format Cells on the context menu. You can also open the Format Cells dialog box by pressing Cmd+1 or choosing Format ➤ Cells from the menu bar.

Controlling How Data Appears by Applying Number Formatting

When you enter a number in a cell, Excel displays it according to the number formatting applied to that cell. For example, if you enter **39250** in a cell formatted with General formatting, Excel displays it as 39250. If the cell has Currency formatting, Excel displays a value such as $39,250.00 (depending on the details of the format). And if the cell has Date formatting, Excel displays a date such as 18 June 2011 (again, depending on the details of the format). In each case, the number stored in the cell remains the same—so if you change the cell's formatting to a different type, the way that Excel displays the data changes to match.

Table 13–1 explains Excel's number formats and tells you the keyboard shortcuts for applying them. You can also apply number formatting by using the buttons on the Standard toolbar, the Number Format pop-up menu and buttons in the Number group of the Home tab of the Ribbon, and the Number tab of the Format Cells dialog box (see Figure 13–8).

Figure 13–8. *Use the Number tab of the Format Cells dialog box when you need access to the full range of number formatting.*

Table 13–1. *Excel's Number Formats*

Number Format	Explanation	Examples	Keyboard Shortcut
General	Excel's default format for all cells in new worksheets. No specific format, but displays up to 11 digits per cell and uses no thousands separator. For any entry longer than 11 digits, General format uses scientific notation (see the "Scientific" entry later in this table).	1234567 Industry	Ctrl+Shift+~ (tilde)
Number	Displays the number of decimal places you choose. You can choose whether to use the thousands separator and how to display negative numbers.	1000 1,000 1,000.00	Ctrl+Shift+!
Currency	Displays the number of decimal places you choose, using the thousands separator. You can choose which currency symbol to display (for example, $) and how to display negative numbers.	$2,345.67 –$2,345.67	Ctrl+Shift+$
Accounting	Displays the number of decimal places you choose, using the thousands separator. You can choose which currency symbol to use. The symbol appears aligned at the left edge of the cell. Negative numbers appear with parentheses around them.	$ 1,000,000 $ (99.999.00)	—
Date	Displays any of a variety of date formats.	2/24/2011 Thursday, February 24, 2011	Ctrl+Shift+#
Time	Displays any of a variety of date formats.	11:59:59 PM 23:59:59	Ctrl+Shift+@
Percentage	Displays a percent sign and the number of decimal places you choose.	78.79% 200%	Ctrl+Shift+%
Fraction	Displays the number as a fraction. Fractions tend to be visually confusing, so use them only if you must—for example, for betting charts.	1/2 1 1/4	—
Scientific	Displays the number in exponential form, with E and the power to which to raise the number. You can choose how many decimal places to use.	1.2346E+08 –9.8765E+07	Ctrl+Shift+^

Number Format	Explanation	Examples	Keyboard Shortcut
Text	Displays and treats the data as text, even when it appears to be another type of data (for example, a number or date).	Champions of Breakfast 18	—
Special	Displays the data in the format you choose: Zip Code, Zip Code + 4, Phone Number, or Social Security Number.	10013 10013–8295 (212) 555-9753 722-86-8261	—
Custom	Displays the data in the custom format you choose. Excel provides dozens of custom formats, but you can also create your own formats.	[Various]	—

UNDERSTANDING HOW EXCEL STORES DATES AND TIMES

Excel stores dates as serial numbers starting from 1 (Sunday, January 1, 1900) and running way into the future. To give you a couple of points of reference, Saturday, January 1, 2011, is 40544, and Sunday, January 1, 2012, is 40909.

You can enter a date by typing the serial number (if you know it or care to work it out), but it's much easier to type a date in a conventional format, because Excel recognizes most of them. For example, if you type **1/1/2011**, Excel converts it to 40544 and displays the date in whichever format you've chosen.

Excel stores times as decimal parts of a day. For example, 40544.25 is 6 a.m. (one quarter of the way through the day) on January 1, 2011.

Older versions of Excel used the starting date January 2, 1904, by default for workbooks. Excel 2011 doesn't do this, but you can set the 1904 starting date manually if necessary (for example, if you're using an older workbook with 1904-based dates). To switch to 1904-based dates, choose Excel ➤ Preferences or press Cmd+, (Cmd and the comma key). In the Excel Preferences dialog box, click the Calculation icon in the Formulas and Lists area to display the Calculation pane. In the Workbook options box, select the Use the 1904 date system check box, and then click the OK button.

Setting the Workbook's Overall Look by Applying a Theme

To control the overall look of a workbook, apply a suitable theme to it by choosing Home ➤ Themes ➤ Themes and then clicking the them you want on the Themes panel

The theme applies a set of colors and a pair of fonts to the workbook. After applying the theme, you can change the colors or fonts by using the Colors pop-up menu or the Fonts pop-up menu in the Themes group on the Home tab of the Ribbon.

Setting Alignment

You can quickly align the contents of cells by using the buttons in the Alignment group on the Home tab of the Ribbon or the controls on the Alignment tab of the Format Cells dialog box (see Figure 13–9):

- *Horizontal alignment.* You can align the text Left, Center, Right, or Justify; apply General alignment, which depends on the data type (left for text, right for numbers); choose Center Across Selection to center the text across multiple cells; or choose Distributed (Indent) to distribute the text across the cell (using wider spaces between words).

NOTE: The Fill horizontal alignment fills the cell with the character you specify.

Figure 13–9. *The Alignment tab of the Format Cells dialog box lets you rotate text to precise angles when needed.*

- *Vertical alignment.* You can align text Top, Center, Bottom, or Justify. You can also choose Distributed to distribute the text vertically, which can be useful when you rotate the text so that it runs vertically.

- *Rotate text.* Use the Orientation box on the Alignment tab of the Format Cells dialog box or the Orientation pop-up menu in the Alignment group.

- *Indentation.* You can indent the text as far as is needed.

- *Wrap.* You can wrap the text to make a long entry appear on several lines in a cell rather than disappear where the next cell's contents start. The disadvantage to wrapping text is that the row height increases automatically to accommodate the wrapped text. (If you set a specific row height that's less than the height needed to display all the wrapped text, only the text that fits appears in the cell.)

- *Shrink to fit.* Select this check box on the Alignment tab of the Format Cells dialog box to shrink the text so that it fits in the cell. Shrinking works well when the text is only a bit too big for the cell. If the text is much too big, shrinking makes it unreadably small.

- *Merge cells.* Use the Merge & Center pop-up menu in the Alignment group to merge selected cells together into a single cell. You can also center an entry across a merged cell. In the Format Cells dialog box, you can merge cells by selecting the Merge cells check box on the Alignment tab.

Choosing Font Formatting

You can quickly format the contents of a cell (or the selected part of a cell's contents) by using the controls on the Standard toolbar, the controls in the Font group on the Home tab, or the Font tab of the Format Cells dialog box (see Figure 13–10).

Figure 13–10. *The Font tab of the Format Cells dialog box gives you a full range of font formatting for the current selection.*

Applying Borders and Fills

To apply borders to a cell, open the Borders pop-up menu in the Font group on the Home tab of the Ribbon, and then click the border type you want (see Figure 13–11).

Figure 13–11. *You can quickly apply borders from the Borders pop-up menu in the Font group of the Home tab (left).*

TIP: If you have displayed the Formatting toolbar, you can apply a border by clicking its Borders pop-up button and then clicking the border type on the panel. After choosing a border type this way, you can apply it quickly to another cell by clicking the main part of the Borders button rather than the pop-up button. You can also tear off the Borders palette to keep it visible so that you don't have to keep opening it. Click the Borders pop-up button, then click the double line at the top of the palette and drag it off the toolbar. When you have finished using the torn-off palette, click the Close button at the left end of its title bar.

For more border options, click the Border Options item at the bottom of the Borders pop-up menu to display the Border tab of the Format Cells dialog box (see Figure 13–12). You can also choose Format ➤ Cells from the menu bar (or press Cmd+1) and then click the Border tab. Use the controls on the Border tab to set up the borders you want, and then click the OK button.

Figure 13–12. *Use the Border tab of the Format Cells dialog box when you need to change the line style or color of borders.*

To apply a fill, use the Fill Colors pop-up menu in the Font group on the Home tab of the Ribbon or the Fill Colors pop-up menu on the Formatting toolbar, or work on the Fill tab of the Format Cells dialog box.

Applying Protection to Cells

The Protection tab of the Format Cells dialog box contains only two controls:

- *Locked.* Select this check box to lock a cell against changes.

- *Hidden.* Select this check box to hide the formula in a cell (the formula's result remains visible).

After selecting either of these check boxes, you must protect the worksheet before the locking or hiding takes effect. You'll learn how to protect a worksheet in the section "Protecting a Worksheet," later in this chapter.

Applying Conditional Formatting to Identify Particular Values

In many worksheets, it's useful to be able to monitor the values in the cells and to pick out values that stand out in particular ways. For example, you may want to see which ten products are bringing in the most revenue, or you may need an easy way to make unusually high values or unusually low values stand out from the others.

To monitor the values in a cell or a range, you can apply *conditional formatting*—formatting that Excel displays only when the condition is met. For example, if you're monitoring temperatures in Fahrenheit, you could apply conditional formatting to highlight low temperatures (say, below 20F) and high temperatures (say, above 100F). Temperatures in the normal range would not receive any conditional formatting.

Understanding Excel's Preset Types of Conditional Formatting

Excel provides five kinds of preset conditional formatting, which you can apply from the Conditional Formatting panel in the Format group of the Home tab of the Ribbon. Figure 13–13 shows the Conditional Formatting panel with the Icon Sets panel displayed.

Figure 13–13. *The Conditional Formatting panel includes sets of icons you can apply to indicate data trends.*

- *Highlight Cells Rules.* This panel gives you an easy way to set up conditional formatting using Greater Than, Less Than, Between, Equal To, Text that Contains, A Date Occurring, or Duplicate Values criteria.

- *Top/Bottom Rules.* This panel lets you apply conditional formatting for Top 10 Items, Top 10 %, Bottom 10 Items, Bottom 10 %, Above Average, and Below Average criteria.

- *Data Bars.* This panel enables you to apply different gradient fills and solid fills.

- *Color Scales.* This panel lets you set up color scales using two or three colors—for example, using green, amber, and red to indicate different levels of risk associated with activities.

- *Icon Sets.* This panel provides different sets of icons, such as directional arrows (up, sideways, down) or a checkmark–exclamation point–cross set, for indicating data trends.

Applying a Preset Form of Conditional Formatting

To apply one of these types of conditional formatting, open the Conditional Formatting panel, display the appropriate panel from it, click the type of formatting, and then specify the details. For example:

1. Select the cell or range you want to affect.

2. Choose Home ➤ Format ➤ Conditional Formatting ➤ Highlight Cells Rules ➤ Greater Than to display the New Formatting Rule dialog box (see Figure 13–14).

Figure 13–14. *Excel's preset conditional formatting types make it easy to apply conditional formatting to cells quickly.*

3. In the Style pop-up menu, you can choose a different style for the conditional formatting if you want. Excel automatically selects the style that suits the type of conditional formatting you chose—in the example, Classic.

4. The Comparison pop-up menu below the Style pop-up menu shows the comparison for the type of conditional formatting—in the example, Format only cells that contain. You can choose a different comparison if necessary, but you won't normally need to do so.

5. On the next line of controls, set up the comparison. In the example, the first pop-up menu is set to Cell value, and the second pop-up menu is set to "greater than" because this is a Greater Than rule. In the third box, you enter the comparison. You can either type in the value or collapse the dialog box, click the cell that contains the value, and then restore the dialog box.

6. In the Format with pop-up menu, choose the formatting you want. Excel provides various canned options, but you can also create custom formatting by clicking the custom format item at the bottom of the list and working in the Format Cells dialog box that opens. (This is a cut-down version of the Format Cells dialog box you met earlier in the chapter—it has only the Font tab, the Border tab, and the Fill tab.)

7. Click the OK button to close the New Formatting Rule dialog box. Excel applies the conditional formatting.

NOTE: If none of the preset conditional formatting rules meets your needs, you can define conditional formatting rules of your own. To do so, choose Home ➤ Format ➤ Conditional Formatting ➤ New Rule, and then work in the New Formatting Rule dialog box that opens.

Using Data Validation to Check for Invalid Entries

When you're entering large amounts of data, it's easy to type an incorrect value by mistake. To help avoid errors in your data, you can use Excel's data validation feature to check entries automatically and flag those that may be wrong. For example, if every entry in a range of cells should be between 250 and 1000 (inclusive), you can validate the data to flag any entry that is not in that range.

CAUTION: Data validation works only when the user types in a value. If the user pastes in a value, Excel doesn't check it.

To apply validation to cells, follow these steps:

1. Click the cell or select the range you want to validate.

2. Choose Data ➤ Tools ➤ Validate (clicking the main part of the Validate button) from the Ribbon or Data ➤ Validation from the menu bar to display the Data Validation dialog box.

3. Click the Settings tab (shown in Figure 13–15 with settings chosen) to bring it to the front of the dialog box if it's not already there.

Figure 13–15. *Set up the validation criteria on the Settings tab of the Data Validation dialog box. The controls that appear depend on the data type you choose in the Allow pop-up menu.*

4.   In the Allow pop-up menu, choose the type of data you want to validate, and then use the controls that appear to set the details.

   ■   *Any value.* Select this item when you want to turn off validation for the cell or range. Even with this setting, you can use the Input Message tab (discussed later in this list) to display a message about the cell or range.

TIP: When setting the criteria for your data validation, you can either type in a value or click the Collapse Dialog button and then click the cell that contains the value. Using a value in a cell enables you to change the value easily without editing the conditional formatting.

   ■   *Whole number.* Select this item to set criteria for a whole number—one with no decimal places. For example, in the Data pop-up menu, click the between item, and then set the minimum value in the Minimum box and the maximum value in the Maximum box.

   ■   *Decimal.* Select this item to set criteria for a number with decimal places. For example, in the Data pop-up menu, click the greater than or equal to item, and then set the minimum value in the Minimum box.

- *List.* Select this item when you need to restrict the cell to a list of valid entries that you specify. You can enter this list in two ways: either type it in the Source box, separating each entry with a comma, or click the Collapse Dialog button at the right end of the Source box, select the worksheet range that contains the data, and then click the Collapse Dialog button again to restore the dialog box. Select the In-cell drop-down check box to make Excel display a pop-up menu with the valid entries in the cell so that the user can enter them easily.

- *Date.* Select this item to set criteria for a date. For example, click the greater than item in the Data pop-up menu, and then enter the start date in the Start date box.

- *Time.* Select this item to set criteria for a time. For example, click the not between item in the Data pop-up menu, and then enter the start time in the Start time box and the end time in the End time box.

- *Text length.* Select this item to set criteria for a text entry or formula. For example, click the less than or equal to item in the Data pop-up menu, and then enter the maximum length in the Maximum box.

- *Custom.* Select this item when you need to enter a formula that returns a logical value of TRUE or FALSE.

5. Select the Ignore blank check box if you want to let the user leave the cell blank. Clear this check box to make the user fill in the cell with valid data.

6. Click the Input Message tab to display it. The left screen in Figure 13–16 shows the Input Message tab with settings chosen.

Figure 13–16. *On the Input Message tab of the Data Validation dialog box (left), enter the message you want the user to see when the cell is active (right).*

7. To display a message when the user makes the cell active, select the Show input message when cell is selected check box. Type the title in the Title box and the message in the Input message box. The right screen in Figure 13–16 shows how the message appears.

8. Click the Error Alert tab to bring it to the front. The left screen in Figure 13–17 shows the Error Alert tab with settings chosen; the right screen in Figure 13–17 shows how the error message appears.

Figure 13–17. *On the Error Alert tab of the Data Validation dialog box (left), set up the error to display when the user enters invalid data in the cell (right).*

9. Select the Show error alert after invalid data is entered check box if you want Excel to display an error message box when the user enters invalid data. Usually, this is helpful.

10. In the Style pop-up menu, choose the icon type for the behavior you want:

    ■   *Stop.* The error dialog box has a Retry button and a Cancel button. If the user clicks the Retry button, Excel selects the entry that failed validation so that the user can change it. If the user clicks the Cancel button, Excel restores the cell's previous entry.

> **NOTE:** On Windows, the Stop, Warning, and Information settings in the Style pop-up menu make the error message box show the different icons that appear under the Style pop-up menu when you make your choice. For example, the Stop style shows the red octagon bearing a white exclamation point that you see on the left in Figure 13–17. On Mac OS X, the error message box displays the same Excel icon (shown on the right in Figure 13–17) for each style, but with different command buttons and behavior.

    ■   *Warning.* The error dialog box ends with a "Continue?" prompt after your message and has a Yes button, a No button, and a Cancel button. If the user clicks the Yes button, Excel accepts the value, even though it has failed validation. If the user clicks the No button, Excel selects the entry that failed validation so that the user can change it. If the user clicks the Cancel button, Excel restores the cell's previous entry.

    ■   *Information.* The error dialog box has an OK button and a Cancel button. If the user click the OK button, Excel accepts the value, even though it has failed validation. If the user clicks the Cancel button, Excel restores the cell's previous entry.

> **TIP:** To force the user to enter valid data, choose the Stop item in the Style pop-up menu on the Error Alert tab of the Data Validation dialog box. The Warning style and the Information style can be useful for when you're providing gentler guidance on how to use the worksheet and the conformity of the data is less critical.

11. Enter the title and error message for the message box.

12. Click the OK button to close the Data Validation dialog box. Excel applies the validation.

Formatting Quickly with Table Formatting and Styles

To save you time with formatting, Excel provides preset formatting that you can apply to a table to give it an overall look. And to save you the effort of applying many different types of formatting over and over again to different cells, Excel includes styles, collections of formatting that you can apply all at once.

Formatting with Table Formatting

When you need to format a table quickly, see if Excel's preset table formatting will do the trick. Select the table, and then choose Tables ➤ Table Styles ➤ Table Styles, and then click the style you want.

NOTE: See Chapter 16 for instructions on creating and working with Excel tables.

Formatting with Styles

As you've seen earlier in this chapter, you can give any cell exactly the formatting you want by using the controls in the Font group, Alignment group, and Number group of the Home tab of the Ribbon, by using the controls on the Formatting toolbar, or by opening the Format Cells dialog box and working on its six tabs. But applying formatting one aspect at a time—font, font size, alignment, and so on—takes ages, and it's easy to apply formatting inconsistently.

To save time and ensure your formatting is consistent, you can use Excel's styles. If you're familiar with Word's styles (discussed in Chapter 7), you'll find Excel's styles a snap, because they work in much the same way.

Each style is a collection of formatting that you can apply to one or more cells. The style contains six types of formatting, one for each tab of the Format Cells dialog box:

- *Number.* For example, General, Currency, or Percentage.

- *Alignment.* Horizontal alignment (for example, General, Center, or Justify), vertical alignment (for example, Top, Center, or Bottom), and any trimmings (such as wrapping the text to the window).

- *Font.* The font, font size, font color, and so on.

- *Border.* Any borders you've applied to the style, or No Borders if it has no borders.

- *Fill.* Any fill you've applied to the style, or No Shading if it's plain.

- *Protection.* Locked, Hidden, both, or No Protection.

Most Excel templates contain plenty of styles to get you started, but you can create your own custom styles as well if you need to.

Meeting Excel's Styles

To see which styles are available in a workbook, choose Home ➤ Format ➤ Styles and look at the Cell Styles panel (see Figure 13–18). This panel lists the styles in the following categories:

- *Custom.* This category appears only when you have created one or more custom styles in the workbook.

Figure 13–18. *The Styles panel displays your custom styles at the top and Excel's built-in styles in different categories.*

- *Comparisons.* This category has Good, Bad, and Neutral styles that you can use to apply color coding to cells. Here is also where you will find the Normal style that Excel applies to any cell that doesn't have another style.

- *Data and Model.* This category contains the Calculation, Check Cell, Explanatory, Followed Hyperlink, Hyperlink, Input, Linked Cell, Note, Output, and Warning Text styles. Most of these styles are used for data modeling. Excel automatically applies the Hyperlink style to cells containing hyperlinks you have not clicked yet, changing their style to Followed Hyperlink once you have clicked them.

NOTE: The Hyperlink style appears in the Data and Model category in the Styles panel only if the workbook contains hyperlinks. Similarly, the Followed Hyperlink style appears only if the workbook contains hyperlinks you've followed.

- *Titles and Headings.* This category contains four styles for descending levels of headings (Heading 1, Heading 2, Heading 3, and Heading 4), the Title style for giving a worksheet a title, and the Total style for easily formatting cells that contain totals.

- *Themed Cell Styles.* This category contains six Accent styles (Accent 1 through Accent 6) featuring six of the theme colors, with four degrees of shading for each. This category appears only if the workbook's template contains themed cell styles.

Applying a Style

To apply a style, choose Home ➤ Format ➤ Styles, and then click the style on the Styles panel. You can also apply the various Number styles (such as the Currency styles, the Percent style, and the Comma style) from the Number group on the Home tab of the Ribbon.

Creating Custom Styles

If none of Excel's styles meets your needs, you can create your own styles. To create a style, follow these steps:

1. Format a cell with the formatting you want the style to have.

TIP: To jump-start your formatting, apply the existing style that's nearest to the look and formatting you want. Then change the formatting so that it looks the way you want.

2. Select the cell you've formatted.

3. Choose Home ➤ Format ➤ Styles ➤ New Cell Style to display the New Cell Style dialog box (shown in Figure 13–19 with settings chosen).

Figure 13–19. *In the New Style Style dialog box, you can quickly create a new style based on the formatting of the selected cell. You can change the formatting as needed by clicking the Format button and working in the Format Cells dialog box.*

4. In the Style name box, type the name you want to give the style.

5. In the "The selected style has formatting for the following properties" area, clear the check boxes for any formatting the cell has that you want to omit from the style. For example, clear the Protection check box to leave out the Locked or Hidden formatting.

> **NOTE:** If you need to alter the formatting, click the Format button to display the Format Cells dialog box. Make the changes needed, and then click the OK button to return to the New Cell Style dialog box.

6. Click the OK button to close the New Cell Style dialog box and create the style. Excel adds the style to the Custom area at the top of the Styles panel.

> **TIP:** Instead of creating a new style, you can modify one of the built-in styles. Choose Home ➤ Format ➤ Styles to display the Styles panel, Ctrl+click or right-click the style you want to change, and then click the Modify item on the context menu. In the Modify Cell Style dialog box, select or clear the check boxes in the "The selected style has formatting for the following properties" area, or click the Format button to display the Format Cells dialog box, and make the changes you need. When you have finished, click the OK button to return to the Modify Cell Style dialog box, and then click the OK button.

Copying Styles from One Workbook to Another

If you have styles in one workbook that you want to use in another workbook, you can copy the styles across. Excel calls this *importing styles*. When you import the styles, the destination workbook receives all the styles from the source workbook—you can't pick and choose (but see the nearby Tip).

To import the styles, follow these steps:

1.   Open the source workbook (the workbook that contains the styles) and the destination workbook.

2.   Switch to the destination workbook by clicking in it.

3.   Choose Home ➤ Format ➤ Styles ➤ Import Cell Styles to display the Import Cell Styles dialog box (see Figure 13–20).

Figure 13–20. *Use the Import Cell Styles dialog box to copy all the styles from one workbook into another workbook.*

4.   In the Copy cell styles from an open workbook list box, click the source workbook.

5.   Click the OK button to close the import Cell Styles dialog box. Excel copies the styles into the destination workbook, and you can then start using them.

> **TIP:** If you need to copy just one style from one workbook to another, apply that style to a cell. Then copy that cell and switch back to the destination workbook. Ctrl+click or right-click a cell you don't mind changing, and then click Paste Special to display the Paste Special dialog box. In the Paste area, select the Formats option button, and then click the OK button. Excel pastes the style onto the cell, and you can then use the style in the workbook.

Deleting Styles You Don't Need

If you no longer need a style, you can delete it. Choose Home ➤ Format ➤ Styles, Ctrl+click or right-click the style in the Cell Styles panel, and then click Delete on the context menu.

> **NOTE:** Excel prevents you from deleting the Normal style.

Adding Headers and Footers to Your Worksheets

Before printing a worksheet or creating a PDF file from it, you'll probably want to add headers, footers, or both to identify the pages. Excel gives each worksheet a separate header and footer, which you can fill with either preset text or custom text. Each header and footer area consists of a left section, a center section, and a right section, so you can easily add several different pieces of information.

You can add information to headers and footers either by using the Header/Footer tab of the Page Setup dialog box or by switching to Page Layout view and working directly in the header and footer areas. We'll start with the Page Setup dialog box, which is the easiest way of adding canned text.

Adding Headers and Footers Using the Page Setup Dialog Box

To add headers and footers to the active worksheet using the Page Setup dialog box, follow these steps:

1. Choose Layout ➤ Page Setup ➤ Header & Footer from the Ribbon or View ➤ Header and Footer from the menu bar to display the Header/Footer tab of the Page Setup dialog box. Figure 13–21 shown the Header/Footer tab of the Page Setup dialog box with a preset header chosen.

Figure 13–21. *From the Header/Footer tab of the Page Setup dialog box, you can quickly add either preset headers and footers or custom headers and footers to the active worksheet.*

2. If you want to add a preset header or footer, open the Header pop-up menu or the Footer pop-up menu, and click the preset. Each pop-up menu has various choices, ranging from just the page number to your name, the page number, and the date. The preset you've chosen appears in the preview box.

3. If you want to create a custom header or footer, click the Customize Header button to display the Header dialog box (see Figure 13–22) or the Customize Footer button to display the Footer dialog box (which is the same apart from the name).

Format text   Insert Page Number   Insert Number of Pages   Insert Date   Insert Time   Insert File Path   Insert File Name   Insert Sheet Name   Insert Picture   Format Pixture

Header

To insert the Page Number, Number of Pages, Date, Time, File Path, File Name, or Sheet Name, click the section you want, and then click the button for the item you want to insert.

To insert a picture, click the Insert Picture button.

To format text, select the text, and then click the Format Text button.

To format a picture, click the section that contains the picture, and then click the Format Picture button.

[OK]

[Cancel]

Left section:

&[Date] &[Time]

Center section:

Page &[Page]

Right section:

General Data 2.xlsx

Figure 13–22. *Use the Header dialog box or Footer dialog box to enter the text, field codes, or pictures you want in the left section, center section, and right section of the header or footer.*

4. Click in the Left section box, and then set up the header or footer you need:

    ■ Click a button on the toolbar in the Header dialog box or Footer dialog box to insert a field code (such as &[Date] for the date), a piece of information (such as the sheet name), or a picture.

    ■ Type in any text needed. (You can also type in field codes if you know them—but using the buttons is usually easier.)

    ■ Format the text as needed by selecting it, clicking the Format Text button, and then working in the Font dialog box.

5. Click in the Center section box, and then enter the information needed, using the same techniques as in step 4.

6. Click in the Right section box, and then enter the information needed.

7. Click the OK button to close the Header dialog box or the Footer dialog box. Excel returns you to the Page Setup dialog box, where the Header preview box or the Footer preview box shows the header or footer you just created.

NOTE: From the Header/Footer tab of the Page Setup dialog box, you can click the Options button to display a different Page Setup dialog box that you use for setting the paper size and orientation.

8. When you've finished creating headers and footers, click the OK button to close the Page Setup dialog box.

Adding Headers and Footers Directly on the Worksheet

Instead of using the Page Setup dialog box as described in the previous section, you can add or edit headers and footers directly on the worksheet. To do so, follow these steps:

1. If the worksheet is in Normal view, switch to Page Layout view by clicking the Page Layout View button at the left end of the status bar or choosing View ➤ Page Layout from the menu bar.

2. Scroll the page so that you can see the header area or footer area you want to edit.

3. Move the mouse pointer over the header area or footer area so that Excel displays a gray box around it and shows the prompt "Double-click to add header" (see Figure 13–23) or "Double-click to add footer."

Figure 13–23. *In Page Layout view, move the mouse pointer over the header area or footer area, and then double-click to open the area for editing.*

4. Double-click to open the header area or footer area for editing. Figure 13–24 shows the header area open and editing underway.

Figure 13–24. *When you open the header area or footer area for editing, Excel displays a toolbar of commands for creating headers and footers..*

5.　Click in the area you want to change, and then add the header or footer by following these techniques:

■　Click a button on the toolbar to insert a field code (such as &[Date] for the date), a piece of information (such as the sheet name), or a picture.

■　Type in any text needed.

■　Format the text as needed by selecting it, clicking the Format Text button, and then working in the Font dialog box.

6.　When you have finished creating or editing the header or footer, click the Close button on the toolbar to close the header or footer. Excel returns you to the worksheet.

Printing Your Excel Worksheets and Workbooks

To print from Excel, you use the Print dialog box, as with the other applications. But before you print, you need to tell Excel which part of the workbook to print. You may also want to check the page setup to make sure the page breaks fall where you want them to fall.

Telling Excel Which Part of the Worksheet to Print

As you learned earlier in this chapter, each worksheet contains billions of cells, so normally you don't want to print the whole of the worksheet—you want to print only the range of cells you've used, or perhaps only a small subset of that range. So when you're printing, the first thing to do is tell Excel which part of the worksheet you want to print. Excel calls this setting the print area. You can set a separate print area for each worksheet.

> **CAUTION:** Until you set the print area, Excel assumes you want to print all the cells you've used on the worksheet—even if there are huge amounts of blank space between them. So, it's a good idea always to set the print area before printing.

To set the print area, follow these steps:

1. Click the worksheet whose print area you want to set.

2. Select the range of cells you want to print.

3. Choose File ➤ Print Area ➤ Set Print Area. Excel displays a dotted blue line around the print area to indicate that it is set.

4. If you need to add a new area to the existing print area, select the range of cells you want to add, and then choose File ➤ Print Area ➤ Add to Print Area.

> **NOTE:** When you create a print area that consists of multiple ranges of cells, the ranges don't need to be contiguous. Excel prints each separate range on a separate page.

If you need to change the print area altogether, select a new range of cells, and then give the File ➤ Print Area ➤ Set Print Area command again.

If you need to clear the print area so that the worksheet has no print area set, click the worksheet, and then choose File ➤ Print Area ➤ Clear Print Area.

Checking the Page Layout and Where the Page Breaks Fall

After setting the print area, check the page layout of the worksheet and adjust it as needed. Follow these steps:

1. Switch to Page Layout view by clicking the Page Layout View button at the left end of the status bar or choosing View ➤ Page Layout.

2. Click the Layout tab of the Ribbon to show its controls. Figure 13–25 shows a worksheet in Page Layout view with the Layout tab displayed.

Figure 13–25. *To see a worksheet's pages laid out, switch to Page Layout view. You can then use the controls on the Layout tab of the Ribbon to refine the layout.*

3. Use the controls in the Page Setup group to change the page setup as needed:

    ■ *Change the margins.* Open the Margins pop-up menu, and then click Normal, Wide, or Narrow. For greater control, click Custom Margins, work on the Margins tab of the Page Setup dialog box, and then click the OK button.

    ■ *Change the orientation.* Open the Orientation pop-up menu, and then click Portrait or Landscape.

    ■ *Change the paper size.* Open the Size pop-up menu, and then click the paper size.

    ■ *Insert a page break.* Click the column before which you want to insert a manual page break. Open the Breaks pop-up menu, and then click Insert Page Break.

NOTE: If you put a page break in the wrong place, click the column after it, and then choose Layout ➤ Page Setup ➤ Breaks ➤ Remove Page Break from the Ribbon. To restore all page breaks to where Excel had placed them, choose Layout ➤ Page Setup ➤ Breaks ➤ Reset All Page Breaks.

When you have finished laying out the pages, it's a good idea to save the workbook—for example, click the Save button on the Standard toolbar, or press Cmd+S—to store the print settings.

Printing a Worksheet or Workbook

After you've set the print area for each worksheet you want to print, you can print a worksheet or workbook like this:

1. If you want to print anything less than a whole workbook, choose what you want to print:

   - *Print a worksheet.* Make that worksheet active. For example, click its worksheet tab.

   - *Print multiple worksheets.* Make all those worksheets active by selecting their worksheet tabs.

   - Selection of cells. Select the cells.

2. Choose File ➤ Print or press Cmd+P to display the Print dialog box. If the Print dialog box opens at its smaller size, click the down-arrow button to the right of the Printer pop-up menu to expand the dialog box to its larger size.

3. Make sure the Copies & Pages item is selected in the pop-up menu under the Presets pop-up menu.

4. In the left column, click Print to display the Print pane.

5. In the Print What area, choose what to print:

   - *Selection.* Select this option button to print only the cells you've selected. This option is useful for printing smaller amounts without resetting the print area.

   - *Active Sheets.* Select this option button to print the active worksheet (if you've selected only one) or active worksheets (if you selected more than one).

   - *Entire Workbook.* Select this option button to print every worksheet in the workbook. Normally, you'll use this option only for small workbooks.

6. Check that the preview of the printout looks right. If you need to change the scaling to make the printout fit the paper better, select the Scaling check box, and then set the number of pages in the Fit to *N* page(s) wide box and the by *N* page(s) tall box. For example, you might choose Fit to 1 page(s) wide by 2 page(s) tall.

7. Click the Print button to print the worksheets.

Sharing Your Workbooks with Your Colleagues

You may create some workbooks on your own, but for others, you'll probably need to work with colleagues to collect, enter, and analyze data. You can either share a workbook on the network so that one person can work on it at a time or turn on Excel's sharing features that enable you and your colleagues to work on the workbook at the same time.

Before sharing a workbook, you may choose to protect it with a password or to allow your colleagues to make only some types of changes to it.

Protecting a Workbook or Some of Its Worksheets

Before sharing a workbook with your colleagues for editing individually on a network, you may want to restrict the changes your colleagues can make in the workbook or on some of its worksheets. Excel calls this *protecting* the workbook or worksheets.

Protecting a Workbook

To protect a workbook, follow these steps:

1. Choose Review ➤ Protection ➤ Workbook from the Ribbon or Tools ➤ Protection ➤ Workbook from the menu bar to display the dialog box shown in Figure 13–26.

Figure 13–26. *When protecting a workbook, you'll normally want to protect the structure but not the windows.*

2. Select the Structure check box to prevent your colleagues from inserting, deleting, or otherwise changing whole worksheets.

3. Select the Windows check box only if you need to prevent your colleagues from changing the number or sizes of windows that you're using for the workbook. Normally, you don't need to do this if your colleagues will work conventionally in the workbook.

4. Type a password in the Password text box and in the Verify text box.

5. Click the OK button to close the dialog box.

6. Save the workbook. For example, click the Save button on the Standard toolbar or press Cmd+S.

NOTE: To unprotect a workbook, choose Review ➤ Protection ➤ Workbook. Excel displays a dialog box prompting you for the password. Type it, and then click the OK button. Save the changes to the workbook.

Protecting a Worksheet

When you need to limit the changes your colleagues can make to a particular worksheet, apply protection to it. Follow these steps:

1. Click the worksheet to activate it.

2. Choose Review ➤ Protection ➤ Sheet to display the Protect the sheet and contents of locked cells dialog box (shown in Figure 13–27 with settings chosen).

Figure 13–27. *Protect a worksheet when you need to prevent your colleagues from making specific types of changes to it.*

3. Type a password in the Password text box and the Verify text box.

4. In the Allow users of this sheet to box, select each check box for actions you want your colleagues to be able to take. Clear each other check box.

5. Click the OK button. Excel closes the dialog box and applies the protection

6. Save the workbook. For example, press Cmd+S or click the Save button on the Standard toolbar.

Sharing a Workbook So That Your Colleagues Can Edit It

When you need to be able to share a workbook with your colleagues, follow these steps:

1. Open the workbook.

2. Choose Review ➤ Share ➤ Share Workbook ➤ Share Workbook to display the Share Workbook dialog box. The left screen in Figure 13–28 shows the Editing tab of the Share Workbook dialog box, which is where you start the sharing process.

Figure 13–28. *On the Editing tab (left) of the Share Workbook dialog box, select the Allow changes by more than one user at the same time check box. You can then choose options on the Advanced tab (right).*

3. Select the Allow changes by more than one user at the same time check box on the Editing tab.

4. Check the Who has this workbook open now list box. It should show only your name and should include the word *Exclusive* to indicate that you've got sole access to the workbook.

5. Click the Advanced tab to display its contents (shown on the right in Figure 13–28).

6. In the Track Changes area, choose how long to keep the change history for the workbook:

   - Normally, you'll want to select the Keep change history for option button and set the number of days in the days box.

   - The default setting is 30 days, but if you develop your workbooks quickly, you may want to reduce the interval to 7 days or 14 days to prevent Excel from keeping large amounts of history you don't need.

   - The alternative is to select the Don't keep change history option button, but usually it's best to keep change history so that you can unravel any mysterious changes.

7. In the Update changes area, choose when to update the changes to the workbook:

   - The default setting is the When file is saved option button, which generally works pretty well.

   - The alternative is to select the Automatically every option button and set the number of minutes in the minutes box. The default setting is 15 minutes; if you work fast, you may want to shorten the interval to 5 or 10 minutes.

   - If you select the Automatically every option button, you can choose between the Save my changes and see others' changes option button (usually the better choice) and the Just see other users' changes option button.

8. In the Conflicting change between users area, choose how to handle conflicting changes to the workbook. Normally, you'll want to select the Ask me which changes win option button so that you can decide which of the conflicting changes to keep. The alternative is to select the option button called The changes being saved win, which tells Excel to overwrite the conflicting changes with the latest changes.

9. In the Include in personal view area, select the Print settings check box if you want to include print settings in your view of the workbook. Select the Filter settings check box if you want to include filter settings. (See Chapter 16 for instructions on filtering an Excel database table.)

10. Click the OK button to close the Share Workbook dialog box. Excel then displays a dialog box telling you that it will save the workbook.

11. Click the OK button. Excel sets up the sharing and adds "[Shared]" to the workbook's title bar so that you can easily see it's shared.

Working in a Shared Workbook

Once you've shared a workbook or someone else has shared it, you can perform basic editing in it much as normal. You can enter data and formulas in cells or edit their existing contents, format cells, and use both drag and drop and cut, copy, and paste. You can also insert rows, columns, and even whole worksheets.

Beyond these basics, Excel prevents you from making changes that may cause problems with the sharing. These are the main restrictions:

- *Apply conditional formatting.* If your workbook needs conditional formatting, apply it before sharing the workbook.

- *Insert objects.* You can't insert pictures, SmartArt, charts, hyperlinks, or various other objects.

- *Insert or delete blocks of cells.* You can insert or delete a whole row or column, but you can't insert or delete a block of cells. You also can't merge cells together.

- *Delete a worksheet.* You can't delete a worksheet from the shared workbook.

- *Protect a sheet with a password.* Any protection you've applied before sharing the workbook remains in force, but you can't apply protection to a sheet in a shared workbook.

- *Outline the workbook.* Excel's advanced capabilities include creating a collapsible outline from a worksheet. (This book does not cover outlining.) You can't create an outline in a shared workbook.

Resolving Conflicts in a Shared Workbook

If you chose the Ask me which changes win option button when sharing the workbook, Excel prompts you to deal with conflicts that arise between the changes you're saving and the changes that your colleagues have already saved. The Resolve Conflicts dialog box (see Figure 13–29) takes you through each of the changes in turn, showing the change you made and the conflicting change.

Figure 13–29. *When you and another user have changed the same cells, the Resolve Conflicts dialog box walks you through each change in turn. You can accept all your changes, all your colleagues' changes, or some of each.*

For each change, you can click the Accept Mine button to accept your change or click the Accept Other button to accept your colleague's change. To clear all the changes at once, click the Accept All Mine button or the Accept All Others button. Excel closes the Resolve Conflicts dialog box automatically when you've finished reviewing the conflicts.

Summary

In this chapter, you learned how to apply all Excel's most useful types of formatting to a worksheet. You know how to manipulate the worksheet's rows and columns to make it fit your data, how to format cells and ranges, and how to save time and worry by using conditional formatting and data validation.

You also went through how to format quickly with table formatting and styles, how to give your worksheets the headers and footers that printouts need, and how to use page breaks to divide a spreadsheet across pages so that they come out right when you print.

Finally, you learned to protect worksheets and workbooks against changes, and you know how to share your worksheets with colleagues—and how to resolve the conflicts that often occur.

In the next chapter, I'll show you how to turn your data into powerful and persuasive charts. Turn the page when you're ready.

Creat...
and P... ...rts

In this chapter, yo... ...sent your data clearly and persuasively. ... ...e charts that fit inside individual cells.

We'll start by goin... ...rent ways you can place them in you... ...nd which types of charts you can cr... ...ng in detail at how you create a chart fro... ...n give it the look it needs—everythin... ...tting components for impact.

After that, I'll sho... ... by either pasting it onto an existing ... ...it. Finally, we'll look at sparklines—wh... ...ke them look them way you want the...

Learning t... ...el

Before you start ... ...place charts in your workbooks, what ... ...d what they show, and the many differer...

Barnes & Noble Booksellers #2804
7325 N. LaCholla Blvd. Ste 100
Tucson, AZ 85741
520-742-6402

TR:2804 REG:005 TRN:5067 CSHR:Dave D

BARNES & NOBLE MEMBER   EXP: 11/30/2011

earn Office 2011 for Ma
9781430233336   T1
(1 @ 39.99) Member Card 10% (4.00)
(1 @ 35.99)   35.99

Subtotal   35.99
Sales Tax T1 (7.099%)   2.55
TOTAL   38.54
VISA   38.54
Card#: XXXXXXXXXXXX2959
Expdate: XX/XX
Auth: 154127
Entry Method: Swiped
MEMBER SAVINGS   4.00

Thanks for shopping at
Barnes & Noble

101.23B   02/03/2011 09:42AM

CUSTOMER COPY

Understanding Embedded Charts and Chart Sheets

In Excel, you can place a chart either on a worksheet (for example, with its data) or on its own chart sheet:

- *Chart on a worksheet.* Excel calls a chart on a worksheet an *embedded chart*—the chart object is embedded in the worksheet. Usually, the worksheet is the one that contains the chart's data, but you can embed a chart on a different worksheet if necessary. Create an embedded chart when you want to look at the chart alongside its data or alongside other information. Figure 14–1 shows an embedded chart.

Figure 14–1. *Create an embedded chart on a worksheet when you want to work on or view the chart alongside its data.*

- *Chart on chart sheet:* Instead of creating an embedded chart, you can create a chart on a *chart sheet*—a separate page in the workbook that contains only a chart. Using a chart sheet gives you more space to lay out the chart and view it. The chart sheet doesn't contain the source data, but you can add a data table showing the source data if you don't mind sacrificing some of the chart sheet's space for the table. Figure 14–2 shows a chart on a chart sheet without a data table.

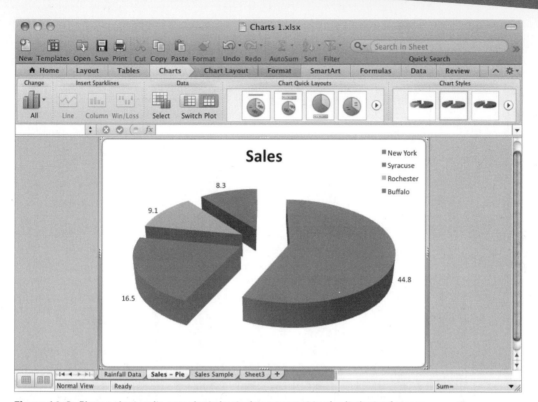

Figure 14–2. *Place a chart on its own chart sheet when you want to give it plenty of space.*

NOTE: You can change an embedded chart to a chart on its own chart sheet, or a chart on a chart sheet to an embedded chart, as needed.

Understanding the Components of a Chart

Excel's charts vary widely in looks and use, but most of them use the same set of components. Figure 14–3 shows a typical type of chart—a 3-D column chart—of rainfall data for six months for seven weather stations, with the main parts of the chart labeled.

NOTE: If you have some sample data you're ready to try turning into a chart, select the data and choose Charts ➤ Insert Chart ➤ Column, and then click a chart type on the Column panel. This will give you a quick column chart that you can experiment with as we go through the components of charts.

The following sections discuss the individual components of charts.

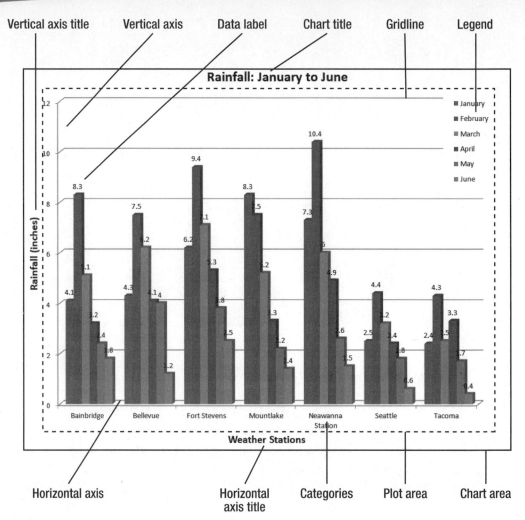

Figure 14–3. *This column chart contains most of the typical elements of Excel charts. The chart area is the whole area occupied by the chart, and the plot area is where the data series are plotted.*

Chart Area and Plot Area

The *chart area* is the whole area occupied by the chart. If the chart has a white background, the easiest way to see the extent of the chart area is to click the chart so that Excel displays a border around it.

The *plot area* is the area of the chart that contains the plotted data—in other words, the main part of the chart area, excluding the areas occupied by the chart title, the axis titles, and the legend (if it appears outside the plot area).

Chart Axes

Most charts have one, two, or three axes:

- *Horizontal axis.* This is the axis along which the data categories are laid out; for example, the weather stations in the sample chart. This axis is also called the *category axis* or the x-*axis*.

- *Vertical axis.* This is the axis along which the data series are laid out. This axis is also called the y-*axis*.

- *Depth axis.* In 3-D charts, this is the axis that provides the third dimension. This axis is also called the z-*axis*.

Each axis has tick marks that show where the values appear on it.

Categories and Data Series

The *categories* are the subdivisions of data that appear on the horizontal axis. For example, in the sample chart, each weather station is a category.

The *data series* are the sets of data used to create the chart. For example, in the sample chart, the data series contain the rainfall measurements.

Chart Title and Axis Titles

The *chart title* is text that identifies the chart as a whole. Normally, you put the chart title at the top of the chart, but you can place it elsewhere if you want.

The *horizontal axis title* is text that explains what is shown on the horizontal axis; for example, the weather stations in the sample chart.

The *vertical axis title* is text that explains what the vertical axis shows; for example, the amount of rainfall in the sample chart.

A 3-D chart can also have a *depth axis title* that explains what the depth axis shows.

> **NOTE:** Chart titles and axis titles are optional, so you can include only those your chart needs. Generally, people viewing your charts will benefit from having clear chart titles and axis titles. But don't feel obliged to include any element that seems to complicate your charts. Remember the saying "if in doubt, leave it out."

Data Markers, Gridlines, and Data Labels

The *data markers* are the points on the chart that show where each data point appears. Each series typically contains several data markers. Depending on the chart type, the data markers may appear as separate points, or they may be linked together.

To make it easy to see how the data markers relate to the axes, you can add *gridlines* to the chart—lines that run across or up from the data markers.

Data labels are text items that display the exact value of data points. You can display data labels when viewers need to see the exact figure for each data point rather than judging the value from the chart.

Understanding Excel's Chart Types and Choosing Which to Use

Excel enables you to create an impressive variety of different types of charts. Some of the charts are widely useful, whereas others are highly specialized. Table 14–1 describes the types of charts that Excel provides and suggests typical uses for them. The table lists the charts in the same order as Excel's Chart panel, which you'll meet shortly and which puts the most widely used chart types first.

Table 14–1. *Excel's Chart Types and Suggested Uses*

Chart Category	Description	Suggested Uses
Column	Displays data in vertical bars.	Comparing equivalent items (such as sales results) or sets of data that change over time (such as rainfall).
Line	Displays each series in a line.	Showing evenly spaced values that change over time, such as temperatures.
Pie	Displays a single data series as a pie divided up by the contribution of each data point.	Showing how much each item contributes to the whole; for example, breaking down expenses by department.
Bar	Displays data in horizontal bars.	Comparing similar items or indicating progress.
Area	Displays data as lines but with the areas between them shaded.	Showing how values have changed over time, especially the contribution of different data points in the series.
Scatter	Displays each data point as a point (or cross, or similar marker) on the plot area. Also known as an XY chart.	Showing values sampled at different times or that are not directly related to each other.
Stock	Displays each data series as a vertical line or bar indicating three or more prices or measurements (for example, high, low, and closing prices).	Showing the daily prices of stocks. Also suitable for some scientific data.
Surface	Displays the data points as a three-dimensional surface.	Comparing two sets of data to find a suitable combination of them.

Chart Category	Description	Suggested Uses
Doughnut	Displays the data series as a sequence of concentric rings.	Showing how much each item contributes to the whole—like a pie chart, but it works with two or more data series.
Bubble	Displays the data points as bubbles of different sizes depending on their values.	Showing the relative importance of each data point.
Radar	Displays the combined values of different data series.	Showing how the combined values of separate data series compare to each other; for example, the sales contributions of several different products over several periods of time.

Creating, Laying Out, and Formatting a Chart

In this section, we'll look at how to create a chart from your data, lay it out with the components and arrangement you want, and apply the most useful types of formatting.

Creating a Chart

To create a chart, you use the commands on the Charts tab of the Ribbon. Follow these steps:

1. Select the data you want to chart, including any row or column headings needed. For example, click the first cell in the data range, and then Shift+click the last cell.

> **TIP:** You can create a chart from either a block range or from a range of separate cells. To use separate cells, select them as usual—for example, click the first, and then Cmd+click each of the others.

2. Click the Charts tab of the Ribbon to display its contents, and then click the appropriate button in the Insert Chart group: Column, Line, Pie, Bar, Area, Scatter, or Other (which contains the Stock, Surface, Doughnut, Bubble, and Radar chart types).

> **NOTE:** If the Excel window isn't wide enough to display multiple buttons in the Insert Chart group, a single pop-up button called All appears. Click this button to display a panel that shows all the chart types. You'll need to scroll down the panel to see most of them.

3. On the panel that opens, click the chart type you want. Figure 14–4 shows the Column panel, which is one of the most widely useful.

Figure 14–4. *To insert a chart, click the appropriate pop-up button in the Charts group on the Insert tab of the Ribbon, and then click the chart type you want.*

Excel creates the chart as an embedded chart in the current worksheet, as shown in Figure 14–1. You can then reposition it, resize it, or move it to a chart sheet as follows:

- *Reposition the chart.* If you want to keep the chart as an embedded chart, move the mouse pointer over the chart border so that it turns to a four-headed arrow, and then drag the chart to where you want it.

- *Resize the chart.* Click to select the chart, and then drag one of the handles that appear. Drag a corner handle to resize the chart in both dimensions; you can Shift+drag to resize the chart proportionally. Drag a side handle to resize the chart in only that dimension; for example, drag the bottom handle to resize the chart only vertically.

- *Move the chart to a chart sheet.* If you want to move the chart to a chart sheet, follow the instructions in the next section.

Changing a Chart from an Embedded Chart to a Chart Sheet

You can change a chart from being embedded in a worksheet to being on its own chart sheet like this:

1. Click the chart on the worksheet it's embedded in.

2. Choose Chart ➤ Move Chart from the menu bar to display the Move Chart dialog box (see Figure 14–5).

TIP: You can also display the Move Chart dialog box by Ctrl+clicking or right-clicking the chart and then clicking Move Chart on the context menu.

Figure 14–5. *Use the Move Chart dialog box to change a chart from being embedded to being on its own chart sheet.*

3. Select the New sheet option button.

4. Type the name for the new chart sheet in the New sheet text box.

5. Click the OK button. Excel creates the new chart sheet and moves the chart to it. The chart is still attached to its source data, so if you change the data, Excel changes the chart too.

NOTE: You can also use the Move Chart dialog box to move a chart from a chart sheet to an embedded chart on a worksheet or to move an embedded chart from one worksheet to another.

Changing the Chart Type

If you find the chart type you've chosen doesn't work for your data, you can change the chart type easily without having to create the chart again from scratch. Follow these steps:

1. Click the chart to select it.

2. Click the Charts tab of the Ribbon to display its contents.

3. In the Change Chart Type group, open the panel for the chart category, and then click the chart type. For example, click the Pie pop-up button to display the Pie panel, and then choose your favorite kind of pie from it.

Switching the Rows and Columns in a Chart

When Excel displays the chart, you may realize that the data series are in the wrong place; for example, the chart is displaying months by rainfall instead of rainfall by months.

When this happens, there's a quick fix: switch the rows and columns by choosing Charts ➤ Data ➤ Switch Plot from the Ribbon. Excel displays the chart with the series the other way around.

Changing the Source Data for a Chart

Sometimes you may find that your chart doesn't work well with the source data you've chosen. For example, you may have selected so much data that the chart is crowded, or you may have missed a vital row or column.

When this happens, you don't need to delete the chart and start again from scratch. Instead, follow these steps:

1. Choose Charts ➤ Data ➤ Select from the Ribbon or Chart ➤ Source Data from the menu bar to display the Select Data Source dialog box (see Figure 14–6).

Figure 14–6. *Use the Select Data Source dialog box to change the source data the chart is using.*

2. In the Chart data range box, enter the data range you want to use:

    ■   Usually, it's easiest to click the Collapse Dialog button to collapse the dialog box, drag on the worksheet to select the right data range, and then click the Collapse Dialog button again to restore the dialog box. (Or you can just work around the Select Data Source dialog box if you prefer.)

    ■   You can also type the data range in the Chart data range box. This is easy when you just need to change a column letter or row number to fix the data range.

3. If you need to switch the rows and columns as well, click the Switch Row/Column button.

4. If your chart data contains empty cells, open the Show empty cells as pop-up menu and choose how to represent them. Your choices are Gaps (the default setting for most charts) or Zero.

5. Select the Show data in hidden rows and columns check box only if you want the chart to include data in hidden rows and columns within the source range. Normally, you'll want to keep these hidden, but it's sometimes useful to show them.

6. Click the OK button to close the Select Data Source dialog box. Excel applies the changes to the chart.

Choosing the Layout for the Chart

When you've sorted out the chart type and the source data, it's time to choose the layout for the chart. For each chart type, Excel provides various preset layouts that control where the title, legend, and other elements appear. After applying a layout, you can customize it further as needed.

To apply a layout, click the chart and then click the Charts tab of the Ribbon. If a suitable layout appears in the Layouts box in the Chart Quick Layouts group, click it. To see the full range of layouts, hold the mouse pointer over the Layouts box in the Chart Quick Layouts group until the panel button appears, and then click the panel button. On the Quick Layout panel that Excel displays (see Figure 14–7), click the layout you want to apply to the chart.

Figure 14–7. *To set the overall layout of chart elements, such as the chart title and legend, open the Layouts panel, and click the layout you want.*

Adding a Separate Data Series to a Chart

Sometimes you may find you need to add to a chart a data series that doesn't appear in the chart's source data; for example, to add projections of future success to your current data.

To add a data series, work from the Select Data Source dialog box. Follow these steps:

1. Click the chart to select it.

2. Choose Charts ➤ Data ➤ Select from the Ribbon or Chart ➤ Source Data from the menu bar to display the Select Data Source dialog box. You can also Ctrl+click or right-click the chart and then click Select Data on the context menu.

3. Click the Add button below the Series list box. Excel adds a new item to the series box, giving it a default name such as Series3 or Series4.

4. Click in the Name text box, and then type the name you want to give the series. If the name appears in a cell on the worksheet, you can click it. When you move the focus out of the Name text box, Excel changes the default name to the name you type.

5. In the Y values text box, type the values for the series inside the braces, putting a comma between the values; for example, **{4.5,8.3,6.2,5.1,4.8,10.2}**. If the values appear in cells on the worksheet, you can enter them by selecting the range.

> **NOTE:** When adding a new data series, you don't normally need to change the contents of the Category (X) axis labels text box. This text box contains the range of cells that provide the labels for the horizontal axis.

6. Click the OK button to close the Select Data Source dialog box.

Applying a Style to a Chart

To control the overall graphical look of a chart, apply one of Excel's styles to it from the Styles box or the Styles panel in the Chart Styles group on the Charts tab of the Ribbon. Click the chart to select it, and then click the Charts tab of the Ribbon to display its controls. Either click a style in the Styles box or hold the mouse pointer over the Styles box until the panel button appears, click the panel button to display the Styles panel (see Figure 14–8), and then click the style.

Figure 14–8. *To give the chart an overall graphical look, apply a style from the Styles box or the Styles panel in the Chart Styles group of the Charts tab of the Ribbon.*

Adding a Title to a Chart

To let viewers know what a chart is about, you'll normally want to add a title to it. To do so, follow these steps:

1. Click the chart to select it.

2. Choose Chart Layout ➤ Labels ➤ Chart Title from the Ribbon, and then choose the title type you want:

    - *No Chart Title.* Choose this item to remove the existing title. You can also click the title and press Delete to delete it.

    - *Title Above Chart.* Choose this time to place the title above the chart, making the chart smaller to provide space for the title. Use this placement when you want to keep the title clearly separated from the chart; for example, because the chart is busy.

    - *Overlap Title at Top.* Choose this item to place the title on the chart, centered over the top. Placing the title on the chart lets you keep the chart as large as possible. If the title lands on top of data, you can click it and drag it to a different position.

3. Triple-click to select the contents of the Chart Title placeholder that Excel adds for you.

4. Type the title for the chart over the default text.

5. If necessary, drag the chart title placeholder to a different position.

6. Click elsewhere to deselect the chart title.

> **TIP:** If you need to format the chart title, double-click the chart title to display the Format Title dialog box.

Adding Axis Titles to the Chart

To make clear what the chart shows, you'll usually want to add titles to the axes. To do so, follow these steps:

1. Click the chart to select it.

2. Choose Chart Layout ➤ Labels ➤ Axis Titles ➤ Horizontal Axis Title ➤ Title Below Axis from the Ribbon to insert a title placeholder for the horizontal axis.

3. Triple-click to select the contents of the placeholder.

4. Type the text for the axis title.

5. If necessary, drag the placeholder to a different position.

6. Choose Chart Layout ➤ Primary Vertical Axis Title from the Ribbon, and then click the placement you want:

   - *Rotated Title.* Click this item to have Excel rotate the axis title 90 degrees counterclockwise so that it runs upward along the axis.

   - *Vertical Title.* Click this item to have the axis title appear vertically, with the letters placed horizontally one above the other.

   - *Horizontal Title.* Click this item to have the axis title appear horizontally. This placement is easiest to read, but it takes up more of the chart's space than the other two placements.

7. Triple-click to select the contents of the placeholder.

8. Type the text for the axis title.

9. If necessary, drag the placeholder to a different position.

NOTE: If the chart has a z-axis, you can add the axis title by choosing Chart Layout ➤ Labels ➤ Axis Titles ➤ Depth Axis Title and then clicking the Rotated Title item, the Vertical Title item, or the Horizontal Title item, as needed.

Changing the Scale or Numbering of an Axis

When you insert a chart, Excel automatically numbers the vertical axis to suit the data range. If you need to change the scale or numbering, follow these steps:

1. Ctrl+click or right-click in the vertical axis titles area, and then click Format Axis on the context menu to display the Format Axis dialog box. The Scale category appears at the front (see Figure 14–9).

Figure 14-9. *You can format an axis to control its values, major and minor units, and whether the chart shows units (such as thousands). Excel applies the changes as you work in the Scale category of the Format Axis dialog box.*

2. Use the controls in the Value axis scale area to set up the values on the axis:

   - *Minimum.* To have Excel set the minimum value on the axis, select the Minimum check box. To set it yourself, click in the text box, and then type in the value; Excel clears the check box for you.

   - *Maximum.* To have Excel set the maximum value that appears on the axis, select the Minimum check box. To set it yourself, click in the text box, and then type in the value; Excel clears the check box for you.

   - *Major unit.* To have Excel decide the interval between major units on the axis, select the Major unit check box. To set it yourself, click in the text box, and then type in the value; Excel clears the check box for you. Depending on how big your chart is, you'll probably want between five and ten major units on the scale you've set by choosing the Minimum value and Maximum value.

■ *Minor unit.* To have Excel decide the interval between minor units on the axis, select the Minor unit check box. To set it yourself, click in the text box, and then type in the value; Excel clears the check box for you. You'll normally want between four and ten minor units per major unit, depending on what the chart shows.

3. In the middle section of the Scale pane, choose whether to display the units the chart uses—for example, choose the Hundreds item, the Thousands item, or the Millions item in the Display units pop-up menu. If you choose to display units, make sure the Show display units label on chart check box is selected, making Excel display a label showing the units. If you don't want to show the units, choose None in the Display units pop-up menu.

4. In the lower part of the Scale pane, choose options as needed:

■ *Logarithmic scale.* If you need the chart to use a logarithmic scale rather than an arithmetic scale, select the Logarithmic scale check box, and then enter the logarithm base in the Base box. For example, enter 10 to have the scale use the values 1, 10, 100, 1000, 10000, and so on, at regular intervals.

■ *Values in reverse order.* For some charts, it's helpful to have the values run in reverse order; for example, lowest values at the top instead of the highest. When you need this setup, select this check box.

■ *Floor crosses at minimum value.* Select this check box if you want the floor of the chart to cross the vertical axis at the minimum value rather than at zero.

■ *Display units*: If you want the chart to show units—Hundreds, Thousands, Millions, and so on—select the unit in this pop-up menu. Excel reduces the figures shown accordingly; for example, 1000000 appears as 1, with Millions next to the scale. This helps make the axis easier to read.

5. In the left pane, click the Ticks item to display the Ticks pane (see Figure 14–10), and then set up the positioning of the tick marks:

■ *Major Tick Mark Type.* In this box, select the Inside option button to have the major tick marks appear inside the chart, the Outside option button to have them appear outside (on the axis side), or the Cross option button to have them appear on both sides. Select the None option button if you do not want major tick marks.

Figure 14–10. *Use the controls in the Ticks pane of the Format Axis dialog box to control how the ticks on the axis appear.*

- *Minor tick mark type.* In this box, select the Inside option button to have the minor tick marks appear inside the chart, the Outside option button to have them appear outside (on the axis side), or the Cross option button to have them appear on both sides. Select the None option button if you do not want minor tick marks.

- *Axis labels.* In this box, select the Next to Axis option button to have the labels appear next to the axis. Select the High option button to have the labels appear on the high side of the chart, or select the Low option button to have them appear on the low side. Select the None option button to suppress the labels.

6. When you're satisfied with the axis, click the Close button to close the Format Axis dialog box.

Adding a Legend to a Chart

Many charts benefit from having a legend that summarizes the colors used for different data series. You can add a legend by selecting the chart, choosing Chart Layout ➤ Labels ➤ Legend, and then clicking the placement you want: Legend at Right, Legend at Top, Legend at Left, Legend at Bottom, Overlap Legend at Right, or Overlap Legend at Left.

Each of the non-"Overlap" items reduces the chart area to make space for the legend. The two "Overlap" items place the legend on the chart without reducing its size, so they're good for keeping the chart as large as possible.

Whichever placement you use for the legend, you can drag it to a better position as needed. You can also resize the legend by clicking it and then dragging one of the handles that appear around it.

If you need to remove a legend from a chart, either click the legend and then press Delete, or choose Chart Layout ➤ Labels ➤ Legend ➤ No Legend.

Adding Axis Labels from a Range Separate from the Chart Data

Depending on how the worksheet containing the source data is laid out, you may need to add axis labels that are in separate cells from the chart data. To do this, follow these steps:

1. Click the chart to select it.

2. Choose Charts ➤ Data ➤ Select from the Ribbon to display the Select Data Source dialog box.

3. Click the Collapse Dialog button to the right of the Category (X) axis labels text box to collapse the dialog box.

4. Drag through the cells in the work sheet that contain the axis labels. Excel enters them in the Category (X) axis labels text box.

5. Click the Collapse Dialog button again to restore the Select Data Source dialog box.

6. Click the OK button to close the Select Data Source dialog box. Excel applies the labels to the axis.

Adding Data Labels to the Chart

If viewers will need to see the precise value of data points rather than just getting a general idea of their value, add data labels to the chart. To do so, click the chart, and then choose Chart Layout ➤ Labels ➤ Data Labels ➤ Value if you want to show the values. The Data Labels pop-up menu offers different options depending on the chart type. For example, for pie charts, you can choose the Series Name item, the Category Name item, the Percentage item, or the Category Name and Percentage item.

CAUTION: Use data labels sparingly. Only some charts benefit from data labels—other charts may become too busy, or having the details may distract the audience from the overall thrust of the chart.

When you add data labels to a chart, Excel displays a data label for each data marker. If you want to display only some data labels, delete the ones you don't need. To delete a data label, click it once to select all data labels, and then click it again to select just the one label. Then either press Delete or Ctrl+click or right-click the selection and click Delete on the context menu.

Choosing Which Gridlines to Display

On many types of charts, you can choose whether to display horizontal and vertical gridlines to help the viewer judge how the data points relate to each other and to the axes.

To control which gridlines appear, follow these steps:

1. Select the chart.

2. Choose Chart Layout ➤ Axes ➤ Gridlines, then click Horizontal Gridlines, Vertical Gridlines, or Depth Gridlines to display the appropriate submenu.

3. Click the menu item for the type of gridlines you want to display:

    ■ *No Gridlines.* Click this item to suppress the display of gridlines.

    ■ *Major Gridlines.* Click this item to display only gridlines at the major divisions in the data series. For example, if your data is in the range 0–25, major gridlines normally appear at 5, 10, 15, 20, and 25.

TIP: When the viewer needs to see clearly where each value falls, use either data labels or major and minor gridlines. If using minor gridlines (with or without major gridlines) makes the chart look cluttered, use only major gridlines. Normally, it's best not to use both horizontal and vertical minor gridlines, because they tend to make charts look confusingly busy—but sometimes your charts may need them.

    ■ *Minor Gridlines.* Click this item to display gridlines at the minor divisions in the data series. For example, if your data is in the range 0–25, minor gridlines normally appear at each integer—1, 2, 3, and so on up to 24 and 25.

- *Major and Minor Gridlines.* Click this item to display both major and minor gridlines. The major gridlines appear darker than the minor gridlines so that you can see the difference between them. Having both major and minor gridlines is usually clearer than having only minor gridlines.

4. Repeat steps 2 and 3 for each other set of gridlines the chart needs.

NOTE: To change the values at which the gridlines appear, format the axis, as described in the section "Changing the Scale or Numbering of an Axis" earlier in this chapter.

Formatting a Chart Wall and Chart Floor

Some charts look fine with a plain background, but for 3-D charts, you may want to decorate the chart walls (the areas at the back and the side of the chart) and the chart floor (the area at the bottom of the chart). You can add a solid color, a gradient, a picture, or a texture to the walls, the floor, or both. Figure 14–11 shows a chart that uses a picture for the walls.

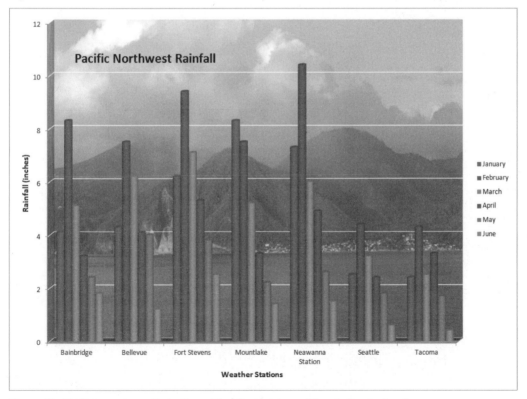

Figure 14–11. *You can give a chart a themed look by applying a picture to the chart walls.*

> **TIP:** Usually, the chart walls and floors are the elements that look best with a custom fill (such as a picture). But you can apply a custom fill to many other chart elements as well. To do so, display the Format dialog box for the element, click the Fill category in the left pane, and then make your choices.

To format the chart wall or the chart floor, follow these steps:

1. Click the chart to select it.

2. Choose Chart Layout ➤ Current Selection ➤ Chart Elements, and then click the item you want to format: Back Wall, Floor, Side Wall, or Walls (to format both the back wall and the side wall).

3. Click the Format Selection button in the Current Selection group to display the Format dialog box for the item you selected. Figure 14–12 shows the Format Walls dialog box with the controls for inserting a picture fill displayed.

Figure 14–12. *Use the Fill pane in the Format dialog box to apply a picture fill to objects such as the chart walls or floor.*

4. Make sure the Fill item is selected in the left pane.

5. In the Fill pane, set up the fill you want:

    - *No fill.* Click the Solid tab to display its contents. Open the Color pop-up menu, and choose the No Fill item if you want the item to be transparent.

- *Solid fill.* Click the Solid tab to display its contents. Open the Color pop-up menu, and then click the color you want. Choose the Automatic item if you want to use the default color. Drag the Transparency slider, or type a value in the text box, to choose how transparent the fill is.

- *Gradient fill.* Click the Gradient tab to display its contents. Open the Style pop-up menu, and choose the gradient style you want: None, linear, Radial, Rectangular, or Path. Use the Angle knob and Direction pop-up menu to set the angle and direction of the gradient if applicable. Then, in the Color and transparency area of the Gradient tab, choose the gradient, color, and transparency.

- *Picture or texture fill.* Click the Picture or Texture tab to display its contents. To use a picture, click the Choose Picture button, click the picture in the Choose a Picture dialog box, and then click the Insert button. To use a texture, choose it from the Texture pop-up palette. Set the degree of transparency by dragging the Transparency slide or entering a percentage in the text box. Then select the Stretch option button if you want to stretch the picture or texture to fill the space, select the Stack option button if you want to tile the picture or texture to occupy the space without distorting it, or select the Stack and scale with *N* Units/Picture option button to tile the picture with the number of units you type in the text box.

- *Pattern fill.* Click the Pattern tab to display its contents. In the Pattern box, click the pattern you want. Then choose the foreground color in the Foreground color pop-up menu and the background color in the Background color pop-up menu.

6. Click the Close button to close the Format dialog box.

Formatting Individual Chart Elements

You can format any of the individual elements of a chart—for example, the legend, the gridlines, or the data labels—by selecting the element and then using its Format dialog box. This dialog box includes the name of the element it affects: the Format Data Labels dialog box, the Format Plot Area dialog box, and so on.

You can display the Format dialog box in either of these ways:

- Ctrl+click or right-click the element, and then click the Format item on the context menu. This is usually the easiest way of opening the Format dialog box.

- *Select the element in the Chart Elements pop-up menu, and then click the Format Selection button.* If it's hard to Ctrl+click or right-click the element on the chart (for example, because the chart is busy), choose Chart Layout ➤ Current Selection ➤ Chart Elements or Format ➤ Current Selection ➤ Chart Elements, and then click the element you want on the pop-up menu. You can then click the Format Selection button (also in the Current Selection group) to open the Format dialog box for the element.

The contents of the Format dialog box vary depending on the object you've selected, but for most objects, you'll find categories such as these:

- *Fill.* You can fill in a solid shape with a solid color, color gradient, picture, or texture. See the section "Formatting a Chart Wall and Chart Floor," earlier in this chapter, for instructions on creating fills.

- *Line.* You can give a shape a color border, gradient border, or no line. You can also choose among different border styles, change the border width, and pick a suitable line type.

- *Shadow.* You can add a shadow to the shape, set its color, and adjust its transparency, width, and other properties.

- *Glow and Soft Edges.* You can make an object stand out by giving it a glow, choosing a color that contrasts with the object's surroundings, and choosing how wide the glow should be. You can also apply soft edges to a shape.

- *3-D Format.* You can apply a 3-D format to different aspects of a shape; for example, setting a different bevel for the top and bottom of the shape.

- *3-D Rotation.* You can apply a 3-D rotation to the object.

- *Font.* For objects that use text, you can control how the text looks.

> **TIP:** If the chart element contains text, you can also format it by using the controls on the Home tab of the Ribbon or keyboard shortcuts. For example, to apply boldface to the data labels, click the data labels, and then choose Home ➤ Font ➤ Bold (or press Ctrl+B). This is often easier than using the Font pane in the Format dialog box for the element.

Copying Chart Formatting

After you set up a chart with all the formatting you need, you can apply that formatting to another chart by using Copy and Paste. Follow these steps:

1. Click the formatted chart to select its chart area.

2. Right-click the border of the chart, and then click Copy on the context menu to copy the chart and its formatting to the Clipboard.

3. Go to the sheet that contains the chart onto which you want to paste the formatting.

4. Choose Home ➤ Clipboard ➤ Paste ➤ Paste Special to display the Paste Special dialog box shown in Figure 14–13.

Figure 14–13. *In the Paste Special dialog box, select the Formats option button to paste just the formatting from one chart onto another chart.*

5. Select the Formats option button.

6. Click the OK button to close the Paste Special dialog box. Excel applies the formatting to the chart.

Reusing Your Own Designs by Creating Custom Chart Types

If you want to be able to reuse a chart design you've created, you can turn it into a custom chart type. Follow these steps:

1. Select the formatted chart either on a chart sheet or on a worksheet.

2. Choose Charts ➤ Change Chart Type ➤ Other ➤ Save As Template from the Ribbon or Chart ➤ Save as Template from the menu bar to display the Save Chart Template dialog box. This is a standard Save As dialog box.

3. If you want, change the folder in which to save the chart type. Excel suggests using the `~/Library/Application Support/Microsoft/Office/Chart Templates/` folder (where ~ represents your home folder). This is good for a template only you will use, but if your colleagues will need to use the template too, you may need to store it in a shared folder on the network.

4. Type a descriptive name for the template in the Save As text box.

5. Click the Save button to close the Save Chart Template dialog box. Excel saves the template in the folder you chose.

To create a chart based on your template, follow these steps:

1. Select the source data for the chart.

2. Choose Charts ➤ Insert Chart ➤ Other to display the Other pane, and then scroll down to the Templates area at the bottom of the pane.

3. Click the template.

Adding Sparklines to Your Worksheets

Charts are great for illustrating medium to large quantities of information, but sometimes you'll want something smaller—a chart that'll fit inside a single cell, giving a quick visual indication of a trend. Excel calls such charts *sparklines*.

Excel provides three kinds of sparklines:

- *Line.* A line sparkline is a straightforward line that runs through the data points, as in the top part of Figure 14–14. A line sparkline is good for showing data that flows from one data point to the next, such as temperatures.

- *Column.* A column sparkline shows the data as a series of columns, as in a column chart. The middle part of Figure 14–14 shows an example. A column sparkline is good for comparing data points that are separate from each other, such as sales results by month.

- *Win/Loss.* A win/loss sparkline shows results as either a win (a positive result) or a loss (a negative result). The lower part of Figure 14–14 shows an example of win/loss sparklines. A win/loss sparkline is good for when you want to take a black-and-white view of results—for example, whether your investments are up or down in a particular month. In a win/loss sparkline, a zero value appears as a blank.

	2010	2011	2012	2013	
Albuquerque	10	12	13	15	
Phoenix	11	17	19	15	
Little Rock	23	21	18	10	
	2010	2011	2012	2013	
Albuquerque	10	12	13	15	
Phoenix	11	17	19	15	
Little Rock	23	21	18	10	
	Q1	Q2	Q3	Q4	
Sacramento	-1	0	-2	3	
Oakland	1	2	3	-3	
Redding	4	-5	2	18	

Figure 14–14. *Sparklines are single-cell charts that you can use to indicate trends or results visually.*

Inserting Sparklines

To insert one or more sparklines in a worksheet, follow these steps:

1. Click the cell or select the range you want to place the sparklines in.

2. Click the Charts tab to display its contents, go to the Insert Sparklines group, and then click the Line button, the Column button, or the Win/Loss button, as needed. Whichever button you click, Excel displays the Insert Sparklines dialog box (see Figure 14–15).

Insert Sparklines

Select a data range for the sparklines:

[|]

Select where to place sparklines:

[F9]

Learn about sparklines   (Cancel)   (OK)

Figure 14–15. *In the Insert Sparklines dialog box, choose the data range for the sparklines and the cells in which to place them.*

3. With the focus in the Select a data range for the sparklines text box (where Excel places it when it displays the Insert Sparklines dialog box), click and drag in the worksheet to enter the range that contains the data for the sparklines.

4. Make sure the Select where to place sparklines text box contains the range in which you want to place the sparklines. If you chose the range before displaying the Insert Sparklines dialog box, it'll be correct. Otherwise, click in this text box, and then drag in the worksheet to select the range.

5. Click the OK button to close the Insert Sparklines dialog box. Excel inserts the sparklines in the cells.

Formatting Your Sparklines

After inserting sparklines, you can format them by using the controls on the Sparklines tab of the Ribbon. Click a cell in the sparklines to select the group of sparklines and make Excel add the Sparklines tab to the Ribbon. If Excel doesn't display the Sparklines tab automatically, click the tab to display it (see Figure 14–16).

Figure 14–16. *Use the controls on the Sparklines tab of the Ribbon to format sparklines to look the way you want them to.*

These are the main moves for formatting your sparklines:

- *Change the source data for a group of sparklines.* Click a cell in the group of sparklines, and then choose Sparklines ➤ Data ➤ Edit from the Ribbon (clicking the main part of the Edit button). Excel displays the Edit Sparklines dialog box, which has the same controls as the Insert Sparklines dialog box.

- *Change the source data for a single sparkline.* Click the sparkline cell, and then choose Sparklines ➤ Data ➤ Edit ➤ Edit Single Sparkline. Excel displays the Edit Sparkline dialog box, which works like the Insert Sparklines dialog box, but affects only the cell you chose.

- *Change a sparkline to a different type.* Click the sparkline cell, and then click the Line button, the Column button, or the Win/Loss button in the Change Type group on the Sparklines tab of the Ribbon.

- *Add markers to the sparklines.* In the Markers group on the Sparklines tab of the Ribbon, select the High check box, the Low check box, the Negative check box, the First check box, or the Last check box as needed—or select the All check box to select all the others. To change the marker color, choose Sparklines ➤ Format ➤ markers, and then work in the Markers dialog box (see Figure 14–17).

Figure 14–17. *Use the Markers dialog box to change the colors of markers and to choose which ones appear on the sparklines.*

TIP: For many kinds of data, the High marker and Low marker are the most useful. Win/loss sparklines use the Negative marker by default, while line sparklines and column sparklines don't use any markers by default.

- *Apply a style to the sparklines.* In the Format group on the Sparklines tab of the Ribbon, either click a style in the Styles box or hold the mouse pointer over the Styles box to display the panel button; then click the panel button to display the Styles panel. Click the style you want.

- *Change the color of the sparklines.* Choose Sparklines ➤ Format ➤ Sparkline to display the Sparkline panel, and then click the color you want.

- *Change the weight of the sparklines.* Choose Sparklines ➤ Format ➤ Sparkline ➤ Weight, and then click the line weight.

- *Change the axes for the sparklines.* Choose Sparklines ➤ Format ➤ Axes to display the Axes dialog box (see Figure 14–18), and then make your choices in it.

Figure 14–18. *You can use the Axes dialog box to choose settings for the horizontal and vertical axes of the sparklines.*

- *Group sparklines together.* If you need to format separate sets of sparklines quickly, group them together. Select each set of sparklines, and then choose Sparklines ➤ Edit ➤ Group from the Ribbon to group them.

- *Clear sparklines.* When you no longer need sparklines, clear them from the cells. Select the sparkline cells you want to clear, and then choose Sparklines ➤ Edit ➤ Clear, clicking the main part of the Clear button. You can also click a single cell and then choose Sparklines ➤ Edit ➤ Clear ➤ Clear Selected Sparkline Groups to clear all the cells in the group.

Summary

In this chapter, you learned how to create powerful and persuasive charts from your data. You know what the separate components of charts are called, how to create a chart, and how to position it either on a worksheet or on its own chart sheet. You can also make Excel show the components you want for a chart and format them as needed. To save time and effort, you also learned to reuse your custom chart formatting either by pasting it onto an existing chart or by creating a custom chart template from it.

You also came to grips with sparklines and can now use them to illustrate results and trends in your worksheets.

In the next chapter, I'll show you to create custom formulas and harness the power of Excel's functions to perform calculations.

Chapter 15

Crunching Numbers with Formulas and Functions

To make your worksheets deliver the information you want, you'll probably need to perform calculations with your data. To perform calculations, you enter formulas and functions in cells, as you'll learn to do in this chapter.

We'll start by going over what functions and formulas are so that you're clear on the difference between them. Then I'll show you how to create your own formulas using Excel's calculation operators. You'll find it easy to get started, because Excel provides plenty of help, but you'll also look at how to troubleshoot common problems that occur with formulas.

In the second half of the chapter, we'll dig into functions: how to insert them in your worksheets using the various tools that Excel provides, how to find the ones you want, and how to point the functions to the data they need for the calculations.

Understanding the Difference Between Formulas and Functions

In Excel, you can perform calculations in two main ways:

- *By using a formula.* A *formula* is a custom calculation that you create when none of Excel's functions (discussed next) does what you need. The word *formula* may sound imposing, but a formula can be a simple calculation; for example, to subtract 50 from 100, you can type **=100-50** in a cell (the equal sign tells Excel you're starting a formula). Formulas can also be more complex. For example, say you need to add the contents of the cells in the range A1:A6 and then divide them by the contents of cell B1. Excel doesn't have a built-in function for doing this, because it's not a standard calculation. So instead, you create a formula such as this: **=SUM(A1:A6)/B1**. (In this example, the / is the keyboard equivalent of the ÷ symbol.)

- *By using a function.* A *function* is a preset formula that performs a standard calculation. For example, when you need to add several values together, you use the SUM() function—for instance, **=SUM(1,2,3,4,5,6)**, which is simpler than **=1+2+3+4+5+6** but has the same effect.

In the following sections, I'll show you how to use each of these methods. But before I do that, let's go over the ways of referring to cells and ranges in formulas and functions.

Referring to Cells and Ranges in Formulas and Functions

To make your formulas and functions work correctly, you need to refer to the cells and ranges you want. This section makes sure you know how to refer to cells and ranges, both when they're on the same worksheet as the formula and when they're on a different worksheet. You can even refer to cells and ranges in another workbook—as long as it will remain in the same place in your Mac's file system.

Referring to a Cell

To refer to a cell on the same worksheet, simply use its column lettering and its row number. For example, use **=A10** to refer to cell A10.

To refer to a cell on a different worksheet, enter the worksheet's name followed by an exclamation point and the cell reference. For example, use **=Supplies!A10** to refer to cell A10 on the worksheet named Supplies. The easiest way to set up such a reference is like this:

1. Start creating the formula. For example, type = in the cell.

2. Click the worksheet tab for the worksheet that contains the cell you want to refer to.

3. Click the cell.

4. Click the Enter button on the formula bar to enter the reference. Excel returns you to the worksheet on which you're creating the formula.

> **NOTE:** Instead of clicking the Enter button on the formula bar in step 4, you can press Return to enter the cell reference. When you do this, Excel returns you to the cell below the formula on the worksheet. You then need to press the up arrow key before taking Step 5.

5. Press Ctrl+U to resume editing the cell.

6. Finish creating the formula as usual.

> **NOTE:** If the worksheet's name contains any spaces, you must put the name inside single quotes; for example, **='Sales Results'!A10** rather than **=Sales Results!A10**. You can also use the single quotes on worksheet names that don't have spaces if you find it easier to be consistent.

To refer to a cell in a different workbook, put the workbook's path and file name in brackets, then the worksheet's name, and then the cell reference. For example, the reference **='Shared:Spreads:[Results.xlsx]Sales!'AB12** refers to cell AB12 on the worksheet named Sales in the workbook `Results.xlsx` in the Shared:Spreads folder.

Unless you happen to know the path, file name, worksheet name, and cell, it's usually easiest to set up the reference by using the mouse. Follow these steps:

1. Open the workbook you want to refer to.

2. In the workbook that will contain the reference, start creating the formula. For example, type = in the cell.

3. Switch to the other workbook. If you can see the other workbook, click it. If you can't see the other workbook, open the Window menu on the menu bar, and then click the appropriate window.

4. Navigate to the worksheet that contains the cell, and then click the cell.

5. Switch back to the workbook in which you're creating the reference, and then complete the formula.

Referring to Ranges

To refer to a range that consists of a block of cells, give the cell addresses of the first cell and the last cell, separating them with a colon. For example, to refer to the range from cell P10 to cell Q12, use **=P10:Q12**.

To refer to a range that consists of individual cells, give the address of each cell, separating the addresses with commas. For example, to refer to cell J14, cell K18, and cell Z20, use **=J14,K18,Z20**.

To refer to a range on a different worksheet or in a different workbook, use the techniques explained in the previous section. For example, if you need to refer to the range P10 to Q12 on the worksheet named Stock Listing, use **='Stock Listing'!P10:Q12**.

> **TIP:** Sometimes you may need to make the contents of one row or column refer to another row or column. For example, say you need to make each cell in row 25 refer to the corresponding cell in row 4, so that cell A25 refers to cell A4, cell B25 to cell B4, and so on. To do this, click the row heading for row 25, selecting the row. Then type **=4:4** to create the reference to row 4, and press Cmd+Return to enter it in all the cells of the selection. Similarly, you can refer to a whole column by entering its letter designation, a colon, and the letter designation again; for example, **E:E**.

UNDERSTANDING ABSOLUTE REFERENCES, RELATIVE REFERENCES, AND MIXED REFERENCES

Using cell addresses or range addresses is straightforward enough, but when you start using formulas, there's a complication: if you copy a formula and paste it, you need to tell Excel whether the pasted formula should refer to the cells it originally referred to, or the cells in the same relative positions to the cell where the formula now is, or a mixture of the two. (If you move a formula rather than copy it, Excel keeps the formula as it is.)

To make references clear, Excel uses three types of references:

- *Absolute reference.* A reference that always refers to the same cell, no matter where you copy it. Excel uses a dollar sign ($) to indicate that each part of the reference is absolute. For example, B3 is an absolute reference to cell B3.

- *Relative reference.* A reference that refers to the cell by its position relative to the cell that holds the reference. For example, if you select cell A3 and enter **=B5** in it, the reference means "the cell one column to the right and two rows down." So if you copy the formula to cell C4, Excel changes the cell reference to cell D6, which is one column to the right and two rows down from cell C4. To indicate a relative reference, Excel uses a plain reference without any dollar signs; for example, B4.

- *Mixed reference.* A reference that is absolute for either the column or the row and relative for the other. For example, $B4 is absolute for the column (B) and relative for the row (4), while B$4 is relative for the column and absolute for the row. When you copy and paste a mixed reference, the absolute part stays the same, but the relative part changes to reflect the new location.

If you're typing a reference, you can type the $ signs into the reference to make it absolute or mixed. If you're entering references by selecting cells, click in the reference in cell you're editing or in the Formula bar, and then choose Formulas ➤ Function ➤ Switch Reference from the Ribbon. Click the Switch Reference button repeatedly to cycle a reference through its absolute, relative, column-absolute, and row-absolute versions.

Referring to Named Cells and Ranges

To make your references easier to enter and recognize, you can give a name to any cell or range. You can then refer to the cell or range by the name.

To create a named range, follow these steps:

1. Select the cell or range.

2. Choose Insert ➤ Name ➤ Define from the menu bar to display the Define Name dialog box (shown in Figure 15–1 with settings chosen).

Figure 15–1. *Use the Define Name dialog box to give a cell or range a name by which you can easily refer to it.*

3. In the Name text box, type the name for the range. Follow these rules:

    ■ The name must start with a letter or an underscore.

    ■ The name can contain only letters, numbers, and underscores. It can't contain spaces or symbols.

    ■ The name must be unique in the workbook.

4. Make sure that the Refers to box shows the right cell or range. If not, click the Collapse Dialog button, select the right cell or range in the worksheet, and then click the Collapse Dialog button again to restore the dialog box.

5.   Click the OK button to apply the name to the range.

After you've named a range, you can use the name in your formulas instead of the cell reference or range reference. Named ranges can be a great time-saver, because the names are much easier to remember and to type than the cell references or range references.

> **NOTE:** To delete a name from a range, choose Insert ➤ Name ➤ Define to display the Define Name dialog box. In the Names in workbook list, click the name. Click the Delete button to delete the name. Click the Close button to close the Define Name dialog box. If you find you've deleted the wrong name, use Undo to restore it.

Performing Custom Calculations by Creating Formulas

When you need to perform a custom calculation in a cell, use a formula rather than a function. All you need to do is type in a simple formula using the appropriate calculation operators, such as + signs for addition and – signs for subtraction. In this section, you'll meet the comparison operators, try using them in a worksheet, and learn the order in which Excel applies them—and how to change that order.

Meeting Excel's Calculation Operators

To perform calculations in Excel, you need to know the operators for the different operations—addition, division, comparison, and so on. Table 15–1 explains the full set of calculation operators you can use in your formulas in Excel.

Table 15–1. *Calculation Operators You Can Use in Excel*

Calculation Operator	Operation	Explanation or Example
Arithmetic Operators		
+	Addition	=1+2.
–	Subtraction	=1–2.
*	Multiplication	=2*2.
/	Division	=A1/4.
%	Percentage	=B1%.
^	Exponentiation	=B1^2 raises the value in cell B2 to the power 2.

Calculation Operator	Operation	Explanation or Example
Comparison Operators		
=	Equal to	=B2=15000 returns TRUE if cell B2 contains the value 15000. Otherwise, it returns FALSE.
<>	Not equal to	=B2<>15000 returns TRUE if cell B2 does not contain the value 15000. Otherwise, it returns FALSE.
>	Greater than	=B2>15000 returns TRUE if cell B2 contains a value greater than 15000. Otherwise, it returns FALSE.
>=	Greater than or equal to	=B2>=15000 returns TRUE if cell B2 contains a value greater than or equal to 15000. Otherwise, it returns FALSE.
<	Less than	=B2<15000 returns TRUE if cell B2 contains a value less than 15000. Otherwise, it returns FALSE.
<=	Less than or equal to	=B2<=15000 returns TRUE if cell B2 contains a value less than or equal to 15000. Otherwise, it returns FALSE.
Reference Operators		
[cell reference]:[cell reference]	The range of cells between the two cell references	A1:G5 returns the range of cells whose upper-left cell is cell A1 and whose lower-right cell is cell G5.
[cell reference],[cell reference]	The range of cells listed	A1,C3,E5 returns three cells: A1, C3, and E5.
[cell or range reference] [space][cell or range reference]	The range (or cell) that appears in both cells or ranges given	=A7:G10 B10:B12 returns the cell B10, because this is the only cell that appears in both the ranges given. If more than one cell appears in the range, this returns a #VALUE! error.
Text Operator		
&	Concatenation (joining values as text)	=A1&B1 returns the values from cells A1 and B1 joined together as a text string. For example, if A1 contains "New York " (including a trailing space) and B1 contains "Sales", this formula returns "New York Sales." If A1 contains 100 and B1 contains 50, this formula returns 10050.

Using the Calculation Operators

Now that you know what the calculation operators are, try the following example of creating a simple worksheet (see Figure 15–2) that uses the four most straightforward operators—addition, subtraction, multiplication, and division.

	A	B	C
1	Gross	$84,000.00	
2	Expenses	$30,000.00	
3	Tax Rate	18%	
4	Tax Amount	$15,120.00	
5	Net	$38,880.00	
6	Months	12	
7	Monthly Net	$3,240.00	
8			

Figure 15–2. *Create this simple worksheet to try using Excel's addition, subtraction, multiplication, and division operators.*

To create the worksheet, follow these steps:

1. Create a new workbook. The quickest way to do this is to press Cmd+N.

2. Type the following text in cells A1 through A7:

   - *A1.* Gross
   - *A2.* Expenses
   - *A3.* Tax Rate
   - *A4.* Tax Amount
   - *A5.* Net
   - *A6.* Months
   - *A7.* Monthly Net

3. Apply boldface to column A by clicking the column heading and then choosing Home ➤ Font ➤ Bold.

4. Apply Currency format to column B by clicking the column heading and then choosing Home ➤ Number ➤ Number Format ➤ Currency.

5. Type the following text in cells B1 through B3:

   - *B1.* 84000
   - *B2.* 30000

■ *B3.* 0.18

6. Apply Percent style to cell B3 by clicking the cell and then choosing Home ➤ Number ➤ Number Style ➤ Percent Style.

NOTE: You can also enter the percentage in Step 6 by typing **18%** and pressing Return. Excel automatically changes the number format to Percentage.

7. Now enter the formula **=B1*B3** in cell B4, like this:

■ Click cell B4 to select it.

■ Type = to start creating a formula in the cell.

■ Click cell B1 to enter it in the formula. Excel displays a shimmering dotted blue outline around the cell and adds it to the formula in the cell and to the Formula bar (see Figure 15–3).

SUM	⊗ ⊘ fx =B1	
	A	B	C
1	Gross	$84,000.00	
2	Expenses	$30,000.00	
3	Tax Rate	18%	
4	Tax Amount	=B1	
5	Net		
6	Months		
7	Monthly Net		
8			

Figure 15–3. When you click cell B1, Excel adds it to the formula in both the cell and the Formula bar and displays a dotted blue outline around it.

■ Type * to tell Excel you want to multiply the value in cell B1. Excel enters the asterisk in the formula and changes the outline around cell B1 to solid blue.

■ Click cell B3 to enter it in the formula. Excel displays a shimmering dotted outline (green this time) around the cell and adds it to the formula in the cell and in the formula bar (see Figure 15–4).

SUM		⊗ ⊘ ⌃ *fx*	=B1*B3	
	A	B	C	
1	Gross	$84,000.00		
2	Expenses	$30,000.00		
3	Tax Rate	18%		
4	Tax Amount	=B1*B3		
5	Net			
6	Months			
7	Monthly Net			
8				

Figure 15–4. *Click cell B3 to add it to the formula.*

- Press Return or click the Enter button (the check-mark button in the Formula bar) to finish entering the formula in cell B4.

8. Enter the formula **=B1-(B2+B4)** in cell B5. Follow these steps:

- Click cell B5 to select it. If you pressed Return to enter the previous formula, Excel may have selected this cell already.

- Type = to start creating a formula in the cell.

- Click cell B1 to add it to the formula.

- Type – to enter the subtraction operator.

- Type **(** to start a nested expression. (More on this shortly.)

- Click cell B2 to add it to the formula.

- Type + to enter the addition operator.

- Click cell B4 to add it to the formula.

- Type **)** to end the nested expression.

- Click the Enter button to finish entering the formula.

9. Enter **12** in cell B6 and apply General formatting to it. Follow these steps:

- Click cell B6.

- Choose Home ➤ Number ➤ Number Format ➤ General.

- Type **12**.

- Press the down arrow to enter the value and move the active cell to cell B7.

10. Enter the formula **=B5/B6** in cell B7. This time, simply type the formula in—lowercase is fine—and then press Return. You'll notice that when you type **b5**, Excel selects cell B5 to let you check visually that you have the right cell.

Now that you've created the worksheet, try changing the figures in cells B1, B2, and B3. You'll see the results of the formulas in cells B4, B5, and B7 change accordingly. Excel recalculates the formulas each time you change a value in a cell, so the formula results remain up to date.

> **NOTE:** If you create a workbook with huge amounts of data, automatic recalculation may make Excel run slowly. If this happens, choose Formulas ➤ Calculation ➤ Settings ➤ Calculate Manually to turn off automatic recalculation. You can recalculate manually when necessary by choosing Formulas ➤ Calculation ➤ Recalculate Sheet (to recalculate just the active worksheet) or choosing Formulas ➤ Calculation ➤ Recalculate All to recalculate the whole workbook.

Understanding the Order in Which Excel Evaluates Operators

In the previous example, you entered the formula **=B1-(B2+B4)** in cell B5. The parentheses are necessary because the calculation has two separate stages—one stage of subtraction and one stage of addition—and you need to control the order in which they occur.

Try changing the formula in cell B5 to **=B1-B2+B4** and see what happens. Follow these steps:

1. Click cell B5.

2. Click in the Formula bar to start editing the formula there. (You can also edit in the cell by double-clicking the cell or pressing Ctrl+U, but editing in the Formula bar gives you more space, so it's often easier.)

3. Delete the opening and closing parentheses.

4. Click the Enter button on the Formula bar.

You'll notice that the Net amount (cell B5) jumps substantially. This is because you've changed the meaning of the formula:

- *=B1-(B2+B4)*. This formula means "add the value in cell B2 to the value in cell B4, and then subtract the result from the value in cell B1."

- *=B1-B2+B4*. This formula means "subtract the value in cell B2 from the value in cell B1, and then add the value in cell B4 to the result."

Click cell B5 and press Ctrl+U to open the cell for editing. Position the insertion point before **B2** and type **(**; then position the insertion point after **B4** and type **)**. Then press Return to enter the formula in the cell.

NOTE: As you type a closing parenthesis in a formula, you'll see that the opening parenthesis momentarily darkens to make the pairing clear. When a cell has complex contents, and contains other nested items, having the corresponding parenthesis darken like this helps you to identify it.

The order in which Excel evaluates the operators is called *operator precedence*, and it can make a huge difference in your formulas—so it's vital to know both how it works and how to override it. Table 15–2 shows you the order in which Excel evaluates the operators in formulas.

Table 15–2. *Excel's Operator Precedence in Descending Order*

Precedence	Operators	Explanation
1	–	Negation
2	%	Percentage
3	^	Exponentiation
4	* and /	Multiplication and division
5	+ and –	Addition and subtraction
6	&	Concatenation
7	=, <>, <, <=, >, and >=	Comparison operators

When two operators are at the same level, Excel performs the operator that appears earlier in the formula first.

Nesting Parts of Formulas to Control Operator Precedence

You can control operator precedence in any formula by nesting one or more parts of the formula in parentheses. For example, as you just saw, using **=B1-(B2+B4)** makes Excel evaluate **B2+B4** before the subtraction.

You can nest parts of the formula several levels deep if necessary. For example, the following formula uses three levels of nesting and returns 180:

```
=10*(5*(4/(1+1))+8)
```

TIP: Nested formulas can quickly become hard to read. If you find a formula is becoming too complex, break it up into intermediate stages, and place each in a separate cell. Excel gives you almost unlimited space, and it's much better to use more cells than to get the wrong result by creating a formula that's impressively complex but wrong.

Entering Formulas Quickly by Copying and Using AutoFill

In many worksheets, you'll need to enter related formulas in several or many cells. For example, say you have the worksheet shown in Figure 15–5, which lists a range of products with their prices and sales. Column D needs to show the total revenue derived by multiplying the Units figure by the Price value.

D2				fx	=B2*C2	
	A	B	C	D		E
1	Product	Units	Price	Total		
2	Emulator	915	$39.99	$36,590.85		
3	Virtualizer	638	$4.99			
4	Video Mule	18	$189.99			
5	Q Leader	1927	$19.99			
6						

Figure 15–5. *When a worksheet needs similar formulas in a column or row, you can enter one formula manually and then use AutoFill or Copy and Paste to enter it quickly in the other cells.*

Each cell in column D needs a different formula: Cell D2 needs =B2*C2; Cell D3 needs =B3*C3, and so on. Because the formula is the same except for the row number, you can use either AutoFill or Copy and Paste to enter the formula from cell D2 into the other cells as well.

To enter the formula using AutoFill, click the cell that contains the formula (here, cell D2), and then drag the AutoFill handle (the blue square at the lower-right corner of the active cell) down through cell D5. Excel automatically fills in the formulas, adjusting each for the change in row.

To enter the formula using Copy and Paste, click the cell that contains the formula, and then give the Copy command (for example, press Cmd+C.). Select the destination cells, and then give the Paste command (for example, press Cmd+V).

NOTE: If you need to copy a formula to a different row or column but have it refer to the original location, create the formula using mixed references. If you need to keep the column the same, make the column absolute (for example, =$B2); if you need to keep the row the same, make the row absolute (for example, =B$2).

Troubleshooting Common Problems with Formulas

Formulas are great when they work, but a single-letter typo or a wrong reference can prevent a formula from working correctly. This section shows you how to deal with common problems with formulas, starting with solutions to the error messages you're most likely to produce.

Understanding Common Errors—and Resolving Them

Excel includes an impressive arsenal of error messages, but some of them appear far more frequently than others. Table 15–3 shows you eight errors you're likely to encounter, explains what they mean, and tells you how to solve them.

Table 15–3. *How to Solve Excel's Eight Most Common Errors*

Error	What the Problem Is	How to Solve It
#####	The formula result is too wide to fit in the cell.	Make the column wider—for example, double-click the column head's right border to AutoFit the column width.
#NAME?	A function name is misspelled, or the formula refers to a range that doesn't exist.	Check the spelling of all functions; correct any mistakes. If the formula uses a named range, check that the name is right and that you haven't deleted the range.
#NUM!	The formula tries to use a value that is not valid for it—for example, returning the square root of a negative number.	Give the function a suitable value.
#VALUE!	The function uses an invalid argument—for example, using =FACT() to return the factorial of text rather than a number.	Give the function the right type of data.
#N/A	The function does not have a valid value available.	Make sure the function's arguments provide values of the right type.
#DIV/0	The function is trying to divide by zero (which is mathematically impossible).	Change the divisor value from zero. Often, you'll find that the function is using a blank cell (which has a zero value) as the argument for the divisor; in this case, enter a value in the cell.
#REF!	The formula uses a cell reference or a range reference that's not valid—for example, because you've deleted a worksheet.	Edit the formula and provide a valid reference.
#NULL!	There is no intersection between the two ranges specified.	Change the ranges to produce an intersection.

Seeing the Details of an Error in a Formula

When Excel identifies an error in a formula, it displays a green triangle at the upper-left corner of the cell that contains the formula. Click the cell to display an action button that you can hold the mouse over to display a ScreenTip explaining the problem (see Figure 15–6) or click to display a menu of actions you can take to resolve the problem.

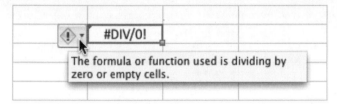

Figure 15–6. *Hold the mouse pointer over the action button for an error cell to display a ScreenTip explaining what's wrong.*

Tracing an Error Back to Its Source

To see which cell is causing an error, click the error cell, then choose Formulas ➤ Audit Formulas ➤ Check for Errors ➤ Trace Error. Excel displays an arrow from the guilty cell or cells to the error cell. The left screen in Figure 15–7 shows a simple example of tracing an error; the more complex the worksheet, the more helpful this feature is. Excel displays a worksheet symbol (see the right screen in Figure 15–7) if the cell reference is on another worksheet or in another workbook.

Figure 15–7. *Use the Formulas ➤ Audit Formulas ➤ Check for Errors ➤ Trace Error command to identify the cell or cells causing an error. If the cell reference is on another worksheet or in another workbook, Excel displays a worksheet symbol, as shown on the right.*

Displaying All the Formulas in a Worksheet

When you need to review or check all the formulas in a worksheet, choose Formulas ➤ Function ➤ Show ➤ Show Formulas, placing a check mark next to the Show Formulas item on the Show pop-up menu. Excel displays the formulas and automatically widens the worksheet columns to give you more space (see Figure 15–8).

Figure 15–8. *Choose Formulas ➤ Function ➤ Show ➤ Show Formulas when you need to see all the formulas in a worksheet.*

When you've finished viewing the formulas, choose Formulas ➤ Function ➤ Show ➤ Show Formulas again, removing the check mark from the Show Formulas menu item. Excel automatically restores the columns to their former widths.

Seeing Which Cells a Formula Uses

To see which cells a formula uses, click the cell that contains the formula, and then choose Formulas ➤ Audit Formulas ➤ Trace Precedents. Excel displays an arrow showing the formula back to its roots. If one of the cells the formula uses contains a formula itself, you can click that cell and click the Trace Precedents button again to display its precedents in turn. Figure 15–9 shows the precedents of cell D6 and one of the cells that it uses, cell D2.

Figure 15–9. *Use the Trace Precedents command to see which cells you're using to produce a formula result. In this example, cells B2 and C2 go to make up the formula in cell D2, which in turn appears in the =SUM(D2:D5) formula in cell D6.*

When you need to look at the problem the other way and see which formulas use a particular cell, click the cell, and then choose Formulas ➤ Audit Formulas ➤ Trace Dependents. Again, Excel displays arrows, this time from the cell going to each of the formulas that use it. Figure 15–10 shows an example of tracing dependent cells.

B1		⊗ ⊘ ⌃	fx	84000		
	A	B	C	D	E
1	Gross	$84,000.00		Monthly	►$7,000.00
2	Expenses	$30,000.00		Deductions	$1,260.00
3	Tax Rate	18%			
4	Tax Amount	$15,120.00			
5	Net	$38,880.00			
6	Months	12			
7	Monthly Net	$3,240.00			

Figure 15–10. *Use the Trace Dependents command to see which formulas use a particular cell's value to produce their results.*

NOTE: You can use the Trace Precedents command and the Trace Dependents command either with formulas displayed or with formula results displayed, whichever you find most useful.

When you've finished tracing precedents and dependents, choose Formulas ➤ Audit Formulas ➤ Remove Arrows (clicking the main part of the Remove Arrows button) to remove the arrows from the screen. If you want to remove just precedent arrows or dependent arrows, click the Remove Arrows pop-up button, and then click the Remove Precedent Arrows item or the Remove Dependent Arrows item on the pop-up menu.

Removing Circular References

Even if you're careful, it's easy enough to create a *circular reference*—one that refers to itself.

Circular references most often occur when you enter a formula that refers to a cell that itself refers to the cell in which you're entering the formula. For example, say cell A1 contains the formula **=B1**. If you enter the formula **=A1** in cell B1, you've created a circular reference: cell B1 gets its value from cell A1, which gets its value from cell B1, and so on.

You can also enter a circular reference by making a cell refer to itself. For example, if you enter **=A1/B1** in cell A1, you've created a circular reference in that cell, because cell A1 refers to itself. This type of circular reference is usually easier to avoid than the previous type.

Circular references can be useful in some specialized circumstances, such as when you need to perform iterations of a calculation, but normally you don't want them in your worksheets, so Excel helps you to get rid of them.

When you create a circular reference that Excel cannot calculate, Excel displays the Excel Cannot Calculate a Formula dialog box shown in Figure 15–11. Click the OK button if you want to open a Help window showing information on how to deal with circular references, or click the Cancel button if you want to go ahead and enter the circular reference in the cell (for example, because you can tell what the problem is and will be able to fix it easily).

Figure 15–11. *Circular references can cause problems in worksheets, so Excel warns you when you enter one. You can click the Cancel button if you're sure you want to create the circular reference.*

NOTE: If you leave circular references in a worksheet, use the Circular readout on the status bar to identify them. This readout shows the location of the most recent circular reference that Excel has identified. When you've dealt with that circular reference, the Circular readout shows the next one, and so on, until there are none left.

Performing Standard Calculations by Inserting Functions

When you need to perform standard calculations in your worksheets, use Excel's built-in functions—predefined formulas that you simply insert in a cell and provide with the data they need.

You can enter functions in four ways:

- *Use the AutoSum button or AutoSum pop-up menu.* The AutoSum button appears on the Standard toolbar and gives quick access to five widely used functions.

- *Use the Insert pop-up menu and the Formula Builder.* The Insert pop-up menu appears in the Function group of the Formulas tab of the Ribbon. When you choose the function you want from the Insert pop-up menu and its submenus, Excel displays the Formula Builder pane in the Toolbox to walk you through inserting the function.

- *Use the Formula Builder pane in the Toolbox.* You can also start work in the Formula Builder pane in the Toolbox without using the Insert pop-up menu first.

- *Type the function in manually.* When you know which function you want, you can type it straight into a cell.

Understanding Function Names and Arguments

In Excel, a function has a name written in capitals followed by a pair of parentheses. Here are three examples:

- *SUM().* This widely used function adds together two or more values that you specify.

- *COUNT().* This function counts the number of cells that contain numbers (as opposed to text, blanks, or other data types) in the range you specify.

- *TODAY().* This function enters the current date in the cell.

Most functions take *arguments*—pieces of information that tell the function what you want it to work on. Excel prompts you to provide the arguments each function needs. For example, when you enter the function in a cell, Excel displays a ScreenTip showing the arguments needed. Figure 15–12 shows an example using the SUM() function.

Figure 15–12. *When you enter a function in a cell, Excel prompts you to supply the arguments it needs.*

The ScreenTip shows that the SUM() function has one required argument and one optional argument, and you can add further arguments as needed:

- *Required argument.* Each required argument appears in bold, like the argument *number1* in the ScreenTip. You separate the arguments with commas. For example, you can use SUM() to add the values of cells in a range: SUM(C1:C10). Here, C1:C10 is a single argument, the required argument.

- *Optional argument.* Each optional argument appears in brackets, like the argument *[number2]* in the ScreenTip. For example, you can use SUM() to add the values of two cells: SUM(C1,C3). Here, C1 is the required argument, and C3 is the first optional argument.

- *Extra arguments.* The ellipsis (...) shows that you can enter extra arguments of the same type. For example, you can use SUM() to add the values of many cells: SUM(C1,C3,D4,D8,E1,XF202). Here, C1 is the required argument, and all the other cell references are optional arguments.

NOTE: A few functions take no arguments. For example, you don't need to tell the TODAY() function which day you're talking about. Similarly, the NOW() function needs no arguments to return the current date and time, and the NA() function simply enters #(N/A) in a cell to indicate that the information is not available.

Inserting Functions with the AutoSum Pop-up Menu

The quickest and easiest way to enter any of five widely used functions—SUM(), AVERAGE(), COUNT(), MAX(), or MIN()—in your worksheets is to use the AutoSum pop-up menu on the Standard toolbar. Follow these steps:

1. Click the cell you want to enter the function in.

2. If you want to create a SUM() function for the cells immediately above or to the left of the selected cell, click the AutoSum button itself. Otherwise, click the AutoSum pop-up button, and then click the function (see Figure 15–13).

NOTE: You can also use the AutoSum pop-up menu on the Standard toolbar to open the Formula Builder pane in the Toolbox. Just click the More Functions item at the bottom of the pop-up menu.

Figure 15–13. *Use the AutoSum pop-up menu on the Standard toolbar when you need to insert the SUM(), AVERAGE(), COUNT(), MAX(), or MIN() function quickly.*

3. Excel inserts the function in the cell you chose and selects the range it thinks you may want to use as the argument. Figure 15–14 shows an example with the AVERAGE() function.

Figure 15–14. *When you insert a function from the AutoSum pop-up menu, Excel selects a range of data it thinks may be suitable.*

4. If you need to change the range, do so in one of these ways:

   ■ Click and drag to select the right range.

   ■ Type the range over the range selected within the parentheses.

5. Add another argument to the formula if needed. For example, type a comma, and then click and drag to select another range.

6. When the formula is as you want it, press Return to enter it in the cell. Excel displays the result of the formula.

Inserting Functions with the Formula Builder

When you need to find the right function to insert or when you need to learn about the arguments for a function, use the Formula Builder to insert the function. The Formula Builder is a pane that appears in the Toolbox and provides a complete list of Excel's functions, together with descriptions and details of the arguments they use.

To insert a function with the Formula Builder, follow these steps:

1. Select the cell in which you want to enter the function.

2. Open the Formula Builder in one of these ways:

   ■ *Standard toolbar.* Click the AutoSum pop-up button, and then click the More Functions item on the pop-up menu.

   ■ *Menu bar.* Choose View ➤ Formula Builder.

   ■ *Ribbon.* Choose Formulas ➤ Function ➤ Formula Builder.

   ■ *Toolbox.* If the Toolbox is already open, click the Formula Builder tab.

3. If you want to search for a function, click in the Search box at the top, type keywords to search for, and then press Return. The Formula Builder displays a list of results, as shown on the left in Figure 15–15.

Figure 15–15. *To find a function, type a search term in the Search pane of the Formula Builder and press Return; the Formula Builder shows a list of results (left). Otherwise, browse the full list of functions, and click the function you want to see information on (right).*

4. Otherwise, browse through the list of functions to find the function you need, as shown on the right in Figure 15–15. The Formula Builder breaks the functions up into the following categories:

    ■ *Most Recently Used.* This category provides quick access to the functions you've used most recently—so if you're looking for a function you've used before, start by looking here.

> **TIP:** You can make the formula list in the Formula Builder window taller or shorter by dragging the sizing handle—the line of three dots below the list—up or down. The Formula Builder window grows or shrinks to accommodate the list.

■ *Arithmetic.* This category doesn't actually show functions, just a single entry called "Add, Subtract, Multiply or Divide." When you select this item, the Arguments pane at the bottom of the Formula Browser (see the right screen in Figure 15–15) displays controls for helping you set up arithmetic formulas.

■ *Database.* This category contains functions for working with databases—for example, returning the average of values in a column or list or the count of cells containing numbers in a field.

■ *Date and Time.* This category contains functions ranging from returning the current date with the TODAY() function to using the WEEKDAY() function to return the day of the week for a particular date.

■ *Engineering.* This category contains functions including the DEC2HEX() function (for converting a decimal number to hexadecimal) and the HEX2OCT() function (for converting a hexadecimal number to octal, base 8).

■ *Financial.* This category contains functions for financial calculations—for example, calculating the payments on your mortgage or the depreciation on an asset.

■ *Information.* This category contains functions for returning information about data, such as whether it is text or a number.

■ *Logical.* This category contains the AND(), FALSE(), IF(), IFERROR(), NOT(), OR(), and TRUE() functions.

■ *Lookup and Reference.* This category contains functions for looking up data from other parts of a worksheet or referring to other cells in it.

■ *Math and Trigonometry.* This category contains mathematical functions, such as the SQRT() function for returning a square root, and trigonometric functions, such as the COS() function for calculating a cosine.

■ *Statistical.* This category contains functions for performing statistical calculations, such as working out standard deviations based on a population or a sample.

■ *Text.* This category contains functions for manipulating text, such as the TRIM() function (for trimming off leading and trailing spaces) and the LEFT() function, which returns the leftmost part of the value.

■ *Compatibility.* This category contains functions included for compatibility with Excel 2008 (Mac), Excel 2007 (Windows), and earlier versions. It's best to use these functions only for compatibility with these older versions; if you're developing worksheets for Excel 2011 or Excel 2010 (Windows), use the newer functions that these versions support—for example, use the new POISSON.DIST() function rather than the old POISSON() function.

5. To learn more about a function, click it. The Formula Builder shows its details at the bottom of the window, as shown on the left in Figure 15–16.

Figure 15–16. *Use the Description area at the bottom of the Formula Builder to identify the function you want (left). When you double-click the function to insert it, the Formula Builder displays the Arguments pane (right).*

6. When you've found the function you want to insert, double-click it. The Formula Builder displays the Arguments pane for the function, as shown on the right in Figure 15–16 (with one argument already entered).

7. Click in the box for the first argument, and then enter the data. You can type in a value or range name, type in a cell reference or range, or use the mouse to choose a cell reference or range in the worksheet (or in another worksheet or workbook).

8. Fill in each of the other arguments for the function. When you have entered all the required arguments, the Result readout in the lower-right corner of the Function Builder window shows the result of the function.

9. Press Return to enter the function in the worksheet.

If you have finished using the Function Builder, close it by clicking its Close button (the button at the left end of its title bar), choosing View ➤ Formula Builder from the menu bar, or clicking the Toolbox button on the Standard toolbar.

Inserting Functions with the Insert Pop-up Menu

When you know which function you want to insert, the easiest way to insert it (unless it's one of the five functions on the AutoSum pop-up menu) is to use the Insert pop-up menu. The Insert pop-up menu helps you pick the function by category and inserts it directly in the cell.

To insert a function using the Insert pop-up menu, follow these steps:

1. Select the cell in which you want to enter the function.

2. Choose Formulas ➤ Function ➤ Insert to display the Insert pop-up menu. This pop-up menu breaks up the functions into ten categories: Database, Date and Time, Engineering, Financial, Information, Logical, Lookup and Reference, Math and Trigonometry, Statistical, and Text. These categories are similar to those that appear in the Formula Builder, as discussed earlier in this chapter. Each category has a submenu.

3. Click the category of functions you want to insert. Excel displays a submenu containing the functions. Figure 15–17 shows the Date and time submenu open.

Figure 15–17. *Use the Insert pop-up menu in the Function group on the Formulas tab of the Ribbon when you want to insert a function by category.*

4. Click the function you want to insert. Excel inserts it in the cell.

5. Enter the arguments for the function as usual.

> **TIP:** If you need help providing the function's arguments, choose Formulas ➤ Function ➤ Formula Builder from the Ribbon or View ➤ Formula Builder from the menu bar to display the Formula Builder. The Formula Builder shows the details of the function you've just inserted.

6. Press Return or click the Enter button on the Formula bar to enter the formula in the cell.

Inserting Functions by Typing Them into a Worksheet

You can also enter functions in your worksheets by typing them into cells. Follow these general steps:

1. Click the cell to select it.

2. Type = to tell Excel that you're creating a formula.

3. Start typing the function's name. Excel displays a list of matching functions (see Figure 15–18).

Figure 15–18. *When you start typing a function name into a cell, Excel lists matching functions. Click the function you want to insert.*

> **NOTE:** You can also keep typing until you've typed enough to identify the function uniquely—or type the whole of the function name if you prefer.

4. To enter a function, double-click it, or move the highlight to it by pressing down arrow or up arrow, and then press Return.

5. Specify the arguments for the function. You can either type in a value or a reference or use the mouse to select a cell or range.

Summary

In this chapter, you learned how to use formulas and functions to perform calculations in your workbooks. You know that a formula is the recipe for a calculation, and you know how to assemble it from its various components—an equal sign, cell or range references, operators, and more. You know how to create the formulas you need and how to troubleshoot them when they go wrong.

You're now also familiar with functions. You know that a function is a preset formula built into Excel, how to insert functions using the various tools Excel provides, and how to furnish functions with the arguments they need to work.

In the next chapter, I'll show you how to create databases and solve business problems.

Chapter 16

Creating Simple Databases and Solving Business Problems

Packed with more than 16,000 columns and more than 1 million rows, each Excel worksheet has enough space to contain serious amounts of data—so it's great for creating a database to store information and quickly find the items you need.

In this chapter, you'll learn first to use Excel to create databases for storing information, sorting it, and filtering it to show the information you need. You'll then learn to use Excel's scenarios feature and its Goal Seek tool to solve business problems by performing what-if analysis.

Creating Databases in Excel

When you need to store a lot of the same type of information in a worksheet, you can create a database. For example, if you run a business, you can make a database of your customers and their orders.

> **NOTE:** Excel refers to databases as *tables*, which can be confusing if you're used to that word's normal meaning in the Office applications. So, this chapter refers to these databases as *database tables* for clarity.

The first step is to set up the database table and to tell Excel that you're creating a database table rather than a regular worksheet. The next step is to add your data to the database, either by typing it into the cells as usual or by using a data-entry form.

Once the data is in the database table, you can sort the table to reveal different aspects of its contents or filter it to identify items that match the criteria you specify.

Understanding What You Can and Can't Do with Excel Database Tables

Before you start creating a database table in Excel, it's important to be clear on what you can and can't do with Excel database tables.

As you know, an Excel worksheet consists of rows and columns. To create a database table on a worksheet, you make each row into a *record*—an item that holds all the details of a single entry. For example, in a database table that records your sales to customers, a record would contain the details of a purchase. You make each column a *field* in the database table—a column for the purchase number, a column for the date, a column for the customer's last name, and so on. Figure 16–1 shows part of an Excel database table for tracking sales to customers.

Figure 16–1. *An Excel database consists of a table, with each row forming a record and each column containing a field.*

This is what's called a *flat-file* database: all the data in the database is stored in a single table rather than in separate tables that are linked to each other.

This means you can use Excel to create any database for which you can store all the data for a record in a single row. Because you have a million rows at your disposal, you can create large databases if necessary, but they may make Excel run slowly.

What you can't do with Excel is create *relational databases*—ones that store the data in linked tables. A relational database is the kind of database you create with full-bore database applications such as FileMaker or Microsoft Access (on Windows). In a relational database, every record has a unique ID number or field that the application uses to link the data in the different tables.

Creating a Database Table and Returning Data

In this section, you'll look at how to create a database table and enter data in it either by using standard Excel methods or by using a data-entry form.

Creating a Database Table

To create a database table, follow these steps:

1. Create a workbook as usual. For example, you can:

   - Create a new blank workbook. Press Cmd+N or choose File ➤ New Workbook from the menu bar.

   - Create a workbook based on a template or an existing workbook. Press Cmd+Shift+P or choose File ➤ New from Template, and then work in the Excel Workbook Gallery dialog box.

2. Name the worksheet on which you'll create the database table. Double-click the worksheet tab, type the name you want (up to 31 characters, including spaces), and then press Return to apply the name.

3. Type the headings for the database table. For example, if the database table will contain customer names and addresses, you'd type fields such as Last Name, First Name, Middle Initial, Title, Address 1, and so on. Try to get all the fields in place at this point; you can add columns to the table later, but you'll then need to add extra data to the existing records.

> **NOTE:** Usually, it's easiest to put the headings in the first row of the worksheet, but if you need to have information appear above the database table, leave rows free for it.

4. Format the headings differently from the rows below them. For example, click the row header for the heading row, and then press Cmd+B to apply boldface.

5. Select the headings and at least one row below them.

6. Choose Tables ➤ Table Options ➤ New from the Ribbon, clicking the main part of the New button rather than the pop-up button. Excel makes the following changes:

   - Creates the table.

   - Gives the table a default name, such as Table1 or Table2.

   - Turns the header row into headers with pop-up buttons.

NOTE: If your headings have the same formatting as the data rows, choose Tables ➤ Table Options ➤ New ➤ Table with Header Rows rather than Tables ➤ Table Options ➤ New. Otherwise, Excel inserts a new row containing headers above your heading row.

- Applies a table style with shading based on the workbook's theme. You can change the style later as needed.

7. Rename your table by following these steps:

- Click the Name pop-up menu at the left end of the Formula bar, and then click the table name. Excel selects the table if it's not still selected.

- Click in the Name text box to select the table name.

- Type the new name for the table. As with chart names, the database table name must be unique in the workbook, must start with a letter or an underscore, and cannot contain spaces or symbols.

- Press Return to apply the table name.

Customizing the Database Table's Looks

At this point, you can start entering data in the database table (as discussed next)—but before you do, you may want to change the way it looks. To do so, follow these steps:

1. Click anywhere in the database table.

2. Click the Tables tab of the Ribbon if it's not already displayed.

3. If a suitable style appears in the Table Styles box on the Ribbon, click it. If not, hold the mouse pointer over the Table Styles box to display the panel button, and then click the panel button to display the Table Styles panel (see Figure 16–2). Click the style you want to apply.

Figure 16–2. *You can format a table quickly by applying one of Excel's table styles from the Table Styles panel on the Tables tab of the Ribbon. Scroll down the panel to see the other styles.*

4. In the Table Options group on the Tables tab of the Ribbon, select the check box for each table style option you want to use:

- *Header Row.* Select this check box to display the header row. This is almost always useful.

- *Total Row.* Select this check box to add a row labeled Total immediately after the database table's last row. This is useful when you need to add a total formula or another formula in the last row. To add a formula, click a cell, click the pop-up button that appears, and then click the formula you want on the pop-up menu (see Figure 16–3).

	Sale Numbe	Date	Last Name	First Name	Initial	Title	Address 1
153	20622		Reyes	Rachel	M	Rev.	4098 Pine
154	20503	11/8/10	Rodriguez	Anthony	O	Mr.	1482 Business Loop
155	20564		Jenkins	Michelle	N	Dr.	1681 Elm
156	Total						
157			✓ None				
158			Average				
159			Count				
160			Count Numbers				
161			Max				
162			Min				
163			Sum				
164			StdDev				
165			Var				
166			More Functions…				

Figure 16–3. *Adding a Total row to a database table lets you quickly insert functions in the row's cells.*

> **TIP:** The pop-up menu in the Total row of a database table gives you instant access to the most widely used functions in databases—Average, Count, Count Numbers, Max, Min, Sum, StdDev (Standard Deviation), or Var (calculating variance based on a sample). You can also click the More Functions item at the bottom of the pop-up menu to display the Formula Builder, from which you can access the full range of Excel's functions. For example, you can insert the COUNTBLANK() function to count the number of blank cells in a column. You might do this to ensure that a column of essential data contains no blanks.

- *Banded Rows.* Select this check box to apply a band of color to every other row. This helps you read the rows of data without your eyes wandering to another row. Some table styles apply banding to the rows automatically.

- *First Column.* Select this check box if you want the first column to have different formatting. You may want to do this if the first column contains the main field for identifying each record (for example, a unique number).

- *Last Column*: Select this check box if you want the last column to have different formatting. Usually, you'll want this only if the last column contains data that is more important in some way than the data in the other columns.

- *Banded Columns.* Select this check box to apply a band of color to every other column. This is sometimes helpful but usually less helpful than banded rows. (Don't use both—the effect is seldom useful.)

When you've finished choosing a style and options for the database table, save your work as usual.

Entering Data in a Database Table

You can enter data in a database table either by typing it in directly or by using a data-entry form. In most cases, the data-entry form is the easier option, as you'll see in a moment.

Entering Data Directly in the Database Table

A database table is essentially an Excel worksheet at heart, so you can enter data in the database table by using the standard techniques you've learned in the past few chapters. For example, click a cell, and then type data into it; or, if you have the data in another worksheet, copy it and paste it in.

When you enter data in the row immediately after the last row in the database table, Excel automatically expands the database table to include that row. To add a row within the database table, click a cell in the row above which you want to add the new row, and then choose Insert ➤ Rows from the menu bar. Again, Excel automatically expands the database table to include the new row.

To insert a column in the database table, click a cell in the column before which you want to add the new column, and then choose Insert ➤ Columns from the menu bar. Again, Excel automatically expands the database table.

> **TIP:** You can quickly select a row, a column, or an entire database table with the mouse. To select a row, move the mouse pointer to the left part of a cell in the database table's leftmost column, and then click with the horizontal arrow that appears. To select a column, move the mouse pointer over a column heading, and then click with the downward arrow that appears. To select the whole database table, move the mouse pointer over the upper-left cell in the database table, and then click with the diagonal arrow that appears.

Entering Data Using a Data-Entry Form

Typing directly into the database table tends to be awkward, especially when the database table contains too many columns to fit in the Excel window with the whole content of each column displayed. When your database has grown beyond a few rows, you can usually enter data more easily by using a data-entry form—a dialog box that Excel automatically tailors to suit your database table.

Choose Data ➤ Form to display the data-entry form dialog box. Figure 16–4 shows this dialog box, whose title bar shows the name of the worksheet you're using (here, Sales) rather than the word *Form*.

Sales		
Sale Number:	20560	2 of 154
Date:	2/5/2011	New
Last Name:	Barnes	Delete
First Name:	Donna	Restore
Initial:	T	Find Prev
Title:	Mrs.	Find Next
Address 1:	1802 Crescent	Criteria
Address 2:		Close
City:	Birmingham	
State:	AL	
ZIP:	35203	
Telephone:	2055552619	
Mobile:	251-555-3124	
E-mail 1:	dbarnes44@hotmail	
E-mail 2:		
Quantity:	1	
Item:	Pain Drill	
Price:	79.99	
Shipping:	9.99	
Total:	89.98	

Figure 16–4. *The Form dialog box bears the name of the worksheet your database table is on (here, Sales) and shows each field in the order they appear in the header row.*

To use the data form, you move to the record you want in one of these ways:

- *Create a new record.* Click the New button to create a new record in the database. When you type the data in the fields, Excel adds the new record after the last current record in the database.

- *Move forward or backward through the records.* Click the Find Next button to display the next record, or click the Find Prev button to display the previous record.

- *Scroll through the records.* Drag the scroll box up or down the scroll bar to move quickly through the records. Click the scroll arrows to move in smaller increments.

■   *Search for a record.* Follow these steps:

1.   Click the Criteria button to switch to the criteria view of the form.
     Excel clears any data in the fields.

2.   Type your search term in the field by which you want to search.
     For example, to search for your customers in Arizona, type **AZ** in
     the State field (assuming your database has this field).

3.   Click the Find Next button to find the next instance, or click the
     Find Prev button to find the previous instance.

Excel automatically switches the dialog box back to Form view when you search. If you
decide you don't need to search after all, click the Form button (which replaces the
Criteria button) to return to Form view.

Once you've created or located the record you want to change, type or edit the data in
the fields in the data-entry form dialog box. Excel enters it in the columns for you.

When you've finished using the Form dialog box, click the Close button to close it.

Resizing a Database Table

When you've created a database table, Excel normally resizes it for you automatically
when you add or delete rows or columns. For example, when you add a record by using
the Form dialog box, Excel expands the database table to include it.

Excel also expands the database table automatically if you add data to the row after the
current last row in a database table that doesn't have a Total row. Excel calls this feature
Table AutoExpansion. If you don't want Excel to do this, click the AutoCorrect actions
button that appears below and to the right of the first cell in the added row, and then
click Undo Table AutoExpansion (see Figure 16–5). Click the actions button again, and
then click Stop Automatically Expanding Tables.

NOTE: When you add a new row to a database table using Table AutoExpansion, Excel makes
the change only when you start typing data in the row. When you do, Excel applies the style to
the row, and you can see that it's part of the database table. But until you start typing, it's just
another plain row.

Figure 16–5. *You can use the AutoCorrect actions button both to undo Table AutoExpansion and to turn it off.*

NOTE: To turn Table AutoExpansion back on, choose Excel ➤ Preferences or press Cmd+, (Cmd and the comma key). In the Excel Preferences dialog box, click the Tables icon in the Formulas and Lists area to display the Tables preferences pane. Select the Automatically expand tables as I type check box, and then click the OK button.

Sorting a Database Table by One or More Fields

When you need to examine the data in your database table, it's often useful to sort it. Excel lets you sort a database table either quickly by a single field or by using multiple fields.

TIP: If you need to be able to return a database table to its original order, include a column with sequential numbers in it. These numbers may be part of your records (for example, sequential sales numbers for transactions) or simply ID numbers for the records. In either case, you can use AutoFill to enter them quickly. To return the database table to its original order, you can then sort it by this column.

Sorting Quickly by a Single Field

To sort a database table by a single field, click any cell in the column you want to sort by, and then choose Data ➤ Sort & Filter ➤ Sort, clicking the main part of the Sort button. This produces a sort in ascending order (A to Z, low values to high values, early dates to later dates, and so on). To reverse the sort to descending order, click the main part of the Sort button again.

NOTE: You can also sort by choosing Data ➤ Sort & Filter ➤ Sort ➤ Ascending, Data ➤ Sort & Filter ➤ Sort ➤ Descending or by one of the other items on the Sort pop-up menu: Cell Color on Top, Font Color on Top, or Icon on Top. Usually, ascending and descending are the most useful kinds of sorting for a database table.

After you sort, the database table remains sorted that way until you change it.

Sorting a Database Table by Multiple Fields

Often, it's useful to sort your database table by two or more fields at the same time. For example, in a customer database, you may need to sort your customers first by state and then by city within the state.

To sort by multiple fields, follow these steps:

1. Choose Data ➤ Sort & Filter ➤ Sort ➤ Custom Sort to display the Sort dialog box. Figure 16–6 shows the Sort dialog box with two criteria entered and a third criterion under way.

Figure 16–6. *In the Sort dialog box, you can set up exactly the sort criteria you need to identify data in your database.*

2. Set up your first sort criterion using the controls on the first row of the main part of the Sort dialog box. Follow these steps:

   ■ Open the Column pop-up menu in the Sort by row, and then click the column you want to sort by first. For example, click the State column.

   ■ Open the Sort On pop-up menu in the same row, and then click what you want to sort by: Values, Cell Color, Font Color, or Cell Icon. In most cases, you'll want to use Values, but the other three items are useful for tables to which you've applied conditional formatting.

   ■ Open the Order pop-up menu on the same row, and then click the sort order you want. If you choose Values in the Sort On pop-up menu, you can choose A to Z for an ascending sort, Z to A for a descending sort, or Custom List. Choosing Custom List opens the Custom List dialog box, in which you can choose a custom list by which to sort the results. For example, you could use a custom list of your company's products or offices to sort the database into a custom order rather than being restricted to ascending or descending order.

■   If you need the sort to be case sensitive (so that "smith" appears
    before "Smith," and so on), click the Options button. In the Sort
    Options dialog box (see Figure 16–7), select the Case sensitive
    check box, and then click the OK button.

Figure 16–7. *Select the Case sensitive check box in the Sort Options dialog box if you want to treat lowercase
letters differently than their uppercase versions.*

3.   Click the Add (+) button to add a second line of controls to the main part of the
        Sort dialog box.

4.   Set up the criterion for the second-level sort on the Then by line using the same
        technique. For example, set up a second-level sort using the City column in the
        database.

5.   Set up any other criteria needed by repeating steps 3 and 4.

6.   Click the OK button to close the Sort dialog box. Excel sorts the data using the
        criteria you specified.

> **NOTE:** When you're sorting data that's not in a database table, there are two main differences.
> First, the My data has headers check box in the Sort dialog box is available, and you must select
> it if the data range you're sorting includes a header row. (Otherwise, Excel sorts the headers into
> the data range.) Second, you can select the Sort left to right option button in the Sort Options
> dialog box to sort columns rather than rows, a choice that's not available in a data table.

Identifying and Removing Duplicate Records in a Database Table

When you've created a large database table, you may need to check it for duplicate
records and remove those you find. Excel provides a Remove Duplicates feature that
saves you having to comb the records by hand.

CAUTION: Two warnings before removing duplicate values. First, make sure you have a backup copy of your database workbook—for example, use Finder to copy the current version of a file to a safe location. Second, be certain you know which fields in the database table should contain unique values and which can contain duplicate values. For example, a customer ID number field must be unique, because each customer has a different ID number; but a customer last name field can't reasonably be unique, because many customers will likely share last names. Most databases need a unique ID number or code of this type.

To remove duplicate records from a database table, follow these steps:

1. Click any cell in the database table.

2. Choose Tables ➤ Tools ➤ Remove Duplicates from the Ribbon or Data ➤ Table Tools ➤ Remove Duplicates from the menu bar to display the window shown in Figure 16–8.

Figure 16–8. *Use this window to locate duplicate values in columns that should contain only unique values. The window's title bar shows the name of the data table.*

3. If the Select All check box contains a check mark, click the check box to remove the check mark, and clear all the check boxes in the Columns box.

4. Select the check box for each column you want to check for duplicates. The readout at the bottom of the dialog box shows the number of duplicates.

TIP: Normally, it's best to check a single column for duplicate values at a time. Make sure that the column is one that must contain a unique value.

5. Click the Remove Duplicates button if you want to remove the duplicates.

6. Repeat the process with another field if necessary.

7. When you have finished removing duplicates, click the × button at the left end of the title bar to close the window.

Filtering a Database Table

When you need to find records in a database table that match the terms you specify, you can *filter* it. Filtering makes Excel display only the records that match your search terms, hiding all the other records.

> **NOTE:** You can also search for records by using Excel's Find feature. Choose Edit ➤ Find from the menu bar or press Cmd+F to display the Find dialog box, type your search term in the Find what box, and then click the Find Next button. Filtering displays all the matching records together rather than spread out in the database table, so it's often more convenient than using Find.

To make filtering easy, Excel provides a feature named AutoFilter. To use AutoFilter, follow these steps:

1. Click a cell in the database table.

2. Click the Data tab of the Ribbon to display its contents.

3. In the Sort & Filter group, make sure that the Filter button is selected so that it looks pushed in; if not, click the main part of the button. Excel normally selects the Filter button when you create a database table, so this button should be pushed in unless you've turned filtering off. Selecting this button makes Excel display a pop-up button on each column heading in the database table.

4. On the column you want to use for filtering, click the pop-up button to display the AutoFilter window (shown on the left in Figure 16–9). The AutoFilter window's title bar shows the name of the field you clicked.

Figure 16–9. *To apply filtering, click the pop-up arrow on a column heading to display the AutoFilter window (left). In the Filter area, open the first pop-up menu, and choose the comparison you want. You can then add further comparisons as needed.*

5.   Click the type of sorting or filtering you want to apply:

- *Sort.* Click the type of sort you want to apply. Normally, you'll want to click either the Ascending button or the Descending button. But if your data table uses colors, you can sort by color instead—just choose the color in the By color pop-up menu in the Sort area.

- *Filter.* If you want to filter the table by color, choose the color in the By color pop-up menu. Otherwise, open the pop-up menu that appears as Choose One in the left part of Figure 16–9, and then choose the comparison from it. For example, choose Equals to set a filter that picks particular states, or choose Begins With to set a filter than selects cities that start with text you specify. Use the fields in the Custom AutoFilter window to set up the rest of the comparison; the right screen in Figure 16–9 shows an example that filters by Equals AK or Equals AL, returning the records that have the state AK or the state AL.

NOTE: The filter comparisons depend on the contents of the column you selected in the database table. For example, if the column contains numbers, the comparisons include the mathematical comparisons Greater Than, Greater Than or Equal To, Less Than, Less Than or Equal To, Between, Top 10, Bottom 10, Above Average, and Below Average. If the column contains dates, the comparisons include Before, After, Between, Tomorrow, Next Week, Next Month, and Next Year.

When you've specified the details of the filter, Excel applies it to the database table and reduces the display to those rows that match the filter. Excel displays a filter symbol in place of the drop-down button on the column that contains the filtering (as on the State column heading in Figure 16–10).

City	State	ZIP	Telephone
Montgome	AL	36119	(335) 555-3912
Huntsville	AL	35813	
Anchorage	AK	99599	(907) 555-8273
Birmingham	AL	35203	(205) 555-2619
Mobile	AL	36601	(251) 555-1298

Figure 16–10. The filter symbol (shown on the State column heading here) indicates that you're filtering the database table by that column.

To remove filtering from a single column, click the filter symbol on the column heading, and then click the Clear Filter button in the AutoFilter window.

To remove filtering from the database table as a whole, choose Data ➤ Sort & Filter ➤ Filter, unpressing the Filter button in the Sort & Filter group.

NOTE: If AutoFilter doesn't give you the flexibility you need, you can also create custom filters manually. To do this, you insert extra rows above the database table to create a criteria range, enter the criteria in the appropriate columns, choose Data ➤ Sort & Filter ➤ Filter ➤ Advanced Filter, and then work in the Advanced Filter dialog box. This topic is beyond the scope of this book, so look it up (online or offline) if you need to perform filtering that AutoFilter can't manage.

Solving Business Problems with Scenarios and Goal Seek

For much of your work with Excel, you'll probably want to manipulate the hard data you already have, as you've been doing so far in this part of the book. But other times, you'll need to ask questions of your data—for example, by how much do you need to raise prices to boost your revenue by a certain amount, or what will happen if you cut 10 percent off your manufacturing costs?

In this section, we'll look at two tools Excel gives you for performing what-if analysis:

- *Scenarios.* Use scenarios when you want to experiment with different data in your worksheet without changing the core data that you already have.

- *Goal Seek.* Use Goal Seek when you need to make one cell's value reach a particular figure by changing one other value.

Examining Different Scenarios in a Worksheet

Often, when you've built a worksheet, you'll want to experiment with different data in it. For example, if you're setting budgets, you may need to play around with different figures for the different departments to get the overall balance you require.

You can experiment with different data by changing the values directly in your worksheet—but then you may need to restore your original values afterward. Another approach is to create multiple copies of the worksheet (or of the workbook) and then change the values in the copies, leaving the original untouched. This works fine, but if you then need to change the original worksheet (for example, adding another column of data), the changes quickly become messy.

Instead of working in these awkward ways, you can use Excel's scenarios. A *scenario* is a way of entering different values into a set of cells without changing the underlying values. You can switch from one scenario to another as needed, and you can merge scenarios from different versions of the same worksheet into a single worksheet.

Creating the Worksheet for Your Scenarios

Start by creating the workbook and worksheet you'll use for your scenarios. If you have an existing workbook with the data in it, open it up. Set up the data and formulas in your worksheet as usual.

> **TIP:** To make your scenarios easy to set up and adjust, define a name for each cell that you will change in the scenario. Click the cell, choose Insert ➤ Name ➤ Define to display the Define Name dialog box, and then work as described in the "Referring to Named Cells and Ranges" section in Chapter 15. For example, type the name in the Names in workbook text box, and then click the Add button to add the name and leave the dialog box open so that you can click another cell and define a name for it too.

Figure 16–11 shows the sample worksheet this section uses as an example. The worksheet summarizes the financial returns from a modest portfolio of rental properties.

Figure 16–11. *To start using scenarios, create a worksheet containing your existing data and the formulas needed.*

Here's what you see on the worksheet:

- The Property Address column shows each property's address.

- The Monthly Rent column shows each property's monthly rent. Cell B10 contains a SUM() formula to produce the total rent. Each of the cells here has a name to make it easy to recognize—Rent_Lincoln, Rent_Pacific_A, and so on.

- The Operating Costs column shows the monthly operating cost for each property, including all mortgage costs and other financial horrors. Cell C10 uses a SUM() formula to produce the total running cost. The numbers in this column are rounded. Each of these cells has a name: Costs_Lincoln, Costs_Pacific_A, and so forth. Again, this is so that we can refer to the cells easily and clearly.

- The Property Profit column shows how much profit each rental unit returns after subtracting the operating cost from the rent (for example, cell D5 contains the sum =B5-C5). The numbers in this column are rounded; that's why cell D5 appears to contain a math error but is in fact correct. Cell D10 uses a SUM() formula to return the total profit.

- The Property Profitability column shows the property's profitability as a percentage. To produce the profitability figure, we divide the Property Profit value by the Monthly Rent value—for example, cell E5 contains the formula = D5/B5. At the bottom of the column, cell E10 uses an AVERAGE() formula to show the average profitability of the properties.

- The Financial Contribution column shows each property's contribution to the total profit as a percentage. To produce the contribution figure, we divide each property's profit by the total profit in cell D10. For example, cell F9 contains the formula =D9/D$10, using a mixed reference to keep the row absolute when copying the formula. Cell F10 contains a SUM() formula that adds the percentages, letting us see that they total 100%.

Times are bad, and the total profit is too low. So, we'll use scenarios to see how we can improve matters by raising rents and shaving costs.

Opening the Scenario Manager Dialog Box

When you're ready to start working with scenarios, choose Data ➤ Analysis ➤ What-If ➤ Scenario Manager from the Ribbon or Tools ➤ Scenarios from the menu bar to display the Scenario Manager dialog box. At first, when the workbook contains no scenarios, the Scenario Manager dialog box appears as shown in Figure 16–12.

Figure 16–12. *At first, the Scenario Manager dialog box contains nothing but a prompt telling you to click the Add button. Do so.*

Creating Scenarios

After opening the Scenario Manager dialog box, you can create your scenarios.

> **TIP:** First, create a scenario containing your original data. This gives you an easy way to go back to the original data when you've finished testing scenarios.

To create a scenario, follow these steps:

1. From the Scenario Manager dialog box, click the Add button to display the Add Scenario dialog box (see Figure 16–13).

Figure 16–13. *Use the Add Scenario dialog box to set up each scenario. First create a scenario for your original data so that you can easily return to it.*

2. In the Scenario name text box, type a descriptive name for the scenario.

3. Click in the Changing cells text box, and then enter the details of the cells that users of the scenario are allowed to change. For the original scenario, we're not making changes; but for a scenario that involves changing the rent, the range is cells B5:B9.

   ■ Click and drag in the worksheet to select a range of contiguous cells. If you need to select noncontiguous cells, click the first, and then Cmd+click each other cell.

NOTE: When you enter a cell or a range of cells in the Changing cells text box by clicking in the worksheet, Excel changes the name of the dialog box from Add Scenario to Edit Scenario. Odd though this seems, it's normal.

- You can also type the name of a range into the Changing cells text box.

- There's a Collapse Dialog button to the right of the Changing cells text box, but you don't need to use it, because Excel automatically collapses the Add Scenario dialog box when you click in the worksheet. After you've selected the changing cells, Excel expands the dialog box again.

4. In the Comment text box, type a comment that explains what the scenario is and how to use it. Excel creates a default comment of *Created by*, your user name (as set in the Office applications), and the date, but a descriptive comment is usually more helpful.

5. Choose settings as needed in the Protection area at the bottom of the dialog box:

   - *Prevent changes.* Select this check box when you need to prevent changes to the scenario. To make the protection take effect, you'll need to protect the worksheet as described in the next section.

   - *Hide.* Select this check box when you need to prevent others from seeing this scenario—for example, because you want them to experiment with their own figures rather than looking at your figures. Again, you need to protect the worksheet.

6. Click the OK button to close the Add Scenario dialog box or Edit Scenario dialog box. Excel displays the Scenario Values dialog box (see Figure 16–14). This dialog box shows a text box for each of the changing cells in the scenario. Here's where you see the benefit of naming the changing cells—each text box is easy to identify. If you haven't named the changing cells, the cell addresses appear, and you may need to refer to the worksheet to see which cell is which.

Figure 16–14. *In the Scenario Values dialog box, enter the values to use for the new scenario you're creating. The cell names produce the labels (Rent_Lincoln and so on), which are much easier to refer to than cell addresses (for example, B5).*

7. Change the values as needed for the scenario.

TIP: You can type formulas into the text boxes in the Scenario Values dialog box. For example, to increase the Rent_Lincoln value in Figure 16–14 by 25 percent, you could change the 1450 value to the formula =1.25*1450. After you enter formulas like this, Excel displays the dialog box shown in Figure 16–15 when you close the Scenario Values dialog box, telling you that it has converted names and results of formulas to values.

Figure 16–15. *After you enter formulas in the Scenario Values dialog box, Excel automatically converts them to values for you.*

8. Click the OK button to close the Scenario Values dialog box. Excel returns you to the Scenario Manager dialog box, where the scenario now appears in the Scenarios list box.

To add another scenario, click the Add button in the Scenario Manager dialog box, and then repeat the previous process.

Applying Protection to Your Scenarios

If you selected either the Prevent changes check box or the Hide check box in the Protection area of the Add Scenario dialog box or the Edit Scenario dialog box, you need to protect the worksheet to make the protection take effect.

To protect the worksheet, follow these steps:

1. If the Scenario Manager dialog box is open, click the Close button to close it.

2. Choose Tools ➤ Protection ➤ Sheet from the Ribbon or Tools ➤ Protection ➤ Protect Sheet from the menu bar to display the Protect the sheet and contents of locked cells dialog box.

3. Type a password in the Password text box and the Verify text box.

4. In the Allow users of this sheet to box, make sure the Edit scenarios check box is cleared.

5. Click the OK button to close the dialog box. Excel applies the protection.

6. Save the workbook. For example, press Cmd+S or click the Save button on the Standard toolbar.

After protecting the scenarios in the worksheet like this, you'll need to turn off the protection before you can edit the scenarios. To turn off the protection, choose Tools ➤ Protection ➤ Sheet from the Ribbon or Tools ➤ Protection ➤ Unprotect Sheet from the menu bar, type the password in the dialog box that Excel displays, and then click the OK button.

Editing and Deleting Scenarios

From the Scenario Manager dialog box, you can quickly edit a scenario by clicking it in the Scenarios list box, clicking the Edit button, and then working in the Edit Scenario dialog box. Excel automatically updates the scenario's comment for you with details of the modification (for example, "Modified by Jack Cunningham on 02/18/2011"), but you'll often want to type in more details, such as what you're trying to make the scenario show.

When you no longer need a scenario, delete it by clicking the scenario in the Scenarios list box and clicking the Delete button. Excel doesn't confirm the deletion; but if you delete a scenario by mistake, and recovering it is more important than losing any other changes you've made since you last saved the workbook, you can recover the scenario by closing the workbook without saving changes (assuming the scenario was already saved in the workbook).

Switching Among Your Scenarios

Once you've created multiple scenarios for the same worksheet, you can switch among them by clicking the scenario you want in the Scenarios list box in the Scenario Manager dialog box (see Figure 16–16) and then clicking the Show button. Excel displays the scenario's figures in the worksheet's cells. The Scenario Manager dialog box stays open, so you can quickly switch to another scenario.

Figure 16–16. *To switch to another scenario, click the scenario in the Scenarios list box in the Scenario Manager dialog box, and then click the Show button.*

TIP: If you need to be able to switch quickly among scenarios, add the Scenario pop-up menu to the Standard toolbar or another convenient toolbar. To customize the toolbar, use the technique described in the "Customizing a Toolbar" section in Chapter 5. On the Commands tab of the Customize Toolbars and Menus dialog box, click the Tools item in the Categories list, and then scroll down the Commands list box to find the Scenario pop-up menu.

Merging Scenarios into a Single Worksheet

If you develop and share your scenarios in a single workbook, you can keep them all together. But other times you may need to develop your scenarios in separate workbooks and then combine them. You can do this easily by using the Merge command in the Scenario Manager dialog box.

To merge scenarios, follow these steps:

1. Open all the workbooks containing the scenarios you will merge.

2. Make active the workbook and worksheet you will merge the scenarios into.

3. Choose Data ➤ Analysis ➤ What-If ➤ Scenario Manager from the Ribbon or Tools ➤ Scenarios from the menu bar to display the Scenario Manager dialog box.

4. Click the Merge button to display the Merge Scenarios dialog box (see Figure 16–17).

Figure 16–17. *In the Merge Scenarios dialog box, choose the workbook and worksheet that contain the scenarios you want to merge into the active workbook.*

5. Open the Book pop-up menu, and choose the open workbook that contains the scenarios you want to merge in. The Sheet list box shows a list of the worksheets in the workbook.

6. In the Sheet list box, click the worksheet that contains the scenarios. The readout at the bottom of the Merge Scenarios dialog box shows how many scenarios the worksheet contains, which helps you pick the right worksheet.

7. Click the OK button. Excel closes the Merge Scenarios dialog box, merges the scenarios, and then displays the Scenario Manager dialog box again.

NOTE: If any scenario you merge into the active worksheet has the same name as an existing scenario in the worksheet, Excel adds the current date to the incoming scenario to distinguish it.

Creating Reports from Your Scenarios

Sometimes you can make the decisions you need by simply creating scenarios and looking at them in the worksheet. Other times, it's helpful to create a report from the scenarios so that you can compare them. Excel gives you an easy way to create either a summary report or a PivotTable report straight from the Scenario Manager dialog box.

To create a report from your scenarios, follow these steps:

1. Choose Data ➤ Analysis ➤ What-If ➤ Scenario Manager from the Ribbon or Tools ➤ Scenarios from the menu bar to display the Scenario Manager dialog box.

2. Click the Summary button to display the Scenario Summary dialog box (see Figure 16–18).

Figure 16–18. *In the Scenario Summary dialog box, choose between a scenario summary and a scenario PivotTable, and then select the result cells for the summary.*

3. In the Report type box, select the Scenario summary option button if you want to create a summary worksheet. If you want to create a scenario PivotTable, select the Scenario PivotTable option button.

4. Click in the Result cells text box, and then enter the addresses of the cells whose results you want the report or PivotTable to show. You can type in addresses or range names or select the appropriate cells in the worksheet.

5. Click the OK button to close the Scenario Summary dialog box. Excel creates the report or PivotTable. Figure 16–19 shows a sample of a summary report, which Excel places on a new worksheet named Scenario Summary at the beginning of the workbook.

Figure 16–19. *Excel places a summary report on a new worksheet named Scenario Summary at the beginning of the workbook.*

Using Goal Seek

When you're planning or forecasting, you'll often need to work backward from your target to derive the figures you need. For example, when planning your next financial year, you may need to find out how much you need to raise the selling price for your widgets to make an extra $30,000 a year.

To work this out, you can try increasing the unit price for the widgets until your revenue figure is $30,000 higher. But you can save time and effort by using Excel's Goal Seek feature to derive the required price automatically by working backward from the revenue figure.

To derive values using Goal Seek, follow these steps:

1. Open the workbook that contains the data, and navigate to the worksheet that contains the calculation.

2. Make active the cell that contains the formula.

3. Choose Tools ➤ Goal Seek from the menu bar to display the Goal Seek dialog box (shown in Figure 16–20 with settings chosen).

Goal Seek

Set cell: B3

To value: 450000

By changing cell: B1

Cancel   OK

Figure 16–20. *Use the Goal Seek dialog box to work backward from your desired result to the figure you need.*

4. Make sure the Set cell text box contains the right cell. (If you selected the cell in Step 2, it will.) If necessary, change the cell either by typing the correct reference or by double-clicking the current contents of the Set cell text box (to select it) and then clicking the right cell in the worksheet. (You can also click the Collapse Dialog button to collapse the Goal Seek dialog box, but the dialog box is so small anyway that it's usually easier to work around it.)

5. In the To value text box, type the value you want to get.

6. In the By changing cell text box, enter the cell whose value you want to change — in the example, the cell containing the price of the widgets. Again, you can type the cell reference or simply click the cell in the worksheet.

7. Click the OK button. Goal Seek calculates the answer, enters it in the worksheet, and then displays the Goal Seek Status dialog box (see Figure 16–21).

Goal Seek Status

Goal Seeking with Cell B3   OK

found a solution.   Cancel

Target value: 450000   Step

Current value: $450,000.00   Pause

Figure 16–21. *When Excel displays the Goal Seek Status dialog box, look at the value in the target cell in the worksheet. Click the OK button if you want to keep the value. Click the Cancel button if you want to revert to the previous value.*

NOTE: If the calculation is straightforward, Goal Seek finds a solution quickly. But if the calculation is more complex, Goal Seek may take a while. If this happens, you can click the Pause button to pause the calculation to see which value Goal Seek is trying at the moment. If you want to follow the individual values Goal Seek is trying, click the Step button to display the next value but keep the calculation paused; keep clicking the Step button as needed to see further values. Click the Resume button when you want Goal Seek to resume the calculation at full speed.

8. Look at the value in the target cell. Click the OK button if you want to keep it. Click the Cancel button if you want to go back to the previous value.

TIP: If you find Goal Seek useful, take a look at the Solver, which you can download for free from the Solver.com web site (`www.solver.com/mac/`). Whereas Goal Seek lets you change only one variable, the Solver lets you change multiple variables. This enables you to ask more complex questions of your data.

Summary

In this chapter, you learned how to create a database table in Excel—a flat-file database rather than the relational type of database that you create with a database application such as Microsoft Access.

You now know how to set up a database table, choose display options for it, and format it to look the way you want. You can add data to the database either by working in the cells as normal or by using a data-entry form to speed the process. You've gained the essential skills of sorting the data into the sort order you need or filtering it to show the records you're interested in.

You also learned how to use Excel's scenarios to explore how different values affect a worksheet and how to use Goal Seek to work backward from a desired result to the value needed to produce it.

Chapter 17

Manipulating Data with PivotTables

In this chapter, we'll look at how you can manipulate the data in your worksheets to draw conclusions from it by creating PivotTables. PivotTables are great for asking questions of your data and looking at the data in different ways without having to enter it multiple times in separate worksheets.

We'll start by going over what PivotTables are and what you can do with them. After that, I'll show you how to create a PivotTable either by using Excel's automated tool or by placing the fields on the PivotTable framework manually, which gives you total control.

After you build a PivotTable, you'll often need to change it so that it shows different data or shows the same data differently. I'll show you several examples of the types of changes you can make easily to a PivotTable once you've constructed it.

When the PivotTable is arranged the way you need it, you can format the PivotTable and choose options to control how it appears. And you can sort and filter the data within the PivotTable to show only the information you're after.

Understanding What PivotTables Are and What You Can Do with Them

A PivotTable is a special kind of report that rearranges the fields and records in a table into a different order so that you can examine their relationships. You *pivot* (in other words, rotate) the columns in a PivotTable to display the data summarized in a different way.

For example, take a look at the worksheet shown in Figure 17–1. This worksheet contains a data table that tracks sales made by a company with four product lines: Hardware, Software, Services, and Supplies. The table uses the following columns:

■ *Sale.* A unique sequential numbers used to identify each sale.

■ *Year, Month, and Day.* The year, month, and day of the sale. Having these items in separate columns makes it easier to filter by time—for example, to compare one month against another or to see which salesperson sold what in January.

■ *Salesperson.* The name of the sales rep who executed the sale.

■ *Line.* The product line of the product sold.

■ *Product.* The name of the product sold.

Sale	Year	Month	Day	Salesperson	Line	Product	Quantity	Price	Total Price	Customer
BD10149	2011	January	2	Lee	Hardware	ThunderPC	2	$499.99	$999.98	Ocean Demographics
BD10150	2011	January	3	Gutierrez	Services	Setup	10	$199.99	$1,999.90	Novelty Appropriations
BD10151	2011	January	5	Dunne	Software	SmartTax	20	$44.99	$899.80	Industrial Disease Associates
BD10152	2011	January	7	Brenger	Supplies	Photo Paper	40	$8.99	$359.60	Helium Partners
BD10153	2011	January	9	Kim	Services	Malware removal	1	$59.99	$59.99	Planned Senescence Service
BD10154	2011	January	11	Price	Services	Restore	4	$29.99	$119.96	Pinion Joiners
BD10155	2011	January	14	Lee	Hardware	BlitzScreen	8	$129.99	$1,039.92	Louisiana Jelly Company
BD10156	2010	January	15	Gutierrez	Software	SecureStream	1	$89.99	$89.99	Lost Angels Cleaning
BD10157	2011	January	16	Dunne	Supplies	Printer Paper	100	$3.99	$399.00	Self-Service Meditations
BD10158	2011	January	18	Brenger	Hardware	ThunderPC	3	$499.99	$1,499.97	Petrolia Milk Company
BD10159	2011	January	20	Kim	Services	Setup	3	$199.99	$599.97	Amalgamated Associates
BD10160	2011	January	21	Price	Software	SmartTax	5	$44.99	$224.95	Ocean Demographics
BD10161	2011	January	22	Lee	Supplies	Photo Paper	10	$8.99	$89.90	Novelty Appropriations
BD10162	2011	January	23	Gutierrez	Services	Malware removal	2	$59.99	$119.98	Industrial Disease Associates
BD10163	2011	January	24	Dunne	Services	Restore	2	$29.99	$59.98	Helium Partners
BD10164	2011	January	25	Brenger	Hardware	BlitzScreen	20	$129.99	$2,599.80	Planned Senescence Service
BD10165	2011	January	26	Kim	Software	SecureStream	2	$89.99	$179.98	Pinion Joiners
BD10166	2011	January	27	Price	Supplies	Printer Paper	50	$3.99	$199.50	Louisiana Jelly Company
BD10167	2011	January	28	Lee	Hardware	ThunderPC	3	$499.99	$1,499.97	Lost Angels Cleaning
BD10168	2011	February	2	Gutierrez	Services	Setup	2	$199.99	$399.98	Self-Service Meditations

Figure 17–1. *The sample table we'll use for creating PivotTables in this chapter*

■ *Quantity.* The quantity of the product sold.

■ *Price.* The unit price of the product sold.

■ *Total Price.* The total price of the products sold (Quantity multiplied by Price).

■ *Customer.* The name of the company or organization that bought the products.

This is all straightforward, and you can use a data-entry form to add the data to the data table or edit existing records. You can also easily see your sum total of sales (for example, by adding the figures in the Total Price column). But when you need to dig into the details, you need a different tool.

This is where PivotTables come in. By creating a PivotTable from a data table such as this, you can quickly find the answers to questions such as these:

- Which is your best-selling product line? And your best-selling product?

- How do this year's sales stack up against last year's?

- Who was your star salesperson for March? And does another salesperson need a quick application of the spurs?

- Which are your key customers? Which of them needs more one-on-one attention to bring sales up to where they were last year?

In the following sections, we'll put together a PivotTable with the data in the data table and then manipulate it to see what it shows.

> **NOTE:** If you want to work through the examples in this chapter, you'll need a database table like the one shown in the screens. You can either create one yourself or (much easier) download the sample workbook from the book's page on the Apress Web site (www.apress.com).

Creating and Laying Out a PivotTable

You can create a PivotTable either from a database table or from a range of data. If you have a database table already, as in the example, you can create the PivotTable from that. Otherwise, create the database table you'll use, or enter the data in a worksheet as usual without creating a database table.

Once your data is ready, you can create a PivotTable either automatically or manually. Which works best depends on your data and what you're trying to do with it, but often you can save time by creating a PivotTable automatically and then adjusting it as necessary. If an automatic PivotTable turns out not to be what you need, you can create the PivotTable manually from scratch instead.

Creating a PivotTable Automatically

To create a PivotTable automatically, follow these steps:

1. Open the workbook and display the worksheet that contains the table or data you'll use in the PivotTable.

2. Click in the table that you'll use for the PivotTable. If you'll use a range rather than a named table, select the range.

3. Choose Data ➤ Analysis ➤ PivotTable from the Ribbon, clicking the main part of the PivotTable button. You can also click the PivotTable pop-up button and then click Create Automatic PivotTable on the pop-up menu, but there's no advantage to doing so. Excel then does the following:

- Inserts an automatic PivotTable on a new worksheet

- Gives the new worksheet a default name such as Sheet5

- Displays the PivotTable Builder window

- Adds the PivotTable tab to the Ribbon and displays it

- Displays some information about PivotTables the first time you create one

Figure 17–2 shows the automatic PivotTable produced from the sample data table, with the PivotTable Builder window positioned in front of the worksheet.

Figure 17–2. *The quickest way to create a PivotTable is to have Excel create it automatically. You will usually need to adjust the PivotTable using the PivotTable Builder window to make the PivotTable show the information you want. Depending on the data you're using, the PivotTable may look substantially different from this one.*

After creating a PivotTable automatically, you'll normally need to adjust it. This is because Excel seldom guesses exactly which information you need where.

To adjust a PivotTable, use the techniques you'll learn in the next section, which shows you how to build a PivotTable from scratch.

Creating a PivotTable Manually

If creating an automatic PivotTable doesn't give a useful result or if you prefer to do things by hand, you can build the PivotTable manually using the PivotTable Builder.

To create a PivotTable manually, follow these steps:

1. Open the workbook, and display the worksheet that contains the table or data you'll use in the PivotTable.

2. Click in the table that you'll use for the PivotTable. If you'll use a range rather than a named table, select the range.

3. Choose Data ➤ Analysis ➤ PivotTable ➤ Create Manual PivotTable from the Ribbon or Data ➤ PivotTable from the menu bar to display the Create PivotTable dialog box (see Figure 17–3). If you're using a named table, you can also choose Tables ➤ Tools ➤ Summarize with PivotTable from the Ribbon; if you're using a range, this command isn't available.

Figure 17–3. *In the Create PivotTable dialog box, choose the table or range of data from which to create the PivotTable. Then choose between putting the PivotTable on a new worksheet or an existing worksheet.*

4. In the Choose the data that you want to analyze area at the top of the Create PivotTable dialog box, select the Use a table or a range in this workbook option button.

> **NOTE:** Instead of creating a PivotTable from data in a worksheet, you can create a PivotTable from an external data source such as a FileMaker database or Access database. To do so, you select the Use an external data source option button in the Choose the data that you want to analyze area of the Create PivotTable dialog box, click the Get Data button, and then choose the data source. Before you can do this, you must install an Open Database Connectivity (ODBC) driver to enable Excel to connect to the data source. To find a suitable driver, search online including the terms *Excel 2011, ODBC driver*, and the type of database you need to connect to.

5. Make sure the Location text box shows the table or range you want to use. If you clicked in the table or selected the range in step 2, you'll be all set. If not, type in the table name or click and drag in the worksheet to select the range (click the Collapse Dialog button first to get the Create PivotTable dialog box out of the way first if necessary).

6. In the Choose where to place the PivotTable area of the Create PivotTable dialog box, choose the appropriate option button:

   - *New worksheet.* Select this option button if you want to place the PivotTable on a new worksheet. This is often clearest, because it gives you plenty of room for the PivotTable.

   - *Existing worksheet.* Select this option button if you want to place the PivotTable on an existing worksheet. Then click in the Location text box, click the worksheet's tab, and then click drag in the worksheet to enter the location.

7. Click the OK button to close the Create PivotTable dialog box. Excel positions a PivotTable framework on a new worksheet or the existing worksheet you chose and displays the PivotTable Builder window. Figure 17–4 shows the PivotTable framework on a new worksheet named Sheet6.

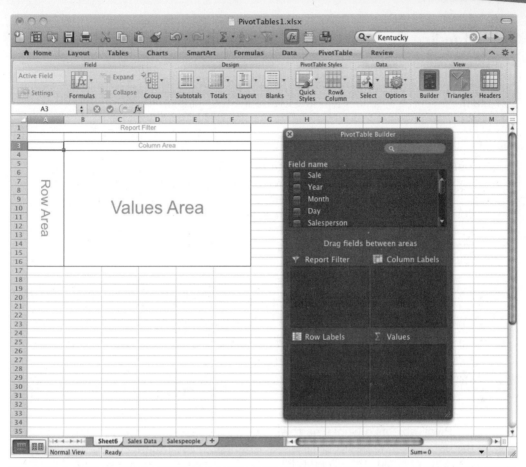

Figure 17–4. *When you insert a PivotTable manually, Excel creates an empty framework on which you lay out the PivotTable the way you need it.*

Now that you've inserted the framework for the PivotTable, you can add fields to it from the Field name list box in the PivotTable Builder window.

Understanding How the PivotTable Framework and PivotTable Builder Window Work

Take a moment to look at the PivotTable framework and the PivotTable Builder window. You use the PivotTable Builder window to arrange the fields on the PivotTable framework.

Here are the essentials you need to know:

- *Field name list box.* This list box in the PivotTable Builder window contains an entry for each of the fields that Excel found in the data table or range you chose. Each item in the list has a check box that you can select to add the field to the PivotTable. The PivotTable framework has no matching area for the Field name list box, because the fields go into the various areas of the PivotTable when you use them.

NOTE: Excel automatically parses the fields in the Field name list box and decides which part of the PivotTable they belong to. Given that Excel has no understanding of what your data table or range contains beyond being able to identify items such as dates, currency, and text, it's pretty smart about this. But you'll often need to move a field from one part of the PivotTable to another by dragging it from one area of the PivotTable Builder window to another.

- *Report Filter.* This area at the top of the PivotTable acts as a filter for the PivotTable as a whole, narrowing down the rest of the table to only the data that matches your filter. For example, if you put the Salespeople field in the Report Filter area by dragging it to the Report Filter box in the PivotTable Builder window, you get a pop-up menu of your salespeople from which you choose whose data you want to show. As you'll see later in this chapter, you can filter by one field, two fields, or more.

- *Row Area.* This area at the left of the PivotTable shows the row headings. You designate those headings by dragging the appropriate field or fields to the Row Labels box in the PivotTable Builder window.

- *Column Area.* This area at the top of the PivotTable shows the column headings. You choose those headings by dragging the appropriate field or fields to the Column Labels box in the PivotTable Builder window.

- *Values Area.* This area in the body of the PivotTable—in most cases, the main part of the PivotTable—contains the values. You specify the values by dragging the appropriate field or fields to the Values box in the PivotTable Builder window.

If this is hard to grasp, don't worry: you'll see how PivotTables work in just a moment.

Adding the Fields to the PivotTable Framework

To create the PivotTable, you add fields to the PivotTable framework by selecting check boxes in the Field name list box or dragging fields to the Report Filter box, the Row Labels box, the Column Labels box, and the Values box in the PivotTable Builder window.

Which fields you need to drag where depends on your data source and what you're trying to make it show. Here's a walk-through using the fields in the data source. If you're using the sample data source, your results should look similar; if your data source is different, they'll look different, but the PivotTable will work in much the same way.

1. In the Field name list box in the PivotTable Builder window, select the Year check box. The data in the Year column in the worksheet is likely the year part of a date, so Excel adds the Year field to the Row Labels box in the PivotTable Builder window and adds the first value in the Year column to cell A5 in the PivotTable (see Figure 17–5).

Figure 17–5. *Select the Year check box in the Field name list box in the PivotTable Builder window to add the Year field to the PivotTable.*

2. Having the years as the row labels can be useful in many PivotTables, but it's not what we want here. In the PivotTable Builder window, click the Year button, and drag it up to the Report Filter box. Excel clears the contents of cell A5, enters Year in cell A1, and creates a pop-up menu for selecting the years in cell B1 (see Figure 17–6).

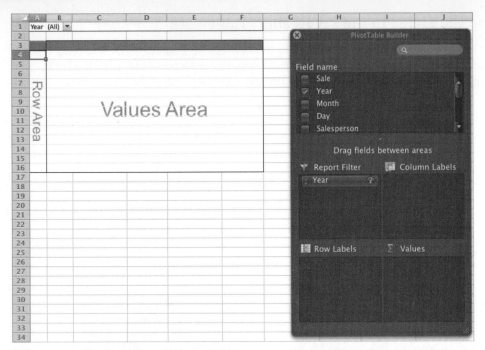

Figure 17–6. *Drag the Year button from the Row Labels box in the PivotTable Builder window to the Report Filter box to create the Year pop-up menu shown in cell B1 here. Excel selects the (All) item in the pop-up menu at first, making the PivotTable show all the years.*

3. In the Field Name list box, select the Salesperson check box. Excel puts the Salesperson field in the Values box in the PivotTable Builder window as a Count of Salesperson button, and adds the corresponding heading in the Values Area of the PivotTable (see Figure 17–7).

Figure 17–7. *When you select the Salesperson check box in the Field name list box in the PivotTable Builder window, Excel adds a Count of Salesperson heading to the Values Area of the PivotTable.*

4. Sometimes you may need a count of salespeople, but it's not what you need here. In the PivotTable Builder window, click the Count of Salesperson button in the Values box, and drag it to the Row Labels box. Excel creates a row label for each salesperson's name (see Figure 17–8).

Figure 17–8. *Moving the Salesperson button to the Row Labels box makes Excel create a row label from each salesperson's name.*

5. Excel's batting zero for two at this point, so add the next field, Line, by dragging it from the Field name list box in the PivotTable Builder window to the Column Labels box. Excel automatically selects the Line check box in the Field name list box and adds the product lines as column labels (see Figure 17–9).

Figure 17–9. *Drag the Line item from the Field name list box in the PivotTable Builder window to the Column Labels area. Excel adds the product lines as column labels and selects the Line check box for you.*

6. Now click the Total Price field in the Field name list box, and drag it to the Values box in the PivotTable Builder window. Excel adds to the PivotTable the values of the items the salespeople sold (see Figure 17–10).

Figure 17–10. *Drag the Total Price field from the Field name list box to the Values box in the PivotTable Builder window to add the totals of each salesperson's sales to the PivotTable.*

This gives us a PivotTable that shows how much of each product line each salesperson sold. At first, the PivotTable shows (All) in the Year pop-up menu in the Report Filter area; to see a breakdown by a year, open the Year pop-up menu, and click the year you want.

So far, so good. But this is just the start.

Changing the PivotTable to Show Different Data

The great thing about PivotTables is how easy they are to change to show different data. You can change a PivotTable by adding different fields to it, removing fields it's currently using, or rearranging the fields among the Report Filter box, the Column Labels box, the Row Labels box, and the Values box in the PivotTable Builder window.

Here are four examples of how you can change the basic PivotTable created earlier in this chapter. These examples work as a sequence, so you'll need to make each change in turn if you want to work through them.

■   In the Field name list box, click the Product field, and drag it to the Row Labels box in the PivotTable Builder window. Excel adds a list of the product names of the products each salesperson has sold (see Figure 17–11).

Figure 17–11. *Drag the Product field to the Row Labels box in the PivotTable Builder window to add a list of the products each salesperson has sold. You can collapse any list by clicking the disclosure triangle to the left of the salesperson's name.*

- In the Row Labels box in the PivotTable Builder window, drag the Salesperson field below the Product field. The PivotTable then shows each product with a collapsible list of the salespeople who have been selling it (see Figure 17–12).

Row Labels	Hardware	Services	Software	Supplies	Grand Total
Sum of Total Price	**Column Labels**				
BlitzScreen	12349.05				12349.05
Brenger	5849.55				5849.55
Lee	6499.5				6499.5
Malware removal		719.88			719.88
Gutierrez		419.93			419.93
Kim		299.95			299.95
Photo Paper				3479.13	3479.13
Brenger				872.03	872.03
Lee				2607.1	2607.1
Printer Paper				3120.18	3120.18
Dunne				1643.88	1643.88
Gutierrez				399	399
Price				1077.3	1077.3
Restore		839.72			839.72
Dunne		359.88			359.88
Price		479.84			479.84
SecureStream			1619.82		1619.82
Gutierrez			899.9		899.9
Kim			629.93		629.93
Lee			89.99		89.99
Setup		2199.89			2199.89
Gutierrez		999.95			999.95
Kim		1199.94			1199.94
SmartTax			5758.72		5758.72
Dunne			3599.2		3599.2
Price			2159.52		2159.52
ThunderPC	20499.59				20499.59
Brenger	13499.73				13499.73
Lee	6999.86				6999.86
Grand Total	32848.64	3759.49	7378.54	6599.31	50585.98

Year: (All)

PivotTable Builder

Field name
- Sale
- ☑ Year
- Month
- Day
- ☑ Salesperson

Drag fields between areas

Report Filter: Year
Column Labels: Line
Row Labels: Product, Salesperson
Values: Sum of To...

Figure 17–12. *Drag the Salesperson field below the Product field in the Row Labels box in the PivotTable Builder window to produce a list of products showing the salespeople who have been selling them.*

■ Drag the Product field from the Row Labels box in the PivotTable Builder window to the Column Labels box. Then drag the Line field from the Column Labels box outside the PivotTable Builder window and drop it, making it disappear from the PivotTable. (You can also clear the Line check box in the Field name list box.) These changes produce a PivotTable showing the salespeople by row and what they've sold of the products in columns (see Figure 17–13).

Year: (All)

Row Labels	BlitzScreen	Malware removal	Photo Paper	Printer Paper	Restore	SecureStream	Setup	SmartTax	ThunderPC	Grand Total
Sum of Total Price	**Column Labels**									
Brenger	5849.55		872.03						13499.73	20221.31
Dunne				1643.88	359.88			3599.2		5602.96
Gutierrez		419.93		399		899.9	999.95			2718.78
Kim		299.95				629.93	1199.94			2129.82
Lee	6499.5		2607.1			89.99			6999.86	16196.45
Price				1077.3	479.84			2159.52		3716.66
Grand Total	12349.05	719.88	3479.13	3120.18	839.72	1619.82	2199.89	5758.72	20499.59	50585.98

Figure 17–13. *Removing the product lines and making column labels of the products produces this PivotTable that shows how much each salesperson has sold of each product.*

■ Make the following changes to see which of your product lines each of your customers bought in a specific period:

1. Drag the Month field from the Field name list box in the PivotTable Builder window to the Report Filter box, placing it below the Year field. You can now filter by month as well as by field. For example, you can choose 2011 as the Year filter and then choose January as the Month filter to see only your January 2011 results.

2. In the Field name list box, clear the Salesperson check box to remove the Salesperson field from the Row Labels area. Then drag the Customer field from the Field name list box to the Row Labels box instead, making the PivotTable show one customer in each row.

3. In the Field name list box, clear the Product check box to remove the Product field from the Column Labels area. Then drag the Line field to the Column Labels box to make the PivotTable show the product lines in the columns. Figure 17–14 shows the resulting PivotTable.

Figure 17–14. *You can add the Month field to the Report Filter box, putting it below the Year field, to filter your PivotTable by first the year (here, 2011) and then the month (here, January). This PivotTable shows how much customers bought from each product line in January 2011.*

When you've finished working with the PivotTable Builder window, you can close it by clicking the Close (×) button at the left end of its title bar or by choosing PivotTable ➤ View ➤ Builder from the Ribbon.

If you need to open the PivotTable Builder window again, choose PivotTable ➤ View ➤ Builder from the Ribbon.

Changing the Function Used to Summarize a Field

When you add values to a PivotTable, Excel tries to automatically use the right function for the calculation that type of data needs. For example, when you add a field that shows prices, Excel uses the SUM() function on the assumption that you want to add the values. And if you use nonnumeric data such as names, Excel uses the COUNT() function, giving you the number of different items.

If you need to change a field to a different function, follow these steps:

1. Click the field, or click a cell containing data that the field produces.

> **TIP:** You can also open the PivotTable Field dialog box for a field by clicking the i button to the right of the field's name in the PivotTable Builder window.

2. Choose PivotTable ➤ Field ➤ Settings from the Ribbon to display the PivotTable Field dialog box (see Figure 17–15).

Figure 17–15. *In the PivotTable Field dialog box, you can change the formula used to summarize the field's data.*

3. In the Summarize by list box, click the function you want to use. For example, click the Average function if you want the field to show an average instead of a sum. Excel automatically changes the contents of the Field Name text box to reflect the function you chose—for example, changing the text from Sum of Total Price to Average of Total Price.

TIP: If you need to present the data in a different format (for example, as the amount of difference from a base value), click the Options button in the PivotTable Field dialog box to expand the dialog box and reveal more options. In the Show data as pop-up menu, choose the format you want—for example, Difference From. Then select the base field in the Base field list box and the base item in the Base item list box.

4. If you want to change the field name, type the change in the Field Name text box.

5. Click the OK button to close the PivotTable Field dialog box.

Controlling the Design of a PivotTable

After setting up the framework for your PivotTable, you can use the tools in the Design group of the PivotTable tab of the Ribbon to choose where to display subtotals and grand totals, choose among the PivotTable layouts that Excel offers, and decide whether to insert blank rows between items to make the PivotTable more readable.

The Design group contains four pop-up menus:

- *Subtotals.* In this pop-up menu, click to place a check mark next to the Show at Bottom item if you want to place the subtotals at the bottom of each group (on a line market Totals). If you prefer to have the subtotals appear at the top of the group, on the same line as the group's label, click to place a check mark next to the Show at Top item instead. Placing a check mark next to one item removes the check mark from the other item—they're alternatives, even though the interface doesn't make this obvious.

- *Totals.* In this pop-up menu, click to place a check mark next to the Show for Rows item if you want to show totals for rows. Click to place a check mark next to the Show for Columns item if you want to show totals for columns. If you don't want the totals, click to remove the check mark. These two items work independently—they're not alternatives.

- *Layout.* In this pop-up menu, click to place a check mark next to the layout you want: Compact Layout (the default; shown at the top of Figure 17–16), Outline Layout (shown in the middle of Figure 17–16), or Tabular Layout (shown at the bottom of Figure 17–16).

Figure 17–16. *You can choose among three layouts for your PivotTables. Compact Layout (left) is good for presenting data in a small space. Outline Layout (right) and Tabular Layout (bottom) take up more space but make the data easier to read.*

■ *Blanks.* In this pop-up menu, place a check mark next to the item called Insert Blank Line After Each Item if you want to have a blank line appear after each item in the PivotTable. Blank lines make the PivotTable take up much more space but can make it far easier to read. If you don't want blank lines, click to place a check mark next to the item called Remove Blank Line After Each Item. (These two controls are opposites: placing a check mark next to one removes the check mark from the other.)

Formatting a PivotTable

To make a PivotTable look good and convey its contents effectively, you can format it. You can apply the formatting at any point, but usually it's best to lay out the framework and fields of the PivotTable first so that you have a fair idea of how it will appear.

Applying a PivotTable Style

As you've seen in the examples so far in this chapter, Excel applies a style to a PivotTable when you create it. The style helps you distinguish the different areas of the PivotTable visually.

To change the way a PivotTable looks, apply a different style to it from the PivotTable Styles group on the PivotTable tab of the Ribbon. You can either click one of the styles in the Quick Styles box or hold the mouse pointer over the Quick Styles box, click the panel button that appears, and then click the PivotTable style you want to the Quick Styles panel.

NOTE: You can also create your own PivotTable styles. To do so, choose PivotTable ➤ PivotTable Styles ➤ Quick Styles ➤ New PivotTable Style, and then work in the New PivotTable Quick Style dialog box that Excel displays. Briefly, you give the style a name in the Name text box, then click an element in the Table element list box, click the Format button, and choose the formatting you want for the element. After you create a new style, you can apply it from the Custom section at the top of the Quick Styles panel.

Choosing Options for a PivotTable Style

After applying a PivotTable style, you can choose options for it by selecting PivotTable ➤ PivotTable Styles ➤ Row & Column and then placing check marks next to the items you want on the Row & Column pop-up menu:

■ *Row Headers.* Place a check mark next to this item to use the style's formatting on the row headers.

- *Column Headers.* Place a check mark next to this item to use the style's formatting on the column headers.

- *Banded Rows.* Place a check mark next to this item to make lines or shaded bands (depending on the style) appear along the rows.

- *Banded Columns.* Place a check mark next to this item to make lines or shaded bands (depending on the style) appear up and down the columns.

Naming a PivotTable and Setting Options for It

When you insert a PivotTable, Excel gives it an automatic name (such as PivotTable1 or PivotTable2) and sets default display options, layout options, and data options. To rename the PivotTable or to choose different options, choose PivotTable ➤ Data ➤ Options to display the PivotTable Options dialog box, and then work with its controls. (If the Excel window is too narrow for the Ribbon to fit, the command is PivotTable ➤ Data ➤ Options ➤ PivotTable Options.)

Figure 17–17 shows the PivotTable Options dialog box with its Display tab at the front.

Figure 17–17. *On the Display tab of the PivotTable Options dialog box, choose whether to show items such as expand/collapse triangles and ScreenTips on the PivotTable and whether to print headings and row labels.*

Renaming a PivotTable

To rename a PivotTable, type the new name over the existing name in the PivotTable name text box at the top of the PivotTable Options dialog box. PivotTable names can include spaces, so you can make them descriptive and readable.

> **NOTE:** When you create a PivotTable on its own worksheet, you'll normally want to rename the worksheet from its default name (for example, Sheet5) to a descriptive name (for example, Sales PivotTable). Double-click the current name on the worksheet tab, type the new name, and then press Return to apply it.

Choosing Display Options for a PivotTable

To control how Excel displays a PivotTable, click the Display tab in the PivotTable Options dialog box to display its controls (shown in Figure 17–17), and then choose the options you want.

These are the options you can choose in the Show area:

- *Expand/collapse triangles.* Select this check box if you want to display the disclosure triangles you click to expand or collapse row labels or column labels. Usually it's useful to display these disclosure triangles, but you can clear this check box if you want to hide them to prevent others from changing the display of a PivotTable.

- *Print expand/collapse triangles.* Select this check box if you want to print the disclosure triangles on printouts of the PivotTables. Printing the disclosure triangles is often useful for PivotTables you print for your own consumption, but you may prefer not to print the triangles on printouts you produce for other people.

- *Contextual ScreenTips.* Select this check box if you want the PivotTable to display ScreenTips for fields and for values when you hold the mouse pointer over a cell. This option is usually helpful.

- *Field captions and filters.* Select this check box if you want captions to appear at the top of the PivotTable and filter pop-up buttons on column labels and row labels. These are usually helpful too.

- *Error values as.* If you want to display standard text in cells that contain errors rather than displaying error messages, select this check box and type the text in the text box.

- *Empty cells as.* If you want to display standard text in empty cells instead of having them simply be empty, select this check box and type the text in the text box.

- *Item labels when no fields are on the table.* This check box is normally selected but dimmed and unavailable, because it applies only to PivotTables created in Excel 2004 (Mac), Excel 2003 (Windows), or earlier versions of Excel. If the check box is available, selecting it makes the PivotTable display item labels even when the Value Area contains no fields.

The Display items with no data area contains two settings that are available only for PivotTables that use an OLAP (Online Analytical Processing) data source:

- *On rows.* Select this check box to display row items that have no values.

- *On columns.* Select this check box to display column items that have no values.

The Print area contains two options for controlling which items print along with the PivotTable:

- *Repeat row labels on each page.* Select this check box to make Excel print the row labels on each page the PivotTable occupies rather than just on the first page. Repeating the row labels makes the PivotTable easier to read, so it's usually a good idea.

- *Page, row and column headings.* Select this check box to repeat the page headings, row headings, and column headings. This too is usually helpful.

Choosing Layout Options for a PivotTable

To control the layout of a PivotTable, click the Layout tab in the PivotTable Options dialog box to display its controls (see Figure 17–18), and then choose the settings you want.

Figure 17–18. *On the Layout tab of the PivotTable Options dialog box, you can set options for the layout, for the report filter, and for sorting.*

These are the settings you can choose in the Layout area of the Layout tab:

- *Allow multiple filters per field.* Select this check box if you want to be able to filter the PivotTable by two or more filters on a single field rather than by just one filter.

- *AutoFit column widths on update.* Select this check box to make Excel automatically resize the column widths to accommodate the data with which you've refreshed the PivotTable. AutoFit is usually helpful.

- *Preserve cell formatting on update.* Select this check box to make Excel retain cell formatting you've applied directly to cells when you update the information in the PivotTable. This option too is usually helpful.

- *Merge and center cells with labels.* Select this check box if you want Excel to merge a label cell with a blank cell next to it and center the label across the cells. Try this look to see whether you prefer it to the regular look.

- *In compact form, indent row labels.* In this pop-up menu, choose the number of spaces by which you want to indent row labels when using the Compact Layout for a PivotTable.

These are the settings you can choose in the Report filter area of the Layout tab:

- *Arrange fields option buttons.* Select the "Down, then over" option button to have Excel arrange the fields downward first and then across to the right. Select the "Over, then down" option button if you prefer to arrange the fields first to the right and then downward.

- *Filter fields per column.* In this pop-up menu, choose the number of fields to display in the report filter before moving to another column or row.

These are the settings you can choose in the Sort area of the Layout tab:

- *Use custom lists when sorting.* Select this check box if you want Excel to sort by your custom lists when it encounters the data in them. For example, if you've created a custom list of your company's offices, select this check box to make Excel sort the PivotTable by the order in that list rather than in ascending order or another standard sort order.

- *Sort A to Z.* Select this option button if you want to sort in ascending order. The alternative is the Sort by data source order option button.

- *Sort by data source order.* Select this option button if you want to sort the PivotTable in the same order as the data source. This is the default setting and is useful if you've laid out the data source in your preferred order. If not, select the Sort A to Z option button instead.

Choosing Data Options for a PivotTable

The Data tab of the PivotTable Options dialog box (see Figure 17–19) lets you control how Excel stores the PivotTable's data from an external connection and whether Excel refreshes the data automatically. For a PivotTable connected to an external data source, you can also choose whether to save the connection password with the Excel workbook and whether to run queries in the background.

Figure 17–19. *On the Data tab of the PivotTable Options dialog box, choose how to handle the PivotTable's data and connection.*

In the Data area of the Data tab, you can choose the following options:

- *Save source data with file.* Select this check box if you want to store the source data from an external data source in the workbook that contains the PivotTable. This setting has no effect on a PivotTable that contains data drawn from its own workbook, because that workbook contains the data already.

- *Enable show details.* Select this check box if you want to be able to drill down in the PivotTable to show details from the data source.

- *Retain items deleted from the data source.* Select this check box if you want Excel to store data that has been deleted from the data source. Storing the data is useful if you are working with older data in a data source that's being updated.

- *Number to retain per field.* Select the Automatic option button to have Excel store the default number of items for each field of data. Select the Max option button to store as many items as possible for each field of data.

■ *Refresh data when opening file.* Select this check box if you want Excel to automatically refresh the data in the PivotTable when you open the workbook. Automatic refreshing is useful when you need to make sure you're working with the latest figures.

In the Connection area, you can choose these two options:

■ *Save password with file.* For an external connection, select this check box to save the connection's password in the workbook. Saving the password means you don't need to enter it manually on each refresh, so you'll usually want to do this unless security dictates otherwise.

■ *Run queries in the background.* For an external connection, select this check box to run queries in the background rather than in the foreground. Running queries in the background typically makes the queries take longer but allows Excel to remain more responsive while a query is running.

When you've finished choosing options in the PivotTable Options dialog box, click the OK button to close the dialog box.

Refreshing the Data in a PivotTable

Even when you create a PivotTable from a data source in the same workbook, the data in a PivotTable remains static rather than updating automatically the way most other Excel objects do.

When you want to make sure your PivotTable contains the latest data from the data source, choose PivotTable ➤ Data ➤ Refresh ➤ Refresh.

To refresh all the PivotTables in a workbook, choose PivotTable ➤ Data ➤ Refresh ➤ Refresh All.

If your PivotTable uses an external data source, and you find the refresh operation is taking too long, choose PivotTable ➤ Data ➤ Refresh ➤ Cancel Refresh to cancel the operation.

Changing the Source of a PivotTable

Sometimes, after building a PivotTable, you may find you need to change its source data. You can do this without deleting the PivotTable and starting again, which is good news.

To change the source data of a PivotTable, follow these steps:

1. From the Ribbon, choose PivotTable ➤ Data ➤ Change Source to display the Change PivotTable Data Source dialog box (see Figure 17–20). If the Ribbon is squashed, you need to choose PivotTable ➤ Data ➤ Options ➤ Change Source.

Figure 17–20. *Use the Change PivotTable Data Source dialog box when you need to switch the PivotTable to a different data source.*

2. In the Location text box, enter the range you want to use instead of the current range. You can type in a table name or a range name; type in a range reference; or click the Collapse Dialog button, select the range in the worksheet, and then click the Collapse Dialog button again.

3. Click the OK button to close the Change PivotTable Data Source dialog box. Excel updates the PivotTable with data from the new data source.

Sorting and Filtering a PivotTable

To make a PivotTable show the data you require, you may need to sort it or filter it.

To sort a PivotTable, click the pop-up button of the field by which you want to sort. Excel displays the sorting and filtering window for that field. The window bears the field's name, as you can see in Figure 17–21, which shows the sorting and filtering window for the Product field. You can then click the Ascending button to produce an ascending sort (from A to Z, from small numbers to large numbers, and from early dates and times to later ones) or the Descending button to produce a descending sort (the opposite).

Figure 17–21. *To sort or filter a PivotTable, open the sorting and filtering window for the field, and then choose options in the Sort area or the Filter area. The sorting and filtering window's title bar shows the field's name (here, Product).*

NOTE: To control how Excel sorts a PivotTable, choose sorting options in the Sort area of the Layout tab of the PivotTable Options dialog box, as discussed earlier in this chapter.

When you apply sorting to a field, the field name pop-up button changes to show an arrow indicating the direction of the sort. For example, in Figure 17–22, you can see an upward arrow indicating a descending sort on the Salesperson field and a downward arrow indicating an ascending sort on the Product field. The Line field shows the regular pop-up button.

4	Sum of Total Price		Line ▼	
5	Salesperson ◤↑	Product ▾↓	Hardware	Services
6	Price	Printer Paper		
7		Restore		479.84
8		SmartTax		

Figure 17–22. *When you sort a PivotTable, the field's pop-up button shows an upward arrow for a descending sort (as on the Salesperson field here) or a downward arrow for an ascending sort (as on the Product field here).*

To filter the PivotTable, click the pop-up button next to the field's name to display the sorting and filtering window, and then choose the filtering criteria in the Filter area. Here are some examples:

- *Filter by label.* To filter by label, open the By label pop-up menu, choose the comparison type, and then specify the data required. For example, choose the Contains comparison to find labels that match the text string you type in the text box that appears, as shown on the left in Figure 17–23.

Figure 17–23. *You can filter a field by its label (as shown on the left here) or by its value. You can also search in the Search box or clear the check boxes of items you want to exclude.*

- *Filter by value.* To filter by value, open the By value pop-up menu, and choose the comparison you want. For example, choose the Top 10 item to create a top-however-many-you-choose filter, and then set the number of items in the left of the two pop-up menus that appears below the By value pop-up menu when it's showing Top 10 (see the right screen in Figure 17–23). In the right of the two pop-up menus, choose Item, Percentage, or Sum as needed for the filtering.

- *Filter by individual values.* To filter by individual values, clear the (Select All) check box in the lower part of the Filter area, and then select the check box for each item you want to use in the filter. To find only particular items so that you can select or clear their check boxes, click in the Search box, and type the search term.

When you apply a filter, the field's pop-up button displays a funnel-like filter symbol, as you can see on the Line field in Figure 17–24.

Line	Month		
Hardware			Hardware Total
January	February	March	April

Figure 17–24. *Excel displays a funnel-like filter on a field's pop-up button to indicate that you've applied filtering to that field.*

To remove filtering, open the sorting and filtering window again, and then click the Clear Filter button at the bottom.

Summary

In this chapter, you learned what PivotTables are and how to create them from your existing tables or other data sources. You know how to start a PivotTable automatically or build it manually, how to rearrange its fields to change the information it displays and the way it displays the information, and how to design and format the PivotTable. Lastly, you learned how to sort and filter PivotTables to make them show the information you need.

This is the end of the book's coverage of Excel. In the next part of the book, I'll show you how to make the most of PowerPoint.

Part IV

Creating Presentations with Microsoft PowerPoint

In this part of the book, you'll learn how to create compelling presentations using Microsoft PowerPoint and either present them live to an audience or deliver them across the Internet.

In Chapter 18, you'll create a presentation document using either a design template or a content template. You'll then learn how to add, delete, and rearrange slides; how to use PowerPoint's views effectively; how to develop the outline of a presentation; and how to break a presentation into separate sections. You'll also gain the skills of collaborating with your colleagues on creating a presentation.

In Chapter 19, you'll learn to create slides that convey your meaning clearly and powerfully. You'll plan your presentation, choose suitable slide layouts (or create a custom layout), and add text and other content to your slides.

In Chapter 20, you'll bring your presentation to life by adding graphics, movies, sounds, animations, and transitions. You'll learn how to hide slides to keep them up your sleeve and how to build custom slide shows that enable you to show only part of a larger presentation.

In Chapter 21, you'll come to grips with delivering the presentation you've created. You can deliver the presentation live in person, broadcast it across the Internet, or create a version of the presentation that you can share via e-mail or in other ways. You'll also learn how to use PowerPoint's Presenter view and how to create a handout for a presentation.

Chapter 18

Starting to Build a Presentation in PowerPoint

In this chapter, you'll learn how to start building a presentation in PowerPoint.

Your first move is to create the presentation document. PowerPoint gives you a wide range of choices, from colorful design themes to sample templates with content that can give your presentation a kick start. You can change the look, colors, or fonts if you don't like what you have, and you can also customize the slide size and orientation if necessary.

Once you've created the presentation, you add slides to it or customize the sample slides that it contains. A PowerPoint presentation consists of a series of slides that you normally play from start to finish. Each slide can contain any of a wide variety of different types of content, from text titles and bullet points through charts, diagrams, and even movies. You'll look at how to add straightforward content in this chapter and how to add more entertaining content types in the next two chapters.

After making sure you know how to add, delete, and rearrange slides, I'll show you how to use PowerPoint's four views to work efficiently on a presentation, how to develop the outline of a presentation quickly, and how to organize a presentation's slides into different sections for convenience.

Last, I'll show you how to collaborate with your colleagues on creating a presentation in PowerPoint—either all editing the presentation at once or editing at your leisure and combining the results.

Creating a Presentation

To create a new presentation, you use the PowerPoint Presentation Gallery dialog box (see Figure 18–1). PowerPoint opens the PowerPoint Presentation Gallery dialog box automatically when you launch the application (unless you've set PowerPoint not to do this), but you can also open the PowerPoint Presentation Gallery dialog box at any time by choosing File ➤ New from Template from the menu bar or pressing Cmd+Shift+P.

NOTE: A presentation template includes sample content that you can use as the basis of your presentation. A presentation theme is a coordinated look for the slides in a presentation but does not contain sample content.

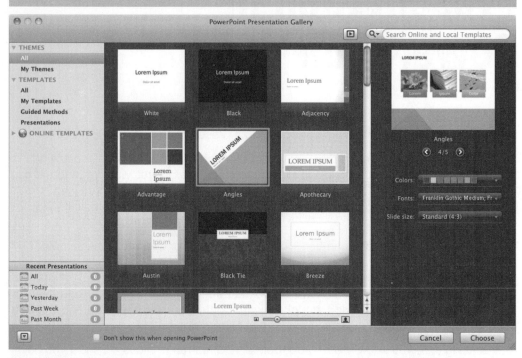

Figure 18–1. *From the PowerPoint Presentation Gallery, you can create a blank presentation or a presentation based on a template, on a theme, or on a guided method.*

From the PowerPoint Presentation Gallery, you can choose among five ways of creating a new presentation:

- *Blank presentation.* To create a blank presentation with a white background, click the White item in the middle box; to create a blank presentation with a black background, click the Black item. Then click the Choose button.

- *Built-in theme.* With the All item selected in the Themes category in the left pane, click the theme you want in the middle pane. PowerPoint displays a preview of the theme in the right pane. You can click the Next (>) button and Previous (<) button to preview the different slide layouts and then use the Colors pop-up menu, the Fonts pop-up menu, and the Slide size pop-up menu to choose how you want the slides to appear. Then click the Choose button to create a presentation using the theme.

- *My Themes.* If you create your own custom themes, click the My Themes item in the left pane, click the theme you want to use, and then click the Choose button.

- *Template on your Mac.* Click the All item in the Templates category in the left pane to display the full list of templates on your Mac. You can also click the My Templates item to display your custom templates, the Guided Methods item to display structured presentations containing sample content you can customize (see Figure 18–2), or the Presentations item to display presentation designs such as photo albums and project status reports. Click the template you want, choose options in the right pane, and then click the Choose button to create the presentation.

Figure 18–2. *Use one of the Guided Methods templates when you need to quickly build a presentation based on an existing structure. You can then replace the sample content with your content.*

- *Online Templates.* When you need a wider selection of templates, click the gray disclosure triangle next to the Online Templates heading to display the list of online templates. Click the type of template you want (for example, Diagrams) to display a list of the available templates (see Figure 18–3). Click the template you want to use, and then click the Choose button to download the template and create a presentation based on it.

Figure 18–3. *For a wider range of templates than you have on your Mac, expand the Online Templates item in the left column of the PowerPoint Presentation Gallery dialog box and browse the items available.*

NOTE: If you need to base a new presentation on an existing presentation, choose File ➤ Open to display the Open: Microsoft PowerPoint dialog box. Select the existing presentation, click the Open pop-up menu and click Copy, and then click the Open button. PowerPoint opens a new presentation file that has the same content as the original presentation. You can then use the File ➤ Save command to save the presentation under a name you specify, just as when you create a new presentation. (By contrast, if you don't choose Copy in the Open pop-up menu, you open the original presentation. You can then use the File ➤ Save As command to save it under a different name or in a different folder—but it's easy to get distracted, forget to use Save As, and then save changes to the original file by mistake.)

Changing a Presentation's Theme, Fonts, or Colors

You can change the look of the presentation by applying a different theme to it. A *theme* is an overall look for a presentation, including a slide background design, a set of colors, and a set of fonts.

To change the theme, click the Themes tab of the Ribbon, and then use the controls in the Themes group. Either click one of the themes displayed in the Themes box on the Ribbon, or hold the mouse pointer over the Themes box to display the panel button, click the panel button, and then click the theme on the Themes panel (see Figure 18–4).

Figure 18–4. *Use the Themes panel in the Themes group on the Themes tab of the Ribbon to quickly change your presentation's theme. For smaller changes within the theme, use the Colors panel, the Fonts panel, or the Background panel.*

When you've applied the theme you want, you can make changes within it:

- *Change the colors.* Choose Themes ➤ Theme Options ➤ Colors, and then click the color set you want to use.

- *Change the fonts.* Choose Themes ➤ Theme Options ➤ Fonts, and then click the fonts set.

■ *Change the background.* Choose Themes ➤ Theme Options ➤ Background, and then click the background.

> **NOTE:** After customizing a theme, you can save it for future use. Choose Themes ➤ Themes ➤ Save Theme from the Ribbon (clicking the main part of the Save Theme button), type a name in the Save As dialog box that opens, and click the Save button. You can then reuse the theme from the My Themes list in the PowerPoint Presentation Gallery dialog box or the Custom section of the Themes panel.

Changing the Slide Size or Orientation

For some presentations, you may also need to change the size or orientation of the slides. Most PowerPoint templates start you off with slides sized for displaying on a regular-format screen in a landscape (wider than high) orientation, which is what you'll most often need. But if you need to create wide-screen slides, slides sized for printing on paper, or slides in a portrait orientation, you'll need to change the setup.

To change the size or orientation, follow these steps:

1. Choose File ➤ Page Setup from the menu bar or Themes ➤ Page Setup ➤ Slide Size ➤ Page Setup from the Ribbon to display the Page Setup dialog box (see Figure 18–5).

Figure 18–5. Use the Page Setup dialog box to change slide size or orientation. You can also switch the notes, handouts, and outlines from portrait orientation to landscape.

2. Open the Slides sized for pop-up menu, and choose the size you need. Here are some examples:

   ■ Choose On-screen Show (16:9) to create slides sized for a screen with a 16:9 aspect ratio.

   ■ Choose Letter Paper (8.5x11 in) to create slides sized for printing on letter paper.

3. If necessary, change the slide size in the Width box and the Height box.

4. Choose the slide orientation by clicking the Portrait button or the Landscape button in the Slides section of the Orientation area.

5. Choose the orientation for notes, handouts, and outlines by clicking the Portrait button or the Landscape button in the Notes, handouts, & outlines section of the Orientation area.

6. Click the OK button to close the Page Setup dialog box. PowerPoint applies your choices to the presentation.

> **TIP:** If you just need to change the slide size to one of the three most frequently used sizes, choose Themes ➤ Page Setup ➤ Slide Size, and then click Standard (4:3), Widescreen (16:9), or Widescreen (16:10), as needed.

Navigating the PowerPoint Window

When you first open a presentation, PowerPoint usually displays it in Normal view. In this view, the PowerPoint window contains three panes, as you can see in Figure 18–6.

■ *Slide pane.* This pane shows the current slide. Click the Fit Slide to Current Window button to zoom the slide as large as it will go and still fit in the pane.

Slides tab   Outline tab   Navigation pane   Slide pane   Placeholder   Notes pane   Fit Slide to Current Window button

Figure 18–6. *In Normal view, the Navigation pane appears on the left and the Notes pane appears at the bottom of the window, leaving the slide pane taking up most of the space.*

■ *Navigation pane.* This pane appears on the left and contains two tabs, Slides and Outline. The Slides tab shows a thumbnail picture of each slide that you can click to display the slide in the Slide pane. The Outline tab displays an outline of the presentation that you can use to quickly develop the presentation's text content. In the Outline tab too, you click a slide to display it in the Slide pane.

NOTE: You can resize the Slide pane, Navigation pane, and Notes pane by dragging the borders that separate them. For example, you may want to widen the Slide pane to make the thumbnail pictures larger so that you can identify the slides more easily. When the Navigation pane is too narrow to display the words *Slides* and *Outline* on the tab buttons, it displays symbols instead.

■   *Notes pane.* This pane appears at the bottom of the window, below the Slide pane. This is where you create notes that you want to accompany the slide. These may be notes that you want to view on-screen as you give the presentation to remind you of what to say, notes you plan to print out for yourself or whoever delivers the presentation, or notes that you turn into a handout for the audience.

> **TIP:** If you want more room to work on your slide, close the Navigation pane by clicking its Close button (the × button) or by dragging its right border all the way to the left side of the window. To display the Navigation pane again, drag the border back to the right. Similarly, you can hide the Notes pane by dragging its border down to the bottom of the window and reveal it again by dragging the border back up.

Add Content to a Slide

Once you've created a slide, you can add content to it. As you'll see in Chapters 19 and 20, PowerPoint slides can contain a wide variety of types of content, from text to audio and movies.

Most slides come with one or more placeholders for adding content. For example, the slide shown in Figure 18–6 has a title placeholder (where it says "Click to add title") and a standard content placeholder for adding text, graphics, tables, or other content. Other slides contain placeholders for other types of content, such as subtitles.

> **NOTE:** Most themes and templates start you off with one or more slides. If your presentation doesn't have a slide at this point, choose Home ➤ Slides ➤ New Slide or press Cmd+Shift+N to insert a slide. See the next section for more details on adding slides.

To add text to a text placeholder, click anywhere in the placeholder. PowerPoint hides the prompt (the "Click to add" text) and displays an insertion point. Type the text you want, and then click outside the placeholder to deselect it.

To resize a placeholder, click to select it. You can then drag a corner handle to resize the placeholder while retaining its original proportions or drag a side handle to resize it in only one dimension.

> **NOTE:** To reset a slide's placeholders to their defaults, click the slide, and then choose Home ➤ Slides ➤ Layout ➤ Reset Layout to Default Settings from the Ribbon. To change the layout of a slide, click the slide, choose Home ➤ Slides ➤ Layout, and then click the layout you want on the Layout panel.

To move a placeholder, first select it by clicking it. Move the mouse pointer over a border so that the pointer changes to a four-headed arrow. Then drag the placeholder to where you want it to appear.

Adding, Deleting, and Rearranging Slides

If you based your presentation on a theme, you'll probably need to add more slides to it now. If you based the presentation on a sample template or a guided method, you may have the opposite problem—the presentation contains too many slides, and you need to delete some of them. Either way, sooner or later, you will likely need to change the order in which the slides appear in the presentation.

Adding a Slide

To add a new slide, select the slide after which you want to insert the new one. Choose Home ➤ Slides ➤ New Slide (clicking the drop-down button on the New Slide button), and then click the slide design on the panel that opens (see Figure 18–7).

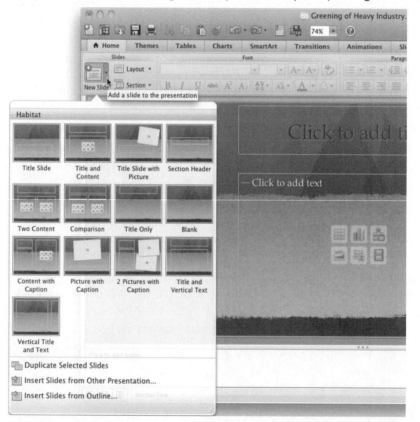

Figure 18–7. *Insert a slide by opening the New Slide panel on the Home tab of the Ribbon and clicking the slide layout you want.*

You can also insert slides in a presentation in three other ways:

- *Duplicate slides from the presentation.* To create new slides based on ones already in your presentation, select those slides, and then choose Home ➤ Slides ➤ New Slide ➤ Duplicate Selected Slides or Insert ➤ Duplicate Slide.

> **TIP:** You can quickly duplicate a slide by Ctrl+clicking or right-clicking it in the Slides pane or in Slide Sorter view and then clicking Duplicate Slide on the context menu. Alternatively, select the slide, and then press Cmd+Shift+D. To duplicate multiple slides, select them before giving the command.

- *Copy slides from another presentation.* You can insert slides from another presentation. Follow these steps:

  1. Select the slide after which you want to insert the copied slides.

  2. Choose Insert ➤ Slides From ➤ Other Presentation from the menu bar or Home ➤ Slides ➤ New Slide ➤ Insert Slides from Other Presentation from the Ribbon to display the Choose a File dialog box (see Figure 18–8).

Figure 18–8. *In the Choose a File dialog box, select the presentation that contains the slides you want to insert in the current presentation. You can insert either all the slides or just some of them.*

  3. Navigate to and click the presentation that contains the slides you want to insert.

4. In the lower-left corner of the dialog box, select the Insert all slides option button if you want to insert all the slides. To insert just some slides, choose the Select slides to insert option button.

5. Click the Insert button. If you chose to insert all the slides, PowerPoint inserts them. If you chose the Select slides to insert option button, PowerPoint displays the Slide Finder dialog box (see Figure 18–9).

Figure 18–9. *In the Slide Finder dialog box, select the slides you want to insert. You can switch between Slide view and Outline view by clicking the buttons in the upper-left corner.*

6. Select the slides to insert. Click the first of the slides you want, and then Shift+click each of the others you want.

7. Select the Keep design of original slides check box if you want to preserve the slides' design. Clear this check box if you want the slides to pick up the design of the presentation into which you're inserting them.

8. Click the Insert button. PowerPoint inserts the slides.

9. Click the Close button to close the Slide Finder dialog box.

- *Insert slides from an outline in a document.* If you've created an outline in a rich text format (RTF) document or a text document, you can create slides based on it. Choose Insert ➤ Slides From ➤ Outline from the menu bar or Home ➤ Slides ➤ New Slide ➤ Slides from Outline from the Ribbon to open the Choose a File dialog box, click the document that contains the outline, and then click the Insert button. PowerPoint tries to break up the content to fit the slides by using the heading styles and formatting, but you will often need to adjust the resulting slides.

Deleting a Slide

You can delete a slide in the Slides pane or the Outline pane in Normal view or in the main pane in Slide Sorter view. (You'll learn about Slide Sorter view in a moment.) Use any of these techniques:

- *Context menu.* Ctrl+click or right-click the slide, and then click Delete Slide on the context menu.

- *Delete key.* Click the slide, and then press Delete.

- *Menu bar.* Click the slide, and then choose Edit ➤ Delete Slide.

NOTE: You can also remove a slide by selecting it in the Outline pane in Normal view or in the main pane in Slide Sorter view and then giving a Cut command—for example, clicking the Cut button on the Standard toolbar, choosing Edit ➤ Cut, or pressing Cmd+X. Cutting the slide removes it from the presentation and places it on the Clipboard, from which you can paste it somewhere else if you want.

Rearranging Slides

You can change the order of the slides in the presentation in either Normal view or Slide Sorter view:

- *Normal view.* In the Slides pane or in Outline pane, click the slide you want to move, and then drag it up or down. PowerPoint moves the other slides out of the way to make space for the slide you're dragging. When the slide appears where you want it, release the mouse button.

- *Slide Sorter view.* Select the slide or slides, and then drag them to the appropriate position. When the slide or slides are where you want them, release the mouse button.

Using Views to Work on Your Presentation

So far in this chapter, you've seen only Normal view, though I've also mentioned Slide Sorter view. Altogether, PowerPoint provides four different views to help you work swiftly and easily on your presentations: Normal view, Slide Sorter view, Notes Page view, and Slide Show view. PowerPoint also provides Presenter view, which you use when running a slide show on two screens (one screen for you, the other for your audience).

You can switch views in any of these ways:

- *Status bar.* Click the appropriate view button in the View Shortcuts group (see Figure 18–10). This group doesn't contain a button for Notes Page view.

Normal   Slide   Slide
view   Sorter   Show
          view   view

Figure 18–10. *Click a view button in the View Shortcuts group on the status bar to change views quickly.*

- *Menu bar.* Choose View ➤ Normal, View ➤ Slide Sorter, View ➤ Notes Pages, or View ➤ Slide Show.

- *Keyboard.* Press Cmd+1 to switch to Normal view, Cmd+2 to switch to Slide Sorter view, Cmd+3 to switch to Notes Page view, or Cmd+Shift+Return to switch to Slide Show view (and start the slide show).

Creating Your Slides in Normal View

As you've seen already, Normal view is the view you use to create your slides and work on their content. Normal view is the view in which PowerPoint usually opens a presentation, and you can give yourself more space to work on a slide by hiding the Navigation pane and the Notes area.

Rearranging Your Slides in Slide Sorter View

When you need to rearrange your slides into a different order, use Slide Sorter view (see Figure 18–11). This view shows a thumbnail picture of each slide laid out in a grid pattern, so you can quickly see where each slide appears in relation to the other slides.

Figure 18–11. *In Slide Sorter view, you can quickly drag a slide or a group of slides to a different place in the presentation, as in the middle of the window here. Drag the zoom slider to change the size at which the slide thumbnails appear.*

NOTE: To select a slide in Slide Sorter view, click it. To select a range of slides, click the first slide, and then Shift-click the last slide; alternatively, click before the first slide, and drag over the slides you want. To select slides that aren't next to each other, click the first slide, and then Cmd+click each of the others.

Slide Sorter view is most useful for these three purposes:

- *Checking the order of slides.* In Slide Sorter view, you can easily see the order your slides are in and change the order if it's wrong. To move one or more selected slides, drag them to where you want them to appear. PowerPoint moves the other slides out of the way, so you can tell where the slides will land when you drop them.

- *Getting an overview of your presentation.* The Slides pane and the Outline pane are good for viewing your presentation as a sequence, but often it's helpful to be able to view all the slides at once.

- *Finding the slide you need to edit.* Once you've located the slide, double-click it to open the slide in Normal view so that you can edit it.

Creating Notes Pages in Notes Page View

When you need to add notes to a slide, switch to Notes Page view by choosing View ➤ Notes Page or pressing Cmd+3. In Notes Page view (see Figure 18–12), you can type the notes you need for each slide.

What kind of notes you'll create depends on the presentation and how you'll deliver it— but here are three typical kinds of notes:

- *Notes for viewing on-screen.* If you will use PowerPoint's Presenter view (which you'll learn to use in Chapter 21) when giving the presentation, you can view notes on your screen without the audience seeing them.

- *Notes to print out for the speaker.* If you (or someone else) will need printed notes to deliver the presentation, you can enter the appropriate information in Notes Page view.

- *Notes to include in handouts for the audience.* If you plan to create a handout for the audience, enter any notes you want to include.

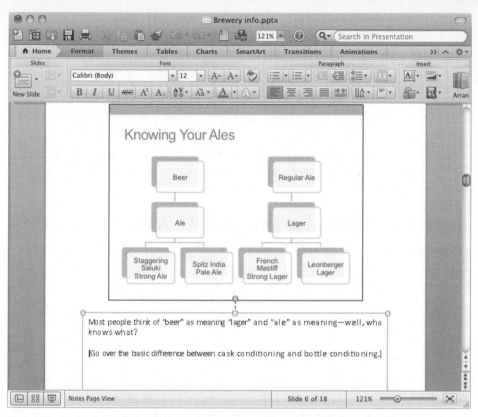

Figure 18–12. *Switch to Notes Page view when you need to create notes for your slides.*

Running a Presentation in Slide Show View

PowerPoint's fourth view, Slide Show view, is the view you use when running a presentation. Slide Show view displays the current slide full screen on the screen you're using for the presentation. If you have a secondary screen (for example, because you've connected your Mac to a projector), you can choose to show your presenter notes on it to help you with the presentation.

You'll see Slide Show view in action in Chapter 21, which covers running slide shows. Chapter 21 also explains how to use Presenter view, which you use to display your notes and upcoming slides on one screen while running a presentation on another screen.

Opening Extra Windows to See Different Parts of the Presentation

Often, it's useful to be able to see two or more different slides at once so that you can compare them or ensure the ideas flow smoothly from one to the other. The easiest way to do this is to open a new window on the presentation and then display the other slide in that window.

To open a new window, choose Window ➤ New Window from the menu bar. You can then position each window wherever you find most helpful and display different slides—or use different views—in the windows.

Creating the Outline of a Presentation

When you need to develop the outline of a presentation quickly, work in the Outline tab of the Navigation pane in Normal view. With the presentation open, click the Outline tab in the Navigation pane to display the outline.

The Outline tab (see Figure 18–13) shows the presentation as a sequence of collapsible slides. Each slide appears as a heading with its ordinal number and the text from the title placeholder (if there is any).

You can expand or collapse a slide by double-clicking its icon in the Outline tab. A collapsed slide shows an underline to indicate that material is hidden, as in slides 3 and 4 in Figure 18–13.

Figure 18–13. *You can quickly enter slide titles and text content by using the Outline tab in the Navigation pane. As you work, PowerPoint enters the information with basic formatting on the slide itself; you can fix it later.*

Use these techniques for working in the Outline tab:

■ *Create a new slide.* Press Return at the end of a paragraph to start a new paragraph, and then press Shift+Tab one or more times (as needed) to promote the paragraph to a slide title.

■ *Create a bulleted paragraph.* After typing a slide title, press Return to start a new paragraph. Then press Tab to demote the paragraph to the first level. You can demote a paragraph to a lower level if needed (for example, to create second-level bulleted paragraphs).

■ *Move a paragraph or selection up or down.* Click at the left end of a paragraph to select it, or click and drag to select multiple paragraphs. You can then drag the paragraph or selection up or down the outline to where you want it to be. For example, you can drag a bulleted paragraph from one slide to another.

■ *Paste in text.* You can paste text into the Outline tab, and then promote or demote its paragraphs to the levels at which you want them to appear.

Organizing Your Slides into Sections

When you add many slides to a presentation, it can become difficult to navigate through the presentation. To simplify matters, you can divide the presentation up into two or more sections. Each section can contain however many slides you need it to, and you can expand or collapse sections as needed.

To add a section, follow these steps:

1. Switch to Normal view if you're using any other view. For example, click the Normal view button in the View Shortcuts area of the status bar.

2. Display the Navigation pane if it's not already displayed.

3. Click the Slides tab of the Navigation pane if the Outline tab is displayed.

4. Click the slide at which you want to start the section.

5. Choose Home ➤ Slides ➤ Section ➤ Add Section from the Ribbon or Insert ➤ Section from the menu bar. PowerPoint creates a new section, names it Untitled Section on the section bar across the top, and displays the Rename Section dialog box (see Figure 18–14).

Figure 18–14. *PowerPoint creates the section, names it Untitled Section, and displays the Rename Section dialog box so that you can rename it. The number in parentheses after each section name shows how many slides the section contains.*

6. Type the section name, and then press Return or click the Rename button to close the dialog box and apply the new name.

NOTE: If the first section you create begins after the first slide, PowerPoint puts the slides before the section into another section named Default Section. Double-click the Default Section heading to display the Rename Section dialog box, type a new name for the section, and then press Return or click the Rename button.

Once you've created your sections, you can manipulate them easily like this:

- *Expand or collapse a section.* Click its disclosure triangle.

- *Expand or collapse all sections.* Ctrl+click or right-click a section heading, and then click Expand All or Collapse All on the context menu.

- *Move a section up or down the list of sections.* Either click the section heading and drag it to where you want the section, or Ctrl+click or right-click the section heading, and then click Move Section Up or Move Section Down on the context menu (see Figure 18–15).

Figure 18–15. *After creating sections, you can use the context menu to rename them, rearrange them, or remove them.*

■ *Remove a section but leave its slides.* Ctrl+click or right-click the section heading, and then click Remove Section on the context menu. To remove all sections, click Remove All Sections.

■ *Remove a section and its slides.* Ctrl+click or right-click the section heading, and then click Remove Section and Slides on the context menu.

Collaborating on a Presentation with Your Colleagues

You'll probably create some presentations on your own, but for others you may need to get input from your colleagues. You can do this in several ways:

■ *Work on the presentation together at the same time.* PowerPoint's "coauthoring" feature enables you and your colleagues to open the same copy of the presentation from a SharePoint site or from Windows Live SkyDrive and work on it together, resolving any conflicts that crop up when two or more people try to change the same part of the presentation at the same time.

■ *Work on the presentation in turn.* If you find coauthoring troublesome or if you don't have a SharePoint site or use Windows Live SkyDrive, you may prefer to save the presentation in a shared folder and work on it in turn. PowerPoint doesn't offer revision marks like Word does, so you may want to have your colleagues provide input by adding comments rather than by changing the slides directly.

■ *Work on separate copies of the presentation, and then compare them.*
The third option is to use two or more separate copies of the
presentation. After you and your colleagues have provided your input,
you can use PowerPoint's Compare feature to flag the differences
between the copies and then decide which changes to keep and
which to reject.

Working on a presentation in turn requires coordinating the various editors but is
otherwise straightforward enough. Coauthoring presentations and comparing
presentations are more involved. The "Editing a Presentation Simultaneously with Your
Colleagues" section discusses coauthoring, and the "Comparing Two Copies of the
Same Presentation" section explains how to compare presentations.

Editing a Presentation Simultaneously with Your Colleagues

When you need to create a presentation quickly, you can edit the presentation
simultaneously with your colleagues. If you can avoid stepping on each other's toes,
coauthoring a presentation can be a fast and efficient way to work, because you can
avoid duplicating effort or working in different directions.

> **TIP:** When coauthoring a presentation, either agree beforehand which slides or which section
> each person will work on or use instant messaging to keep in touch as you work. As far as
> possible, avoid working on the same slide as one of your coauthors—otherwise, it's all too easy
> to create conflicting changes that you then need to resolve.

Here's how to coauthor a presentation with your colleagues:

■ *Create the presentation.* One of you creates the presentation in the
normal way—for example, by basing it on a theme, as described
earlier in this chapter, or by cloning an existing presentation (likewise).
You save the presentation either to a SharePoint site on your local
network or to Windows Live SkyDrive.

> **NOTE:** If you have the choice between using a local SharePoint site and using Windows Live
> SkyDrive, choose the SharePoint site—it'll give much better performance, especially if you
> create a large and complex presentation.

- *Open the presentation.* The first person opens the presentation as usual. Then, whenever another person opens the presentation, PowerPoint displays a pop-up message telling them who else is working on it. The first person also sees a corresponding pop-up message (see Figure 18–16).

Figure 18–16. *The Authors readout on the left side of the status bar shows you when another author opens the presentation for editing.*

- *See the current list of editors*: To see the full list of people editing the presentation, click the Authors readout on the status bar to display the Authors editing this document pop-up menu. From here, you can click an author's name to display a pop-up panel (see Figure 18–17) containing ways to contact that person—for example, e-mail or instant messaging.

Figure 18–17. *Click the Authors readout on the status bar to see the list of people editing the document. You can then click one of the people to display options for contacting him or her.*

- *Edit the presentation.* You can work as normal using almost the full range of PowerPoint's features. The main limitation is that only one person can edit any given element at a time. For this reason, the most practical approach is to work on different slides than your coauthors are editing.

- *Update the presentation.* When you've made changes you want to share with your coauthors or when you're ready to see what changes they've made, click the Save button on the Standard toolbar or press Cmd+S to save the presentation. PowerPoint uploads your changes to the document on the SharePoint site or on SkyDrive and merges them with your coauthors' changes; if your changes conflict with a coauthor's changes, you'll need to resolve them, as described later in this chapter. PowerPoint downloads your coauthors' changes and displays them for you.

- *Resolve conflicts.* If you and another author change the same element at the same time, PowerPoint displays the dialog box shown in Figure 18–18 to whoever saves the document after the other. Click the Conflicts Only button, and then work in the Compare Changes pane, as described later in this section.

Other authors have made changes that conflict with some of your recent changes. Do you want to review the conflicts only?

To review all changes by other authors, click All Changes.

Conflicts Only   All Changes

Figure 18–18. *If PowerPoint displays this dialog box, click the Conflicts Only button, and then use the Compare Changes pane to work through the conflicting changes.*

NOTE: If PowerPoint displays the Refresh Required bar across the top of the document window below the Ribbon, click the Save button. PowerPoint then normally displays the dialog box shown in Figure 18–18, warning you there are conflicting changes.

- *Review your coauthors' changes.* When you save your changes as described a moment ago, PowerPoint merges your coauthors' changes into the presentation you're viewing and flags them for you. To review the changes and choose which to accept, follow these steps:

    1. Click the Updates Available button on the status bar to display the pop-up menu (see Figure 18–19).

Figure 18–19. *Open the Updates Available pop-up menu on the status bar and click the Save and Review item to start reviewing your coauthors' changes.*

2.   Click the Save and Review item to display the dialog box shown in Figure 18–20.

Figure 18–20. *Click the Review Changes button in this dialog box to review the changes your coauthors have made to the presentation.*

3.   Click the Review Changes button to display the Merge tab of the Ribbon and the Compare Changes pane (see Figure 18–21). The first of the changed slides appears in the Slide pane.

Figure 18–21. *Use the controls on the Merge tab of the Ribbon and in the Compare Changes pane to review—and accept or reject—the changes your coauthors have made to the presentation.*

4. In the Compare Changes pane, click the slide for which you want to see the changes. Expand the list of changes as needed by clicking the disclosure triangles so that you can see the details of the changes.

5. Move to each change in turn, and deal with it by clicking the Accept button or the Reject button in the Compare group of the Merge tab of the Ribbon. You can click the Previous button or Next button in the Compare group to move to another change, or you can click the change in the Compare Changes pane.

6. Choose Merge ➤ Compare ➤ End to close the merge view and return to editing the presentation.

■ *Close the presentation.* When you have finished working with the presentation, save any unsaved changes that you want to keep. Then close the presentation as usual—for example, choose File ➤ Close.

Comparing Two Copies of the Same Presentation

If you use two or more copies of the same presentation to gather input, use PowerPoint's Compare feature to compare the copies and identify the differences so that you can review them.

> **TIP:** When comparing presentations, keep the original presentation clean (unedited) as the basis for the comparison. You can then compare each edited version in turn to the original presentation and identify all the changes. The result is much clearer than comparing one person's edited version with your edits of the original version.

To compare two copies of a presentation, follow these steps:

1. Open one copy of the presentation in PowerPoint as usual.

2. Choose Review ➤ Compare ➤ Compare from the Ribbon to display the Compare Presentations dialog box. This dialog box is the Open dialog box under a different name.

3. Navigate to the other copy of the presentation, and then click it.

4. Click the Compare button to close the Compare Presentations dialog box. PowerPoint merges the changes from the second presentation into the first presentation and displays the Revisions pane. Figure 18–22 shows a presentation with changes merged into it and the reviewing process underway.

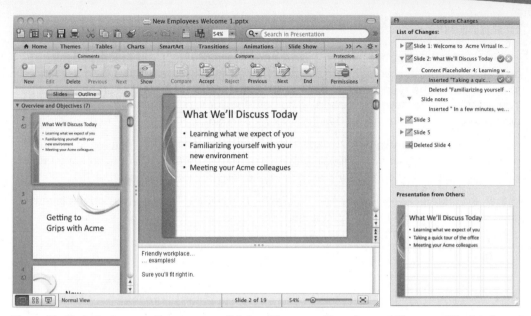

Figure 18–22. *In the Compare Changes pane, click the slide you want to review, and then expand the list of changes to see the details of what has changes. Click the green checkmark button to accept the change, or click the red × button to reject the change.*

5. In the Compare Changes pane, click the slide you want to review. Then use the disclosure triangles to display the level of changes you want.

6. Click the green check mark button to accept a change, or click the red × button to reject the change.

7. When you have finished reviewing the changes, choose Review ➤ Compare ➤ End to stop the review. You can then save the presentation.

Make sure you review all the changes before you choose Review ➤ Compare ➤ End. Otherwise, PowerPoint displays the dialog box shown in Figure 18–23 warning you that some changes have not been reviewed yet and that PowerPoint will discard any changes you haven't yet dealt with. Click the Cancel button if you want to check through the remaining changes, accepting those you want to keep and rejecting the others.

Figure 18–23. *If PowerPoint displays this dialog box when you try to end the comparison, you'll usually want to click the Cancel button so that you can go back and review the remaining changes.*

Summary

In this chapter, you learned how to create a new PowerPoint presentation by basing it on a sample template, on a design theme, or on an existing presentation. You saw how to add slides to the presentation, rearrange them, and delete ones that aren't needed. You grasped the techniques for adding content to slides, developing the outline of a presentation, and organizing slides into different sections.

I also showed you how to use PowerPoint's powerful collaboration features to work on presentations with your colleagues—either sharing the same copy of the presentation or working on separate copies and then integrating the changes from each.

In the next chapter, we'll look at how to create compelling slides by making the layouts and the content work effectively together.

Chapter 19

Creating Clear and Compelling Slides

In this chapter, I'll show you how to create slides that convey your meaning clearly and powerfully to your audience.

I'll begin where you'll probably want to start your presentation—by looking at how to plan the slides it will contain. Then you'll see which of PowerPoint's built-in slide layouts suits which type of content—and how you can create a custom slide layout when none of the built-in layouts fits the bill.

After that, you'll learn how to add text to your slides and format it to look good. Finally, I'll show you how to add tables, charts, SmartArt graphics, and hyperlinks to your slides.

Planning the Slides in Your Presentation

As you plan your presentation and as you create the slides for it, keep the audience in mind. Whether you'll deliver the presentation in person, via an Internet broadcast, or by distributing digital copies of the presentation, you'll want to make sure your slides are easy to read, are attractive to look at, and convey your meaning clearly.

For most presentations, follow these general rules when planning and creating your slides:

- *Keep your text concise*. Some presentation experts suggest following the "6×6 rule" for text slides—each slide should have about six bullet points of around six words each. The name is catchy, but the exact numbers are less important than the wider point: it's fine to have anywhere from four to eight bullets, as long as each of them is fairly short and your slide is easy to read.

NOTE: For most presentations, you'll have things that you definitely want to say to the audience but that don't fit directly in the text of your slides. Put these items in your notes for the slide. Also put in the notes any things you may need to add—for example, statistics to mention if audience members ask questions you've anticipated about the slides.

- *Keep your slides uncluttered.* If you need to choose between fitting in more information on an existing slide and adding a slide, it's usually best to add the extra slide. Don't feel you need to fill up each slide— it's fine to leave blank space on a slide. You're not short-changing the audience by making the presentation easy for them to assimilate.

- *Illustrate your points.* When you make a point, drive it home by illustrating it with an example that catches your audience's imagination. For example, don't just say you're now selling half a million gizmos a year—point out that's enough for everyone in Albuquerque to have one.

- *Use your strongest material—not all your material.* Many presentations suffer from too much detail. Usually, you can convince your audience that you have the facts and figures with just a couple of well-chosen examples; you don't need to numb them with a complete rundown of the data.

TIP: You may find it useful to keep extra material in reserve by using hidden slides or by creating custom slide shows that let you show a series of extra slides when you need to do so. See Chapter 20 for details on both these topics.

- *Provide visual interest—but don't overdo it.* Even with the liveliest presenter, a text-only presentation can be dull as ditch water. As you'll see in this chapter and the next, PowerPoint makes it easy to add tables, charts, graphics, videos, and animations to your slides, so it's a good idea to include visually interesting and relevant information to give the audience something to look at. You can also use audio in your presentations.

- *Put a Welcome slide at the start of the presentation.* Many presentations benefit from having a Welcome slide that gives the audience something to look at on entering the room and waiting for stragglers. A Welcome slide is good for you too, because you can see that you have the presentation up and running correctly.

- *Give your presentation a final slide.* Often, when you spend ages creating a presentation, finishing it is such a relief that you don't notice it ends with a bump with the final slideful of content. For many presentations, it's helpful to have a final slide that you can leave on the screen. This slide may be as simple as a single line—for example, "Questions?" or "Coffee and cookies in the lobby"—or even a colored screen with no text at all.

Choosing Slide Layouts to Suit the Contents

To get your material onto a slide and to make it look good, you need to choose a suitable layout. You can either use one of PowerPoint's built-in slide layouts or create a custom layout of your own.

Using PowerPoint's Built-in Slide Layouts

You'll probably want to start by using the standard slide layouts that PowerPoint provides on the Home ➤ Slides ➤ New Slide panel. The exact list of layouts depends on the theme or template you're using. Table 19–1 lists the most common layouts and explains when to use each.

Table 19–1. *PowerPoint's Standard Slide Layouts and When to Use Them*

Slide Layout	When to Use It
Title Slide	To start your presentation or to introduce a new section of it.
Section Header	To start a new section of the presentation. In most designs, this slide has a substantially different look from other slides to suggest the change.
Title and Content	To display a content item such as a table, chart, or picture.
Two Content	To display two content items—for example, two pictures or two tables—but without necessarily comparing them to each other.
Comparison	To display two content items (for example, two charts) and compare them to each other. The Comparison layout is like the Two Content layout but has an extra text box above each item that you can use to highlight the differences.
Content with Caption	To display a content item (such as a table or chart) over most of the slide, with a title and explanatory text alongside it.
Picture with Caption	To display a picture over most of the slide, with a title and explanatory text alongside it. The Picture with Caption layout is almost identical to the Content with Caption layout but is customized for pictures rather than other content types.
Title and Vertical Text	To display a horizontal title (as usual) and then vertical text items. This layout is useful for specialized purposes.

Slide Layout	When to Use It
Vertical Text and Title	To display the title vertically on one side of the slide and the text items vertically on the other side. This layout can be useful for highly specialized purposes.
Title, Content and Text	To display a title on the top, content (such as a picture or table) on the left, and explanatory text on the right. This layout is widely useful.
Title Only	To add only a title to a slide or to have a title followed by content you place manually.
Blank	To create your own layout or to insert a blank slide as a pause in your presentation.
Background Only	To display only a background on the slide. You can add other content as needed or simply show the background as a visual interlude.

You can change a slide's layout at any time by clicking the slide, choosing Home ➤ Slides ➤ Layout, and then clicking the layout you want. And you can snap a slide's layout back to its default settings by choosing Home ➤ Slides ➤ Layout ➤ Reset Layout to Default Settings.

NOTE: If you change a slide's layout by applying a layout that has fewer placeholders than the number of placeholders you're currently using, PowerPoint leaves the extra placeholders on the slide so that you can deal with them.

Creating Custom Slide Layouts

When none of PowerPoint's built-in slide layouts is exactly what you want, you can create a custom slide layout in either of these ways:

- Apply the closest slide layout to what you want, and then customize it. For example, you can delete a placeholder by clicking it and then pressing Delete, or you can copy a placeholder by clicking it and then Option+dragging to where you want the copy.

- Start with a blank slide layout, and then add the objects you need.

TIP: After you create a custom slide layout, you can reuse it by selecting the slide and then duplicating it. For example, Ctrl+click or right-click the slide and then click Duplicate Slide on the context menu, or press Cmd+Shift+D.

Formatting Text on Your Slides

You can format text on PowerPoint slides quickly by using the controls in the Font group and the Paragraph group on the Home tab of the Ribbon. You'll be familiar with most of these controls from the first part of the book, but Figure 19–1 points out several key controls and PowerPoint-specific controls that you'll use in this section.

Figure 19–1. *You can apply many types of text formatting quickly by using the controls in the Font group and Paragraph group on the Home tab of the Ribbon.*

NOTE: To change the formatting of all the text in a placeholder, select the placeholder itself. To change the formatting of just some of the text, select that text.

Changing the Font, Font Size, and Alignment

You can easily change the font, font size, and alignment of text:

- *Change the font size.* Click the placeholder that contains the text, and then click the Increase Font Size button or the Decrease Font Size button in the Font group on the Home tab or open the Font Size pop-up menu and click the size you want.

NOTE: If you find the Ribbon awkward, you can apply the most widely used types of text formatting from the Standard toolbar instead.

- *Change the font.* Click the placeholder, open the Font pop-up menu in the Font group on the Home tab, and then click the font you want. The Theme Headings item and Theme Body item at the top of the list show the primary fonts used for the theme or template—so you may want to use them for consistency.

- *Change the alignment.* Click the placeholder or click in the paragraph you want to affect, and then click the Align Text Left button, the Center button, the Align Text Right button, or the Justify button in the Paragraph group on the Home tab of the Ribbon.

To reach the full range of options for formatting text, choose Format ➤ Font from the menu bar. PowerPoint opens the Format Text dialog box with the Font category displayed (see Figure 19-2). To set widely used font formatting options, work on the Font tab in the Font category. If you need to space characters farther apart or place them closer together, use the Character Spacing tab in the Font category.

Figure 19-2. *When you need full control over text formatting, open the Format Text dialog box, and then click the appropriate category in the left column.*

KEEPING YOUR TEXT EASY TO READ

Like most applications, PowerPoint gives you such a wide variety of fonts that it's easy to make poor choices.

When choosing fonts and font sizes for your slides, put clarity foremost. If the audience can't read the text on a slide because you've chosen an unsuitable font or too small a font size, your words of wisdom will be wasted. After creating a slide, make sure that even the smallest text on it will be easy to read from the back of the audience—and by someone with less than perfect eyesight.

Often, it's tempting to use a striking or "designy" font to look different. But in most cases, the best fonts are those that people barely notice because they're simply easy to read, such as the Calibri font used in the Office design. Unless you're presenting to designers, you're usually better off with straightforward fonts rather than fonts that set out to catch the eye.

Above all, keep the number of fonts to a sensible minimum. Using many different fonts can make your presentation look like an old-style ransom note.

Changing the Indentation and Line Spacing of Text

To make text look right on a slide, you'll often need to adjust its indentation and line spacing. You can change these as follows:

- *Change the indentation.* Click the Decrease Indent button or the Increase Indent button. To take direct control, choose Format ➤ Paragraph from the menu bar to display the Paragraph category in the Format Text dialog box (see Figure 19–3), and then use the controls in the Indentation area.

Figure 19–3. *Use the Paragraph category in the Format Text dialog box when you need close control over the indentation and spacing of paragraphs.*

- *Change the line spacing.* Click the Line Spacing button, and then make your choice from the pop-up menu, which offers a range of choices from 0.5 lines to 3.0 lines. For greater control, click the Line Spacing Options item on the pop-up menu to display the Paragraph category in the Format Text dialog box, and then use the controls in the Spacing area.

Rotating Text

For some slides, you may want to rotate text either in two dimensions or in three dimensions.

To rotate text simply, click the text placeholder, choose Home ➤ Paragraph ➤ Text Direction from the Ribbon, and then click one of the directions on the pop-up menu (see Figure 19–4):

- *Horizontal.* Choose this item to restore text to normal horizontal orientation.

Figure 19–4. *Use the Text Direction panel in the Paragraph group on the Home tab of the Ribbon to turn text sideways or make it run in a stack down a slide. For other types of rotation, click the Text Direction Options item to open the Text Box category in the Format Text dialog box.*

- *Rotate Clockwise.* Choose this item to turn the text on its side so that it reads from top to bottom.

NOTE: To rotate the text box freely rather than in 90-degree increments, click the text box, and then drag the green rotate button above it to the left or right, as for any other graphical object.

- *Rotate Counterclockwise.* Choose this item to turn the text on its side so that it reads from bottom to top.

- *Stacked.* Choose this item to make the text read from top to bottom but without rotating the letters. This arrangement is good for adding narrow labels to graphical items.

> **CAUTION:** Use text rotation only for special effects. Don't rely on rotated text to convey important points, because the audience may find it difficult to read.

If you need rotate text in other ways, follow these steps:

1. Choose Home ➤ Paragraph ➤ Text Direction ➤ Text Direction Options from the Ribbon or Format ➤ Text Direction from the menu bar to display the Text Box category in the Format Text dialog box (see Figure 19–5).

Figure 19–5. *In the Text Box category of the Format Text dialog box, open the Text direction pop-up menu, and choose the text direction you want.*

2. In the Text Layout area at the top, open the Vertical alignment pop-up menu, and choose the alignment for the text—Top, Middle, Bottom, Top Centered, Middle Centered, or Bottom Centered.

> **NOTE:** If you've rotated the text vertically, the Text Layout area of the Text Box category in the Format Text dialog box shows the Horizontal alignment pop-up menu instead of the Vertical alignment pop-up menu.

3. Open the Text direction pop-up menu and choose the direction for the text—Horizontal, Rotate to 90° Counterclockwise, Rotate to 90° Clockwise, or Stacked.

4. In the left column, click the Text 3-D Rotation category to display the Text 3-D Rotation controls.

5. Set up the 3-D rotation you want by using the Type pop-up menu and the controls in the Rotation area. See Chapter 4 for details on rotating shapes.

6. In the Text area, make sure the Keep text flat check box is cleared so that PowerPoint rotates the text rather than just the shape around it.

7. Click the Close button to close the Format Text dialog box.

> **TIP:** If you need to display text upside down, put it in its own container, and then rotate the container so that it is upside down.

Using Bulleted Lists

Many PowerPoint slides use bulleted lists, because they can be a great way of presenting your content clearly—provided you get them right.

This section shows you how to handle the mechanics of bulleted lists and suggests ways to make your content easy for your audience to grasp.

Creating a Bulleted List

Creating a bulleted list is easy. When you start typing text in a placeholder that has bullets applied, PowerPoint automatically gives the paragraph a bullet. When you press Return to create the next paragraph, PowerPoint displays a bullet for that paragraph too.

To move the current paragraph down to the next lower level of bulleted list, press Tab at the beginning of the paragraph or choose Home ➤ Paragraph ➤ Increase List Level. Figure 19–6 shows a slide with three levels of indentation.

To move the current paragraph up to the next higher level, press Shift+Tab at the beginning of the paragraph or choose Home ➤ Paragraph ➤ Decrease List Level.

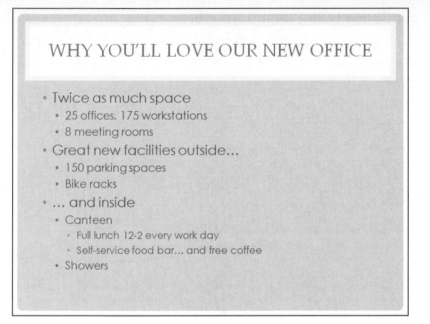

Figure 19–6. *You can create a sublist by pressing Tab or by choosing Home ➤ Paragraph ➤ Increase List Level.*

Making Sure Your Bulleted Lists Are Readable

The fonts and font sizes PowerPoint uses for text depend on the slide design. Many bulleted slides start off in a small enough font size to enable you to type five or six bullets of two lines each—so if you have fewer bullets on a slide or if each is less than a single line, it's often a good idea to increase the font size to make the words easy to read.

When you start a bulleted sublist, PowerPoint reduces the font size. This makes the hierarchy of the bullet points clear, but it can easily make the text too small to read. You may need to increase the font size of the bulleted sublist points as well to keep them readable. The extra indentation and different bullets will still indicate the hierarchy.

CAUTION: PowerPoint lets you create pretty much as many levels of sublist as you want—just keep pressing Tab at the start of a line or clicking the Increase List Level button to go to the next level. But if you go past two levels of bullets, that should raise a red flag to indicate that your slide is becoming too complex. If some content is that far subordinate, either cut it or break the material up onto several slides.

Livening Up Your Slides with Custom Bullets

One way to make your slides look different is to change from the default bullet characters. PowerPoint provides a wide range of bullet characters, but you can also create your own.

To customize bullets, follow steps:

1. Click the text placeholder in which you want to use the bullets.

2. Choose Format ➤ Bullets and Numbering from the menu bar, or Home ➤ Paragraph ➤ Bullets ➤ Define New Bullet, to display the Bullets and Numbering category in the Format Text dialog box. PowerPoint shows the Bullets tab at the front (see Figure 19–7).

Figure 19–7. *Use the Bullets tab in the Bullets and Numbering category of the Format Text dialog box to set up custom bullets for a list.*

3. If you want to create a custom bullet based on an existing bullet, follow these steps:

    ■ Click the bullet style you want to start with.

    ■ Open the Color pop-up palette, and then click the color you want. To choose a color that doesn't appear, click the More Colors button, and then work in the Colors dialog box; click the OK button when you've chosen the color.

■ Use the Size box to increase or decrease the bullet's size relative to the text. For example, set the bullet to 150% of text to make the bullet one and a half times the base height of the text.

4. If you want to use a different bullet character, open the Custom bullet pop-up menu and see whether any of the characters on it is suitable. If not, follow these steps to choose a different character, or go to step 5 if you want to use a picture:

■ From the Custom bullet pop-up menu, choose Character to display the Characters window (see Figure 19–8).

Figure 19–8. *In the Characters window, you can pick from a wide range of symbol characters available in the various fonts. You can expand the Character Info and Font Variations areas by clicking the gray disclosure triangles.*

■ In the View pop-up menu, make sure Roman is selected unless you want a different character set, such as Japanese or Korean.

■ In the left list box on the By Category tab, click the category of symbols you want to view—for example, Miscellaneous. The symbols appear in the right list box.

■ Click the symbol you want to insert.

■ Click the Insert button. PowerPoint adds the bullet to the Custom bullet box in the Format Text dialog box.

TIP: If you want to be able to reuse a character easily as a bullet, add it to your Favorites list. Click the character in the list box on the By Category tab. Then click the Action button (the cog button in the lower-left corner of the Characters window), and click Add to Favorites. You can access your favorites by clicking the Favorites tab at the top of the Characters window.

- Click the Close button (the red button at the left end of the title bar) to close the Characters window.

5. To use a picture as a bullet, follow these steps:

   - From the Custom bullet pop-up menu, choose Picture to display the Choose a Picture dialog box.

   - Navigate to the folder that contains the picture you want to use, and then click the picture file.

   - Click the Insert button. PowerPoint closes the Choose a Picture dialog box and displays "Picture…" in the Custom bullet box.

6. Click the OK button to close the Format Text dialog box. PowerPoint applies the bullet you chose to the placeholder.

Adding Tables, SmartArt, Charts, and Hyperlinks to Slides

PowerPoint makes it as easy as possible to add graphical content to your slides. If the slide has a content placeholder (see Figure 19–9), click the appropriate icon in it, and then use the dialog box or pane that PowerPoint opens to identify the item you want. If the slide doesn't have a content placeholder, use the commands on the Ribbon, the menu bar, or the toolbars. Here are some examples:

- *Insert a table.* Choose Tables ➤ Table Options ➤ New from the Ribbon or Insert ➤ Table from the menu bar.

- *Insert a picture.* Click the Media Browser button on the Standard toolbar to display the Media Browser. Then use the Photos pane or the Clip Art pane to add a picture. Alternatively, use the Clip Art Gallery as described in Chapter 3.

- *Insert a chart.* Click the Charts tab of the Ribbon, go to the Insert Chart group, click the chart category, and then click the chart type. Or choose Insert ➤ Chart from the menu bar.

Figure 19–9. *Click one of the six icons in a placeholder to start adding that type of content, or click the "Click to add text" prompt to start typing text.*

Adding Tables to Slides

You can create a new table on a slide, but you can often save time by importing a table from Word or by creating it from cells in an Excel worksheet.

Creating a Table from Scratch

To create a table from scratch, follow these steps:

1. Click the Insert Table icon in a placeholder to display the Insert Table dialog box (see Figure 19–10).

> **NOTE:** If the slide doesn't have a content placeholder, choose Insert ➤ Table from the menu bar to display the Insert Table dialog box. Alternatively, choose Tables ➤ Table Options ➤ New from the Ribbon, and then choose the table dimensions on the grid.

Figure 19–10. *To insert a new table, click the Insert table icon in a placeholder, and then specify the number of columns and rows in the Insert Table dialog box.*

2. In the Number of columns box, set the number of columns. Unless each data item is very short, you'll usually need to keep the number low (for example, three or four columns) to make sure the text is readable.

3. In the Number of rows box, set the number of rows. You can add further rows as needed, so it's fine to start with just a few.

4. Click the OK button to close the Insert Table dialog box. PowerPoint inserts the table and gives it a design that works with the presentation's color theme.

5. Type the contents of the table, pressing Tab to move from one cell to the next. Figure 19–11 shows a table with sample data entered.

Trends in Girl Baby Names

Name	2009 Rank	2010 Rank	2011 Rank
Emily	1	2	2
Emma	2	1	3
Abigail	3	3	4
Elizabeth	8	4	1
Samantha	6	7	5

▶ 7

Figure 19–11. *At its default size, table data is often too small for comfortable reading from a distance.*

6. Resize the table and its contents as needed—for example:

   ■ If the table occupies only part of the slide, drag the handle at the bottom of its container downward, or drag the lower-right handle down and to the right, to expand the table. PowerPoint increases the row height to take up the extra space.

   ■ With the table container selected, adjust the fonts to make the text easy to read. For example, click the Increase Font Size button a few times to pump up the font size. Figure 19–12 shows the same table taking up the full slide and with the text at a better size.

Trends in Girl Baby Names

Name	2009 Rank	2010 Rank	2011 Rank
Emily	1	2	2
Emma	2	1	3
Abigail	3	3	4
Elizabeth	8	4	1
Samantha	6	7	5

▶ 7

Figure 19–12. *To make a table more readable, give it as much of the space on the slide as it needs, and then increase the font sizes.*

7. Change the design of the table as needed. For example, choose Tables ➤ Styles and then click the table style you want to apply, or choose Table ➤ Table Options ➤ Table Options and then apply formatting such as a header row or banded rows.

Importing a Table from Word

If the table you need to use in PowerPoint is already in a Word document, you can quickly reuse it in PowerPoint—but you may need to reformat it. Follow these general steps:

1. In Word, open the document that contains the table.

2. Select the table, and then copy it to the Clipboard. For example, click in the table, and then choose Table ➤ Select ➤ Table. Then Ctrl+click or right-click in the selection, and click Copy on the context menu.

3. In PowerPoint, navigate to the slide on which you want to place the table, and then create a table that has the same number of rows and columns as the table you've copied.

4. Again in PowerPoint, Ctrl+click or right-click in the table you've just created, and then click Paste on the context menu. PowerPoint pastes the copied data straight into the new table.

5. Format the table as needed in PowerPoint. Here are some examples:

- Resize the table's container to the size you need.

- Choose Tables ➤ Table Styles ➤ Table Styles, and then click the style you want to apply.

- Still on the Tables tab, choose any options in the Table Options group. For instance, select the Total Row check box if the table needs different formatting for a total row at the bottom.

Creating a Table from Excel Worksheet Data

When a PowerPoint slide needs a table of data that you have in an Excel worksheet, copy the data across and paste it in. Don't waste time retyping the data and maybe introducing mistakes into it.

To create a PowerPoint table from Excel worksheet data, follow these steps:

1. In Excel, select the cells you want, and then copy them. For example, Ctrl+click or right-click in the selection, and then click Copy on the context menu.

2. In PowerPoint, select the slide on which you want to place the data.

3. Insert a table in one of these ways:

    - If the slide has a placeholder displaying the content icons, click the Insert Table icon. Either set the exact number of rows and columns your Excel selection will occupy or (easier) insert a smaller table—for example, 2 columns by 2 rows. Click the OK button. PowerPoint automatically adjusts the number of columns and rows to fit the data you pasted.

    - Choose Tables ➤ Table Options ➤ New, and then click the table size. Again, either set the right number of rows and columns or create a smaller table.

4. Click to place the insertion point in the first cell in the table.

5. Paste in the data. For example, click the Paste button on the Standard toolbar or press Cmd+V.

6. Format the table as needed in PowerPoint. Here are some examples:

    - Resize the table's container to occupy more of the slide.

    - Choose Tables ➤ Table Styles ➤ Table Styles, and then click the style you want to apply.

    - Also on the Tables tab of the Ribbon, choose options in the Table Options group. For instance, select the Header Row check box to add header row formatting.

■   Open the Home tab of the Ribbon, and use the controls in the Font group on the Home tab of the Ribbon to change the font sizes as needed. For most slides, you'll need to increase the font size considerably from the size used in Excel to make the data easy to read in PowerPoint.

Adding SmartArt Graphics to Slides

You can add a SmartArt graphic to a slide by using the techniques explained in Chapter 4. For example, you can add an org chart like this:

1. Select the slide on which you want to add the SmartArt graphic. Create a new slide if necessary.

2. If there's a content placeholder, click the Insert SmartArt Graphic icon to display the SmartArt tab of the Ribbon. Otherwise, click the SmartArt tab or choose Insert ➤ SmartArt Graphic.

3. In the Insert SmartArt Graphic group, click the pop-up button for the type of SmartArt item you want to create. For example, click the Hierarchy pop-up button to display the Hierarchy panel, which includes organization charts and similar diagrams.

4. On the panel, click the type of graphic—for example, Name and Title Organization Chart. PowerPoint inserts the graphic on the slide.

5. If PowerPoint doesn't display the Text Pane window, click the Text Pane button at the upper-left corner of the SmartArt graphic to display the Text Pane window.

6. Type the text for each item in the Text Pane window.

7. Resize the SmartArt graphic to suit the slide best. For example, you may want to make it as big as will fit on the slide to enable the audience to read it easily.

Adding Charts to Slides

A chart can be a great way of presenting complex or detailed information in a manner that's instantly clear on a slide. In PowerPoint, you can add a chart to a slide in two ways:

■   *Create a chart on an embedded worksheet.* Click the Insert Chart icon in a content placeholder, or click the Charts tab of the Ribbon, and then choose the chart type by using the pop-up buttons and panels in the Insert Chart group. PowerPoint then opens Excel for you and creates a new workbook so that you can enter the chart data and create the chart. The workbook is embedded in the PowerPoint presentation, so it becomes part of that file.

- *Copy a chart from an Excel workbook.* Create your chart in Excel using the techniques described in Chapter 14. Then copy the finished chart and paste it into your PowerPoint slide. You can choose whether to embed the chart's data in the PowerPoint presentation or just to insert it as a picture or PDF file.

Here's how to choose when to create a new embedded workbook, embed an existing workbook, link back to a workbook, or insert a picture:

- *Create a new embedded workbook.* Do this when you don't yet have the data for the chart in Excel and you need to keep the chart's data with the PowerPoint presentation. For example, you'll send the presentation to someone else who will need to work on the chart data too.

- *Embed an existing chart and its data.* Do this when you have the data for the chart or the chart itself in a workbook in Excel and you need to keep the chart's data available in the PowerPoint presentation. After embedding the chart and its data, you can open the chart from PowerPoint in Excel and edit it there.

- *Link back to a workbook.* Do this when you want to be able to change the chart or its source data in Excel and then automatically bring those changes into PowerPoint by updating the chart. Linking requires the workbook to stay in the same relative place in the computer's file system to the presentation so that the presentation can find the updated data. Moving the presentation to a different computer breaks the link.

CAUTION: Linking a chart can be great when it works—but links can fail at the most awkward times. Before giving a presentation that includes linked charts, double-check that the links are working. That way, you'll have a chance to fix any problems rather than discovering them when your audience sees them.

- *Insert a picture.* Do this when you don't need to keep the connection between the chart and its source data and you will not need to edit the chart in the presentation.

Creating a Chart in a New Embedded Workbook

To create a chart on a worksheet in a new workbook embedded in your PowerPoint presentation, follow these steps:

1. On the slide where you want to create the chart, click the Insert Chart icon in a placeholder or simply click the Charts tab of the Ribbon. Either way, PowerPoint displays the Charts tab of the Ribbon.

2. In the Insert Chart group, click the pop-up button for the category of chart you want to create. For example, click the Column pop-up button to display the Column panel.

3. On the pop-up panel, click the chart type. PowerPoint creates a chart of that type on the slide and launches Excel, which creates a new workbook, embeds it in the presentation, and gives it a name such as Chart in Microsoft Office PowerPoint.

4. Change the chart range and the sample data (see Figure 19–13) to the data your chart needs. PowerPoint automatically updates the chart to match the data in the Excel worksheet.

Figure 19–13. *Excel enters sample data on the first worksheet in the embedded workbook. Change this data to create your chart.*

5. When you have finished changing the data, close Excel. For example, click the Close button (the red button at the left end of the title bar) or choose Excel ➤ Quit Excel.

NOTE: Excel saves the data in the embedded workbook automatically, so you don't need to save it while you're working in the Excel window.

6. Use the controls on the Charts tab and the Chart Layout tab of the Ribbon to format the chart the way you want it. Figure 19–14 shows a slide containing a chart with formatting under way.

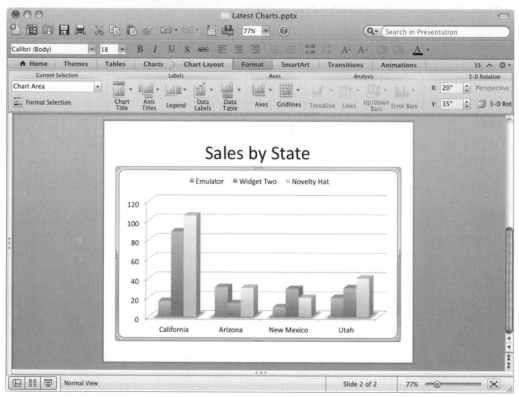

Figure 19–14. *After inserting a chart using an embedded workbook, use the controls on the Charts tab and the Chart Layout tab of the Ribbon to format the chart.*

7. Save your presentation.

NOTE: To edit the data on your chart again, choose Charts ➤ Data ➤ Edit from the Ribbon, clicking the main part of the Edit button. PowerPoint opens Excel, which displays the embedded worksheet.

Pasting a Chart from Excel into a PowerPoint Slide

If you have a chart already created in Excel or if you have a workbook containing the data from which you will create the chart, you can paste the chart into PowerPoint. Follow these general steps:

1. Create the chart using the techniques explained in Chapter 14.

2. Click the chart to select it.

3. Copy the chart to the Clipboard. For example, click the Copy button on the Standard toolbar or press Cmd+C.

4. Switch to PowerPoint, and then navigate to the slide on which you want to insert the chart.

5. Paste in the chart from the Clipboard. For example, click the Paste button on the Standard toolbar, or press Cmd+V.

6. Click the Paste Options button at the lower-right corner of the chart, and then click the appropriate option button in the upper group on the Paste Options pop-up menu (see Figure 19–15):

    ■ *Chart (linked to Excel data).* Select this option button to link the chart back to the Excel workbook it came from.

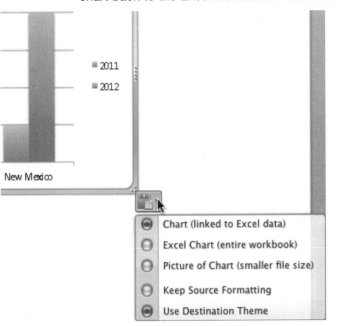

Figure 19–15. *When pasting a chart from Excel into a PowerPoint slide, click the Paste Options button, and use the option buttons on the pop-up menu to choose how to paste the chart.*

    ■ *Excel Chart (entire workbook).* Select this option button to embed the entire Excel workbook in the PowerPoint presentation.

    ■ *Picture of Chart (smaller file size).* Select this option button to insert a picture of the chart. As the name says, inserting the picture helps keep the presentation file size down, but you can't edit the picture.

7. If you want the chart on the slide to use the original formatting you gave it in Excel, click the Paste Options button again, and then select the Keep Source Formatting option button. Otherwise, leave the Use Destination Theme option button selected, and the chart will pick up the formatting from the presentation.

8. Use the controls on the Charts tab or the Chart Layout tab of the Ribbon to format the chart the way you want it. (If you inserted the chart as a picture, use the controls on the Format Picture tab of the Ribbon.)

9. Save the presentation.

To edit the data in either an embedded or linked chart, choose Charts ➤ Data ➤ Edit, clicking the main part of the Edit button.

Adding Hyperlinks to Slides

You can add hyperlinks to PowerPoint slides using the standard technique explained in detail in Chapter 3.

1. Place the insertion point where you want to insert the hyperlink.

2. Choose Insert ➤ Hyperlink from the menu bar to display the Insert Hyperlink dialog box.

3. Choose the destination for the hyperlink, and specify the text to display on the slide.

4. Click the OK button to close the Insert Hyperlink dialog box and insert the hyperlink.

In your presentations, you'll typically use hyperlinks on slides for two purposes:

- *Link to other slides in the presentation.* To make it easy for the presenter or someone browsing the presentation to move to another slide, add a hyperlink to it. Follow these steps after opening the Insert Hyperlink dialog box:

    1. Click the Document tab to display its contents.

    2. In the Anchor area, click the Locate button to display the Select Place in Document dialog box (see Figure 19–16).

Figure 19–16. *Use the Select Place in Document dialog box to create a link to another slide in the same presentation. This is a great way of enabling the viewer to navigate quickly about the presentation.*

3. In the Select an existing place in the document box, click the slide you want to display.

4. Click the OK button to close the Select Place in Document dialog box and return to the Insert Hyperlink dialog box

5. Edit the text in the Display box as needed.

6. If you need to provide additional information about the hyperlink, click the ScreenTip button, type ScreenTip text in the Set Hyperlink ScreenTip dialog box, and then click the OK button.

7. Click the OK button to close the Insert Hyperlink dialog box and insert the hyperlink.

■   *Link to a web site.* You'll often want to include a link to your web site. In a live presentation, you can click the hyperlink to display your web site directly from a slide. In a presentation you share with others, they can click the hyperlink to go to the web site or to find out how to contact you.

Summary

In this chapter, you learned how to plan and put together attractive and compelling slides. You now know how to use PowerPoint's built-in slide layouts effectively, how to create your own custom layouts, and how to add graphical elements such as table, charts, and SmartArt to your slides.

In the next chapter, I'll show you how to add graphics, movies, and sounds to your presentations; how to animate the objects on a slide; and how to apply transitions between slides.

Adding Life and Interest to a Presentation

In the previous two chapters, you learned how to create a presentation and how to fill it with good-looking slides that convey the message you want.

In this chapter, you'll look at how to inject life and interest to a presentation by adding graphics, movies and sounds, animations, and transitions. You'll also learn to hide slides so that they don't appear during a slide show, allowing you to keep them in reserve, and how to create custom slide shows within a presentation so that you can show only specific parts of it.

Adding Pictures to a Presentation

Many slides benefit from having pictures—graphics or photos—to illustrate or offset their text content. You can easily add a picture in these ways:

- *Use a content placeholder.* If the slide includes a content placeholder, click the Insert Picture from File icon to display the Choose a Picture dialog box. Click the picture file, and then click the Insert button.

- *Use the Insert ➤ Photo ➤ Picture from File command.* If the slide doesn't have a content placeholder, choose Insert ➤ Photo ➤ Picture from File to open the Choose a Picture dialog box. Click the picture file, and then click the Insert button.

- *Drag a photo from the Photos Browser pane of the Media Browser.* If the photo is in iPhoto, open the Photos Browser pane, and then drag the photo to the slide.

- *Drag a picture file from a Finder window.* You can also open a Finder window to the folder that contains the picture file and then drag the picture file to a slide in the PowerPoint window.

NOTE: To add a clip art picture, choose Insert ➤ Clip Art ➤ Clip Art Browser or Insert ➤ Clip Art ➤ Clip Art Gallery. You can then work in the Clip Art Browser or the Clip Art Gallery as discussed in Chapter 4.

Once you've added a graphic or photo to a slide, you can work with it using the techniques discussed in Chapter 4. For example, you can click the picture and drag it (see Figure 20–1) to where you need it to appear. Or you can use the commands in the Adjust group on the Format Picture tab of the Ribbon to correct the picture's colors, apply filters, or remove the background.

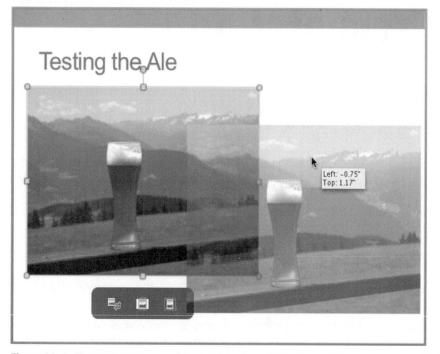

Figure 20–1. *The quick way to reposition a picture on a slide is to drag it to where you need it. The ScreenTip shows the details of the picture's position.*

As you can see at the bottom of Figure 20–1, PowerPoint displays a pop-up control bar when you select a picture. This bar contains three buttons (see Figure 20–2) for quickly cropping and resizing pictures:

- *Manually Reposition, Resize, or Crop Picture in Placeholder.* Click this button to display cropping handles around the picture. You can then drag a cropping handle to resize the picture, drag a sizing handle to resize it, or drag the picture to a different position on the slide.

- *Crop Picture to Fill Placeholder.* Click this button to crop the picture so that it fills the whole placeholder. PowerPoint typically cuts off part of the picture to make it fit, but it doesn't distort the picture. This is usually the best choice for photographs.

- *Resize Picture to Fit Inside Placeholder.* Click this button to resize the picture horizontally, vertically, or both so that the whole picture fits inside the placeholder. Doing this often distorts the picture, so it's not a good choice for most photographs.

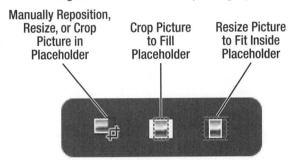

Manually Reposition, Resize, or Crop Picture in Placeholder   Crop Picture to Fill Placeholder   Resize Picture to Fit Inside Placeholder

Figure 20–2. *Use the three buttons on the pop-up control bar to control how the picture fits in its placeholder.*

Adding Movies and Sounds to a Presentation

Graphics and photos can make a big difference to a presentation, but you may also want to add movies and sounds. This section shows you how to do both.

Adding a Movie to a Slide

You can add a movie file to a slide so that you can play the movie as needed during the presentation. If the movie is in the Movie Browser pane, you can add it from there. Otherwise, you can add the movie from a file in your Mac's file system.

Adding a Movie from the Movie Browser

To add a movie from the Movie Browser, follow these steps:

1. Click the Media Browser button on the Standard toolbar or choose View ➤ Media Browser from the menu bar to display the Media Browser.

2. Click the Movies button in the toolbar to display the Movie Browser pane.

3. Click the movie you want, and then drag it to the slide.

Adding a Movie from a File

To add a movie file to a slide, follow these steps:

4. Select the slide on which you want to add the movie. Add a new slide if necessary.

> **NOTE:** At this writing, PowerPoint can't play YouTube files or Flash files.

5. If the slide has a content placeholder, click the Insert Movie from File icon to display the Choose a Movie dialog box. If not, choose Insert ➤ Movie ➤ Movie from File to open this dialog box.

6. Navigate to the folder that contains the movie file, and then click the file to select it.

7. If you want to link the movie file rather than insert it, select the Link to file check box.

> **TIP:** Linking keeps down the size of the presentation (because the presentation file contains the link rather than the whole movie), but the movie will play only when the movie file is in the same place in the file system as when you created the link. Generally, this means that if you move the presentation to a different Mac, the movie won't play (the exception is if the movie is in the same place in the other Mac's file system—for example, on a USB stick or a shared network drive).

8. Click the Insert button. PowerPoint closes the Choose a Movie dialog box and places the movie on the slide.

Making the Movie Look and Play the Way You Want

After inserting a movie, you can change both the way it appears on the slide and how it plays back. To do so, follow these steps:

1. Click the movie to select it. PowerPoint adds the Format Movie tab to the Ribbon (see Figure 20–3).

Figure 20–3. *After inserting a movie on a slide, use the controls on the Format Movie tab of the Ribbon to make it appear the way you want.*

2. Adjust the movie file's appearance as needed by using the controls on the Format Movie tab:

- Click the movie file to select it, and then drag it into the right position on the slide.

- If necessary, resize the movie frame by dragging a corner handle. You can also crop it by choosing Format Movie ➤ Adjust ➤ Crop and then dragging a corner handle with the cropping pointer.

- To correct the movie's brightness and contrast, choose Format Movie ➤ Adjust ➤ Corrections, and then click the balance of brightness and contrast you want.

- To change the movie's color balance, choose Format Movie ➤ Adjust ➤ Color, and then click the color option you want. For example, you can apply a sepia hue or make the movie black and white.

- To choose which frame of the movie appears on the slide until you play the movie, use the playback controls to move the movie to the frame you want. Then pause the movie and Format Movie ➤ Movie Options ➤ Poster Frame ➤ Current Frame.

TIP: Instead of using a frame from the movie as the poster frame, you can use a still picture. Choose Format Movie ➤ Movie Options ➤ Poster Frame ➤ Picture from File, select the picture in the Choose a Picture dialog box, and then click the Insert button.

- To put the movie in a frame, hold the mouse pointer over the Movie Styles box on the Format Movie tab of the Ribbon until the panel button appears. Click the panel button to display the Movie Styles panel, and then click the frame you want.

- To crop the movie to a shape, choose Format Movie ➤ Adjust ➤ Crop ➤ Mask to Shape, and then choose the shape from the Mask to Shape submenus.

- To customize the border for the movie, choose Format Movie ➤ Movie Styles ➤ Border, and then click the type of border you want.

3. In the Start pop-up menu in the Movie Options group on the Format Movie tab, choose On Click if you want to start the movie playing by clicking it. If you want the movie to start playing automatically, choose Automatically.

4. To control how the movie plays back, open the Playback Options pop-up menu in the Movie Options group on the Format Movie tab. You can then click an option you want to use, placing a check mark next to it. These are the four options:

   - *Play Full Screen.* Turn on this option to display the movie full screen rather than just in the area it occupies on the slide. This setting is useful for giving the movie full impact without devoting a full slide to it.

   - *Hide While Not Playing.* Turn on this option to make PowerPoint hide the movie any time it's not playing.

   - *Loop Until Stopped.* Turn on this option to make the movie keep playing over and over again until you stop it. Looping the movie can be useful for presentations used at trade shows and the like, but it's cruel and unusual treatment for a regular audience.

   - *Rewind After Playing.* Turn on this option to make PowerPoint rewind the movie to the beginning when it reaches the end. Automatic rewinding is useful if you may need to play the movie again.

5. Click the Play button (choose Format Movie ➤ Preview ➤ Play) to play the movie and check that everything is how you want it to be.

Adding a Sound to a Slide

Depending on the type of presentation you're creating, you may find it helpful to add sounds to some slides. For example, you can add music that plays automatically when the slide it's on is displayed or insert a sound file that you can play as needed by clicking its icon.

> **NOTE:** Make sure the audio you add to your slides enhances them rather than distracting the audience. For example, playing background audio with your introductory slide displayed can help set the scene while your audience is arriving and getting settled, but in a typical spoken presentation, most slides will not need background audio.

You can add a sound to a slide by using the Audio Browser pane, by adding a sound directly from a file, or by recording audio into a slide. The following sections give you the details.

> **CAUTION:** If you add to a presentation an audio file that you've bought from Apple's iTunes Store in a protected audio format (such as AAC), you'll be able to play the audio back only on computers authorized for your iTunes account. When you move a presentation to a different computer, double-check that your audio files play correctly before you give a presentation.

Adding a Sound from the Audio Browser Pane

If the sound you want to use is in your iTunes library or in GarageBand, you can add it by using the Audio Browser pane. Choose Insert ➤ Audio ➤ Audio Browser to display the Audio Browser pane in the Media Browser, locate the sound you want, and then drag it to the slide.

Adding a Sound from a File

If the sound you want to use isn't in your iTunes library or in GarageBand but rather in a file in your Mac's file system, follow these steps to add it to a slide:

1. Select the slide on which you want to add the audio.

2. Choose Insert ➤ Audio ➤ Audio from File to display the Choose Audio dialog box.

3. Navigate to the folder that contains the file you want to insert, and then click the file.

4. If you want to link the audio file rather than embedding it, select the Link to file check box. Normally, you'll want to do this only when you will deliver the presentation on the same Mac you're using to create the presentation.

5. Click the Insert button. PowerPoint adds the sound to the slide.

TIP: You can also add a file from a sound by dragging the sound file from a Finder window to a slide.

Recording Audio into a Slide

Using a prerecorded sound works well for many slides, but you may also want to record custom audio for other slides. PowerPoint's Record Audio feature lets you record audio directly onto a slide using your Mac's microphone or other audio hardware you've connected.

NOTE: Recording audio via the microphone is fine for adding narration to individual slides. But if you need to create high-quality recorded audio, use an application such as GarageBand to create a sound file and process it as needed. Then add the finished file to the presentation by using the Audio Browser pane.

To record audio onto a slide, follow these steps:

1. Select the slide.

2. Choose Insert ➤ Audio ➤ Record Audio to display the Record Sound dialog box (see Figure 20–4).

Figure 20–4. Use the Record Sound dialog box when you need to record audio directly onto a slide.

3. In the Name text box, type the name you want to give the sound. PowerPoint suggests the generic "Recorded Sound," but a more descriptive name is usually more helpful.

4. Make sure the Sound input device pop-up menu shows the sound input you want to use. If not, open the pop-up menu and click the right device.

5. Similarly, make sure the Input source pop-up menu shows the right device. If not, select it.

6. Select the Play sound through output device check box if you want PowerPoint to play the sound through your Mac's output device as you record. Normally you'll want to do this only if you're using headphones to monitor the recording.

7. Click the Record button to start the recording. Speak or perform the audio, and then click the Stop button to stop recording.

8. Click the Play button to play back the audio and check that it has come out acceptably. Re-record it if necessary.

9. Click the Save button to save the audio on the slide. PowerPoint closes the Record Sound dialog box and adds the sound to the slide.

Positioning the Sound and Setting Its Volume

Whichever of the previous three ways you use to add the sound to the slide, PowerPoint inserts an audio icon (see Figure 20–5) representing the sound.

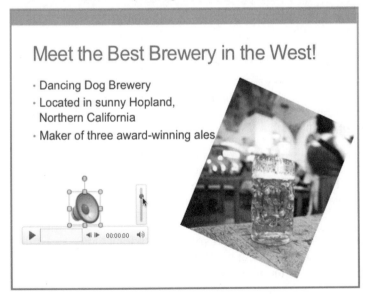

Figure 20–5. *PowerPoint inserts an audio item as a speaker icon. Click the icon to display controls for testing the audio and setting the volume.*

Select the icon by clicking it, and then drag it to where you want it to appear. Then, with the icon still selected, use the pop-up controls to test the audio clip and set the volume at which you want it to play.

Adding Transitions to Slides

Instead of having a straightforward switchover from one slide to the next, you can set PowerPoint to play a *transition*—an effect that smoothes, animates, or dramatizes the change of slides. You can set a different transition for each side if necessary. You specify the transition by selecting the slide and choosing the transition to play when the slide appears (as opposed to setting the transition for when PowerPoint changes the slide to the next).

PowerPoint provides a wide range of transitions that you can apply from the Transitions tab of the Ribbon (see Figure 20–6).

Figure 20–6. *The Transitions tab of the Ribbon gives you one-stop access to the key controls for setting up transitions between slides.*

> **NOTE:** Depending on the presentation template or design you're using, some or all of the slides in the presentation may already have transitions applied to them.

PowerPoint breaks up the transitions into three categories:

- *Subtle.* Use these transitions when you don't need to draw the audience's attention to the transition. The first transition in the Subtle category is the None transition, which you apply when you don't want a transition effect between slides.

- *Exciting.* Use these transitions when you want to make sure the audience notices the transition. For example, you can use an effect such as Vortex or Shred to dramatize the switchover from one slide to another that uses a similar look and so might be mistaken for the previous slide.

- *Dynamic Content.* Use these transitions when you want to draw attention to the transition. For example, the Ferris Wheel transition makes the incoming slide go around as if it were moving on a Ferris wheel.

TIP: PowerPoint's transitions are easy and fun to apply, but don't go hog wild with them. In a typical presentation, not every slide benefits from a transition; and when you do use a transition, one of the Subtle transitions often gives the best effect. Keep the Exciting and Dynamic Content transitions for those rare occasions when you actually want to draw your audience's attention to the transition rather than to the content of the slides.

To apply a transition, follow these steps:

1. Click the slide to which you want to apply the transition.

2. Click the Transitions tab to display its contents.

3. Apply the transition you want:

    - If the transition appears in the Transitions box, click it. You can also scroll the list of transitions to the left or right to make other transitions appear in the box. PowerPoint plays a preview of the transition in the Slide pane.

    - If the transition doesn't appear, hold the mouse pointer over the Transitions box until the panel button appears, and then click the panel button to display the Transitions panel (see Figure 20–7). Click the transition you want. Again, PowerPoint plays a preview of the transition in the Slide pane.

Figure 20–7. *Open the Transition panel to access the full range of transitions all at once.*

4. To choose options for the transition, choose Transitions ➤ Transition to This Slide ➤ Effect Options, and then click the option you want on the panel that opens.

    ■ The choices on the Effect Options panel vary depending on the transition you've selected. For example, the Vortex transition has four directional options (From Left, From Top, From Right, and From Bottom), while the Honeycomb transition has no options.

    ■ PowerPoint plays a preview of the effect after you select it. To preview the transition again, choose Transitions ➤ Preview ➤ Play.

5. If you want to add a sound to the transition, choose Transitions ➤ Transition to This Slide ➤ Sound, and then click the sound on the pop-up menu. You can make the sound keep playing until the next sound starts (open the Sound pop-up menu, go right to the bottom, and then click the Loop Until Next Sound to place a check mark next to it), but this is not usually a good idea.

NOTE: To use a sound other than PowerPoint's built-in sounds, choose Transitions ➤ Timing ➤ Sound ➤ Other Sound, click the sound file in the Choose a Sound dialog box, and then click the Insert button.

6. If you want to change the duration of the transition, set it in the Duration box in the Transition to This Slide group on the Transitions tab. PowerPoint automatically sets the duration to a suitable length for the transition you choose, but you may need to change it to make your presentation's timing work.

7. In the Advance Slide group on the Transitions tab, choose how to advance the slide to the next slide:

   - *On Mouse Click.* Select this check box if you want to click the mouse to move to the next slide.

   - *After.* To display the next slide automatically, select this check box, and then set the timing in the text box.

8. Preview the transition again to make sure it gives the effect you want, and then click the Save button on the Standard toolbar to save your changes.

NOTE: If you want to apply the same transition to all slides, choose the transition and its options, and then choose Transitions ➤ Apply To ➤ All Slides from the Ribbon. You may want to apply the same transition to all slides at first, and then apply a different transition or different effects to a few slides that deserve special attention.

Adding Animations to Slides

When you need to bring a slide to life, you can animate one or more of the objects on it. For example, you may need to make an object appear on a slide, draw attention to itself at a key point, or disappear from view when its role is over—or all three.

You can also use animations to reveal only part of a slide or part of an object at a time, which can help keep the audience focused on your current point rather than reading ahead to the end of the slide.

Understanding the Essentials of Animations

To add an animation to a slide, you apply it to an object on the slide—for example, a picture or a text placeholder. Any object can have one or more animations, and you can arrange them into the order you need.

CAUTION: As with transitions, it's easy to go over the top with animations. Resist the temptation! Animations will have more effect in your slides if you use them sparingly and only at the appropriate times. When you do use animations, make sure the ones you choose work together; PowerPoint provides a wide variety of animations to help you achieve different effects, not to suggest you should use them all in the same presentation.

PowerPoint provides a wide range of animations in four categories:

- *Entrance Effects.* These animations bring the object onto the slide. For example, the Appear animation makes the object appear in place, while the Swivel animation makes the object appear and swivel several times.

- *Emphasis Effects.* These animations help draw the audience's attention to the object. For example, the Pulse animation makes the object pulse visibly, and the Spin animation makes the object revolve around its axis.

- *Exit Effects.* These animations remove the object from the slide. For example, the Disappear animation makes the object vanish, while the Shrink & Turn animation makes the object turn sideways as it disappears into the distance.

- *Motion Paths.* These animations make the object move around and then return to its original position.

The next section shows you how to add a straightforward animation to an object. The section after that shows you how to create more complex animations.

Adding an Animation to an Object

To add a straightforward animation to an object on a slide, follow these steps:

1. Click the object to select it.

2. Click the Animations tab of the Ribbon to display its controls.

3. Add an Entrance Effect, an Emphasis Effect, or an Exit Effect by following these steps. The example adds an Entrance Effect.

    - Hold the mouse pointer over the Entrance Effects box to display the panel button.

    - Click the panel button to display the Entrance Effects panel (see Figure 20–8).

    - Click the effect. PowerPoint applies the effect and plays a preview of it.

Figure 20–8. *You can quickly apply an animation to an object by using the Entrance Effects panel, the Emphasis Effects panel, the Exit Effects panel, or the Motion Paths panel.*

- Apply any options the effect needs by choosing Animations ➤ Animation Options ➤ Effect Options and then clicking the appropriate item on the Effect Options panel. The options available depend on the effect you've chosen; for example, many animations offer direction options such as From Bottom, From Bottom-Left, From Left, From Top-Left, From Top, From Top-Right, From Right, and From Bottom-Right. Some effects have no options.

4. To control when the animation runs, use the controls on the left side of the Timing group:

- Open the Start pop-up menu, and choose when to start the animation: On Click (in other words, when you click the mouse), With Previous (at the same time as the previous animation), or After Previous (after the previous animation has finished).

- In the Duration text box, set the number of seconds and hundredths of seconds you want the animation to run—for example, 1.50 for one and a half seconds.

5. Repeat steps 3 and 4 to add further animations as needed. For example, if you've already added an Entrance Effect to an object, you may want to add an Exit Effect as well.

> **NOTE:** If you need to change the order of animations you've applied to an object, work as described in the next section.

6. Click the Preview button in the Preview group to preview the animation and see whether you need to make further changes.

Changing the Order of Animations

When you apply multiple animations to the same slide, you may need to change the order in which they occur. To do so, click the Reorder button to display the Custom Animation pane in the Toolbox. Figure 20–9 shows a slide that contains six animations, including all those applied to the text container, with the Custom Animations pane in the Toolbox open.

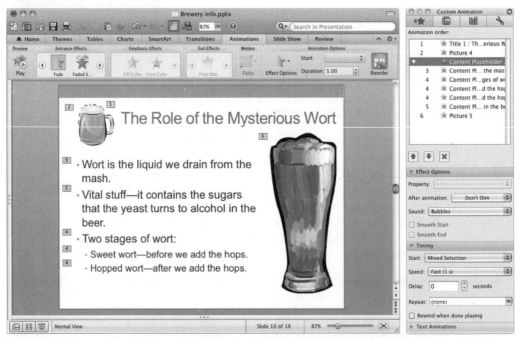

Figure 20–9. *Use the Custom Animation pane in the Toolbox to examine the animations and to control which plays when.*

These are the main actions you can take in the Custom Animation pane:

- *Play an animation.* In the Animation order list box, Ctrl+click or right-click the animation, and then click Play on the context menu.

- *Change the order of the animations.* In the Animation order list box, click an animation to select it, and then click the Up button or the Down button to move it up or down the list.

- *Expand or collapse a container's animations.* Click the disclosure triangle to expand or collapse the list of a container's animation. In Figure 20–9, the list for the Content Placeholder is expanded.

- *Change an animation's effect options.* Click an animation to select it, and then work in the Effect Options pane.

- *Change an animation's timing.* Click an animation to select it, and then work in the Timing pane.

When you have finished using the Custom Animation pane, close it by clicking its Close button (the red button at the left end of its title bar) or by clicking the Toolbox button on the Standard toolbar.

Using Animation to Display Bulleted Paragraphs One at a Time

When you have several bulleted paragraphs in a text placeholder, you can use animation to display them one at a time. This helps prevent the audience from reading ahead of you and missing the point you're explaining.

To display bulleted paragraphs one at a time, follow these steps:

1. Click the container that holds the bulleted paragraphs.

2. Apply the animation to the container from the appropriate Effects panel. For example, apply the Fly In animation from the Entrance Effects panel.

3. If the animation offers different directions, choose Animations ➤ Animation Options ➤ Effect Options, and then click the direction you want. For example, click From Right.

4. Choose Animations ➤ Animation ➤ Effect Options again, and this time click the Sequence option you want:

   - *As One Object.* PowerPoint animates the whole object at once.

   - *All at Once.* PowerPoint animates each top-level paragraph separately but runs the animations all at once. Depending on the animation, this can look very similar to As One Object, but it can also look different.

- *By Paragraph.* PowerPoint animates each top-level paragraph separately. This is usually the most useful setting.

5. Click the Play button (choose Animations ➤ Preview ➤ Play) to preview the effect.

6. If the text has different levels, and you need to control their paragraphs separately, click the Reorder button to display the Custom Animation pane in the Toolbox.

7. In the Animation order list box, click the container that holds the bulleted paragraphs. PowerPoint displays the Text Animations pane at the bottom of the Custom Animation pane (see Figure 20–10).

Figure 20–10. *In the Group text pop-up menu in the Text Animations pane of the Custom Animation window, choose the level of paragraphs by which you want to animate the object.*

8. Open the Group text pop-up menu and choose the animation you want: All paragraphs at once, 1st level, 2nd level, 3rd level, 4th level, or 5th level. For example, if the container has two levels of paragraphs, and you want to control both separately, choose 2nd Level.

NOTE: In the Text Animations pane in the Custom Animation pane of the Toolbox, you can also choose to animate text by word or by letter rather than all at once. Open the Animate text pop-up menu, and then choose By word or By letter, as needed.

9. Click the Toolbox button on the Standard toolbar to close the Toolbox.

Animating SmartArt Graphics, Charts, and Tables

You can apply animations to SmartArt graphics, charts, and tables just as you can to other objects in PowerPoint. Animations are especially useful when you want to reveal only part of one of these objects at a time, gradually building up to showing the whole object.

Animating a SmartArt Graphic

PowerPoint enables you to animate the component parts of a SmartArt graphic in sequence, so you can choose between displaying the whole object at once, displaying all the objects at a particular level, or displaying one object at a time.

To choose how to display a SmartArt graphic, follow these steps:

1. Select the SmartArt graphic by clicking it on the slide.

2. Apply the animation to the graphic as a whole from one of the Effects panels. For example, apply the Fade animation from the Subtle section of the Entrance Effects panel. Fade makes the whole graphic appear at once with the animation.

3. Choose Animations ➤ Animation Options ➤ Effect Options, and then click the way you want to animate the graphic:

    - ■ *As One Object.* This option displays the graphic as a single object, so it all appears in one animation.

NOTE: The selection of options on the Effect Options pop-up menu depends on the object you're animating. For example, the Level at Once option and the Level One by One option appear only for objects that have levels.

    - ■ *All at Once.* This option treats the graphic as separate objects but runs the animation on all the objects at once.

    - ■ *One by One.* This option treats each component of the graphic as a separate object. In many cases, this is the most useful option.

■ *Level at Once.* This option treats each level of a hierarchical SmartArt graphic as a separate object. Choose this option when you want to display one level of the graphic at a time.

■ *Level One by One.* This option treats each level of a hierarchical SmartArt graphic as a separate object and treats each object within the level as a separate object. Choose this option when you want to display the graphic one object of a level at a time.

4. Click the Play button (choose Animations ➤ Preview ➤ Play) to preview the effect.

5. If you need to change the order, choose Animations ➤ Animation Order ➤ Reorder. PowerPoint displays the Custom Animation pane in the Toolbox.

6. In the Animation order list box, click the container that holds the SmartArt object. PowerPoint displays the SmartArt Animation pane at the bottom of the Custom Animation pane.

7. Open the Group graphic pop-up menu, and then click the option you want. The options available depend on the type of SmartArt graphic, but these are typical:

■ *As one object.* Choose this option to display the whole SmartArt graphic at once.

■ *All at once.* Choose this option to display all the components of the SmartArt graphic at once.

■ *One by one.* Choose this option to display one component at a time.

■ *By branch one by one.* Choose this option to display each branch of a graphic such as an org chart separately, showing one component at a time.

■ *By level at once.* Choose this option to display each level of a graphic separately, showing the whole level at once.

■ *By level one by one.* Choose this option to display each level of a graphic separately, showing one component at a time.

8. If you want to reveal the SmartArt graphic in reverse order, select the Reverse order check box.

9. Click the Toolbox button on the Standard toolbar to close the Toolbox.

Animating a Chart

When you're displaying a chart, it's often helpful to use an animation to show part of it at a time rather than displaying the whole chart at once. To do this, follow these steps:

1. Select the chart by clicking it on the slide that contains it.

2. Apply the animation to the chart as a whole from one of the Effects panels. For example, apply the Appear animation.

3. Choose Animations ➤ Animation Options ➤ Effect Options, and then click the way you want to animate the chart:

    - *As One Object.* This setting displays the chart all at once, so you probably won't want to use it.

    - *By Series.* This setting displays one full data series at a time and is good for contrasting the data series to each other.

    - *By Category.* This setting displays one whole category at a time and is good for comparing the categories.

    - *By Element in Series.* This setting displays each element in a series at a time, then the next element in the series, and so on, until the series is finished. This setting is great for focusing on the individual elements in the series.

    - *By Element in Category.* This setting displays each element in a category at a time, then the category's next element, and so on. Use this setting to zero in on the individual elements in the categories.

NOTE: If you insert a chart as a picture, you can't animate its components.

4. If necessary, choose Animations ➤ Animation Options ➤ Reorder to display the Custom Animation pane in the Toolbox, click the chart's placeholder in the Animation order list box, and then adjust the settings. For example, if you've chosen the By Element in Series option, you can set the elements in a series to display automatically one after the other, using a short delay between them.

5. Preview the animation and make sure that the objects appear as you want them to appear.

Animating a Table

When you're displaying a complex table on a slide, it's often helpful to display the rows, columns, or even cells one at a time to keep the audience's attention on the data you're currently talking about. PowerPoint's animations don't work for rows, columns, or cells, so you need to take matters into your own hands.

Here are two approaches you can use:

- *Create two or more separate tables.* Create two or more separate tables and position them next to each other so that they appear to be a single table. You can then animate each of the tables separately, giving the effect of animating different parts of the same table. This approach sounds clumsy, but it's easy to do, and it's effective visually.

- *Hide parts of the table.* Create a single table, and then cover those parts you want to hide with shapes (for example, rectangles) colored the same as the slide's background. You can then reveal a hidden part of the table by running an Exit animation on the shape that's covering it.

> **TIP:** Sometimes you'll want to trigger each animation manually so that you can control the timing, but it can be handy to string other animations together so that when one animation ends, the next runs automatically. For example, when you click to display the next bullet point, you can make a picture appear automatically on the slide. To do this, select the animation you want to run automatically, and then choose Animations ➤ Animation Options ➤ Start ➤ After Previous. If you want to run an animation simultaneously with the previous one, choose Animations ➤ Animation Options ➤ Start ➤ With Previous.

Keeping Extra Information Up Your Sleeve with Hidden Slides

In many presentations, it's useful to have extra information that you can summon up to deal with points you don't want to cover unless the audience raises them. To meet this need, PowerPoint lets you hide any slide so that it doesn't appear unless you specifically choose to display it.

To hide a slide, Ctrl+click or right-click the slide in the Slides tab of the Navigation pane or in Slide Sorter view, and then click Hide Slide on the context menu. You can also choose Slide Show ➤ Hide Slide from the menu bar.

PowerPoint indicates a hidden slide by dimming it and showing a circle with a diagonal line (see Figure 20–11) in the Slides tab in Normal view and in the slides area in Slide

Sorter view. On the Go to Slide menu in Slide Show view, a hidden slide appears with parentheses around its slide number.

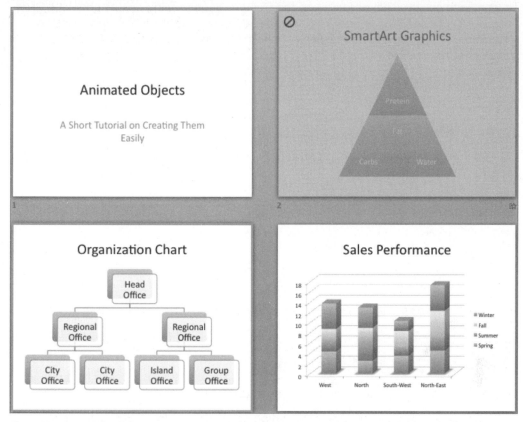

Figure 20–11. *In Slide Sorter view and on the Slides tab of the Navigation pane, a circle with a diagonal strikethrough (as in the upper-left corner of the upper-right slide here) indicates a hidden slide.*

To change a slide back from hidden to normal, Ctrl+click or right-click the slide, and then click Hide Slide again, turning off the hiding.

Creating Custom Slide Shows Within a Presentation

Hidden slides can be great when you want to keep some information in reserve, but if you find yourself hiding many slides within a presentation, you may need to take the next step—creating a custom slide show.

A custom slide show is an arrangement of slides within a presentation. You can choose which of the presentation's slides to include in the custom show, and you can change the order in which they appear. You can create as many custom slide shows within a presentation as you need.

Opening the Custom Shows Dialog Box

To work with custom shows, first open the Custom Shows dialog box by choosing Slide Show ➤ Play Slide Show ➤ Custom Shows ➤ Edit Custom Shows from the Ribbon or Slide Show ➤ Custom Shows ➤ Edit Custom Shows from the menu bar. Figure 20–12 shows the Custom Shows dialog box with two custom shows already created.

Figure 20–12. *From the Custom Shows dialog box, you can create, launch, and manage custom slide shows within a presentation.*

Creating a Custom Slide Show

To create a custom slide show, follow these steps:

1. Create all the slides for the presentation or as many of the slides as you can create at this point. (You can add other slides later, but it's easiest to start with all your slides if you've created them.)

2. Choose Slide Show ➤ Play Slide Show ➤ Custom Shows ➤ Edit Custom Shows from the Ribbon or Slide Show ➤ Custom Shows ➤ Edit Custom Shows from the menu bar to display the Custom Shows dialog box.

3. Click the New button to display the Define Custom Show dialog box (shown in Figure 20–13 with settings chosen).

Figure 20–13. *Use the Define Custom Show dialog box to name a custom show, add slides to it, and put the slides in the order you want.*

4. In the Slide show name box, type the name you want to give the custom show. Usually, you'll want to make the name as descriptive as possible while keeping it short enough to fit fully in the Custom shows box in the Custom Shows dialog box—40 characters or so at most.

5. In the Slides in presentation box, select the slides you want to add to the custom show, and then click the Add button. After clicking a slide to select it, you can Shift+click another slide to select all the slides between the two, or you can Cmd+click individual slides to add them to the selection. Or, if you prefer, add a single slide at a time.

6. Once you've added the slides you want to the Slides in custom show box, rearrange them into the order needed. To move a slide up or down the order, click it, and then click the up arrow button or the down arrow button, as needed.

7. When you've finished creating the custom show, click the OK button to close the Define Custom Show dialog box. PowerPoint returns you to the Custom Shows dialog box, where the Custom shows box includes the custom show you just created.

TIP: To create another show based on a custom show you've created, click the existing show in the Custom Shows dialog box, and then click the Copy button. PowerPoint creates a new custom show called *Copy of* and the existing show's name—for example, *Copy of Brewery Introduction*. With the copy selected, click the Edit button to open the copy in the Define Custom Show dialog box. You can then rename the copy and change its contents.

Playing a Custom Slide Show

After you've created a custom slide show, you can play it in either of these ways:

- Choose Slide Show ➤ Play Slide Show ➤ Custom Shows, and then click the custom show's name on the Custom Shows pop-up menu.

- Open the Custom Shows dialog box, click the show in the Custom shows list, and then click the Show button.

Editing or Deleting a Custom Slide Show

To edit a custom slide show, open the Custom Shows dialog box, click the custom show's name in the Custom shows list, and then click the Edit button. You can then use the Define Custom Show dialog box to change the selection of slides in the show or alter their order as needed.

To delete a custom show, click its name in the Custom shows list in the Custom Shows dialog box, and then click the Remove button. PowerPoint removes the show without confirmation.

Summary

In this chapter, you looked at how to add graphics, movies, and sounds to your slides. You also learned how to smooth or dramatize the switchover from one slide to another by choosing a suitable transition to introduce the next slide and how to bring the elements of a slide to life by applying animations and setting them to run the way you want.

You can now also hide slides that you want to keep in reserve and create custom slide shows consisting of only some of the slides from a presentation.

By now, you know how to put together a powerful and convincing presentation. The next stage is to deliver the presentation. You'll learn how to do this in the next chapter.

Chapter 21

Delivering a Presentation Live or Online

By this point, chances are that you've created a powerful and compelling presentation stuffed with great content. Now it's time to deliver that presentation.

With PowerPoint, you can deliver a presentation in a handful of ways. The most straightforward way is by giving it live to your audience, showing the slides on a screen. This can be a challenge, but PowerPoint helps greatly by providing Presenter view, which puts your notes and essential controls where you can see them but the audience can't.

To help your audience enjoy your presentation and retain its message, you can print a handout or create a PDF file for distribution, and if you need to distribute a presentation rather than deliver it personally, you can record narration to fit the slides.

Later in the chapter, I'll show you how to export and share your presentations. Apart from using means of sharing that you already know, such as e-mailing a presentation or saving a presentation to a SharePoint site or Windows Live SkyDrive, you can broadcast a slide show live on the Web to however big an audience you can muster, save the slides as a series of picture files that you can use separately, or create a movie of the presentation.

We'll start by going over how to prepare to deliver a presentation—setting up the display, arranging Presenter view, practicing your presentation, and (if you need to) recording automatic timings.

Getting Ready to Deliver a Presentation in Person

Before you deliver a presentation, you'll need to set up the computer you'll use with the projector or display on which you'll show the presentation. You will likely want to use PowerPoint's handy Presenter view if possible to keep your notes and controls on-screen. You will almost certainly want to practice your presentation before you actually have to give it. And you may want to record automatic timings for the slides so that the presentation automatically advances itself while you perform.

Setting Up Your Display and Choosing the Resolution

Start by connecting your Mac to the display or projector on which you'll give the presentation, and then get the displays set up. Here's an example using a MacBook:

1. Connect the display or projector to the MacBook's external display port.

> **NOTE:** Check the kind of connector cable you need to connect the projector or display to your Mac's external display port. Most current Macs use a Mini DisplayPort for output, while older Macs use a Digital Visual Interface (DVI) or Mini-DVI port. Recent projectors use a High-Definition Multimedia Interface (HDMI) or DVI port, while many older projectors use a Video Graphics Array (VGA) port; current displays use Mini DisplayPort, DVI, or HDMI. Unless your Mac has the same connector type as the projector or display, you'll need a converter cable—for example, a Mini DisplayPort to HDMI converter. You can get these from the Apple Store (http://store.apple.com) or other online or real-world computer stores.

2. Turn on the projector or display.

3. Turn on the MacBook, and log on.

4. Choose Apple ➤ System Preferences to display the System Preferences window.

5. Choose View ➤ Displays from the menu bar to switch to the Displays preferences pane. Mac OS X shows two Displays windows—one for the MacBook on its screen and one for the projector or external display on the other screen.

6. In the MacBook's Displays window, click the Arrangement tab to display its contents (see Figure 21–1).

Figure 21–1. *Start by setting up the projector or the external display in the Displays pane in System Preferences.*

7. Make sure both the displays appear in the Arrangement pane. If not, check the connection of the projector or external display, make sure it is receiving power, and then click the Detect Displays button.

8. Drag the display icons to match how the displays are physically positioned. For example, if the projector will be projecting onto a screen that you'll see over the top of your MacBook's display, drag the icon for the projector so that it is above the icon for the MacBook's display. Positioning the displays like this helps you avoid confusing them.

9. Make sure the Mirror Displays check box is cleared so that you can use Presenter view on the MacBook.

10. If you need to change the resolution for the projector or external display, click the Displays window for that display. On the Display tab, choose the resolution in the Resolutions list. You can also adjust the Brightness slider if necessary.

11. When you've finished, click the Close button (the red button at the left end of the title bar) on one of the Displays windows or press Cmd+Q to quit System Preferences.

Using Presenter View

Next, if you're using two screens, turn on Presenter view. In PowerPoint, click the Slide Show tab of the Ribbon, go to the Setting for Two Displays group, and then click the Presenter View button so that it appears pushed in (see Figure 21–2). Then, when you start the slide show, PowerPoint displays Presenter view on the monitor that's not showing the slides to the audience.

Figure 21–2. *In the Setting for Two Displays group on the Slide Show tab of the Ribbon, you'll normally want to select the Presenter View button.*

Presenter view is perhaps PowerPoint's biggest aid to you in giving an effective presentation. While the audience sees only the slide you're currently displaying in Slide Show view, Presenter view (see Figure 21–3) shows your current slide, the next slide or object that will appear, and the slide's notes. Normally, you'll use Presenter view on your laptop's screen, so you're the only one who can see it, and show the slides for the audience on the projector or external monitor.

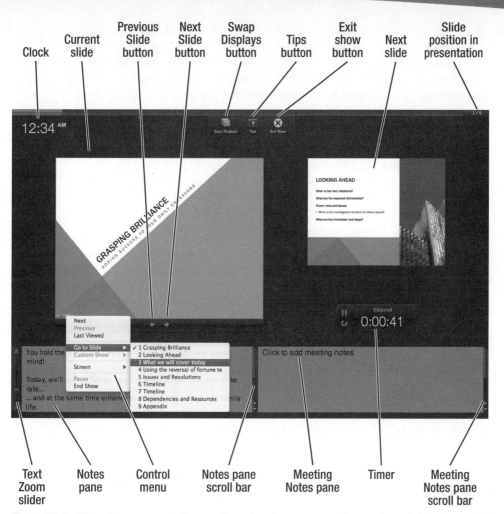

Figure 21–3. *When giving a presentation, use Presenter view on a second screen to control the presentation, display your notes, and navigate quickly from slide to slide.*

In Presenter view, you can take the following actions:

- *View the current slide.* The current slide appears in the upper-left part of the window.

- *View the next slide or object.* The next slide, or the next object that will appear on the current slide, appears in the upper-right corner of Presenter view.

- *Consult your notes.* The notes for the current slide appear in the Notes pane in the lower-left part of the window. You can drag the Text Zoom slider to adjust the text to a comfortable size for viewing, or you can use the scroll bar on the right side of the Notes pane to scroll up and down.

- *Take notes on the meeting.* Click in the Meeting Notes area, and then type the information you want to record. This feature is great for capturing items you need to follow up on, names of audience members you want to talk to after the presentation, or extra information you need to shoehorn into the presentation for the next time you deliver it.

- *Display another slide.* Click the Next Slide button to move along to the next slide, or click the Previous Slide button to move back to the previous slide. To move in bigger steps, click the icons in the lower-left corner of the current slide to display the control menu, click or highlight Go to Slide, and then click the slide you want on the submenu that appears (see Figure 21–3).

TIP: To move to another slide that you identify visually, move the mouse pointer to the bottom of the screen in Presenter view. PowerPoint displays a bar containing thumbnails of the presentation's slides. Click the slide you want to display.

- *End the slide show.* Click the End Show button. You can also press Esc.

NOTE: If you don't have a second monitor for presenter view, you'll need to fall back on traditional means of handling your notes—memorizing them, printing them on cards, or writing them on the palm of your hand or on your cuff.

Practicing Your Presentation

To make sure your presentation goes well on the day, practice it until you're confident you know your material and you can speak fluently from the notes you've given yourself. If you find your notes need more detail, rearranging, or other improvements, work on them too.

Ideally, you will rehearse your presentation in the room in which you will deliver the presentation, using the same equipment. Sometimes you can do this; for example, if you'll be speaking in your company or organization, you may be able to book the conference room for your run-through. But if you will deliver the presentation elsewhere, as is often the case, you will need to practice wherever you find most convenient— preferably somewhere you can speak aloud with interruption or drawing unwelcome attention.

To practice your presentation, use Presenter view (if you'll use it during your presentation) or your notes. You may also want to set timings for slides, as discussed next.

Rehearsing Timings for Slides

For some presentations, you may need to set automatic timings for slides so that you don't need to cue them manually. To set timings, use PowerPoint's Rehearse Timings feature like this:

1. Choose Slide Show ➤ Presenter Tools ➤ Rehearse. PowerPoint starts the slide show using Presenter view but displays a different timer (see Figure 21–4).

Pause/Resume button   Restart Slide Timing button

Figure 21–4. *Use the controls on the timer to set automatic timings for slides or to control the recording of your narration.*

2. Go through your presentation, setting the timings like this:

    ■ *Display the next slide.* Click the Next Slide button to display the next slide.

    ■ *Pause and resume the timer.* Click the Pause/Resume button on the timer to pause timing. Click the button again to restart timing.

    ■ *View the time.* The Current Slide readout on the timer displays how long the current slide has been displayed for. The Total readout on the timer shows how long the presentation has been running for.

    ■ *Restart timing for the current slide.* Click the Restart Slide Timing button to start recording the timing for the current slide again.

3. When you finish going through the presentation, PowerPoint displays a dialog box (see Figure 21–5) giving the total show time and asking whether you want to apply the timings to the slide show.

Figure 21–5. *Click the Yes button in this dialog box to apply the timings you've recorded to the slide show.*

4. Click the Yes button to apply the timings to the slide show.

5. Save the presentation. For example, click the Save button on the Standard toolbar.

Delivering a Presentation to a Live Audience

When you're ready to deliver the presentation live (or when you're practicing), use the commands and techniques explained in this section to start the presentation and display the slides. If necessary, you can annotate the presentation or display a black screen or white screen instead of your slides. You can also run the presentation from the keyboard rather than using a mouse.

Starting a Presentation

When you're ready to launch the presentation, choose Slide Show ➤ Play Slide Show ➤ From Start from the Ribbon or Slide Show ➤ Play from Start from the menu bar. You can also press Cmd+Shift+Return.

If you need to start from a slide other than the first, select that slide, and then choose Slide Show ➤ Play Slide Show ➤ From Current Slide from the Ribbon or Slide Show ➤ Play from Current Slide from the menu bar. You can also press Cmd+Return to start from the current slide.

Displaying the Slides You Need

To give the presentation smoothly and effectively, you'll need to display slides in the order you want. The most straightforward way is to start at the beginning of the presentation and run straight through to the end, but in many cases, you'll need to change the order. For example, you may need to go back to an earlier slide, skip ahead to a particular slide by name or number, or display a hidden slide.

PowerPoint provides plenty of different ways to move from slide to slide. The following ways tend to be the most convenient:

- *Run the next animation or display the next slide.* Click the mouse button, or press the spacebar.

NOTE: You can also move forward or back by holding the mouse pointer over the lower-left corner of the slide and then clicking the Next button or the Previous button on the row of controls that appears.

- *Return to the previous slide.* Press P; or either Ctrl+click or right-click the current slide, and then click Previous on the context menu.

TIP: In Presenter view, Ctrl+click anywhere on the current slide, or click the icons in the lower-left corner of the current slide, to display the context menu for navigation.

- *Go to a slide by name or number.* Ctrl+click or right-click the current slide, click or highlight Go to Slide on the context menu (see Figure 21–6), and then click the slide on the submenu. PowerPoint truncates long slide names, but it's usually easy enough to identify the slides.

NOTE: Parentheses around a slide's number on the Go to Slide submenu indicate that the slide is hidden.

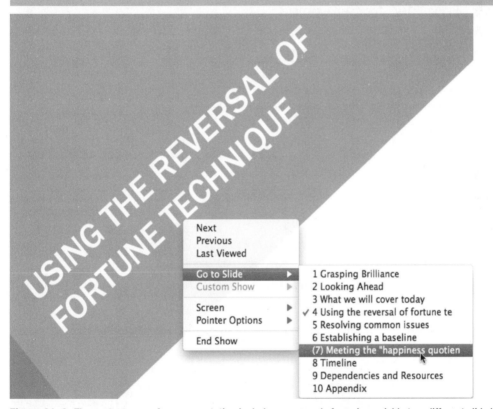

Figure 21–6. *The context menu for a presentation includes commands for going quickly to a different slide by name or number, returning to the last slide viewed, or switching to a custom show.*

- *Return to the last slide viewed.* Ctrl+click or right-click the current slide, and then click Last Viewed on the context menu.

Annotating the Slides

Sometimes you may want to annotate a presentation to make sure your audience grasps your most important points. PowerPoint gives you the following choices on the Pointer Options submenu of the context menu:

- *Automatic.* Choose this item to let PowerPoint change the pointer automatically depending on where you move it.

- *Hidden.* Choose this item when you want to hide the mouse pointer—for example, so that it doesn't distract the audience.

- *Arrow.* Choose this item when you want to restore the mouse pointer to its normal arrow so that you can point to items on slides.

- *Pen.* Choose this item when you want to write or draw on a slide. Figure 21–7 shows an example.

Staffing Requirements

Office	2011	2012
Sacramento	24	28
San Luis Obispo	4	6
San Jose	31	39
Redding	2	2
Yreka		

Figure 21–7. You can use PowerPoint's annotation features to mark up slides during a presentation. PowerPoint doesn't save your annotations.

- *Pen Color.* From this submenu, choose the pen color you want—for example, Red.

NOTE: To erase the annotations from the slide, display the context menu, and choose Screen ➤ Erase Pen.

Controlling a Presentation Using the Keyboard

If you're at your Mac when you're giving the presentation, you can control the presentation by using keyboard shortcuts. Table 21–1 explains the keyboard shortcuts you can use; you'll find the most useful ones explained elsewhere in the text as well. Several of the actions have two or more keyboard shortcuts. Each works the same; the one I've listed first is usually the easiest, but try them all, and use whichever you find most convenient.

Table 21–1. *Keyboard Shortcuts for Running a Presentation*

Action	Keyboard Shortcut
Run the presentation from the first slide	Cmd+Shift+Return
Run the presentation from the current slide	Cmd+Return
End the slide show	Esc or – (numeric keypad)
Display the next slide or trigger the next animation	N, Return, spacebar, Page Down, down arrow, or right arrow
Display the previous slide or trigger the previous animation again	P, Backspace, Page Up, up arrow, or left arrow
Display the next slide if it's hidden	H
Toggle on or off a white screen with no content	W or , (comma key)
Toggle on or off a black screen with no content	B or . (period key)
Go to a slide by specifying its number	*Number key* followed by Return (for example, 8 and then Return)
Start or stop an automatic slide show	S
Change the mouse pointer to a pen	Cmd+P
Restore the normal mouse pointer	Cmd+A
Erase all annotations from the current slide	E

Displaying a White Screen or Black Screen

When you need to focus your audience's attention on you rather than on your slides, display a white screen or a black screen (whichever best suits the lighting conditions under which you're giving the presentation). To do so, open the context menu, and then choose Screen ➤ Black Screen or Screen ➤ White Screen, as needed.

Press Esc or click to go back from the black screen or white screen to the slides.

Creating a Handout for a Presentation

When you're delivering a presentation live, it's often useful to create a handout that provides your audience with material to browse before you start, to scribble notes on as you proceed, and to take home for further reference afterward.

To create a handout, follow these steps:

1. Open the presentation if it's not already open.

2. Choose File ➤ Print or press Cmd+P to display the Print dialog box.

3. Open the Print What pop-up menu, and choose the Handouts item you want: Handouts (2 slides per page), Handouts (3 slides per page), Handouts (4 slides per page), Handouts (6 slides per page), or Handouts (9 slides per page). PowerPoint displays a quick preview on the left side of the Print dialog box (see Figure 21–8).

> **TIP:** If you want your audience to be able to take notes easily, choose Handouts (3 slides per page). This layout puts the three slides in a vertical stack on the left side of the page, with a lined area to the right of each slide for taking notes, as you can see in Figure 21–8.

Figure 21–8. *In the Print dialog box, choose the layout and content you want for your handout.*

4. In the Slide Show pop-up menu, choose which slides to print handouts for:

■ *Print handouts for all slides.* Select All Slides in the Slide Show pop-up menu, and make sure the All option button in the Slides area is selected.

■ *Print handouts for a range of slides.* Select All Slides in the Slide Show pop-up menu. Then select the From option button, and type the starting number in the text box next to it. Type the ending number in the To text box.

NOTE: If you need to print a handout for only some of the slides in a presentation but those slides aren't in sequence, select those slides before opening the Print dialog box. You can then select the Selected Slides option button in the Slides area to print handouts for only those slides.

■ *Print handouts for a custom show.* Select the custom show by its name in the Slide Show pop-up menu.

5. In the Output pop-up menu, choose the kind of output for the handouts: Color, Grayscale, or Black and White.

6. Select the Scale to Fit Paper check box if you want PowerPoint to resize the slides to fit the paper better. The preview shows you the effect of this change so you can tell whether it will be helpful.

7. Select the Print Hidden Slides check box if you want to include hidden slides in the handout. If the selection or presentation contains no hidden slides, this check box is unavailable.

8. Select the Frame Slides check box if you want PowerPoint to put a frame around each slide. This is useful if the slides use a light-colored or white background that will disappear on the printout without a frame.

9. If you want to print the handouts, click the Print button. If you want to create a PDF file that you can then print from another computer (or distribute as a PDF), click the PDF pop-up button, and choose click Save as PDF. In the Save dialog box, specify the file name and folder for the PDF, and then click the Save button.

Recording Narration into a Presentation

When you can't deliver a presentation in person, you can record your narration for the presentation and create a file that your audience can play back. This is great for creating a presentation that you will share on the Web or on a CD or DVD.

Unless you're a pro at speaking off the cuff or you can already deliver this presentation in your sleep from relentless practice, you'll probably want to write a script of what you'll say. Having a script helps you avoid the pauses that pass unnoticed in a live presentation but stick out uncomfortably in a recorded presentation. When using a script, avoid the trap of lapsing into a monotone—deliver your lines with all the life and conviction you'd give to a live audience.

NOTE: To record narration, you'll need a suitable microphone. In a pinch, you can use the microphone built into your MacBook or iMac, but such a microphone will usually pick up ambient noise (even if you use PowerPoint's noise-cancellation feature). Usually, you'll be better off using a microphone that you can position freely, such as a handheld microphone or one on a stand, and best off with a noise-canceling microphone mounted on a headset.

To record a presentation, follow these steps:

1. Set up your microphone and check that it's working. What you need to do depends on your setup, but these steps are typical:

    ■   Choose Apple ➤ System Preferences from the menu bar to open the System Preferences window.

- Choose View ➤ Sound from the menu bar to display the Sound preferences pane.

- Click the Input tab if it's not already displayed.

- Make sure the right microphone or input is selected in the Select a device for sound input list box.

- Speak into the microphone, and make sure the Input level meter shows a suitable level. If not, drag the Input volume slider to set the input volume.

- Select the Use ambient noise reduction check box if you want the Mac to try to tune out as much ambient noise as possible.

- Click the Close button (the red button at the left end of the title bar) or choose System Preferences ➤ Quit System Preferences to close the System Preferences window.

2. In PowerPoint, select the slide from which you want to start recording. For example, if you want to start recording from the beginning, click the first slide.

3. Choose Slide Show ➤ Presenter Tools ➤ Record Slide Show from the Ribbon or Slide Show ➤ Record Slide Show from the menu bar. PowerPoint switches to Presenter view, displays the slide you chose, and starts recording your audio and the timings for moving from slide to slide and from animation to animation.

4. Speak your narration for the presentation, advancing the slides and animations as needed.

> **NOTE:** If you need to pause the recording, click the Pause/Resume button on the timer; click this button again when you're ready to resume. If you need to start over for the current slide, click the Restart Slide Timing button in the lower-left corner of the timer.

5. When you reach the end of the presentation, PowerPoint automatically stops recording the narration and prompts you to save your timings. Click the Yes button.

Exporting and Sharing a Presentation

Apart from delivering a presentation in person, PowerPoint gives you several ways to get the presentation to other people across the Internet:

- *Send the presentation via e-mail.* The most direct way to get a presentation to somebody else is to e-mail it to them, as discussed in Chapter 2. E-mail works well for small presentations, but many presentation files are too large for mail servers to handle. In this case, you're better off using a different means of distribution.

■ *Save the presentation to SkyDrive.* You can save the presentation to a shared folder on Windows Live SkyDrive, as discussed in Chapter 2. Anyone with permission to view the folder can then download the presentation and view it. This is an effective way to distribute presentations across the Internet.

■ *Save the presentation to a SharePoint site.* If you have a SharePoint site, you can save the presentation to it. Anyone with permission to view the folder on the SharePoint site can then view the presentation. In many cases, this is the best way to distribute a presentation within a company or organization that uses SharePoint.

■ *Broadcast a slide show.* In broadcasting, you give the slide show live on the Web. Beforehand, you create a link to where you will broadcast the slide show. You send this link to the potential audience, and any of them can click the link to tune in to the slide show at the appointed time. The following section explains how to broadcast a slide show.

NOTE: Broadcasting a slide show works well even with a modest-speed Internet connection. Before you start the broadcast, you upload the presentation file to the broadcast server; if the presentation is large and your Internet connection slow, this can take a while, but you need do it only once. Similarly, the audience doesn't need a screaming-fast Internet connection to watch the broadcast—but if you broadcast audio at the same time, it's a good idea to use a relaxed tempo for the presentation so that you can be sure the audience is seeing the slide you're talking about. Rapid-fire changes of slide can get parts of the audience out of sync.

■ *Save the presentation as pictures.* If you need to share the presentation with extra comments on a web page or send individual slides to people, you can save it as pictures. When you do this, you lose the transitions and animations—so make sure that the slides don't rely on them. The "Saving a Presentation as Pictures" section explains how to save a presentation as pictures.

■ *Save the presentation as a movie.* If you need to share the presentation with people who don't have PowerPoint, you can turn it into a movie. The "Saving a Presentation as a Movie" section explains how to save a presentation as a movie.

Broadcasting a Slide Show

When you need to share a slide show with a large audience over the Internet, you can broadcast it. Broadcasting involves you giving the presentation live (or playing back a recorded presentation) at a scheduled time and your audience tuning in to watch it in their web browsers. To provide audio, you can arrange a conference call with the participants.

To broadcast a slide show from PowerPoint, you use Microsoft's PowerPoint Broadcast Service or an equivalent service. The PowerPoint Broadcast Service is free to anyone who has a Windows Live ID, so you'll probably want to try it unless you have a different broadcast service available (for example, one your company or organization runs on its own network).

NOTE: A Windows Live ID is the identifier that Microsoft uses for Windows Live Mail, Hotmail, MSN, and other services. If you have an account with one of these services, you already have a Windows Live ID that you can use for the PowerPoint Broadcast Service. If not, you can sign up for a Windows Live ID using your existing e-mail address; either click the Get a Live ID button in the Windows Live Sign In dialog box the first time you use the PowerPoint Broadcast Service feature or go to http://home.live.com, click the Sign Up link, and fill in the form.

To broadcast a slide show, follow these steps:

1. Open the presentation if it's not already open.

2. Choose File ➤ Share ➤ Broadcast Slide Show. PowerPoint displays the Broadcast Slide Show dialog box (see Figure 21–9).

Figure 21–9. *Use the Broadcast Slide Show dialog box to set up a slide show broadcast on Microsoft's PowerPoint Broadcast Service or another broadcasting service.*

NOTE: If your company uses another broadcast service, choose it in the Broadcast service pop-up menu in the Broadcast Slide Show dialog box.

3. Click the Connect button. If you're using the PowerPoint Broadcast Service, PowerPoint prompts you for your Windows Live ID. Type your e-mail address and password, select the Save password in my Mac OS keychain check box if you want to use automatic sign-in from now on, and then click the Sign In button.

4. Next, wait while PowerPoint prepares the slide show for broadcast. This can take several minutes for a slide show with many slides and complex content.

5. When PowerPoint displays the Broadcast Slide Show dialog box shown in Figure 21–10, the slide show is ready to go. You now need to share the link for the slide show in one of these ways:

   ◼ Click the Copy Link item to copy the link so that you can share it—for example, by pasting it into an instant message.

Broadcast Slide Show

Share this link with remote viewers, and then click Play Slide Show to start broadcasting.

Broadcast Link

http://sn1-
pptbroadcast.officeapps.live.com/
PowerPointBroadcast.aspx?
pptbid=ce30175e-f4fe-43c6-a67f-
b62e462f68f3

(Send in E-mail...)

(Copy Link)

(Close)   (Play Slide Show)

Figure 21–10. *From this Broadcast Slide Show dialog box, you can copy the slide show's link or create an e-mail message containing it.*

■ Click the Send in Email link to create an e-mail message containing the link and a subject line derived from the presentation's name. You can then add other details as needed (for example, details about the conference call that will provide the audio component of the presentation), address the message, and then send it.

6. If you're providing audio with a conference call, set it up. You can do this on landlines, cell phones, or Internet telephony services.

7. When you're ready to start giving the presentation, click the Play Slide Show button. PowerPoint switches to Slide Show view (and displays Presenter view on your second screen if you're using it), and you can start giving the presentation.

TIP: Until you start giving your presentation, viewers see a blank screen telling them that the presentation will start soon. Instead of leaving them in suspense, create a first slide that shows the time the presentation will start (include the time zone for clarity) and gives some useful information (for example, the URL of your web site). Click the Start Slide Show button in the Broadcast Slide Show dialog box to display this first slide, and leave it on-screen until you're ready to start the slide show for real.

8. Deliver the presentation as usual. When you have finished, click the End Broadcast button on the Broadcast View bar (see Figure 21–11) or choose Home (Broadcast) ➤ Broadcast ➤ End to tell the broadcast service that the presentation is over.

Figure 21–11. *PowerPoint displays the Home (Broadcast) tab of the Ribbon while the broadcast is going on. Click the End Broadcast button on the Broadcast View bar to end the broadcast.*

9. In the confirmation dialog box that PowerPoint displays (see Figure 21–12), click the End Broadcast button. Viewers then see a message saying that the broadcast is over.

> All remote users will be disconnected if you continue. Do you want to end this broadcast?
>
> Cancel   End Broadcast

Figure 21–12. *Click the End Broadcast button in this dialog box to confirm that the broadcast is over.*

Saving a Presentation as Pictures

If you need to use individual slides separately rather than as part of the presentation, you can save the slides as picture files.

To save a presentation as picture files, follow these steps:

1. Open the presentation if it's not already open.

2. Choose File ➤ Save as Pictures. PowerPoint displays the Save As dialog box and selects the JPEG item in the Format pop-up menu.

3. If you want, change to a different picture format by opening the Format pop-up menu and making the appropriate choice:

    - *JPEG*. Joint Photographic Experts Group (JPEG) files are widely used for everything from digital photography to web pages. JPEG files use *lossy* compression—the application that creates a JPEG file discards some of the image data to make the file smaller—so they're not full quality.

    - *PNG*. Portable Network Graphics (PNG) files are full quality and have relatively small file sizes. PNG files are a good choice for most uses.

- *GIF.* Graphics Interchange Format (GIF) is an old file format that uses only 256 colors. GIF files are small, but you lose so much quality that the trade-off is seldom worthwhile.

- *BMP.* Windows Bitmap (BMP) format retains full quality at the expense of a large file size. PNG is usually a better choice.

- *TIFF.* Tagged Image File Format (TIFF) files are full quality and are widely used in publishing, but they're less good for web pages than PNG.

4. In the Save As text box, type the name of the folder you want PowerPoint to create and put the files in.

5. If you want to put the new folder in a different folder than the current folder, navigate to the folder you want.

6. Click the Save button. PowerPoint exports the slides as pictures, naming them Slide01, Slide02, and so on. It then displays a dialog box telling you which folder to find the files in.

7. Click the OK button. You can now distribute the presentation—for example, by zipping the folder and sending it via e-mail or by posting slides on your web site.

> **TIP:** You can also use the Save as Pictures command to give a presentation in Second Life. In this case, use the JPEG format for the pictures.

Saving a Presentation as a Movie

If you need to share a presentation with people who don't have PowerPoint and who won't (or can't) watch a live broadcast on the Web, you can save the presentation as a movie. You can then send the movie via e-mail or put it on a CD that you give or send to whomever needs it.

> **NOTE:** PowerPoint creates movies in the QuickTime (MOV) format. Any Mac or PC that has QuickTime Player installed can play these movies. All Macs have QuickTime Player installed, as does any PC that has iTunes installed (Apple bundles QuickTime with iTunes). Other PC users may need to download and install iTunes and QuickTime in order to view the movie. You can use iTunes or iMovie to change the QuickTime movie to another format if necessary.

To save a presentation as a movie, follow these steps:

1. Open the presentation if it's not already open.

2. Choose File ➤ Save as Movie. PowerPoint displays the Save As dialog box for saving a movie.

3. In the Save As text box, type the name you want to give the movie.

4. Choose the folder in which you want to save the movie.

5. Click the Movie Options button to display the Movie Options dialog box. This dialog box has two tabs; the left screen in Figure 21–13 shows the Movie Settings tab.

Figure 21–13. *On the Movie Settings tab (left) of the Movie Options dialog box, choose the size and quality, the media settings, and which presentations to apply them to. On the Credits tab (right), enter the details of those responsible for the movie.*

6. Choose options in the Size and quality area of the Movie Settings tab:

   ■ *Optimization.* In this pop-up menu, choose how to optimize the movie. Try the default setting, Automatic (Normal), first. If the results aren't satisfactory, choose whichever of Size, Smooth playback, or Quality is most important.

   ■ *Movie dimensions.* Choose the movie size by selecting the 640 × 480 option button, the Current screen size option button, or the Custom option button; for the last, enter the dimensions you want. The 640 × 480 resolution is usually the best place to start.

7. Choose options in the Media settings area of the Movie Settings tab:

■ *Slide transitions.* In this pop-up menu, choose Follow Slide Show settings if you want to use the transitions set in the presentation. Choose [None] if you want the movie to omit the transitions.

NOTE: PowerPoint discards animations when creating a movie from the presentation.

■ *Background soundtrack.* In this pop-up menu, choose [None] if you want the movie to have no soundtrack. To add a soundtrack, click the Select soundtrack item, click the soundtrack file in the Choose a Soundtrack dialog box, and then click the Choose button.

■ *Loop movie.* Select this check box if you want the movie to run over and over. This is occasionally useful, but usually you'll want to make sure this check box is cleared.

■ *Show movie player controls.* Select this check box to make the movie player show its playback controls while the movie is playing. Having the controls displayed is usually helpful.

8. In the Save area of the Movie Settings tab, select the Apply these settings to all new presentations option button if you want to use these settings for all new presentations you turn into movies. Otherwise, leave the Apply these settings to the current presentation option button selected to make PowerPoint use these settings for only this presentation.

9. Click the Credits tab to display its controls. The right screen in Figure 23-13 shows the Credits tab.

10. Enter the credits information for the movie.

11. Click the OK button to close the Movie Options dialog box and return to the Save As dialog box.

12. Click the Save button. PowerPoint exports the presentation to a movie file using the settings you chose and then returns you to the presentation.

Summary

In this chapter, you learned how to deliver a PowerPoint presentation to a live audience either in person or by broadcast across the Internet. You know how to prepare for the presentation by setting up your displays and using Presenter view, and you can record either timings or full-on narration for the presentation's slides. You can also create a handout for your audience and publish slides to a slide library for your colleagues.

At this point, you're good to go with PowerPoint. In the next chapter, you'll start exploring Outlook, Office's powerful application for managing e-mail, your schedule, and more.

E-mailing and Organizing with Outlook

In this fifth and final part of the book, you'll learn how to use Outlook to send, receive, and manage your e-mail and to organize your contacts, calendar, and tasks.

In Chapter 22, you'll set up Outlook to work with your ISP or e-mail provider's servers. Once Outlook is working, you'll learn how to get around its complex user interface, how to send and receive e-mail, and how to manage your messages.

In Chapter 23, you'll see how to create contacts either from scratch or by importing them from your address books, spreadsheets, or other sources. You'll also learn how to view and sort your contacts, add or update their contact information, and quickly create communications to your contacts.

In Chapter 24, you'll get up to speed with Outlook's Calendar interface, customize it to suit the way you work, and use its views effectively. After that, you'll learn to create one-shot appointments and repeating appointments, schedule meetings, and respond to meeting requests.

In Chapter 25, you'll learn to use Outlook to set down the tasks you need to complete and track your progress on completing them. You'll also see how to use Outlook's Notes feature to jot down information as you work.

Using E-mail Effectively

In this part of the book, you'll learn to use Outlook, Office's heavy-duty e-mail and organizer application.

Outlook covers four main areas:

- *Mail.* Outlook calls it Mail, but most of us call it e-mail—and it's the most important part of Outlook. I'll cover e-mail in this chapter.

- *Contacts.* Outlook provides a digital address book on steroids for storing the details of your contacts and keeping in touch with them. Chapter 23 explains how to work with contacts in Outlook.

- *Calendar.* Outlook can help you keep tabs on your appointments, whether they occur once only or at regular intervals. Chapter 24 shows you how to manage your calendar with Outlook.

- *Tasks.* Outlook provides a robust task list that you can use not only to track your own commitment but also offload them onto your colleagues. Chapter 25 teaches you how to organize your life with tasks.

So in this chapter, you'll learn how to use Outlook to send and receive e-mail and attachments.

You'll start by setting up Outlook to work with your e-mail account (or accounts). You'll then take a tour of the Outlook interface, because Outlook packs a host of controls into its window in order to handle all its different roles and tasks.

Once you know what's what, I'll show you how to send and receive messages and attachments; reply to messages and forward them to others; and delete the messages you don't want to keep and file those you do. Then you'll look at how to quickly add standard closings to your messages by creating and using signatures. Finally, you'll learn how to deal with spam, or unwanted e-mail.

Setting Up Outlook

First, you need to set up Outlook to work with your e-mail account. To do this, you need to know your e-mail address and password. You may also need to know which types of mail servers your ISP uses and their addresses.

If you have your e-mail accounts set up with a different e-mail application already, you can import the accounts into Outlook. You can also choose whether to use Outlook as your primary e-mail application or stick with the application you're currently using.

NOTE: If you've set up Outlook already, go to the section "Meeting the Outlook Interface."

Launching Outlook

Start by launching Outlook. The easiest way to launch Outlook is to click the Microsoft Outlook icon on the Dock.

If there's no Outlook icon on the Dock, click the Desktop, choose Go ➤ Applications, and then open the Microsoft Office 2011 folder. Double-click the Microsoft Outlook icon. If this is the first time you've run Outlook, the application displays the Welcome to Outlook for Mac dialog box (see Figure 22–1).

Figure 22–1. *The first time you run Outlook, the Welcome to Outlook for Mac dialog box appears. From here, you can set up your e-mail accounts.*

TIP: If you find Outlook vital to your computing life, add the Microsoft Outlook icon to the Dock. After you've launched Outlook, Ctrl+click or right-click the Outlook icon on the Dock, and then choose Options ➤ Keep in Dock from the context menu. If you want Outlook to start automatically each time you log in, Ctrl+click or right-click the Outlook icon on the Dock, and then choose Options ➤ Open at Login, placing a check mark next to this item.

Adding an E-mail Account to Outlook

To start adding an e-mail account to Outlook, click the Add Account button In the Welcome to Outlook for Mac dialog box. Outlook displays the Accounts pane of the Outlook Preferences window (see Figure 22–2).

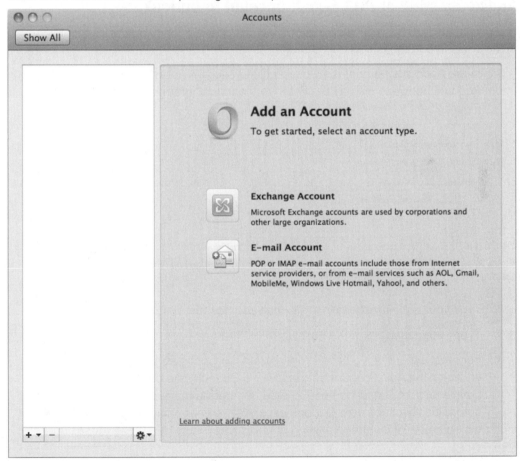

Figure 22–2. From the Accounts pane of the Outlook Preferences window, you can add either an Exchange account or another type of e-mail account.

From here, you can add either a Microsoft Exchange account or a regular type of e-mail account (IMAP or POP). We'll start with regular accounts and then look at Exchange accounts.

> **NOTE:** The main difference between an IMAP account and a POP account is that an IMAP account stores your messages on the mail server, while with a POP account your e-mail application (for example, Outlook) keeps your messages on your computer. IMAP is good for when you need to check your e-mail from multiple computers, because you see the same inbox and folders from each computer as a result of the folders being on the server. POP gives better performance if you use a single computer.

Adding an IMAP or POP E-mail Account to Outlook

If you have an IMAP or POP e-mail account rather than an Exchange account, follow these steps to add the account to Outlook:

1. In the Accounts pane of the Outlook Preferences window, click the E-mail Account button to display the Enter your account information dialog box (see Figure 22–3).

Enter your account information.

E-mail address: chris_smith@mac.com

Password: ••••••••••

☑ Configure automatically

Cancel   Add Account

Figure 22–3. *In the Enter your account information dialog box, you can set up most IMAP and POP accounts by entering just your e-mail address and password.*

2. Type your e-mail address in the E-mail address text box.

3. Type your password in the Password text box.

4. For most accounts, you can simply select the Configure automatically check box and click the Add Account button to have Outlook take care of the configuration details for you. But if you need to enter the details manually, clear the Configure automatically check box. Outlook expands the Enter your account information dialog box to show the remaining controls (see Figure 22–4).

Enter your account information.

E-mail address: chris_smith@mac.com

Password: ••••••••••

☐ Configure automatically

User name: chris_smith

Type: IMAP ▲▼

Incoming server: mail.mac.com : 143

☐ Override default port
☐ Use SSL to connect (recommended)

Outgoing server: smtp.mac.com : 25

☐ Override default port
☐ Use SSL to connect (recommended)

(Cancel) (Add Account)

Figure 22–4. *If you need to configure e-mail account settings manually, clear the Configure automatically check box, and then work with the extra controls that the Enter your account information dialog box displays.*

5. Change the default settings as needed:

- *User name.* In this text box, type the user name for the e-mail account.

- *Type.* In this pop-up menu, choose IMAP or POP. If you're not sure which type your e-mail account is, ask your e-mail provider.

- *Incoming server.* In the left text box, type the name of the incoming mail server.

- *Override default port.* Select this check box if your e-mail provider has told you to use a specific port for the incoming mail server. Type the port number in the right text box on the Incoming server line.

- *Use SSL to connect.* Select this check box if your e-mail provider provides Secure Sockets Layer (SSL) connections and you want to use a secure connection for incoming mail.

- *Outgoing server.* In the left text box, type the name of the outgoing mail server.

- *Override default port.* Select this check box if your e-mail provider has told you to use a specific port for the outgoing mail server. Type the port number in the right text box on the Outgoing server line.

- *Use SSL to connect.* Select this check box if your e-mail provider provides SSL connections and you want to use a secure connection for outgoing mail.

6. Click the Add Account button. Outlook adds the account and displays it in the Accounts pane (see Figure 22–5).

Figure 22–5. *After you have added the account, it appears in the Accounts pane. You can change further settings if necessary.*

7. Change any of the settings needed. These are the settings you're most likely to need to change here:

- *Account description.* Type the name you want Outlook to show for the account rather than the generic name that Outlook chose.

NOTE: In the Accounts pane of the Outlook Preferences window, you can change many of the same settings as in the expanded version of the Enter your account information dialog box. For example, you can enter the name of the incoming mail server or outgoing mail server, override the default mail port on the server, and use SSL to connect.

- *Full name.* Type your name the way you want Outlook to use it—for example, Jack Frederickson or John T. Frederickson.

- *Always use secure password.* Select this check box if you want always to use secure password authentication (SPA) when connecting to the mail server.

8. If you need to use different credentials for connecting to the outgoing mail server than for connecting to the incoming mail server, click the More Options button to display the Settings dialog box shown in Figure 22–6.

Settings for: smtp.mac.com

Authentication: User Name and Password

User name:

Password:

Unqualified domain:

Learn about IMAP settings   Cancel   OK

Figure 22–6. *Use the Settings dialog box when you need to provide different credentials for connecting to the outgoing mail server than for connecting to the incoming mail server.*

9. Open the Authentication pop-up menu, and choose User Name and Password instead of the default setting, Use Incoming Server Info.

10. Type your user name in the User Name text box and your password in the Password text box.

11. If the mail server requires you to enter an unqualified domain name, type it in the Unqualified domain box.

12. Click the OK button to close the Settings dialog box and return to the Accounts pane.

If you need to set up another e-mail account, click the Add (+) button in the lower-left corner of the Accounts pane, and then click the Exchange item or the E-mail item on the pop-up menu, depending on the type of account. Outlook displays the Enter your account information dialog box, and you can enter the information as discussed in this section.

When you have finished setting up accounts, click the Close button (the red button at the left end of the title bar) to close the Preferences window. You'll then see the main Outlook window, usually with the Inbox displayed. Go on to the section "Meeting the Outlook Interface."

Adding a Microsoft Exchange Account to Outlook

Microsoft Exchange is a mail server used by many corporations and organizations. To add a Microsoft Exchange account to Outlook, follow these steps:

1. Click the Exchange Account button in the Accounts pane to display the Enter your Exchange account information dialog box (see Figure 22–7).

Enter your Exchange account information.

E-mail address: [   ]

Authentication ————————————————

Method: [User Name and Password ‡]

User name: [DOMAIN\username   ]

Password: [   ]

☑ Configure automatically

(Cancel) (Add Account)

Figure 22–7. *In the Enter your Exchange account information dialog box, type your e-mail address and enter your authentication details for Exchange.*

2. In the E-mail address text box, type your full e-mail address.

3. In the Method pop-up menu, choose your authentication method:

    ■ *User Name and Password.* This is the normal choice for most networks. Type your domain and user name (for example, CORP\agreen) in the User name text box and your password in the Password text box.

    ■ *Kerberos.* If your network uses Kerberos for authentication, select Kerberos in the Method pop-up menu, and then open the Kerberos ID pop-up menu (which appears below the Method pop-up menu) and click the Kerberos ID.

NOTE: If you're not sure whether to choose User Name and Password or Authentication, ask your network administrator.

4. Make sure the Configure automatically check box is selected.

NOTE: If your network administrator tells you to enter the server name for the Exchange account, clear the Configure automatically check box. The Enter your Exchange account information dialog box then displays a Server text box above the two buttons. Type the server's address in this text box.

5. Click the Add Account button. Outlook adds the account.

Importing an Existing E-mail Account

If your Mac already contains the e-mail account you want to use with Outlook, you can import the account into Outlook. To do so, click the Import button in the Welcome to Outlook for Mac dialog box to launch the Import assistant.

On the Begin Import screen (shown on the left in Figure 22–8), click the option button for the type of operation you want to perform, click the right arrow button in the lower-right corner, and then follow through the screens to specify the details.

For example, to bring in an account from Apple Mail, select the Information from another application option button. When you click the right arrow button in the lower-right corner, the Import assistant displays the Choose an Application screen (shown on the right in Figure 22–8). You would then select the Apple Mail option button and choose which items to import—messages, accounts, rules, or signatures.

Figure 22–8. *You can use the Import assistant to import an existing e-mail account from Apple Mail or another e-mail application.*

Meeting the Outlook Interface

When Outlook opens, you'll see a window such as Figure 22–9. Outlook normally displays your Inbox at first, on the basis that you'll want to start by checking your e-mail. If Outlook is displaying a different item, click the Mail button in the lower part of the Navigation Pane, and then click the Inbox item.

Figure 22–9. *Outlook's interface uses many different components to provide access to your information and its features.*

> **NOTE:** This chapter introduces you to the Mail aspect of Outlook's interface. The following chapters show you how to use the Calendar aspect, the Contacts aspect, and the Tasks aspect.

The following sections explain how to use the main components of the Outlook interface—and how to change those you're most likely to want to change.

Using the Toolbar, Ribbon, and Menu Bar

Like the other Office applications, Outlook uses three main means of control: the toolbar across the top of the window, the Ribbon below the toolbar, and the menu bar across the top of the Mac's display (or primary display if it has more than one).

By default, the toolbar contains six buttons for standard operations—Send/Receive, Undo, Redo, Print, My Day (which displays the My Day view), and Help—plus the Search box. You can customize the toolbar by choosing View ➤ Customize Toolbar.

The Ribbon contains three tabs: the Home tab, the Organize tab, and the Tools tab. Unlike in the other Office applications, Outlook's Ribbon doesn't divide each tab into groups; instead, it has the controls (for example, buttons and pop-up menus) directly on the Ribbon. The contents of the Home tab and the Organize tab change to suit the category of items you're working with; for example, the Home tab contains different control when you're working with Mail than when you're working with the Calendar. The contents of the Tools tab remain the same.

The menu bar provides access to commands as normal.

Using and Customizing the Navigation Pane

The Navigation Pane appears on the left side of the Outlook window by default. You use this pane to navigate to the items you want to work with.

Normally, your first navigation move is to display the Outlook area you want to work in: Mail, Calendar, Contacts, Tasks, or Notes. To do so, you click the appropriate button in the lower part of the Navigation Pane.

Once you've displayed the area, the upper part of the Navigation Pane displays controls for navigating about that area. Here are some examples:

- *Mail*. The Navigation Pane displays your e-mail folders so you can quickly click the folder whose contents you want to display.

- *Calendar*. The Navigation Pane displays a list of your calendars so that you can easily switch from one calendar to another.

- *Contacts*. The Navigation Pane displays your Address Book and the groups it contains. You can click the group of contacts you want to work with.

- *Tasks*. The Navigation Pane shows the Tasks list, broken down by category. You can click the task you want to manipulate.

- *Notes*. The Navigation Pane shows your Notes, broken down by category.

TIP: You can switch quickly among Outlook's areas by using keyboard shortcuts. Press Cmd+1 to display Mail, Cmd+2 to display Calendar, Cmd+3 to display Contacts, Cmd+4 to display Tasks, or Cmd+5 to display Notes in the Navigation Pane.

Normally, you use the Navigation Pane all the time in Outlook, so it's a good idea to spend some time setting up the Navigation Pane so that you can work quickly in it.

Your first choice is how wide to make the Navigation Pane. You want to strike a balance between being able to read the longest item in the Navigation Pane (whichever area you're working in) and keeping as much space as possible for the rest of the Outlook window.

To change the width of the Navigation Pane, move the mouse pointer over the sizing handle (the three vertical lines) in its lower-right corner so that the pointer displays a two-headed arrow, and then drag to the left or right. You can also drag the right border of the Navigation Pane.

To hide the Navigation Pane, choose View ➤ Navigation Pane from the menu bar. Give the same command when you want to bring the Navigation Pane back.

If you're working with a long list of items, you can display small buttons instead of large buttons for the different areas of Outlook—Mail, Calendar, Contacts, Tasks, and Notes. To display the small buttons, drag the horizontal divider bar above the buttons down to the bottom of the Navigation Pane. As you drag, Outlook buttons to a row at the bottom of the Navigation Pane (see Figure 22–10).

Figure 22–10. *You can drag the horizontal divider line down to reduce the buttons to small buttons across the bottom of the Navigation Pane. Drag the divider line back up to restore the buttons.*

Using and Customizing the Message List and Reading Pane

To the right of the Navigation Pane is the Message List, which shows the messages in the selected mailbox (for example, the Inbox). To the right of the Message List is the Reading Pane, which shows the contents of the selected message (or part of the contents). To view a message in the Reading Pane, click it in the Message List.

NOTE: Outlook provides the Reading Pane to help you plow through your messages quickly. But you can also open a message in a separate window if you prefer. To do so, double-click the message in the Message List. Opening a message in a separate window is useful when you need to compare the contents of two or more messages at once.

Arranging and Sorting the Message List

To enable you to quickly find and read the messages you need, Outlook lets you sort the Message List in several different ways. This section runs you through the main ways of sorting the Message List, but you will want to spend some time experimenting with the various options to see which types of sorting you find most helpful for the tasks you perform with e-mail and the ways you prefer to approach them.

The easiest way to set up the Message List is to use the Arrange By pop-up menu at the top of the Message List (see Figure 22–11). You can also use the View ▶ Arrange By submenu on the menu bar.

Figure 22–11. *Use the Arrange By pop-up menu at the top of the Message List to set up the Message List the way you want it. Start by choosing the overall sort order in the top part of the list—for example, by Conversations or by Date Received.*

In the Arrange By pop-up menu, choose from the following arrangement settings:

- *Account.* Sorts the items by the e-mail account to which they've been sent. This gives a similar effect to the To arrangement, but it uses only e-mail account names rather than your name.

- *Attachments.* Sorts the items into a Has Attachments group and a No Attachments group. This setting is good for locating messages with attachments that you need to deal with.

- *Categories.* Sorts the items into the categories you've applied—for example, Manager, Team, and Junk. You can customize the categories that Outlook uses.

- *Conversations.* Sorts the items into conversations by date. (You'll learn about conversations shortly.)

- *Date Received.* Sorts the items by the date and time Outlook received them.

- *Date Sent.* Sorts the items by the date and time the messages indicate they were sent.

- *Flag Status.* Sorts the items into a Flagged group and a No Flag group by the flags you've applied to them. (For example, you can flag a message for follow-up tomorrow.)

- *Folder.* Sorts the items by the folders that contain them. If you're looking at your Inbox, sorting by folders isn't helpful, but if you've searched and found messages in various folders, sorting can be useful.

- *From.* Sorts the items by the sender. This setting is good for locating messages from important people.

- *Priority.* Sorts the items by their Importance tag into High, Normal, and Low groups; items deemed junk go into a Junk group below the Low group. This setting can be useful if your colleagues use the Importance tag sensibly and consistently, but you may find so many people give their messages High priority that the result is meaningless. What you may find more useful is to set the priority on messages you receive— for example, assigning High priority to those from your boss.

- *Size.* Sorts the items by their size. This setting is handy for quickly locating messages with large attachments. You can also use the Attachments setting (discussed earlier) to locate all messages with attachments.

- *Status.* Sorts the items into groups including Unread, Sent or Read, Replied To, and Calendar.

- *Subject.* Sorts the items by their subject lines. This setting is useful for locating an item whose subject line you can remember but whose other details you can't. (You can also search for the item, as described shortly.)

- *To.* Sorts the items by the recipient's name or e-mail address. This setting is useful if you have Outlook checking different e-mail accounts, because it lets you separate the messages by account. Items sent to you by name (for example, Chris Smith) appear separately from those sent to the e-mail address.

Changing the Sort Order

Within each arrangement, you can change the sort order by clicking the right column heading in the Message List and choosing the order you want. For example, if you sort by Date Received, you can choose between Newest on Top and Oldest on Top; if you sort by Subject, you can choose between A on Top and Z on Top; and if you sort by Attachments, you can choose between With on Top and None on Top.

Choosing Whether to Group Items

For each arrangement, you can choose whether to show the items in groups or as a series. The groups vary depending on the arrangement. For example, when you sort by Date, Outlook uses groups such as Today, Yesterday, Last Week, and Last Month; when you sort by From, the groups are the senders (by name when it appears and by e-mail address when it doesn't); and when you sort by Size, the groups are Small, Medium, Huge, and Enormous.

To choose whether to group items, open the Arrange By pop-up menu, and then click the Show in Groups item. If a check mark appears next to Show in Groups, grouping is on, and you click to turn it off; otherwise, click to place the check mark and turn grouping on.

Viewing Conversations

If you use e-mail to discuss topics with your colleagues, you'll probably get back-and-forth exchanges of messages about many topics. To view these exchanges easily, arrange the messages by Conversations in the Arrange By pop-up menu.

When you do this, Outlook presents each exchange of e-mail messages as a separate section, enabling you to see the sequence of messages clearly and to determine who said what when without having to trawl through your Inbox and other mail folders. You can expand a conversation by clicking the horizontal gray disclosure triangle to its left, or you can collapse a conversation by clicking the downward gray disclosure triangle. Figure 22–12 shows a conversation.

Figure 22–12. *When you need to see the sequence of an e-mail exchange, display the messages in conversations.*

Using and Customizing the Reading Pane

When you click a message in the Message List, Outlook displays the message's contents in the Reading Pane so that you can read it.

At first, Outlook displays the Reading Pane to the right of the Message List. If you prefer, you can position the Reading Pane below the Message List by choosing Organize ➤ Reading Pane ➤ Below from the Ribbon. Figure 22–13 shows this arrangement. (To put it back, choose Organize ➤ Reading Pane ➤ Right.) You may prefer this layout, because it gives you a better view of the Message List (but not as much of it).

You can also control the Reading Pane from the menu bar or keyboard: choose View ➤ Reading Pane ➤ Right or press Cmd+\ to place the Reading Pane on the right, choose View ➤ Reading Pane ➤ Below or press Cmd+Shift+\ to place the Reading Pane at the bottom, or choose View ➤ Reading Pane ➤ Hidden or press Cmd+Option+\ to hide the Reading pane.

> **TIP:** If your Mac has a small screen or if you need more space for the Message List, you may prefer to hide the Reading Pane and read messages in a separate window instead. To hide the Reading Pane, choose Organize ➤ Reading Pane ➤ Hidden. To read a message in a separate window, double-click the message in the Message List.

Figure 22–13. *Positioning the Reading Pane below the Message List can make the Message List easier to navigate.*

To control how Outlook interprets your opening a message in the Reading Pane, follow these steps:

1. Choose Outlook ➤ Preferences or press Cmd+, (Cmd and the comma key) to display the Outlook Preferences window.

2. In the E-mail section, click the Reading icon to display the Reading preferences pane (see Figure 22–14).

Figure 22–14. *In the Reading pane of the Outlook Preferences window, use the options in the Mark as read area to control when Outlook decides you've read an item.*

3. In the Mark as read area, select the appropriate option button:

- *Mark items as read after being previewed for* N *seconds.* Select this option button if you want Outlook to mark a message as read when you open it in the Reading Pane and don't move the focus for the number of seconds specified. The default is two seconds, but you may want to use a longer period so that you can glance through a message without having Outlook mark it as read. If you want Outlook to mark a message as read the instant you open the message, choose 0 (zero) seconds.

- *Mark item as read when selection changes.* Select this option button if you want Outlook to mark an item as read when you display it in the Reading Pane and then display another item. In this case, the trigger for marking the item as read is your changing the selection, not the length of time you spend looking at the item.

- *Mark items as read only when they are opened.* Select this option button if you want Outlook to mark an item as read only after you open the item in its own window.

4. Click the Close button (the red button in the upper-left corner) to close the Reading pane of the Outlook Preferences window.

Sending and Receiving Messages

When you have Outlook set up and working right, you'll probably want to start by using Mail. This section shows you how to create and send messages, how to receive messages, and how to read your messages.

Sending an E-mail Message

To send an e-mail message, you create a message, address it, and add contents. You may also want to choose options for the message, such as setting its reply-to address to a different e-mail address than the one you're sending from.

Creating a New Message

You can create a new blank message in any of these three ways:

- *Keyboard.* Press Cmd+Option+N.

> **NOTE:** When you've selected the Mail category, you can also press Cmd+N to create a new e-mail message. Cmd+N is the keyboard shortcut for creating a new item of whichever kind you're currently using—for example, when you're using Calendar, pressing Cmd+N creates a new appointment. But you can use the Cmd+Option+N shortcut to create a new e-mail message from anywhere in Outlook.

- *Ribbon.* Choose Home ➤ E-mail from the Mail category or Home ➤ New ➤ E-mail Message from any category.
- *Menu bar.* Choose File ➤ New ➤ E-mail Message.

Whichever way you give the command, Outlook opens a new message window. The message window's title bar at first shows Untitled, but then it displays the subject line you give the message. Figure 22–15 shows a message window with a new message open. As you can see, the Ribbon in the message window contains the Message tab and the Options tab.

Figure 22–15. *A new message opens in a window named Untitled at first.*

Choosing Which Account to Send the Message From

If you have set up Outlook to use multiple e-mail accounts, check which account appears in the From pop-up menu. Outlook uses the account you're working in, but sometimes you may need to change accounts. To do so, open the From pop-up menu, and then click the account you want to use.

Addressing the Message

You can add the components of a message in any order that suits you, but what you'll usually want to do is address the message first. To do so, you enter the primary recipients in the To box and any Cc (carbon copy) recipients in the Cc box.

You can enter the e-mail addresses in three main ways:

- *Type or paste in an e-mail address.* If you know the e-mail address, you can click in the box (for example, the To box) and simply type it in. Or if you've copied from a document or a web page, you can paste it in.

- *Type the name and have Outlook complete the address for you.* Click in the box, and start typing the name. When Outlook suggests a match (see Figure 22–16), press Enter to accept it. If Outlook suggests several matches, click the right address; or move the highlight to the right one by pressing Down arrow or Up arrow, and then press Return.

Figure 22–16. *Outlook automatically suggests matching contacts for names you start typing.*

■ *Use the Contacts Search window*: Click the button to the right of the
   To box or the button to the right of the Cc box to display the Contacts
   Search window (see Figure 22–17), and then work like this:

   1. Start typing the search term in the search field at the top of the
       window. The main part of the window displays matching results.

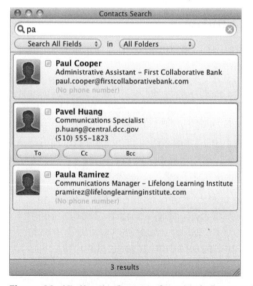

Figure 22–17. *Use the Contacts Search window to select e-mail recipients from your contacts list to a message.*

   2. If you need to restrict the search to just names rather than all
       fields, open the left pop-up menu, and then click Search Names
       Only instead of Search All Fields.

   3. If you need to restrict the search to a particular address book,
       click the right pop-up menu, and then choose the address book.
       For example, choose Address Book in the On My Computer area
       of the pop-up menu to use your Mac's Address Book.

4.   Click the address you want.

5.   Click the To button to add the address to the To box, click the Cc button to add it to the Cc box, or click the Bcc button to add it to the Bcc box.

> **NOTE:** Bcc stands for *blind carbon copy*. You use the Bcc field to add recipients whose names the To recipients and Cc recipients will not be able to see. This is sometimes useful in business situations. It's also useful when you're sending a message to a group of people who may not want to disclose their e-mail addresses to each other—for example, when you send a change-of-address message to your acquaintances. By putting your own address in the To field and all the other recipients' addresses in the Bcc field, you can prevent each recipient from seeing others' addresses.

6.   When you've chosen all the addresses you want, click the Close button (the red button at the left end of the title bar) to close the Contacts Search window.

Adding the Subject Line and Message Contents

In the Subject box, type the subject of the message. This is the text that appears in the recipient's Inbox to help them identify the message.

> **TIP:** Make your subject lines as clear as possible while keeping them short enough to fit in the narrow columns that appear in a typical e-mail application window. Your message will most likely be competing for the recipient's attention with many other messages, so making the subject clear will help it get read.

In the main box of the message window, enter the text of the message. Many e-mail messages require only plain text, which you can enter by typing as normal (or by using other standard text-entry techniques, such as pasting text or expanding AutoCorrect entries). Other messages need formatted text, pictures, or other graphical items.

> **NOTE:** Outlook lets you format the message content as plain text or as HTML. To choose which, choose Options ➤ Format in a message window, clicking the Format switch to move it to the HTML position or to the Plain position. You can also choose Draft ➤ HTML Format from the menu bar (clicking to place a check mark next to the HTML Format item or to remove the check mark) or press Cmd+Shift+T. Choose Plain Text when you want the text to have no formatting. Choose HTML when you want to use formatting that is compatible with most e-mail applications.

The easiest way to apply formatting to a message is to use the controls on the Message tab of the Ribbon. You can also apply formatting from the Format menu and its submenus or by using keyboard shortcuts (for example, press Cmd+B to apply bold, Cmd++ to increase the font size, or Cmd+– to decrease the font size).

> **NOTE:** You can mark a message as being important by choosing Message ➤ High Priority from the Ribbon or Draft ➤ Priority ➤ High from the menu bar (or you can choose Message ➤ Low Priority or Draft ➤ Priority ➤ Low to mark a message as being unimportant). But be warned that high importance has been so widely abused in e-mail messages that many people ignore it.

Choosing Options for a Message

The Options tab of the Ribbon in a message window (see Figure 22–18) contains a range of options for making a message look and behave differently from normal.

Figure 22–18. *The Options tab of the Ribbon in a message window lets you change the message's look and behavior.*

Click the Bcc button if you need to add the Bcc field to the message so that you can add Bcc recipients directly. (You can also add Bcc recipients by using the Select Contacts window, as discussed earlier.)

To add a background color to the message, click the Background Color button, and then click the color in the Colors window that opens. To add a background picture, click the Background Picture button, browse to the picture in the dialog box that opens, and then click the Open button.

> **NOTE:** To remove a background picture, choose Background Picture ➤ Remove, click the pop-up button next to the Background Picture button and then click Remove on the pop-up menu.

The Permissions pop-up menu lets you set restrictions on a message you're sending to another Outlook user on your e-mail system. For example, you can set the Do Not Forward restriction on a message to prevent the recipient from forwarding the message.

CAUTION: The options on the Permissions pop-up menu work on only some mail servers (such as Microsoft Exchange servers).

The Security pop-up menu contains two commands:

- *Digitally Sign Message.* Use this command to apply a digital signature to the message, proving that the message came from someone who holds the digital certificate you specify. (Normally, you'll specify your digital certificate so that the recipient can tell the message comes from you.)

- *Encrypt Message.* Use this command to encrypt this message so that it can be decrypted only by someone who holds the appropriate digital certificate.

SETTING UP DIGITAL CERTIFICATES FOR SIGNING AND ENCRYPTION

Before you can use the Digitally Sign Message command or Encrypt Message command on the Security pop-up menu on the Options tab of the Ribbon in a message window, you must set Outlook up with the digital certificates it needs for signing and encryption.

To tell Outlook which certificates to use, follow these steps:

1. Choose Tools ➤ Accounts from the menu bar to display the Accounts pane of the Outlook Preferences dialog box.

2. In the Accounts list on the left, click the account for which you want to set up the certificates.

3. Click the Advanced button at the lower-right corner of the account information to display the Advanced dialog box.

4. Click the Security tab to display its contents (see Figure 22–19).

Figure 22–19. *If you need to digitally sign and encrypt messages, set up Outlook with digital certificates on the Security tab of the Advanced dialog box for the account.*

5. In the Digital Signing area, open the Certificate pop-up menu, and then click the certificate you want to use for digital signing.

6. In the Signing algorithm pop-up menu, leave the default selection, SHA-256, selected unless an administrator has told you to use a different signing algorithm.

7. If you need to sign all the messages you send on this account, select the Sign outgoing messages check box. Otherwise, leave this check box cleared, and use the Security pop-up menu to sign individual messages as needed.

8. Select the Send digitally signed messages as clear text check box if you want to ensure recipients can read your e-mail messages even if they're using a mobile e-mail client or a Web-based e-mail service.

9. Select the Include my certificates in signed messages check box to make Outlook include your certificate's public key in the messages. Sending the public key enables the recipients to send you encrypted messages, which is usually helpful.

10. In the Encryption area, open the Certificate pop-up menu, and then click the certificate you want to use for encryption.

11. In the Encryption algorithm pop-up menu, leave the default selection, AES-256, selected unless an administrator has told you to use a different encryption algorithm.

12. Select the Encrypt outgoing messages check box only if you want to encrypt every message you send from this account. Otherwise, clear this check box, and then apply encryption from the Security pop-up menu to individual messages as needed.

13. Click the OK button to close the Advanced dialog box.

14. Click the Close button (the red button at the left end of the title bar) to close the Accounts window.

Checking the Spelling in a Message

Outlook checks spelling and grammar as you type unless you turn off the spelling checker and grammar checker, so you can easily resolve spelling and grammar queries as you create the message.

If you choose not to check spelling and grammar as you work, you can start a check by clicking the Spelling button on the Options tab of the Ribbon in a message window, choosing Edit ➤ Spelling and Grammar ➤ Check Document Now, or pressing Cmd+; (Cmd and the semicolon key).

NOTE: To control whether Outlook checks spelling and grammar, choose Edit ➤ Spelling and Grammar, and then place or remove the check mark next to the Check Spelling While Typing command or the Check Grammar With Spelling command on the Spelling and Grammar submenu.

Sending the Message

When you're ready to send the message, click the Send button at the left end of the Message tab on the Ribbon.

Receiving and Reading Messages

Normally, Outlook automatically checks your incoming mail server for messages and collects those sent to you. You can also force Outlook to check all your accounts for e-mail at any point by clicking the Send/Receive button on the toolbar or choosing Tools ➤ Send & Receive ➤ Send & Receive All or pressing Cmd+K.

To send and receive messages for only one account, choose Tools ➤ Send & Receive, and then click the account name on the Send & Receive submenu.

CONTROLLING HOW FREQUENTLY OUTLOOK CHECKS FOR NEW MAIL

To control how frequently Outlook checks for new mail, follow these steps:

1. Choose Outlook ➤ Preferences to display the Outlook Preferences window.

2. In the E-mail area, click the Schedules icon to display the Schedules preferences pane (see Figure 22–20).

Figure 22–20. *From the Schedules pane in the Outlook Preferences window, you can adjust the schedule on which Outlook checks for messages on your e-mail accounts.*

3. Double-click the Send & Receive All schedule to open it in the Edit Schedule dialog box (see Figure 22–21).

Figure 22–21. *Use the Edit Schedule dialog box to change the interval at which the Send & Receive All schedule repeats.*

4. In the Every text box and pop-up menu in the When group box, enter the interval you want. For example, set 5 Minutes instead of 10 Minutes.

5. Click the OK button to close the Edit Schedule dialog box.

6.   Click the Close button (the red button at the left end of the title bar) to close the Outlook Preferences window.

Once you've received your messages, click the Inbox to display them. You can then read the messages either in the Reading Pane or in a separate window. The Reading Pane is often easiest, because it's designed to enable you to quickly triage your messages. Open a message in a separate window when you need more space to concentrate on it or when you need to compare the contents of two or more messages side by side.

Click the message you want to read, or press the down arrow or up arrow to move the highlight to the message so that Outlook displays it in the Reading Pane.

> **TIP:** When reading messages in the Reading Pane, press the spacebar to display the next screen of the message. When you reach the end of this message, press the spacebar again to display the next message. You can also press Shift+spacebar to display the previous screen of the current message or (from the beginning of the current message) to display the previous message.

To read a message in a separate window, double-click the message in the Message List. In the message window, you can then display the next message by clicking the Next Item button at the right end of the toolbar or by pressing Ctrl+] or display the previous message by clicking the Previous item button on the toolbar or by pressing Ctrl+[.

To close a message window, click its Close button (the red button at the left end of the title bar), choose File ➤ Close from the menu bar, or press Cmd+W.

After reading a message, you can reply to it, move it to a folder, or delete it, as discussed later in this chapter.

> **TIP:** As discussed in the section "Using and Customizing the Reading Pane" earlier in this chapter, Outlook normally marks a message as having been read after you view it for two seconds (or the number of seconds you set) in the Reading Pane. If you turn off this automatic marking of messages as read, you can manually mark messages as read. From the keyboard, press Cmd+Option+T to mark a message as read or press Cmd+Shift+T to mark a read message as unread. With the mouse, Ctrl+ click or right-click the message in the Message List, and then click Mark as Read on the context menu; to mark a read message as unread, Ctrl+click or right-click the message, and then click Mark as Unread on the context menu.

Sending and Receiving Attachments

E-mail is a great way of sending messages quickly, but it's also useful for transferring files from one computer to another. To send a file via e-mail, you attach it to a message that you then send as usual; and when someone sends you a file, it comes to your Inbox as part of the message that brings it. You then detach the file from the message and store it in a folder.

Sending a File As an Attachment

To send a file as an attachment, start a message as usual. Then choose Message ➤ Attach from the Ribbon or choose Draft ➤ Attachments ➤ Add from the menu bar to display a dialog box for selecting the file. Click the file you want, or select multiple files by Shift+clicking or Cmd+clicking, and then click the Choose button. Outlook adds an attachment box below the Subject box in the message window showing the file's name and its size (see Figure 22–22). You can then add other files from other folders by repeating the process.

Figure 22–22. *Outlook displays the attachment box below the Subject box when you attach one or more files to a message.*

> **TIP:** You can also attach a file to a message by dragging the file from a Finder window to the message window.

Receiving a File as an Attachment

When you receive a file as an attachment, it arrives in your Inbox with its message. You'll see a paperclip icon on the message's listing in the Message List and the attachment's file name at the top of the Reading Pane (see Figure 22–23).

Figure 22–23. *The Message List displays a paperclip icon to indicate that a message has an attachment. The attachment's name appears at the top of the Reading Pane.*

To display a preview of the attachment, click the Preview button in the Reading Pane. Outlook displays the preview using Mac OS X's Quick Look feature.

To save an attached file to a folder, Ctrl+click or right-click the attachment's name at the top of the Reading Pane, and then click Save As on the context menu. In the dialog box that opens, navigate to the folder in which you want to save the file, change the file name if necessary, and then click the Save button. You can then open the file either from a Finder window or from the application you use for that type of file—for example, Word for a word processing file or Excel for a spreadsheet file.

> **CAUTION:** The pop-up menu for dealing with attachments includes an Open item, but don't open an attachment directly from Outlook. This is because the file opens in read-only mode, in which you cannot save changes you make to the file. You then need to use a Save As command to save the file under a different file name or in a different folder. Saving the file from Outlook and then opening it using the appropriate application saves time and confusion.

After you've saved an attachment to a folder, you can either remove it from the message or leave it in the message for reference. Removing attachments is usually a good idea because otherwise your mailbox can become huge, but you may sometimes need to keep attachments in messages as a safety net.

To remove an attachment from a message, Ctrl+click or right-click the attachment icon in the Reading Pane, and then click the Remove item on the context menu. In the confirmation dialog box that Outlook displays (see Figure 22–24), click the Delete button.

Are you sure you want to permanently delete the attachment Raw Data.xlsx?

You cannot undo this change.

Cancel   Delete

Figure 22–24. *Outlook confirms your removal of an attachment from a message.*

Replying to and Forwarding Messages

To reply to a message you've received, choose Home ➤ Reply from the Ribbon or Message ➤ Reply from the menu bar, or press Cmd+R. To reply to all the recipients of a message you've received, choose Message ➤ Reply All from the Ribbon, choose Message ➤ Reply All from the menu bar, or press Cmd+Shift+R.

> **TIP:** To include only part of the message in your reply, select that part of the message before giving the Reply command or Reply All command. This trick helps you keep your messages concise and easy to understand.

Outlook opens a message window for the reply, adding "Re:" to the subject line to indicate that it is a reply, and showing the original message and sender information below the insertion point (see Figure 22–25). You can then enter the text of the reply— and any other objects needed—and click the Send button to send it.

Figure 22–25. *Outlook adds "Re:" to the subject of a reply and includes the original message.*

To send a message you've received to someone else, forward it by choosing Home ➤ Forward from the Ribbon or Message ➤ Forward from the menu bar; from the keyboard, press Cmd+J. Outlook opens a message window containing the forwarded message, adding "FW:" to the subject line to indicate that the message is forwarded, and placing the original message below the insertion point. You can then address the message, type whatever information you need to add to the forwarded message (for example, why you're forwarding it), and then click the Send button.

> **TIP:** Sometimes it's useful to forward a message as an attachment so that the recipient can see it as it originally appeared. To do this, choose Home ➤ Attachment from the Ribbon or Message ➤ Forward Special ➤ As Attachment from the menu bar. You can also press Cmd+Ctrl+J from the keyboard to forward a message as an attachment.

Deleting, Storing, and Organizing Messages

When you don't need to keep an e-mail message, you can delete it by selecting it and pressing Delete or choosing Home ➤ Delete from the Ribbon or Edit ➤ Delete from the menu bar. But chances are that you'll need to keep many—perhaps most—of the messages you receive. That means creating a structure of folders in which you can place the messages and then moving each message to the appropriate folder.

Moving a Message to a Mail Folder

The quick way to move a message to a mail folder is to drag the message from the Message List to the folder in the Navigation Pane. This technique works well when you have few enough folders to fit easily in the Navigation Pane; if you have a longer list of folders, you can drag down to the bottom of the Navigation Pane to make it scroll further, but even so, getting to the folder you want can be awkward.

The next way of moving a message is to select it, open the Move pop-up menu on the Home tab of the Ribbon, and then click the destination folder on the menu (see Figure 22–26).

Figure 22–26. *You can quickly move the selected message to a folder that appears on the Move pop-up menu. If the folder doesn't appear, click the Choose Folder dialog box.*

TIP: You can also move a message to a folder using the menu bar. Select the message, choose Message ➤ Move, and then click the folder on the Move submenu.

If the folder you want doesn't appear on the Move pop-up menu, click the Choose Folder item to display the Search dialog box (see Figure 22–27). Type the first few letters of the folder name, click the folder in the list of results, and then click the Move button.

Figure 22–27. *When you have many folders, you may find it easier to search for the folder to which you want to move the message.*

Creating a New Mail Folder

To create a new mail folder, follow these steps:

1. In the Navigation Pane, Ctrl+click or right-click the folder in which you want to create the new folder, and then click New Folder on the context menu. Outlook adds a new folder named Untitled Folder and displays an edit box around the name.

> **NOTE:** To create the new folder as a subfolder of an existing folder, right-click the existing folder, and then click New Folder on the context menu.

2. Type the name for the folder, and then press Return to apply the name.

To rename an existing folder, Ctrl+click or right-click it in the Navigation Pane, and then click Rename Folder on the context menu. Outlook displays an edit box around the name. Type the new name, and then press Return (or click elsewhere) to apply it.

Adding Consistent Closings to Your Messages with Signatures

When you send a message, you often need to let the recipient know standard information about you—for example, your name and phone numbers or your company name and address, plus your position in it. To save you having to retype the same information over and over again, Outlook provides a feature called *signatures* that lets you set up one or more standard closings for inserting in your messages.

TIP: If you find signatures awkward, you can create a signature as an AutoCorrect entry and enter it by typing its abbreviation. See Chapter 2 for coverage of AutoCorrect.

To set up your signatures, follow these steps:

1. Choose Outlook ➤ Preferences or press Cmd+, (Cmd and the comma key) to display the Outlook Preferences window.

2. In the E-mail area, click the Signatures icon to display the Signatures pane (shown in Figure 22–28 with a signature being created).

Figure 22–28. *Set up one or more standard signatures in the Signatures pane of the Outlook Preferences window.*

3. To add a signature, click the Add (+) button in the lower-left corner of the Signatures pane. Outlook adds a new signature named Untitled to the left box. Double-click the Untitled name to display an edit box, type the name for the signature, and then press Return to apply the name.

4. To edit a signature, click it in the left list. Outlook displays the signature in the right box. You can then edit the existing text, type in additional text, or apply extra content. The Signature pane looks Spartan, but you can apply formatting by using the Format menu on the menu bar or by Ctrl+clicking or right-clicking and then choosing Font ➤ Show Fonts on the context menu.

TIP: You can add a picture to a signature if necessary: choose View ➤ Media Browser from the menu bar to display the Media Browser, click the Photos tab, and then drag the picture you want to the right side of the Signature pane. To keep down the burden on mail servers, it's best to use only small pictures, and even then only when necessary.

5. In the list of signatures, select the check box for each signature you want to use as one of your random signatures. (More on random signatures in a moment.)

6. To control which signature Outlook uses by default, click the Default Signatures button. Outlook displays the Default Signatures dialog box (see Figure 22–29). Open the Default signature pop-up menu for each account in turn, and click the signature you want to use. When you're done, click the OK button to close the Default Signatures dialog box.

Figure 22–29. *Use the Default Signatures dialog box to set the default signature for each account. You can also choose None if you prefer to choose a signature manually each time, or you can choose Random to have Outlook pick a signature from your Random group.*

NOTE: Sometimes it's useful to create a group of signatures and have Outlook apply different ones to your messages. To do this, create the signatures, and select the check box for each in the Signatures pane. Then click the Default Signatures button to open the Default Signatures dialog box, open the Default signature pop-up menu for the account, and choose Random. For each message you then create with that account, Outlook picks a random signature from your Random group.

7. When you've finished creating signatures, click the Close button (the red button at the left end of the title bar) to close the Outlook Preferences window.

Now create a new message using the account you set up to use a signature, and make sure that Outlook inserts the signature you chose.

If you prefer to insert a signature manually, click in the body area of the e-mail message, choose Home ➤ Signatures from the Ribbon, and then click the signature you want on the Signatures pop-up menu. Alternatively, choose Draft ➤ Signatures from the menu bar, and then click the signature on the Signatures submenu.

Dealing with Spam

E-mail monitoring companies report that more than nine out of ten e-mail messages are *spam*, or unsolicited commercial messages. ISPs and e-mail providers generally do a great job of preventing most spam from reaching us, but even so, plenty of spam messages evade the filters and make it to inboxes.

To help you deal with spam, Outlook automatically monitors your incoming mail and puts any suspected spam in the Junk E-mail folder. It's a good idea to visit this folder every day or two to rescue any messages that Outlook has falsely accused and to get rid of the rest.

Removing Nonspam Messages from the Junk E-mail Folder

If your Junk E-mail folder contains a message that's not junk, Ctrl+click or right-click the message in the Message List, and then choose Junk Mail ➤ Mark as Not Junk from the context menu. Outlook moves the message to the Inbox.

After checking that all the messages in your Junk E-mail folder are spam, Ctrl+click or right-click the Junk E-mail folder, and then click Empty Folder from the context menu. Alternatively, select the messages in the folder, and then choose Home ➤ Delete or press Delete to delete them.

Marking Spam Messages as Junk

If you receive a spam message in your Inbox, Ctrl+click or right-click it, and then choose the appropriate action from the Junk Mail submenu on the context menu:

- *Block Sender*. Outlook adds the sender's name to your Blocked Senders list, but leaves the message in your Inbox.
- *Mark as Junk.* Outlook moves the message to the Junk E-mail folder.

Changing Your Junk E-mail Protection Settings

Outlook uses a filter consisting of a set of rules to determine which messages to treat as junk. If you're getting too many junk messages in your Inbox, you can increase the sensitivity of the filter, and if you find yourself having to retrieve too many innocent messages from the Junk E-mail folder, you can turn down the sensitivity.

To change your junk e-mail protection settings, follow these steps:

1. Choose Tools ➤ Junk E-mail Protection to display the Junk E-mail Protection dialog box with the Level tab at the front (see Figure 22–30).

Figure 22–30. *On the Level tab of the Junk E-mail Protection dialog box, choose the overall level of sensitivity for the junk mail filter. You can also choose to delete old messages automatically.*

2. Select the None option button, the Low option button, the High option button, or the Exclusive option button, as needed. Low and High are usually the most useful settings, but if you're getting severe amounts of junk messages, using Exclusive to restrict senders to those in your Address Book, in the Safe Domains list, and in the Mailing List Manager may be helpful.

3. Select the Delete messages from the Junk E-mail folder older than *N* days check box if you want Outlook to get rid of old messages automatically. Set the number of days in the text box.

4. Click the OK button to close the Junk E-mail Protection dialog box.

Creating a List of Safe Domains for E-mail

To make sure you receive messages from people you trust, you can create a list of safe domains—address blocks the junk e-mail filter should treat as being safe. For example, if you want to receive all messages sent from addresses at apple.com, you can add apple.com to the Safe Domains list.

To set up your Safe Domains list, follow these steps:

1. Choose Tools ➤ Junk E-mail Protection to display the Junk E-mail Protection dialog box.

2. Click the Safe Domains tab to display it (see Figure 22–31).

Figure 22–31. *Type in a list of safe domains on the Safe Domains tab of the Junk E-mail Protection dialog box.*

3. In the Safe Domains box, type in the list of domains, separating them with commas.

4. Click the OK button to close the Junk E-mail Protection dialog box.

Removing Senders You've Blocked by Mistake

As you saw earlier in this chapter, Outlook maintains a Blocked Senders list to which you add addresses by blocking individual senders. If you block a sender and then realize you shouldn't have, follow these steps to remove the sender from the Blocked Senders list:

1. Choose Tools ➤ Junk E-mail Protection to display the Junk E-mail Protection dialog box.

2. Click the Blocked Senders tab to bring it to the front (see Figure 22–32).

Figure 22–32. *On the Blocked Senders tab of the Junk E-mail Protection dialog box, you can remove senders you've blocked by mistake or add entire domains to block.*

3. In the Blocked Senders list, select the address of the sender you've blocked by mistake, and then press Delete to delete it.

4. Add other addresses as needed, separating them with commas. You can add either a specific address (for example, bill@spamming123.com) or the whole domain (for example, spamming123.com).

5. Click the OK button to close the Junk E-mail Protection dialog box.

Summary

In this chapter, you learned how to get around the Outlook interface and how to use Outlook's features for managing your e-mail.

You set up Outlook to work with your e-mail account, and you know how to send and receive e-mail and attachments. You can reply to messages, forward messages to others, delete messages you don't want, and store those you want to keep. You can create and use signatures, and you know how to deal with spam—both identifying messages as spam and recovering those that Outlook has mistakenly sent to the Junk E-mail folder.

In the next chapter, I'll show you how to use Outlook to organize your contacts.

Chapter 23

Keeping Your Contacts in Order

In this chapter, I'll show you how to use Outlook to keep your contacts in order.

We'll start by going through how to create contacts either from scratch or by importing your existing contacts from sources such as address books or spreadsheets. After that, we'll examine how to work with contacts: viewing and arranging your contacts to reveal the ones you need, editing contact information when necessary, and quickly starting communications to your contacts.

Creating Contacts

What you'll probably need to do first is create some contacts in Outlook. You can create contacts by entering the information manually, by merging your Address Book or MobileMe contacts with Outlook, or by importing existing contacts from other sources. We'll look at each option in turn.

Creating a Contact from Scratch

If you have a contact's details on a hard copy (for example, a business card or paper) rather than in an electronic form, you'll probably need to enter the details manually. To do so, create a contact from scratch by following these steps:

1. Click the Contacts button in the Navigation Pane if it's not already selected.

2. Choose Home ➤ Contact from the Ribbon or File ➤ New ➤ Contact from the menu bar, or press Cmd+N, to open a new contact window. Figure 23–1 shows a contact window with a contact's name entered. Until you enter the name, the window's title bar is blank.

Figure 23–1. *When you type in the contact's name, Outlook displays it in the title bar of the contact window.*

3. Type the contact's first name in the First Name field. Outlook adds the name to the title bar.

4. Press Tab to move to the Last Name field.

5. Type the contact's last name. Outlook adds this to the title bar too.

6. Press Tab to move to the Job Title field, or click in another field to move directly to that field.

7. Continue entering the contact's information. Fill in the Office, Department, and Company fields if you have the relevant data.

8. If you have a photo of the contact, add it like this:

    ■ Click the Picture placeholder to display the dialog box shown in Figure 23–2. The empty frame in the middle is the *image well*.

    ■ Add a photo by dragging it from iPhoto or a Finder window to the image well or by clicking the Choose button, selecting the photo in the Open dialog box, and then clicking the Open button.

Figure 23–2. *Add a photo by dragging it to the image well from iPhoto or a Finder window or by clicking the Choose button and using the Open dialog box. Then use the Size slider to make the photo the right size.*

- Drag the Size slider to make the face the right size.

- Click inside the image well and drag the photo so that the face appears in the frame.

- Click the Set button to close the dialog box and add the photo to the contact record.

9. Enter the contact's phone numbers in the Phone area. Outlook gives you a Mobile entry and a Work entry by default. To change one of these to a different type of entry, click the pop-up button to the right of the name (for example, Mobile), and then click the type you want (for example, Home). You can add other phone numbers by clicking the Add (+) button next to the Phone heading and then clicking the type of number: Work 2, Home, Home 2, Work Fax, Home Fax, Pager, Primary Assistant, Phone 1, Phone 2, Phone 3, or Phone 4.

10. Enter the contact's e-mail address or addresses in the Internet area. Outlook displays a Work E-mail item at first, but you can add other addresses by clicking the Add (+) button next to the Internet heading and then clicking the type of address: Work E-mail, Home e-mail, Other E-mail, IM Address, Work Web Page, or Home Web Page.

TIP: You can start creating a contact quickly by holding the mouse pointer over the sender's name in an e-mail message or in the Reading Pane and then clicking the Open Outlook contact icon on the pop-up panel. Figure 23–3 shows an example of this move.

Figure 23–3. *In a message window or the Reading Pane, hold the mouse pointer over the sender's name, and then click Open Outlook contact on the pop-up panel to start creating a new contact for that person.*

11. In the Address area of the contact window, enter the contact's addresses. Outlook displays a Work address at first, but you can add home address fields by clicking the Add (+) button next to the Address heading and then clicking Home.

12. To add personal information, click the Add (+) button next to the Personal heading at the bottom of the General tab, and then click the field you want to add—for example, Middle Name, Spouse/Partner, or Title—on the pop-up menu (see Figure 23–4). Outlook adds the field to the Personal section, and you can type the relevant information in the box.

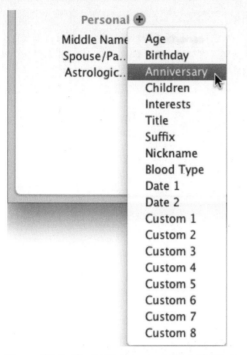

Personal ⊕

Middle Name	Age
Spouse/Pa..	Birthday
Astrologic..	Anniversary
	Children
	Interests
	Title
	Suffix
	Nickname
	Blood Type
	Date 1
	Date 2
	Custom 1
	Custom 2
	Custom 3
	Custom 4
	Custom 5
	Custom 6
	Custom 7
	Custom 8

Figure 23–4. *The Add (+) pop-up menu in the Personal area provides a wide variety of fields. As you add each field to the Personal area, Outlook removes it from the pop-up menu.*

13. On the other four tabs of the Contact window, fill in further information about the contact as needed:

■ *Organization tab.* If your Mac is connected to a Lightweight Directory Access Protocol (LDAP) server, you can enter organization information here.

■ *Details tab.* If your Mac is connected to an LDAP server, you can enter details here.

■ *Notes tab.* This tab contains a text box for entering notes about the contact. You can format the notes by using the commands on the Format menu on the menu bar or on the context menu (Ctrl+click or right-click the selection you want to format).

■ *Certificates.* On this tab (see Figure 23–5), set up the default certificate you want to use for encrypting e-mail messages to this contact. If a contact has a single certificate, as is often the case, Outlook automatically makes that certificate the default one. If a contact has multiple certificates, and the wrong one is marked Default in the Encryption certificates list, click the certificate you want to use, click the Action button in the lower-right corner, and then click Set as Default on the pop-up menu.

NOTE: Normally, Outlook acquires digital certificates automatically when your contacts send you encrypted messages. But you can also add a certificate to a contact manually by clicking the Add (+) button in the lower-left corner of the Certificates tab and then following the prompts.

Figure 23–5. On the Certificates tab of the contact window, make sure Outlook has identified the correct digital certificate for encrypting e-mail messages.

14. If you want to assign a contact to a particular category of contacts—for example, Professional, Social, or Family—choose Contact ➤ Categorize, and then click the appropriate category. Outlook gives the categories generic names, but you can customize the names and colors associated with the categories by choosing Contact ➤ Categorize ➤ Edit Categories and working in the Categories dialog box.

15. When you've finished entering the contact's details, choose Contact ➤ Save & Close from the Ribbon to save the contact record and close the window.

Importing Contacts from Other Address Books

Often, you'll have contact data in an address book already—so instead of typing it laboriously into new contacts one by one in Outlook, you can import it. This section shows you how to import data from the data sources you're perhaps most likely to have: your Mac OS X Address Book, Yahoo! Contacts, Google Contacts, Microsoft Entourage, or an Excel worksheet containing contacts.

Broadly speaking, you have four main options for importing contacts:

- *Use Outlook's Sync Services feature to import addresses.* Sync Services is the easiest way of getting contacts from the Mac OS X Address Book and from MobileMe into Outlook. Better yet, after you merge the contacts, Outlook keeps them synchronized for you, so any changes you make or new contacts you create in Outlook appear in Address Book, and vice versa.

- *Create vCard files, and then import them.* A vCard file is a file that contains the virtual address card of one or more contacts. For data sources for which you can't use Sync Services, using vCard files is usually your best bet for getting contacts into Outlook, because each of the fields is clearly mapped, so there's no confusion about which piece of information goes where.

NOTE: Most address-book and contact-management applications support the vCard standard, making vCards a straightforward way to transfer contact information from one application to another.

- *Import an existing address book from Entourage.* If your contacts are in Microsoft Entourage (the e-mail and organizer client from earlier versions of Office for Mac), you can import the address book into Outlook, either on its own or with other data.

- *Create a comma-separated values (CSV) file, and then import it.* Comma-separated values, abbreviated to CSV, is a standard format for exchanging data between spreadsheets or databases. The values are separated from each other with commas. When importing CSV files, you may need to adjust the field mapping manually to get each piece of information in the right place.

Importing Contacts from Address Book and MobileMe with Sync Services

To import contacts from the Mac OS X Address Book or from MobileMe, follow these steps:

1. Choose Tools ➤ Sync Services to display the Sync Services pane in the Outlook Preferences window (see Figure 23–6).

Figure 23–6. *Use Outlook's Sync Services feature to merge your Outlook contacts with those in your Mac OS X Address Book and MobileMe.*

2. Select the Turn on Sync Services for contacts.

3. In the Select the accounts to sync list box, select the check box for each account you want to sync.

4. In the Add new contacts to Outlook folder pop-up menu, choose the Outlook folder to add new accounts to. The default setting is On My Computer/Address Book; depending on your Mac's setup, this may be the only choice.

5. Click the Close button (the red button at the left end of the title bar) to close the Outlook Preferences window. Outlook displays the You have enabled Contacts sync dialog box (see Figure 23–7).

Figure 23–7. *Click the OK button in this dialog box to make Outlook synchronize your contacts.*

6. Click the OK button. Outlook merges your contacts and thereafter keeps them synchronized.

> **NOTE:** If a contact you're merging have the same name as an existing contact, Outlook displays the Conflict Resolver dialog box. Click the Review Now button to expand the Conflict Resolver dialog box and make Outlook display the first conflict. Click the card containing the correct information, and then click the Next button (if there's another conflict for you to resolve) or the Done button (if you've resolved the final conflict). When Outlook prompts you to save your conflict resolution changes, do so.

Creating and Importing vCard Files from Address Book

Sync Services may be great, but in other situations you may not want to keep your Mac OS X Address Book synchronized with your Outlook contacts. In this case, you can create vCard files from Address Book and import them into Outlook.

To create vCard files from your Address Book, follow these steps:

1. Open Address Book. For example, click the Address Book icon on the Dock, or open the Applications folder and then double-click the Address Book icon.

2. Select the contacts you want to export as vCards. To select all the contacts, choose Edit ➤ Select All or press Cmd+A.

3. Click anywhere in the selection, and drag the contacts to your desktop or to a Finder window. Address Book creates a vCard file containing all the contacts.

> **NOTE:** Instead of dragging the contacts to your desktop or to a Finder window, you can Ctrl+click or right-click in the selection in Address Book and then click Export vCard on the context menu. In the dialog box that opens, choose the folder, specify the file name, and then click the Save button.

4. Drag the vCard file to the Contacts area. in Outlook. Outlook adds the contacts from the file.

Creating and Importing vCard Files from Yahoo! Address Book

If you use Yahoo! Mail, chances are that you have contact information stored in Yahoo!'s Contacts feature. To get this data into Outlook, export it to a vCard file by following these steps:

1. Sign into Yahoo! and go to Contacts.

2. Click the Tools button, and then click Export on the pop-up menu to display the Export screen.

3. On the vCard Single File line, click the Export button.

4. On the Please answer the following to verify you are not a robot screen, type the text of the CAPTCHA test, and then click the Export Now button. Yahoo! exports the contacts to a vCard file named yahoo_ab.vcf in your Downloads folder.

5. Open the Downloads folder in a Finder window.

6. Drag the vCard file from the Finder window to the Contacts area in Outlook. Outlook imports the contacts from the file.

> **NOTE:** The Yahoo! Export screen also offers an option named Outlook for exporting your contacts to a CSV file. You can use this option too for getting the contacts into Outlook, but generally, the vCard file is the easier choice. (The Outlook option is mostly for Windows versions of Outlook, which can handle single-person vCard files but not multi-person vCard files.)

Creating and Importing vCard Files from Google Contacts

If you use Gmail or Google Mail, you can export your contact data to a comma-separated values (CSV) file that you can then import into Outlook. Follow these steps:

1. Sign into Gmail or Google Mail, and then go to the My Contacts area.

2. Click the More Actions button to display the pop-up menu, and then click Export to display the Export contacts dialog box.

3. In the Which contacts do you want to export? area, select the All contacts option button if you want to export all your contacts. Otherwise, select the option button called "The Group Only," and then choose the appropriate group in the pop-up menu—for example, Friends.

4. In the Which export format? area, select the vCard format option button.

5. Click the Export button. Google exports the contacts to a vCard file named contacts.vcf in your Downloads folder.

6. Open the Downloads folder in a Finder window.

7. Drag the vCard file from the finder window to the Contacts area in Outlook. Outlook imports the contacts from the file.

Importing Contacts from Entourage

If your contact information is in Entourage for Mac, you can import it quickly into Outlook. Follow these steps:

1. Choose File ➤ Import from the menu bar to launch the Import assistant. The assistant displays the Begin Import screen.

2. Click the Entourage information from an archive or earlier version option button.

3. Click the right-arrow button in the lower-right corner to display the Choose an Application screen (shown on the left in Figure 23–8).

Figure 23–8. On the Choose an Application screen (left) of the Import assistant, select the version of Entourage from which to import the contacts. On the Import Items screen (right), select the Contacts check box and the check boxes for other items you need.

4. Select the Entourage archive option button, the Entourage 2008 option button, or the Entourage 2004 option button, as appropriate.

5. Click the right-arrow button in the lower-right corner to display the Import Items screen (shown on the right in Figure 23–8).

6. Select the check box for the Contacts item and the check boxes for other items you want. Clear the check box for each item you don't want.

7. Click the right-arrow button in the lower-right corner to display the Select an Identity screen.

8. Click the identity from which to import the items.

9. Click the right-arrow button in the lower-right corner, and then follow through the remainder of the import process.

Importing Contacts from a CSV File

When you've created a CSV file containing your contacts, follow these steps to import them into Outlook:

1. In Outlook, choose File ➤ Import to launch the Import assistant. The assistant displays the Begin Import screen.

2. Select the Contacts or messages from a text file option button.

3. Click the right-arrow button in the lower-right corner to Choose a File Type screen (shown on the left in Figure 23–9).

Figure 23–9. *To import contacts from a CSV file, select the Import contacts from a tab- or comma-delimited text file option button on the Choose a File Type screen of the Import assistant.*

4. Select the Import contacts from a tab- or comma-delimited text file.

5. Click the right-arrow button in the lower-right corner to display the Import Text File dialog box.

6. Select the CSV file, and then click the Import button. The Import assistant displays the Import Contacts dialog box (see Figure 23–10).

Figure 23–10. *In the Import Contacts dialog box, check the mapping choices the Import assistant has made. If necessary, change them.*

7. In the upper-left corner of the Import Contacts dialog box, the Map fields using pop-up menu normally shows Automatic Mapping at first. Until you create a custom mapping, as discussed later in this section, Automatic Mapping is your only choice.

8. Also in the upper-left corner, make sure the First record contains field names check box is selected if the first line of your CSV file contains field names (as is usually the case). If the Mapped fields list box shows a list of contact data rather than field names, you'll need to clear this check box.

9. Also in the upper-left corner, select the Import unmapped fields to "Notes" check box is selected if you want to put information from any unmapped fields into the Notes category. This setting is often helpful, but you'll want to map as many fields as possible.

10. Look at the Unmapped fields list box, and see which of the fields from the CSV file you want to map to fields in your Outlook contacts. To map a field, drag it from the Unmapped fields list box to the appropriate field in the Mapped fields list box (see Figure 23–11).

Figure 23–11. *To map a field, drag it from the Unmapped fields list box to the appropriate field in the Mapped fields list box.*

11. When you have finished mapping the fields, click the Import button. The Import assistant imports the contacts into Outlook and displays the Import Complete screen.

NOTE: If you change the field mapping, Outlook displays a dialog box prompting you to save the current field mapping settings. If you will import more contacts from the same kind of source, click the Save button, enter a name in the Enter Mapping Name dialog box, and click the OK button. On subsequent imports, you'll be able to select your custom mapping in the Map fields using pop-up menu in the Import Contacts dialog box. If you don't want to save the mapping, click the Don't Save button instead.

12. Click the Finish button to close the Import assistant.

Importing Contacts from vCard Files

When you create vCard files or receive them from others, you can quickly add them to your contacts list in Outlook. Follow these steps:

1. Open Outlook, and then click Contacts in the Navigation Pane to display your contacts.

2. Open a Finder window to the folder that contains the vCard file or files.

3. Arrange the windows so that you can see both.

4. Drag the vCard file or files from the Finder window to the contacts list in Outlook.

Importing Contacts from an Excel Worksheet

If you've created a contact database in Excel, you may need to import contacts from it into Outlook. To do so, you need to save the appropriate worksheet as a CSV file, and then import it as described in the previous section.

To save a worksheet as a CSV file, follow these steps:

1. Open the workbook in Excel.

2. Activate the worksheet that contains the addresses. For example, click its sheet tab in the sheet tabs bar.

3. Choose File ➤ Save As to display the Save As dialog box.

4. Open the Format pop-up menu and click Comma Separated Values (.csv).

5. In the Save As text box, type the name you want to give the CSV file. Excel suggests the workbook's current name, but you'll often want to change it.

6. If necessary, use the Where pop-up menu or the navigation panes to navigate to the folder in which you want to save the CSV file.

7. Click the Save button. Excel displays the dialog box shown in Figure 23–12, telling you that the workbook cannot be saved in the selected file format because it contains multiple sheets. This appears to be a problem, but it's fine and normal.

Figure 23–12. *If Excel displays this dialog box when you're exporting a spreadsheet page to a CSV file, click the Save Active Sheet button to save just the active sheet.*

8. Click the Save Active Sheet button. Excel displays the dialog box shown in Figure 23–13, warning you that the workbook contains features that will not work or that may be removed if you use the CSV format. This too is normal.

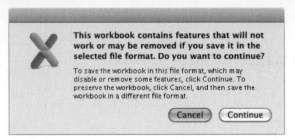

Figure 23–13. *If Excel warns you that the workbook contains features that won't work in the CSV format, click the Continue button.*

9. Click the Continue button. Excel now saves the active worksheet as a CSV file under the name you chose.

10. Choose File ➤ Close from the menu bar to close the CSV file.

You can now import the CSV file into Outlook using the technique explained in the previous section.

Working with Contacts

After creating contacts or importing them into Outlook, you can work with them. Outlook makes it easy to view your contacts, sort them in different ways, edit the information in a contact record, organize your contacts into groups, and communicate with them.

Viewing Your Contacts

To view your list of contacts, click the Contacts button in the Navigation Pane. Outlook displays the contacts with the Reading Pane on the right of the window at first (see Figure 23–14), showing the details of the selected contact. If you prefer to have the Reading Pane at the bottom of the window, choose Organize ➤ Reading Pane ➤ Below from the Ribbon or choose View ➤ Reading Pane ➤ Below from the menu bar as usual (or press Cmd+Shift+\).

Figure 23–14. *Click the Contacts button in the Navigation Pane to display your contacts. The Reading Pane appears on the right at first, but you can choose Organize ➤ Reading Pane ➤ Below to move it to the bottom of the window.*

Arranging Your Contacts

You can arrange your contacts by whichever field you find most convenient. For example, you can arrange the contact list by First Name or by Last Name; by Work State or Work City; or by Birthday or Job Title.

The easiest way to choose the arrangement is to open the Arrange By pop-up menu at the top of the contacts list and then click the field you want. To use this view as the default for your contacts, open the Arrange By pop-up menu again, scroll all the way down to the bottom, and then click the Make This the Default View item.

You can also change the arrangement by using the Organize ➤ Arrange By command on the Ribbon or the View ➤ Arrange By submenu on the menu bar.

To reverse the sort order, click the Ascending item or the Descending item at the top of the contacts list to switch to the opposite order.

Searching for a Contact

To search for a contact, follow these steps:

1. Click in the Search box on the toolbar.

2. Start typing your search term. As you type, Outlook a pop-up panel to let you choose among matches for the name, for the company, for e-mail addresses, or for the category (see Figure 23–15).

Figure 23–15. *Type a search term in the Search box, and then click the category of result you want.*

3. Click the item you want—for example, click the name item to display name matches.

Editing Contact Information

As you interact with your contacts and learn more about them, you'll often need to take notes, add further details, or change the information you've already entered.

To edit a contact's information, double-click the contact record in the contacts list. Outlook opens the contact in a contact window, where you can edit the information freely.

When you've finished editing a contact record, choose Contact ➤ Save & Close to save the contact record and close it.

Communicating with Your Contacts

When working in the main Contacts window or a individual contact window, you can quickly start a communication with one of your contacts by giving the appropriate command:

- *E-mail.* Choose Home ➤ E-mail (in the main Contacts window) or Contact ➤ E-mail (in an individual contact window) to create a new message to the contact.

- *Meeting.* Choose Home ➤ Meeting (in the main Contacts window) or Contact ➤ Meeting (in an individual contact window) to start a meeting invitation to the contact.

- *Instant Message.* Choose Home ➤ IM (in the main Contacts window) or Contact ➤ IM (in an individual contact window) to start an instant message to the contact.

NOTE: You can also start a communication by Ctrl+clicking or right-clicking the contact in the contacts list and then choosing New E-mail to Contact, New Meeting with Contact, or New IM to Contact from the context menu.

Summary

In this chapter, you learned how to work with contacts in Outlook. You now know how to create contacts from scratch or import your existing contact data into Outlook. And you know how to view and arrange your contacts, edit their contact information, and quickly and easily start communications to them.

In the next chapter, I'll show you how to use Outlook to manage your schedule.

Managing Your Calendar

In this chapter, you'll look at how to use Outlook to schedule your appointments and keep your calendar in order.

First, you'll meet the Calendar interface, learn to display the dates you want, and customize the calendar settings. I'll discuss the different types of time commitments Outlook uses—appointments, events, and meetings—and then I'll show you how to use the Calendar's different views.

After that, we'll go through how to create one-shot appointments (or events) and ones that repeat on a regular schedule. Finally, we'll look at how you use Outlook to schedule meetings and how you respond to meeting invitations you receive.

Meeting the Calendar Interface

To get started working with the Calendar, click the Calendar button in the Navigation Pane, choose View ➤ Go To ➤ Calendar from the menu bar, or press Cmd+2. Outlook first displays the Calendar in Week view (see Figure 24–1), giving you an overview of the whole calendar week.

These are the main parts of the Outlook window:

- *Navigation Pane.* The Navigation Pane shows your calendar with a list of the categories it contains. You can display the categories by clicking the sideways disclosure triangle or hide the categories by clicking the downward disclosure triangle.

NOTE: As usual, you can hide the Navigation Pane by choosing View ➤ Navigation Pane (clicking to remove the check mark from the Navigation Pane item on the View menu). Give the command again when you want to restore the Navigation Pane.

Figure 24–1. *Outlook first opens showing the current week's appointments.*

- *Time bar.* This vertical strip shows the times of day, with the hours marked. You can change the number of hours shown by dragging the Hours slider in the lower-right corner of the window to the left or right. The minimum number of hours you can display is 4; the maximum number is 24.

- *Hours slider.* Drag this slider to the left to decrease the number of hours shown in the Time bar or to the right to increase the number of hours shown.

- *Previous button.* Click this button to display the previous time unit— the previous day when the Calendar is in Day view, the previous work week when the Calendar is in Work Week view, and so on.

- *Go to Today button.* Click this button to move quickly to the current day without changing the view. For example, if the Calendar is in Week view, clicking the Go to Today displays the current week with the current day selected.

- *Next button.* Click this button to display the next time unit displayed— the next day, the next work week, the next month or whatever.

Displaying the Dates You Want

After you switch Outlook to show the Calendar, what you'll probably want to do first is display the dates you need to work with.

Make sure the Home tab of the Ribbon is displayed—if not, click the Home tab. Then click the button for the arrangement you want:

- *Day.* Click this button to display a single day at a time. This view gives you an in-depth view of that day.

- *Work.* Click this button to display the days of the work week—Monday to Friday by default, but you can change the days as needed, as you'll see in a moment. This view can be highly useful for planning your time at work.

- *Week.* Click this button to display a full week—Sunday through Saturday (you can change the start day of the week as needed).

- *Month.* Click this button to display the full month, including any days from the previous month and next month needed to make up the full weeks.

Customizing the Calendar Settings

Outlook comes with standard calendar settings, but you can often save time and effort by taking a few minutes to customize the settings to suit your work schedule and your needs. For example, you may need to use different start times and end times for work, change the work week to show different days than Monday to Friday, or start the week on a different day than Sunday.

To customize the calendar settings, follow these steps:

1. Choose Outlook ➤ Preferences, or press Cmd+, (Cmd and the comma key), to display the Outlook Preferences dialog box.

2. In the Other area, click the Calendar item to display the Calendar preferences pane (see Figure 24–2).

Figure 24–2. *In the Calendar pane in the Outlook Preferences window, set your work schedule, reminder interval, and default time zone.*

3. To change your work hours, set the appropriate times in the Work day starts pop-up menu and the Work day ends pop-up menu. In Day view, Work view, and Week view, Outlook shades the hours outside work hours to help you avoid scheduling appointments in them (for example, a 3 a.m. meeting instead of a 3 p.m. meeting).

4. To change the days Outlook displays for your work week, click the buttons in the Work week bar to switch them between dark gray (part of the work week) and light gray (days of freedom). If you set a day within your work week to be a nonworkday, Outlook still displays that day in Work view but shades the day to indicate it's not a workday.

5. To set the day Outlook treats as the start of the week, open the First day of week pop-up menu and click the day you want. For example, choose Monday to start the week on Monday rather than the default day, Sunday.

6. If you want to use a default reminder interval before appointments, select the Default reminder check box, and then choose the interval in the pop-up menu. Outlook offers intervals ranging from 0 Minutes to 2 Weeks. Doing this sets a reminder for each new appointment you create, but you can turn off the reminder, or use a different interval, for any appointment.

7. In the Default time zone for new events pop-up menu, select the time zone in which most of your events will occur.

8. When you've finished choosing calendar settings, click the Close button (the red button at the left end of the title bar) to close the Outlook Preferences window.

Understanding Appointments, Events, and Meetings

Outlook's Calendar uses three different types of time commitments:

- *Appointment.* An appointment is an item on your schedule that requires only you, not other people you need to invite or resources (for example, a conference room or projector) that you need to reserve. The Calendar creates appointments by default unless you choose to create an event or a meeting. An appointment occupies the appropriate time slots in your schedule. For example, if you create a three-hour meeting starting at 10 a.m., Outlook displays the appointment taking up the time slots from 10 a.m. to 1 p.m.

- *Event.* An *event* is simply an appointment that lasts for 24 hours or more. Instead of taking up all of a day's time slots by displaying an event right across them, Outlook displays events in the banner area at the top of the schedule.

- *Meeting.* A meeting is an appointment to which you invite other people or for which you schedule resources.

NOTE: You can change any of the three types of time commitments to another type by editing its details. For example, you can change an appointment to a meeting by inviting someone else to it.

Creating Appointments and Events

This section shows you how to create appointments and events. The following section explains how to schedule meetings.

NOTE: At this writing, you cannot synchronize Outlook Calendar with other calendars, such as Mac OS X's iCal or online calendars such as Google Calendar.

Creating One-Shot Appointments

In a typical schedule, many of your appointments will occur only once rather than at regular intervals. You can create such one-shot appointments either quickly, providing a minimum amount of information, or by using an Appointment window to enter full details.

Creating a One-Shot Appointment Quickly

To create a one-shot appointment quickly, follow these steps:

1. Drag through the appropriate slot in the schedule to select it. As you drag, Outlook increases the length of the appointment by a quarter-hour at a time.

2. Type the name of the appointment (or as much detail as you need, but it all goes into a single field). Figure 24–3 shows an example of creating an appointment like this.

Figure 24–3. *You can create a one-shot appointment quickly by dragging through the time period and then typing the details into the box that Outlook displays. The bell in the lower-right corner shows that Outlook has added a default reminder, as set in Calendar preferences.*

3. Press Return to apply the appointment.

Creating a One-Shot Appointment or Event with Full Details

Creating a one-shot appointment quickly as discussed in the previous section is often handy, but other times you'll need to enter full details for a one-shot appointment. To do so, follow these steps:

1. Double-click in the schedule at the point where you want the appointment to start. Outlook opens an Appointment window (shown in Figure 24–4 with some settings chosen).

Figure 24–4. *Open an Appointment window when you want to specify the appointment's details beyond the subject and the times.*

NOTE: You can also start an item by Ctrl+clicking or right-clicking the time in the schedule and then clicking the New Meeting item, the New Appointment item, or the New All-Day Appointment item on the context menu.

2. In the Subject box, type the subject of the appointment or event.

3. In the Location box, type the location for the appointment or event.

4. Use the controls on the Starts line to adjust the date and start time of the appointment if necessary. If you got the date and time right in step 1, these controls will already be set right.

5. Use the controls on the Ends line to set the date and end time of the appointment. For most appointments, the easiest way to do this is to open the Duration pop-up menu and choose one of the preset durations. If you need a duration that doesn't appear on the Duration pop-up menu, type the exact end time in the time box on the Ends line.

6. If you want to create an all-day event rather than an appointment, select the All day event check box.

7. Type any notes for the appointment in the box at the bottom of the Appointment window. For example, you may need to prepare materials to take with you.

8. In the Status pop-up menu on the Ribbon, Outlook automatically selects Busy when you create the appointment. Instead, you can choose Out of Office, Tentative, or Free. Outlook displays a shaded bar on the left side of the appointment or event in the Calendar so that you can easily see the status you've set.

9. In the Reminder pop-up menu on the Ribbon, choose whether and when Outlook should play a reminder for you about the appointment. The default setting is 15 minutes (or the interval you set in the Calendar preferences pane), but you can choose None to turn off the reminder or any length of time between 0 minutes and 2 weeks.

10. If you need to change the time zone for the appointment, click the Time Zones button on the Ribbon. Outlook displays a time zone pop-up menu below the Ends time line. Choose the time zone you need.

> **CAUTION:** When changing the time zone for a repeating appointment, event, or meeting, check through the sequence of items to make sure the new dates are correct. At this writing, Outlook has a bug that sometimes causes the dates to change incorrectly.

11. If you need to create a recurring event, click the Recurrence button, and then work as described in the section "Creating Repeating Appointments" later in this chapter.

12. If you need to categorize the appointment, open the Categorize pop-up menu on the Ribbon, and then click the category you want—for example, Manager or Team. You can apply multiple categories if you need to do so.

13. If this is a private appointment, click the Private button on the Ribbon to prevent others from seeing the appointment's details when you share your calendar.

14. Click the Save & Close button on the Ribbon to save the details of the appointment and close the window.

Creating Repeating Appointments

If your work life involves repeating appointments, you can set them up easily in Outlook. Follow these steps:

1. Open an Appointment window, and set up the other details of the appointment as described in the previous section. Or, if you've already set up an appointment and now need to change it to a repeating appointment, double-click the appointment to open it in an Appointment window.

2. Click the Recurrence button on the Ribbon to display the Recurrence pop-up menu (see Figure 24–5).

Figure 24–5. *You can set up straightforward repeating appointments using the Recurrence pop-up menu. For more options, click the Custom item.*

3. If you want one of the recurrence types that appears on the pop-up menu, click it—for example, Every Thursday or Day 20 of Every Month—and skip the rest of this list. (The items in the pop-up menu vary depending on the appointment's context.) Otherwise, click the Custom item to display the Recurrence dialog box (see Figure 24–6).

Figure 24–6. *Use the Recurrence dialog box when you need to create a repeating appointment.*

4. Set up the recurrence like this:

    ■ In the Repeats pop-up menu, choose Daily, Weekly, Monthly, or Yearly, as needed. Outlook displays the appropriate controls in the Every area of the dialog box.

    ■ Use the controls in the Every area to set up the recurrence. For example, for a weekly appointment, you can set the number of weeks in the Every *N* week(s) box, and then click the day in the On bar (for instance, click the second T button for Thursday). For a monthly appointment, use the controls in the On line to set the repetition—for example, On First Monday or On Day 20.

> **TIP:** To set a weekly appointment to recur on multiple days, select those days in the On bar. For example, click the W button and the F button to create an appointment that recurs on Wednesdays and Fridays.

    ■ In the Start box, enter the start date. Outlook uses the date you've specified for the appointment; you can change it if necessary.

    ■ In the End date pop-up menu, choose None, After, or By. For After, specify the number of occurrences—for example, After 10 occurrences. For By, pick the end date.

5. Click the OK button to close the Recurrence dialog box and return to the Appointment window, which is now called Appointment Series. The Recurrence line appears below the other details giving the details of the recurrence (see Figure 24–7).

Figure 24–7. *When you set up a repeating appointment, Outlook shows the details of the recurrence on the Recurrence line. You can click the rotating arrows icon at the right end of the Recurrence line to display the Recurrence dialog box.*

6. Click the Save & Close on the Ribbon to close the window and save the changes.

NOTE: If you need to stop an appointment from recurring, open the Recurrence pop-up menu, and then click the Once only item.

Scheduling Meetings

As you'll remember from earlier in this chapter, Outlook considers an appointment that involves inviting other people or scheduling resources to be a meeting. Chances are you'll need to schedule meetings of your own and respond to meeting invitations that other people send you.

Setting Up a Meeting

To set up a meeting, follow these steps:

1. Ctrl+click or right-click the meeting time in the schedule, and then click New Meeting on the context menu to open a Meeting window (see Figure 24–8).

Figure 24–8. In the Meeting window, enter the recipients, the subject, the location, and the date and time for the meeting. On the Message tab at the bottom, enter any message needed.

2. In the To box, enter the recipients for the meeting invitations. You can either type in the names (with Outlook suggesting matches) or click the button at the right end of the To box to display the Contacts Search window, and then search as discussed in Chapter 22.

3. Type the subject for the meeting request in the Subject box—for example, the name of the meeting.

4. Type the meeting's location in the Location box.

5. Type any message about the meeting in the text box on the Message tab at the bottom. For example, you may want to make clear what the meeting will cover, what attendees need to prepare, and so on.

6. If you want to check schedule information, click the Scheduling Assistant tab in the lower part of the Meeting window. On the Scheduling Assistant tab (see Figure 24–9), you can see the information available about each participant's schedule, which should help you pick a suitable time for the meeting. The information is available only if the participant gives you access to their schedule— for example, in a company calendaring system.

Figure 24–9. *Use the Scheduling Assistant tab in the lower part of the Meeting window to identify a suitable time for the meeting. You may be able to access schedule information for only some participants.*

7. When you've finished setting up the meeting invitation, click the Send button to send the meeting invitation.

Tracking the Status of Meeting Invitations You've Sent

After you send a meeting request, you receive the responses that the invitees send. Outlook tallies the acceptances and refusals for you. To see a summary of the responses, double-click the meeting in your calendar to open it in a Meeting window, and then click the Scheduling Assistant tab at the bottom to see the current status of the attendees:

- A gray circle containing an ellipsis (...) indicates No Response.

- A green circle containing a check mark indicates Accepted.

- A blue circle containing a question mark indicates Tentative acceptance.

- A red circle containing a cross indicates Declined.

Normally, you'll let Outlook manage the status for you. But if an invitee gives you a verbal response, you can update the status manually by clicking the button next to the invitee's name and then clicking the appropriate item on the pop-up menu (see Figure 24–10).

Figure 24–10. You can update the status for an invitee manually if necessary. Click the Refresh button to the right of the All Attendees heading to refresh the information with the latest updates.

Dealing with Invitations to Meetings

When someone sends you an invitation to a meeting, you receive an e-mail message with the details of the message and with a built-in mechanism for replying. Double-click the meeting message to open it in a Meeting window (see Figure 24–11).

Figure 24–11. When you receive an invitation, you can accept it, tentatively accept it, or decline it. Each pop-up menu lets you choose among responding with comments, responding without comments, and not sending a response.

Click the Accept button, the Tentative button, or the Decline button to display the associated pop-up menu, and then click the appropriate command:

- *Respond With Comments.* Click this item to start creating a message to which you can add comments before sending it.

- *Respond Without Comments.* Click this item to send the response without adding comments.

- *Do Not Send a Response.* Click this item to accept, tentatively accept, or decline this item in your calendar but not send a response to the person who invited you to the meeting. This action is occasionally useful for meetings that don't need to receive your response, but most people find it confusing.

Summary

In this chapter, you learned how to use Outlook to schedule your appointments and keep your calendar in order.

You now know how to navigate the Calendar interface and make it show the dates you want in the way you want them to appear. You understand the difference between an appointment and an event, and you know not only what distinguishes a meeting from an appointment but also how to set up meetings and respond to meeting invitations.

In the next chapter, I'll show you how to work with tasks and notes in Outlook. Turn the page when you're ready to start.

Working with Tasks and Notes

In this chapter, I'll show you how to work with tasks and notes in Outlook.

Outlook's Task feature helps you get organized by defining tasks you need to complete and organizing them by priority, due date, or other criteria. You can create either one-shot tasks or recurring tasks, keep notes in them, and mark them as complete when you finish them.

Outlook's Notes feature is useful for jotting down information as you work and then sharing your notes with other applications.

Creating Tasks

In this section, you'll learn how to work with Outlook's Tasks feature. You'll first meet the interface Outlook provides for working with tasks. You'll then create new tasks and manage your tasks.

> **NOTE:** At this writing, you must create each new task in Outlook. You can't import or sync tasks from other sources, such as your To-Do items in Mac OS X's iCal application or your tasks in Google Tasks.

Meeting the Tasks Interface

To get started with tasks, click the Tasks button in the Navigation Pane or press Cmd+4. Outlook displays the Tasks folder (shown in Figure 25–1 with several tasks added).

Navigation   Check box   Priority   Reading   Search
   Pane   column   Task List   column   Pane   box

Figure 25–1. *Click the Tasks button in the Navigation Pane to display the Task List.*

By default, Outlook displays the Reading Pane on the right of the Task List. When you click a task in the Task List, the details of the task appear in the Reading Pane. You can move the Reading Pane to the bottom of the Outlook window by choosing Organize ➤ Reading Pane ➤ Below from the Ribbon, choosing View ➤ Reading Pane ➤ Below from the menu bar, or pressing the Cmd+Shift+\ keyboard shortcut. You can hide the Reading Pane by choosing Organize ➤ Reading Pane ➤ Hidden from the Ribbon, choosing View ➤ Reading Pane ➤ Hidden from the menu bar, or pressing the Cmd+Option+\ keyboard shortcut. When you need to return the Reading Pane to the right side, choose Organize ➤ Reading Pane ➤ Right from the Ribbon, choose View ➤ Reading Pane ➤ Right from the menu bar, or press Cmd+\.

Creating One-Shot Tasks

Outlook lets you create either one-shot tasks—tasks that occur only once—or repeating tasks that recur on a schedule. This section explains how to create one-shot tasks; the next section covers creating repeating tasks.

To create a task, you open a Task window and enter the details. Follow these steps:

1. Open a Task window (Figure 25–2 shows an example) in one of the following ways:

2. Choose Home ➤ Task on the Ribbon.

3. Choose File ➤ New ➤ Task from the menu bar.

4. Press Cmd+N after clicking the Tasks button.

Figure 25–2. *Enter the details of the task in the Task window.*

5. In the upper text box, type the task's subject or description—for example, **Buy white paint**.

6. Open the Due pop-up menu, and choose the date the task is due to be completed.

7. If you want to enter a start date, open the Start pop-up menu, and choose the date the task will start. Setting a start date makes Outlook hide the task until the start date, which helps keep your Task List from being overwhelming.

8. If you want to set a reminder for the task, click the Reminder control, and then set the time and date for the reminder.

9. Type any notes about the task in the main box. You can apply formatting by using the context menu (Ctrl+click or right-click in the main box to display the context menu) or by using the Format menu.

10. If you need to create a recurring task, click the Recurrence button, and then work as described in the section "Creating Recurring Tasks" later in this chapter.

11. If necessary, change the task's priority by clicking the High Priority button or the Low Priority button on the Ribbon. If you need to remove the priority you've set, click the button again.

12. If you want to assign the task to one or more categories, click the Categorize button on the Ribbon, and then click the category you want, placing a check mark next to it. Repeat this move to add other categories as needed.

13. Click the Save & Close button on the Ribbon to save the task and close the task window.

Creating Recurring Tasks

If your job includes tasks that repeat at regular intervals, you can set up recurring tasks to have Outlook remind you of them. Follow these steps:

1. Create a task as described earlier in this chapter.

2. Open the task in a Task window.

3. Click the Recurrence button on the Ribbon to display the Recurrence pop-up menu (see Figure 25–3).

Figure 25–3. *You can set up straightforward repeating tasks using the Recurrence pop-up menu. For more options, click the Custom item.*

4. If you want one of the recurrence types that appears on the pop-up menu, click it—for example, Every Monday or Day 28 of Every Month—and skip the rest of this list. (The items on this pop-up menu vary depending on the context.) Otherwise, click the Custom item to display the Recurrence dialog box (see Figure 25–4).

Figure 25–4. *Use the Recurrence dialog box to set up the schedule for a repeating task. The options vary depending on the item you choose in the Repeats pop-up menu.*

5. Set up the recurrence like this:

 - In the Repeats pop-up menu, choose Daily, Weekly, Monthly, or Yearly, as needed. Outlook displays the appropriate controls in the Every area of the dialog box.

 - Use the controls in the Every area to set up the recurrence. For example, for a weekly task, you can set the number of weeks in the Every *N* week(s) box and then click the day in the On bar (for instance, click the second T button for Thursday). For a monthly task, use the controls in the On line to set the repetition—for example, On Second Tuesday or On Day 20.

 - In the Start date box, enter the start date. Outlook uses the date you've specified for the task.

 - In the End date pop-up menu, choose None, After, or By. If you choose After, specify the number of occurrences—for example, After 10 occurrences. If you choose By, pick the end date.

6. Click the OK button to close the Recurrence dialog box and return to the task window. The Recurrence line appears below the other details giving the information about the recurrence (see Figure 25–5).

Figure 25–5. *Outlook displays the details of a repeating task on the Recurrence line in the task window. To edit the recurrence, click the rotating-arrows icon at the right end of the Recurrence line.*

7. Click the Save & Close button on the Ribbon to close the window and save the changes.

Now that you've applied recurrence, the task recurs on the schedule you set.

> **NOTE:** If you need to stop a task from recurring, open the Recurrence pop-up menu, and then click the Once only item.

Viewing, Arranging, and Filtering the Task List

If you have only a handful of tasks in the Task List, you'll probably find it easy enough to view them all at once. But when you have many tasks, you may want to view only particular ones—for example, those that are overdue or those you've given high priority.

Choosing Which Columns to Display in the Task List

To work quickly with the Task List, you'll probably want to choose which columns appear in it. Outlook starts you off with a widely useful set of columns—Completed Status, Due Date, Item Type Icon, Priority, and Title—but you may well need to add other columns.

To choose which columns appear, Ctrl+click or right-click any of the column headings displayed in the Task List. The context menu that opens (see Figure 25–6) shows a check mark next to each column that's currently displayed. Click a column that doesn't have a check mark to display that column, or click a column that does have a check mark to remove that column.

Figure 25–6. *You can customize the columns displayed in the Task List by Ctrl+clicking or right-clicking a displayed column heading and then placing or clearing check marks on the context menu of columns.*

NOTE: You can also choose View ➤ Columns from the menu bar and then click the items on the Columns submenu to add or remove check marks.

Rearranging the Columns

When you've displayed the columns you want to see, you can rearrange the columns into a different order if necessary.

To rearrange the columns, drag a column heading to where you want that column to appear. Outlook moves the other columns out of the way (see Figure 25–7).

Figure 25–7. *You can rearrange the columns by dragging a column heading to where you want that column to appear.*

Filtering Tasks to Show the Ones You're Interested In

To view only the tasks you want to see, you can apply filters. For example, you can display only your High Priority tasks so that you can concentrate on them.

To filter the tasks, choose Home ➤ Filters to display the Filters pop-up menu, and then click the filtering you want. For example, choose Due Date ➤ Today (see Figure 25–8) to view tasks whose due date is today, or click the High Priority item on the Filters pop-up menu to display tasks you've flagged with High Priority. You can also use the View ➤ Filters submenu to set filters.

Figure 25–8. *To display only particular types of tasks, open the Filters pop-up menu on the Ribbon, and then choose which tasks you want to see—for example, tasks whose due date is today.*

When you want to see all your tasks again, choose Home ➤ Filters ➤ Clear All Filters from the Ribbon or View ➤ Filters ➤ Clear All Filters from the menu bar.

NOTE: Another way to narrow down the list of tasks displayed is to go to the Navigation Pane and clear the check boxes for the categories you don't want to see.

Viewing Your Tasks in the My Day Window

To view your tasks for the current day, click the My Day button on the Standard toolbar, choose Tools ➤ My Day from the Ribbon, or choose Window ➤ My Day from the menu bar; you can also press Cmd+9. Use the Tasks tab and Completed tab at the bottom of the My Day window to switch between tasks you need to do and tasks you've already done.

Managing Your Tasks

To keep your Task List in order, you'll need to plow through it regularly, adding details to tasks, marking them for follow-up, and—when the time comes—marking them as complete.

> **TIP:** After you open a task in a Task window, you can quickly display the next task by clicking the Next button at the right end of the toolbar or the previous task by clicking the Previous button.

Editing an Existing Task

Often, you'll need to edit an existing task—for example, to add further details or to change the due date or priority.

To edit an existing task, either work in the Reading Pane or double-click the task in the Task List to open a task window showing the details of the task. You can then change whichever aspects of the task you need to change. When you've finished, click the Save & Close button on the Ribbon to save the changes and close the task window.

Marking a Task for Follow-Up

If a task needs further action, you can mark it for follow-up at the appropriate time. You can quickly mark it for follow-up today, tomorrow, this week, next week, on no due date, or at a custom date of your choosing.

- *Task List*. Click the task, choose Home ➤ Follow Up from the Ribbon, and then click the follow-up date.

> **CAUTION:** The follow-up date is the due date for the project. If you don't want to change the project's due date, don't mark the task for follow-up—instead, set a reminder to the appropriate time. If you change the due date by marking the task for follow-up, the task moves further down your Task List if you're sorting by date.

■ *Task window.* Choose Task ➤ Follow Up from the Ribbon, and then click the follow-up date.

TIP: You can also set follow-up for the current task by using the Task ➤ Follow Up submenu on the menu bar.

■ *Keyboard.* Press Ctrl+1 to mark the selected task for follow-up today, Ctrl+2 for follow-up tomorrow, Ctrl+3 for follow-up this week, Ctrl+4 for follow-up next week, Ctrl+5 for follow-up with no due date, or Ctrl+6 to open the Dates and Reminder dialog box for setting a custom date for follow-up.

When you need to set a different date than any of the preset buttons offers, click the Custom item, and then use the Dates and Reminder dialog box (see Figure 25–9) to set the details of the follow-up.

Figure 25–9. *Use the Dates and Reminder dialog box to set a follow-up flag using the exact date and time you want.*

Marking a Finished Task as Complete

When you have finished a task, select its check box in the Task List or in the task window. You can also click the Mark Complete button on the Home tab of the Ribbon for the Task List or on the Task tab of the Ribbon in a task window.

NOTE: You can delete a task by clicking it in the Task List and pressing Delete or choosing Home ➤ Delete from the Ribbon.

Taking Notes

When you're working in Outlook, you'll often find it handy to have a place to jot down scraps of information that you need to deal with later. To do this, you can use Outlook's Notes feature.

Meeting the Notes Interface

To start using Notes, click the Notes button in the Navigation Pane, or press Cmd+5. Outlook displays the Notes pane (shown in Figure 25–10 with two notes created).

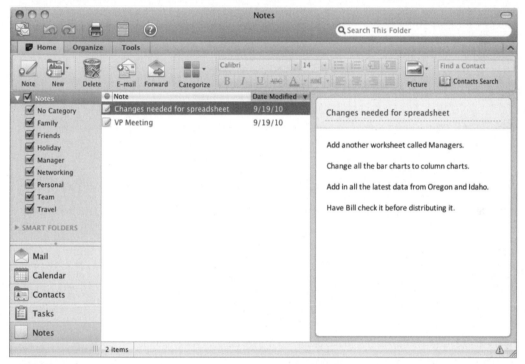

Figure 25–10. *Use Outlook's Notes feature to take quick notes as you work.*

By default, Outlook displays the Reading Pane on the right of the Notes List; the Reading Pane displays the text of the current note. You can move the Reading Pane to the bottom of the Outlook window by choosing Organize ➤ Reading Pane ➤ Below from the Ribbon, choosing View ➤ Reading Pane ➤ Below from the menu bar, or pressing the Cmd+Shift+\ keyboard shortcut. You can hide the Reading Pane by choosing Organize ➤ Reading Pane ➤ Hidden from the Ribbon, choosing View ➤ Reading Pane ➤ Hidden from the menu bar, or pressing the Cmd+Option+\ keyboard shortcut. When you need to return the Reading Pane to the right side, choose Organize ➤ Reading Pane ➤ Right from the Ribbon, choose View ➤ Reading Pane ➤ Right from the menu bar, or press Cmd+\.

Creating a Note

To create a new note, follow these steps:

1. Choose Home ➤ Note from the Ribbon, or press the Cmd+N keyboard shortcut with the Notes List displayed. Outlook creates a new note in a Note window. Figure 25–11 shows a new note with a title and some information entered.

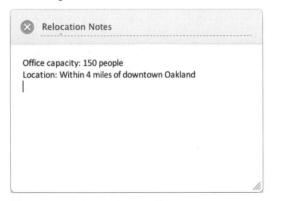

Figure 25–11. *Choose Home ➤ Note to create a new note, and then type the information in the note window.*

2. In the box at the top, type the subject of the note.

3. In the lower box, type the detail of the note.

4. Click the Close button (the × button). Outlook prompts you to save the note (see Figure 25–12).

Figure 25–12. *Click the Save button in this dialog box to save the note you're closing.*

5. Click the Save button. Outlook closes the note and adds it to the Note List.

TIP: You can also press Cmd+S to save the note as you create it and press Cmd+W to close the Note window when you've finished working with the note.

Editing and Using Your Notes

To edit a note, click it in the Notes List. The note's contents appear in the Reading Pane, and you can edit them there.

If you need to edit two or more notes at once, open each in a separate window by double-clicking the note in the Notes List.

You can use the information you've saved in a note in any of these ways:

- *Copy and paste a note's contents.* Copy the contents of the note, and then paste them into whichever application you want to use them in—for example, Microsoft Word or Microsoft PowerPoint.

- *Send a note as an e-mail message.* Click a note, and then choose Home ➤ E-mail to create a new e-mail message containing the text of the note. Address and send the message as usual.

- *Forward a note.* Click a note, and then choose Home ➤ Forward to create a new e-mail message with the contents of the note attached as a file in the HTML format. Address the message as usual, type any covering message needed, and then click the Send button to send the message.

Summary

In this chapter, you learned to work with tasks and notes. You now know how to organize your commitments by creating tasks, managing them, and marking them as complete. And you can quickly and easily take notes as you work and share them with other applications.

Index

G

◼ H

O

■S

▌W

You Need the Companion eBook

Your purchase of this book entitles you to buy the companion PDF-version eBook for only $10. Take the weightless companion with you anywhere.

We believe this Apress title will prove so indispensable that you'll want to carry it with you everywhere, which is why we are offering the companion eBook (in PDF format) for $10 to customers who purchase this book now. Convenient and fully searchable, the PDF version of any content-rich, page-heavy Apress book makes a valuable addition to your programming library. You can easily find and copy code—or perform examples by quickly toggling between instructions and the application. Even simultaneously tackling a donut, diet soda, and complex code becomes simplified with hands-free eBooks!

Once you purchase your book, getting the $10 companion eBook is simple:

❶ Visit **www.apress.com/promo/tendollars/**.

❷ Complete a basic registration form to receive a randomly generated question about this title.

❸ Answer the question correctly in 60 seconds, and you will receive a promotional code to redeem for the $10.00 eBook.

233 Spring Street, New York, NY 10013

Offer valid through 6/11.